NIETZSCHE ON TRAGEDY

Nietzsche on tragedy

M. S. SILK
Lecturer in Classics, King's College London

AND

J. P. STERN
Professor of German, University College London

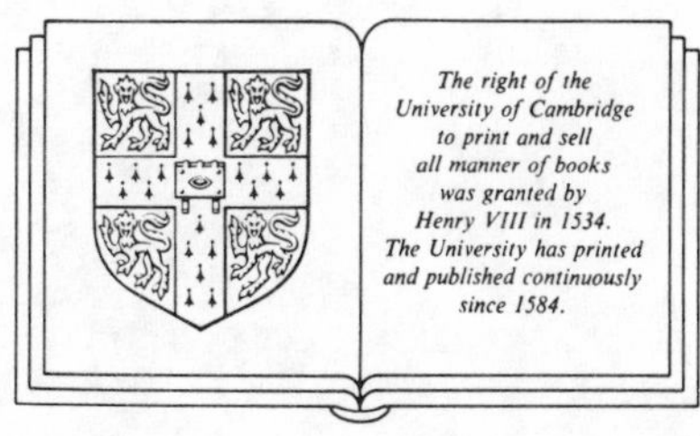

CAMBRIDGE UNIVERSITY PRESS

CAMBRIDGE

NEW YORK NEW ROCHELLE MELBOURNE SYDNEY

Published by the Press Syndicate of the University of Cambridge
The Pitt Building, Trumpington Street, Cambridge CB2 1RP
32 East 57th Street, New York, NY 10022, USA
10 Stamford Road, Oakleigh, Melbourne 3166, Australia

First published 1981
First paperback edition 1983
Reprinted 1984, 1987

Printed in Great Britain at the University Press, Cambridge

British Library Cataloguing in Publication Data
Silk, Michael Stephen
Nietzsche on tragedy.
1. Nietzsche, Friedrich. Geburt der Tragödie
aus dem Geiste der Musik
2. Tragic, The
3. Greek drama (Tragedy) – History and criticism
I. Title II. Stern, Joseph Peter
882′.01′01 B3313.G43 80-40433
ISBN 0 521 23262 7 hard covers
ISBN 0 521 27255 6 paperback

TO THE MASTER AND FELLOWS OF

ST JOHN'S COLLEGE

CAMBRIDGE

Hinter mir sind dunkle Chöre,
Wälder rühren sich und Meere;
und es nimmt mir alle Schwere,
dass ich hinter dem Geschehn
manchmal einen Athem höre
breiter als den meinen gehn.

Und dann weiss ich voll Vertraun,
dass die Hände mir nicht lügen
wenn sie neue Formen fügen –
dass sie alle Last ertrügen
um zu diesen Athemzügen
eine tiefe Brust zu baun.

[Behind me are dark choirs, forests stir and seas; and all heaviness falls from me; for sometimes I hear a breath greater than mine behind the course of things.

Then I am sure my hands do not betray me as they fashion new forms, but would bear any burden to frame unto this breath a mighty breast.]

lines written 18 March 1900 by
Rainer Maria Rilke in the margin
of his copy of *The Birth of Tragedy*

Contents

Preface

Nietzsche on Tragedy is a study of Nietzsche's first book, *The Birth of Tragedy*. It is not a commentary on his philosophy as a whole, although it does take account of his other writings – letters and notes as well as books – where these have a bearing on the discussion. For anyone concerned with an understanding of the ancient world or the history of modern culture or ideas, with Nietzsche and the evolution of his philosophical idiom, with Wagner or with drama, especially Greek drama, *The Birth of Tragedy* is an important book. But although it is widely read and although it has been extremely influential, it has never been discussed as a whole (or, in some aspects, discussed at all), and it has been much misunderstood. The chief cause of both misunderstanding and partial treatment is the particular way that the book combines the perspectives of German thought with the knowledge of a Greek scholar. Being concerned with these two spheres in their daily work, and having a common interest in Nietzsche's book, the authors felt that together they might contribute in a concerted way to its appreciation. Their collaboration, under the circumstances, was bound to be a close one; in the event, it has been unusually close. In the first instance the Greek and the biographical material was worked by M. S. S., the material pertaining to German literature and thought by J. P. S. But each stage of the writing was preceded by so much discussion and followed by so much intensive rewriting on both sides, that the final version cannot be regarded as anything other than the joint effort of the two authors, who accept equal responsibility for it. When they first mooted the idea of a collaboration (at the institution to which this book is dedicated), the authors did not, as a matter of fact, share a common view of their subject. The final version is the product of mutual correction and convergence.

The authors wish to thank all those who assisted them during several years' work on this book, among them Professor Mazzino Montinari, who generously provided material and advice concerning the unpublished portions of Nietzsche's *Nachlass* in Weimar, and Michael Tanner, who read the proofs.

For this 1983 printing we take the opportunity of making a few minor corrections and thanking our reviewers and other readers for their comments.

September 1982 M.S.S. J.P.S.

Note

The reader's attention is drawn to the following points:

Abbreviations

BT denotes *The Birth of Tragedy*, while § followed by a number without further explanation denotes a section of *BT*: e.g. § 15 = *The Birth of Tragedy*, section 15. For other abbreviations, see pp. 381 and 429.

Translations

Translations from both Greek and German are in general to be taken as our own, but we have sometimes made use of existing translations, in whole or part, notably those by Kaufmann (*Friedrich Nietzsche, The Birth of Tragedy and The Case of Wagner* (translation with commentary, Random House Inc., New York, 1974) and Middleton (*Selected Letters of Friedrich Nietzsche*, University of Chicago Press, 1969).

Dates

Our discussions range in time over two millennia B.C. and two A.D. In cases of doubt, unspecified single figure centuries (ninth to first) are to be taken as B.C., double figure centuries (tenth to twentieth) as A.D.

1

Germany and Greece

THEORIES OF TRAGEDY

Friedrich Nietzsche's book, *The Birth of Tragedy*, appeared in 1872. It is a book that can be related closely to the age in which it was written, and especially the personal circumstances of its author, then a young classical scholar. It can be related, again, to the mature philosophy of its author's later years. It must, obviously, be considered in relation to the actual matters it is concerned with, of which Greek tragedy is the most specifiable. And in respect of this main concern, it is also to be related to a particular tradition within German thought, which provides us with our starting point: a tradition of theoretical enquiry into the nature of tragedy – Greek tragedy, above all. This tradition goes back at least to Herder and Lessing in the eighteenth century;[1] and it continues beyond Nietzsche to Johannes Volkelt and Bertolt Brecht in our own time. Common to all the contributors, up to and including Nietzsche, is their profound interest in the literature of ancient Greece. They all take issue, in a variety of different ways, with the classic theory of tragedy propounded in Aristotle's *Poetics*; they all, in the wake of Herder, make some attempt to relate the achievements of the Greek tragedians to the religious or social facts of Greek life; and they all consider the dramas of Aeschylus, Sophocles and Euripides to form one of the summits of world literature. About the other summit there is less agreement: it is not always Shakespeare. But while the reasons for 'the tyranny of Greece over Germany' are many, the belief in the paramount value of these Greek plays as in some sense forming one of humanity's fundamental documents is always present.

Why the interest in *theory*? It is true that preoccupation with theoretical accounts of phenomena of all kinds is characteristic of German culture at least since the days of Leibnitz at the beginning of the eighteenth century, but in this instance there is a more specific reason. The need for a German theatre, as part of a wider literary and philosophical programme for Germany, arises at the point where Herder sets out to emphasize the Englishness of

Shakespeare and the French character of the court of Louis XIV and its drama, and where he begins to point to the absence of a comparable phenomenon in the 'Germany' – that is, the conglomeration of German principalities and duchies – of his own day. To the articulation of this need are added proposals for a specific programme and conscious, often self-conscious, attempts to create the repertoire of a national theatre. The theory of Greek drama is intended to provide the guide-lines for such a theatre, for there is an idea prevalent in Germany that a special affinity links German thought of the period with classical Greek thought. Above all, there is a feeling that the metaphysical and religious thinking revealed in the Greek dramas is specially relevant to German thought about the relation of man to the cosmos and the forces that rule it.

Lessing – for us the first of these theoreticians – is quite frank about the strictly functional purpose of his concern with Aristotle. It is to gain authority from the *Poetics* for his 'bourgeois tragedy' (*bürgerliches Trauerspiel*) by arguing that with the reduction in the social standing of the characters of his plays must come a corresponding reduction in the intensity of the emotions displayed by them and the reversals of fortune that they experience. His aim might unkindly be described as the creating of rococo tragedy with Aristotle's support. For Schiller, Greek tragedy poses a problem which he approaches from the point of view of Kantian ethics. If, in the age of the Enlightenment, a transcendent religious authority no longer provides an objective sanction for men's deeds and a punishment of their misdeeds, and if a common belief in such an authority is no longer there to provide the theatre with a cultural-religious function and to give unity to its public, then that authority must be replaced by the voice of individual conscience. The 'political' dramas of the Greeks are seen as, and become the authority for, dramas of psychological conflict; and this innovation, which is not always fully conscious, is hardly modified in Schiller's attempts in his last plays to re-establish supra-individual objectivity by the use of the ancient chorus.

Next comes Schelling, the most uncompromisingly metaphysical of our theoreticians, and the one least concerned with the theatrical side of the programme. He offers an interpretation of Greek drama, in some ways anticipating Hegel's, which brings to the fore the question of tragic guilt. The aim is to acknowledge the guilty nature of the hero according to one set of criteria, those of ordinary morality, but to stress at the same time that his guilty act is a source of pride and value of an altogether different, non-moral, antinomian kind. As far as the Greek stage is concerned, Schelling's emphasis on the hero is bound to entail a diminution of interest in the chorus, that problematic but inescapable feature of ancient drama. While in Schiller the attempt to re-establish (and perhaps re-interpret) the function of the chorus never gets very far, in Schelling this concern is abandoned altogether in favour of a wholly individualistic view of the hero, whose very solitude is the source of his strength and tragic predicament alike.

Hegel's life-long love of Sophocles and his profound historical preoccupations issue in a novel view of the relationship between chorus and hero. It may be described as the dialectical relationship between the broad objectivity of the socio-political circumstances of an age, embodied in the chorus, and the assertive subjectivity of the individual. Here, as in Schelling, something like the notion of pride in suffering is validated on the side of the hero, but, as against that, the validity of the point of view of the socio-political complex is asserted with equal force and disastrous – necessarily tragic – consequences. Finally, for Schopenhauer Greek tragedy has a significance that must be comprehended in terms of his particular brand of pessimism: it provides a powerful demonstration of the vanity of all desires of the 'will', its foolish stubbornness, and the unworthiness of all its goals. In so doing, tragedy teaches us to contemplate with equanimity, indeed with serene detachment, that which we cannot change and should therefore speedily abandon. It must be said, though, that in Schopenhauerian eyes the Greeks are in fact less compelling instructors than Shakespeare; and that tragedy as a whole is not much more than one of several 'quietives of the will' which it is the function of art in general to provide.

Were we to adhere strictly to the interpretation of our tradition as 'theoretical', there would, for our purposes, be no need to go beyond Schopenhauer. But with Nietzsche in mind, we can hardly conclude this section without mention of Richard Wagner: a figure of central importance to Nietzsche, albeit one of only peripheral relevance to the tradition in itself. With Wagner the theatrical part of the programme reappears in a pure form. The product is a new German drama – *music*-drama – which, with its re-integration of long separated arts, its mythic basis and its aspiration towards a socially organic function, evokes, at least in intention, several of Greek tragedy's most distinctive characteristics. But notwithstanding a strong attachment to Schopenhauerian doctrine, Wagner does not evince any serious theoretical interest in tragedy as such; and therefore he cannot, one might add, effectively reassert the special claims of tragedy, especially Greek tragedy, which Schopenhauer himself had tended to discount. For the decisive reassertion of these claims, we must wait for Nietzsche, Wagner's young friend and admirer who, like Wagner himself, had the deepest respect for Schopenhauer's ideas, but, unlike the composer, also possessed the capacity to reappraise those ideas and challenge them.

GERMAN HELLENISM

The German preoccupation with the theory of tragedy is bound up with a more general German admiration for Greece, to which we have alluded already. The question that needs some consideration now is: why *Greece*? What did the German writers of the century preceding Nietzsche's book hope to find in Greek antiquity? The short answer is: a superior alternative to the contemporary world and the situation of Germany in it. They might, as we have suggested, feel confident of some affinity between their own world of ideas and the Greeks', and so think themselves particularly well equipped to explore this alternative. This apart, their characteristic posture was not one of confidence about the world they lived in. They were apt to see contemporary man in a radically alienated situation: estranged from his divine origins, from nature, from his fellow-men. In the culture of ancient Greece, as they saw it, man was the 'whole man', with precisely that integrity of experience and that experience of psychic integrity which they missed in the world around them. Such enthusiasm, for all its passing likeness to the Renaissance esteem of the 'universal man', is something new in Europe, something axiomatically Romantic, the *exile's* enthusiasm. It is (in Nietzsche's words) 'thoroughgoing romanticism and yearning for home [*Heimweh*]...: it is the desire for the best that ever was. One is no longer at home anywhere, so in the end one longs to be back where one can somehow *be* at home because it is the only place where one would *wish* to be at home: and that is the world of Greece!' The value and dignity of German Hellenism, therefore, lay in 'reclaiming the soil of antiquity' and strengthening Germany's 'bond with the Greeks', the 'highest type of the species "man" so far achieved'.[2]

To Johann Joachim Winckelmann (1717–68), son of a Saxon cobbler, who rose to be a friend of cardinals and custodian of their books and antiquities, belongs the honour of having been the first and, in some ways, the most influential of these 'thoroughgoing Romantics'.[3] To appreciate his achievement, we must bear in mind that in his time Europe in general and Germany in particular had remarkably little awareness of Greece or Greek culture as *distinctive* entities, and insufficient enthusiasm for things Greek (as opposed to things Greco-Roman) to feel such unawareness as a deficiency. The Renaissance had provided western Europe with a handsome collection of hitherto lost Greek texts, literary, philosophical and historical, to be studied by scholars, admired by the cultivated (generally in translation), and imitated, in part, by contemporary writers; but insofar as the Renaissance was actually a 'rebirth' of anything past, it was predominantly a rebirth of Rome and the spirit of Rome, not of Greece; and the remains of Greek antiquity were treated, and well into the eighteenth century continued to be treated, largely as if they belonged to some kind of extension of the now assimilated world of Rome. Germany, moreover, had been comparatively little touched by the Renaissance and so by even the limited Renaissance cognizance of Greece. Yet in the person of Winckelmann it was Germany that now initiated a quite new passion for the Greek world and an equally new sense of its distinctiveness.

In ancient Greece, Winckelmann saw the embodiment of an ideal: an ideal of visual beauty and, more particularly, of a whole mode of life dominated by visual beauty. His ideas derived partly from his youthful reading of Greek literature, but largely from his studies of Greek statuary – or, in most cases, later copies of Greek statuary – in Germany and Rome. From the contemplation of these copies he distilled 'the spirit of Greek art', which became, for him and his successors, not only the characteristic of *all* Greek art (poetic as well as visual), but also the criterion of aesthetic value-judgements in general. The perfection this 'spirit' reveals is a perfection of static harmony. It is displayed (Winckelmann affirms) in the Laocoon group, that famous sculpture of the Trojan priest and his sons in the grip of the sea god's serpents: and this example, certainly surprising,[4] is used over and over again by subsequent theorists. His description of the group culminates in the famous formulation of the 'perfect law of art' of which it is said to be the embodiment:

> The universal, dominant characteristic of Greek masterpieces, finally, is noble simplicity and serene greatness [*edle Einfalt und stille Grösse*] in the pose as well as in the expression. The depths of the sea are always calm, however wild and stormy the surface; and in the same way the expression in Greek figures reveals greatness and composure of soul in the throes of whatever passions. This spirit is depicted in Laocoon's face, and not in the face alone, in spite of the most violent sufferings. The pain which is manifest in all the muscles and sinews of the body...does not express itself with any violence either in the face or in the position as a whole. This Laocoon, unlike the hero in Virgil's poem, is raising no dreadful cry....The pain of the body and the greatness of the soul are equally balanced throughout the composition of the figure and seem to cancel each other out. Laocoon suffers; but he suffers like Sophocles' Philoctetes; his misery pierces us to the soul; but we should like to be able to bear anguish in the manner of this great man.[5]

Are there any manifestations of Greek art which are not informed with this spirit? Once Laocoon, an effigy of the utmost suffering, physical and mental, has been accommodated within the scheme, almost anything, seemingly, can be. There is, Winckelmann concedes, 'Aeschylus' tragic muse' with its dark hyperboles and lurid dramatic effects; Greek drama, he admits, does contain 'the high-flown and the astonishing', 'the hasty and the evanescent'. But whenever something does not fit his 'spirit of Greek art', he has a notion – and for eighteenth-century aesthetics it is a disturbingly new notion – of *development* to fall back on. And so he ascribes all the dark aspects of Presocratic drama to the imperfection of a young and immature culture. Yet the heartland is safe: 'Greek literature of the best period, the writings of the Socratic school', are once again validated by that solemn phrase, 'noble simplicity and serene greatness'. The fact that this particular 'best period' had seemed to some of its leading figures a fallen world is not allowed to affect the conclusion.

Winckelmann's influence was enormous. When Goethe, in a scene of *Faust* I written in Rome, evokes the travail of modern man and shows it being assuaged by the contemplation of the 'silver figures of the ancient world' (*der Vorwelt silberne Gestalten*),[6] these shapes are the ideal models of Greek man which Winckelmann had set up in his historico-aesthetic studies; and when, in his 'classical' drama *Iphigenia in Tauris*, Goethe's fervent heroine is eventually victorious and the play resolves itself into a serene and harmonious close, it is the spirit of Winckelmann that triumphs. In the sphere of aesthetics, Lessing, Herder, and, a generation later, Friedrich Schlegel not only base their diverse theories on material or formulations put into currency by Winckelmann, but might be said to owe to him, as Schlegel put it, 'the very idea of a history of art',[7] conceived as the development of a series of individual works towards a perfect beauty. And even Nietzsche – whose vision of Greece was formulated, as we shall see, in conscious opposition to Winckelmann's – generously acknowledged his great feat of imaginative scholarship as the foundation of a true German national culture. Generously, but also nostalgically: the national culture thus founded reaches an immediate peak in the Weimar classicism of Goethe and Schiller at the end of the eighteenth century, but the innocence and cultural purpose of that epoch are strengths no longer to the fore among the Germans of Nietzsche's own day – the modern barbarians and 'cultural philistines' (*Kulturphilister*) of the Wilhelminian *Reich*.

The Greek ideal as founded by Winckelmann implied something more than a purely scholarly pursuit. It implied a quest for perfection: a quest that could inspire an astonishing quantity of new translations of Greek authors, original literature on Greek models, and theoretical writing informed by the Greek achievements; and a quest that could be interpreted by subsequent generations in a variety of ways. If the Greeks had, for instance, thought through the deepest problems of life and if Germans aspired to emulate their profundity, the Greeks had also possessed a rich and much admired language which was likewise not beyond emulation. There was (as indeed there still is) a strange belief that the German language showed a particular affinity with Greek and was, among other things, uniquely placed to achieve effects associated with the ancient system of quantitative metre. This theory, already prefigured by Klopstock, was worked out at inordinate length by the poet, scholar and translator Johann Heinrich Voss (1751–1826) and, erroneous though it was, it served to fuel the growing fire of Hellenism by stimulating the imitation of Greek metres in German poetry. There were those, again, in Germany as elsewhere, for whom the terms 'Hellas' and 'liberty' were axiomatically linked: a link symptomatized and strengthened by the warm interest taken by many German writers in the Greek struggle for independence, whose fruition followed in the wake of the French Revolution. One of these writers, the poet Hölderlin, claims our particular attention here for the new attitude towards Germany that his commitment to the Greek ideal entails – and also for his intuitive awareness of a greater complexity underlying 'the spirit of Greece' than Winckelmann or his immediate successors had been able to recognize.

Hölderlin was born in 1770, two years after Winckelmann's death. Like many German poets of his age, he came from a clerical family and was intended for the church. The passion of his life, however, was Greece. For Hölderlin, the assimilation of classical Greece is conceived of as a blueprint for the German nation. Criticisms of Germany had hitherto been largely implicit in the philhellenic perspective. It is Hölderlin who first articulates them fully in his letters, in his epistolary novel *Hyperion* and, above all, in his poetry; and his central target is the imbalance of German culture – as compared with the supposed perfection of Greece. It is, in particular, the unnerving intellectuality of the life around him that Hölderlin attacks, the overvaluation of philosophizing and the promise of action that never comes, the substitution of books and words for deeds, the excessive introspection and lack of worldly competence (the criticism has a special poignancy in that these are character traits he is intimately familiar with, which at times become part of his self-criticism).[8] When he speaks of Greece, it is not always clear whether he has in mind the fifth century or the timeless present in which Hyperion lives, but it is always Greece that provides the contrast. For Greece is the golden mean between this northern introversion and the passionate spirit of exotic lands:

> The north drives...its pupils back into themselves too soon; and while the spirit of the fiery Egyptian hurries out into the world, too intent on the journey, in the north the spirit prepares to retire into itself before it is ready to travel. In the north you must be wise even before you have a mature emotion...; you must develop your self-assurance before you have become a man, you must be intelligent before

you are a child; personal harmony and beauty are not allowed to thrive and mature....[9]

Hölderlin's vision of Greece is, like Winckelmann's, idyllic, but not in precisely the same way. Like Winckelmann he still speaks of 'harmony' and 'beauty', but the ultimate source for his interpretation of these ideal values is not Greek sculpture, but Greek literature of the classical period, especially Plato and Pindar. The Greece that these writers evoke for him is a whole culture, a mode of life in which there is no division between material and spiritual, gods and men:

And the people [of Hellas] came out of their doors and felt the spiritual stir in the air lightly move the soft hair across the forehead and cool the ray of [divine] light, and gladly they loosened their robes to take it to their breast: they breathed more sweetly, touched more fondly the light, clear, caressing sea in which they lived and moved.[10]

'Felt the spiritual stir': the breath of the Spirit itself is tangible, is *felt*. The opposites are reconciled in an overriding harmony. Hölderlin, then, has significantly modified Winckelmann's notion of a homogeneous 'Greek spirit': the harmony is the product of opposing forces. It can also be said that, unlike Winckelmann, Hölderlin has some intuitive appreciation of the Greek spirit's darker depths to which Nietzsche will later attach the name 'Dionysiac' – although Hölderlin gives them no such definition, and only in the last draft of his unfinished dramatic poem, *The Death of Empedocles*, do these depths receive a comparably urgent emphasis. His own urgent concern is the material–spiritual harmony which he sees as something lost and never again recovered: here, certainly, he agrees with Winckelmann. In his own interpretation, it is the advent of Christianity and its repudiation of the material that destroyed the harmony – at which point Hölderlin's Christian allegiance engenders, in his greatest poetry, an antithesis, if not an actual conflict between his Greek ideal and the purely spiritual aspiration appropriate to his own Protestant background. This dilemma may well have been one of the factors that precipitated his eventual madness, which began in 1802: that possibility adequately suggests the existential seriousness of the Greek ideal for the German writers under its spell.

After the first decade of the nineteenth century the German concern with Greece can be seen to undergo a change in character. Schiller died in 1805. By 1810 Hölderlin's active life was over. And Goethe – although he retained his admiration for the Greeks, and not least for the three tragedians, right up to his death in 1832 – mostly looked in other directions for his inspiration after the unfinished drama *Pandora* of 1810. Sixty odd years separate this work from *The Birth of Tragedy* and compared with the similar span of years since Winckelmann's revolutionary study of Greek art, the later period, viewed as a period of German Hellenism, is anti-climactic. This is not through any lack of distinction on the part of the writers of the time or those of their works that show the Greek influence; nor is there any lack of such works. On the contrary, the poetry of von Platen, Mörike and Heine attests the continuing influence of ancient Greece at a high level of poetic achievement. And in other spheres too, such as philosophy, a figure like Schopenhauer (to choose a single example particularly relevant to our general concern) can be taken to represent the respect for Greek literature general among the intellectual élite of the time: in his case, Plato, above all, was not merely an interest but an important influence – if not quite to the extent he claimed himself – on his own work. But these are *individual* writers or thinkers responding to, and making use of, ancient Greece for their own *individual* purposes; whereas in the earlier period there was the constant hope, at least, of something more, something evoked by such of our phrases as 'quest for perfection', 'superior alternative to the present', 'blueprint for the German nation'. The Greek achievement represented an ideal: special, superior, but still largely remote and mysterious; Germany's own new culture was to evolve by coming to terms with it; and a *collective* effort was to be the means of realizing that aim. In the age of Winckelmann and Weimar, therefore, the sense of purpose depends on there being a common cause to guide the nation's culture; and it is this that wanes.

CLASSICAL SCHOLARSHIP

One aspect of the change of character within German Hellenism – and, to an extent, one of the complex causal factors in the change – needs special consideration: the development of German classical scholarship. The quest for Greece initiated by Winckelmann was not (we have said) a purely scholarly pursuit. Nevertheless, it did have important consequences within the scholarly study of antiquity itself. If his notion of Greek serenity and harmony induced writers to look to Greece for their standard of perfection, it also coloured the interpretation of Greece current among professional students of the Greek world. If his studies in ancient sculpture succeeded in making the notion of 'art history' a public possession, they also gave a particular impetus to the study of ancient artefacts in their own right and to the *historical* study of antiquity as a whole. In short, Winckelmann epitomizes an intimate relationship between classical scholarship on the one hand and living culture and thought on the other. And in this he was renewing a tradition which had once existed (albeit primarily outside Germany): the Renaissance tradition, which had weakened during the intervening centuries, and which was to lapse again almost beyond recall within the hundred years after his death.

The Renaissance was essentially a rebirth of Rome. Its driving force was the aspiration to make classical Latinity – not merely literature, but culture overall – an integral part of contemporary life. That aspiration was realizable, in Italy above all, and to a substantial degree was realized; and in its realization scholarship and contemporary cultural activity were inseparable. We might think back, for example, to the fourteenth century, and its dominant figure, Petrarch. Here was a creative writer of great historical importance in vernacular Italian, as also in neo-Latin; one who played a crucial role in the promulgating of manuscripts of lost classical texts which embodied the ancient culture and could propagate that culture anew in his own time; whose creative writing variously reflected the new access to ancient literature; and whose overall achievement helped to ensure that classical scholarship, in its work of reclaiming the ancient world, became not merely a prestigious activity, but a central and formative activity in contemporary culture as a whole. But if Winckelmann's activities evoke this Petrarchan world, they do so only momentarily. The differences between the Italian Renaissance and the German Hellenizing movement initiated by Winckelmann are far greater than the similarities. One relevant difference is that whereas the Renaissance aspiration to assimilate Rome was realizable, no analogous aspiration was possible for Germany *vis-à-vis* Greece. Germany could not assimilate Greece – perhaps because Greece was simply too great, certainly because Greece was too alien. For all the suppositions of 'affinity', Germany – and western Europe in general – had no direct linguistic or cultural continuity with the ancient Greek world. If only for this reason, it was inevitable, as the nineteenth century wore on, that the sense of purpose once associated with German Hellenism must be lost.

But whatever else was lost, the impetus that Winckelmann had given to Greek scholarship in Germany survived; and if we wish to understand its subsequent history and the remarkable growth of German classical scholarship as a whole, we should not forget his formative contribution, even though much of the impending development can hardly be traced directly back to him. This development can be briefly outlined. In the mid-eighteenth century, Germany was not – and never had been – a notable centre of classical studies, and least of all a centre of Greek studies. German scholarship had done little to add to, and nothing to disrupt, the traditional European pattern of 'philology', as the study of classical antiquity was widely called (and for a long time continued to be called). 'Antiquity' for philological purposes was conceived primarily as the two ancient languages and the literature written in them; and its 'study' was, generally speaking, the province of learned individuals concerned, above all, with the restoration and exegesis of the ancient texts. Thanks, initially, to Winckelmann, Greece and thereby the whole ancient world took on a new fascination which resulted in a new kind of scholar with a new kind of scholarly aim: the reconstruction of antiquity in *all* its real detail. And such was the momentum of the new German scholarship that by the beginning of the nineteenth century Germany had become *the* European centre for classical studies, traditional as well as new, and an unprecedented growth in the scale of scholarly work of a host of different kinds was well under way.

To reconstruct antiquity in all its real detail was the aim; and in this connection 'real' is the appropriate word to use. The movement that began with Greek sculpture rapidly added other new areas of study to the familiar territories of language and literature, issuing in a serious concern not simply with 'the classics', but with ancient civilization in all its aspects: aspects that might well centre on the 'facts' of ancient life, its physical relics, its customs and institutions: all of which to be summed up in the German word *Realien*. This is one major innovation developed in Germany. A second, of even greater significance, was closely associated with it. To its increased range, scholarship added a new 'scientific' method. Techniques that went back to the age of Aristotle and the scholars of Alexandria were married to contemporary notions, among them the idea, conceived in the time of Leibnitz, of a historiography based on the study of original documents;[11] and the marriage bore fruit. The ancient world, its texts and its history, were submitted to critical analysis with an unprecedented thoroughness, sense of system and concern for evidence that was, in intention at least, dispassionate and (in the spirit of Kant's moral and aesthetic philosophy) disinterested. Learning was superseded by research; and if the work was pursued with the enthusiasm of a Winckelmann, that enthusiasm was not to be allowed to affect the outcome of the pursuit itself.

A further innovation was prefigured, as we have noted, by Winckelmann himself: the historical approach. Where the works of antiquity had once been treated as timeless products of a homogeneous whole, ancient civilization was now conceived historically and its diverse elements related to their precise period. To take a simple instance: in the heyday of the Enlightenment, Homeric poetry would have been treated primarily like its Virgilian equivalent – as a work of a certain kind (epic), embodying given characteristics of its genre or of poetry as a whole. Homer was, of course, the best part of a millennium earlier than Virgil and his chief model; and Homer, like Virgil, might naturally allude to contemporaneous, or earlier, events or individuals; but 'history' hardly impinged beyond this. In contrast, it would now be a consideration of primary and pervasive significance that the two epics were produced in quite different epochs and were, perhaps correspondingly, composed in quite different ways. This was bound to entail a new evaluation, which (we may note) might not necessarily be to Homer's advantage, for all the undoubted 'harmony' and 'beauty' of the early epic. Like Winckelmann and Hölderlin, many later Hellenists felt those favourite qualities to be best represented in the literature of the mature classical period from Sophocles to Plato (roughly 450 to 350), which was almost exempt from criticism. The later Greek literature of the Hellenistic period, the literature of Rome and the literature of earlier Greece, even Homer, were not so favoured.

Our Homeric example was not chosen at random. The man who posed the 'Homeric question' in this, its modern, form was Friedrich August Wolf (1759–1824), a scholar of representative significance in the development of classical studies in Germany. Wolf produced his *Prolegomena to Homer* in 1795, while professor at the University of Halle. Partly because of this book his lectures became famous; and in them his aim, as the standard English history of classical scholarship puts it, was 'not to communicate knowledge, but to stimulate and suggest. The spirit of critical inquiry...breathed through all his lectures...symbolized by the fact that the sole ornament of his lecture-room was a bust of Lessing.'[12] But Wolf's concern for 'stimulus' and 'suggestion' was, ultimately, a means to an end that might be defined very much in terms of 'knowledge' and not at all in terms of cultural purpose such as one would associate with a figure like Lessing. For Wolf was 'the first to present a systematic description of the vast fabric that he called by the name of *Altertumswissenschaft*, to arrange and review its component parts and to point to a perfect knowledge of the many-sided life of the ancient Greeks and Romans as the final goal of the modern study of the ancient world. He raised that study to the rank of a single comprehensive and independent science, and thus deserved to be reverently regarded by posterity as the eponymous hero of all the long line of later scholars.'[13] *Altertumswissenschaft*, the 'scientific' study of antiquity (Wolf's use of this expression has, in retrospect at least, a symbolic significance) becomes 'a single comprehensive and independent science' – with its autonomy implicit in its scientific stance.

This new autonomy, fostered by German scholarship, was its most decisive innovation of all; and the fact that most areas of knowledge were just then involved in methodological developments of one kind or another does not lessen its importance. In the context of German Hellenism as a whole, what it meant was an ever-widening gulf between classics as a study and the creative art and life of the time. Previously, 'the classics' (or some of them) were a possession of the educated classes in general and for those classes they constituted a natural part of experience, forming a continuum with modern literatures and ideas. 'Classics' henceforth is an isolatable, delimitable entity and classical philology a discontinuous academic *subject*. In 1777 Wolf himself, then a prospective student at Göttingen, had to fight to be allowed to enrol for philology: there *was* no such 'subject' then. A generation later, such battles are a thing of the past. Classical philology is a subject and institutionalized as such. Research is conducted by specialists in organised fashion, often in university programmes, on a systematic basis; knowledge accumulates; philological periodicals and societies multiply to absorb and facilitate the accumulation. And as knowledge expands, the next tendency is towards specialization within 'the subject' itself. Language, literature, thought, art, politics and society become separate territories and are occupied by separate specialists, until it becomes increasingly hard to find any scholars with pretensions to competence over the whole field: K. O. Müller from Göttingen, active in the 1820s and thirties, is one notable exception, but there were few to approach his breadth then or subsequently.

On its own terms, meanwhile, the new philology went from strength to strength. Its most important triumph, perhaps, was not in fact on new ground at all; indeed, it was on the most traditional of all grounds: textual criticism. In the first half of the nineteenth century, the age-old struggle to reconstitute an ancient text from imperfect manuscript copies was, for the first time, given a proper basis: methodical study of the manuscripts' interrelationships. Scholars of impressive energy and fine acumen established the new 'science' and formulated its principles.[14] Wolf's treatise on Homer laid the foundations at the end of the eighteenth century and a celebrated edition of Lucretius by Karl Lachmann represents the completion of the edifice in 1850. Ever since the ancient Alexandrians, textual criticism had been a highly valued activity; it now acquired a new lustre. Young scholars gravitated towards it, to concern themselves, generally, with the practicalities, and especially the problems, of single texts. The solution of such limited problems might be seen as a triumph of 'method' as much as a source of new knowledge.[15] But in any case the cost of the progress of 'the subject' was, as usual, more specialization. It would be idle to deny that great progress was made; but equally idle to deny that a price was paid for it.

The fragmentation of classical studies from 'life outside' and the further fragmentation within classical studies itself ironically symbolize the much wider disintegration which had been deplored by the Romantic philhellenes and which had evoked their yearning for Greece in the first place. And, ironically again, the increasing specialization of Greek scholarship made it increasingly more problematic for German writers to draw on Greek literature and its *topoi* as wholeheartedly as they once had. Specialization thus emerges as a contributory factor to the loss of momentum suffered by German Hellenism as a cultural force after Weimar. The Hellenic ideal – or ideals – that German intellectuals and writers hoped to live by could hardly command full allegiance without some support from the professionals in the field and perhaps some modification from their new ideas. But to the new professional researcher a Hellenic ideal was something that belonged to the modern world outside; and while he might privately approve, his professional concern was with a self-contained world of antiquity. Furthermore, the new notions about antiquity that he was professionally concerned to propagate would very likely be conceived without reference to that modern world and expressed in such dauntingly esoteric form, with such a massive presupposition of specialist information, as to repel the amateur, however willing. Any interplay between scholarship and life, under such circumstances, was bound to be exceptional and random.

Wolf himself, poignantly enough, did not evince this inward-looking spirit. On the contrary, he exemplified perfectly the interplay which was shortly to disappear: his own scholarly work was of immediate interest to – and readily assimilated by – the finest minds of the day. Not that all of those minds were equally receptive to his theories on the ancient epic. The poets Klopstock, Wieland and Schiller were among those who listened but dissented, as was the versatile Voss, himself a good example of the interplay: his *œuvre* included verse in classical metres (*Luise*, 1795) which influenced Goethe's *Hermann and Dorothea*, scholarly work on Latin as well as Greek, and a celebrated translation of the *Odyssey* (1781). Even so, they listened, and their disapproval of Wolf was in any case balanced by the enthusiasm of von Humboldt, the brothers Schlegel and, for a time, Goethe too, who 'drank to his health' in 1796 in celebration of the study of Homer,[16] corresponded with him, and attended his lectures.

But the fact remains that Wolf and the tendency Wolf represented made an inward-looking discipline possible and, ultimately, respectable. By the eighteen fifties and sixties, a generation after his death, the classical philologist's separatism is something normal and generally unquestioned, and interplay between classical studies and life as a whole is an ideal as little in prospect as the 'wholeness' of life itself.

2

Biographical Background I: Nietzsche and his early interests*

LIFE AND CLASSICAL CAREER

The main external events in Nietzsche's life that concern us here are easily summarized.[1] Friedrich Wilhelm Nietzsche was born in 1844 into a pious Protestant family at Röcken in Saxony. His father, the local parson, died in 1849, leaving, in all, three children, one of whom died shortly afterwards. The survivors were Nietzsche himself and a younger sister. This sister, Elisabeth, was to count for a good deal in Nietzsche's later life, favourably and otherwise: she eventually became the custodian of all his surviving works during the long period of incapacity that preceded his death and continued in that influential rôle, which she executed in a highly questionable way, for thirty-five years afterwards.

In 1850, with his mother, sister and – to add to the regiment of women – two aunts and a grandmother, Nietzsche moved to nearby Naumburg. He soon showed academic promise and in 1858, at the age of fourteen, went to the famous boarding school of Pforta, not far from Naumburg, where he excelled in most subjects, the chief exceptions being art and mathematics. The standing of this school, established in 1543 and before that a Cistercian Abbey, was considerable. Its distinguished pupils over the years had included such famous names in German cultural life as Klopstock, Fichte, Ranke, and Friedrich Schlegel; and not the least of its products was a series of remarkable classical scholars, beginning with Ernesti in the early eighteenth century and proceeding through Böttiger, Thiersch, Doederlein, Dissen, Meineke, Otto Jahn, Nauck, Breitenbach, Bonitz and Wachsmuth to the illustrious Wilamowitz, four years Nietzsche's junior.

Classics was also to be Nietzsche's chosen profession and his rise in it was rapid. From Pforta in 1864 he went to the University of Bonn to read classical

* There exists no adequate discussion of Nietzsche's developing attitudes in youth and early manhood or of the genesis of *BT*. The following account is based both on newly published evidence and on an independent interpretation of long known material.

philology and theology, but he stayed only for a single year. A bitter personal feud had developed there between the two eminent classics professors, Otto Jahn (like Nietzsche from Pforta) and Friedrich Ritschl; and in 1865 Ritschl left, followed by some of his students, to take up a post at the University of Leipzig. Nietzsche was among those who went with Ritschl; and under Ritschl at Leipzig his career blossomed. He now dropped theology to concentrate entirely on classics. He rapidly achieved prominence among his contemporaries and in the winter of 1865 was one of the founders of a University Classical Society, the *Philologischer Verein*. At a meeting of the Society in January 1866 he read a paper on the formation of the *Theognidea*, a collection of poems traditionally ascribed to the sixth-century Greek poet Theognis. Ritschl was impressed and urged him to turn the paper into an article for publication. There followed regular contact between student and professor and more published work by Nietzsche on Greek subjects: besides reviews, there were articles on the lyric poet Simonides, the historian of philosophy Diogenes Laertius and the anonymous quasi-biographical piece known as the *Contest of Homer and Hesiod*.[2] His unpublished contributions to the Leipzig Classical Society included scholarly studies in other Greek fields, such as the Aristotelian corpus, while at Leipzig he also worked extensively on the philosopher Democritus.[3]

Taken together, these studies comprise a substantial body of work notable for its diversity, its competence and its orthodoxy. They show us Nietzsche collating manuscripts, emending texts or (in more discursive, literary-historical vein) investigating date, authorship, provenance or genesis of ancient writings. In short, these studies exhibit all the familiar features of nineteenth-century 'scientific' scholarship. They also evince an obvious preference for Greek, as against Latin, as an object of study – a preference that can be traced back to Nietzsche's schooldays, which produced a noteworthy essay on Sophocles' *Oedipus Rex* (1864).[4]

In 1867, the young scholar's career was temporarily interrupted by a period of military service which resulted in a serious chest injury. There followed a period of convalescence in Naumburg, and in the autumn of 1868 Nietzsche returned to Leipzig to continue his independent studies. Ritschl, by now increasingly confident of his protégé's abilities, recommended him for a vacant chair of classics at the University of Basle in Switzerland. In January 1869, on the strength of his published work and Ritschl's glowing reference, he was offered the chair despite his youth and lack of the usually mandatory doctorate and 'habilitation'; he took up the post in April 1869.[5] This was the only regular employment he was ever to have. It lasted until 1879, when ill health compelled his premature retirement. Thereafter, apart from a small private income, he subsisted on a university pension for a further ten years, during which time he produced the bulk of his philosophical works, at that time largely unknown, until in January 1889 all creative work ended abruptly with his mental breakdown; he died in 1900. At the time of Nietzsche's move to Basle, none of his major works were yet conceived, but it is the winter of this year, 1869–70, to which we can trace the genesis of *The Birth of Tragedy*, his first. In May 1869 he gave his inaugural lecture on Homer, but his classical interests were now turning towards Greek tragedy. After a break during the Franco-Prussian war, in which he was actively involved, though not as a combatant, his thoughts on tragedy took final shape in 1871. The book appeared in early 1872, beset with controversy from which – with good reason, one may think – it has never been free.

SCHOPENHAUER

The genesis of *BT* in the first years at Basle is, we shall see, problematic. To understand it, we need first to look at the development of Nietzsche's inner life: the particular temperament and range of interests without which the controversial book would never have been written at all. A few quotations from his correspondence to friends during the years before its appearance will serve to introduce the main interests and traits in question: 'Three things are my relaxations, but infrequent ones: my Schopenhauer, Schumann's music, and solitary walks' (from 1866); 'It is only too natural that... concentrating on a particular field of knowledge all day long should somewhat blunt one's untramelled receptivity and attack the philosophic sense at its root. But I flatter myself that I can meet this danger more calmly and securely than most philologists; my philosophical seriousness is already too deeply rooted, the true and essential problems of life and thought have been too clearly shown to me by the great mystagogue Schopenhauer...' (1869); 'I love the Greeks more and more...[but]...the philologist's existence... seems to me more and more anomalous' (1870); 'For me, everything that is best and most beautiful is associated with the names Schopenhauer and Wagner, and I am proud and happy to share this feeling with my closest friends' (1870 again); and from the close of the same year, 'Let us drag on in this university existence for a few more years; let us take it as a sorrowful lesson...I realize what Schopenhauer's doctrine of university wisdom is all about.... We shall create a new Greek academy.... You will know of Wagner's Bayreuth plan. I have been quietly considering if we too should not likewise break with philology...as practised till now'.[6]

Three preoccupations stand out clearly: music (especially, though not at first, Wagner), philosophy (the ubiquitous Schopenhauer), and the Greeks – the Greeks not merely as a professional concern, but as a personal ideal in conflict with professional norms: here, as will become apparent, Nietzsche is a whole-hearted successor of the earlier generations of Romantic Hellenists. In addition, we can point to certain temperamental facts: most obviously, the youthfully ardent seriousness; then the self-consciousness of the gifted and isolated individual – a consciousness of his own giftedness, one might add, which shades into a growing concern with the problems surrounding genius as such, and which helps to intensify an already strong impulse to express himself articulately in writing; and, finally, a compulsion to relate his music, his philosophy, his Greece to each other. This last characteristic is of central importance: this, above all else, is what associates him with the earlier philhellenes and their quest for wholeness, and sets him against his own scholarly profession. The creative work to which his life will be devoted is the expression of a sensibility which makes it increasingly distasteful, and eventually impossible, to keep any one area of experience permanently apart from any other. Even that commonplace academic distinction between 'intellectual' and 'emotional' becomes ever more unreal. Years later he will note: 'I have at all times written with my whole body and my whole life. I do not know what "purely intellectual" problems are.'[7] *BT* is, in fact, the first of his works for which these words are true.

The other relevant facts about the gifted and isolated individual can be left, for the moment, to emerge from a more detailed discussion of his major preoccupations. To take the philosophical one first, it was actually Nietzsche's isolation at a critical period of his life that helped to create the need which Schopenhauer was to satisfy. But certainly his interest in 'the true and essential problems of life and thought' had begun long before. His first apprehension of such large issues as 'problems' seems to have been during his schooldays at Pforta. After a pious and seemingly untroubled Christian upbringing, he was duly confirmed in 1861 at the age of sixteen, but within a year was already casting a cold eye on the case for a 'literalistic attitude' towards Christian doctrine and asserting that 'the existence of God, immortality, the authority of the Bible, inspiration and other things will always remain problems'.[8] By 1864 his interest in Christianity and his deference to family expectations were still strong enough to lead him to the choice of theology as one of his two subjects at Bonn; but there is no doubt that *belief* was a thing of the past. The next summer he wrote from Bonn to his sister: 'If you want to gain peace of mind and happiness, have faith; if you want to be a disciple of truth, search.'[9]

With hindsight, we can see this loss of faith as one of the formative facts of his life: much of his subsequent thinking is precisely a 'search' for something to fill the void or, more characteristically, for a way of honestly confronting the void. Whether at the time Nietzsche himself felt the loss as so momentous is not clear. At all events, he was unsettled by it and, partly for this reason, was not happy at Bonn. He achieved little in his work and dissipated much of his time in an uncongenial student fraternity. On his arrival at Leipzig in the autumn of 1865, with a largely wasted year behind him and no fixed bearings for the future, he was in low spirits. Cut off from close friends and sympathetic counsellors, and without any creed to turn to for support, he was in an ideal condition to respond to a new spiritual guide: his discovery of Schopenhauer when browsing one day in a Leipzig bookshop seemed like an event preordained. In an autobiographical account written a couple of years later, he described himself as having been 'absolutely alone, full of the most painful experiences and disappointments'; and of his first response to 'Schopenhauer's masterpiece' he wrote that 'in this book, in which every line cried out renunciation, denial and resignation, I saw a mirror in which I espied the whole world, life and my mind depicted in frightful grandeur'.[10]

But the appeal that Schopenhauer had for Nietzsche was far from being merely dependent on temporary circumstances, and it survived the return to everyday optimism that his life at Leipzig gradually produced. There was certainly a specifically doctrinal attraction, which, for a time, was almost overwhelming. In the ensuing months, his letters, glowing with a convert's fervour, faithfully reflect the tenets of Schopenhauerian philosophy: the illusoriness of empirical reality, with all its individual phenomena; and the recognition, behind our illusory world of an ultimate reality that brings no joy, no god, no providence, no ordained meaning, no rational basis to life or to death. Only a blind will-to-exist fills the universe, and the only salvation from it lies in the surrender of the individual will through self-denial. The appeal of such a doctrine for the young Nietzsche was bound to be intensified by Schopenhauer's conception of aesthetic, especially musical, experience as a main escape route from the domination of the will. For Nietzsche's 'aesthetic, especially musical, experience' was already of special importance to him.

Nietzsche, then, became a Schopenhauerian in a state of mind engendered by isolation, although he was soon 'proud and happy' to share his new creed with friends. 'Creed' was, indeed, to some extent how the convert himself saw it at the time: witness the acknowledgement in letters of 1866 and 1867, that such philosophical tenets are not philosophically demonstrable, but are acceptable as art or for their edifying power or simply as faith.[11] Implicit in this admission, however, is the possibility of a more critical stance, and this was not long forthcoming. Uncritical adherence was clearly out of the question by 1868, as appears from various sober notes on the logical problems that he saw in Schopenhauer's system.[12] The bare notion of the will remained important for him and, along with it, the presupposition of irrational nature and the special value of art, but much of the doctrine was no longer operative in this thinking. Nevertheless, his allegiance did not suddenly evaporate and by 1869, on the eve of his departure for Basle, he was still happy to be the central member of a small circle of devotees. The most important of these was Erwin Rohde, a fellow-classicist and contemporary of his at Leipzig. In the late 1860s, Rohde, a sensitive and highly intelligent person, was Nietzsche's closest friend and so kindred a spirit that ambitious, albeit abortive, joint plans were regularly mooted: a collaborative book on Greek literature in 1868 or a year studying together in Paris (scheduled for 1869 and frustrated by Nietzsche's appointment at Basle).[13]

But Schopenhauer could not have had his potent influence on the young scholar without an additional *aesthetic* quality which, in Nietzschean eyes, made him virtually a one-man cultural ideal. From remarkably early in his life, Nietzsche had a strong awareness, visionary rather than analytical, of the problematic nature of modern culture, although initially his perspective could hardly be called original. It was derived in the first place from Goethe and Goethe's Hellenist contemporaries; and it was modified only by the conviction that the ailments which artists and thinkers of that period had identified in the Germany of their day were now more virulent than ever, while an additional threat was posed by the new diseases of mediocrity and the cult of 'progress' (often associated with politicking and liberalism), from which the age of Goethe had been relatively free. Amidst all the complexities of modern culture in which Nietzsche could only see 'desolation and exhaustion', Schopenhauer was 'a Dürer knight', a spiritual guide 'pursuing his terrible path' alone.[14] To Nietzsche he was a thinker who not only valued the right things, notably art, but also embodied them himself: a philosopher with an artist's power of words. He was an upholder of the supreme value of individual genius and its special insights as against everything ordinary and 'philistine'; an *honest* thinker, whose philosophical composure was strenuously acquired, so unlike the easy optimism of his age; a man equipped to inspire a nation, 'the philosopher of a reawakened classicism, a Germanic Hellenism, the philosopher of a regenerated Germany'.[15] Above all, he was seen by the young Nietzsche as the proponent of a *total* philosophy, a vision of life that called for a personal, not merely an intellectual, commitment – a vision that stimulated, and even promised to satisfy, the yearning to be a personal whole attuned to the ultimate values, or non-values, of life. So intently did Nietzsche interpret Schopenhauer's 'personal' relevance at this time, that he could locate the vital centre of the philosopher's system in its therapeutic power to help with the practical crises of living. In a letter of 1867 to a friend on the death of the latter's brother he writes: 'You have experienced at first hand...why our Schopenhauer exalts suffering and sorrow as a glorious fate, as the *deuteros plous* [second way] to the negation of the will...This is a time for you to test for yourself what truth there is in Schopenhauer's doctrine...If [it]...does *not* have the power to raise you up...to that mood where one sees the earthly veils pull away from oneself – then I too want to have nothing more to do with this philosophy.'[16]

GREECE

Schopenhauer's status as total philosopher and cultural ideal lasted longer, in the event, than the doctrinal appeal of his metaphysics. To understand why it should have attracted Nietzsche so strongly at this time, we must turn to the background of his academic specialization, and his great love for Greece. Nietzsche's school, Pforta, had its impressive classical tradition, but his own decision to specialize in classics did not come early or easily. In 1859 the self-conscious schoolboy had written that the most important rule of school life should be 'to educate oneself equally in all sciences, arts, faculties and ensure that body and mind go hand in hand. One should guard against specializing in one's studies'; and in himself he noted 'an extraordinary craving for knowledge and universal culture'[17] – something like an instinct for 'wholeness' was clearly, if naively, operative. Soon, however, restlessness and some undefined ambition began to be apparent. 'I started to feel a revulsion against this desultory wandering over all the departments of knowledge; I wished to force some limitation on myself, so as to probe individual subjects more deeply and thoroughly. I was able to realize this desire agreeably by means of a small scholarly society which I formed with two friends.'[18]

This group, with the grandiose name of *Germania*, was founded in 1860 and survived until 1863. Its concerns were intellectual and cultural. The three members contributed regular essays, or else original compositions, and criticized one another's work at group meetings. Nietzsche's varied contributions included poems, essays on historiography and discussions of the medieval *Nibelungen* saga, but mostly consisted of musical compositions, an indication of his predominant artistic interest at the time. By comparison with music, the visual arts barely touched him (a fact presumably connected with the poor eyesight he had from birth), but he possessed a strong feeling for poetry, especially Romantic poetry. Among other signs of this is a lecture on Byron for the *Germania* and, during the same period, a remarkable 'letter to a friend'[19] in praise of Hölderlin, who was at this time little read. Concomitantly, he felt great enthusiasm for Shakespeare, long since appropriated by the German Romantics as an honorary ancestor. These artistic predilections went hand in hand with a marked interest in aesthetic theory. His notebooks of 1862–3, for instance, contain comments under the heading 'On the Essence of Music', which are probably notes for a two-part *Germania* essay on 'The Demonic in Music', and, again, a set of Emersonian reflections on Nature, beauty and art.[20]

It was during the *Germania* period that Nietzsche's inclination towards ancient Greece seems to have taken its first definite shape, although his distaste for specialization remained. The two attitudes can be found side by side in the letter on Hölderlin, which was written in 1861. 'Nowhere has the longing for Greece been revealed in purer tones', proclaimed Nietzsche, and a few lines earlier, in equally heartfelt terms, he spoke of Hölderlin's 'bitter truths' to his countrymen on the subject of their cultural inadequacies: 'In *Hyperion* he hurls sharp and cutting words at German "barbarism"' – and, above all, 'he hated in Germans the mere specialist, the philistine'. It is evident that even at seventeen Nietzsche took life and his own views on it with great seriousness; also, that implicit in those views was an uneasy relationship, here in its first stage, between the inevitable 'mere specialism' of the professional classical scholar and a growing 'longing for Greece'. As late as 1863 he could still assure his mother that he might turn his attention to almost any subject,[21] but it must have been around this time that a first decision in favour of classics was taken, even though it was not until 1865 at Leipzig that his academic specialization became complete. Bearing in mind the strength of his views on 'mere specialists', we may surely see more than coincidence in the swiftness with which this final commitment was followed by the conversion to Schopenhauer.[22] He opts for a single fragment of European culture and, by way of compensation, he must at once reaffirm that ideal of personal and cultural wholeness which on various grounds he now sees immediately symbolized in Schopenhauer – and not least because Schopenhauer, for all his scorn of the contemporary world, unquestionably belongs to it. The older philosopher offers the young Nietzsche a lifeline between his scholarly avocation and the world outside.

But Nietzsche's motive in opting for classical philology, when he finally did so, was not simple. It was not just the love for the Greeks that he acknowledged later, although certainly that was already present: an autobiographical essay of 1864, for instance, expresses in warm tones his feeling for Greek poetry, including Sophocles and Aeschylus, and for Plato.[23] It was also a desire for therapy, a wish to subordinate himself to the specific kind of 'scientific' discipline that, over the previous half century, classical philology had everywhere become. Looking back on the decision a few years later, he interpreted it in these terms: 'What I wanted was some counterweight to my changeable and restless inclinations, a science that could be pursued with cool impartiality, with cold logic, with regular work, without its results touching me at all deeply.'[24] A peremptory demand for 'wholeness', a specialist 'science' requiring 'cool impartiality', and strong personal feelings for the object of that science – this was a combination which could hardly be stable for long. In the event, what happened was a strengthening of those personal feelings ('I love the Greeks more and more'). This was accompanied by a desire to relate the feelings and their object to the wider issues of life and by a growing resentment of philology as currently practised. The very qualities that had recently prompted him to opt in its favour were now distasteful: its methodical impersonality and the inherent compartmental separateness from 'life' that its impersonal, scientific character presupposed – and with it the all too familiar compartmentalization within the subject itself.

In later years Nietzsche came to have a more favourable attitude to these aspects of classical studies, but for the time being his dissatisfaction was almost unqualified. Thus, from a letter of 1867: 'most philologists lack that elevating total view of antiquity, because they stand too close to the picture and investigate a patch of paint, instead of gazing at the big, bold brushstrokes of the whole painting and – what's more – enjoying them...'; and '...our whole mode of working is quite horrible. The hundred books on the table in front of me are so many tongs that pinch out the nerve of independent thought...one cannot go one's own way independently enough'; and, from 1868, a sardonic dismissal of 'the philologists of our time' for 'their joy at capturing worms and their indifference to the true problems, the urgent problems of life'.[25] The earlier letter reveals, incidentally, how closely his complaint against contemporary philology was related to distaste for contemporary intellectual life in general. His correspondent had lately left the academic world for military service; and with his own bookish situation, so detrimental to 'independent thought', Nietzsche contrasted and, in part, commended his friend's active life: '...not that I applaud your present profession as such, but only insofar as it is the negation of your previous life...With such contrasts, soul and body stay healthy and do not produce those inevitable diseases that result from the preponderance of scholarly activity and from the excessive predominance of physical activity as well... The Greeks were no scholars, but they were also not mindless athletes. If it is so necessary for us to opt one way or the other, is it perhaps that here too Christianity has caused a split in human nature of which the people of harmony knew nothing?' The formulation of the criticism recalls Hölderlin's *Hyperion*, but its intensity arises from Nietzsche's own experience.

And yet, for all his reservations, Nietzsche continued to devote time and energy to orthodox classical scholarship; and he was still prepared for an academic career, albeit with the special aims appropriate to one so sceptical of the established order. He wrote to Rohde in 1868, encouraging his friend to follow suit: 'we must do it simply because we cannot do anything else ...[but]...for our part let us see to it that young philologists are brought up with the necessary scepticism, free from pedantry and the over-valuation of their profession, and behave as genuine promoters of humanistic studies. *Soyons de nôtre siècle*, as the French say – a stance that no one forgets more easily than the trained philologist.'[26] Accordingly, when the call to Basle came in 1869, he accepted. Indeed, despite his disillusion with the present reality and underneath the modest ambition he communicated to Rohde, he cherished an almost missionary hope that if and when he was himself in a position to exert influence, the future of his subject might look altogether different. What he envisaged was an access of 'philosophical' seriousness: the positive alternative to a discredited *status quo* was 'Schopenhauerian'. 'To permeate my discipline with this new blood, to transmit to my listeners that Schopenhauerian seriousness..., this is my wish.'[27] But Nietzsche's use of such terminology tends to mask the actual nature of the alternatives in question. A diagrammatic note of early 1869[28] is closer to the ground: on the one side, academic philology (*Universitätsphilologie*) with its goal of the 'scientific' study of history and language; on the other, classical *education* (*klassische Bildung*) with its acknowledgement of the ancient world as a standard or model for life. Restated in this way, the two aspirations are clearly familiar: the latter is Winckelmann's, the former is Wolf's.

MUSIC: THE CONVERSION TO WAGNER

Nietzsche's great interest in music began early in life. 'Through a peculiar accident, I began to take a passionate interest in music in my ninth year and even started composing immediately.'[29] His devotion to music seems in fact to have been even stronger than his feeling for words: 'there are times when everything...that cannot be grasped in terms of musical relations actually fills me with disgust and horror'.[30] In his *Germania* days before university he may have entertained thoughts of a musical career[31] and, as we have noted, his contributions to that forum were usually musical. In music, unlike literature, he was largely self-taught, but during his schooldays he developed a facility both for improvisation on the piano and for attractive small-scale compositions.

In view of Nietzsche's subsequent adulation of Wagner, it is important to recognize that in these early years his predilections lay elsewhere. Musical opinions among the educated circles of the time tended towards a polarization. On the one side, lovers of the traditional harmonic idiom and formal structuring in which German music had excelled since Handel and Bach favoured such modern representatives of that tradition as Schumann and, a little later, Brahms. On the other side were the proponents of a new 'music of the future' (*Zukunftsmusik*), represented by Berlioz, Liszt, and above all, Wagner, whose restless chromatic explorations, culminating at this period in *Tristan und Isolde* (finished in 1859) and the tetralogy *Der Ring des Nibelungen* (1854–74), most radically undermined traditional diatonic stability. Wagner's compositions, furthermore, involved a dramatic 'programme' on which the full significance of the music was to depend. This represented a challenge to the conventional presupposition of self-contained musical structures, hitherto heeded even by 'dramatic' grand opera. For in that traditional genre, which Wagner set himself to transcend, dramatic action was customarily relegated to the dialogue or recitative, whereas throughout the arias the musical element was hardly less dominant than in any 'absolute' music. The operas of Gluck and Donizetti, Mozart and Meyerbeer, however unlike in other ways, were at one in this: music and drama usually alternated, and the Wagnerian ideal of music as a means to a dramatic end was only occasionally in view.

In university circles there was for a long time little sympathy for the innovators, and in his younger days Nietzsche's own tastes inclined the same way. He knew something of the new music, but neither the movement as a whole nor Wagner's particular achievement within it meant anything special to him. During the early and middle sixties he was firmly attached to such composers as Bach, Haydn and, especially, Schumann. For a time he showed a certain curiosity about Liszt and something of the same kind about Wagner.[32] He evidently found the new idiom interestingly problematic,[33] but not attractive enough to compel his full attention.

In the autobiographical *Ecce Homo*, written in 1888, Nietzsche asserted flamboyantly: 'From the moment when there was a piano score of *Tristan* – my compliments, Herr von Bülow – I was a Wagnerian.'[34] This claim has been shown to be a considerable misstatement.[35] It was through the *Germania* that Nietzsche encountered the piano score of *Tristan* in 1861, and though this and other Wagnerian topics figured prominently in *Germania* discussions, they had little place in Nietzsche's own contributions. It is true that he seems to have been sufficiently interested to use Wagner as the extreme example of 'the demonic in music' for his *Germania* paper on that theme; and also that, following his exposure to the music of *Tristan*, some of his own compositions of 1861 have a marked Wagnerian flavour (in eccentric combination with formally archaic polyphony) – but this flirtation was short-lived and not repeated until his conversion to Wagner seven years later.[36] We may well find it significant that there is no evidence during this period of any attempt on his part to acquaint himself with Wagner's own voluminous theoretical prose.[37]

During the mid-sixties, Nietzsche's traditionalism seems even to have stiffened: certainly his attitude towards anything Wagnerian became explicitly antipathetic. During his year at Bonn (1864–5), he came under the influence of the distinguished music critic Eduard Hanslick who was, where Wagner's experiments were concerned, largely a traditionalist and a sceptic. From Nietzsche's private notes of the period, it appears that his conservative inclinations were reinforced by Hanslick's insistence on traditional formal principles of composition and the orthodox ideal of autonomous musical structures; and it is no surprise to find distinct hostility in Nietzsche's recorded comments on the new piano score of *Die Walküre* in 1866.[38] In the meantime, of course, he had become a Schopenhauerian, the relevant effect of which can only have been to confirm the validity of his preoccupation with music and his suspicion of the new musical idiom. For while Schopenhauer gave music a gratifyingly important rôle within his scheme of things, the music on which he based his theories was primarily the formally respectable tradition that he saw represented in Haydn and Mozart; and the importance he gave to music turned to a large extent on its supposed capacity to foster the right – dispassionate and otherworldly – response. And while conservative, 'Hanslickian', music might, at least in part, elicit such a response, the new music was likely to lead in the opposite direction. If a dispassionate response was obligatory, then Wagnerian music, in particular, with its irresistibly sensuous-emotional appeal, was bound to seem wholly illegitimate. In addition, the rôle of the words in Wagner's music drama would be open to damaging criticism on Schopenhauerian grounds, although this further problem only impinged fully on Nietzsche at a later date, when his interest in Wagner was of a different order altogether.[39]

Nietzsche's musical attitudes remained more or less constant until the summer of 1868, when the conversion to Wagner began. Unlike his earlier conversion to Schopenhauer, this one involved no sudden, overwhelming revelation, but rather a gradual heightening of interest and enthusiasm over several months. The catalyst of the change was the much publicized premiere of *Die Meistersinger* in Munich in June. Nietzsche was not present, but whereas the premiere of *Tristan* in 1865 had not prompted any discernible reaction in him, on this occasion he took a much livelier interest and during the following months familiarized himself with the work through the score. In view of the terms in which he was later to express his enthusiasm for Wagner, it is interesting to note what it was that first seriously attracted him: nor the morbid metaphysical-flavoured world of romance, the hypnotic emotional intensity and musical 'modernity' of *Tristan*, representing, at the time, the high point of Wagner's most distinctive line of development; nor indeed the available parts of the similarly 'modern', but emotionally more robust, *Ring*; rather, the musically 'reactionary' *Meistersinger* that deferred to traditional expectations of harmony, tonality and musical organization and depicted through the medium of 'healthy' comic opera the successful struggle of artistic genius against stifling Hanslickian convention.

Signs of Nietzsche's growing enthusiasm are visible in his correspondence during the summer. An enigmatic reference to *Meistersinger* in a letter to Rohde in August[40] is followed two months later by an avowed relish for the emotive Wagnerian ethos to which *Meistersinger* presents, comparatively, such a contrast. His comments here, interestingly enough, were occasioned by a reading of some essays on musical topics by Otto Jahn,[41] Ritschl's former colleague and opponent at Bonn. 'Recently I also read...Jahn's essays on music, including the ones on Wagner. You have to have some enthusiasm to do such a person justice, whereas Jahn has an instinctive antipathy to him and listens with his ears half stopped up. Still, I grant him many points, particularly his maintaining that Wagner is representative of a modern dilettantism that sucks up and swallows everything of any artistic interest; but precisely from this standpoint, one cannot be astonished enough at... a disposition that allies indestructible energy with many-sided artistic gifts... Moreover, Wagner has a sphere of feeling totally hidden from O. Jahn, one of those "wholesome provincials", to whom the *Tannhäuser* saga and the *Lohengrin* atmosphere are a closed world. In Wagner, as in Schopenhauer, I like the ethical air, the Faustian odour, cross, death, grave etc.'[42]

These remarks show Nietzsche's attitude a stage further on, but still in a state of transition. Wagner's appeal is becoming stronger and more general and the association of his name with Schopenhauer's[43] indicates a new degree of commendation. At the same time, Nietzsche's stance, though extremely favourable, is still critical, and his enthusiasm is qualified by a certain self-conscious humour: witness the blandly ironic use of 'wholesome' (*ein Gesunder*) and the self-deflating 'etc.', which in the German original is preceded by an extravagantly formulated double rhyme: *die ethische Luft, der faustische Duft, Kreuz, Tod und Gruft etc.* Furthermore, at the time of writing it was still the 'healthy' *Meistersinger* that in fact came first in his esteem. It is therefore slightly ironic that it should have been this same *Meistersinger* which now finally stirred his feelings to the point where any 'healthy' critical stance became impossible. In late October he wrote again to Rohde: 'This evening I was at the Euterpe Society, which has started its winter concerts, and refreshed myself with the Prelude to *Tristan und Isolde* as well as the Overture to *Die Meistersinger.* I cannot get myself to react with critical coolness towards this music; every tissue, every nerve vibrates in me and it is a long time since I had such an enduring feeling of rapture as when listening to the latter overture.'[44] *Meistersinger*, then, still came before *Tristan*, but such distinctions were fast losing their significance. Wagnerian music in general had now taken its hold and was irresistibly leading Nietzsche to admit a response diametrically opposed to the objectivity that had commended itself to him before.

It is possible that for all its lofty consequences, Nietzsche's willingness to expose himself to *Meistersinger* in the first place arose out of nothing loftier than social contacts: the coincidence that a sister of Wagner's living in Leipzig was friendly with Professor Ritschl and his wife, with whom Nietzsche was on excellent terms at the time. At all events, it was through this channel that in early November he engineered[45] a meeting with Wagner. From a famous letter to Rohde we know of the powerful effect that the meeting had on him.[46] He felt himself to be in the presence of a creative genius and experienced 'enjoyments of such peculiar piquancy that today I am not quite my old self...'. The composer's liveliness and wit impressed him and, not least, his enthusiasm (unsuspected by Nietzsche) for Schopenhauer: 'You will understand how much I enjoyed hearing him speak of Schopenhauer with indescribable warmth, what he owed to him, how he is the only philosopher who has understood the essence of music.' Wagner, for his part, was equally taken with his gifted young admirer and, as Nietzsche explained to Rohde, 'when we were getting ready to leave, he shook my hand warmly and with great friendliness invited me to visit him, in order to make music and talk philosophy.' Contact with the man Wagner now kindled an interest in Wagner the theorist and within a few weeks Nietzsche was writing again to Rohde to impress on his friend his high opinion of Wagner's *Opera and Drama*,[47] a treatise written nearly twenty years before, but apparently now providing Nietzsche's first direct acquaintance with any of Wagner's theoretical works.[48] In January 1869 he travelled to Dresden to attend the local premiere of *Meistersinger*, whose special place in his affections was unchanged,[49] and on 17 May, now at Basle, he was finally able to accept Wagner's invitation and visit him at Tribschen, his house near Lucerne in Switzerland.

Why the conversion to Wagner in 1868–9? It was not simply the attraction of Wagner's music: Nietzsche, after all, had known some Wagnerian music, including the quintessentially Wagnerian *Tristan*, for years without feeling any overwhelming pull. We can better appreciate the conversion by thinking back to the philosopher Schopenhauer, with whose name Nietzsche was now so assiduously coupling Wagner's as twin deities, *dei maximi*.[50] By 1868 Schopenhauer remained a central fact of life for Nietzsche, but hardly, in himself, a source of fresh inspiration; if anything, Nietzsche's more critical attitude towards this first *deus maximus* had left something of a vacuum. Once he had been won over by *Meistersinger*, with its triumphant portrayal of genius, Wagner began to assume in his mind a heroic, aesthetic, *Schopenhauerian* status, so that it was natural for him to couple the two even before he had any reason to suppose that Wagner was at all interested in the philosopher.[51] Wagner's profession of sympathy for Schopenhauer at the November meeting could only have come as the happiest of coincidences, while, in general, this first experience of the composer's powerful personality confirmed and added to his new status: Wagner was at one with Schopenhauer and he was (to Nietzsche's way of thinking) an artist such as Schopenhauer himself would have wished him. 'Wagner, as I now know him from his music, his poetry, his aesthetic, not least from that fortunate meeting with him, is the flesh-and-blood illustration of what Schopenhauer calls a genius.'[52] It was, naturally, a substantial part of Wagner's appeal that he was 'flesh and blood', a living genius, unlike Schopenhauer (who had died in 1860). It also seems likely that Wagner, thirty-one years Nietzsche's senior and born in the same year as Nietzsche's long dead father, was in some sense a father-figure and additionally attractive on this account. The passion of Nietzsche's attachment – and, still more, of his later assertion of independence – becomes more explicable in this light; and 'passion', Nietzsche wrote years afterwards, 'is the only word for it'.[53] In some ways, too, the relationship smacks of a Platonic love-affair – in the fullest sense of that word, with the young man learning wisdom at the feet of the older.

But something is still needed to explain Nietzsche's willingness to commit himself so totally at this particular time; and the November meeting, usually taken to be the cause, cannot by itself have been sufficient. The answer, we suggest, is that Wagner now represented precisely what Schopenhauer had been before: a lifeline to save himself from drowning in his professional specialization, as he went further and further out into it. The propriety of coupling the two names, therefore, could hardly be more complete. It was no accident that Nietzsche's move to Leipzig, implying the decision to specialize in classics, was followed by an overnight conversion to Schopenhauer; and no accident, again, that his final acceptance of a classical career should have been so closely associated in time with his commitment, after so many years of desultory acquaintance, to Wagner. Nietzsche's first news of the offer of a chair at Basle came in January 1869 and we have on record, as it happens, his immediate reaction. A letter to Rohde contains, half-way through, the sign 'N.B.' and, at the end, the following: 'At the point marked N.B., a message came calling me into town as soon as I reached the foot of the page; now returned, I am trembling all over and cannot free myself of it even by pouring out my heart to you. *Absit diabolus*! *Adsit amicissumus Erwinus*! [The devil leave me! Friend Erwin be with me!]'[54] It was with Rohde that Nietzsche had intended to spend the forthcoming year in Paris on what might have amounted to a non-classical refresher course.[55] In November 1868 he had written to Rohde: 'I intend to get through all the business of habilitation by Easter [sc. 1869] and finish my doctorate at the same time.' Then would come the journey to Paris, after which (as he noted in another connection in the same letter) 'it will be all right in this academic career'.[56]

'*Absit diabolus*': the strength of Nietzsche's feelings needs no commentary. In the light of the order of events involved in the earlier conversion to Schopenhauer, we can surely point to this moment as decisive. If Nietzsche was to come to terms with a specialized academic career, his need of a compensatory allegiance was extreme. Since June 1868 his enthusiasm for Wagner and his works had been steadily growing. The allegiance he needed was now to hand. From this moment, but only from this moment, he was 'a Wagnerian' without any qualification.

3

Biographical background II: the genesis of *The Birth of Tragedy*

BASLE, TRIBSCHEN, AND THE FIRST PLANS FOR A BOOK

Up to this point in our narrative, it has been possible, with some difficulty, to keep the three main strands of Nietzsche's life apart. With the beginning of his Basle period, it is virtually impossible to separate these or any aspects of his life or work, including the complicated genesis of *BT*. Everything converges – and Nietzsche himself does everything possible to ensure that it should. The convergence, in fact, reflects his first full-scale, and characteristically self-conscious, attempt to oppose fragmentation in favour of a whole response to experience. As he puts it, with a certain dispassionate irony, in a letter of early 1870: 'I observe how my philosophical, moral and scholarly endeavours strive towards a single goal and that I may perhaps become the first philologist ever to achieve wholeness.'[1] And how should he achieve it? Throughout this early period, 'Schopenhauer' is the device behind which Nietzsche is mustering his increasingly independent thinking. And so he can still express his aspiration towards that 'wholeness' in terms of a unifying Schopenhauerianism. In September 1869 he writes: 'I really do stand now at a centre from which Schopenhauerian threads reach out into all parts of the world'; and it was in April, on the eve of his departure for Basle, that he had expressed the ambition to infuse his own philological discipline with 'that Schopenhauerian seriousness...; I should like to be something more than a drill-master for competent philologists – the generation of present-day teachers, the care of the growing younger generation, this is what I have in mind.'[2]

Despite these protestations, however, it can hardly be denied that Nietzsche's main enthusiasm, and the main stimulus to his enthusiasms in general, was no longer Schopenhauer, but the composer whose devotee he was and whose intimate friend he shortly became. 'Intimate' is not, perhaps, the right word. There is a case for saying that Nietzsche's relationships, though often intense, hardly ever permitted the degree of self-revelation, at least on his side, that true intimacy presupposes. His friendship with Rohde might be an exception here; his relationship with Wagner was probably not. Nevertheless, there is no doubt that this relationship flourished. The visit to Wagner's Swiss home, Tribschen, in mid-May was the first of over twenty such visits made between 1869 and 1872, the year in which first *BT* appeared and then, a few months later, Wagner, with his wife Cosima, moved to Bayreuth in preparation for the foundation of the *Festspielhaus*. Cosima, illegitimate daughter of Franz Liszt and wife of Wagner's friend Hans von Bülow, eloped with Wagner in 1866 and married him in 1870. A woman of character and finesse and blessed with a total devotion to her new husband, she played a large part in setting the artistic tone at Tribschen, which Nietzsche was to remember with admiration all his life.

The first years at Basle were, for Nietzsche, the Tribschen years. His rapport with the Wagner household comes across vividly from letters to Rohde in the late summer of 1869: 'Just recently I've paid four visits there in quick succession and a letter takes wing in the same direction almost every week'; 'On the visit before last, during the night, a baby boy called Siegfried was born. On my last visit there, Wagner had just finished his composition *Siegfried* and was full of the most exuberant sense of his artistic strength.'[3]

The proximity of Tribschen to Basle obviously made contact easier, but it was undoubtedly Nietzsche's new professional eminence that made it particularly welcome to Wagner and led to a rapid development of the relationship between the two. It is clear that Wagner became genuinely fond of Nietzsche, but for all the young professor's admiration of him as a person, Wagner – it is a notorious fact – was a supremely egocentric man; it is easily inferred that he glimpsed in Nietzsche a means of gaining respectability in hitherto hostile academic circles, and that it was this glimpse, as much as anything, that encouraged his fond feelings to grow. At the same time the young scholar's concern with large aesthetic-cultural questions and his deep interest in Schopenhauer were felt as a stimulus by Wagner himself. Nietzsche was therefore made increasingly welcome. He became a party to household secrets and to Wagner's cherished artistic plans. He was shown unpublished essays and given his own room to work in. Not surprisingly, his enthusiasm knew no bounds. In August 1869 he wrote to his mother: 'I have never felt happier than during the last few days. The warm, hearty and increasing closeness with Wagner and Frau von Bülow, the complete agreement between us on all the questions that chiefly interest us, Wagner absolutely in the prime of his genius...'[4] In Wagner he could see an 'absolute immaculate greatness' and a 'depth of seriousness' such that at Tribschen he felt 'in the presence of one of the century's elect'.[5] 'Dear friend', he wrote to Rohde in September, 'what I learn there, and see, and hear, and understand, is indescribable. Schopenhauer, Goethe, Aeschylus and Pindar still live, I assure you.'[6] In 1888, a decade after total estrangement had come between them, Nietzsche was still able to look back to his days with Wagner at Tribschen as 'days of trust, optimism, sublime accidents, profound moments'.[7]

Nietzsche's Wagnerian experience affected him profoundly and pervasively. If Schopenhauer had given him the notion of a personal vision of life, Wagner gave him first-hand knowledge of a creative talent and the ambition to emulate its cultural achievements. At the same time, the experience was formative in a more immediately practical way. In the first place, Wagner and the ideal of his music drama directly influenced the direction of Nietzsche's classical thinking. Not that he was suddenly drawn into entirely new areas of interest: it was more a matter of being drawn back, with a new urgency, into old ones. The fact was that Wagnerian music drama claimed a relationship with Greek tragedy and that the new status of music drama in Nietzsche's thoughts sufficed to activate and inform an interest he had taken in the Greek tragedians years before: witness his Pforta dissertation on the *Oedipus Rex* (which, prophetically enough, actually alluded at one point[8] to the analogy between Wagner and the Greeks). But hitherto that interest had been merely one among many; his temperament had precluded any drastic specialization, and he worked on an almost random variety of Greek topics, with a discernible bias only towards philosophy. Now his professional interests began to assume a pointed interrelation. He chose, for example, to lecture to his students largely on Greek subjects which were associable, however indirectly, with the new enthusiasm. Between the summer of 1869 and the winter of 1870–1 his lectures included courses on metrics, a field fundamental to the consideration of Greek music; on two tragedies, Aeschylus' *Libation Bearers* and Sophocles' *Oedipus Rex*; and on lyric poetry, which in Greece was originally and characteristically *sung* poetry and which included the dithyramb, that special kind of sung poetry originally employed in the orgiastic worship of the fertility god, Dionysus, and conventionally regarded as ancestral to Greek tragedy. And his notes for the course on lyric (prepared in the spring of 1869)[9] show him devoting ten times more space to the dithyramb, of which next to nothing had survived from antiquity, than to the epinician, the kind immortalized by Pindar and the only kind that *had* survived in any bulk.[10] It is clearly a new preoccupation with tragedy that explains the disproportion – tragedy *and its origins*: in the historically minded nineteenth century, no one with intellectual pretensions could think of an entity without also looking to its origins, however remote or obscure.

Outside the Hellenic sphere, too, Wagner's influence materialized in the form of a revival of earlier preoccupations: a renewal of Nietzsche's old interest in large problems of aesthetics and art as a whole. But for Nietzsche 'art as a whole' and 'the Hellenic sphere' were simply not separable, any more than they had been for Winckelmann. Any thought he had about Greek art was a thought about art *per se*: a Greek instance was not, for pragmatic purposes, *an* instance but *the* instance. But if Nietzsche stood with the earlier philhellenes in this way, he was explicitly against them in another. For thanks once more to his Wagnerian experience, he was beginning to formulate a new interpretation of art, art as a whole, and, in accordance with the given pragmatic logic, a new interpretation of the 'Hellenic sphere' as well: a view of Greece and Greek art in direct opposition to the traditional view of which Winckelmann was a prime source. Nietzsche himself was, as usual, self-consciously aware of what was going on. In October 1869 he wrote to Rohde: 'a whole lot of aesthetic problems and answers have been bubbling inside me for the last few years...Of course, Wagner is in a very pregnant sense beneficial, especially as an example incomprehensible on the basis of traditional aesthetics...'; and a few months later he was proclaiming to another correspondent a 'marvellously new and changed...Greek world'.[11]

The 'traditional aesthetics' which Wagner was, in Nietzsche's eyes, helping to bring into question had its roots in the aesthetics of Winckelmann and, among others, of Lessing, whose classic discussion of poetry and the plastic arts, *Laocoon* (1766), Nietzsche had studied privately in 1865.[12] Whatever Lessing's disagreements with Winckelmann, he had shared Winckelmann's estimate of *beauty* as the goal and supreme achievement of Greek art. It was this principle that seemed now to be inadequate. If beauty was sovereign for Greece, it was sovereign everywhere. But Wagner's art, so irresistible and so much to the fore in Nietzsche's thinking, seemed to presuppose some value other than – or in addition to – beauty: and was this not also true of Greek art, on the basis of which the theory of beauty had been largely formed? Having declared the new music to be 'incomprehensible on the basis of traditional aesthetics', Nietzsche at once went on to sum up the task he saw before him: 'the thing above all is to get beyond Lessing's *Laocoon*'.[13] In saying this, it is likely that he had in mind not merely Lessing's criterion of beauty, but his fundamental contrast between poetry and the visual arts. Nietzsche was soon to substitute a new opposition, whose polar extremes were occupied by visual art and *music*. But that was still to come. For the time being, his dissent from 'traditional aesthetics' was very much a matter of finding his way among various alternative sets of ideas. From as far back as late 1868 items in his notebooks show this happening. One sequence of entries, for instance, seemingly associates the words 'aesthetic' and 'tragedy'; another connects Greek drama with 'optimism and pessimism', a new polarity destined to exercise his mind for years to come; and another, after a list of topics that includes 'development of tragedy' and 'Lessing, Winckelmann', offers a brief theoretical discussion of 'development' that refers to 'music', 'opera', and another notion of significance for the future, 'instinct'.[14] The associations among these items, however, serve to remind us once more of Nietzsche's relation with earlier German theorists, Winckelmann among them. 'Aesthetics' in these exploratory notes is not confined to art, not even to 'art as a whole'. It runs into history, psychology and moral philosophy, into life itself. We can see in this Nietzsche's aspirations towards a total philosophy of life. We can also note that the relating of the artistic to the existential is characteristic of a long line of German writers. The word 'aesthetic' itself acquired its modern academic denotation in eighteenth-century German philosophy – in the writings of Alexander Gottlieb Baumgarten and his disciple Immanuel Kant;[15] but the most significant of German 'aesthetic' enquiries have invariably moved beyond 'aesthetic' in the narrow sense, and often into a quest for the 'whole man'. Schiller's *On the Aesthetic Education of Man* (1795) represents one of Nietzsche's most celebrated precedents.

The new direction of Nietzsche's interests was first made public in early 1870 in two lectures with the suggestive titles, 'Greek Music Drama' and 'Socrates and Tragedy'.[16] In these lectures we can identify the beginnings of *BT*. Not only do they represent the first substantial draft of much of the material that was to be more fully worked out there. They also open up a breach with scholarly orthodoxy which *BT* was to make final. Nietzsche's inaugural lecture, it is true, had alarmed Ritschl by suggesting that 'all philological activity should be embraced and defined by a philosophical outlook',[17] but that (in a lecture on Homer) was merely a statement of intent. Now, however, Nietzsche was making his first serious attempt to put into practice the 'wholeness' he aspired to. He was treating 'the classics' as one coherent entity and, without apology, bringing that new entity and his extra-classical orientations together. Personal involvement was implicit in the tone and the procedures involved: the matters under consideration were treated as if they did matter; epochs and makers of epochs were sharply characterized and subjected to urgent evaluation.

The first lecture was given in mid-January. In it Nietzsche attempted to illuminate Greek tragedy with a modern parallel, grand opera. Greek tragedy, he impressed on his audience, had been a total art form, a *Gesamtkunst* (Wagner's slogan, although Wagner's name was not mentioned), to suit an age of whole men: a poetic drama that made use of architecture (the theatre), painting (scenery and costume), song, dance and music; a drama created amid 'perfection and harmony' by 'artistic man',[18] who, at least in the earlier part of the fifth century, the time of Aeschylus, was poet, composer, conductor, producer and actor in one; a drama performed at the communal festival of Dionysus before an audience which brought to the theatre something of the instinctive, rapturous spirit from which, in the Dionysiac celebrations, tragedy had originated in the first place. For tragedy and true art in general must (this was implicit) be essentially the product of instinct. Despite the absence of Wagner's name, it must have been sufficiently evident that the real parallel offered was not with opera as such, but with Wagner alone: an insistence on traditional opera's inherent inferiority and a brief allusion at the end of the lecture to its new rival 'music drama' were enough. Nietzsche, however, made no attempt to demonstrate the aptness of his particular parallel, and the plausibility of the detailed propositions was not thereby enhanced.

The second lecture, closely connected with the first and, like the first, closing with a portentous allusion to contemporary music drama, was given at the beginning of February, and dealt with the mysterious 'death' of tragedy at the end of the fifth century. Its chief heterodoxy, ironically enough, was the large theory of Greek cultural development invoked to explain the mystery: ironically, because the view of Greek culture actually advanced was based – with explicit acknowledgement – on ideas familiar to all classical scholars and accepted by them without demur, but accepted only as a purely historical phenomenon. Their source was Aristophanes, comic poet, critic of his times, and younger contemporary of Sophocles and Euripides, the two tragedians whose almost simultaneous deaths inspired his comedy, *The Frogs* (405). From this play, taken in conjunction with earlier comedies, an interpretation of Athenian culture can be extracted which is, in essence, coherent and credible – even though there is considerable room for argument about how seriously the comic author might have liked the interpretation to be taken. At all events, the great age of Athens, on this reading, was the age of the Persian wars in the early years of the fifth century, a time of supreme political endeavour and a time when the grandest of all tragic dramatists, Aeschylus, was there to provide the spiritual leadership of the city. By comparison, the Athens of Aristophanes' own day, at the end of the century, was a city fallen from greatness, and not only because of the protracted destruction brought about by the Peloponnesian war. That war had, rather, intensified the real causes of decline: social and cultural changes that were already operative and that were, almost uniformly, changes for the worse. Prominent among these developments was the rise of a new *intellectual* attitude towards the traditional, stable bases of Greek life, above all, its instinctive religious basis. The new intellectualism, represented in different spheres by the 'modern' tragedian Euripides and the philosopher Socrates, was both disturbing and destructive. As regards tragedy, spiritually the city's focal point, Euripides was not and could not be a spiritual guide as Aeschylus had once been, although the need was, no doubt, greater than in Aeschylus' time. Most melancholy fact of all, however, there was no going back. Euripides (and with him the more 'traditional' Sophocles) was dead, and degenerate as he might have been, the scale of his artistic gifts was not in doubt; but there was no successor of equivalent stature to mend matters: like Athens herself, tragedy was in decline.

Building on this Aristophanic foundation, in the second of his lectures Nietzsche sharpened the relationship between Euripides, Socrates, and tragedy's demise. Euripides, the intellectual Euripides, was the 'poet of Socratic rationalism' and tragedy did not simply die *after* him: it was 'Socratism' in its Euripidean embodiment that killed it, although this destructive tendency preceded Socrates himself and affected even Sophocles. As in the earlier lecture, therefore, the most positive valuation was given to Aeschylus, while the harshest words of all were reserved for Socrates' pupil Plato, who translated into paradoxically artistic form his master's rationalistic distrust of instinct and instinctive art. But it was not only its a-rational basis that damned tragedy in Socratistic eyes. It was also its insight into the a-rational nature of life itself. Inherent in Socratism was the optimistic insistence that life must make rational sense, whereas true tragedy was pessimistic and found in life only 'terror' and 'absurdity'.[19]

These propositions are large and open to a variety of possible objections. They are also inextricably bound up with evaluations which were at the time extremely unfashionable: not so much the depreciation of Euripides, who, although the most admired of the tragic poets in later antiquity, hardly approached that popularity again until the twentieth century (and who, in any case, had been subjected to a famous critique in the lectures of A. W. Schlegel as long ago as 1808);[20] rather, the elevation of 'primitive' Aeschylus above even Sophocles, and the disrespect shown towards Socrates and the 'divine' Plato. Apart from anything else, the dethronement of Sophocles – and Plato – in favour of Aeschylus represented a challenge to the ideals on which German Hellenism had been founded and to which academic circles in general still generally adhered. As against the classical, the serenely beautiful, Nietzsche was opting for the archaic.[21]

One novelty Nietzsche did spare his audience, a new antithesis that was not yet fully worked out, but was, no doubt, the object of much private thought at this time: the Apolline (*das Apollinische*) and the Dionysiac (*das Dionysische*).[22] This celebrated polarity was not actually invented by Nietzsche, but derives its fame from his very particular and original use of it in *BT*. The distinction concerns, in the first instance, the two Greek gods Apollo, lawgiver and god of light, and Dionysus, a god of life and yet a sinister, 'dark', force. As Nietzsche uses them, however, the names denote not merely this pair of very different Greek deities, but two large, supra-historical, and diametrically opposite aspects of art and existence in general. It was these two terms that he was to use in *BT* to symbolize his alternative to the single Winckelmann–Lessing principle of 'beauty'. But in his two lectures he contented himself with a couple of scattered references to 'Apolline clarity' and tragedy's – actually Shakespearean tragedy's – 'Dionysiac' quality.[23] The audience was given no hint that he was envisaging the terms as an antithesis, let alone that he was feeling his way towards significant categories of thought, although from various notes from the winter of 1869–70 it is clear that he was now doing just that.[24] Nevertheless, the world of classical scholarship was left in no doubt about one thing. On top of his other heterodoxies, Nietzsche's criticism of 'Socratism' implied, as he was only too well aware, a question mark against pure intellectual inquiry as such, against *Wissenschaft*. And with their given tone and range, the two lectures proclaimed that *Altertumswissenschaft*, the pure intellectual and compartmental study of antiquity, was not the least of his particular targets. Here, then, were the first tangible fruits of his aspirations towards 'wholeness'.

That last, familiar, word was used by Nietzsche himself precisely in this context and at this time : 'I observe how my philosophical, moral and scholarly endeavours strive towards a single goal and that I may perhaps become the first philologist ever to achieve wholeness.' So much we have already quoted. The continuation of the passage is to the point: 'How marvellously new and changed history looks to me, especially the Greek world! I would like to send you my most recent lectures, the second of which ("Socrates and Tragedy") has been understood here as a chain of paradoxes and has aroused hatred and anger in some quarters. Offence must come. I have, by and large, already stopped taking any notice.'[25] Nietzsche, then, was as aware of the dangers on his path as of its necessity. In a memorable letter to Rohde, written at the same time, he envisaged his eventual goal: 'I gave a lecture here on "Socrates and Tragedy" which excited terror and incomprehension. On the other hand, it has strengthened the ties with my Tribschen friends even more...Richard Wagner has also most touchingly indicated the aim he sees mapped out for me. This is all very frightening. You know what Ritschl has said about me. But I refuse to be tempted: I really have no literary ambition at all; I don't need to conform to a prevailing stereotype in the search for distinguished and illustrious positions. But when the time comes, I shall express myself with as much seriousness and freedom of mind as possible. Scholarship [*Wissenschaft*], art and philosophy are now growing together inside me so much that in any case I'll be giving birth to centaurs one day.'[26]

What Ritschl had said one can gather from his testimonials that had helped to bring Nietzsche to Basle: his pupil was 'a phenomenon' who would simply be able to do anything he chose to do.[27] Wagner's comments, made on reading the two lectures, were more specific. Full of admiration and impressed above all by the signs of Nietzsche's originality of mind and literary power, he saw in him a new kind of worker for the cultural cause with which he identified his own ambitions: 'Now you must show what philology is for, and help me bring about the grand "renaissance"...' And Wagner spelled out the means: 'I should like to advise you not to touch on such incredible views in short essays written...for popular effect, but...to concentrate on a larger and more comprehensive work on this subject.'[28]

Years afterwards, in fact decades afterwards, when Nietzsche himself was no longer available for comment, his sister repeatedly asserted that as a young professor he had always intended to produce a 'large' book on Greece, not one dealing with, or centred on, a single topic, but a book that would deal comprehensively with various aspects of Greek civilization.[29] Although widely accepted, the claim is hard to substantiate, not so much because of Nietzsche's professed lack of 'literary ambition' (a somewhat disingenuous profession in any case), but for want of any decisive evidence in, for instance, the copious private notes surviving from his first years at Basle. In his notebooks of 1869–71 we find an extraordinary profusion of plans for a book:[30] one or two are lists of wide-ranging topics arranged to form a more or less coherent whole;[31] most are variations on the theme of tragedy. In itself, a plan, even a coherent plan, can easily imply a vague aspiration rather than a definite commitment; and it seems that, though not averse to the occasional vague aspiration, Nietzsche was in fact committed to nothing – except to the book on tragedy that eventually materialized.

What we do know is that in the autumn of 1869 Nietzsche *was* contemplating a large book, but one of a different kind. On 16 October he wrote for advice to his mentor, Ritschl. He felt he ought now to be thinking of writing a book – but on what? A major work on a coherent subject seemed out of the question, with much of his time fragmented by preparation for lectures and classes. What he could do, if Ritschl thought it a plan worth pursuing, was put together a book of miscellaneous bits and pieces, part literary history, part 'new ideas and views' (*neue Ansichten und Aussichten*) of an as yet unspecified nature, part textual criticism. And he added his hope that in about two years he would have a more straightforward kind of book ready, developing his published studies on Diogenes Laertius, and possibly also an edition of Aeschylus' *Libation Bearers* (on which he had been lecturing earlier in the year).[32] Without any direct reference to this last suggestion, Ritschl, in his reply a few weeks later,[33] implicitly endorsed it. To the idea of a miscellany he gave a firm no. There was no hurry and for a first book something unified was essential: a couple of years' delay was of no importance. Nietzsche took the advice. He gave the miscellany no further thought.[34]

The subjects of Nietzsche's two public lectures were already chosen by the time of his letter to Ritschl, as we can see from a letter to a friend in late September.[35] But the letter to Ritschl (if we take it at face value, as we presumably should) shows that Nietzsche had as yet no thought of *basing* a book on these subjects, although something pertinent to 'Greek music drama' or 'Socrates and tragedy' would, no doubt have been among the various matters envisaged for the miscellany in the 'literary history' or the 'new ideas and views'.[36] When first envisaged, then, the lectures were not seen as the core of a forthcoming book, even though (with their Wagnerian connection) they bore on his current preoccupation – and even though he was currently casting around for a subject for a book. But we can surely reconstruct the pattern of events whereby the lectures did become the basis of the book that in fact materialized. Once Ritschl had scotched the idea of a miscellany, only something 'unified' would do. The material of the two lectures, though not originally envisaged in this connection, provided the starting point – but only in the light of Wagner's flattering advice to 'concentrate on a larger and more comprehensive work on this subject'. Wagner's suggestion that such a book would help to usher in a new 'renaissance' must have made his advice irresistible.

Wagner's rôle in the genesis of *BT* has not hitherto been accurately defined. It was twofold: first, the material of the book had a Wagnerian stimulus behind it and a discernible 'Wagnerian connection'; and secondly, the decision to write a whole book on the basis of that material was prompted by Wagner's personal advocacy. Having emerged from this complex background, the book evinced an eccentric fidelity to Ritschl's advice, when it duly appeared after the suggested 'couple of years'. Compared with the rejected miscellany, it was even less what that orthodox scholar could approve, but it was certainly 'unified' – in more senses than one.

THE PROBLEM OF THE GENESIS

It will already be apparent from our narrative that the genesis of *BT* is far from straightforward. It is as well at this point to confirm that it is so and to add that there are further complications, bibliographical and biographical. In the first place, our picture of the genesis to a large extent depends on the interpretation and dating of Nietzsche's literary remains (the *Nachlass*), and specifically on the mass of plans, fragments and isolated notes which survive in notebooks from his first years in Basle. This material has recently (1978) been published in its entirety for the first time,[37] but many problems remain unsolved – or insoluble. The corpus relevant to *BT* numbers hundreds of separate items and fills about four hundred printed pages; it is contained in fourteen different notebooks, written over a period of two years (autumn 1869 to autumn 1871).[38] The notebooks are datable, but each one may cover a month, a few months, or a year or more, and many of them were used concurrrently. This means that the individual items in each notebook can rarely be dated with any precision and that notes in one notebook may, and often do, presuppose plans in another; even within single notebooks it is not always possible to determine whether items in a sequence belong together.[39] Nor is it always clear whether a given list of topics constitutes an actual plan for a book or not, or whether a given note pertains to *our* book at all.[40] Furthermore, the dating of a notebook need not be the same as dating its contents. On the one hand, an item may be a later insertion, and therefore postdate its apparent context; on the other, it may be a more or less faithful copy of earlier, perhaps discarded, material, and may thus predate its apparent context.[41]

The second complication is biographical. There is a traditional picture of the genesis of *BT* whose main lines depend, substantially, not on any direct evidence, but on the later recollections of Nietzsche's sister, which were first set out in one volume of a biography of her brother published in 1897. But her evidence by itself is of very little value. It has for some years been established beyond doubt that Elisabeth used her long period as custodian of her brother's works and papers (during which time she wrote and rewrote his biography, as well as overseeing the editing of his works) to misrepresent important aspects of his life and thought and, in extreme cases, to falsify letters and unpublished writings.[42] Her motives were various and not always dishonourable, but chief among them was the desire to glorify her brother's reputation: to represent him, in fact, as supremely original genius, complete intellect (she made an exception of his mathematical capabilities, but, by way of compensation, emphasized his standing as a classical scholar), perfect human being and, eventually, tragic hero. And although there is no question of any actual tampering with the unpublished material that pertains to *BT*, Elisabeth is no more reliable as a biographer for our period than for any other. In the first place, there is the time factor: her first biography was begun over twenty years after the publication of *BT* and even honest sisters' memories would be fallible at such a distance. Secondly, it is not even probable that she would have known much about the progress of the book at the time, except in the most general terms: she was not often in her brother's company and his letters to her during these years do not suggest that details of such matters formed any part of their common ground. Thirdly, it does not inspire confidence in her work to find it not simply going *beyond* the independent evidence we have, but often going *against* it. And finally, her particular motive for deception is surely not far to seek: the crucial consideration is that Nietzsche's relationship with Wagner, with which the genesis of the book is bound up, was for her a sensitive issue in which her brother's reputation was particularly at stake. This is, indeed, confirmed by differences between her various accounts of the biographical aspects of the genesis ('how did the "Wagnerian connection" come about?'), generally in line with a characteristic of hers, that in sensitive areas of her brother's biography her memory for convenient detail improved as she got older.[43]

An apt description of Elisabeth's cast of mind in the very years when her first biography was planned and written was given by Rudolf Steiner in 1900. He had been invited to give her 'private lessons in her brother's philosophy' which (as she had rightly decided) would help her to propagate the Nietzschean cause. His caustic comments included the following: 'Frau Förster-Nietzsche[44]...lacks any sense of objectivity...She *believes* at every moment what she says. She convinces herself today that something was red yesterday that most assuredly was blue.'[45] Yet although her capacity for distortion is well known and although her account of the genesis has been questioned (Erich Podach has called it 'untenable', *nicht haltbar*),[46] its substance is still widely accepted – by her brother's latter-day detractors no less than his admirers. Representatively, Martin Vogel's recent large-scale – and extremely hostile – study of Nietzsche and the Apollo–Dionysus polarity relies heavily, at certain points, on her testimony.[47]

The genesis of *BT* must be reconstructed from contemporary documents: Nietzsche's plans and fragments, especially if datable, and correspondence. After re-examining this evidence, we have come to conclusions that differ in certain respects from received opinion. Received opinion, based unduly on the word of sister Elisabeth, has it that Nietzsche began with the idea of a large book on Greek culture which, under Wagner's influence and against its author's real inclinations, was gradually whittled down to a book on Greek tragedy – and Wagner. Our conclusion, overall, is rather that a large book on Greece was not a serious possibility for long, if at all; that the actual book written was, in an important sense, Wagnerian from the start; but that, notwithstanding the extent of Wagner's influence, there is no good reason to suppose that Nietzsche ever went against his own inclinations for Wagner's sake, whether by adding material, changing it or suppressing it. On this last point, it is worth emphasizing, in advance of the evidence, that Nietzsche did certainly reject a quantity of material before the final draft, but that few of the 'suppressed' passages are at all long and none are strikingly impressive. In later years, we shall find Nietzsche looking back at this first book, and especially its Wagnerian dimension, with very mixed feelings. It is particularly significant that none of his many critical comments on the book from that period suggest any mixed feelings at the time when the book was actually being planned and written. But it is presumably these later criticisms, made long after his emancipation from Wagner, that inspired Elisabeth to explain away the Wagnerian connection as merely secondary; while her claims about her brother's real intention to produce a 'large' book about Greece (and nothing but Greece) would seem to be prompted by a desire to enhance his scholarly image; for no other kind of book (she decided) would have satisfied his 'scholar's conscience'.[48]

NEW PLANS, WAR, 'PHILOSOPHICAL CREDENTIALS'

By the spring of 1870 the new project had its first name. In April Nietzsche announced to Rohde: 'The theme and title of the coming book [*Zukunft-buch*, perhaps with allusion to Wagner's *Zukunftsmusik*] is "Socrates and Instinct".'[49] From our knowledge of Nietzsche's earlier thinking on that subject, we would naturally take such a title to imply a central concern with tragedy and its demise, but it is certainly significant that the word 'tragedy' is not itself part of the title. Nietzsche, it seems, was at a transitional stage. He had not yet finally committed himself to subordinating all his other interests to tragedy, but was still toying with ideas of a wider scope.[50] The book, as we gather from a plan in his notebooks of the same period,[51] was to deal with four large areas: ethics; aesthetics; religion and mythology; and politics, law and education. Of the forty-odd subheadings in the plan only two point explicitly towards drama, 'Socratism in tragedy' (under 'aesthetics') and 'The tragedians and the state' (under 'politics...'), although in the retrospective light of *BT* a considerable number of the others can be seen as bearing specifically on the tragic ethos: for instance, 'music and poetry', 'Aristotle's aesthetic', 'ecstatic art in Greece', 'Dionysus and

Apollo'. Nevertheless, the plan is too wide for a tragedy-centred book even on Nietzsche's terms, and, as such, it is certainly a piece of evidence in favour of his sister's postulate of a full-scale book about Greece.[52] The width of the Greek material can be gathered from the presence of such diverse names as Plato, Homer, Alcibiades, Herodotus and the Stoics. On the other hand, even in this plan the book was not to be simply 'about Greece'. For one thing, there were some headings of a still wider generality: for instance, 'Art in the service of the will', where the orientation towards Schopenhauer points, if not away from Greece, at least *past* Greece; and in a separate note the whole plan was subtitled, without reference to Greece, 'A contribution to the philosophy of history'.[53] There were also one or two indications of expressly non-classical matters, including allusions to the 'Jewish–Christian world'.

But in any case, bare titles give us no indication of the strength of their author's commitment to them. If we suppose that Nietzsche did feel committed to the plan's extra-tragic Greek aspects (ethics, politics and the rest), we must make that supposition without much in the way of supporting evidence. The notebooks show that Nietzsche was prepared to rethink the precise shape of the book well into 1871,[54] but almost all of the numerous plans there – including some which appear to be *earlier* than 'Socrates and Instinct'[55] – point to a book centrally concerned with tragedy and recognizably related to *BT*. So too do most of his other notes and jottings and – more important – most of the substantial pieces of work that he wrote during this period. The chief exception is a group of extended fragments generally known under the title 'The Greek State' and ascribed to early 1871, which correspond roughly to some of the 'political' sections of the 'Socrates and Instinct' plan.[56] Here at last, it may be, Nietzsche shows a serious interest. But these fragments stand alone. It is surely a powerful confirmation of his underlying concern with tragedy throughout the whole of 1870–1 that in this period we find, again and again, lengthy drafts and preliminary studies for one part or other of *BT*, but no other sizeable fragments ascribable to a 'large' book 'about Greece' and falling outside the actual book's eventual range. There are some pieces – the most notable is usually known as 'On music and words'[57] – which were apparently meant for the book and later rejected, but which fall *within* the scope of *BT*, and so have no bearing on the question. The same goes for Nietzsche's very limited work on such topics as his 'Homer's Contest', apparently begun in 1871 and quite unrelated to the material of *BT*, but arising out of his earlier philological studies.[58]

In the light of our discussion, it comes as no surprise to find another, abbreviated plan for 'Socrates and Instinct' with a question mark against the heading 'politics',[59] which, of all the main headings, would seem the furthest removed from Greek drama. But whatever the real significance of the plan's extra-dramatic aspects, they hardly square with any talk of a 'scholar's conscience'. Here, as elsewhere, heterodoxy was built into the whole conception, as Nietzsche intimated in the letter to Rohde: 'I'm afraid it won't look philological; but who can go against his own nature?'[60]

During the spring and summer of 1870, Nietzsche rethought his ideas on tragedy. The results are preserved in some notes for a course of undergraduate lectures on Sophocles' *Oedipus Rex* and an essay called 'The Dionysiac Philosophy',[61] in both of which Greek tragedy is the primary object of attention. Here, then, are two more of the group of 'preliminary studies' from which *BT* was to emerge; and indeed a letter to Wagner later that year refers to 'The Dionysiac Philosophy', in precisely such terms, as a *Vorstudium*.[62] Whatever remains of the course on *Oedipus Rex* itself is as yet unpublished. All that we have available is the notes for the first part of the introduction, written, presumably, in the spring, and consisting of a highly condensed discussion of Greek tragedy and its development.[63] The material is more extensive than that of the two earlier lectures, but the general orientation much the same. In particular, Nietzsche lays stress on tragedy's origin, its musical element and its chorus, and devotes a separate section to the topic of 'classical tragedy and opera', which, among other details, briefly names Wagner as a successful instance of the redevelopment of classical tragic norms.[64] There is also, unheralded and essentially unexplained, a first public appearance of Nietzsche's new antithesis. Early on, contrasting Greek lyric and epic poetry, he notes: 'Lyric, from which Greek tragedy developed, was Dionysiac, not Apolline. This distinction of style holds good for the whole of Greek art...'[65]

From now on, Nietzsche's antithesis was to figure prominently in all the studies leading up to *BT*. The next of them, 'The Dionysiac Philosophy', was largely devoted to it. This essay was a theoretical account of Apollo and Dionysus in their various guises: as deities within Greek religion; as expressions of opposing attitudes to, or philosophies of, life; and as artistic forces in Greece and elsewhere. Under the last heading, music and lyric poetry were characterized as Dionysiac, sculpture and epic as Apolline, and tragedy as a rare fusion of the two. (Lessing, we recall, had made *his* contrast between poetry and plastic art: Nietzsche had now, in his own words, 'got beyond Lessing's *Laocoon*'.) In calling 'The Dionysiac Philosophy' a preliminary study, Nietzsche did not say preliminary to *what*, but in the light of the essay's range, the end product as envisaged could hardly be anything very different from *BT* as it in fact emerged. In his preface to the book, written at the close of 1871, he signified, albeit in flamboyantly veiled language, that this essay was indeed the effective starting point.[66] We may say, then, that by the summer of 1870 he was committed to a book centred on, and organized with reference to, Greek tragedy – although its exact scope still remained to be determined.

In August 1870 Nietzsche's work was brought to a temporary halt by the Franco-Prussian war, which had begun in July. On moving to Switzerland, he had forfeited his German citizenship and was therefore ineligible for active service, but an exception was made for him, and as a German patriot he was allowed to volunteer in the capacity of medical orderly. His service was itself cut short by illness. He contracted severe dysentery and diphtheria and after a partial recovery returned to Basle in October. The recovery was to remain partial: his permanent ill-health dates from this time.

The experience of war and its suffering affected Nietzsche deeply. In August, near Wörth, he sent his mother 'a memoir of the horribly devastated battlefield, scattered all over with countless mournful remains and reeking with dead bodies';[67] and in December he wrote to a friend: 'if one is to avoid losing all courage, one must not think of these frightful things any more'.[68] It is apparent how far removed this mood was from any chauvinistic or militaristic fervour – nor would we particularly expect any such fervour (despite long established misconceptions about Nietzsche's attitudes) from one whose ideas of German nationhood were moulded so largely by the cultural preoccupations of a Hölderlin or a Schopenhauer. In fact, the war gave him a new sombreness of attitude to match his stark experience of the 'essential problems of life'; and inevitably this sombreness communicated itself to his continued thinking about the problems of tragedy. 'Before the walls of Metz, in cold September nights, while on duty as medical orderly, I thought through these problems.'[69] His feelings reached their bitter climax a few months later, when the war was over and the defeated French were in the throes of the Commune rising. The Tuileries were destroyed by fire and it was rumoured that the Louvre had been burned down as well. Nietzsche wrote: 'When I heard of the fires in Paris, I felt annihilated for some days and was overwhelmed by fears and doubts; the whole academic [*wissenschaftlich*], philosophical, artistic world seemed an absurdity, if a single day could wipe out the most glorious works of art, even whole periods of art; I clung with earnest conviction to the metaphysical value of art, which cannot exist for the sake of poor human beings, but has higher missions to fulfil.'[70]

His feelings thus transcended any straightforward patriotism. With his high cultural ideals he had, in any case, strong and growing suspicions about the worth of a Germany united under Prussian domination and dedicated to narrow military and materialistic goals. Set against these were what he took to be the essential strengths and cultural possibilities of the German spirit, which in recent generations – and most clearly in the age of Goethe – had been partially realized and whose full realization was an ever-present dream. His letters of 1870–1 are scattered with remarks pointing up the contrast: on the one side 'our *German* mission' and 'old Germanic health', on the other 'that fatal anti-cultural Prussia' and 'our whole threadbare culture'.[71] His hopes for Germany and its culture were, of course, vested most particularly in Wagner, whose Bayreuth ideal of a spiritual centre for German culture was something he could support unreservedly. It was, therefore, extremely relevant to him that Wagner had a less complicated view of the age they lived in and found it possible to regard the rise of the new *Reich* as the outward expression of, precisely, Germanic health and strength. And under the Master's spell, Nietzsche too was able to ease himself out of his suspicions into something more like Wagner's optimism. To Wagner, therefore, he could write in a different tone: 'I prefer not to say a word about the German victories: these are the letters of fire on the wall, intelligible to all peoples.'[72] Perhaps the war might, after all, have some deep artistic meaning or goal.[73] In Wagner himself, at all events, he continued to see only the image that Wagner wished to project: an 'idealistic cast of mind', an 'incredible seriousness and German depth' in his view of life and art, an epitome of 'our German mission' in every way.[74] Years before, Nietzsche had written: 'the past is dearer to me than the present; but I believe in a better future'.[75] With Wagner in mind he could say it now.

The sobering experience of war, which now determined Nietzsche's general outlook, affected his thoughts about the tragic spirit that were to be embodied in the coming book. It also precipitated changes of plan regarding the book's scope. When first setting out for Basle, he had expressed the conviction that his grasp of life's 'true and essential problems' was already strong enough to meet the threat to his 'philosophic sense' posed by academic specialization.[76] The scholar's separation of the Greek experience from the modern world had always seemed a frivolity; now it was intolerable. His 'philosophic sense' required to be given a freer play and a more adequate expression. Accordingly, in the autumn of 1870, under the new title 'Tragedy and the Freethinkers', he drew up the first main plan whose scope, in both space and time, went substantially beyond Greece.[77] While still centred on Greek tragedy and associated topics, the plan began and ended with a wide range of other subjects from Buddhism to modern culture and education, from Schiller and Goethe and their drama to the generalities of 'art', 'religion' and 'science'; the Greek items went from 'Dionysus and Apollo' to 'Plato against art', via the central 'music and drama'.[78] The plan contained no Greek items unrelated to tragedy, or the birth and death of tragedy, which makes it the earliest of Nietzsche's plans to define the scope of the Greek material as eventually realized in *BT*. Many of the other subjects, Buddhism and the rest, were also there to stay – although *BT* was to deal with them in extremely summary or allusive form.

Nietzsche's capacity to stick to a plan, however, was no greater than before, and at or towards the end of the year he produced a spate of alternatives. Some were simply modified versions of 'Tragedy and the Freethinkers'.[79] Some involved quite new titles: 'Tragic Man', 'Greek Serenity', 'Tragedy and Greek Serenity'.[80] 'Greek Serenity' was itself the title for a series of plans – here too Nietzsche kept chopping and changing – and despite the presence of 'Greece' and the absence of 'tragedy' in the title, the book was still, unmistakably, a 'comparative' tragedy book in all its versions.[81] In the most detailed of these, the plan had six main sections, beginning with 'tragic thought' and ending with 'science and art' and 'metaphysics of art'.[82] The unqualified generality of these two headings confirms Nietzsche's insistence on looking beyond Greece, even if specifically non-Greek items, like those on Buddhism and Goethe in the previous plan, were no longer explicit. A greater concentration on Greece, however, was envisaged in the remaining parts, whose headings were 'the tragic masks' (meaning, among other things, tragic *characters*), 'the death of tragedy', and 'the means used by the Hellenic will to achieve its goal, the genius'.[83]

That last heading is of special interest. Concealed beneath the opaque wording about the 'Hellenic will' was another attempt – as it proved, Nietzsche's last attempt – to discuss some of the socio-political aspects of the Greek world as part of his first book. The heading was subdivided into eight separate sections on such subjects as slavery, women, Plato's ideal state and the mysteries, and Nietzsche was sufficiently interested in it to produce a draft version for the bulk of the sequence. The result was the fragments, four in number, to which the name 'The Greek State' has traditionally been given: that name was actually attached to one of the eight sections themselves.[84] In these four passages Nietzsche's sister saw a prime piece of evidence for her brother's 'real' intention to write a big book about Greece rather than a short one about tragedy.[85] That idea can be dismissed out of hand. The eight sections deal only with a small fraction of what a 'big book about Greece' must have entailed, and the portions written (covering most of those sections) would add only about one fifth to the eventual modest length of *BT*.[86] Furthermore, Nietzsche very soon decided that these particular sections of the book did not belong with the rest. One of the 'Greek

Serenity' plans attempts to subsume them under 'tragedy itself'; a memorandum elsewhere suggests rewriting them; another of the plans seems to omit them altogether.[87] And if we look at the actual fragments, it is all too clear that Nietzsche was right. A few sequences were eventually used in *BT* in modified or abbreviated form.[88] The rest is fundamentally alien both to *BT* as we have it and to any of its earlier versions,[89] even the version implicit in the extended 'Greek Serenity' plan to which it relates. As far as *BT* itself is concerned, the discrepancies are not simply those of subject: the fragments are strangely different from the book in attitude, in idiom and, not least, in quality.[90] All in all, it is in no way surprising that Nietzsche should have put them to one side soon after writing them at the turn of the year.[91] From the terms in which he subsequently refers to the longest of the fragments, we can confirm that 'The Greek State' represents a short-lived attempt to widen the scope of a book whose central concern with tragedy was already determined.[92]

Whatever their other fluctuations, Nietzsche's latest plans had one thing in common: their lists of topics, however long or diverse, contained no explicit reference to Wagner. And although it is true that Wagner could, if required, have figured under various of their headings, it seems that the decision to lay any emphasis on the relevance of Wagner's work to his own ideas represented a further and final development.[93] This step came soon enough. Something approaching a personal crisis had been building up since Nietzsche's return from the unforgettable distress of war. If the contemporary world as a whole seemed to be more flawed than ever, academic life, in particular, was irredeemably so. We have already quoted part of the letter to Rohde, written in December, which gives the best testimony to Nietzsche's state of mind: 'Let us drag on in this university existence for a few more years...A completely radical institution for truth is not possible here... Afterwards we can become real teachers...by becoming not only wiser, but also better human beings.... So one day...we shall create a new Greek academy...You will know of Wagner's Bayreuth plan. I have been quietly considering if we too should not break with philology as practised till now and its educational perspective. I am preparing a big *adhortatio* for everyone who has not yet been utterly suffocated and swallowed up by the present age.'[94] Only three days earlier, however, he had written to another correspondent in less drastic tones: 'give me a few more years and you should sense a new influence on classical studies'.[95] The note of personal ambition here is reminiscent of that zeal which the young professor-elect had felt, among other feelings, on setting out for Basle. His aspiration then had been to inject a 'Schopenhauerian seriousness' into his subject, and the ideal had never been abandoned. But alongside it he felt a deep disillusion with the actuality that confronted him, and a growing restlessness.

With the new year, his restless feelings were given, for the time being, a specific object to focus on: an opportunity of a new kind presented itself and he espoused it eagerly. The chair of philosophy at Basle became vacant and in January 1871 he applied for it. In a remarkable letter of application,[96] he set out his reasons in detail. He began with his poor health. This, he had eventually decided, was caused by the diversity of his present academic work, which was especially taxing in that one of his university duties was a daily round of language-teaching at the local high school, the *Pädagogium*. These commitments were constantly distracting him from what he called 'my real, philosophical task, to which, if necessary, I must *sacrifice my career*'. Elliptically relating this 'philosophical task' to academic philosophy (including the history of philosophy), he declared himself to be better qualified for a philosophical chair than a purely philological one. His dominant inclination (he wrote) had always been towards philosophy, 'and even in my philological studies I have been most attracted by those topics which seemed important for the history of philosophy or for ethical and aesthetic problems'. His 'solid training in classical philology' was surely an asset: it was important to 'stimulate among the students an interest in the careful interpretation of Aristotle and Plato'. He had indeed already announced two forthcoming lecture courses on ancient philosophy (on the Presocratics and on Plato) and could also point to work he had published in this field (on Diogenes Laertius). Of modern philosophers he had studied Kant and Schopenhauer 'with particular interest'. For his own successor he suggested Rohde, 'the ablest of all the younger philologists I have known', and with a disarming naïvety he added: 'I cannot express how profoundly my life here in Basle would be alleviated by the presence of my best friend.'

As far as the stress on his philosophical bent is concerned, we can certainly grant (and not only with hindsight) that Nietzsche was substantially correct. Diogenes Laertius was not the only ancient philosopher he had worked on in his later Leipzig days: he had also grappled with the Aristotelian corpus and, especially, with the Presocratic, Democritus.[97] And as regards modern philosophy, in 1868, before the summons to Basle, he had actually considered writing his doctoral dissertation on Kant, although he subsequently rejected the subject as unsuitable.[98] The electors to the philosophy chair might also recall, as symptomatic of his inclinations, that striking formula from his inaugural lecture: 'all philological activity should be embraced and defined by a philosophical outlook'.[99] And, again, they might call to mind a passage from Ritschl's eulogistic reference that had made Nietzsche's earlier appointment possible: 'His studies so far have been weighted towards the history of Greek literature...with special emphasis, it seems to me, on the history of Greek philosophy. But I have not the least doubt that, if confronted by a practical demand, with his great gifts he will work in other fields with complete success.'[100] On the other hand, it should be borne in mind that for all his adolescent encyclopaedic zeal and his years of cultural enthusiasms, his familiarity with European culture was largely restricted to two areas: classical antiquity and the modern period, especially the previous hundred years. This was as true in philosophy as elsewhere. Schopenhauer and, to a lesser extent, Kant he might claim to know, but his knowledge of any pre-Kantian, post-classical, philosophy – nearly two millennia of European thought – was at this time quite superficial.[101]

Nietzsche's letter to the authorities at Basle included one cryptic sentence which we have still to mention: 'I shall be able, soon enough, to show publicly my competence for an appointment in philosophy.' The meaning emerges from another letter to Rohde, written some weeks later, at the end of March. The crucial appointment had not, to his knowledge, been decided yet and was still in the forefront of his thoughts. The passage in question, revealing on various counts, deserves to be quoted at length: 'I have no idea how the business is coming on...I must establish my philosophical credentials a bit; to that end I have finished, except for a few touches, a short work, "The Origin and End of Tragedy" [*Ursprung und Ziel der Tragödie*]. ...I live in reckless estrangement from philology – a worse alienation is unimaginable...So gradually I am claiming my philosophical estate and already believe in myself; it wouldn't even surprise me if I turned into a poet. I have no compass to tell me what I am destined for; and yet, when I look back, everything seems to fit as well together as if I'd been following a benevolent daimon all along.... What a feeling to see your own world, a pretty ball, growing round and full before your eyes! Now I see a part of some new metaphysics growing, now a new aesthetic...Everything I learn now finds its proper place in some corner of whatever's already there. And I feel the growth of this world of mine most of all when I consider, not coolly but calmly, all the so-called "world-history" of the last ten months.'[102] The book, then, was once again in progress, under a new title,[103] and evidently progressing in a spirit that might be called 'philosophical', and specifically 'metaphysical' or 'aesthetic', and perhaps even 'poetic'; but *not* philological. It was nearing completion, and its completion embodied the hope of that now familiar wholeness so precious to its author: everything seemed to fit together, *all* experience could at last be integrated.

One important corollary of this new integration Nietzsche had not mentioned in his letter to Rohde. The book was at last to deal specifically with Wagner. The new 'philosophical' perspective meant that Nietzsche could feel free to give all his enthusiasms, classical and non-classical, their due public expression. Subtitled 'an aesthetic essay', the work was to begin with a preface to Wagner and, after discussion of the birth and death of Dionysiac art in Greece, to end (apparently) with its rebirth in Wagner's music.[104] The aim of the book was set out in the preface (which, unlike many items in these plans, was actually written).[105] The object, Nietzsche explained, was to find appropriate terms for his insight into the 'weighty problem' of tragedy's origin and goal. Greek tragedy belied the prevalent notion of a Hellas grounded in serene optimism: its lesson was that a beautiful surface may conceal terrible depths. To appreciate this was to see the problem as ultimately a problem of living, and as uniquely relevant to a recently unified and politically ascendant Germany. For Germany now had the chance to bring her new strength of purpose to bear against her real enemy – at which point Nietzsche introduced a reinterpretation of politics in cultural and philosophical terms which was to become characteristic of his mature thinking: the 'real enemy' was modern superficiality, and Germany's chance was to destroy it by relearning 'tragic cognition' from the Greeks. In this way she might foster a new creative generation and a 'German rebirth of the Hellenic world'.

WAGNER AND THE CONCLUDING PHASE

In established classical-scholarly terms, Nietzsche's heterodoxy was now complete, in exact proportion to his commitment to Wagner. Without question the period between autumn 1870 and the close of 1871 was the high point of Wagner's direct influence on him, as can almost be demonstrated without reference to *BT* at all. There was, for instance, a project for a 'music drama' that Nietzsche began in the autumn of 1870, and there was a new and strong Wagnerian flavour in his musical compositions of 1871:[106] the *explicit* emphasis on Wagner in the developing book is in no way an isolated phenomenon.[107] At the same time it needs to be stressed that despite his close relations with Wagner the man and his reverence for Wagner the artist, Nietzsche's first-hand acquaintance with his idol's artistic achievements was in one important respect limited: experience of Wagnerian music drama in its proper theatrical setting was largely denied him. He had access to scores and opportunities of hearing orchestral excerpts in concert, but at the time of the publication of *BT* the only Wagnerian work he had seen performed remained *Meistersinger*.[108]

'. . . I have finished, except for a few touches, a short work, "The Origin and End of Tragedy"...' Those words, just quoted, were written at the end of March, not from Basle, but from Lugano, and it was in Lugano that the new plans for the book had been translated into this continuous draft. Nietzsche's health had not improved, and in February he had left Basle for two months of convalescence. He returned to Basle in April to find the hopes he had left there come to nothing: he was not to have a philosophy chair[109] (nor Rohde his own chair), and so he was obliged to remain, at least nominally, a philologist. Precisely what effect the disappointment had on Nietzsche himself and the book in progress is not clear. For himself, he may well have decided that his cavils against classical philology applied equally to academe in general, so that, wounded pride apart, he was hardly worse off than before.[110] As for the book, there was at least no drastic change of plan, but rather a continuation of work already done: the 'short work' was surely not all that 'finished' by the end of March.[111] At the end of April, however, it *was* near enough to completion for Nietzsche, at last, to send the first part of the manuscript to a publisher, Engelmann, in Leipzig. In his covering letter he mentioned yet another title and gave the Wagnerian aspect an unexpected prominence: 'I have written a pamphlet...which is to have the title "Music and Tragedy", and I am sending you the beginning of it in manuscript. As you will see, I am attempting to explain Greek tragedy in a completely novel way, in that for the time being I disregard all philological approaches to the question and keep only the aesthetic problem in view. The real task, however, is to throw light on Richard Wagner, the extraordinary enigma of our age, in his relation to Greek tragedy. I think I can claim that the whole last part is bound to make an impact on our musical public; at least, if I compare it with what has been said recently on the same problem by Hanslick and others..., I cannot help believing that the most discerning public must be interested in this work. In order to make myself comprehensible to them, I have taken particular pains with the style and clarity of the exposition...'[112]

In speaking of Wagner as an 'enigma', Nietzsche was not resorting to empty rehetoric. 'Hanslick and others' had indeed found it difficult to place Wagner's achievements, and furthermore Wagner's own explicit interpretation of his ideal had in recent years been shifting in an enigmatic way that impelled his articulate young admirer to offer his own clarification: here was one of those 'aesthetic problems' which had been occupying his mind for some time. The task was not simply to come to terms with Wagner's music drama, but to reconcile his theory of it with his actual practice.

Intermittently throughout his long career, Wagner attempted to formulate his aspirations in prose. The first phase of his theorizing was represented by a group of essays, including the celebrated *Opera and Drama*, that were written as far back as 1849–51, before much of his most distinctive music was yet composed. It was in these essays that he pronounced Attic tragedy, and especially the tragedy of Aeschylus, to be the complete form of art, the original *Gesamtkunstwerk* whose spirit must be recreated in a German context. Unhampered by his lack of scholarly acquaintance with Aeschylus, or indeed any Greek author, he saw himself (it was evident) as the German Aeschylus who could reinterpret in tragic poetry and music the ancient gods, heroes and heroic legends that comprised the national mythology. (We can see how the new Aeschylean note that Nietzsche had been sounding since his lectures of 1870 was, like much else, in harmony with Wagner's aspiration.) But Aeschylus, however close to the Wagnerian ideal, was no more than a spiritual ancestor. The immediate source of inspiration was much more modern – it was Beethoven. Ignoring his considerable debt to Meyerbeer and the Parisian grand opera without which his early works, especially *Rienzi* (1838–40), would have been inconceivable, Wagner claimed descent from Beethoven and, in particular, the Choral Symphony. For it was there that Beethoven had enhanced the German grandeur of his music with the words of Schiller's *Ode to Joy* and thus took the first step towards reintegrating poetry and music as equal partners in a new and sublime unity. This, for Wagner, was the goal, and a goal which he, as supreme poet-composer, was destined to reach: a perfect harmony between word and music, with music as emotional expression of the verbal line and verse as regulating element in the composite whole.

Such was Wagner's first position and it satisfied him, if not his critics, for a decade. What eventually brought him to reconsider his theory was not the critics' doubts. If, for instance, Hanslick found it impossible to take his libretti seriously as poetry, so much the worse for Hanslick. The impetus came partly from a growing interest in Schopenhauer's theory of music,[113] and partly from an uncomfortable sense that his own artistic practice was diverging further and further from the theoretical postulates of which it was supposed to be the realization. On both counts it was, above all, the status of the word that was brought into question – and thereby the *Gesamtkunst* ideal as a whole. In *Das Rheingold*, finished in 1854, and, up to a point, in *Die Walküre*, begun in the same year, Wagner came as near as he was ever to come to giving his theories practical effect. The work that really belied the ideal was *Tristan und Isolde*. Finished eight years after *Opera and Drama* in 1859 (though not performed until 1865), *Tristan* was the most impressive of his works up to that time, and yet one in which the music, irrespective of its dramatic significance, dominated the word utterly. Impassioned sequences in which the 'poetry' consisted of nothing more than strings of synonyms were merely the extreme example of a tendency that was apparent throughout the work.

Wagner's relationship with Schopenhauer was a curious one. Paradoxically, it dates from the very period in which *Tristan* was conceived; in fact the *Tristan* drama itself was planned and its words written under Schopenhauerian influence – but influence of an ethical, rather than an aesthetic, kind. 'Apart from making slow progress with my music', Wagner wrote to his future father-in-law, Franz Liszt, in 1854, 'my sole concern recently is a man who has come like a gift from heaven...into my solitude. This is Arthur Schopenhauer, the greatest philosopher since Kant...The German academics very prudently ignored him for forty years; but lately, to the disgrace of Germany, he has been discovered by an English critic. All the Hegels etc. are charlatans beside him. His central idea, the ultimate negation of the will to live,...[offers] the only salvation possible' – and turning to his own artistic activities, present and prospective, he added, 'I have in my head *Tristan und Isolde*...; with the "black flag" that flutters at the end of it I shall shroud myself to die.'[114] Wagner, that is, contrived to regard his hymn to love and love's fulfilment in death as an enactment of Schopenhauerian renunciation, and even sent the elderly philosopher a copy of the libretto, which was finished in 1857. On the aesthetic side, the dominance of the musical element in *Tristan* did, as it happens, bring Wagner's art somewhat into line with Schopenhauer's theories, although, as we have already pointed out, the sensuous-emotional appeal of Wagnerian music, at its most extreme in *Tristan*, directly flouted the philosopher's denial of all worldly values. But in any case, Schopenhauer's terms of reference were such that the poet-composer could never properly comply with them, for the simple reason that they reduced the role of the word in a musical context to nothing more than a necessary evil. For Schopenhauer, valuable as all the arts were, music was the art which uniquely penetrated the depths of metaphysical reality and expressed the essence of that reality, the will, directly: 'the composer reveals the innermost nature of the world and expresses the deepest wisdom in a language which his rational faculty does not understand'.[115] Words, on the other hand, like the instruments of reason that they are, could only intrude from the secondary world of physical phenomena, with which true music was not concerned. Folk-song was a special case: here words were said to aspire to the condition of music. But in general, and especially at the highest creative level, words were redundant. It is not entirely surprising that Wagner's gift of the *Tristan* poem elicited no response.

It seems clear that Wagner perceived the lack of congruence between his own theory and Schopenhauer's as uncomfortably as the gulf between his own theory and practice. Being the child of a system-ridden age, he must have a theory. Being vain, however, and temperamentally unable to reject outright any of his earlier pronouncements, he could not admit, to the world or to himself, the contradictions in which Schopenhauer involved him.[116] Instead, he groped towards some formula into which he might recast his earlier aesthetic while obscuring the reasons for doing so: a task made easier by his tortuous prose style. The first fruit of this endeavour was *Music of the Future* (*Zukunftsmusik*). In this treatise, written a year after the completion of *Tristan* and, as it happened, in the month of Schopenhauer's death (September 1860), he continued to represent music drama as a harmonious union of music and poetry, but the equal status of the two had gone. The function of music now was to express pure feeling on an ideal, unverbalizable, metaphysical level (Schopenhauer's influence is plain); the task of the poetic word was to reinterpret that 'feeling' in terms of 'thought' and so help mediate the metaphysical world to an earth-bound, concept-bound audience.

In the next decade Wagner complicated his position by returning, in *Meistersinger*, to the tradition of grand opera with which his career had begun, and, incongruously enough, by adding further Schopenhauerian elements to his theory. *On State and Religion* (1864–5), a political treatise with forays into aesthetics, showed a new preoccupation with creative illusion and dream images, *Wahn* and *Wahngebilde*, clearly visible also in *Meistersinger* (the victorious *Prize Song* itself arises from a dream) and, at least in part, derived from Schopenhauer's *Parerga and Paralipomena* (1851). These notions recur in Wagner's essay *Beethoven*, a thickly and explicitly Schopenhauerian mixture of ideas, written in late 1870, and a companion piece, *The Destiny of Opera*, written in early 1871. By this time, however, Wagner and Nietzsche had explored areas of mutual interest in many conversations and had begun to exercise a reciprocal influence on each other's thinking. The two essays, accordingly, reveal Wagner's influence on Nietzsche and equally his own debt to him – one unmistakable sign of this being a casual allusion in *The Destiny of Opera* to the Apolline–Dionysiac polarity, as to a pre-existing conceptual entity.[117]

Compared with its earlier forms, Wagner's theory had gained in complexity, but not, perhaps, in perspicuity, from its new influences. Poetry, it appeared from *Beethoven*, was now a very junior partner to music ('the union of music and poetry must always end in...a subordination of the latter')[118] and served chiefly to stimulate the composer's creative process. The two elements that mattered were the music and the drama (meaning the stage action, which Wagner, unlike Schopenhauer, now saw as a thing independent of words). The relation between these two major elements was far from clear. Wagner differentiated them by associating drama with visionary illusion and music with dreams, but also made an attempt at establishing parity between them by pronouncing drama 'the visible counterpart of music'[119] and by stressing the equal greatness of Beethoven's music and Shakespearean drama. If the reader was nevertheless left with the feeling that music counted for most, it was partly because the bulk of the long treatise was in fact about music and nothing else. *The Destiny of Opera* discussed the special rôle of the performers in the ideal work and offered some further thoughts concerning the three elements, but without modifying their relative status. The supremacy of music was not challenged.

One might be forgiven the thought that Wagner's theoretical position had at this point compounded too many incongruities to make criticism necessary. The theory, in all its latest elusiveness, might suit *Tristan*, more or less, but continued to stand in a highly problematic relation to Wagner's musical *œuvre* as a whole – an *œuvre* surely too varied for any useful all-embracing formula. Meanwhile, the Schopenhauerian aspects of his theory contradicted his own earlier doctrines without in fact bringing them properly into line with Schopenhauer's aesthetic itself. Few of Wagner's admirers can have been satisfied. Nietzsche, in particular, was not – but, unlike most of Wagner's admirers, he was willing to take the master's prose voice sufficiently seriously to contemplate positive action on its behalf. Since his first meeting with Wagner in 1868 he had known of the latter's conviction that Schopenhauer was 'the only philosopher who had understood the essence of music'. On Nietzsche's return from the war in late 1870, Wagner sent him a copy of *Beethoven*. Nietzsche's letter of acknowledgement evinced unqualified loyalty, but did so without one word of unqualified praise for Wagner's latest effort. He stressed first how important it had been to him to get to know Wagner's philosophy of music and that his own 'Dionysiac Philosophy' reflected that debt. With awe he noted the remoteness of Wagner's new range of thought, where everything was surprising and astonishing. 'But', he added, 'I am afraid that to the aestheticians of these days you will seem like a sleepwalker, whom it is inadvisable, not to say dangerous, and, above all, impossible to follow.' There was a 'deep harmony' between Wagner's thinking and Schopenhauer's, but even experts in Schopenhauerian philosophy would mostly be incapable of grasping the connection either intellectually or emotionally. 'I would think that to follow your thought in this instance is only possible for one to whom the message of *Tristan*, in particular, has been revealed.'[120]

From the tone of these comments it is easy to see that, for Nietzsche, Wagner's work was still a problem in urgent need of a solution.[121] It was, in fact, 'the enigma' on which, he now assured the publisher Engelmann, his book might shed new light. It is not so easy to gauge what his emphasis on the book's Wagnerian aspect really implied. We might infer simply that

Nietzsche supposed this aspect was the most likely to interest the general public. Did he intend to give the impression that it was the central aspect? Such a characterization would certainly not fit *BT* as we have it, nor any of the various plans leading up to it. It is apparent, however, that at the 'Music and Tragedy' stage of his thinking, Nietzsche did envisage a larger rôle for specifically Wagnerian matter than eventually materialized.[122] It will have been in this connection that he wrote the discarded pieces 'On music and words', which largely rework part[123] of 'The Dionysiac Philosophy' of the previous year, but whose copious references to Schopenhauer, opera and Beethoven's Choral Symphony relate directly to one side of the Wagner problem, though without any explicit stress on that fact.[124] The Schopenhauerian character of these fragments is striking and serves, incidentally, to align them with *BT*. In the work on tragedy done *before* Wagner's *Beethoven* Schopenhauer's influence is less evident. We may infer that Nietzsche, although now somewhat distanced from the detail of Schopenhauer's doctrines, had shortened the distance under the stimulus of Wagner's interest in the philosophy of music.

When it comes to the appraisal of new writing, publishers are generally more cautious than authors, and Engelmann, apparently unmoved by Nietzsche's self-confidence, deferred a decision. In June, with understandable disappointment, Nietzsche withdrew the manuscript[125] and conceived the idea of dismembering the new whole and having the pieces published separately as pamphlets or articles. The only fruit of this plan, however, was the private publication in that month of the book's central portion under the title 'Socrates and Greek Tragedy';[126] and it is clear that Nietzsche continued to regard the book as one continuous work.[127] In October he took the manuscript to Wagner's publisher, E. W. Fritzsch. The book had now at last acquired its final title, *The Birth of Tragedy*, or in full, with qualifying subtitle, *The Birth of Tragedy from the Spirit of Music* (*Die Geburt der Tragödie aus dem Geiste der Musik*);[128] and on 16 November, under this title, it was accepted.[129] The manuscript, however, was not entirely ready for publication,[130] and during the next few weeks Nietzsche submitted it to a final revision. The book's central part, represented by 'Socrates and Greek Tragedy', had already been well worked and, apart from some reordering, was left virtually as it was; the rest required more attention, but on 12 December he was able to send off the final portions of the manuscript, including a new, short, preface to Wagner.[131] This introductory piece was little more than an extremely abbreviated version of the February preface. The relation of *BT* itself to its earlier versions was more complicated. The book comprised twenty-five sections of varying lengths. 'Socrates and Greek Tragedy' was the immediate source of the central part (§§ 8–15), but was more a final than a preliminary version. Looking further back, we can see the book as very largely a composite of earlier extended drafts. The beginning (§§ 1–10) is substantially based on the essay of summer 1870, 'The Dionysiac Philosophy', although one sequence (§§ 5–6) is more closely related to the lectures on Sophocles' *Oedipus Rex* (also from 1870) and the rejected fragments 'On music and words'. The next portion (§§ 11–14) can be traced directly to the lecture 'Socrates and Tragedy' (February 1870), but the rest of the book (§§ 15–25) is a less tidy amalgam. Apart from a few parts which seem to lack any antecedents, it derives variously, but less closely, from the compositions just mentioned, from the lecture on 'Greek Music Drama' (January 1870), from the fragments on 'The Greek State' and, in a few places, from the earlier preface to Wagner.

Less than a month separates the publisher's acceptance of the book and Nietzsche's completion of the revision; and during part of this time he was busy preparing lectures on Plato and, unexpectedly enough, on Latin epigraphy.[132] However, Nietzsche's first editors (1895), then his sister (1897), and subsequently the world at large have asserted that the scale of this last revision was substantial and, specifically, that of the book's eventual twenty-five sections, he *added* at this time the final six (§§ 20–25), which are partly (though not, as is often said, *largely*) concerned with Wagner.[133] The point is of some importance: it would seem to follow that the end of the book was a hasty after-thought. It is necessary, therefore, to point out that there does not seem to be any decisive evidence in favour of the assertion.[134] We would do better to accept that we cannot say precisely how much of the book dates from this last stage, although there were, no doubt, changes of various kinds, including deletions. It is worth stressing once more that most consequential points or passages in *BT* are prefigured, sometimes loosely, sometimes almost verbatim, in one or other of the preliminary versions of 1870 and the extended fragments of 1870–1. This means that most of *BT* is a rewriting and as such embodies considered judgements, not 'hasty afterthoughts'. And for the bulk of the last six sections, the general pattern of correspondence (in this case, loose correspondence) to earlier versions is unchanged. The chief exceptions seem to be the final two sections (§§ 24–5), which in large part reformulate points already made, and a page-long discussion (§ 21) of the relation between the drama and the music in *Tristan*, which, apart from passing references, is actually the only discussion of any Wagnerian work in *BT*. It is not hard to imagine Nietzsche adding passages of this modest length in the final weeks, especially if he had continued to work on the 'whole last part' of the book during the summer; any late additions would then have been based on that work.[135] Be that as it may, our main conclusion must be that the traditional claim about the last ('Wagnerian') part is unsubstantiated; and such other evidence as we have does not give it much plausibility.[136] In discussing the 'Wagnerian' aspect of the book, we should in any case remember that during the later part of 1871 Nietzsche actually *reduced* the extent of Wagner's presence in it, rather than increased it.

If some uncertainty surrounds the last stage of the book's genesis, we can at least say something about its author's state of mind on the eve of publication. He went through a quick succession of very different feelings. Now finally assured of a publisher and a book, he could forget his earlier disappointments and even indulge, briefly, in a degree of euphoria: he envisaged a spectacular success and had 'the greatest confidence' that the book would have huge sales.[137] Within a few days, however, anxiety had set in and he was confiding in Rohde his fear that a book that crossed so many conventional demarcation lines might deter all his prospective specialist readers: 'the philologists won't read it because of the music, the musicians because of the philology, the philosophers because of the music and the philology...'; and regarding the classical readership in particular, Rohde would know 'how offended the philologists are bound to be at anything not published by Teubner[138] and without the paraphernalia of critical notes'.[139] After four more weeks, with the last amendments now seen to and the last portions of the manuscript finally delivered, his mood was more settled. While still hoping for general public success, he anticipated some hostility, especially to the 'Wagnerian' end of the book, but about the book's merits and its personal necessity he felt no doubts at all. Among other things there is no sign of any late qualms about his reliance on the Apollo–Dionysus formula: as he had remarked to Rohde a few months earlier, 'I really believe I can get a great deal out of the polarity.'[140] Shortly before Christmas and in the middle of correcting the proofs, he wrote to Rohde again: 'The whole last part, which you do not know,[141] will certainly astonish you; I have been very daring, and I can cry out to myself in an altogether enormous sense, *animam salvavi* [I have saved my soul]; for which reason I think of the book with great satisfaction and am not worried if it turns out to cause the greatest possible offence and in some quarters a "cry of outrage" greets its publication. Moreover, I feel wonderfully assured in my musical perceptions and convinced of their rightness – thanks to what I experienced this week at Mannheim with Wagner.'[142]

This last remark referred to a Wagner Society concert that had included, among other works, the preludes to *Lohengrin* and *Meistersinger* and the prelude and *Liebestod* of *Tristan*. Nietzsche was more enthusiastic about Wagner's music than ever: 'What are all other artistic memories and experiences compared with this latest one! I felt like a man whose presentiments have at last come true.'[143] Appropriately enough, then, the last few days before the book's appearance were touched with the same rapture that had helped to prompt its creation. 'Scholarship, art and philosophy', Nietzsche had presciently written nearly two years earlier, 'are now growing inside me so much that I'll be giving birth to centaurs one day.'[144] The 'centaur'[145] in question, child of Nietzsche's yearning for wholeness, meeting-point of his diverse interests, and his 'salvation' from philistine compartmentalism, made its due appearance in January 1872. Rapturous as the circumstances of its conception may have been, the genesis as a whole could only, in retrospect, seem an extraordinarily painful business, as he intimated to Rohde shortly after the book was out: 'No one has any idea how such a book comes into being: the trouble and torment it is to keep oneself as clear as this of *other* ideas pressing in from all sides; the courage needed to conceive of it and the honesty needed to carry it through; and above all, perhaps, my tremendous task *vis-à-vis* Wagner, which has certainly been the cause of many heavy clouds in my heart[146] – the task of being independent even here, of taking up an, as it were, alienated stance.' Nevertheless, as he went on to say, 'my friends at Tribschen assure me that, to their amazement, I have succeeded in this even where the problem is at its most extreme, with *Tristan*...It is precisely on this point that I feel proud and happy and am convinced that my book will survive.'[147]

4

The argument of *The Birth of Tragedy*

The argument of *BT* is large, complicated, allusive and often elusive as well. In this chapter we provide a detailed summary as a practical aid, to help the reader to see precisely what Nietzsche is saying. The summary follows its original uniformly, section by section (§§), except in the following ways: (i) Nietzsche frequently alludes, without explaining the allusions, to more or less well-known features of Greek tragedy or the Greek world; he gives virtually no dates for artists, thinkers, or events, ancient or modern; and he sometimes makes points that rest, clearly enough, on unstated presuppositions, but points that cannot readily be summarized without reconstructing each presupposition and making it fully explicit. In all these cases we have supplied explanatory or factual material within square brackets: [ ] We have also supplied headings and subheadings (Nietzsche provides none), likewise within square brackets. (ii) Nietzsche sometimes alludes to a topic without explanation in one section, but adds the necessary explanatory matter in another (or in more than one other). In such cases, we have transposed the explanatory matter *out of its proper section* to the main discussion that presupposes it, but have enclosed it inside pointed brackets: ⟨ ⟩. We have then indicated in the margin *ad loc.* from which section or sections such matter actually derives, using the symbol <, so that (e.g.) '<§10' means 'this matter comes from §10'. (iii) Where necessary, we have provided footnotes, containing explanatory editorial comments. However, editorial additions of all kinds are kept to a minimum. In particular, it is not our business in this chapter to pass judgements on Nietzsche's suppositions, arguments or conclusions. (iv) In many sections, Nietzsche's points are not presented in what one might take to be their natural order. *Within sections*, therefore, we have reordered his material, without warning, in the interests of the argument. (v) All unattributed quotations are from *BT*, but in this chapter and thereafter all quotations from the book follow the standard (1874) text.[1]

Preface to Richard Wagner The aesthetic problem considered in this book is central to the hopes for Germany today. Those who find it objectionable that an aesthetic problem should be taken so seriously may be assured that art represents the highest task and the true metaphysical activity of this life: witness the illustrious pioneer on my path, to whom I dedicate this essay.

[I THE BIRTH AND DEATH OF GREEK TRAGEDY]

[§§ 1–4 *The Apolline and the Dionysiac*]

§ 1 All true art is either Apolline or Dionysiac or both. The Apolline and the Dionysiac are to be thought of as antithetical artistic tendencies or impulses; and the nature of any art at any time varies according to which of the two is operative. The names of the two impulses are derived from the Greek art deities, Apollo and Dionysus. [Like all the Greek gods, these two have many differing spheres of activity and areas of special interest, but taken together they present a particular contrast. Apollo is in various ways a god of higher *civilization*: he is, for instance, the god of medicine. Dionysus, on the other hand, is a god of *nature* and natural fertility, associated with wine and 'uncivilized', orgiastic worship. Some of his mythical exploits are equally remote from civilized life:] ⟨among the events recounted are his < § 10
dismemberment by primitive powers, the Titans, and subsequent rebirth⟩.

The Apolline and the Dionysiac are the only genuine art impulses. They often operate singly, the classic instances being sculpture, which is pure Apolline art, and music, which, ⟨at least in its highest form⟩, is pure Dionysiac (⟨for Apolline music and music of a third, 'inartistic' kind do exist < §§ 2, 17,
as well⟩). But there are also instances of the synthesis of the two tendencies; and the classic instance here is Greek tragedy.

Higher art is not the only sphere in which the Apolline and the Dionysiac are to be found. They find expression also, on an elemental level, in dreams (Apolline) and intoxication (Dionysiac).

Dreams are, by their nature, imagistic. They give us an immediate apprehension of *form*, albeit with a residual sense that the forms apprehended are illusory. For the dreamer this illusion represents a deep and pleasurable necessity – which accounts for the well-known state of mind in which a dreamer can say, 'It is a dream: I want to go on dreaming it.' The dream seems to have one kind of reality and yet is felt, at the same time, to have another, deeper reality underlying it. In this it is analogous to reality itself; that is, the ordinary individuated reality in which we, as individuals, live. For that reality too may be reinterpreted philosophically as an illusion, a world of appearances, what Schopenhauer calls 'the veil of maya', interposed between ourselves and the ultimate reality – by which is meant the ground of being, the primordial oneness or unity of all individual things.

Apollo is the bright sun-god, the symbol of all brightness, all appearance, all plastic energies that express themselves in individual shapes. The Apolline is the sphere of *individuation*, restraint, form, beauty, *illusion*. Apollo is also
< §2 the soothsaying god, ⟨the god of the Delphic oracle⟩; but though Apolline images seem to offer higher truth, they are and remain mere appearance.

In a state of intoxication, an individual loses himself. This is the basis of the Dionysiac experience: *the collapse of individuation*. In its fuller forms this is an ecstatic experience with mystical implications, and an experience of supreme intensity: rapturous, but also terrifying. Dionysiac emotions may be aroused directly, especially among unsophisticated peoples, by intoxicants and also by the approach of spring, with its promise of the rebirth of natural life and fertility. In particular, they tend to find *collective* expression, as with the medieval dances of St John and St Vitus; the wild and orgiastic festivities of ancient near-Eastern religion, with their song and dance and sexual licence; and, in Greece, the choruses that sang and danced in the worship of the fertility god, Dionysus. In his Dionysiac state a man feels that all barriers between himself and others are broken in favour of a rediscovered universal harmony. Between himself and nature, too, all things are as one. There is, in fact, no place for any distinctions, for anything that sets one thing off against any other thing: limits, forms, conventions, individuals.

§2 In the first phase of [historic] Greek culture, [the 'Homeric' period (VIII B.C. and earlier),] the Apolline impulse was entirely dominant. There was no [overt] Dionysiac worship among the Greeks at this time; and though they must have known of the near-Eastern festivals, the savage excesses of those cults were totally alien to them, at least on a conscious level, and were rejected uncompromisingly. The pure Apolline tendency of this phase, clearly present in the Homeric epics, found its purest expression in Doric art [(sculpture and architecture) of a rather later period], but [meanwhile] irresistible Dionysiac impulses began to appear spontaneously in Greece itself. The result was a compromise. The Dionysiac cult was established throughout Greece and a symbolic reconciliation with Dionysus was effected in Apollo's chief cult at Delphi; at the same time, Dionysus' cult in its Greek shape lost the wildness of its Asiatic equivalents, although its other features – above all, its song – were retained.

By this means, Dionysiac music was introduced into Greece [(VII B.C.?)]
< §6 and rapidly became a potent force. ⟨Its characteristic instrument was the flute and⟩ the cult-song to the new deity was the *dithyramb*. Apolline music, played on the lyre and characterized by regular rhythm and overall restraint, was

already familiar in Greece. Dionysiac music – music proper – introduced the emotional power of tone, melody and harmony.

Dionysiac religion was a religion of initiates, ⟨a mystery religion⟩, and < §10
at the centre of its worship was the mystical evocation of nature's awesome
unity, the primal unity concealed by our dismemberment into individuals,
and the worshippers' yearning for a recovery of that unity. In the dithyramb,
the potent Dionysiac music and the accompanying movements of the dance
symbolized the agony and the joy of this aspiration.

§3 Although the Apolline tendency was dominant in early Greece, this state of affairs was not, in fact, original, as a closer examination reveals.

Apollo, unlike Dionysus, is one of the *Olympian* deities, familiar to us
from Homer, and these deities are, in general, Apolline in the given sense.
Olympian religion, lacking in moral elevation and other-worldly spirituality,
is an exuberant and indiscriminate deification of good and evil, suggestive
of an extreme enjoyment of life. But actually the Greeks in their most creative
period knew only too well that the basis of existence is horrific. Beneath its
Olympian surface, Greek culture evinces an unmistakable and unique
sensitivity to the painful truth about life: the *Dionysiac truth* ⟨that the < §§4, 6,
underlying reality of existence is unchanging contradiction, pain and excess, 9, 17
represented to our immediate experience as the 'curse of individuation' – our
subjection, as impotent individuals, to the change and suffering that befall
us from birth to inevitable death⟩. As evidence of the Greeks' Dionysiac
perception, we can point to the dark side of their mythology: Titanic wars
and heroes; the agonies of Prometheus, Oedipus, Orestes; and the definitive
wisdom of Silenus, the satyr companion of Dionysus: the best thing is not
to be born – the next best is to die soon.

These Dionysiac elements within Greek mythology must be regarded as its earliest stratum, [*pre*-Hellenic in origin (second millennium B.C.);] while the Olympian mythological apparatus, along with the world of art that depicts it, is a later development. This fact is reflected in Greek myth, which commmemorates the victory of the Olympians over the Titans. The Titanic terror, then, precedes the Olympian joy. The terror, in fact, *necessitates* the joy. In other words, the Olympian world that overtakes the Titans was created by the Apolline instinct for beautiful illusion, *in order to make life bearable*.

The Olympian gods satisfy a profound need. They vindicate life and make it desirable by living it themselves more gloriously. It is they who make possible the 'naïve' Homeric identification with living and pain at the idea of death. Contrary to Romantic misconceptions, such *naïveté* is not 'natural', but achieved. It represents the sublimation* of suffering into beauty, the formation of a beautiful illusion to conceal the painful truth. Homeric *naïveté* is the complete victory of the Apolline.

§4 Naïve art, then, is a secondary phenomenon. It must also, like dreams, be regarded as a psychological necessity: its visionary illusion is needed to redeem the horror and suffering of existence. It may even be regarded as a *metaphysical* necessity, in that the primal unity, 'eternally suffering and contradictory', likewise needs the visionary illusion *for its own redemption*. And if the value of Apolline art is that it redeems existence, the value of the suffering inherent in existence is that it impels the creation of this art.

In early Greece, where the Apolline tendency was dominant, the redemptive vision almost entirely overlaid the horrific truth it was created to redeem. Above all, it imposed norms of order and limitation to conceal the Dionysiac revelation of contradiction and excess as ultimate realities. Moderation became a central ideal in human affairs, requiring observance of the limits of the individual. Hence the celebrated commandments of Delphic Apollo, 'know thyself' and 'nothing in excess'. And hence, inevitably, the hostility towards any manifestations of excessive self-assertion, whether those of the pre-Hellenic, pre-Apolline, world of Titans, or comparable tendencies among the 'barbarian' peoples outside Greece. But despite the Apolline code, the Dionysiac impulse could not be permanently repressed.* With the introduction of Dionysiac worship, either the Apolline gave way entirely; or the repression was intensified, as in the Dorian world (witness the defensive rigidity of Dorian Sparta as well as Doric art); or, thirdly, a compromise was reached.

The observations made so far may be summed up in terms of four historical phases throughout which Hellenic creativity was dominated by the two impulses. Phase one: the [pre-Hellenic] Dionysiac world with its dark mythology and the austere wisdom of Silenus [(second millenium B.C.)]. Phase two: the Apolline world of Homeric *naïveté* [(X–VIII B.C.)]. Phase three: the influx of Dionysus-worship [(VII B.C.)]. Phase four: the Dorian reassertion of the Apolline [(VII–VI B.C., although during this period]
< §10 ⟨Apolline culture was undermined by a growing trivialization of its religion and mythology⟩). Attic tragedy [(*fl.* late VI and V B.C.)] represents a further, climactic, stage in which the two conflicting tendencies were united.

* Not Nietzsche's own term.

[§§ 5–6 *Lyric poetry*]

§5 Greek tragedy originated in lyric poetry. Greek lyric was established as a literary genre by Archilochus [(VII B.C.)], whom the Greeks accordingly regarded as a creative originator on a par with Homer [(*c.* VIII B.C.)],* the creative genius of Greek epic. To appreciate the significance of the lyrical origin of tragedy, we must first elucidate lyric poetry as such.

Lyric poetry has been misleadingly categorized as 'subjective' art. All true art, however, must entail objectivity and the 'silencing of the individual will'. Lyric poetry is not subjective in the ordinary sense; and in its freedom from subjectivity it should be thought of in the same terms as *music*. Greek lyric poetry was [literally] musical: it was sung to music and inseparable from its music. The lyric poet [in general] is a *composer* first and foremost and, as such, a Dionysiac artist who surrenders his egoistic subjectivity to identify himself with the true metaphysical reality and reflect it in music. He now comes under Apolline influence and is therefore able to symbolize the music, in turn, in the form of specific *ideas* and *language*. This sequence of events is already prefigured in a claim made by Schiller that he used to conceive his own poetry in and through a 'musical mood'.[2] In other words, *music precedes the idea*. Epic poetry, like sculpture, is an Apolline art, and all such art involves a quite different creative process. Like a dreamer, the Apolline artist is absorbed in contemplation of something outside himself and does not identify with it. The ideas of the lyric poet, on the other hand, are projections of himself (whence the lyric 'I'), *but* a self indistinguishable from the ground of being, with which the poet is now one.

This explanation of lyric makes use of Schopenhauerian categories, although Schopenhauer himself was unable to deal satisfactorily with the problem of 'subjectivity'. The whole subjective–objective distinction is irrelevant here. Schopenhauer's position was that lyric combines contemplation and the individual will. But, on the contrary, the lyric poet, as artist, is released from his individual will and becomes a *medium* through which the ground of being makes its appearance. We are not, after all, the ultimate creators of the realm of art: we are ourselves *part* of it. We are works of art, belonging to a world that is itself an aesthetic phenomenon; and this is our highest claim to dignity, 'for only as an aesthetic phenomenon can existence and the world be eternally justified'. Of course, our conscious

* Readers unfamiliar with classical scholarship should be warned that the dating of ancient personages or events may be, as here, quite approximate. In other instances, reassuringly exact dates may well be merely conventional and conventionally acceptable – even in the case of celebrated authors' births and deaths.

rationalizations of our own significance and the significance of our art are bound to be quite illusory. Only the Dionysiac artist in the act of creation has any direct knowledge of the truth, thanks to his identity with the ultimate reality and the ultimate creator.

§6 Archilochus' specific contribution was to introduce *folk-song* into literature. Folk-song is the direct ancestor of lyric poetry, and the simplest artistic form that unites the Apolline and the Dionysiac. As with lyric proper, the music (the Dionysiac element) is primary and the words (the Apolline element) are secondary reflections of the music. The music, therefore, may be variously objectified in the verbalization. This explains the strophic form of folk-song, whereby one melody generates a succession of different lyrics. One may also adduce the fact that a Beethoven symphony often impels its audience to interpret the music pictorially, but in no one single way.

The distinction between the two main streams of Greek verse represented by Homer and Archilochus can now be restated in a way that, incidentally, takes account of the essential differences of phraseology between Homeric §§13, 17 poetry and the lyric tradition that begins with Archilochus and ⟨ends⟩ with Pindar [(V B.C.)]. In Homeric epic, language symbolizes the world of *phenomena*; in the new poetry, it symbolizes the world of *music*. In Schopenhauerian terms, this means that music becomes will, or rather that music, which cannot *be* will, makes its appearance as will. In sum, lyric poetry is dependent on the spirit of music, while music itself is independent of language. For music, unlike language, symbolizes ultimate reality, beyond and prior to all phenomena.

[§§7–10 *The origin and essence of tragedy*]

§7 [Greek tragedy is generally assumed to have had an original connection with Dionysus. It was performed at the festival of Dionysus in Athens and is said by Aristotle in his *Poetics* (*c.* 330 B.C.) to have originated in the Dionysiac dithyramb. Beyond this, however,] its origin has hitherto been an insoluble problem: the explicit evidence of the ancients is notoriously inadequate and various different theories have been constructed from it. The main task is to establish the nature of the tragic *chorus*, since it is clear from the ancient tradition that tragedy originated in the chorus and once consisted of nothing but the chorus. For this reason, among others, we must reject A. W. Schlegel's interpretation of the chorus as the 'ideal spectator',[3] there being originally no spectacle for it to be spectator of. We should also reject [Hegel's] idea that it represents the populace as against the aristocratic heroes of the drama proper:[4] in origin and essence, tragedy is purely metaphysical and not socio-political. There is more value in Schiller's insight[5] that the chorus is essentially anti-naturalistic and serves to uphold tragedy's ideal ground and poetic freedom. The chorus of primitive tragedy did indeed have such a basis. Originally it was the satyr chorus of the Dionysiac dithyramb. That is, it originally comprised the band of Dionysus-worshippers who, in their ecstatic state, saw themselves as the god's goatlike attendants, fictitious nature spirits in a fictitious natural state. But the 'fiction' had its own reality and credibility on a religious level.

Greek tragedy, like all true tragedy, leaves its audience with the feeling that despite all superficial changes, 'life is at bottom indestructibly joyful and powerful'. This feeling was originally conveyed in manifest form by a chorus of primeval beings, close to nature, who permanently retain their natural shape, irrespective of any changes in civilization. In their presence, the audience could feel its civilized surface annulled and replaced by a consoling sense of unity with nature. And the reason why the Greeks should have needed such consolation is that in their Dionysiac ecstasies they had looked into the painful essence of life. Like Hamlet, they had come face to face with its essential horror and absurdity. Such knowledge by itself leads to a Buddhistic negation of the will. It induces nausea and thereby inaction, since nothing can be done to affect the essential condition: action requires illusion. The salvation and solace for this state of mind is *art*, which converts thoughts of loathing into ideas it is possible to live with: horror is tamed and made *sublime*, while what had been disgusting absurdity becomes *comic*. [Like tragedy, its 'sublime' sister art, the 'Old' (Aristophanic) Comedy of classical Athens is generally regarded as having originated in the worship of Dionysus. Aristotle derives it from 'phallic songs', which were a common constituent of Greek fertility ritual and would have been sung to or for a particular fertility god: this would usually, though not perhaps invariably, have been Dionysus.] The Greeks, 'uniquely susceptible to the tenderest and deepest suffering', were saved from total Dionysiac nausea by the artistic mediation of the Dionysiac satyr-chorus.

§8 The Greek satyr represented nature in a pre-cultural state, but without any 'idyllic' sentimentality or artificiality and (for all his goat-like appearance) without being a mere animal either. As sympathetic companion of the suffering god, the satyr embodied man's highest and most intense emotions. He was a source of wisdom and a symbol of nature's sexual omnipotence. The satyr-chorus of the dithyramb represented what poetry always aspires to represent, the real truth of nature. The contrast between this truth and the false 'reality' of civilization is equivalent to the contrast between the eternal ground of being and the world of appearance.

In their ecstatic state, the Dionysiac worshippers saw themselves as satyrs. These visions constitute the starting point of tragic drama and must not be confused with the Apolline visions of the epic poet[6] (or equally those of the visual artist). In his mind's eye the epic narrator visualizes the personages and events that he is to describe, and sees them as something independent of and outside himself. In contrast, the Dionysiac chorus, like unconscious actors, enter into and lose themselves in the characters that their collective ecstasy impels them to conjure up. We must also contrast the dithyramb with the other kinds of choral song developed by the Greeks, all essentially Apolline, in which there is no 'entering into' and the singers remain 'themselves', retaining their names and keeping a sense of their ordinary civic status. In the dithyramb, but only in the dithyramb, the chorus are oblivious of everyday existence: in their ecstatic state they identify entirely with their proto-dramatic part.

A second visionary experience was required to create the world of the archetypal stage, the *skēnē*, and with it make true drama possible. In his ecstasy, the worshipper saw himself as a satyr and 'as a satyr, in turn, he saw his god'. That is, the Dionysiac vision of himself as satyr was complemented by an Apolline vision of events outside himself, i.e. the sufferings of Dionysus; and these visionary events constitute the origin of the *skēnē* with its dramatic action and speech. Tragedy remained *pre*-dramatic, however, so long as Dionysus himself, the hero of the vision, was purely visionary. Drama began when a masked actor was introduced to represent the god [in the sixth century, from which time] the Dionysiac experience of visionary transformation into satyrs was represented artistically. This meant that the Dionysiac participants were divided into two separate groups, worshippers [(making up a new and smaller chorus)] and spectators. The chorus now had the task of moving the spectators to see, not an actor, but the visionary figure that the actor stood for. A special relationship between the two groups remained, and the physical conditions of the Greek theatre [as it subsequently evolved] continued to ensure that the two groups were never in actual opposition to each other. [The theatre, always open-air, consisted in the first place of a circular dancing-floor (*orkhēstra*), where the chorus danced and sang, and the *skēnē*, behind the *orkhēstra*, was later added for the actors. The audience sat in tiers round the front half of the *orkhēstra*, which thus served to separate them from the *skēnē*.] The spectators could therefore still feel themselves as one with the chorus performing immediately below them and ignore the 'reality' of the real world all around.

We can now explain tragedy's familiar alternation of choral lyrics and dramatic dialogue as the Dionysiac chorus with its repeated objectifications in Apolline form. We can also now account, genetically, for two qualities that characterize the chorus of classical tragedy: *passivity* and *wisdom*. In their Apolline vision, the dithyrambic chorus see Dionysus as their lord and master: they are his servants. But in their Dionysiac experience, they become participants in the god's suffering and thereby in his understanding: as such they can 'proclaim the truth from the heart of the world'. In so far as the action of tragedy is originally a vision, seen only by the chorus, the chorus may, in a special sense, be regarded as its 'ideal spectator'.

§9 In classical tragedy as we know it, [the tragedy of Aeschylus (525–456) and Sophocles (496–406)], the drama, as represented in the dialogue, gives a uniformly Apolline impression of form, precision, lucidity and beauty, much like Homeric epic. But the heroes who convey this impression are merely embodying the Apolline response to life's horror: the attempt to make that horror acceptable. *This* is the real meaning of the famous 'Greek serenity', so often misrepresented as some kind of untroubled cheerfulness.

Consider the serenity achieved in Sophocles' two Oedipus plays. In these, Sophocles presents the hero as the noble man who is doomed to error and misery despite his wisdom and all his efforts (*Oedipus Rex*), but who, through his great suffering, eventually wins the magical power of benediction beyond his death (*Oedipus at Colonus*). The structure of the first play has an intricate, and quite exquisite, logical basis, a peculiarity that contrives to lend the work a 'note of superior optimism'. In *Oedipus at Colonus* the optimism is raised to a religious plane. It is implied here that however destructive they may be, the actions of a noble man cannot involve sin and that the apparent passivity to which the hero is eventually reduced is actually his highest activity. This whole conception is undeniably optimistic; *and yet* the myth underlying it is gruesome. Oedipus, who solved the riddle of the Sphinx, murdered his father and married his mother. This is to say that the man who solves the riddle of nature must also violate the most sacred natural law, and even that wisdom as such is a crime against nature. The serenity, then, belongs to the poet, not to the myth: it lies precisely in the poet's attempt to palliate the dark truths that the myth represents. The myth in itself is deeply pessimistic.

The glorification of action in Aeschylus' *Prometheus Bound* is the antithesis of Sophocles' endorsement of saintly passivity, but it rests on the same pessimistic basis. The Aeschylean Titan, who, to his own cost, gives man fire and thereby civilization, has an artist's confidence in the sufficiency of his own capacities and an artist's readiness to suffer for it. In him we see man himself, risen to Titanic stature, creating civilization by his own efforts. But the mythical basis for these gratifying notions is, once again, deeply disturbing. The control of fire is the mark of the civilization man aspires to, but constitutes a kind of sacrilege, a 'robbery of divine nature', that must be paid for with immense suffering: human aspiration must inevitably bring man into conflict with the divine realm.

The Prometheus myth is not specifically Greek. It is in fact of native Aryan origin and, with the dignity it confers on the crime against nature, it presents a marked contrast to the equivalent Semitic myth, the myth of the Fall. In the Aryan conception, human evil (guilt and suffering) is traced to active sacrilege, which is masculine (*der Frevel*) and committed by a man. In the Semitic myth, evil originates in feminine weakness (*die Sünde*). The central insight of the Prometheus myth evinces an Aryan instinct for the tragic interpretation of life, whereby human evil is justified pessimistically. Man's aspiration to transcend his limits entails sacrilege and suffering, being at bottom an attempt to reimpose the original unity of life. The cost of that
< §16 heroic effort is the ⟨annihilation of the individual hero⟩: 'he suffers the primordial contradiction in his own person'. This is Dionysiac wisdom, and in this respect Prometheus is certainly a Dionysiac figure. The *Aeschylean* Prometheus, however, expresses at the same time an Apolline demand for justice characteristic of his author. The clash between human and divine presents us with two spheres, each with right on its side, pointing forward to a reconciliation in line with the Aeschylean view of 'Fate enthroned above gods and men as eternal justice'. The poet's conception is, once again, more optimistic than the myth.

§10 We know from ancient tradition that in its earliest form Greek tragedy always dealt with the mythical sufferings of Dionysus. We may therefore imagine performances centring, as the Dionysiac mysteries did, on his dismemberment by the Titans and his hoped-for rebirth, which would be presaged in the worshippers' songs of triumph. The meaning of this myth is clear. The god experiences the agony of individuation in himself, symbolizing the shattering of the original unity and its transformation into a multiplicity of elements and their individual forms. It is understood that individuation is the ultimate source of all suffering, and the end of individuation, implicit in the vision of the god's rebirth, is intensely desirable;
< §21 ⟨for only by [a second shattering], the destruction of the individual, can the original unity be restored.⟩ We have here all the elements of the 'mystery doctrine of tragedy': the ultimate unity of all things, individuation as the source of evil, and art as an augury of eventual reintegration.

[It was in the second half of the sixth century that the primitive tragedy practised by the Dionysiac worshippers developed into true drama, and, in the same period,] the cult was accepted as a public cult in Athens. Dionysiac wisdom was now promulgated openly, [sometimes through its own mythology, although more often] it was mediated through the *Olympian* mythology associated with Homeric epic. For the post-Homeric Dionysiac movement that culminated in tragedy supplanted Olympianism to the extent of taking over epic mythology to express its own insights. In this sense, *all* the diverse myths of classical tragedy are equally Dionysiac, and the same applies to the tragic heroes: for a long time, Dionysus had been the only character represented in the early drama, its only hero, and, until Euripides, all the different suffering heroes of tragedy were still 'mere masks of this original hero'. This accounts for the fact that the Aeschylean and Sophoclean heroes are never represented as individuals, but have an 'ideal' character.

[By the beginning of the fifth century] the Olympian religion and its mythology were in a state of crisis. In particular, the mythology was coming to be regarded as *history* – the first step towards trivialization and eventual nullity. But for the time being the whole field of myth was reinterpreted in terms of Dionysiac pessimism and thereby revitalized, gaining a new weight and significance. The catalyst that made this possible was Dionysiac music.

[§§ 11–14 *The death of tragedy: Euripides and Socratic optimism*]

§ 11 As a serious force, Greek tragedy came to a sudden end with the death[s] of [Sophocles and] Euripides [(480–406) at the end of the fifth century]. Euripides was its last great figure, and it was his innovating genius that
destroyed it – ⟨myth, music and all⟩. Once tragedy was dead, its only heir < § 10
was the 'New Comedy' [of the late fourth and third centuries] and it is, again, Euripides to whom the innovations represented by this degenerate form must be traced back.

Euripides' importance for New Comic poets like Menander [(342–293)] and Philemon [(368–267)] lay, above all, in his introduction of mundane naturalism, through which it became possible, for the first time, to stage the mediocrity of ordinary life: 'Euripides brought the *spectator* on stage.' His heroes had none of the traditional grandeur appropriate to demigods and he reduced the customary high language of the genre accordingly. His positive contribution in this sphere was to give his characters the ability to 'speak' in a special sense – to debate and to philosophize. This is the origin of New Comedy's characteristic *cleverness*, its 'perpetual triumphs of cunning', its glorification of the good-natured, cunning slave. And this good nature has its own enormous importance. It is representative of a new outlook on life. There is no more of the *profound* serenity that had characterized the Greek spirit in its greatest period, and, above all, in the sixth century, which had produced the [religious] movement of the mysteries, tragedy, and [the 'religious' philosophers,] Pythagoras and Heraclitus. Instead we have the cheerfulness of a slave without responsibilities or aspirations, and a satisfaction with the easy enjoyment of the passing moment. Such superficiality became a legitimate target for the early Christian thinkers, under whose influence Greek antiquity *as a whole* has been misrepresented as superficial ever since.

If Euripides brought the spectator onto the stage, it was not because he enjoyed popular favour in his lifetime. Unlike Aeschylus and Sophocles, he was not consistently popular, and his innovations did not arise from any desire to pander to the public. They were prompted by his *critical spirit*. Like Lessing in modern times, he had an extraordinary critical talent, which constantly stimulated his productive artistic impulse. To such a man the traditional basis of tragedy must be essentially alien. For Euripides, understanding generated all enjoyment and creation, but at the heart of tragedy he saw something inexplicable and altogether 'incommensurable' with the workings of reason. Accordingly, he formulated a new conception of drama to suit his own inclinations.

§12 What Euripides wanted was to make tragedy *reasonable*. He therefore aspired to remove its 'original and all-powerful Dionysiac element'; and his aspiration was fulfilled. It is true that his late play, the *Bacchae* [(produced in 405 B.C., a year after his death)], dealing expressly with Dionysus and the early opposition to his worship in Greece, is to be interpreted as a belated recognition that such opposition is in fact inadvisable: Pentheus, who opposes the god, is destroyed, and the poet impresses on us that Dionysus is too powerful to be ignored. But thanks to Euripides' earlier efforts, the Dionysiac element in tragedy had been negated already. This elimination of the Dionysiac might, at best, have resulted in some kind of dramatized Apolline epic (like Goethe's projected *Nausikaa*, perhaps); but in fact Euripides did
< §10 not achieve even this: ⟨having abandoned Dionysus, he was in turn abandoned by Apollo⟩. Like the latter-day rhapsode of Plato's *Ion*, he intruded his own personality into his work and, instead of the requisite epic detachment, showed an intense involvement with his heroes and heroines. [This is the source of] the two new, suspect [and barely compatible] ingredients that he added in order to give his drama any life at all: hot emotional outbursts and cold thoughts and paradoxes – poor substitutes for
< §9 Dionysiac ecstasy and Apolline ⟨lucidity and precision⟩. The extreme

naturalism with which his characters' thoughts and emotions were portrayed was the final inartistic touch. The fact was that, driven by an impulse that was not artistic at all, but critical, Euripides could only produce work that was thoroughly inartistic itself. But *quite apart from* these subsidiary deficiencies, it is clear that Euripides' rejection of the Dionysiac was bound to make the true tragic effect unattainable.

And yet the Euripidean spirit cannot be regarded as the ultimate cause of tragedy's downfall. It is itself a manifestation of something deeper: a new *rationalism*, epitomized by Euripides' great contemporary, the philosopher *Socrates* [(469–399)].

In Euripidean drama, we see the results of 'aesthetic Socratism', the outlook that makes intelligibility a prerequisite of beauty – a counterpart to Socrates' notion that only the man of knowledge can be virtuous. With this criterion Euripides adjusted all the elements of the drama: language, characters, structure and choral music. His treatment of the prologue is representative. Euripidean drama commonly has an expository prologue whose function is to outline the forthcoming action of the play. This action is not itself the centre of interest, however. The effective centre of interest is intense emotion, embodied above all in the new 'rhetorical-lyrical scenes' that featured the 'passion and dialectic of the protagonist'. To ensure that the spectators would be totally absorbed in these scenes, there must be no missing links or unexplained aspects of the story to act as distractions. On such characteristically conscious grounds, he employed the prologue.

[According to a well-known anecdote quoted by a writer of late antiquity,[7]] Sophocles said that Aeschylus did what was right, although he did it unconsciously. Euripides would probably have said that what Aeschylus did was *wrong because* he did it unconsciously. For Euripides, as for Socrates, too, conscious intelligence was everything.

§13 Euripides and Socrates were persistently associated by ancient writers. Socrates had a contempt for tragedy; yet we hear anecdotes about him helping Euripides with his plays and only watching tragedy at the theatre if there was a new play by Euripides on. Especially important is the way that [their younger contemporary], Aristophanes [(d. 385 B.C.)], brackets the two as instigators of a suspect enlightment; and likewise the decision of the Delphic oracle that the wisest of men was Socrates, followed by Euripides, with Sophocles third – a decision clearly based on the new estimate of conscious intelligence. Socrates' own comment was that all men were equally ignorant, but he alone was aware of the fact; and even those expert in their own fields (poets among them) had no conscious understanding of their calling but worked 'only by instinct'. The implied contempt for instinct, together with his excesssive logical faculty, explains why Socrates should have depreciated all known art and ethics and aspired with 'divine *naïveté*' to put them right. At the same time, some special factor is necessary to explain his extraordinary self-confidence and strength of purpose, evinced even in the face of death – the death that he himself engineered and then suffered with such calm that the image of 'the dying Socrates' became a new ideal.

The special factor is Socrates' *daimonion*. In moments of crisis, Socrates was guided by the utterances of a divine voice, which invariably warned against any further pursuit of knowledge. In his case, that is to say, instinctive wisdom manifested itself only on exceptional occasions and as a purely inhibiting agency. And even though he insisted on the divinity of his inner voice, the essential perversity remains: in him, instinct, which should be a creative-affirmative force, becomes the critic, and consciousness, which should be critical-dissuasive, becomes the creator.

§14 To Socrates, the only acceptable kind of literature was the fable – a straightforward medium for conveying necessary truths. At the opposite extreme, tragedy seemed unreasonable and dangerous: it was full of incongruities and had no concern with 'truth' at all. Following Socrates, the young Plato [(429–347)], who had aspired to be a tragedian himself, repudiated tragedy and art in general, even burning his own plays. Nevertheless, he was led by a strong artistic instinct and the personal impact of Socrates himself to create a new art-form related to those he now despised. Plato's main (if misguided) objection to traditional art was that it represented only the limited reality of the empirical world. His new art attempted to represent instead the underlying *idea* and so transcend the pseudo-reality – which is in fact precisely what traditional art, in its own way, had always done. The new form was the Platonic dialogue, in which the traditional modes of poetry survived, albeit in an eccentric reconstitution. It was a cross between prose and poetry, a mixture of narrative, lyric and drama. By this means, Plato provided the model of a new art-form, the novel, which might be regarded as 'an infinitely enhanced Aesopian fable', with poetry in strict subordination to rationality: as in Euripides, the Apolline was reduced to 'logical schematism'. The new art-form also had a hero, Socrates: a 'dialectical hero', reminiscent of the argumentative Euripidean protagonist.

The Socratic dialectical tendency, found alike in Euripides and Plato, is inherently untragic, because it is inherently optimistic: it presupposes that essential problems of existence can be solved by the activities of the rational mind. 'Virtue is knowledge, all sins arise from ignorance, the virtuous man is the happy man': in these Socratic maxims we see the formulae of a rationalistic optimism that was – and is – incompatible with tragedy. It is in accordance with such optimism that Euripides should have turned the suffering hero of earlier tragedy into a dialectician and the transcendental justice of Aeschylus into the 'poetic justice' dispensed by the *deus ex machina* who appears at the end of so many of his plays.

The central target of the new rationalism, however, was the chorus, which now came to be seen as an anomalous relic of the past. That process is, in fact, already apparent in Sophocles, who no longer gives the chorus the major rôle; instead, he limits its sphere to that of one of the characters, which (*pace* Aristotle) destroys its meaning. After this the chorus degenerates further in Euripides and all but disappears a century later, in New Comedy. [There it merely provides musical interludes between acts, a pattern foreshadowed in some odes of Euripides.][8] But without the chorus and its music the Dionysiac impulse – and thus the very essence of tragedy – cannot survive.

In the light of this discussion, we can see that even before Socrates there was a spirit hostile to the Dionysiac. Socrates was simply its most magnificent expression. We can also see that Socrates himself cannot be regarded merely as an agent of destruction, despite the immediate responsibility of the Socratic impulse for the dissolution of tragedy. The new art-form developed by Plato would not have existed without Socrates, who, in any case, seems to have felt some misgivings about the sufficiency of rationality himself. It appears that he had a recurring dream in which he was told, 'Socrates, be an artist',[9] a command which he ignored at first, supposing that nothing could be a higher 'art' than his own philosophizing, but eventually complied with by writing some poetry while waiting for death in prison. Is it that Socratism and art are not incompatible after all? Might art be Socratism's necessary correlative? And might they even be combined in one person? – is an 'artistic Socrates' a possibility?

[§ 15 *The Socratic spirit in the modern world*]

§ 15 Having granted that Socrates is far from being a purely destructive force, we must now go further and acknowledge the full extent of his positive cultural significance.

Greek culture has provided the creative exemplars of all subsequent cultures, including our own, and Socrates is one of its principal figures. He represents *theoretical man*, a type of existence previously unheard of, but one which our culture has elevated above all others. Like the artist, theoretical man takes an 'infinite delight in all that exists' and is thereby protected against pessimism. The two types differ primarily in respect of their attitude towards truth and the uncovering of truth. Whenever truth is uncovered, the artist's pleasure lies in contemplating whatever is still unexplained, whereas theoretical man finds pleasure in something already explained and, above all, in the attempt to explain still further. In fact, ultimately (as 'the most honest theoretical man', Lessing, perceived)[10] he cares more for the search after truth than for truth itself. And this attitude is explained by the 'sublime metaphysical illusion' peculiar to theoretical man, his 'unshakable faith' that by rational thought he can penetrate the depths of existence and even *correct* existence itself.

Socrates lived by reason and died by reason. He symbolizes man liberated by reason from the fear of death, the optimist for whom all truth is rationally accessible and knowledge of the truth a panacea. Over the centuries, this Socratic spirit has extended its influence, and in our culture that influence has reached its peak with a universal demand for knowledge and the triumphs of *Wissenschaft* – philosophy,[11] science and learning – by which our culture endeavours to make existence comprehensible and therefore justified. As the progenitor of this movement of ideas, Socrates must be regarded as the turning point in the whole history of civilization. Without his influence, the vast energy expended on *Wissenschaft* over the centuries might have been used for purposes of individual or national aggrandizement. The result would have been world wars and migrations and eventually a weakening of life-instincts in favour of a self-destructive ethic of murder and suicide like that of the Fijians.

But for all the triumphs of the Socratic spirit, its true significance is that it repeatedly prompts a regeneration of art – 'art in the metaphysical sense', which is its widest and deepest sense. For *Wissenschaft* has its limits, and the 'unshakable faith' in its power ensures that its most gifted followers press on until they reach those limits and discover for themselves its ultimate powerlessness to solve the problem of existence. At this point optimism makes way for a new kind of awareness, *tragic* awareness, which can only be borne through art in the shape of myth. Thus myth is the necessary consequence of science, even its purpose; and the demand for knowledge which on a lower level is hostile to art ultimately becomes a need for art.

Such is the critical situation at the present day, but the outcome is still unclear: a new triumph of art (albeit under the name of religion or *Wissenschaft* itself)? a new barbarism? new kinds of genius – even perhaps the 'artistic Socrates'?

[II RESTATEMENT: HOPES FOR THE REBIRTH OF TRAGEDY IN GERMANY]

[§§ 16–20 *Music and the crisis in modern culture*]

§ 16 The aim of the discussion so far has been to show that tragedy arises from the spirit of music and is bound to perish without it. What follows is an amplification of matters already discussed with an emphasis on contemporary culture and the conflict at its summit between the resurgent tragic impulse and the rationalistic spirit of *Wissenschaft*.

The origin of my inquiry was Schopenhauer's insight about music, [recently] approved by Wagner in his essay, *Beethoven*. It was this that prompted me to scrutinize Greek tragedy and thereby gain the new view of the Hellenic spirit that I have been putting forward. To recapitulate: what Schopenhauer demonstrated is that music differs in character and origin from the other arts because they represent phenomena, while music represents metaphysical reality directly. This truth is to be reinterpreted in the light of my principle that art does not derive from a single impulse (i.e. the Apolline impulse towards beauty), but from two: the Dionysiac as well as the Apolline. From these starting points we can come to understand the dual effect of Dionysiac music on our Apolline capability. Music stimulates us to realize the Dionysiac metaphysical world in Apolline symbolism, which then, under the influence of music, acquires its highest significance. Hence the capacity of music to engender myth, especially the tragic myth that symbolizes Dionysiac wisdom.

The tragic spirit, with its joy in the annihilation of the individual, cannot be explained simply in terms of the traditional principle of beauty. The beauty associated with tragedy represents Dionysiac wisdom translated into Apolline images. Tragedy affirms, not the illusory beauty of this world, but the eternity of the metaphysical world, even through the negation of the hero. ⟨It < § 17
reconciles us to the destructibility of the individual by an evocation of indestructible (albeit, for the individual, terrifying) unity.⟩ It is only Apolline art that seeks to replace suffering by beauty. The 'eternity' promised here is the eternity of the phenomenon. In Apolline art beauty replaces truth.

§ 17 My theory of tragic myth provides the first acceptable explanation of the chorus of Greek tragedy. It has to be admitted, though, that the real meaning of tragic myth was never consciously articulated by the Greek tragedians who used it. Their plots and theatrical effects reveal a deeper wisdom than they themselves could verbalize. (It is the same with Shakespeare, whose Hamlet, for instance, 'talks more superficially than he acts'.) But it must be remembered that the choral music of Greek tragedy, now lost, might have conveyed the requisite metaphysical depth.

The mythopoeic power of music has already been shown to be a decisive force in Greek literary history. The first such objectification of music in myth was in Greek lyric poetry [(from VII B.C.)]; the last, climactic, one was in Attic tragedy [(VI–V B.C.)]; after tragedy, [(in fact, from IV B.C.)], thanks to the new rationalism, the faculty for creating myth disappeared from Greek art, although a mythic expression of the Dionysiac world-view lived on in
< §12 a debased form in the mystery religions underground, ⟨later to re-emerge in the shape of 'a secret cult which gradually covered the earth'⟩.

Mythopoeia began to decline [in the middle of the fifth century]. We see this in the music of the New Dithyramb [(from *c.* 470–460)], a degenerate form of the dithyramb proper and rightly opposed by Aristophanes. Where Dionysiac music expresses truth on a universal and metaphysical scale and engenders myth as the instance of that truth, the aim of the New Dithyrambic composers was to imitate particular *phenomena* (natural or human) in the manner of a tone-painting. The result was to make the music an even poorer thing than the phenomenon itself, and to nullify the music's mythopoeic power. It is not surprising that this movement had the sympathy of Euripides, who made considerable use of its tricks and mannerisms.

[During this same period,] an analogous tendency was operative in the sphere of tragic character-portrayal. [In Aeschylean tragedy] the characters had been eternal types representing the universal laws implicit in myth. Sophocles still portrayed complete characters, but used the myths to suggest individual peculiarities. In Euripides the characters are *purely* individuals, with their prominent traits delineated to suit a proto-scientific 'truth to nature'. The process culminates in New Comedy's recurrent stock characters, each one based on a single stereotyped peculiarity – cunning slaves and so on. From now on, music could be no more than tone-painting or else a stimulant for jaded nerves, where the words hardly mattered (as was already the case in Euripidean lyrics).

The clearest instance of all involves the dénouements of the new drama. Genuine [mythic] tragedy characteristically ended on a note of metaphysical comfort, the purest instance being Sophocles' *Oedipus at Colonus*. The new drama pioneered by Euripides and perfected as New Comedy [rejected the implications of tragic myth and] was obliged, *faute de mieux*, to look for 'an earthly resolution of the tragic dissonance'. After due suffering, the hero was rewarded with a marriage or some token of divine favour. The *deus ex machina* took the place of metaphysical comfort.

These are all signs of the new 'Greek serenity' which excluded the Dionysiac and dominated the Greek world from Socrates onwards. Apart from its survival in underground religion, the tragic outlook was overwhelmed by a 'senile love of life', unproductive and sharply distinct from the Apolline *naïveté* of the early period, which was an *achievement*, a triumph over suffering. The optimism of theoretical man, with its aspiration to 'confine the individual within a limited circle of soluble problems', was the noblest form of the new outlook. For all its worldly achievements, however, such optimism cannot prevent the re-emergence of the tragic outlook for ever.

§18 At its higher levels, what we call culture is made up of three formative elements: Socratic love of knowledge; [the Apolline impulse towards] the beauty of art; and [Dionysiac] metaphysical [faith] in the essential indestructibility of life. All three are [in different degrees] *illusions*, which make the weight of life bearable – to those of sufficient stature to feel its weight in the first place. Depending on which one of the three is dominant, we have a predominantly *Socratic* or *artistic* or *tragic* culture – or, in historical terms, *Alexandrian** or *Hellenic* or *Buddhistic*.

Up to the present day, modern culture has been almost totally Alexandrian. Distrustful of action, it is preoccupied with the expansion of knowledge, and theoretical man is its ideal. It education is geared to producing such men. Its religion has degenerated into scholarship. Even its poetry has developed from scholarly imitations. The quest for knowledge and the assumption of the limitless power of rationality have shaped our civilization; above all, they have imbued it with its optimistic view of life.

But modern culture is now proving to be vulnerable on two counts, one social, one intellectual. In the first place, its survival requires the existence of a slave class, whereas its optimistic outlook obliges it to deny the necessity of such a class. Without some fundamental change of outlook, this internal contradiction must eventually be fatal: slaves who have learned to regard their existence as an injustice will look for a terrible vengeance. In the second place, the claim of rational thought to limitless applicability has been disproved. Such great thinkers as Kant and Schopenhauer have used the apparatus of *Wissenschaft* to demonstrate the limits of *Wissenschaft*. The optimistic belief that the essence of reality can be explored by scientific laws

* Referring to the post-classical Greek culture centred on Alexandria in Egypt in the last three centuries B.C. Alexandria, founded by Alexander the Great in 332, is famous not for its art (although Alexandrian writers of note came to have a formative influence on the later literature of Rome), and still less for any expression of metaphysical insight, but for its unique library and the copious scholarship and research associated with it.

has been exposed as a failure to see that the mere phenomenon is not the sole reality. With this insight, a tragic culture is inaugurated. In such a culture, knowledge is superseded by *wisdom*, which looks for a total view of life, seeking to come to terms with its essential suffering and aspiring [in Goethe's words] to 'live resolutely in wholeness and fulness'.[12] To educate the new and heroic seriousness of the coming generation, a new art will be needed, the art of metaphysical consolation: tragedy.

Meanwhile, Socratic culture, shaken from two directions, has lost its self-confidence: witness its present obsession with novelty, coupled with a fear of any change of direction that would contradict its own premises. The crisis is indicated by the state of modern art, which is eclectic and derivative, scholarly but unsatisfying, without joy or strength. In place of a Socratic self-assurance, modern man has a Faustian yearning.

§19 Modern culture can be regarded as the culture of the opera: in this superficial art its essence is revealed most clearly.

The primary need that opera was invented to satisfy was a non-artistic need. That explains how such externalized music – recitative, *stilo rappresentativo* and all – could have arisen in an age [(XVI A.D.)] which had produced the 'ineffably sublime and sacred music of Palestrina'. The new music was characterized by alternations of emotionally charged speech (half-sung) and passionate lyrical interjections (wholly sung). The 'speech' emphasized the sense of the words, whereas the lyrical parts invited a musical response. Such an unprecedented mixture had no inspiration from Apolline or Dionysiac principles. And yet it was intended as a re-creation of the music of ancient Greece; that is, as an evocation of a primitive and pure world.

Operatic music is essentially *idyllic*. It sets up an ideal world of nature, which is nevertheless represented as attainable reality (to use a formula of Schiller's).[13] In other words, it is constructed on the false premise that man is archetypally good and naturally artistic (witness the absurd convention of the eternally virtuous hero forever bursting effortlessly into song). As such, it represents a trivialization of nature and an optimistic glorification of man to suit an Alexandrian-theoretical culture. Opera is, indeed, the invention of theoretical man, the *critical layman*, not the artist. It stems from experiments in Renaissance Florence based on the demand of unmusical amateurs that, above all else, the words must be understood. Lacking any sense of the Dionysiac depths of music, they assumed that the words took precedence and, as with the New Attic Dithyramb, their music aspired to nothing higher than tone-painting, in imitation of the world of phenomena.

Under the influence of opera and the culture it represents, most modern music has been reduced to the level of entertainment and deprived of its Dionysiac seriousness – *except in Germany*. For in the recent course of German music from Bach to Beethoven and Beethoven to Wagner, we see the re-awakening of the Dionysiac spirit, albeit misinterpreted in terms of 'beauty' by such as Otto Jahn,[14] and, in general, uncomprehended by its contemporaries. This movement is aligned with the recent advance of German philosophy. Thanks to the Kantian-Schopenhauerian critique of Socratism, an infinitely more profound view of ethics and art has been developed, which amounts to a conceptualized form of Dionysiac wisdom.

In these developments of music and philosophy, we can foresee a new form of existence. The rebirth of the Dionysiac spirit in art presages the rebirth of culture as a whole, in the shape of a new tragic age. This is shown by the Hellenic prototype, thanks to which we can see that we are now recreating the Hellenic epochs, but in reverse order, passing from the Alexandrian to the tragic. At the same time, in these new developments the German spirit is rediscovering its own true self. Germany must now reject the alien influence of Romance culture, to which she has been subservient, and develop her full creative potential; and for this purpose, Hellenism, as an educational and cultural force in our society, is more necessary than ever.

§20 Since the time of Winckelmann, Goethe and Schiller, the German attempt to recreate the achievement of ancient Greek culture has grown increasingly feebler because of a failure to penetrate into the essence of the Greek spirit. The result is that belief in Hellenism as a cultural force has been almost abandoned. The Hellenic ideal is either patronized, or else upheld with vacuous rhetoric about 'Greek harmony', 'Greek beauty', 'Greek serenity'; while professional scholars, opting for a comfortable scepticism, have been content to pervert their subject by limiting its aim to textual and linguistic studies or the 'historical' assimilation of antiquity.

The critical state of Hellenic studies in Germany is a particular, central, instance of our general educational and cultural crisis. The educative power of our academic institutions has never been lower: it is *journalism* that gives the lead. The intelligentsia and true art have never been further apart. Our entire Socratic–Alexandrian civilization is exhausted and desolate. Even Goethe and Schiller failed to renew it. Even Schopenhauer could do no more than persist in a hopeless search for truth. Unless we place our hope in the rebirth of true Hellenism through tragic music, there is no hope anywhere.

[§§21–24 *The tragic effect and tragic myth*]

§21 Only from the Greeks can we understand what a rebirth of tragedy must mean to the inner life of a nation. The Persian wars [(490–479, in the time of Aeschylus)] were fought by men who were inspired by tragedy and in turn revived by it. In its pure form, the Dionysiac impulse leads to apathy and hostility to any political action, and eventually to a total, Buddhistic withdrawal from the public world in pursuit of mystical self-negation. The antithesis of this is the extreme secularization of the Roman Empire, in which the institutional and political instincts (these being essentially Apolline impulses that define the place of the individual) were credited with absolute validity. 'Placed between India and Rome', the Greeks in their greatest period achieved a third mode of existence thanks to an extraordinary combination of political and Dionysiac instincts; and the remedial power that prevented either instinct from overwhelming the other, the power that stimulated, purified and relieved the people at this time, was tragedy. To comprehend all that was involved here, one must experience the full force of tragedy at first hand; and here Act III of *Tristan* can be pointed to as a prime specimen of tragic art.

Tragedy's specific effect depends on the interaction of its two components, the Apolline drama and the Dionysiac music. There is a fashionable but crude notion that music and drama are related like body and soul.[15] In fact the relationship between the two is intricate. The chief function of the Apolline elements is to shield the spectator against the full impact of the music; and it is actually the presence of this shield that permits the highest potential of music to be realized. By itself such music would be shattering with its evocation of primordial universality, but the Apolline particularity of the tragic myth makes the evocation bearable by giving us sublime individuals to feel for and to satisfy our sense of beauty. Instead of the negation of all individuality, we are offered a parable of a single individual who, in his heroic struggle, 'takes the whole Dionysiac world on his back and thus relieves us of that burden'. In its turn, the music activates the Apolline component to the highest degree. The drama acquires a supreme vividness unattainable by words and action alone: words and ideas are made to convey their suggestions sensuously, and the movements and characters of the drama are illumined from within. But this triumph of the Apolline is qualified by the predominance of the Dionysiac in the total effect. Through the music the tragic myth acquires an intense metaphysical significance, [whereby] it gives the spectator intimations of a supreme joy and a higher existence to be attained through the annihilation of the individual. In the last analysis, therefore, the Dionysiac, as the more powerful element, forces the Apolline to communicate its own wisdom. Thus the intricate relation between the two elements in tragedy is resolved by a synthesis: 'Dionysus speaks the language of Apollo and Apollo, finally, the language of Dionysus: and so the highest goal of tragedy and all art is attained'.

§22 ⟨Of all the peculiar effects of musical tragedy, the most remarkable is < §24
the co-existence of opposite impressions.⟩ Whereas visual art and epic poetry
invite a purely contemplative response and an uninterrupted delight in the
phenomena as portrayed, the spectator of tragedy ⟨experiences a satisfying < §24
sense of illumination,⟩ even of omniscience, ⟨together with an impulse to < §24
find a more intense satisfaction in something deeper.⟩ In one sense he accepts
the world of the stage, in another he denies it. The tragic hero appears before
him with an epic clarity and beauty, and yet he rejoices at the hero's
annihilation. ⟨He feels compelled to see, and yet at the same time he yearns < §24
for something beyond sight.⟩

Tragedy can only be fully explained in such ⟨metaphysical⟩ terms. It is < §24
not to be thought of as a mere 'imitation of nature'. With its creation and destruction of individuals, it offers us a presentiment of the primordial unity that lies behind the world of phenomena. But our aestheticians have no inkling of this. Their notion of the essence of tragedy is 'the struggle of the hero with fate' [(like Schelling)] or 'the triumph of the moral world-order' [(like Schiller)] or 'the discharge of the emotions' [(like Lessing and other neo-Aristotelians)].[16] One can only suppose that they are incapable of the proper response to tragedy: that is, an *aesthetic* response to a work of art.

Previous theories of the tragic effect are misplaced. It is quite wrong to posit a pathological process, as Aristotle does with his theory of *katharsis*, whereby the audience is purged of pity and fear by the solemn events of the play. And it is equally inadequate to suggest that the audience should only respond morally, elevated by the supposed triumph of good over evil – even though for many people now this is undoubtedly the effect of tragedy.

The Greeks, as Goethe divined, were attuned to experience intense feeling in the spirit of *an aesthetic game*. But until now the members of our theatre-going public have not been so attuned: a public brought up with entirely false expectations, a public of 'critics' evincing a half-moral, half-scholarly, predisposition. The reaction of the more serious dramatists of our era to this public was to appeal to irrelevant moral-religious feelings or to use contemporary material to arouse equally irrelevant socio-political emotions like patriotism. But these well-meant attempts were bound to fail from the sheer perversity of the enterprise. The attempt to use the theatre for purposes of moral education, still practised in Schiller's time, was soon discredited. With critics and journalists in positions of influence in the worlds of culture and education and in society as a whole, art has degenerated into a mere topic of inconsequential chit-chat, and criticism, correspondingly, into the cement of a worthless social milieu. But even in such an unfavourable atmosphere, a work like Wagner's *Lohengrin* [(first produced in 1850)] might succeed in momentarily startling the more sensitive members of the public into a true response. In the absence of any informed critical guidance, it is true, they would be unable to go any further: the experience would remain isolated and leave nothing behind it. Nevertheless, in such experiences 'the aesthetic audience' has been reborn along with tragedy itself.

§23 Only a spectator with a truly aesthetic capacity can respond properly to myth. For him, myth is a concentrated image of the world, which is serious and effective notwithstanding the way it breaches causality by introducing miracles. The Socratic-critical spectator finds miracles on stage arbitrary or childish; and, in fact, most of us in the modern world are incapable of feeling any myth as a credible reality unless it is mediated through the abstractions of scholarship: our own mythology has been all but destroyed. But without myth every culture loses its creative power and its unity. Only myth provides direction for man's imaginative powers; it is myth that matures the child's mind and helps the adult to interpret his mature experience, and myth that sanctifies the state. In our age, Socratism, despising myth, has reduced everything to abstraction: education, morality, law, the state, culture. Our insatiable demand for knowledge and frantic interest in other cultures, past and present, stem from the loss of myth and the consequent absence of any stable consecrated basis for our own culture.

A people may or may not identify itself with the dominant culture. In France, such an identification was a source of strength when the culture was itself strong, but now it is a source of weakness. Fortunately, the German spirit that found expression in the Reformation, and with it gave rise to the first German music, has never yet fully lost itself in the dominant Alexandrianism. It is still uncorrupted and the hope is that it can now generate the rebirth of German myth.

The destruction of Greek *tragedy* went hand in hand with a nullification of Greek *myth* and a degeneration of the Greek *national character*. These correlations must be insisted on. Hitherto, the Greeks had instinctively interpreted their experience through their myths and so given it 'the stamp of the eternal'. The worth of any people depends on its capacity to do this.

Only in this way can it express its unconscious conviction of 'the relativity of time and the true, *metaphysical* meaning of life'. Conversely, when a nation begins to see itself historically and destroys its mythology, the result is secularization and spiritual malaise. Greek art and especially Greek tragedy delayed the destruction of myth. Once myth was destroyed, the metaphysical drive survived at best in attenuated form in the Socratic search for knowledge; and at worst in a religious syncretism that led only to complete triviality or exotic superstition.

The Renaissance was a rebirth of the Alexandrian–Roman spirit, and it has taken us on the same path. We now exhibit the same symptoms of the same disease, the loss of myth. To ensure the regeneration of her spirit, Germany must recover her own mythic roots and, if necessary, reject alien mythic elements implanted in her culture. It may be that our first target should be Romance elements and, if so, our victory in the recent war may be taken as a good augury. But the inner spiritual effort is what really matters. We must restore German myth and make ourselves worthy of our great predecessors – Luther, as well as our artists and poets; but we can only do so under the direction of the Dionysiac impulse.

§24 The co-existence of opposite feelings experienced by a spectator during a performance of tragedy is shared by the tragic artist himself. Despite the pleasure he finds in appearances, he negates it for the higher satisfaction of their destruction. And it is in terms of just such a co-existence of opposites that tragic myth arises. The content of tragic myth is, in the first instance, a pleasurable epic glorification of the hero. The hero's destruction, on the other hand, is ugly and discordant. The positive inclination [of the Greeks] towards this discordance can only mean [that they found] a higher pleasure in it – especially as [the period in question was] the period of [their] youth and vigour. It cannot be explained on the grounds that ordinary life is just as tragic (art is *not* merely imitation of life) or by reference to moral feelings or pity and fear.

Mythic discordance is analogous to musical dissonance: in fact, the two derive from the same source and arouse the same joy. The tragic myth's ugly content stimulates a higher, *aesthetic* pleasure. The explanation of this can only be in metaphysical terms, namely that 'only as an aesthetic phenomenon are existence and the world seen to be justified'. The function of tragic myth is to show that all things, even such ugly discordance, are part of an 'artistic game' played at the heart of things.

The Dionysiac capacity of a nation is revealed equally by its music and its tragic myth. The development of the new German music drama, therefore, fully attests our latent Dionysiac capacity. For here we have the most profound music and tragic myth to supersede the 'entertainment' represented by opera. We may now hope that, with the rebirth of our own mythology from music, the abstractions and the shallow optimism that have degraded the German genius for so long will make way for a new strength and joyful seriousness.

[§25 *The Dionysiac and the Apolline: Conclusion*]

§25 The Dionysiac is the basic ground of the world and the foundation of all existence. In the final analysis, it must be thought of as the eternal and original artistic power that calls into being the entire world of phenomena. The Apolline is secondary, the source of those illusions with which the Dionysiac world must, for our sakes, be transfigured. As far as human awareness is concerned, the two impulses manifest themselves in a strict relation: only so much Dionysiac experience is permitted to the individual consciousness as can be controlled by the Apolline and translated into its life-sustaining terms. The present emergence of the Dionysiac thus implies the co-presence of the Apolline and, in turn, an efflorescence of Apolline art in the years ahead. The scale and perfection of the Apolline manifestations among the Greeks, conversely, attest the powerful hold that the Dionysiac must have had among them. Let us bear in mind how much they must have suffered to achieve such beauty. Above all, let us acknowledge the two principles, Dionysiac and Apolline, as the basis of tragedy, their highest achievement.

No summary can be perfect. In one respect ours falls particularly short of perfection: it gives very little idea of Nietzsche's style. This is an inevitable consequence, not merely of the need to anglicize Nietzsche's German phraseology, but of the special nature of that phraseology itself. From start to finish, *BT* is written in a remarkable idiom, whose precise effect a summary cannot convey. In later chapters we shall give this aspect of the book closer attention. Here we need only point out that for most of Nietzsche's first readers – even readers familiar with his public lectures of 1870 – the style must have been quite unexpected. For whereas in subject-matter and perspective those lectures clearly prefigure the final work, stylistically they still bear some of the marks of academic decorum from which *BT* is entirely removed. Compared with the lectures, the book is condensed, elliptical and impatient. Methodical presentation of evidence and scholarly citation of references are proscribed. Without warning or apology, interpretation of the historical past alternates with bold evaluation of past and present, and with large theories about eternal truths of art and life. With its ubiquitous Dionysus and Apollo and a mass of imagery besides, the language has a high coloration and a strong emotional charge. For better or worse, Nietzsche had developed an idiom for his book that was no less distinctive than its contents and their range.

5

The aftermath

FIRST REACTIONS, WILAMOWITZ, ROHDE

The advance copies of *BT* appeared in the last days of 1871. On 2 January 1872 Nietzsche sent one to Wagner at Tribschen. In his covering letter he stressed, with extreme deference, the close relation of his book and its theories to Wagner's creative achievements: 'if I myself think that in essence I am right, then that only means that *you* with your *art* must be eternally right...I feel proud that...now people will always link my name with yours.' At the same time, in the lofty tone appropriate to communication with the Master on such an occasion, he alluded to his misgivings about the public's response: 'God have mercy on my philologists if they insist on learning nothing now.'[1] To Rohde, we recall, only a few weeks earlier, he had expressed the more general concern that the book's multifariousness would alienate all his prospective specialist readers, but the philologists above all. On that occasion he had, in fact, put it to his friend that, as far as the philological fraternity was concerned, his book (the central part of which Rohde had now seen) would be in dire need of some 'higher advertising' ('*höhere Reklame*' – Nietzsche's inverted commas), and he had suggested that the solution might be an open letter about the book from Rohde, preferably in some scholarly journal.[2] Rohde gladly offered his services: the idea had already occurred to him, although his inclination was to try a less specialized journal, the *Litterarische Centralblatt*.[3]

Bypassing any such anxieties for the moment, Tribschen responded in tones of ecstasy. Here was its supreme vindication. Wagner wrote by return: 'I have never read a finer book than yours. It is utterly magnificent.' And Cosima: 'How beautiful your book is! How beautiful and how profound – how profound and how daring!...You have conjured up spirits I thought only the Master had at his service.'[4] As her diary records, she and Wagner spent several days on the book, reading it, discussing it, and enthusing over it.[5] In addition, she indicates that they too were privately uneasy about the public reaction, albeit not quite for Nietzsche's reasons. The entry for 4 January runs: 'in the evening we had another reading from N's book, Richard is more and more pleased with it, but we ask each other what the readership for it will be.' Tribschen, one infers, was concerned not so much that the book might alienate the specialists, but that it was not calculated to reach a wide audience. Wagner – here, as elsewhere, the driving force behind Cosima's every word and thought – could not see the book making sufficient impact to inform and give momentum to the great Wagnerian cause.[6]

There was at any rate little doubt about the enthusiasm of Nietzsche's other friends and of his fellow-Wagnerians, among them Cosima's father, Franz Liszt.[7] Rohde, of course, belonging to both categories, was already committed; for him the book represented 'a brilliantly lucid and exhaustive expression' of his own deepest experiences.[8] But all this was commendation from those predisposed either by friendship or sympathy with the causes propounded. Within a few weeks of publication it was clear to Nietzsche and his friends that their worst fears had been realized. The book was being received with silent disfavour in the philological world as a whole, and it was not making any great impact anywhere else. On 16 January (as Cosima noted in her diary) she and Wagner wondered how they might 'protect the book from a conspiracy of silence'. Two days later she reported, on the authority of a nephew in Leipzig, that there the book was greeted with incomprehension.[9] On the 28th Nietzsche wrote to Rohde: 'the things I have heard about my book are quite incredible...I am profoundly sobered by all I hear of it, because in such voices I divine the fate in store for what I have to do. This life will be very hard. In Leipzig there is bitterness everywhere. Nobody writes me a word from there. Not even Ritschl.'[10]

Ritschl's silence was particularly hurtful. As an elderly and unwaveringly orthodox scholar who had even felt uneasy after Nietzsche's inaugural lecture, he would hardly have welcomed such a book with open arms. But some positive reaction, Nietzsche must have felt, would surely be forthcoming from the man who had done more than any other to further his career, who knew the strength of his enthusiasms as well as the direction of his intellectual powers, and who had not lost faith in him on that account in the past. After a month Nietzsche broke the silence himself. On 30 January he wrote to Ritschl: 'You will not take amiss my astonishment at not having heard a single word from you about my recent book – or, I hope, my candour in telling you of this astonishment. The book, after all, is something of a manifesto, and the last thing it invites is silence. Perhaps you will be surprised at the reaction I anticipated from you, my revered teacher. I thought that if you had ever met with anything hopeful in your life, it might be this book, full of hope for our classical studies, full of hope for the German spirit, even if a number of individuals should be ruined by it...I seek nothing for myself, I hope to achieve something for others. Above all, I am concerned to win over the younger generation of philologists, and I would consider it a disgrace if I failed in this...I hope I may remain assured of your goodwill...'[11]

The precise reasons for Ritschl's silence are a matter for conjecture. They must certainly have included embarrassment; perhaps also a feeling of personal injury, in so far as he himself was a prime instance of 'Alexandrian man', characterized by his protégé in *BT* (§18) as a 'critic without joy or strength,...at bottom a librarian and proof-corrector, wretchedly going blind from the dust of books and printers' errors'. His immediate reaction to the book, however, had been quite generalized. His diary for 31 December 1871 contained a sweeping dismissal: 'Nietzsche's Birth of Tragedy – ingenious dissipation' (*geistreiche Schwiemelei*). His reaction to Nietzsche's letter was no less curt: 'Amazing letter from Nietzsche – megalomania' (*Grössenwahnsinn*).[12]

'Megalomania': what took Ritschl aback was the unashamed sense of *mission* in Nietzsche's words to him. With the whole of Nietzsche's career in mind, it is tempting to relate this moment of self-revelation to various later chapters in his life, among them the staggering self-dramatization that was to characterize his very last, heated writings and herald his breakdown. In the letter to Ritschl, though, there was no such menace and no sense of strain. Rather, it was the very calmness of his pretensions that startled the older man: 'I thought that if you had ever met with anything hopeful in your life, it might be this book, full of hope for our classical studies, full of hope for the German spirit...' Ritschl had simply had no idea that, beneath his superficial acceptance of the rules of the academic philological game, Nietzsche had for years been nursing ambitions which an orthodox career could never contain or satisfy – even if he had been content to remain more or less within the fold so long as those ambitions were not yet fully defined.

As we have seen, the enlargement of Nietzsche's ambition had been closely associated with his relationship with Wagner, and it is no coincidence that his letter to Ritschl followed another visit to Tribschen and a re-affirmation of that relationship. Cosima's diary for 20 January indicates a joyful reunion, and Nietzsche's letter to Rohde a week later speaks majestically of 'an alliance with Wagner' and adds, 'you cannot imagine how close we are now and how our plans coincide'.[13] And while 'alliance with Wagner' heightened his personal aspirations, opposition to the book served to convince him that his cause – the fight for true culture and the enhancement of the individual – was more urgent than ever; the effect was to strengthen his determination to do and say openly whatever those aspirations demanded. Ritschl was the first surprised recipient of this new openness. Under the circumstances, his answer to Nietzsche was mild in tone. He did indeed continue to regard his pupil with goodwill, but had not thought a personal communication necessary. He was at one with him in a profound reverence for ancient Greek culture, but an Alexandrian scholar like himself could hardly be expected to abandon (as he put it) *knowledge* for *art*. His perspective was historical: he was too old to cope with a new, philosophical conception of life. With regard to Nietzsche's hopes of influencing 'the younger generation of philologists', he rather feared that most young men would find in Nietzsche's views the pretext for an immature disregard for scholarship, rather than the means to an enhanced perception of art.[14]

If Ritschl's comments seemed to Nietzsche not entirely discouraging,[15] it was because Ritschl's delicately expressed observations compared well with the open disrespect shown by others. Nietzsche received his letter in the middle of February, by which time it was apparent that Rohde's attempt to promote the book had run into trouble. The review, two thousand words of enthusiastic paraphrase, had been written and duly sent off in January, but was not to be published.[16] 'It's becoming very hard for my book to get a hearing', Nietzsche wrote to another friend on 4 February: 'An excellent review Rohde did for the *Litterarische Centralblatt* was rejected by the editorial staff. There went the last chance that a serious voice in a learned journal would speak out in support of it. From now on I expect nothing but malice and stupidity.' And with the now familiar sense of mission, this time accompanied by the conviction of ultimate success: 'but I'm counting on a slow, quiet journey – centuries long, I'm convinced. For some eternal truths are spoken here for the first time. There are bound to be reverberations'.[17] Some days later, Nietzsche, though professedly very pleased with Rohde's review, suggested that it would be better not to write on his behalf after all.[18] Rohde abandoned the review, but went ahead, nevertheless, and prepared a second piece of 'higher advertising'.

As early as April 1871 Nietzsche had suggested to Engelmann, at that time his prospective publisher, that his 'real task' was 'to throw light on Richard Wagner'.[19] And he knew perfectly well that whatever hostility the book aroused would stem partly, and for some primarily, from the 'Wagnerian connection'. Even so, in the early months of 1872 it came as an unpleasant surprise to find that the book was being interpreted as Wagnerian literature and he himself as a Wagner propagandist *tout court*, a rôle which in this instance he rejected with some distaste. A letter to Rohde in the autumn contains two comments that can stand as representative of his feelings throughout the year. On the one hand: 'for one spectator like Wagner I would forgo all the garlands the present could afford, and to gratify him stimulates me more and raises me higher than any other power'. On the other: 'I am told that the *Nationalzeitung* recently had the cheek to count me among "Wagner's literary lackeys".'[20] To Tribschen the difference between authentic writing related to Wagner and mere Wagner-literature was hardly so clear-cut. A comment in one of Nietzsche's earlier letters to Rohde is revealing here. Apropos Rohde's first, ill-fated review, he noted that Wagner found it 'excellent' and Cosima too, but she 'would like you to have drawn attention to the act rather than the work'.[21] Clearly, Rohde's review had concentrated too much on the detail of Nietzsche's book. More significant to the Wagnerian cause was its championship by a classical scholar: Cosima's emphasis on 'the act' meant just this.

The book in any case was not simply meant for Wagner or for Wagnerians as a whole, or for any single category of readers. Nietzsche, of course, had hoped for a varied readership, however grandly he might now resign himself to the comfort of posthumous recognition. The question arises, nevertheless: was there any one category of readers at whom the book, with all its facets, could be said to have been *primarily* directed? It is striking that during 1871 and 1872 – from the time when the book was assuming its final form to the period of publication and disappointment – Nietzsche's letters contain a series of contradictory answers to this question. In April 1871 Engelmann was to believe that the main concern of the book was with Wagner and, by implication, that the musically literate public was the prime target; Rohde, a month earlier, had been assured that the idea was to establish the author's 'philosophical credentials' among philosophically minded circles; Nietzsche's pained letter to Ritschl singled out 'the younger generation of philologists'; and by November 1872 he was explaining to a new friend, 'I did not write for the philologists, although they – if only they *could* – might learn even some purely philological matters from my book.'[22]

In interpreting these claims, we should allow for some disingenuousness, such as might be felt to underlie the last disclaimer, motivated presumably by wounded vanity. We should also consider the possibility that Nietzsche really did change his mind, especially during the actual writing of the book in 1871. What seems to be beyond reasonable doubt is that during the winter of 1871 and the larger part of 1872 he behaved in keeping with his words to Ritschl: the book had been written, above all, for classicists. Hence the fact that while Rohde was content to advertise the book in a less specialist organ, Nietzsche preferred a classical journal; and hence the remark in his dedicatory letter to (of all people) Wagner, 'God have mercy on my philologists if they insist on learning nothing now' – the only allusion to any specifiable public on that occasion. In the same spirit he told Rohde in February of his hope that 'everyone concerned with antiquity [should] *have* to read it, as a matter of duty. We do not want to make it so easy for the good philologists by chasing them away.'[23]

In its final form, *BT* itself surely points the same way. Its subject matter is diverse, but the book presupposes its classical background as it presupposes none of its other backgrounds. It aspires to subvert old ideas, and to convert those holding them to new ones, but it hardly reads like an attempt to convert (for instance) philosophically minded Wagnerians to a love of Greece. Nietzsche's aspiration was to convert his fellow-classicists, especially those not yet set in their ways, to his own philosophical and aesthetic perspective. If (as is often said) the Nietzsche of *BT* was a classical scholar turning his back on scholarship, he was *not* turning his back on classical scholars as well.

By May 1872 a single review of the book had appeared – in the Italian *Rivista Europea*.[24] The book was selling reasonably well,[25] but the world at large and the classical world in particular remained silent. Towards the end of the month Rohde's second article at last appeared in a non-specialist journal of Wagnerian sympathies, the *Norddeutsche Allgemeine Zeitung*.[26] Almost twice the length of the first, abortive review, thanks largely to several expansions of points in Nietzsche's argument, it hailed the book as representing a new profundity in aesthetics and offering insights of permanent value into the eternal primacy of Greece and Greek art. *BT*, Rohde suggested, was a book for all serious readers, particularly those already cognisant with 'the wonderfully harmonious ideas' of Schopenhauer and Wagner.[27] It was a book that bore comparison with Schopenhauer on its philosophical ground and was worthy to stand with Wagner as a cultural force for good in the new Germany.

Within a few days of Rohde's review, the silence of classical orthodoxy was broken. *Philology of the Future! A reply to Friedrich Nietzsche's "Birth of Tragedy"*, a pamphlet by the young scholar Ulrich von Wilamowitz-Moellendorff, appeared on 1 June, published in Berlin. The title, *Zukunftsphilologie*, with its sarcastic allusion to Wagner's *Zukunftsmusik*, set the tone of the piece, which in twenty-eight breathless pages attempted a total demolition of Nietzsche's book and its author's classical credentials.[28] Wilamowitz was twenty-four, four years younger than Nietzsche, and had recently gained his doctorate. He and Nietzsche had been at Pforta together and so knew each other personally, although not at all well; he had in fact visited Nietzsche in company with their old headmaster in 1871. *Philology of the Future* was his first publication; many more were to follow.

It is not easy to summarize what Wilamowitz objected to in *BT* except with the one word, *everything*. He attacked the tone of the book; its style (a mixture of preaching, journalese, and general imprecision); its logic; above all, its lack of scholarship. Here he charged Nietzsche with both ignorance and dishonesty. In Nietzsche's 'metaphysics' he professed no interest, except that the metaphysician was also attempting to purvey wisdom about the ancient world attained by some non-scholarly, intuitive means. That was unacceptable. To Wilamowitz, Nietzsche was not simply bypassing scholarly method and relying on unstated evidence. He was evading scholarship because there was no evidence to support his arguments, and their plausibility, such as it was, depended on suppressing any discussion of the evidence: he stood accused of a myriad of errors of principle and of detail. With a flurry of citations Wilamowitz endeavoured to show that whether dealing with the Greek satyr or Greek dreams, Greek music or Greek literary history, he was an ignorant charlatan. In the one area in which he seemed to have made any attempt at historical research, the origin of tragedy, he was no better than elsewhere.

With much sound and fury Wilamowitz attacked Nietzsche's betrayal of historicism. When interpreting the past, the only proper procedure was to 'comprehend each historical event solely in terms of the assumptions of the times in which it developed'; while 'aesthetic evaluation' was likewise held to be possible 'only in terms of the attitudes of the time'. The use of Schopenhauerian theory and Wagnerian practice to illuminate the finite world of ancient Greece was methodologically untenable – and particularly offensive (one was to gather *en passant*) in view of the fact that to Wilamowitz Schopenhauer and Wagner were both risible figures in their own right. Of course (he concluded, with heavy irony), it might be that Nietzsche was not really concerned with history and criticism, but only with creating some kind of Dionysiac–Apolline work of art of his own. If so, he was welcome to try – provided that he abandoned his professional position, 'the professorial chair from which he should be dispensing *Wissenchaft*'.[29]

Whatever the justification for its criticisms, *Philology of the Future* does not make pleasant reading. It jeered at Nietzsche's scholarship, though (as its author had soon to admit) its own was not beyond reproach; at his style, though it was itself abysmally turgid and clumsy; and at his vatic tone, where its own monotonously shrill invective, both arrogant and (often) petty, was anything but exemplary. Nonetheless, Wilamowitz knew he had arguments on his side, and the profession as a whole was only too ready to respond to them. Nietzsche's hopes, as expressed to Ritschl, had been grossly disappointed.

Nietzsche was pained at the attack, but not unduly.[30] Wilamowitz, he supposed, had been egged on by his superiors at Berlin who preferred not to criticize him directly;[31] and someone as alienated from his profession as Nietzsche's convictions had already made him could not be particularly offended, or even surprised, if by expressing those convictions he offended the establishment in turn. It was his friends who felt a greater sense of outrage. Wagner, in the first place, evidently took the attack on Nietzsche as an affront to himself and to everything he stood for. On reading Wilamowitz, he drafted – apparently on his own initiative – an open letter in Nietzsche's defence, which appeared, like Rohde's review, in the *Norddeutsche Allgemeine Zeitung* for 23 June.[32] The gist of the letter was the observation that contemporary classical scholarship appeared to have no contact whatsoever with contemporary artistic or literary life or even with the work of the other professions. It was surely impoverished by its lack of inspiration from the cultural world at large, which, in its turn, waited in vain for the philologists to offer it the product of their accumulated learning. As it was, the elaborate paraphernalia of classical scholarship epitomized by Wilamowitz seemed to exist as an end in itself. Nietzsche was to be commended not just for his insights into Greek tragedy, but for 'speaking to us and not to [other] scholars'.[33]

Wagner's point about the hermetic isolation of philology was unassailable, but one effect of his argument was undoubtedly to give the impression that Wilamowitz was right to dissociate Nietzsche from other professional classicists and his book from any professional concern of theirs. Wagner's biographer, Newman, comments: 'whatever harm had been done to Nietzsche in academic circles by the attack of Wilamowitz must have been a flea-bite compared to the damage done him by Wagner's maladroit championship'.[34] This, however, is misleading. Inwardly, Nietzsche had been at odds with conventional philology and philologists even before he took the chair at Basle. The writing and publishing of *BT* represented (among other things) the public affirmation of that state of mind. He was fully aware of that, and equally aware that to publish such a book would compromise him in the eyes of his colleagues. 'Offence must come. I have, by and large, already stopped taking any notice' – he had said that in the early months of 1870, and he had since said as much to Ritschl: *BT* offered a hope to classical studies, 'even if a number of individuals should be ruined by it'.[35] He had anticipated the 'damage' all along, and the damage was, after all, self-inflicted. If Wagner was now making that damage worse, it was by spreading the impression that classical scholars could safely ignore *BT* because it was not meant for them. And needless to say, Nietzsche was human and had his pride. However much 'offence' he might have anticipated, as soon as any materialized, it gave him no pleasure to find the dignity of his position undermined, whether by Wilamowitz deliberately or Wagner unwittingly. On this count, as much as on the other, it was obvious that his book needed a new champion.

If Nietzsche's classical colleagues were to be persuaded after all that a *bona fide* scholar should take the book seriously, there was only one way to do it: one of their number must be *seen* to be taking it seriously. Rohde had written two reviews and Rohde it was that now offered his services again with a new pamphlet *contra* Wilamowitz. The essay was composed by Rohde alone, but after consultations and many suggestions from Nietzsche, most of which Rohde incorporated.[36] The title – invented by Nietzsche's friend, the church historian Franz Overbeck[37] – was *Afterphilologie*, a sarcastic multiple pun designed to pay Wilamowitz back in kind: *pseudo-* or *false* philology (*After-* as in *Afterrede*, 'slander') on the model of Schopenhauer's dismissive expression for academic philosophizing, *Afterphilosophie*, with additional suggestions deriving from the proper sense of *After* ('anus') and, in evocation of Wilamowitz's own title, from its use in compounds referring to futurity (*After-* as in *Afterheu*, 'aftermath').

The pamphlet, roughly the length of the three previous published contributions to the debate put together, was published by Fritzsch and appeared in October in the ostensible form of another open letter: *Pseudo-philology. Towards the Elucidation of the Pamphlet published by Ulrich von Wilamowitz-Moellendorff Ph.D.: 'Philology of the Future!' Open Letter from a Classicist to Richard Wagner.*[38] This form of counter-attack had been suggested by Nietzsche: a public 'explanation' to Wagner of Wilamowitz's otherwise inexplicable attack would serve to reassert the 'direct relationship with Wagner' which was 'precisely what terrifies the philologists most and gives them most food for thought'. At the same time 'the slaughter of Wilamowitz must be done on purely philological lines', since 'what they will least expect, the most terrible feature of it all, will be that a qualified scholar should come to my support. The confidence that this could never happen explains the superlatively impudent tone of this young man from Berlin.'[39] As it turned out, however, the posed address to Wagner must have looked remarkably like a crude attempt to conceal the obvious reason for writing at all. It was not Wagner who needed to be told that Nietzsche had been right all the time; it was Nietzsche's professional colleagues and other 'friends of antiquity',[40] who might otherwise too readily acquiesce in Wilamowitz's prejudices and conclusions.

Pseudo-philology was as totally hostile to Wilamowitz as *Philology of the Future* had been to Nietzsche, and in its tone it was no more edifying than Wilamowitz's essay. The young man from Berlin (Wagner was to understand) was an ill-informed and presumptuous nobody; slanderous and malevolent (being especially given to wilful misrepresentation of Nietzsche's exact words), critically incompetent and banally complacent. More pointedly, Rohde noted that Wilamowitz had largely ignored the intellectual content of the book and confined himself to Nietzsche's scholarship. Nietzsche had been compelled by the nature of his book to state his argument without scholarly references. (Nietzsche himself had said as much to Rohde[41] – although it occurred to neither to question whether, if that was so, 'the nature of the book' might not be open to attack.) It was simply Wilamowitz's immaturity that prevented his identifying Nietzsche's supporting evidence.

However, what had affronted Wilamowitz (Rohde continued) was not this, but the seriousness of Nietzsche's attempt to put his classical learning to a higher use than the usual cultivation of sharp-wittedness and memory. And it was sad but true that in the world of contemporary classics even genuine scholars (which, Rohde repeatedly explained to Wagner, Wilamowitz was not) would be suspicious on finding that Nietzsche had any extra-scholarly purpose, and above all when they gathered what that purpose was : 'the understanding of the noblest works of art' as a guide towards an 'artistic existence'.[42] They would also react with horror on learning that the original inspiration of Nietzsche's theory of Greek art was Schopenhauer. The modern scholar believed in an 'objective' interpretation of the past, achieved only by exclusive reliance on 'evidence', unaware that in classics, as in life, the significance of isolated phenomena was accessible only to a unified interpretative vision which must have some positive source outside the phenomena themselves. This (he argued) was not only defensible, but essential. The alternative was not 'objective interpretation', but the unconscious reading in of modern prejudices.[43] In any case, what Schopenhauer had said (and Wagner himself had confirmed) carried a special weight, beyond all scholarly findings. Not that (Rohde hastened to add) Nietzsche actually had neglected the relevant philological evidence – and at this point he embarked on a systematic refutation of Wilamowitz's detailed criticisms: it was Wilamowitz, he maintained, who was in the wrong, over and over again. In his conclusion, Rohde looked again to the cultural goal of Nietzsche's book. The purpose of classical studies was more than the cultivation of a harmless luxury. Its true purpose was to perpetuate the memory of the richest period of antiquity to serve as our constant cultural example, as it had served in the time of the poet Schiller and the scholar F. A. Wolf. In committing himself to the cause of contemporary culture, Nietzsche was not nullifying his subject, but living up to it.

These battles of long ago: why go over them again? Because they are no battles of frogs and mice, fit only for a condescending smile. We have here a classic confrontation, the epitome of all controversy between the defenders of 'pure' scholarship and the spokesmen for learning in the service of art and life.

In retrospect, the oddest aspect of this dispute was the eventual stature of the various participants, now so busy belittling one another. Wagner, of course, had been an artist of international importance for years, although he had yet to achieve the established place in German culture that his theatre at Bayreuth and the efforts of his supporters – not least Nietzsche's efforts in *BT* – were to give him. But Nietzsche himself was not at the time well known outside his profession, and neither Wilamowitz nor even Rohde inside it. Rohde, in fact, had made the first important advance in his career earlier in the year by being appointed to a chair at the University of Kiel. His subsequent work, not prolific but of consistently high quality, was to place him in the front rank of classical scholarship. Two major books eventually stood to his credit, one on the late Greek novel (*Der griechische Roman und seine Vorläufer*, first edition 1876) and the other – a work of lasting importance in its field – on Greek religious beliefs (*Psyche*, first edition 1891–4).

Wilamowitz's career was to be altogether grander. As an extraordinarily prolific writer who maintained, over a long career, an unflagging interest in virtually every aspect of the Greek world and who possessed an amazing range of learning to bring to bear to the study of any of its products, he became (by general consent and in Gilbert Murray's words) the 'greatest Hellenist of our time'.[44] In scores of articles and books, he produced editions, commentaries, textual discussions and interpretations, translations and discursive studies, dealing with early, classical, Hellenistic and later Greek literature, from Homer to Callimachus, from the newly discovered Aristotelian *Constitution of the Athenians* to the lexicon of the Byzantine scholar Photius. He worked on epigraphy and papyrology, on metrics, on ancient history and archaeology, on Greek political and religious institutions and beliefs. Eduard Fraenkel characterized him as 'radiant with the joy of life and the light of a sublime intellect, a scholar of boundless learning, who yet could not for a moment seem bookish'.[45] In many ways he was a greater successor to Wolf, the inaugurator of the 'scientific' study of the ancient world and the spokesman for the interrelation of its diverse elements. In the field of textual criticism, above all, he was one of the scholarly elect. In this most traditional of philological skills he was, said the poet-scholar A. E. Housman in 1927, 'a very great man, the greatest now living and comparable with the greatest of the dead'.[46]

At the same time, Wilamowitz had striking limitations, and limitations of some relevance to his criticisms of Nietzsche's book. Housman's encomium, as it happens, was produced in correspondence with Sir James Frazer, who, with his own anthropological interests in mind, had described Wilamowitz as 'a sophist with an infallible instinct for getting hold of a stick by the wrong end' ('Wilamowitz', Housman replied, 'may be all that you say in your sphere; but where I come across him, in verbal scholarship and textual criticism, he is a very great man...').[47] Exaggerated though Frazer's judgement is, few would credit Wilamowitz with the sureness of touch in any area of cultural interpretation that he showed elsewhere. Moreover, despite a keen interest in Greek philosophy, his own mind was in no sense philosophical. In particular, aesthetics was never one of his preoccupations. Any such interest would inevitably have conflicted with his historicist scruples about relating elements of the ancient world to their modern analogues; but even purely ancient theories of art were not his province.

As a literary scholar Wilamowitz excelled in so-called 'exact scholarship': in textual criticism, in metrics and in the various techniques of editorial interpretation. For literary criticism he never showed any qualifications. Like many students of *Altertumswissenschaft* before and since, he sought to avoid that aspect of his profession as an 'unscientific' indulgence, never admitting that literary-critical finesse, not necessarily articulated, is a pre-requisite for many of the interpretative activities of the literary scholar. The young research worker, so inflexibly attached to his historicist principle of examining a work of art *only* according to the canons of its time, was in any case not well placed even to develop the particular delicacy or intellectual curiosity required to recognize his own limitations in this field. In practice, however, Wilamowitz repeatedly, if unwittingly, violated his own ordinance as well. A classic instance is his monumental study, *Pindaros* (1922), which, by reading fifth-century choral lyric poetry as autobiography, constitutes a gross misinterpretation of an ancient *œuvre* in terms heavily influenced by the Romantic preoccupation with 'the author'. Rohde's dismissal of 'objective' interpretation as the unconscious importation of modern prejudices was in this respect prophetic; and in recent years Wilamowitz's book on Pindar has been cited more as a cautionary tale than as a repository of accumulated, and strictly 'objective', learning.

In 1908, thirty-five years after the confrontation with Nietzsche, Wilamowitz gave a lecture at Oxford in which he touched once again on the question of scholarly objectivity. He made no explicit mention of the earlier argument, but its echoes can still be heard. Commenting on the respective roles of 'imagination' and sober scholarship ('Mr Dryasdust') in the study of the past, he declared:

> It may be that Mr Dryasdust is no very agreeable companion, but he is indispensable. It is the curse of ancient historical writing that it neglected him. Very famous persons have tried to do the same in our own days. The result is the same, but they have the less claim upon our forgiveness... Yet let us be honest. We ourselves, when once Dryasdust has done his work within us, and we advance to the shaping of our scientific results – from that time forth... we use our free formative imagination. The tradition yields us only ruins. The more clearly we test and examine them, the more clearly we see how ruinous they are; and out of ruins no whole can be built. The tradition is dead; our task is to revivify life that has passed away. We know that ghosts cannot speak until they have drunk blood; and the spirits whom we evoke demand the blood of our hearts.

Having made this concession to the revivifying imagination, Wilamowitz at once reverted to the convictions he had upheld against Nietzsche in his youth. He proceeded to offer a qualification that opposed imagination to 'truth' – to the detriment of the former. If the spirits we evoke demand the blood of our hearts, 'we give it to them gladly; but if they then abide our question, something from us has entered into them; something alien that must be cast out, cast out in the name of truth!'[48]

The striking image of the ghosts takes on a special interest for us when we set it against its apparent but unacknowledged source, a passage from one of Nietzsche's later books, *Human, All Too Human* (1878). The author of *BT* was surely one of the 'very famous persons' in Wilamowitz's mind; and equally it was Nietzsche who had few qualms about putting 'our questions' to works of art from earlier ages. Very much in the spirit of his first book, Nietzsche writes:

> These works can only survive through our giving them our soul, and our blood alone enables them to talk to *us*. Real 'historical' discourse would talk ghostly speech to ghosts. We honour the great artists less by that barren timidity that leaves every word, every note as it is than by energetic endeavours to aid them continually to a new life.[49]

On Wilamowitz's behalf, it may be said that there is no need for revivification to operate totally at the expense of Dryasdust's insistence on keeping every note of the original intact – no need, that is, for 'imagination' to be given free rein at such an early stage in the construction of a thesis as we shall find

Nietzsche doing in *BT*. On the other side, Wilamowitz's apparent (and to him comforting) belief in the possibility of an impersonal imagination which revivifies *without* introducing 'something from us' can only be called absurd. As Nietzsche and Rohde saw, the choice that faces the custodian of the past is harder than that.

The scholarly antagonists, Rohde and Wilamowitz, had one thing in common: both in their different ways pleaded the cause of scholarship, but in neither instance was the motivation one of scholarly disinterestedness. With Rohde this was evident to all, Wilamowitz included. In defending *BT*, Rohde was inevitably defending Nietzsche's name as a scholar, but he was doing so as a friend and a devoted admirer. To Rohde Nietzsche in his student days and his early years at Basle was a human being of a very superior kind: 'I cannot express the emotion with which I always feel the nobility of his nature affect me and a quite peculiar poetry in his whole atmosphere...' Rohde wrote that about Nietzsche in 1873; and in 1890 he remembered 'what a magnificent man, and what a new revelation of humanity [Nietzsche] was at that time'.[50]

It was this intense, generous admiration for Nietzsche that impelled Rohde to become his public advocate, and it was the same intensity of feeling that prevented his advocacy from being dispassionate. He knew well enough that whatever odium *BT* had brought upon his friend would be directed at himself as well, that therein lay serious risks to his own professional career (although ultimately no harm was done), and that, nevertheless, he had no choice. 'I could not look on in silence at my friend, whom I love,...being punished by his colleagues with coy silence and pilloried like a criminal.'[51] And while Rohde was as much in sympathy with Nietzsche's book as with its author, he granted in private what he preferred not to say in public, 'I am not so naïve as to take his book as the documentary truth' – and in a notebook a year later he described *BT* as a 'didactic poem' (*Lehrgedicht*).[52] The open expression of such thoughts, however, was precluded by a reluctance to make any concession to the enemy.

In the light of recent biographical work by W. M. Calder, it is clear that Wilamowitz's attack on Nietzsche was equally prompted by personal factors. To Nietzsche 'the young man from Berlin' was a misguided novice put up to it by his superiors (who incidentally included the great historian, Theodor Mommsen). The idea of publication was indeed suggested to Wilamowitz,[53] but what he wrote was activated entirely by his own feelings. Wilamowitz, like Nietzsche, was a product of Pforta. Their careers there overlapped from 1862 to 1864, when Nietzsche left for Bonn before moving on (a year later, with Ritschl) to Leipzig. In 1867 Wilamowitz too left for Bonn where the leading figure was now Ritschl's enemy, Otto Jahn. Wilamowitz became a keen supporter of Jahn and stayed at Bonn until the latter's death in 1869. Given an academic tradition of rival 'schools' headed by eminent scholars dispensing their own brand of wisdom to a succession of loyal young disciples, it is conceivable that simply by virtue of his allegiance a follower of Jahn might react with disfavour to the work of a favourite pupil of Ritschl. Nor would any follower of Jahn take kindly to Nietzsche's castigation (§ 19) of the 'latter-day aestheticians' who assign music to the sphere of 'the beautiful': '..."Beauty! Beauty!" Do they really bear the stamp of nature's darling children who are fostered and nourished at the breast of the beautiful, or are they not rather seeking a false cloak for their own coarseness, an aesthetic pretext for their own insensitive sobriety? – and here I am thinking of Otto Jahn, for example.'

But Wilamowitz's feelings towards Nietzsche were much stronger than disfavour; and – as Calder's work shows – they dated not from his years at Bonn, but from his schooldays at Pforta.[54] Whatever the 'radiance with the joy of life' that he showed in later years, Wilamowitz, it seems, had a tormented youth, not least because his academic leanings were repudiated by most of his aristocratic family. The classics, at which he shone, became his salvation, and he was determined to overcome all obstacles to his success in the subject. At Pforta he and Nietzsche were the two best pupils in living memory, and it was therefore against Nietzsche that he pitted himself. For his rival he felt a mixture of admiration and jealousy, but for a variety of reasons jealousy became uppermost. *BT* – a betrayal, as he saw it, of the scholastic training that he, unlike Nietzsche, espoused uncritically – incensed him beyond endurance. We have here the explanation, not of his objections to the book (most philologists shared the objections), but of the almost pathological tone of detestation, sometimes marked by personal abuse, that he reveals in his pamphlet.

In *Philology of the Future* we find disparaging allusions to Nietzsche's competence as lecturer; even to his family background;[55] but above all to his school record at Pforta where, we recall, he had excelled at all subjects except mathematics and had produced, *inter alia*, an extended essay on Sophocles' *Oedipus Rex*. For instance, apropos Nietzsche's idea that the dark side of Greek mythology was the early, pre-Homeric side, Wilamowitz writes: 'The curse on the house of Atreus etc. is supposed to be Homeric, pre-Homeric even! What shame, Herr Nietzsche, you bring on mother Pforta! It must appear that no one has ever given you *Iliad* II. 101 to read, or the relevant passage in Lessing's *Laokoon*; and Schneidewin's introduction to Sophocles' *Oedipus Rex* is another piece of wisdom from the first six months of the Pforta primer. You will make the excuse that you were only a couple of centuries out, and that counting is vulgar mathematics; but since Plato (and despite Schopenhauer) there is an inscription above the portals of philosophy [*über der Philosophie Pforten*], *mēdeis ageōmetrētos enthad' eisitō* [no one unversed in geometry is to enter here]. And I only wish that they had kept to that text at Pforta [*ich wollte nur, man hätte in Pforte*...], at least with the version *enthend' exitō* [no one...is to leave here].'[56] The criticism in fact misrepresents Nietzsche's point,[57] although it becomes hard to attend to the argument in such a storm. What is obvious is that for Wilamowitz Pforta embodied academic respectability, and he, Wilamowitz, embodied Pforta. With hindsight, the possessive punning on the name *Pforte* evokes its author's personal stake in the affair.

Nietzsche was delighted with Rohde's response to the challenge. 'I am as happy as a child with your present...What you have done for me is beyond words.'[58] In his eyes Rohde had provided both a demonstration of solidarity for the cause and a vindication of the actual argument of the book.[59] But *Pseudo-philology* was aimed primarily at professional classical scholars, and their attitude was not appreciably affected. By the end of the year only a handful of them had managed to find a good word of any kind for the book, although it was an interesting handful. Apart from Rohde, there was his new mentor, Otto Ribbeck, a distinguished Latinist and himself author of a recent essay on the cult of Dionysus; the elderly Ernst von Leutsch, in his time editor of two journals of unimpeachable virtue, *Philologus* and *Philologischer Anzeiger*; Nietzsche's distinguished colleague in Basle, Jacob Burckhardt, primarily historian of the Renaissance, but also author of a notable history of Greek culture; and the brilliant Jacob Bernays, another of Ritschl's pupils, whose important published work included the classic discussion of Aristotelian *katharsis* fifteen years earlier.[60]

But these, with their varying degrees of sympathy, were the exceptions. The rule was exemplified by Hermann Usener, an eminent scholar in the fields of Greek literature and religion. As Nietzsche wrote to Rohde in October, 'the good Usener in Bonn, whom I greatly respect, has revealed to his students...that my book is sheer nonsense, quite useless, that anyone writing like that is professionally dead.'[61] And a fortnight later he confessed to another correspondent: 'the philologists...seem to think I have committed a crime...Even what Rohde has done will have no effect, for nothing can bridge the enormous gap.'[62] This was so. Orthodoxy was unmoved by Rohde, and Nietzsche had to resign himself to the fact. But now his notoriety had an unexpected consequence. 'There is one thing that upsets me terribly at the moment', he wrote to Wagner in November: 'our winter semester has begun, and I have no students at all! Our classicists have not turned up! ... The fact is so easy to explain – I have suddenly acquired such a bad name in my field that our small university suffers from it!'[63]

Whatever else this situation seemed to call for, there was no question of any further polemics on Nietzsche's behalf: the public verdict was settled. Only Wilamowitz still felt that there was business outstanding. His personal animus had not been spent, and Rohde had provoked him all over again. Early in 1873 he produced a second pamphlet, *Philology of the Future! Part II* (*Zukunftsphilologie! Zweites Stück*).[64] Subtitled 'A reply to the attempted rescue of F. Nietzsche's *Birth of Tragedy*', it was shorter and, if not sweeter, certainly less frenetic than either his or Rohde's earlier pieces, despite the fact that he was now under attack himself. He had been sobered, perhaps, by the wholeheartedness of the 'attempted rescue' and the recognition that at least some of Rohde's points against him were good ones. He must also have appreciated that the scholarly world was broadly behind him, and the sense of dignity that this knowledge carried with it may have communicated itself to the tone.

Wilamowitz began the second round with an ironic review of the state of play. Wagner's contribution he dismissed with some disdain, noting drily, as he did so, that there was no essential difference between his and 'the Master's' assessment of Nietzsche's distance from classical orthodoxy. As for Rohde's pamphlet, he detected in it a fury and a haste which suggested that his blows had struck home. As far as classicists were concerned, Nietzsche's missionary enterprise had failed – although, as Wilamowitz correctly pointed out, that was not *his* doing: they had mostly decided against Nietzsche's book before he had entered the fray. Reviewing Rohde's arguments, he granted him a number of points of detail (and tacitly admitted various others), but on essentials he stood firm. Overall (Wilamowitz continued) Rohde's defence was weak, for the simple reason that it was based not on argument, but on loyalty to his friend. If one read between the lines, it was clear that really Rohde agreed with him about the book's inadequacies. After berating these (and the weaknesses in Rohde's defence) over again, he suddenly broke off. He was weary of wasting time and energy on the pitiful idiocies of 'a couple of addled brains'. He was more interested in the classics than in Nietzsche and Rohde. The wrangling over details was not the heart of the matter. What was at stake was the whole question of the approach to art and the status of scientific method – in fact, as he spelt out for the first time, a whole attitude to life. On his own initiative (he insisted) and without any prospect of personal gain, he had entered the lists to speak up for his highest ideals. It was in this cause that – he rather graciously, if euphemistically, admitted – he might perhaps have committed some errors of taste.[65]

But there was no question of Wilamowitz softening his attitude towards the objectionable book. In a final, eloquent declaration, he identified Nietzsche's ultimate and totally unforgivable offence as his attack on the great tradition of western rationality. 'For me the highest ideal is the development of the world in accordance with law, life and reason [*Vernunft*]. With gratitude I look up to the great intellects who, step by step, have wrested its secrets from it. In awe I seek to come closer to the light of eternal beauty which every work of art in its own way gives forth; and in scholarship [*Wissenschaft*], which fills my life, I strive to follow in the footsteps of those who liberated my judgement within me, as I willingly submitted myself to them. And here I saw the development of thousands of years falsified; the revelations of philosophy and religion snuffed out to let a wishy-washy pessimism make its sweet-and-sour faces in the waste-land; the images of the gods with which poetry and art peopled our heavens smashed to pieces so that the image of the false god [*Götzenbild*] Richard Wagner could be worshipped in their dust.'[66]

Nietzsche's overt response to his latest condemnation was flippant. 'I have read Wilamowitz's second piece...I found it jolly enough and completely self-negating.'[67] Had he felt inclined, he might have seen some cause for a wry satisfaction. In his closing attack on Nietzsche's pessimism and the false god Wagner, Wilamowitz had tacitly shifted his ground. His initial assault had been directed against Nietzsche's historical scholarship. The objection to Nietzsche's metaphysics and aesthetics at that time was that they were alien to the historical milieu of ancient Greece, and so could safely be ignored. His complaint now was that they challenged rationality and as such must be exposed as obnoxious and false *per se*. But in asserting this, he inevitably found himself in the position of the thinker depicted in Nietzsche's book (§ 15) as the man who stands at the boundary of thought, where 'logic coils up and finally bites its own tail'. In drawing attention to Nietzsche's large perspective, Wilamowitz had made one of Nietzsche's underlying points for him: that the scholar cannot come to terms with the past without raising wider, and ultimately philosophical questions, one of which is the status of scholarship and rational thought itself.

THE LATER YEARS AT BASLE AND THE BREAK WITH WAGNER

In June 1879 Nietzsche resigned his chair. During the seven and a half years since the publication of *BT* he had changed his position drastically on several of the most important issues dealt with in the book. In December 1875 he could still speak of 'the constant joy of having found educators in Schopenhauer and Wagner and the daily objects of my work in the Greeks',[68] but such a simple tally of allegiances no longer represented his position. He had begun to emancipate himself from Schopenhauer well before the completion of *BT*; by 1875 the same process was under way with Wagner; and from now on Greece was no longer at the forefront of his thoughts, although Greece, like Wagner, continued to retain a great exemplary significance for him.

Nietzsche's reputation as a classical scholar was not (*pace* a widespred misconception) destroyed by Wilamowitz. After a brief lull caused by *BT*, a steady stream of new classics students requested his services at Basle, and continued to do so until his retirement.[69] His earlier published philological work was still respected: it was his larger designs on Greek culture that aroused disapproval. In 1875, for example, a long review of his work on the 'Contest of Homer and Hesiod' in *Bursian's Jahresbericht* concluded with the comment: 'we leave the essay, which occupies an important place in the literature on Hesiod, with the hope that its talented author may very soon carry out the plans [for future investigations] mentioned in his conclusion ...and turn his back on his present "music and philology of the future"'.[70]

While his health permitted, Nietzsche continued to perform his professorial duties, lecturing on a wide variety of topics from Hesiod's *Works and Days* to Greco-Roman rhetoric. But as far as philological investigations were concerned, he was no longer active. Whether his interest in scholarship might have revived, had it not been for the estrangement between him and his colleagues in the wake of *BT*, it is impossible to know. The logic of his development, however, suggests that it would not. His sights were already fixed on other targets when he came to Basle in 1869. And the effect of the Wilamowitz episode was not so much to widen the gap between Nietzsche and scholarship, as to widen the gap between him and his fellow-scholars. It was this skirmish that finally convinced him of the futility of looking among the philologists for the shock troops of a new culture;[71] thereafter he looked elsewhere for allies.

The lack of support Nietzsche received from his colleagues marks the final closing of the long era in which classical studies and classical scholars – and not merely classical ideals – occupied a place in the vanguard of western culture. Winckelmann, like the scholars of the Renaissance, was a major figure both in the classical world of his day and in the world of intellect and culture as a whole, and in his time a distinction between 'classics' and 'culture' would have had no meaning. The distinction was established between Winckelmann's time and Nietzsche's generation, and (as Wagner saw) made rigid by classical scholars in the interests of scholarly purism. In the years after *BT*, Wilamowitz, who in scholarly terms was to become a much greater figure than Nietzsche, played an important part in dismantling the barriers between the various aspects of the subject which had been erected in the decades of specialization after Wolf. However, the barrier between the subject itself and contemporary cultural life was not dismantled. It was not Wilamowitz who put it up, but neither he nor his profession showed any serious interest in removing it.

Nietzsche's concern with Greece, at all events, remained intense for some time yet, expressing itself in projects which had much in common, both in spirit and perspective, with *BT* – although, unlike *BT*, none of them reached the stage of publication. Two notable fragments survive, both from 1872–3: a short essay on the significance of the agonistic spirit among the ancient Greeks ('Homer's Contest') and a long and (by Nietzschean standards) rather plain historical survey of the Presocratic philosophers in what he called 'the tragic age' of Greece.[72] In one respect these pieces do differ strikingly from *BT*. The Apolline–Dionysiac polarity to which he attached so pervasive a significance while working on tragedy has vanished. There was a conscious decision here:[73] the formula had apparently served its purpose and could now be dispensed with; and although Dionysus is still a significant figure in Nietzsche's later thinking, the antithesis is hardly ever alluded to again in his published works.[74] One other difference deserves to be noted, which also helps to distinguish *BT* from all his later writings. The centre of that book is Greek tragic drama. The word 'tragic' reappears in the title of the essay on the Presocratics, but not in any dramatic connection. The blunt fact is that after *BT*, and apart from the special case of Wagnerian music drama, he never again shows any marked interest in drama, Greek or any other. The later works, and the unpublished notes, contain a number of brief comments on drama or dramas, but nothing more.

Nietzsche was, at any rate, eager that his published discussion of tragic drama should be as adequate as possible. When the opportunity arrived for a second edition of the book, he made a number of minor corrections, especially to the early part. The edition was ready in 1874, although for commercial reasons it was not published until 1878. It is the revised text of this edition which has almost invariably been reprinted and used for purposes of citation and translation, ever since Nietzsche was first institutionalized in a collected edition in the 1890s.

One other unpublished work deserves special mention, a collection of *sententiae* entitled 'We Philologists'.[75] These caustic thoughts, sometimes bare notes, were set down in 1875, although most of them had been on Nietzsche's mind for years. The predominant theme is the sad contrast between, on the one hand, contemporary philology and philologists and, on the other, the supreme object of their study, Greece and its creative individuals. As in *BT*, Nietzsche's interest in Greece is inseparable from his hopes for modern culture (and his faith in modern creativity), but here with a more specific emphasis on education. 'It is not true that we can attain culture through antiquity alone', he writes. And again: 'Think how much Goethe understood about antiquity: certainly not as much as any philologist, and yet quite enough to enable him to engage in fruitful competition with it...Let us try to live in the manner of antiquity...Our philologists never show that they are trying to emulate antiquity at all; that is why *their* antiquity remains without effect on the schools...The essence of study lies in this: that we should study only what we feel we should like to imitate...But imitation can create nothing...It is only as creators that we shall be able to take anything from the Greeks.'[76]

'We Philologists' (despite that 'we') marks the end of Nietzsche's active Hellenism. For although his later writings continue to show the influence of the ancient world, this is his last piece of work specifically related to it. From 1873 onwards his philosophical development proceeds on its own terms. With *Thoughts Out of Season* (*Unzeitgemässe Betrachtungen*, 1873–6) and *Human, All Too Human* (*Menschliches, Allzumenschliches*, 1878–9), the philosopher clearly emerging in *BT* has reached maturity. The subject matter of these works – and the range of experience behind them – was less and less related to Nietzsche's academic situation. By the last of the *Thoughts Out of Season* (*Richard Wagner in Bayreuth*, 1876) his professional career and his real work were quite separate things. On the purely personal level, too, the classical world ceased to provide him with new sources of inspiration. In the late 1870s even his friendship with Rohde began to wane, partly as a result of the new developments in his thought, which were not to Rohde's taste.[77]

Now that Nietzsche's lecturing was his only contact with pure philology, and as the visionary Hellenism which had been his only link between philology and philosophy ceased in its turn to activate his thinking, his position at Basle became more anomalous than ever. It was probably only the lack of any obvious alternative that led him to keep it for as long as he did, especially in view of his bad health. This was of serious concern throughout the 1870s, and repeated violent attacks (usually migraine and stomach disorders) led him, over and over again, to question the wisdom of his staying at Basle. A lament in a letter to his sister in 1877 is typical: 'out of fourteen days, I spent six in bed with six major attacks, the last one quite desperate...In the long run, my university career at Basle cannot go on; to carry it through would mean abandoning all my important projects and still sacrificing my health completely.'[78]

Like his friendship with Rohde, Nietzsche's friendship with Wagner also changed, but more dramatically. If the growth of this relationship had been among the most momentous and formative episodes in his life, its decline was no less so, but also painful in the extreme. The long sequence of events has often been discussed,[79] and we need not rehearse it in all its complications here. What matters is the difference between Nietzsche's attitudes to Wagner before and after the estrangement, and the reasons why the estrangement took place at all.

In the letter of January 1872 that Nietzsche sent Wagner with his copy of *BT*, he proclaimed: 'if I myself think that in essence I am right, then that only means that *you* with your *art* must be eternally right'.[80] Whether one cares for the adulatory tone of this remark or not, its meaning is clear: in *BT* he was (among so many other things) attempting to express the experience of the creation of art that he had gained through his knowledge of Wagner's music and his relationship with Wagner himself at Tribschen.

In April 1872 the Wagner household moved from Tribschen to Wahnfried in Bayreuth in preparation for the founding of the *Festspielhaus*. Nietzsche described the last day before the move: 'Last Saturday was a sad and deeply moving farewell to Tribschen. Tribschen is all over now. We wandered about as if among ruins. Nostalgia lay everywhere, in the air, in the clouds. The dog wouldn't eat, the servants couldn't stop sobbing whenever anyone spoke to them. Together we packed the manuscripts, the letters, the books – it was so sad! These three years I have spent near Tribschen, in which I paid twenty-three visits there – what they mean to me! What would I be without them? I am glad that I have petrified that Tribschen world for myself in my book.'[81] Nietzsche's relationship with Wagner was closely associated with Tribschen and it could hardly survive the move to Wahnfried. Now that the two men were physically much further apart, frequent visits from disciple to master were out of the question; while Wagner was increasingly preoccupied with his new world in Bayreuth, and Nietzsche with his new world of ideas.

It was, in any case, natural that Nietzsche would now find his own posture of discipleship unwelcome. Notwithstanding his colleagues' hostility towards his first book, he had to continue the search for his philosophical identity, and it soon became very obvious to him that the assertion of that identity consisted precisely in liberating himself from his deference to Wagner and from the attitudes that deference entailed. For some masters such a development on the part of their disciples might be acceptable: the relationship might survive on the basis of mutual respect and agreement to differ; but not for Wagner. From the first, Wahnfried was reserved about Nietzsche's new trains of thought:[82] he should have been attending to his reinterpretations of Greece, and if he took time off, he should have taken it only for the purpose of doing something directly for Bayreuth – as indeed he did by means of various promotional activities.

For a year or two more, Nietzsche was still regarded by Wagner as his 'most loyal follower',[83] and Wagner and Cosima continued to care a good deal about him.[84] But they had always cared, not so much as friends, but in the manner of overbearing parents. They would give him errands; they would expect him to visit at their convenience; they would assume his willingness to be tutor to their son or editor of a new Bayreuth review. Wagner's biographer Newman (not noted for his charity towards Nietzsche) nicely characterizes their attitude. They were both 'so blind...to the individuality of the young genius whom the Fates had thrown into Wagner's orbit, so blind to the despotic nature of his daemon. He was to be theirs and theirs alone, body and soul: a tight hand would have to be kept on the jesses lest the young hawk should take a flight on his own account and bring down another prey than the one they had worked out for him. No man of anything like Nietzsche's calibre had ever come into such close relation with Wagner's own intellectual life; yet towards no one else did he ever behave so imperiously.'[85] Wagner could not accept his right to develop. Therefore, Wagner could not be peacefully outgrown: sooner or later he must be violently rejected.

On 22 May 1872, the foundation stone was laid for Wagner's theatre in Bayreuth. Nietzsche was there, his intense devotion to the cause still unchanged. In 1875 he wrote *Richard Wagner in Bayreuth*, which was published a year later as the fourth of his *Thoughts Out of Season*. A perceptive eye would have 'deconstructed' the celebration of Wagner and noted the tensions in this piece, which Nietzsche did his best to conceal. Wagner saw nothing but 'a magnificent essay'.[86] Since 1872, perhaps under the pressure of the need to assert himself, Nietzsche had begun to see negative features in Wagner's make-up, his art, and, not least, in the whole ambience of Wagnerian Bayreuth. In *BT* he had proclaimed his hopes for Bayreuth; in April 1872 he had even thought of leaving Basle for a time to become a migrant lecturer drumming up support for Bayreuth.[87] Now disillusion set in. Far from being a realization of his hopes for true culture, the new cult gave every sign of fostering the spirit of national self-congratulation and opulent superficiality which he found so distasteful in contemporary

Germany: it was, in a word, *reichsdeutsch*.[88] And there was something about Wagner himself that was distasteful too, and even about his music. Any balanced criticism of Wagner must admit a coarse side to his personality and his art. While under Wagner's personal spell, Nietzsche had idealized or overlooked his coarse traits – from the theatricality of some of his musical effects to his rabid anti-Semitism (which Wagner shared with Nietzsche's sister and her future husband).[89] With the spell now over, Nietzsche had to see that coarseness for what it was. Given his predisposition to dramatize all his experiences, he was bound to see it as a more painfully distorted version of what it was. And as his dissatisfaction with the whole Wagner phenomenon grew more intense, so did his resentment of the older man's domination over him. In one way that domination was more evident than ever. For though he now knew that his own integrity was at stake, that there was no hope of an acceptable recasting of the relationship, and that a decisive break was inevitable, he still could not bring himself to say anything openly.

The summer of 1876 was the season of the first Wagner music festival at Bayreuth. Tormented by headaches and sickened by the proceedings – perhaps sickened, most of all, by the effort of concealing his distaste for them – Nietzsche came briefly and left to begin work on *Human, All Too Human*, the work which marks his emancipation from his Wagnerian past. In November he met Wagner for the last time, in Sorrento. For Nietzsche the relationship had passed its crisis and seemed now over. Wagner, meanwhile, was still blissfully unaware of any change.[90] In December 1877 he sent Nietzsche the libretto of his new work, *Parsifal*. Nietzsche's reaction (still withheld from Wagner) was highly critical.[91] The psychology was 'fantastic'; the action would be 'insupportable' on stage; the language sounded like 'a translation from a foreign tongue'; above all, it was 'all too Christian'. Despite a good word for 'the situations and the way they unfold', Nietzsche's attitude shows less sympathy than he had shown towards any product of Wagner's mind since the mid-1860s. In the spring of 1878 *Human, All Too Human* was published. Among many other indications of a change in Nietzsche's attitudes, it contained a thinly disguised critique of Wagner (referred to as 'the artist'). It is a comment on Wagner's insensitivity as well as on his good-will (though also a comment on the extent of Nietzsche's concealment) that this was the first he knew or suspected of any hostility towards him on Nietzsche's part.[92] The crisis was a crisis for Nietzsche, not for Wagner. The rupture was Nietzsche's doing, and the grounds for it – as usual with him, inextricably personal and intellectual – were felt to be such by him alone.

Nietzsche's act of apostasy from Wagner corresponded with, and entailed, a whole set of other shifts in his attitudes. His sympathies now no longer lay with Germany, its metaphysics and its Romanticism, but with France and its Enlightenment: *Human, All Too Human* aptly opens with a dedication to Voltaire. It is in this connection that Nietzsche parts company with Schopenhauerian pessimism, after a graceful tribute in the third of his *Thoughts Out of Season* (*Schopenhauer as Educator*, 1874); how permanent, and how real, this emancipation was to be is another question. At the same time, freed from the Wagnerian embrace, Nietzsche turns to reflect on the artistic experience and all that it seems to entail for morality and the meaning of life. An attempt at an extra-moral, 'aesthetic' interpretation of the world is, as we shall see, prefigured in *BT* itself. In Nietzsche's later years, his preoccupation with this endeavour will become more explicit and his interest in 'aesthetics' will be largely determined by it.

Another, related, change in his attitudes concerns religion, and specifically Christianity, towards which the Nietzsche of *BT* had on the whole preserved an inscrutable silence, not exactly hostile and punctuated by a few, more or less complimentary, characterizations: in §11 the fathers of the early church are 'profound and formidable', while in §23 Luther is named as a 'sublime champion' of the German spirit. This apparent respect gives way to a growing antipathy – hence one of his objections to Wagner's *Parsifal*, a work reflecting its author's late enthusiasm for religion. And not the least important mark of the emancipated thinker is a new form of writing. From *Human, All Too Human* onwards, the aphorism and the short note – both very different from the expansiveness of *BT* – are Nietzsche's characteristic modes.

Not everything in his outlook or methods changed: there are striking continuities from his first work to his last. Nevertheless, the Nietzsche who gave up his classical chair in 1879 was a very different Nietzsche from the author of *BT*. Even so, we should not rush to explain his retirement by the changes he had undergone in the meantime, any more than by the consequences of the academic controversy over his first book seven years before. We need look no further than the severe deterioration in his health which was the obvious and accepted reason for his retirement at the time, although that condition must have been exacerbated both by the strains of his professional life at Basle and by the breach with Wagner. From now on he was to move from one spot in Europe to another, perpetually looking for some resort or retreat that would be kind enough to his physical system to permit him to carry on with his writing. Even for one without his pressing ambitions, to continue a conventional career would have been impossible.

At all events, once the last thread attaching him to the philological world had been snapped, Nietzsche never afterwards showed the slightest regret.

Admiration for Greece was one thing. Scholarship as a profession was quite another, and he now took it as axiomatic that, for him, being a Greek scholar had been 'an eccentricity', no less than being a Wagnerian. 'It is the humour of my situation', he wrote a few years later, 'that I should be mistaken for the former Basle professor Dr Friedrich Nietzsche. The devil take him! What has this fellow to do with me?'[93]

THE LAST ACTIVE YEARS: NIETZSCHE'S AFTERTHOUGHTS

For another ten years after his retirement, despite appalling health, isolation and minimal encouragement from the outside world, Nietzsche pursued his philosophical undertaking. He did this in works of reflections and aphorisms like *The Gay Science* (*Die Fröhliche Wissenschaft*, 1882), in the poeticizing and quasi-biblical *Thus Spake Zarathustra* (*Also sprach Zarathustra*, published 1883–92) and in the autobiographical *Ecce Homo* (not published until 1908). This last book was written during 1888, the year before his mental breakdown. To the same extraordinarily productive year belong *The Wagner Case* (*Der Fall Wagner*), *Twilight of the Idols* (*Die Götzendämmerung*), *The Antichrist* (*Der Antichrist*), and *Nietzsche Contra Wagner*. These last works contain a good deal that in one way or another looks back to *BT* or invites reference to it, and viewing Nietzsche's career, as we are, in the perspective of that first book, we must ascribe to this late group a special interest. The books of 1888 also share an extremity of tone, a curiously confidential and sometimes startling private idiom, and – despite a good deal of concomitant irony – a striking lack of modesty and inhibition: witness the very title of the autobiography.

These characteristics may be explained by the release of ordinary constraints that presages madness (although in other respects these late works exhibit the incisive sanity characteristic of Nietzsche); by the demands of his hermit-like existence which contributed to that eventual collapse; or by the lack of a public to adjust his thoughts to. But all these considerations are overshadowed by his conscious choice – a choice at once literary and philosophical – in favour of a new philosophy in a new style. As to the question of his readership, it is certainly true that from *BT* onwards he had to reckon with a small and unreliable audience for his ideas. The subtitle of *Zarathustra* is 'A book for all and for none', and one is tempted to give the 'none' a very simple interpretation, alongside any more profound significance. Ironically enough, it was in 1888, at the time when the last and most 'private' books were being written, that the first signs of his impending fame began to appear.

As far as Nietzsche's thought is concerned, these ten years are marked by the emergence of most of the explicit doctrines (or slogans) generally associated with him: the 'will to power', the 'eternal recurrence of the same', the 'superman', 'master morality' (*Herrenmoral*), *amor fati* and the 'yes-saying' to life. Also visible is an accentuation of the antagonisms that were articulated in the last years of the seventies, along with a tendency to see his particular targets as symptoms of almost cosmic disorder. The world, for Nietzsche, will always offer enticements to human weakness; but the modern world, as he now sees it, is riddled with weakness, disease and decadence, whether we call it Christianity (or its latest mask, socialism), the liberal conscience, Germany or Wagner.

In the case of Wagner the process of generalization is very obvious. The composer died in 1883, and his death brought Nietzsche 'the greatest relief'. It was hard (he wrote to a friend) 'to be for six years the opponent of a man one has admired above all others.'[94] What Nietzsche continued to admire was Wagner's situation as it had been when he first met him: the genius struggling to express itself with all integrity and independence of spirit in the teeth of a hostile world. Here, he hoped, he would be Wagner's true heir.[95] In Wagner's music, despite large reservations, he still heard or remembered some features of unsurpassable art, the 'sweet infinity' of *Tristan* and (more surprisingly) the 'perspicuity that cuts through the soul like a knife' of *Parsifal*.[96] Wagner the man he remembered with gratitude from the days at Tribschen. There Nietzsche had been 'indescribably happy': they were 'the best days of my life'.[97] It was Wagner ('the fullest human being I have known') who had in the first instance helped him grow ('to him I am indebted for some of the strongest incitements to intellectual independence').[98] At the same time, it was Wagner's 'nerve-shattering music' that had, at least symbolically, 'ruined my health'; and it was Wagner whose refusal to have the growing plant grow in its own soil had driven him to a 'rediscovery of myself, which...was among the hardest and most melancholy things that have ever been my lot'.[99]

In Nietzsche's last writings Wagner – this artist of whom he had so complex and so composite a knowledge – regularly appears as the supreme instance of modern culture and all its tendencies; *his* good and *his* bad features – but especially the bad features – make up *its* physiognomy. Wagner, then, is 'the artist of decadence... *Wagner est une névrose*... Wagner is *the modern artist par excellence*... In his art everything that the modern world requires most urgently is combined in the most seductive manner: the three great stimulants of an exhausted people – *brutality*, *artificiality* and *innocence*.' But Wagner is not to be simply dismissed and dispensed with: 'the philosopher is not free to do without Wagner...Confronted with the labyrinth of the modern soul, where could he find a guide more initiated...? Through Wagner modernity speaks most intimately, concealing neither its good nor its evil – having forgotten all sense of shame...Wagner sums up the modern world.'[100] There is a relentless insistence in the late books on Wagner and his real – that is, exemplary – significance, and often, as here, it is heavily coloured by irony. As the foil to Wagner and his decadence Nietzsche offered Bizet: French, free of metaphysical pretensions, unsullied by 'the baroque art of over-excitement'.[101] Here (in his own words) was a suitable 'ironic antithesis'.[102]

In terms of writings and ideas, the ten years after Nietzsche's retirement were a period of rich achievement. As far as his personal relationships were concerned, they were a disaster. Bad health, incessant wanderings, and dedication to his philosophical mission combined to isolate him from old acquaintances and did little to provide him with new ones. Among the many sad events during this time was the final disintegration of his friendship with Rohde. After several years in which contact had consisted of no more than intermittent correspondence, they last met in 1886. Rohde reacted with considerable discomfort to the effects of Nietzsche's increasing isolation. His old friend had about him 'an indescribable atmosphere of strangeness...It was as if he came from a land which no one else inhabits.'[103] The final breach came a year later after an angry exchange of letters.[104] There was a clash of ideas. In his general outlook Rohde still stood more or less where he and Nietzsche had once stood together. Nietzsche's development, along with Nietzsche's insistence on its rightness, was distasteful to him; above all, he deprecated the notion of 'master morality' (*Herrenmoral*).[105] He was enthusiastic about some of Nietzsche's work, notably *Zarathustra*, for he had 'always seen the artist and poet in Nietzsche';[106] but there were not enough other signs of what he took to be the real Nietzsche to retain his loyalty. All he could do was stay loyal to the memory of that earlier friendship, if only by maintaining an unremitting hostility to Wilamowitz.[107]

Through all his other changes, Nietzsche preserved the positive valuation of Greece. Even here, however, there were differences: he no longer located the summit of Greek achievement quite where he once had or for the same reasons. The Nietzsche who could now assert that 'drama occupies a lower rank than epic' had deserted not merely Aristotle's *Poetics*, where the opposite case is argued in detail, but his own *BT*.[108] Plato provides another instance. In *BT* Plato was condemned for his collusion with Socrates' anti-tragic rationalism. In the latest books Plato is still regarded as a traitor to the Greek spirit, but for his 'moralistic and idealistic swindle', his 'Christianity', to which the antidote is not so much tragedy as the 'realism' of Thucydides and the Sophists.[109] (Plato's master Socrates, on the other hand, is the object of curiously mixed feelings, as he was already in *BT*.)[110] Greece – the true pre-Platonic Greece – opposed to Christianity: this becomes one of the *topoi* in Nietzsche's later writings. Greece is opposed also to Romantic modernity and (reversing the equation of *BT*) to Wagner, but to Christianity above all. In this connection the name *Dionysus* takes on an immense symbolic significance for the Nietzsche of the later 1880s, no longer in antithesis to Apollo and not in precisely the sense it had had in that antithesis.[111] 'Have I been understood?' – *Ecce Homo* ends – '*Dionysus versus the Crucified*.'

And what of *BT* itself? Not surprisingly, Nietzsche's views of his first book underwent considerable change. There were certainly some positions taken up there from which he never moved, among them his view of the psychology of the tragic effect.[112] But he was far from reticent with his criticisms. During his last active years, besides various incidental references in books and unpublished notes,[113] he produced two extended discussions of *BT*. The first was in 1886. In that year he brought out a new edition of the book (although the others were still in print), which differed from the second version by the addition of a preface and a new sub-title: no longer *The Birth of Tragedy from the Spirit of Music*; instead *The Birth of Tragedy or: Hellenism and Pessimism* (*...oder: Griechentum und Pessimismus*). The preface, made up of seven short sections and running to a dozen pages in all, is a critique of remarkable verve and candour, fittingly entitled *Attempt at a Self-Criticism* (*Versuch einer Selbstkritik*). If its points are not all equally cogent, it nevertheless remains a document of the greatest importance for any reader of Nietzsche's book.

'Whatever may be at the bottom of this questionable book', the preface began, 'it must have been an exceptionally significant and fascinating question, and deeply personal at that: the time at which it was written, *in spite of* which it was written, bears witness to that – the exciting time of the Franco–Prussian war...' (§ 1). Nietzsche went on to define this 'question' in terms of two related existential problems. The first was the problem of a 'pessimism of strength'. '*The Birth of Tragedy from the Spirit of Music*. – From music? Music and tragedy? Greeks and the music of tragedy? Greeks and the art-form of pessimism? The best-favoured, most beautiful, most envied, most life-inspiring type of humanity to date, the Greeks...how could it be that they of all people stood *in need* of tragedy – or indeed of art? Greek art – what was it for? The reader will guess where the large question mark concerning the value of existence had thereby been placed. Is pessimism *necessarily* a sign of decline, decay, degeneration, weary and weak instincts – as it once was in India and now is, to all appearances, among us "modern" men and Europeans? Is there a pessimism of *strength*?' (§ 1). The second problem was the problem of science (*Wissenschaft*), 'science considered *as* a problem, as questionable'. 'What is the significance of all science when seen as a symptom of life?...Is the scientific disposition perhaps only a fear of, an escape from, pessimism? A subtle defence against – *truth*?' (§§ 1–2).

To the reader familiar with *BT* – and especially the reader more familiar with *BT* than with Nietzsche's later ideas – this account of the book must seem striking not only for what it says, but also for what it minimizes or ignores. Nietzsche's retrospective comments offer an answer to a question which, reduced to its most banal terms, would run: what is *BT* really *about*? And his answer, in effect, is: about those issues ('value of existence', 'pessimism of strength', 'symptom of life', 'defence against truth') which matter most to the Nietzsche of the 1880s. The objection that in *BT* such issues are subsidiary to others, or merely implicit in them, is not considered.

Nietzsche's review, then, involved a reinterpretation of *BT* in terms of his subsequent outlook. But this did not mean that he was in any danger of glossing over those aspects of the book which were out of line with his later thoughts or methods. On the contrary, he went out of his way to draw attention to them, and it was on their account that he found the whole book 'questionable'. 'Constructed from a lot of premature, all-too-green personal experiences, all of them close to the limits of communication', it was 'marked by every defect of youth' (§ 2). He elaborated: 'Today I find it an impossible book: I consider it badly written, ponderous, embarrassing, image-mad and image-confused, sentimental, in places saccharine to the point of effeminacy, uneven in tempo, lacking the will to logical exactitude, quite convinced and therefore disdainful of proof, mistrustful even of the *propriety* of proof, a book for initiates...an arrogant and rhapsodic book that right from the outset sought to exclude the *profanum vulgus* of "the educated" even more than "the mass"...What found expression here was...a *strange* voice, the disciple of a still "unknown God", one who concealed himself for the time being under the scholar's hood, under the gravity and dialectical ill-humour of the German, even under the bad manners of the Wagnerite. Here was a spirit with strange, still nameless needs, a memory bursting with questions, experiences, secrets, after which the name of Dionysus was added as one more question mark. What spoke here – this much was admitted, not without suspicion – was something like a mystical, almost maenadic soul...that stammered with difficulty...as if in a strange tongue, almost undecided whether it should communicate or hide. It should have *sung*, not spoken, this new soul. What I had to say then – what a pity that I did not dare to say it as a poet: perhaps I had the ability. Or at least as a philologist: even today practically everything in this field remains to be discovered and unearthed by philologists! Above all, the problem that there *is* a problem here – and that so long as we lack an answer to the question, "what is Dionysiac?" the Greeks remain as unknown and unimaginable as ever' (§3).

The implication of this critique is clear. Nietzsche had repudiated his 'centaur'. In *BT* he had attempted to produce a work that would at one and the same time give expression to his ideas about the ancient world and satisfy his philosophical and artistic aspirations. What he had succeeded in producing was a work unconstrained by the norms of classical scholarship or abstract philosophy, and yet indefinable in terms of any ordinary art-form. That was what the Nietzsche of 1886 rejected, and in rejecting it he tacitly accepted at least some of the criticisms levelled at him years before by Wilamowitz. At the same time, he went a stage further in his reinterpretation of the book. 'The name of Dionysus was added as one more question mark' – so runs the retrospective gloss. But this again is to recall selectively, for in *BT*, of course, the focus of attention is a *polarity* between Dionysus and *Apollo*. Now, however, in line with his later, changed, usage of the name and the idea, *Dionysus* is given pride of place and Apollo is not mentioned once – a consequence of which is to give a rather different impression of the relationship between the Apolline and the Socratic (here simply called 'art' and 'science').

Nietzsche went further still. The ultimate target of the book (he wrote) could be inferred from 'the careful and hostile silence with which Christianity is treated throughout the whole book'. 'In the book itself the suggestive sentence is repeated several times that the existence of the world is *justified* only as an aesthetic phenomenon', but 'nothing could be more opposed to the purely aesthetic interpretation and justification of the world as expounded in this book than Christian teaching, which is and must be *exclusively* moral.' Christianity with 'its absolute standards' that engender 'hatred of "the world", condemnation of the passions, fear of beauty and sensuality' exhibits 'a *hostility to life*...dressed up as faith in "another" or "better" life... Confronted with morality (especially Christian, or unconditional, morality), life *must* continually and inevitably be in the wrong, because life *is* something essentially amoral....It was *against* morality that my instinct turned with this questionable book so long ago; it was an instinct that aligned itself with life and that discovered for itself a fundamentally opposite doctrine and valuation of life – purely artistic and *anti-Christian*. What was I to call it? As a philologist and a man of words I baptized it, not without taking some liberty – for who can tell the real name of the Antichrist? – in the name of a Greek god: I called it *Dionysiac*' (§5).

The obvious comment invited by this vivid prose is that there is certainly continuity between *BT* and Nietzsche's later works; and that these dicta are relatable to at least one passage in the book; but that Nietzsche is barely talking about *BT* and *its* Dionysus or *its* attitude to Christianity at all. Any reader of the *Self-Criticism* tempted to accept its comments at face value must be taken aback on looking up the passage in the book to which the vivid prose most directly relates. In *BT* § 3 we read: 'Anyone contemplating these Olympians with another religion in his heart, searching for moral elevation, even for sanctity, for disincarnate spirituality, for loving glances of compassion, will soon be forced to turn his back on them, discouraged and disappointed. For there is nothing here that suggests asceticism, spirituality or duty. We hear nothing but the accents of an exuberant, triumphant existence in which all things, good or evil, are deified.' As in the *Self-Criticism*, the opposition is between Greek religion and Christianity (although the latter is not mentioned by name). The Greek religion in question, however, is Olympian religion – which Nietzsche has just declared to be *Apolline* and not Dionysiac at all. Furthermore, from other contexts in the book it is apparent that not only is Christianity *not* regarded with straightforward hostility (we have already made the point); it is not even opposed to Dionysus.[114] Christianity itself is taken to be an expression of the Dionysiac impulse, possibly a deviant or 'degenerate' expression (§ 17), but an expression nevertheless. In § 12, for instance, Nietzsche describes Dionysus, banished from tragedy because of 'Socratic' opposition, seeking refuge in 'the mystical flood of a secret cult which gradually covered the earth'. There is a similar passage in § 17, and in both passages the 'secret cult' can hardly be anything other than Christianity. Later on in the book, in § 23, he refers to the 'abyss from which the German Reformation came forth; and in its chorale the future tune of German music resounded for the first time. So deep, courageous, and spiritual, so exuberantly good and tender did this chorale of Luther sound – like the first Dionysiac luring-call breaking forth from dense thickets at the approach of spring.' Even without the explicit mention of Dionysiac 'luring-calls', the association of Reformation and 'the future tune of German music' – that is, the movement that culminates in Wagner – would be conclusive. We may add the description of the 'ineffably sublime and sacred' – and totally Christian – music of Palestrina (§ 19), which, like 'German music', is opposed to the counter-Dionysiac genre of opera. These references are certainly very scattered; for the rest we have the silence that Nietzsche now, plausibly, calls 'careful' and also, less plausibly, 'hostile'. There is clearly more to be said by way of interpreting this silence – but we, and not Nietzsche, must do the saying.

If Nietzsche's critique ended at this point, his censure would fall only on the book's style, its tone, and its procedures. Inevitably, he also has criticisms to make of its content, and, above all, its Schopenhauerian and Wagnerian aspects – although it would be true to say that so far as possible he deals with these aspects of the book too in stylistic or procedural terms. *Not*, then, that such and such arguments in the book were *wrong*, but – 'How I regret now that in those days I still lacked the courage (or immodesty?) to permit myself a language of my own for views and adventures so very much my own – and that I tried laboriously to express by means of Schopenhauerian and Kantian formulae strange and new valuations which were essentially at odds with the spirit of Kant and Schopenhauer – and at odds with their taste. What, after all, did Schopenhauer think of tragedy? "What gives everything tragic its peculiar elevating force...is the realization that the world and life can never give real satisfaction and hence are *not worthy* of our affection: this constitutes the tragic spirit – which therefore leads to *resignation*." How differently Dionysus spoke to me! How far removed I was from all this resignationism! But there is something far worse in my book, something I now regret still more...: namely, that I utterly ruined my insight into the magnificient Greek problem...by dragging in the most modern things! That I appended hopes where there was no ground for hope, where everything pointed all too plainly to an end! That on the basis of the latest German music I began to fantasize about "the German spirit"....Meanwhile I have learned to look without any hope or mercy on this "German spirit", and also on contemporary *German music*, which is romanticism through and through and which, apart from being the most un-Greek of all possible art-forms, is also a first-rate poison for the nerves, doubly dangerous for a nation which loves drink and honours unclarity as a virtue...' (§6).

The whole 'centaur' is repudiated, then: not only the mixed stylistic mode of the book; also its interrelating of ancient and modern. Ultimately, both disclaimers belong with Nietzsche's strategy of reinterpretation. The real core of *BT*, he would have us believe, is the same as that of his mature philosophy; and the very considerable residue left after that core has been abstracted is dismissed as adolescent bad taste, rather than as the set of thought-out and coherent positions that he had once taken it to be and that, on the whole, it surely is.

Nietzsche's reinterpretation has been influential, and in some ways its influence has been unfortunate. What he disdained so eloquently, subsequent readers (admirers and detractors alike) have assumed is of secondary importance or no importance at all – without any clear warrant for the assumption from *BT* itself. Above all, it is probably his retrospective contempt for the modern, Wagnerian, aspect of the book that has fed (perhaps even created?) the myth that he had *never really meant any of that*: whence the tacit agreement of most modern critics not to *count* his discussion of Wagner, and then not to take any of his thoughts on music at all seriously either. The change of title (not...*from the Spirit of Music*, but...*Hellenism and Pessimism*) is obviously a deliberate incitement to his readers to make light of the musical aspect in this way.

It is true that the *Self-Criticism* concludes with a highly indirect admission that the Wagnerian facets of the book are as organic to it as any other. For in basing such hopes on romantic music, that misguided young author had only been stating a romantic presupposition of the whole book – after all (and here Nietzsche appeals to an imaginary sceptic), 'my dear sir, what is romantic if *your* book isn't? Can profound hatred of "the present day", of "reality" and "modern ideas", be pushed further than you pushed it in your artists' metaphysics?...Is your pessimists' book not itself a piece of anti-Hellenism and romanticism?' (§7). But this conclusion still provides no adequate corrective to the impression built up so powerfully earlier on. *BT* was (among other things) a conceptualization of Nietzsche's Wagnerian experience, and he had now rejected the 'romantic' conceptualization and very nearly the 'premature' experience too. Thanks to his eloquence, the book continues to be seen as its author's first, immature, work, in which, however, the seeds of his mature thinking have already germinated and begun to grow above ground – alongside other, lusher plants which, to the eye trained by the later Nietzsche, are merely weeds.

Nietzsche's second substantial discussion of the book belongs to 1888 and the autobiography *Ecce Homo*, in which he offers a review of all his main works in turn. There may be room for argument about how far the *Self-Criticism* is a trustworthy guide to *BT*. There can be no doubt that the discussion in *Ecce Homo*[115] needs to be read with extreme caution. Not only is it, in part, cavalier reinterpretation, like the *Self-Criticism*; it is also imbued with the tone of excessive exaltation that characterizes much of Nietzsche's very last work.[116] At the same time, it is in some ways more down-to-earth than the *Self-Criticism*. It makes the book sound decidedly more *about Greece* than that piece had (it even mentions Apollo, beside the now hyper-Nietzschean Dionysus), and in any case it offers several new insights into the book's many facets.

Nietzsche began his last review of the book, four sections long, by restating his repudiation of its Wagnerism. 'Several times I saw this book cited as "The Rebirth of Tragedy from the Spirit of Music": what people had ears for was only a new formula for the art, the intentions, the task of *Wagner* – and what was really valuable in the essay was ignored. "Hellenism and

Pessimism" would have been a less ambiguous title – a first explanation of how the Greeks got the better of their pessimism, how they *overcame* it. It is precisely their tragedies that prove that the Greeks were not pessimists: Schopenhauer went wrong at this point, as he went wrong everywhere.' The rejection of 'Schopenhauer the educator' is total, then, and in view of that Nietzsche adds a new thought on his 'educator's' influence on the book: in essence (he now claims) *BT* was not actually a Schopenhauerian book at all. Rather, 'it smells offensively Hegelian, and the cadaverous perfume of Schopenhauer clings only to a few formulae. An idea [*Idee*] – the Dionysiac–Apolline antithesis [*Gegensatz*] – translated into the realm of metaphysics; history itself as the development of this idea; in tragedy this antithesis elevated into a unity...' (§ 1).

On the credit side he notes 'two decisive innovations', which correspond approximately to the two 'problems' specified in the *Self-Criticism* as the existence of 'a pessimism of strength', and the question of science as a problematic 'symptom of life'. First, there is the elucidation of 'the Dionysiac phenomenon among the Greeks: for the first time a psychological analysis of this phenomenon is offered and it is considered as one root of the whole of Greek art' (§ 1). Secondly, there is 'the understanding of Socratism: Socrates is recognized for the first time as an instrument of Greek disintegration, as a typical decadent. "Rationality" *against* "instinct". "Rationality" at any price as a dangerous force that undermines life' (§ 1). With these words Nietzsche tacitly revises his assessment of where the centre of the book lies. He redirects his readers to his interpretation of Greece, its art and its disintegration, and in so doing he makes a claim for the value of that interpretation that is more decisive than any such claim in the *Self-Criticism*. After which, pursuing the theme of 'life' and its enemies, he reverts to his reinterpretation of the book, offering perhaps the most extreme example of all: 'profound, hostile silence about Christianity throughout the book. It is neither Apolline nor Dionysiac; it negates all aesthetic values – the only values recognized in *BT*: it is nihilistic in the most profound sense, while in the Dionysiac symbol the ultimate limit of affirmation is attained' (§ 1). The anti-Christianity has here become more speciously schematic than it was in the *Self-Criticism* ('neither Apolline nor Dionysiac'), but it is no less false to the book.[117]

Among various other striking, but more or less reinterpretative, passages in the review, Nietzsche included a brief comment on his Wagnerian experience. In the *Self-Criticism* that experience had been dismissed as 'premature' and barely communicable. He now approached it in quite different terms. 'I had discovered the only parable and parallel in history for my own inmost experience', which was how 'I became the first to comprehend the wonderful phenomenon of the Dionysiac' (§ 2). However, 'a psychologist might still add that what I heard as a young man listening to Wagnerian music really had nothing to do with Wagner; that when I described Dionysiac music I described what *I* had heard' (§ 4) – but what Wagner had not written. His Wagnerian experience *was*, then, a vital ingredient of the book and its Dionysus after all – only the Wagnerian Dionysiac was really the *non*-Wagnerian Dionysiac all the time. This claim, incredible if taken literally, is not altogether absurd when we recall that Nietzsche's experience of Wagner's music rapidly became inseparable from his experience of the visionary and the man. The incomparable works of Wagner's maturity make a strange misalliance with the turpitude of some of his theories and the scandals of his life. Only by an extraordinary projection of his own ideals onto Wagner could the young Nietzsche see that miracle of incompatibilities as an undifferentiated primal force.

In the context of his comments on the Dionysiac, Nietzsche included also a discussion of his theory of tragedy, quoting a passage from one of the other late books in which he restated for the last time the opposition between tragedy and pessimism. 'How I had thus found the concept of "the tragic" and at long last knowledge of the psychology of tragedy, I have explained ... in *Twilight of the Idols*: "Saying Yes to life even in its strangest and hardest problems; the will to life rejoicing over its own inexhaustibility even in the very sacrifice of its highest types – this is what I called Dionysiac, this is what I understood as the bridge to the psychology of the tragic poet. Not in order to get rid of terror and pity, not in order to purge oneself of a dangerously strong feeling by its vehement discharge – Aristotle misunderstood it that way – but in order to be oneself the eternal joy of becoming, beyond all terror and pity – that joy which includes even joy in destroying." In this sense I have the right to understand myself as the first *tragic philosopher* – that is, the most extreme opposite and antipode of a pessimist' (§ 3).

BREAKDOWN AND FAME: MODERN OPINIONS

Nietzsche's career as writer and thinker came to an abrupt and permanent stop with his mental collapse (from causes that are still a matter for conjecture) in January 1889. In the next few years, unknown to him, the writings of the obscure 'tragic philosopher' were, for the first time, widely disseminated, discussed, and acclaimed. His importance was now established. It was during this period that his sister Elisabeth took custody of him and began to devote herself to her new mission: promoting his works, publishing his *Nachlass*, and spreading more or less distorted notions of his life and his philosophy. For better or worse, his new fame was partly the result of her promotional activities. Their growth and the growth of her brother's reputation now proceeded into the twentieth century, both unaffected by his death in 1900.

Among classical scholars, the new fame of their eccentric ex-colleague made it harder to ignore him, although for a time no easier to accept him as a Hellenist worthy of serious attention; and it was not for some years that there was any real enthusiasm about *BT* from members of the profession. One of the first to speak up for Nietzsche's book was the English scholar F. M. Cornford, in whose important study of early Greek thought, *From Religion to Philosophy* (1912), it was pronounced 'a work of profound imaginative insight, which left the scholarship of a generation toiling in the rear'.[118] That, from a disinterested and informed source, is the kind of response Nietzsche had hoped for forty years before; and if anything is calculated to make one wonder whether his career might have taken a different course, it is the thought of such a response coming *then*.

Among all the various attitudes to Nietzsche shown by classicists in the years of his insanity, Rohde's inevitably has a special interest. Rohde was very affected by the breakdown, by any news of Nietzsche, and by the evocation of their earlier friendship as he reread their old correspondence at Elisabeth's request.[119] Above all, he was ready to reassert to close friends his unqualified admiration for the Nietzsche of the *BT* period. Whatever Nietzsche now was, he had then been a 'magnificent man', a 'new revelation of humanity'.[120] He was glad of Nietzsche's belated recognition and eager to help if possible, not only in connection with the correspondence, but also by sifting through Nietzsche's philological *Nachlass* – a mass of notes from the 1860s and seventies – with a view to possible publication.[121]

Rohde's feelings about *BT* in this new situation were not so straightforward, and he evidently preferred to keep to himself his thoughts on a work that had been so intimately bound up with such a special friendship. In the absence of direct evidence, we are obliged to draw inferences from the great work of his later life, *Psyche*. The book, whose first edition was published in two parts, in 1891 and 1894, deals (in the words of its subtitle) with 'the cult of souls and belief in immortality among the Greeks' (*Seelenkult und Unsterblichkeitsglaube der Griechen*) and in its discussions of Homer, tragedy, and Dionysiac religion inevitably covers some of the ground demarcated by *BT*, albeit from a different perspective and in a very different spirit. To Otto Crusius it was clear that *Psyche* shows the influence of Nietzsche and especially of his first book.[122] And although Crusius also noted important differences between Rohde's conception of Dionysus and

Nietzsche's, it is actually Nietzsche's *later* usage of the name that is so distinct.[123] In any case, what is more revealing is the presence in *Psyche* of passages which evoke *BT* in idiom or cast of thought, sometimes so markedly as to suggest actual paraphrase. In Rohde we read, for instance, that Homeric religion

> ...had no leaning towards anything resembling an excited emotional worship like that practised by the Thracians in their orgiastic cult of Dionysus. The whole movement, wherever it came to their notice, must have struck Homer's Greeks as strange and barbaric, attractive only through the interest always attached to the unknown. And yet – the fact is certain – the thrilling tones of this enthusiastic worship awoke an answering chord deep in the hearts of many Greeks; in spite of all that was strange they must have recognised a familiar accent in it...[124]

and we remember from *BT* §4 how

> the effects wrought by the Dionysiac also seemed 'titanic' and 'barbaric' to the Apolline Greek, while at the same time he could not conceal from himself that he, too, was inwardly related to [it]...

and from §2, in similar vein, that

> the song and pantomine of [the Dionysiac cult] was something new and unheard-of in the world of Homeric Greece; and Dionysiac music in particular excited awe and terror...[for] the votary of Dionysus is understood only by his peers. With what astonishment must the Apolline Greek have beheld him! With an astonishment that was all the greater the more it was mingled with the shuddering suspicion that all this was actually not so very alien to him after all...

Hostility or indifference on Rohde's part towards *BT* would have precluded such conscious echoes – and conscious they must have been in view of his familiarity with the book and his feelings about its author. A continuing sympathy for the work he had once championed is the only explanation.

And yet, as has often been noted, nowhere in *Psyche* does Rohde refer explicitly to *BT*. This silence too must have been deliberate, and there seem to have been two reasons for it.[125] In the first place, his theses were in some respects at odds with the presuppositions of Nietzsche's book. If, for instance, he agreed with Nietzsche in ascribing to Homeric man a deep 'familiarity' with the Dionysiac, he certainly did not agree that the whole Homeric–Olympian apparatus was generated by Dionysiac experience in the past. Furthermore, his whole method and perspective, unlike Nietzsche's, were academic and historical. In the preface to the first edition, discussing the interpretation of ancient religious practices, he even went out of his way (reversing his erstwhile scorn for 'objective' scholarship) to refer slightingly to the 'complete unprofitability of the attempt to make use of the shifting ideas and tendencies of modern civilization to explain underlying motives'. Granted such differences, Rohde would have been obliged to comment critically, if he was to have commented explicitly on *BT* at all. But even though Nietzsche himself in the *Self-Criticism* had been as dismissive of the modern analogies, at least, as Rohde could have wished, Rohde's relationship with him was too personal and (in the shadow of Nietzsche's insanity) its memory too painful to permit him to make a dispassionate appraisal for public consumption, least of all an adverse appraisal. And the fact that in his own book Rohde had occasion to touch on the question of madness in connection with Dionysiac worship in Greece[126] would only have added to his pain.

But in any case – the second reason – Rohde was embarrassed. Not that Nietzsche's views embarrassed him, whatever his objections to them. It was rather that he was embarrassed by the memory (inseparable in his mind from Nietzsche) of his own *Pseudo-philology*. That pamphlet was a large romantic gesture in support of two causes, friendship and German Hellenism. Rohde had been and remained in many ways very romantic in his general outlook, and his ideals had hardly changed; but increasingly he shrank from any direct expression of them.[127] Unlike Nietzsche, he preferred to keep the private and public domains quite separate. By the time of his death, two years before Nietzsche's own in 1898, he had done everything he could to advance his old friend's cause, short of involving himself in public.

In our century, despite intermittent fluctuations in his reputation, Nietzsche has been generally accepted as a major writer, thinker and intellectual influence on the modern West. In *BT*, readers without an extensive classical background – which means most readers – have found primarily a theory of tragedy and (within the Nietzschean canon) the fascinating, but immature, prefiguration of the philosopher's later ideas which his own *Self-Criticism* has encouraged them to find. On either count, it is fair to say, most readers have also found its 'classical' subject matter a source of some difficulty, although obstacles of that kind have not impeded its recognition (on the first count) as 'one of the most suggestive and influential studies of tragedy ever written'[128] – or its immense influence, not only on other theorists, but on creative writers and poets. An account of that, however, in English, French and Scandinavian literature as well as German, would be a vast undertaking and (given the book's many readings) intractably disparate.[129] Among classicists, the interest taken in the book and estimates of it have varied enormously (Cornford's eulogy has never represented the norm), partly because of differing attitudes to Nietzsche's mature philosophy. On the negative side, a 1937 volume of the classical scholar's bible, the Pauly-Wissowa *Real-Encylopädie der klassischen Altertumswissenschaft*, could assure its users, without much in the way of qualification, that 'the criticism of the young Wilamowitz remains essentially correct'.[130]

A few years earlier, 'the young Wilamowitz' himself, having long since become the elder statesman of Greek scholarship, had delivered his final verdict on the controversy of his youth in his memoirs (*Erinnerungen*, 1928). The account given is striking for various shifts in his position over the years; for an obvious embarrassment about the whole affair (perhaps his chief point of contact with Rohde); above all, for the rancour towards Nietzsche which after more than half a century (and despite the embarrassment) still found him looking to score points, rather than cultivating an elder statesman's detachment. The account deserves to be quoted at length:

Rudolf Schöll, who was then lecturer [*Privatdozent*] at Berlin and was soon to go for a short time as professor to Greifswald,...prompted me to make a premature public appearance: by myself I should not have thought of it. Nietzsche's *Birth of Tragedy* appeared, and made me furious. So Schöll, who was fond of a joke, met me, and invited me to write a review which he could get into the Göttingen *Anzeigen*. I was led astray by him, and at Markowitz, almost without books, wrote *Philology of the Future*. Schöll was more than satisfied: it would not do for the *Anzeigen*, but it must be printed. I soon found a publisher, and bore the expense, which was defrayed by the sale of the second part, to which I was impelled by Rohde's *Pseudo-philology* when I was in Rome, in another and purer world.

Nietzsche had excited my moral indignation chiefly by an impudent attack on Otto Jahn. Moreover, everything seemed to be degraded which I had carried away from Pforta as inviolably sacred. An old Pforta boy should not lay hands on that. Nietzsche had counted for something out of the common, though eccentric; we who were slightly his juniors looked up to him. Not quite without exception, for it was said that Paul Deussen, though Nietzsche was and continued to be a superior friend to him, had to help him in his Greek, in which Deussen beat all others, and his mathematics, for which Nietzsche notoriously had no head. He had followed Ritschl from Bonn to Leipzig (hence the attack on Jahn) and through Ritschl's influence got the professorship at Basle and the honorary degree of doctor. I cannot conceive how anyone can excuse this nepotism, an unheard-of favour to a beginner, which could not be justified at all. What he wrote in the *Rheinisches Museum* did not even contain much that was correct...This I could not then judge; Usener had praised it highly in the seminar, and so one was proud of the success of one's fellow-scholar. When immediately after the war [1871] I visited my old headmaster, I also paid my respects to the Basle professor at Naumburg. A few months afterwards *BT* appeared. The violence done to historical facts and all philological method was clear as daylight, and impelled me to fight for my threatened science. It was desperately naïve of me. No scientific knowledge was aimed at by the book: it really did not deal with Attic tragedy, but with Wagner's music drama, for an estimate of which I for my part had no special qualification. Once again the Greeks, as the absolute pattern of an artistic people, were to be shown to have lived, felt, created what modern theory would prove to be absolutely perfect. Apolline and Dionysiac are aesthetic abstractions like naïve and sentimental poetry in Schiller, and the old gods only supplied sonorous names for the contrast, in which there is some truth, however many trivial stupidities half-educated derivative prattle dishes up with the words. Apollo, not Dionysus, inspires the seer and the sibyl to clairvoyant frenzy, and it is the ecstatic music of the flute, not the *kithara* of the god, which prevails in his Delphic cult. Nietzsche had learnt something about Dionysus from Erwin Rohde; for it is one of the chief merits of this eminent scholar to have recognized that with the alien god there came in a new form of religious feeling and action alien to the old worship of the Hellenes. Also it is true that there is a Dionysiac spirit in the rapturous poems to which Nietzsche subsequently rose. This is just why he has always been not only alien but hostile to the truly Hellenic.

Juvenile as much of that work of mine is, with the conclusion I hit the bull's-eye. He did what I called on him to do, gave up his teaching post and scholarship and became the prophet of an irreligious religion and an unphilosophical philosophy. His daemon justified him in that: he had the genius and strength for it. Whether self-worship and blaspheming against the teaching of Socrates and Christ will give him the victory, let the future show.

My book should not have been printed...I was an inexperienced youngster... But I have no reason to repent, for I followed my daemon; honourably and courageously I bore 'the sword in the myrtle bough', as our Bonn society's motto bade me do, for my science, which I thought to be in danger.[131]

The bizarre suggestion that one brief allusion to Wilamowitz's mentor Otto Jahn[132] had been the prime cause of his anger thinly conceals the real cause, his old jealousy of Nietzsche. That jealousy, however, surfaces in the pettiness of his concern with Nietzsche's mathematics, his appointment to Basle, and his retirement; in the spurious attempt to credit his ideas about Dionysus to Rohde[133] (the posthumous tribute to whom is quaint enough); even perhaps in the attempt (diametrically opposed to Nietzsche's position in the *Self-Criticism* and *Ecce Homo*) to detach him entirely from Greece and see *BT* as really about *Wagner*. Having thereby removed the book far enough from his own territory to render further consideration of it endurable, he felt able, at last, to admit what he had denied fifty-five years earlier, that he had been led to initiate one of the most celebrated controversies in the history of classical studies by the promptings of a senior colleague – who had suggested it for a joke.

Wilamowitz's more substantive points – about the Greeks, scientific method, Apollo and Dionysus – will require individual consideration along with the matter of his earlier critiques, although it can safely be said that most classical scholars (like the contributor to *Pauly*) have remained broadly behind him. His estimate of Nietzsche's alienness to 'the Hellenic', however, has not been generally accepted. On the contrary, there has been an increasing willingness to grant that, for all the attendant eccentricities, Nietzsche's ideas about Greece – and the book that most fully embodies them – have a special value. To many of the most thoughtful scholars of the last few decades, Nietzsche is (in Ludwig Edelstein's words) 'one of the most penetrating modern interpreters of the Greek mind',[134] while *BT* is now widely seen as a book to admire, whatever its defects. To Bruno Snell it was a book that showed 'a fine sympathy with the elemental power of inchoate tragedy'; to Werner Jaeger it was 'brilliant', even if 'uneven'; and to G. F. Else, 'a great book, by whatever standard one cares to measure it'.[135] Synthesizing the two sides of the argument, Hugh Lloyd-Jones has recently commented: 'with all its appalling blemishes, it is a work of genius and began a new era in the understanding of Greek thought'.[136] We can now turn to the book's eccentricities, its blemishes and its claims to genius.

6

Nietzsche's account of Greece

THE BIRTH OF TRAGEDY AND CLASSICAL SCHOLARSHIP

The Birth of Tragedy is not a work of classical scholarship. It does contain a good deal of incidental material which only a scholar would be likely to know; and it takes a good deal for granted in a way that only a scholar could find natural. It could only have been written by one who, whatever else he was or wanted to be, was a scholar. And if there is any single group of readers that it seems to presuppose, it can only be a select group of sympathetic, or at least open-minded, classical scholars. But the book is still not a work of scholarship. Not only does it denounce from the pulpit, with all the strident vigour at its author's command, the heresy of Socratism, of which all science and scholarship are expressions. It also practices what it preaches by flouting most of the obvious norms of scholarly prose and striving after other, less 'Socratic', virtues. And yet it represents a significant contribution to the appreciation of the cultural and spiritual realities of the ancient world. As such, and despite Wilamowitz, it has come to exert a considerable influence on subsequent Greek scholarship. Eduard Fraenkel – one of the foremost scholars of our own century and himself a pupil of Wilamowitz – once suggested that 'the most powerful factor in the difference of outlook between Wilamowitz and [Fraenkel's] own generation was the influence of Nietzsche'.[1] *BT* has been the main source of that influence, and it continues to deserve the attention of serious students of antiquity today.

As a comment on Greek culture Nietzsche's book is an extraordinary composite of brilliant insight, expressed with unforgettable force, conventional wisdom, sloppiness, speciousness, distortion and (for lack of a better name) artistic construct. It would have been convenient to use Wilamowitz as an expert adviser to help separate the ingredients of this strange mixture. Unhappily, Wilamowitz, in the violence of his objection to Nietzsche's explicit assault on scholarship and unbalanced by his own personal interest, evaded or denied Nietzsche's insights and misrepresented his procedures. That unspeakable book (Wilamowitz assured the world) was *all* sloppiness, speciousness, distortion – and furthermore (he added half a century later) its unspeakable author had no scholarly credentials anyway. The later claim was actually as false as the earlier: Nietzsche was a *bona fide* scholar whose capacities have been attested by many less prejudiced voices since,[2] and whose failure to produce any major scholarly publications was not the result of incompetence but of profound disinclination. It might well be added that Wilamowitz himself was in no sense a model of cautious scholarly rectitude, and even at the height of his maturity was wont to produce – in Fraenkel's words, again – 'pieces of magnificent scholarship...intermixed with things which are thoroughly bad'.[3] *Philology of the Future*, which is definitely not a work of his maturity, has more than its fair share of errors,[4] albeit errors committed with the self-assurance that Wilamowitz retained until the end of his life.

But even had it been true, the claim that Nietzsche was no scholar was bound to obscure the real issues raised by a work which had not been writen as a work of scholarship in the first place. It is here that Rohde could have dispelled at least some of the fog by sharing with the reading public his awareness that the book was essentially and ineradicably a hybrid, a 'centaur' as Nietzsche himself had called it, a 'didactic poem' (*Lehrgedicht*) in his own formulation. Instead, Rohde too distracted attention from the composite character of the book: on *his* reading it was all insight and undifferentiated wisdom from start to finish. His contributions, like those of Wilamowitz, certainly raised various pertinent points of detail. Overall, however, the polemics merely succeeded in ensuring that many fundamental questions about the book and its formulations were never raised, except perfunctorily, in clear daylight. Either such questions were supposed to have been settled one way or the other already, or else those with an incipient interest in the questions were deterred from pursuing them by the scholarly complications of the controversy and its overheated tone. The result has been that, for all the influence of Nietzsche's book on classicists, as on others, a hundred years after its publication the questions have still never been properly posed and answered.

The first point to make is that there are some respects in which *BT* is simply bad scholarship. Apart from anything else, the presentation of the argument is not just unsystematic (as our précis has shown), but sometimes gratuitously and offensively slovenly. For instance, within the space of a few pages (§§ 8–9) Nietzsche offers a derivation of proto-tragedy from satyr-chorus, from which it might (but should not) be inferred that the chorus of *classical* tragedy is still in some sense 'satyric'; a characterization of the dithyramb which suggests that, contrary to earlier indications, the victory odes (epinicians) of Pindar are not Dionysiac, but Apolline; and a simultaneous interpretation of a play by Aeschylus and a poem by Goethe in which it is left to the reader to gather what is Goethe, what Aeschylus, and what Nietzsche himself.[5] Again, the book makes certain assumptions of obvious importance to its argument which are demonstrably false: for instance that Greek music involved any kind of harmony or counterpoint comparable with those of modern music.[6] And again, the book often fails to offer adequate evidence – or any evidence at all – for positions that are sound or at least tenable, even where those positions are unorthodox or new. Nietzsche's remark on the Greek attitude to sexuality (on which Wilamowitz heaped some ill-advised abuse) is a case in point,[7] and the existence of such cases is important. False and essentially unsupported positions might invite the inference – which Wilamowitz for one was very ready to draw – that Nietzsche was eschewing argumentation because there were no arguments for him to use. The presence of sound but equally unsupported positions suggests that Nietzsche's avoidance of argument is due to some other cause.

The second point is that *BT* has various characteristics whose common effect (or, as Nietzsche himself might have said, whose common *aim*) is to complicate the task of assessing its contents in conventional scholarly terms and sometimes to confer on an assessment made in those terms a disquieting sense of unreality. The highly charged and coloured language of the book is the most obvious of these features. Another is Nietzsche's unremitting insistence on evaluation: every mode and aspect of human life, it seems, is to be weighed in the balance, and the mere accident of pertaining to a past culture in no way serves to exclude any facet of ancient Greece from the same scrutiny. Another is a corollary of Nietzsche's reluctance to argue through evidence, even where the evidence is in his favour: a marked inclination to use statement and assertion as a complement or alternative to argument. One other characteristic is perhaps the most important of all. Nietzsche's main theses involve some entities which scholarship is used to dealing with (such as the dithyramb, or Archilochus, or Greek dreams) – and others which seem to defy its customary procedures of proof and disproof. Nietzsche's idea (Lloyd-Jones has remarked) 'that tragedy originated through a synthesis of Apolline and Dionysiac elements, is as a statement of fact to say the least unprovable'.[8] Such a comment betokens no lack of goodwill, but simply the distance of these entities from the scholarly norm.

The exact status of Nietzsche's aberrant entities is one particular problem. Less problematic conceptually, but no easier to deal with in practice, is the mass of inadequately substantiated positions taken up in the book. The task of sifting these into true (or suggestive or tenable) and false is a large one.

In the first place Nietzsche is dealing with a wide variety of highly controversial aspects of the ancient world – aspects that are still controversial in our own day. In the second place, some of Nietzsche's points look rather different (though not necessarily worse) in the light of subsequent research. Not only has scholarship progressed in its various traditional ways since his day. It has also profited from a huge access of new material, above all in the spheres of archaeology, epigraphy and papyrology: far more is now known about Greek prehistory and Greek lyric poetry – to take only two of the many fields within which he invites us to share his views. In other areas classics has acquired new perspectives and technical sophistication: Greek religion (on the study of which modern anthropology, in various forms, has been a major influence), Greek art-history, and the linguistic science of comparative philology are cases in point. One consequence of this new scholarly equipment is that Nietzsche is sometimes liable to seem methodologically naïve in the extreme. 'Side by side on sculptures, gems etc.', he writes in §5, 'the ancients put the faces of Homer and Archilochus, as the forefathers and torchbearers of Greek poetry', indulging, evidently, in a now happily outmoded practice of *ad hoc* identification of ancient portraiture. The truth is that the subjects of many ancient portraits cannot be specified, either for want of evidence, or because the portrait represents a type not an individual, and that there seems to be no evidence in *any* visual medium of *any* certain portrait of Archilochus in company with Homer.[9] To castigate Nietzsche here, however, is really to criticize nineteenth-century scholarship as much as to criticize him for betraying it.

What with all the diversity and complexity of Nietzsche's Greek material and the quite separate complications provided by his problematic treatment of it, there can be no question of our attempting a comprehensive discussion of every aspect of his view of Greece. Just how formidable such a task would be may be gathered from a sample commentary on another few words from his discussion of Archilochus in §5. It is in this section that Nietzsche introduces the elaborate antithesis between the Apolline epic with its 'forefather' Homer and the Dionysiac lyric with *its* progenitor Archilochus – that lyric being the 'germ' of classical tragedy. The section begins:

> We now approach the real goal of our investigation, which is directed towards knowledge of the Dionysiac – Apolline genius and its art-product, or at least towards some feeling for, and understanding of, this mystery of union. Here we shall begin by seeking the first evidence in Greece of *that new germ which subsequently developed into tragedy and the dramatic dithyramb.* The ancients themselves give us a symbolic answer, when they put the faces of Homer and Archilochus, as the forefathers and torchbearers of Greek poetry, side by side...

The italics are ours, and a remotely adequate commentary on those few italicized words in their context, even a commentary largely stripped of proper substantiation and references, discussion of alternative positions and Nietzsche's sources, would have to be substantial – for instance:

The 'new germ' is lyric poetry (or, in the first instance, folk-song). In view of Nietzsche's subsequent references to modern lyric verse (Schiller etc.), it is essential to bear in mind the meaning of the term 'lyric' in a Greek context: viz. any poetry sung to music (not necessarily the lyre) by a solo performer (monody, personal lyric) or a chorus (choral lyric).

The 'dithyramb' was the traditional ritual hymn to Dionysus, sung by a chorus (hence a species of choral lyric), and since Aristotle generally regarded as the source of tragedy. In its early form, its 'dramatic' potential supposedly consisted in the separation from the chorus of the chorus-leader, producing a rudimentary independent actor. Nietzsche's 'dramatic' evidently refers to the dithyramb at a hypothetical later stage. His 'and' is vague, but implies (or conceals) a development from an early (simpler) dithyramb to tragedy via the later ('dramatic') dithyramb (see e.g. the end of §8), in line with the orthodox, Aristotelian account. Nietzsche now abandons orthodoxy by stressing that dithyramb is a type of lyric and claiming that lyric in general, and specifically personal lyric, is Dionysiac in spirit. The claim is confusing, because (i) dithyramb – but no other species of lyric – is literally *Dionysiac, (ii) dithyramb is not personal lyric but choral lyric. His pretext is the multifarious status of Archilochus of Paros (VII B.C.), traditional founder of artistic lyric and, in particular, the first known personal poet and composer of dithyrambs (Arch.* fr. *120 West, 'I know how to lead Lord Dionysus' fair song, the dithyramb, when my wits are thunderstruck with wine'), hence literally the first known Dionysiac poet. In fact the literal link between Dionysus and Archilochus was stronger than Nietzsche knew. An inscription of the third century B.C., first published in 1952, indicates that the poet 'tried to introduce a fertility cult of Dionysus into Paros and was opposed. Then the men became sterile, and when they consulted the Delphic oracle they were told to honour Archilochus, which presumably means that he was allowed to introduce the cult.... It is tempting to suppose that Archilochus also composed his dithyramb for the new cult' (T. B. L. Webster).*[10]

If a comprehensive discussion is out of the question, what we can attempt is a critical survey of the main areas of Greek culture that Nietzsche deals with, one by one. Even that programme entails difficulties of its own, partly because the organic world of ancient Greece does not break into neatly separate pieces, partly because of Nietzsche's own refusal to compartmentalize. Nevertheless, we can isolate five aspects of his account of the Greek world. One of these, his critical and theoretical interpretation of Greek tragedy, along with his critical-aesthetic treatment of art in general (especially literature and music), we reserve for a later consideration. There remain four areas: music; various aspects of *mores* and religion; literary and intellectual history; and the origin of tragedy, which is largely separable from Nietzsche's discussion of actual tragedies and tragedy – with an imaginary capital 'T' – as such. Of these four, and contrary perhaps to the layman's expectations, religion is the one which shows Nietzsche at his best and the one which needs the most extensive examination. He is at his worst with Greek music, and, for the rest, simply uneven. His 'best', no one familiar with Nietzsche will be surprised to hear, is generally the product of intuitive insight; the kinds of slovenliness (and so on) subsumed under the 'worst' have already been indicated.

GREEK MUSIC

We start with one of the areas named in *BT*'s original title. Most of Nietzsche's comments under this heading are conditioned by his evident desire to create the impression that Greek music was somehow like Wagner – 'metaphysical' and 'mythopoeic' (§ 16). The construction to be put on this endeavour (self-deception? – it was certainly not ignorance)[11] is for the moment less important than the sheer extent of the misrepresentation involved. A summary of the general character of Greek music may serve to put Nietzsche's ideas of its metaphysical, mythopoeic, capacities in perspective.[12] In the first place, it is clear that music played an important part in the *social* life of the Greek world as a regular ingredient of a multitude of different social occasions, from private dinners and funerals to festivals of the gods. Its most characteristic association was with poetry. In the archaic and classical periods, and in fact until the third century B.C., most Greek poetry was *performed*, rather than read privately, and a good deal of it was performed to music. More specifically, much poetry was sung (i.e. lyric, or, strictly, *melic* poetry), or had once been sung (such as elegy and iambus),[13] and an important part of the rest was chanted or declaimed to the lyre, as was the case with Homeric epic. Very little verse, therefore, was entirely divorced from music, with the important exception of the spoken dialogue or monologue (usually iambic) of drama. Furthermore, there was very little scope for music without words: 'pure' music was rare. It is apparent, then, why the Greek word *mousikē* should have meant 'music and poetry' and not just 'music'. It would be hard to argue that there was any real sense of music as a fully autonomous activity until the fourth century.

Being tied to the word, Greek music was very limited instrumentally. Percussion was used in various specific contexts, but for the most part the music was made on the *aulos* – a 'pipe', played approximately like an oboe or clarinet, but conventionally mistranslated 'flute' – or the lyre. The latter is not in fact to be taken as the name of a single instrument, but as a cover term for several, of which the most important were the *lura* (whence our word 'lyre') and *kithara* (whence our 'cithern', 'zither' and 'guitar'). Not only was the range of instrumentation small; the instruments themselves were normally restricted to solo accompaniment, and not used in any remotely 'orchestral' combinations. It will be obvious why there is general agreement that Greek music was not merely tied to the word, but subordinate to it (a notion that is in any case enunciated as a principle by more than one classical source);[14] that situation held good until the last decades of the fifth century, when the old order was overthrown by a musical revolution associated with – and often, for convenience, known as – the New Dithyramb. It will be obvious also how remote that old order was from the world of nineteenth century instrumental music, the concert orchestra, and the unashamed supremacy (*pace* Wagner's earlier theories) of music over word. Nietzsche's pervasive attempt to predicate of Greek *mousikē* the dominant role of modern music is idle and (being made as much by innuendo as by frontal argument) less than fully honest.

Yet just *how* unmodern, and how utterly un-Wagnerian, Greek music was one can only comprehend in the light of its internal limitations. Even with so few types of instrument and a tradition of restricting them to solo accompaniment, there would have been latitude for a certain exploitation of (to use the musical jargon) heterophony. It is beyond dispute, however, that the Greeks employed no harmony, no counterpoint, no polyphony worth the name.[15] For our model of progress in the mythopoeic art, Nietzsche refers us to German music's 'vast solar orbit from Bach to Beethoven, from Beethoven to Wagner' (§ 19). But at every point in the orbital development of Greek music, however varied and affecting the rhythmic and melodic elaborations may have been, that additional dimension of sound without which the effects of Bach, Beethoven and especially Wagner would be unthinkable, was quite unknown. In a faintly uncomfortable discussion of Greek music in § 17, Nietzsche grants – as well he might – that music in its modern form is 'infinitely richer', but nevertheless contrives to ascribe the effect of that richness to a music that lacked its necessary cause. On one occasion (§ 2) he goes so far as to credit the music of the primitive Dionysiac dithyramb not only with 'the emotional power of tone' and 'the uniform flow of melody' but also with 'the utterly incomparable world of harmony'. No evidence is offered in support of the claim and, apart from a little special pleading, none could be.[16]

The dithyramb, of course, occupies a critical place in Nietzsche's scheme of things. It is the cult-song of Dionysus and the putative source of tragedy. On ancient evidence, it is generally accepted that its musical component had a distinctive, ecstatic character, this being engendered in the most typical cases by wild dancing, the emotive 'flute' and exotic percussion – especially distinctive, perhaps, in the period before Arion (*c.* 600 B.C.), who is credited with various changes that amount to the instutionalization of the form.[17] Our knowledge here, however, is strictly limited. It is possible, for instance, that, being 'wilder' than Greek music in general, the early dithyramb will have been music-dominant and verbally simple,[18] and, as such, a remote spiritual ancestor of modern music – but we have virtually no direct evidence of the nature of the dithyramb (its words, let alone its music) earlier than the fifth century. The dithyrambic parts of Nietzsche's thesis are not erroneous so much as speculative; and his equation between the cultic ecstasies of early Greece and the rapturous response of a modern sensibility to a great composer's subliminal effects, though ingenious, rests on little more than an act of faith.

In the absence of heterophonic richness, Greek music concentrated on the exploitation of melody and rhythm, and Nietzsche is also open to criticism for failing to make this clear. As far as the rhythmic factor is concerned, we know enough to be able to say that the rhythms of Greek music (which we customarily refer to as the metres of Greek lyric verse) were developed to a far higher level of complexity than is usual in nineteenth-century music. In the case of melody, this is not likely to have been the case, although here we are on less certain ground. Our information is largely concerned with the celebrated *harmoniai*, usually translated 'modes'. The nature of the modes has been, and remains, a controversial and difficult subject,[19] not least because it seems to have changed during the period between the early Greece of Homer and Archilochus and the intellectualized society of the music theorists (from the fourth century B.C. onwards) who are our chief source of information. It is safe, nevertheless, to say that at one time or another modality involved identifiable patterns of tones or intervals (as in scales) or motifs or indeed actual melodies; and that from an early period the Greeks attached an ethical significance to the various modes – 'manliness', for instance, to the Dorian, a 'passionate' character to the Phrygian. A corollary of this is that in what Warren Anderson calls the period of 'true modality', from the seventh century to the mid-fifth, the modes were kept distinct. According to one ancient tradition,[20] there were three original modes, the Dorian, Phrygian and Lydian (whose ethnic names are presumably indicative of an actual origin, Hellenic or non-Hellenic), while other names, like the Mixolydian, came later. From Aristotle, however, we learn that according to general belief 'there are two kinds, the Dorian and the Phrygian; the others are comprehended under one or other of these two'.[21] The modes were to some extent correlated with literary forms, i.e. with lyric species. The dithyramb, for instance, was traditionally associated with the Phrygian, the nome (a song usually in honour of Apollo) with the Dorian, while the lyrics of tragedy were normally in the Mixolydian, although other modes (including Phrygian) were occasionally employed.[22]

One conclusion to be drawn from these complexities is that, with melody as with rhythm, the generalizations to be made about Greek *mousikē* are totally different from those appropriate to modern music. Another is that even if Nietzsche's vision of the 'Wagnerian' powers of the dithyramb was entirely convincing, his attempt to read those same qualities into the music of tragedy would be untenable in the light of the quite different modal affiliations of the dithyrambic and tragic genres, Phrygian and Mixolydian respectively. Even less tenable (if that were possible) is the idea that music with those qualities is *the* representative Greek music. Nietzsche avoids spelling out this remarkable notion; nevertheless, it permeates §§2–6.

The tale of Nietzsche's distortions is completed by his treatment of the revolutionary effects of the 'new' music.[23] There were many signs of a new order, among them: a greater play of emotion; confusion of forms (the nome and dithyramb, in particular, switched modes);[24] a fashion for reproducing sounds (musical or non-musical) in a spirit of 'naturalism'; 'free verse' in place of traditional strophic construction; the development of music as a solo activity giving scope for virtuoso musicianship; and in song, a distinct tendency to develop the musical (and specifically melodic) element at the expense of the word. Nietzsche's examination of the new music (which he discusses under the heading of the New Dithyramb) comes in §§17 and 19. It is, to say the least, selective. While fully recognizing the fact and importance of the revolution, Nietzsche nevertheless characterizes it virtually without reference to any of its manifestations listed above, except one, the fashion for musical *mimesis*. In his terms we are asked to see the whole significance of the movement in its perversion of metaphysical truth-telling (his idea of which is heavily influenced by Schopenhauer) into degenerate tone-painting. That the tone-painting existed is not in doubt. A nice instance is attested with reference to the *Nauplios* dithyramb of Timotheus (*c.* 400) 'in which the attempt to represent a storm by means of the flute roused the ridicule of the flute-player Dorion, who said that he had seen a bigger storm in a boiling saucepan'.[25] However, even if we are disposed to accept Nietzsche's premise that *some* music has a special metaphysical propensity, its attribution to the original dithyramb remains entirely speculative.

Whatever else is uncertain, it is at least possible to surmise one reason for Nietzsche's having touched so selectively on the movement's innovations. The overall direction of those innovations is more or less parallel to what he was soon to see as the path taken by Wagner's own 'music of the future': the release of music from all limiting factors – whether constraints of formal structure, or domination by the word, or simply traditions of emotional restraint – in the cause of expressive effect. For all his present insistence on Wagner's music as the fulfilment of a 'metaphysical' rôle, Nietzsche can hardly have overlooked the resemblance entirely. However reluctantly he may have sensed it, and however staunchly he may have rejected it, this resemblance must have helped to engender his lopsided depiction. Committed as he was *to* Wagner and *against* the self-conscious art of the Socratic age, he concentrated his fire on the safest target, the revolutionaries' mimetic excesses. The composer of – to take one among many instances – the fire music in the third act of *Walküre* was himself no stranger to the art of programmatic effect; but in Nietzsche's eyes all that was in the service of the musico-dramatic complex whose 'metaphysical' depth belied any suggestion of *mere* 'imitation of phenomena'. That charge, then, could safely be laid at the door of those earlier histrionic innovators.

There are certainly aspects of Nietzsche's treatment of Greek music that invite no criticism: his stress, for instance, on the unity of music and word in Greek lyric (§§5–6). And despite our lack of information about the early dithyramb, there is no reason to reject his fundamental opposition between that 'wild' *aulos* music and the more widespread strains of the lyre. (We shall see that this opposition of instruments is not quite as significant as he would have us suppose; but the special position of dithyrambic music is not in doubt.) For Nietzsche both kinds of music – and music as such, except for degenerate 'Socratic' music (§§17, 19) – are further opposed to anything smacking of rational consciousness. This opposition, as Martin Vogel has noted,[26] runs up against the close relation between Greek music and mathematics (attested in the person of Pythagoras as early as the late sixth century). The objection is not quite as damaging as it sounds, when one recalls that in Greece mathematics was as easily associated with mysticism (witness again Pythagoras, and through him, the Plato of the myth of Er) as with any rationalistic science. Nevertheless, here as elsewhere it is apparent how few areas of real identity exist between Greek music and its modern counterpart, and how misleading it is to impose a single label, 'music', on both.

THE ORIGIN OF TRAGEDY

For its modern interpreter, Greek music, though a subject full of unknowns, is at least one in which there exists a reasonable measure of agreement about most of the basic questions. The same cannot be said of the origin of tragedy. It is hard to escape a feeling of helplessness when one contemplates the range and number of modern theories[27] – that range and that number testifying not only to the inherent fascination of the question, but also (one fears) to its insolubility. As G. F. Else has pointed out,[28] Nietzsche's own suggestions have appreciably affected some of the suggested answers; and one might add that his book has helped to stimulate interest in the question in any case.

Like Nietzsche, most modern theorists have derived tragedy from the worship of the god Dionysus. This is in effect what Aristotle did (*Poetics*, Ch. 4) by tracing it back to the dithyramb, and it is undeniable that classical tragedy itself had a real, if external, connection with the god. It was performed at the Great Dionysia, one of his annual festivals in Athens, and at that festival each playwright, in formal competition, submitted three tragedies followed by a satyr-play, whose connection with Dionysus is unmistakable: the satyr is the god's mythical attendant, and the satyr-play – the Greek masque – involves light-hearted treatments of various mythological plots, but always with a chorus of satyrs. It is widely supposed that the overt connection of tragedy with Dionysus had once been greater and that its gradual reduction was the reason for an ancient proverb, 'nothing to do with Dionysus'.[29] Of the theories purporting to explain *how* that connection could have been greater, the least controversial is that early tragedy (like the primitive dithyramb) involved exclusively Dionysiac subjects – in other words, the birth and sufferings of the god. One of the more problematic theories is that the original (i.e. dithyrambic) chorus of proto-tragedy was in fact a satyr-chorus – the authority for this idea being another remark made by Aristotle in *Poetics*, Ch. 4, according to which tragedy developed *ek saturikou*, 'from a satyricon', or 'from the satyr-play' or 'from an entity in some way akin to the satyr-play'.

In 1927, in an important book, *Dithyramb Tragedy and Comedy*, A. W. Pickard-Cambridge summed up the evidence and ideas about the pre-history available at the time, and offered a sober and scrupulous evaluation both of the evidence and of earlier theories. His conclusion was that tragedy, like the satyr-play and the dithyramb, originated in the worship of Dionysus; it did not, however, develop from either of the other two Dionysiac forms, but from immemorial, unrecorded rustic performances of semi-dramatic choral dance and song, which in the mid-sixth century the Athenian Thespis revolutionized by the addition of an actor's part. The newly developed drama was now transferred to the spring festival of Dionysus (*c.* 534 B.C.), and came under the influence of various sophisticated literary and musico-literary traditions. (One of these involved a supposed 'tragic' style of lyric composition, ascribed to the dithyrambist Arion, about 600 B.C.) As a result of these influences, and in the hands of creative talents like Aeschylus, tragedy developed into the mature form of which every extant play (from Aeschylus' *Persians*, 472 B.C.) is an example.[30]

Among the views Pickard-Cambridge rejected was Ridgeway's theory that tragedy derived from the Greek cult of the dead (usually known as hero-cult), the proto-drama having supposedly evolved from ritual lamentations at the dead hero's tomb. Another was Gilbert Murray's idea that the original form was a species of ritual belonging to the worship of what he, after Jane Harrison, called the 'eniautos-daimon', or 'year-spirit'. By that was meant a notional undifferentiated fertility-deity, of which both Dionysus and the heroes familiar from Greek mythology were particular forms, and whose ritual (nowhere actually attested in Greece but ascribed by Murray to the primitive dithyramb) began with a contest between the year-spirit and its enemy, and proceeded through the sacrificial death of the spirit to its glorious resurrection or epiphany – the whole ritual symbolizing the cyclic death and rebirth of Nature.[31] Pickard-Cambridge rejected also the neo-Aristotelian theories propounded by many scholars (especially German scholars) both before and after Nietzsche, including the attempt to combine the two main Aristotelian data (the dithyrambic origin and the development from a 'satyricon') in terms of a composite 'satyric dithyramb'.

Not only is the neo-Aristotelian theory the predominant one of modern times. It is also the basis of Nietzsche's own account, as we gather when he confronts us with 'the satyr chorus of the dithyramb' in §7. '*The Birth of Tragedy*', writes G. F. Else, 'does not present any new theory of the origin; it simply visualizes, *visionalizes*, an outline of events suggested in Aristotle's *Poetics*.'[32] Accordingly, whatever its other merits or demerits, Nietzsche's account is open to the objections which apply to the neo-Aristotelian theory as a whole. Chief among these is a lack of evidence that the dithyramb was ever in fact performed by satyrs – that is, by a chorus singing and dancing in satyr-costume[33] – or that it had any dramatic or proto-dramatic characteristics at any relevant (i.e. early) date.[34]

In 1962 T. B. L. Webster brought out a revised edition of Pickard-Cambridge's book. As far as the origin of tragedy was concerned, one discernible departure from the first edition was a shift towards the neo-Aristotelian position, accompanied by an attempt to reconcile that position with Gilbert Murray's theory in a modified form. Another was the use of a considerable quantity of new archaeological evidence, including depictions of choral performances on vases of the archaic period and material from the Mycenaean age of the second millennium which suggested the existence at that time of fertility worship of the 'eniautos-daimon' type, perhaps associated with the god Dionysus himself, and involving performances by a dancing chorus. The significance of the new evidence was that the prehistory of the tragic genre might be traceable back even beyond Homer. Webster suggested that it was indeed so – not, however, in the sense that the Mycenaean rituals were the immediate ancestor of classical drama, but rather that they were the ancestral rituals to those in the archaic age from which the proto-drama did develop. He suggested further that it was this fertility worship of the Mycenaean age that generated the myth of the suffering Dionysus and other myths of that type – myths whose rhythm was 'so satisfying that stories from other mythological cycles were approximated to it',[35] thus finding a natural place alongside Dionysiac mythology as material for the tragic drama of the classical age. From the remote world of pre-Homeric Greece, Webster meanwhile traced the line of descent through the seventh-century 'satyric dithyramb', via Arion and others to Thespis, from whose time the tragic chorus was complemented by an actor's part – the source of true drama – and the tragic material diversified further and further away from its Dionysiac (or equivalent) beginnings.[36]

If Murray's theory (or Webster's revised version of it) recalls *BT*, this is no accident; it is a theory that was evolved in a Nietzschean context. Murray's ideas were originally set out in an excursus to Jane Harrison's *Themis* (1912), a book whose author proclaimed herself a 'disciple of Nietzsche' and one that also contained a contribution by F. M. Cornford, whose rapport with Murray and Murray's theory helps to explain his own eulogy of Nietzsche's book, quoted above.[37] The extent of Nietzsche's direct influence on Murray, however, should not be overstated. The idea of a ritual origin in the dithyramb is common to both, but was accepted long before Nietzsche. An emphasis on *primitive* ritual is another point in common, but here Murray's perspective derives immediately from J. G. Frazer and the new science of anthropology. The most significant resemblance is rather the inner logic of the hypothetical ritual sequence, which (according to Murray's reconstruction) involves a movement from the ritual death of the god to his resurrection, and hence an 'extreme change of feeling from grief to joy'.[38] One might compare the description in *BT* § 10 of the 'suffering Dionysus' and the 'hymns of joy' that anticipated his rebirth, which Nietzsche relates to that 'metaphysical consolation – with which every true tragedy leaves us – that at the bottom of things, despite all the changes of appearances, life is indestructibly powerful' (§7).

What is a little surprising about the Nietzschean side of Murray's theory is that it does not appear to include Nietzsche's idea of possession as a key to dramatic impersonation, even though the idea would have been eminently compatible both with Murray's theory and with the expositions of mystery ritual which bulk large in Jane Harrison's book. As Nietzsche indicates (§8), Dionysus, unlike the Olympian gods, takes possession of his dithyrambic worshippers, 'who consider themselves and one another transformed', each one surrendering his own *persona* as an 'unconscious actor';[39] the actor in the Greek theatre, who (like his counterpart on the modern stage) formally exchanges his own personality for another, is seen to be only a step away.[40] The omission is worth noting, because Nietzsche's idea was not part of the standard account at the time, although it has been widely repeated in our century, and neo-Aristotelians such as Walther Kranz have affirmed it with some force.[41] By way of enforcing this point, one might compare Nietzsche's version with that of J. W. Donaldson, a learned English neo-Aristotelian, well acquainted with German ideas about Greece. Writing a dozen years earlier than Nietzsche, Donaldson duly relates tragic drama to 'those enthusiastic orgies which spring from a personification of the powers of nature', and specifically to the dithyramb, in which it seems to him 'a reasonable conjecture that the Coryphaeus [i.e. chorus-leader] occasionally assumed the character of the god himself, while the rest of the chorus...represented his noisy band of thyrsus-bearing followers.'[42] From such 'mimicry' Donaldson derives theatrical impersonation. When, however, it comes to explaining *why* 'mimicry should enter largely into such a worship', he can only suggest that 'a religion which recognizes a divinity in the great objects of nature...is essentially imitative in all its rites'.[43]

Murray's theory has had a considerable following, especially in the English-speaking world and among a non-specialist public, but neither in its original form nor in Webster's modified version has it achieved a consensus among scholars. There is in fact no more sign of a consensus now than ever. Recent years have seen yet more neo-Aristotelian juggling acts with dithyrambs, satyrs, Arion *et al.* from J. A. Davison in 1968, Wolfgang Schadewaldt in 1974, and others; an impressive argument from Walter Burkert in 1966 for relating tragedy specifically to *sacrificial* ritual; a massive study by F. R. Adrados in 1972 dealing with a ritual complex of a much larger kind; and an etymological diversion *contra* Burkert by Szemerényi in 1975, looking towards Anatolian song-dance proto-drama of the eighth or seventh centuries B.C.[44] The most original theory, however, has undoubtedly been that of the distinguished American commentator on Aristotle's *Poetics*, G. F. Else.

Else's study, *The Origin and Early Form of Greek Tragedy* (1965), is a sparkling book, and the theory propounded in it is not merely original, but (by comparison with virtually all other theories) extremely coherent. Unfortunately, originality and coherence are achieved at the high cost of arguing away a large part of what has generally been taken to be the relevant ancient evidence. Else's premise is that *post eventum* assertions by the ancients about the prehistory of tragedy rest not on evidence, accessible to them but now lost, but on speculative theorizing which is not, in principle or in practice, superior to our own. Accordingly, he discards the testimony of Aristotle and others and proclaims that tragedy has indeed (in the words of the proverb) 'nothing to do with Dionysus' – or with any other religious ritual either. Noting how strong and pervasive the attachment to a ritual origin is, he ascribes a large share of the responsibility for it to Nietzsche. 'If', writes Else, 'any single impression concerning the origin of tragedy is fixed in the minds of most literate members of Western society, it is that tragedy stems from Dionysus and satyrs. This dominant impression is the joint work of as unlikely a pair of collaborators as ever lived: Aristotle and Friedrich Nietzsche.' Then, having noted that *BT* (in his words) 'simply *visionalizes* an outline of events suggested in Aristotle's *Poetics*', he adds: '*BT* has cast a spell on almost everyone who has dealt with the subject since 1871. Even those who reject Dionysus and satyrs and look for other points of origin tend to feel – unconsciously, perhaps – that these must belong to the same order of being as Dionysus, that is, that they must go down to the deepest and most primitive levels of Greek religion.'[45]

Tragedy, Else declares, evolved late – in sixth and fifth-century Athens – or rather, it did not 'evolve' at all: it was invented in a series of two creative acts, by Thespis and by Aeschylus. What Thespis did was not to add iambic speaking parts to a pre-existing chorus, but to invent a new form with actor and chorus, in which the choral lyric part looked back to the established *artistic* choral lyric tradition (including the now literary dithyramb), and the actor's speaking part to the iambic and trochaic verse of the Athenian poet-statesman Solon (*fl.* early sixth century). Under the influence of the Homeric epics, which from the sixth century were publicly recited at the Panathenaic festival in Athens, the predominant content of the new form was heroic myth and legend. The sole connection of Thespis' new creation with Dionysus was external and accidental. Athens' enlightened tyrant Pisistratus, who had also been responsible for the development of the Panathenaea, founded a new festival for the popular god Dionysus not long before his own death in 527. The central feature of the new Dionysia was Thespian tragedy, which continued to be composed for the festival henceforth. In due course, a generation later, Thespis' great successor Aeschylus took the second step by adding a second actor (here at least Else follows Aristotle) and, thereby, the various interactions between individuals and interests that drama in its truest sense implies.

Else has demonstrated conclusively (if it needed demonstrating) how open the question of the origin of tragedy still is. No theory, his own included, is free from objections. If it is a fair comment on Else that the ancient testimony he rejects as speculative *may* have rested on older and more secure foundations (and ancient speculators had far more tragedy, including early tragedy, to speculate from than we do), the alternative theories are open to the charges of hypothesizing unattested ritual (as even the cautious Pickard-Cambridge did) or unsubstantiated connections between the presumed stages of development. But it is much easier to find the faults in the conflicting theories than to remove them. Our evidence is in various ways both contradictory and insufficient – a fact that obviously needs to be taken into account in any assessment of Nietzsche's version of events. The particular deficiencies of his version may be more evident or more idiosyncratic than most, but he is not to be condemned for having a version with any deficiencies at all.

Strong as the 'spell' cast by *BT* may have been, Nietzsche's theory is not such as to have encouraged the book's admirers to accept it *tout court* (Walter Otto has perhaps come closest to doing this).[46] It is *too* idiosyncratic for that and too intimately connected with the book's idiosyncratic philosophy. But as with so many aspects of *BT*, the difficulties it raises have not been publicly aired, except in single dismissive sentences or else (in Wilamowitz's case) in a thoroughly distorted form. We have already alluded to one of the sensitive spots: the 'satyric dithyramb'. This notion Nietzsche shares with the neo-Aristotelian theory in most of its guises. At the same time, his version raises special difficulties, because in his eyes satyric experience is all vision, impersonation, ritual drama – the kind of ritual drama attested in the mysteries of Demeter at Eleusis, where the goddess's search for her lost daughter was ritually re-enacted by the priestess and the initiates. What Nietzsche has in effect done is identify the Dionysiac worship represented in the early dithyramb (of which we know very little) with another problematic entity, the 'Dionysiac mysteries',[47] and interpret the supposed satyric aspect of the former with reference to the presumed characteristics of the latter. If we grant (as many have not granted) both the existence and the co-existence of the two entities, a connection is possible, even likely, but it remains hypothetical in the extreme.

Among the problems inherent in the notion of a 'satyric dithyramb' is a discrepancy between the seriousness of the dithyramb as we know it and the apparent frivolity of the satyr as represented in, for instance, Euripides' *Cyclops*. As Else puts it: 'the actual satyrs of Greek legend and drama were subhuman, "good-for-nothing" creatures distinguished above all by braggadocio, cowardice, and lechery. If the original tragic chorus was made up of them, tragedy must have undergone a drastic change of tone and theme somewhere along the way.'[48] Of the various attempts that have been made to overcome this difficulty, none has been so startlingly direct as Nietzsche's, according to which the satyr's characteristics are subjected to a reinterpretation that in one way looks back to Rousseau and, in another, forward to Freud to yield the seriousness required. The satyr now is not 'lecherous', but the sublime symbol of nature's sexual potency; no longer 'subhuman', but the primitive archetype of man; no longer *lower*, but *deeper*, than civilized men (§8). Like much else in Nietzsche's theory, the reinterpretation is highly problematic. What he has done (as Wilamowitz observed) is conflate the satyrs with Dionysus' other half-animal attendants, the Sileni.[49] Both satyrs and Sileni were originally independent fertility spirits, but by the sixth century both had been drawn into the Dionysiac circle, and by the fifth they were confused by the Greeks themselves. One important distinction, however, was that the Silenus had a connection with *wisdom*. A traditional figure, in satyr-plays and elsewhere, was 'the old Papposilenus, who has many weaknesses, but also has intellectual talents. He is entrusted with the education of Dionysus, and even voices a proverbial philosophy in Pindar...and in the story of Midas. The comparison of Socrates with Silenus is based not only on common ugliness...but also on common irony and wisdom.'[50] The close relationship between satyrs and Sileni in the classical period is illustrated by the tendency for that same Papposilenus to be regarded as the satyrs' father. The two types are nevertheless distinct. It is the Silenus, not the satyr, who has connections with wisdom, as in the Midas anecdote, which Nietzsche retells with considerable emphasis (§3). It is, on the other hand, the satyrs, and not the Sileni, who have the putative connection with proto-tragedy. Nietzsche's wise, half-animal chorist is his own invention.

In some ways Nietzsche has simplified the neo-Aristotelian position: various of the well-known 'stages' in the development of the tragic embryo find no mention in his account. There is, for instance, no Arion in *BT*, no Thespis even, and one cannot be sure whether the suppression of an item like Arion's dithyramb implies scepticism about its relevance or even existence, or simply indicates Nietzsche's reluctance to weary his readers with inessential detail. In other ways, however, he has elaborated the inherited argument. This is particularly obvious in the case of the 'visionary' aspects of his theory, whose detailed exposition is given in §8. There he tells us that

The revelling throng, the votaries of Dionysus, jubilate under the spell of these moods and insights whose power transforms them before their own eyes till they imagine that they are beholding themselves as restored geniuses of nature, as satyrs. The later constitution of the chorus in tragedy is the artistic imitation of this natural phenomenon, though of course at this point the separation of Dionysiac spectators and magically enchanted Dionysiac [worshippers] became necessary.

One wonders whether the 'point' mentioned is not partly logical, rather than strictly chronological, but the depiction is, in itself, realizable and plausible. When, on the other hand, Nietzsche turns his attention to explaining how the dramatic *events* (rather than their spectators) originate, his words defy the literal understanding that they seem to require:

The magic transformation is the presupposition of all dramatic art. In this magic transformation the Dionysiac reveller sees himself as a satyr, *and as a satyr, in turn, he sees the god*, which means that in his metamorphosis he beholds another vision outside himself, as the Apolline complement of his own state. With this new vision the drama is complete... *Dionysus*, the real stage hero and centre of the vision, is ...not actually present at first, in the very oldest period of tragedy; he is merely imagined as present, which means that originally tragedy was only 'chorus' and not 'drama'. Later the attempt is made to show the god as real and to represent the visionary figure together with its transfiguring frame as something visible for every eye – and thus 'drama' in the narrower sense begins. Now the dithyrambic chorus is assigned the task of exciting the mood of the audience to such a Dionysiac degree that, when the tragic hero appears on stage, they do not see the awkwardly masked human being but rather a visionary figure, born as it were from their own rapture.

It is clear enough how the ecstatic worshipper could feel himself to be the daemonic servant of his god. It is clear enough how he might, in his ecstatic state, *see* his god. And it is a brilliant stroke of ingenuity (which does not, in itself, make it true) to assert that the stage events originated from that vision of the god. What is not at all clear is why the vision of the god should have to come *after* an initial metamorphosis into the satyr. That vision – the object of the whole exercise – would more likely be the first or the only distinct event, the 'metamorphosis' being in the first instance a self-induced impersonation whose realization would presumably be coincident, temporally and otherwise, with the vision. Why then is Nietzsche so insistent on his order of events – first the satyr, then the god? Simply because his whole metaphysico-aesthetic theory of the Dionysiac and Apolline prescribes it – and it is at this point that the intimate connection of his theory with the higher reaches of his own philosophy becomes apparent. The Dionysiac is ontologically, and *therefore* chronologically, prior to the Apolline; an ecstatic transformation of status is a Dionysiac event, whereas visions of anything outside the visionary (even visions of the god Dionysus himself) are Apolline; *therefore* the Dionysiac 'vision' (so-called) comes before the Apolline; and the 'before' and 'after' are not strictly chronological at all. When one compares Nietzsche's silence about Arion and Thespis with the effort he has evidently put into *this* argument, it becomes clear that his interest in the genesis of tragedy depends on a deeper concern with aesthetics, psychology, even metaphysics – but, for better or worse, not literary history. If by 'theory of the origin of tragedy' we understand a contribution to literary history, Nietzsche's 'visionalization' of Aristotle, whatever else it may be, is no theory at all.

LITERARY HISTORY

In view of Nietzsche's essential unconcern with the origin of tragedy as a literary-historical development, it is not surprising to find that much of his treatment of Greek literary and intellectual history in its other aspects consists of barely substantiated *dicta*, often magisterially brief, on diverse periods and authors. To judge from Wilamowitz, Nietzsche was not simply cursory; he misunderstood every chapter of Greek literary history. There are in fact various trivial errors – like taking as contemporaneous the late story that the Delphic oracle had not only, as Plato said, pronounced Socrates wisest of men, but also made Euripides and Sophocles runners-up.[51] There are also some of a more serious nature. The first of these, chronologically speaking, concerns the literature of the pre-Homeric period, Nietzsche's comments on which are (to say the least) somewhat hazy. This, however, is essentially the fault of his age. For the eighteenth century, European literature began with Homer. With the researches of Wolf at the end of the century, it became apparent that Homer was not a 'writer' in the modern sense, but either a specially creative member of a centuries-long epic tradition or else the convenient personification of that tradition as a whole. In Nietzsche's time, however, very little was known of the earlier phases of this tradition, nor could it be known without the developments of the next hundred years in various areas of the subject and, above all, in archaeology. If these developments begin with Schliemann's search for Troy in the 1870s (and while Nietzsche was writing *BT*, Schliemann had already begun his excavations), they may be said to have reached their climax with the decipherment of the Linear B script in 1953 and the identification of the language written in it as Mycenaean Greek. Where Nietzsche had only the vaguest notions of a 'bronze age' and a 'folk philosophy' (§4), it is now widely agreed that Greek speakers had reached Greece *circa* 2000 B.C. and that Greek culture, assimilating to itself the culture of the pre-Greek Minoans, was established over a wide area by the middle of the second millennium.

These and other new sources of knowledge have made possible a tentative reconstruction of two Greek literary traditions, stretching back from Homer to the second millennium: oral epic and lyric, the latter having a good claim to actual priority.[52] Nietzsche, as one gathers from §§2–6, acquiesces in the traditional view that epic came first, even though it would have suited his argument better to give the Dionysiac art the priority. For him lyric begins with Archilochus, who is preceded only by pre-literary folk-song. The importance he gives to Archilochus as the father of Greek lyric is striking, although in line both with ancient tradition (which did, as Nietzsche says in §5, bracket him with Homer)[53] and with a good deal of modern opinion. The attention he devotes to Archilochus takes on a further interest, however, when one contrasts it with his total silence about such historically important members of the lyric tradition as Alcman and Stesichorus (seventh and sixth centuries B.C.), and his relative indifference to one of the greatest of all the poets of ancient Greece, Pindar.

Nietzsche's concern with Archilochus at the expense of the rest of the lyric tradition presupposes a literary-historical judgement about Archilochus' importance, but also something more fundamental – a judgement akin to his later conception of Wagner as the image of modern decadence. It is ultimately the result of a desire for an archetype: a single, symbolic figure who sums up the whole drift of a movement, a whole constellation of forms or ideas; a figure capable of symbolizing its origin and its essence alike. Archilochus *is* Greek lyric and therefore parallel to Homer who *is* Greek epic. For Nietzsche has done exactly the same with Homer, using him as the personalized embodiment and symbol of his genre. 'With Archilochus', he writes in §6, 'begins a new world of poetry, fundamentally opposed to the Homeric'; but elsewhere we have 'Homer, the naïve artist' (§3), 'Homer as a dreaming Greek' (§2), an 'unutterably sublime' Homer as an 'individual being' (§3). The two poets confront each other as individuals, not only on alleged 'sculptures, gems etc.', but in Nietzsche's own formulations: 'compared with Homer, Archilochus appals us by his cries of hatred and scorn, by his drunken outbursts of desire' (§5).

Nietzsche, then, has invested the two names with a particular status. If this is less obvious in the case of Homer, it is because the two great Homeric poems, the *Iliad* and *Odyssey*, completely overshadow the many other epics (long since lost) from early Greece. For this reason it has always been common, even in sober scholarship, for 'Homer' and 'the early Greek epic' to be used almost interchangeably. In setting up his symbolic construction, Nietzsche has traded on this habit.

The difficult questions of the authorship and composition of the two epics – the question, among others, who, or *what*, was 'Homer'? – have been posed, reformulated, and variously answered from the time of Wolf to the present. In the nineteenth century there were supporters of multiple authorship and (at the other end of a spectrum) proponents of a 'unitarian' position – for them Homer was *one* poet who, under whatever circumstances, composed the two long poems virtually as we have them. (The two positions have subsequently been more or less reconciled by means of Milman Parry's theory of oral-formulaic composition.) As his inaugural lecture on Homer shows, Nietzsche was not in fact a strict unitarian,[54] but from the language of *BT* one could be forgiven for supposing he was. The anti-unitarian Wilamowitz, who made just such a supposition, poured scorn on Nietzsche's naïvety.[55] He would hardly have been less scornful had he understood the real reason for Nietzsche's writing as he did, and the indifference to literary history of which it provides further evidence.

Apart from the – almost incidental – correctness of his stress on Archilochus, Nietzsche cannot be said to have made much headway with Greek lyric. He indulges in the most amazing Schopenhauerian and anti-Schopenhauerian contortions in order to evade the proposition that 'personal' lyric poetry is not only personal, but also 'subjective' (§5). (A comparison between, say, Sappho's dispassionate representation of her erotic malady[56] and some sample of modern effusive egoism would have been a better way of upholding his conviction.) His antithesis between the Dionysiac–Archilochian–Pindaric mode of language 'in imitation of music' and the Apolline–Homeric 'in imitation of phenomena' (§6) is equally Schopenhauerian and no less imponderable, and it appears to land him in complete confusion as to whether Pindar's epinician odes would count as Dionysiac–Archilochian or not. In §6 we are given 'Homer and Pindar' as an antithesis equivalent to 'Homer and Archilochus', and we are specifically assured that there are linguistic differences in 'colour, syntactic structure and vocabulary' between Homer and Pindar which reflect the former's 'imitation of phenomena' and the latter's 'imitation of music'. In §8, on the other hand, Nietzsche impresses on us a contrast between the dithyramb and 'all other choral odes' (of which Pindar's epinicians provide the most extensive and the best-known instances), and tells us that, as against the dithyramb, 'all the other choral poetry of the Hellenes is merely a tremendous intensification of the Apolline solo singer'.

The point may simply be that there are gradations, that the non-dithyrambic choral lyric of the victory odes is less Dionysiac than the dithyramb, though of course more Dionysiac than Homer. If so, Nietzsche fails to say so, let alone to explain to what degree, and in what respect, the best preserved Greek lyric is actually Apolline after all. It would be interesting to know. For one thing, it might shed some light on a very dark area of Nietzsche's treatment of Greek poetry, the relation between personal and choral lyric.

For instance: is the choral lyric of Archilochus' unrecorded dithyrambs not only more Dionysiac than the choral lyric of Pindar's victory odes, but also more Dionysiac than the personal lyric which contains Archilochus' own 'cries of hatred and scorn'? It is, at least, apparent that by choosing as his archetype Archilochus, who is *both* individual author of personal lyrics *and* participator in the collective dithyramb, Nietzsche has successfully concealed this problem. It is further apparent that his tortuous dealings with Greek lyric overall are among the weakest parts of his treatment of Greek art, and indeed of his book as a whole.

In the light of what Nietzsche has to say about Archilochus and Homer, it may be easier to comprehend his notion of 'Socratism', especially in its application to Euripides. For Socrates too has been made into a symbolic figure, and one of appreciably greater significance. He is the archetype of rationalism: the spirit whose essence is seen by Nietzsche as an unalloyed confidence in the human intellect and its power to convert life into a 'soluble problem' (§17); the spirit which in his eyes is irrevocably, or almost irrevocably, opposed to true art; the spirit under whose influence Euripides subverted the art of true tragedy. Nietzsche's representation of these two figures and their interrelation has not been correctly understood. Euripides (he tells us in §12) is 'the poet of aesthetic Socratism'; Euripides is 'only a mask', and 'the deity that spoke through him was an altogether unknown daemon called Socrates'; it was 'in alliance' with Socrates that Euripides 'dared to be the herald of a new mode of art'. These expressions are not intended to mean that the historical Socrates actually made Euripides what he was. Nietzsche would have been as well aware as Wilamowitz (who predictably pointed the finger here) that the main characteristics of Euripides' work were in evidence well before Socrates, nearly twenty years his junior, seems to have formed his own outlook.[57] Nor primarily do they mean (as Lloyd-Jones has suggested) that Nietzsche saw a 'community of opinion' between the two men which is also, in Lloyd-Jones' words, 'wholly unacceptable'.[58] What they mean is that Socrates and Euripides are both 'children of the new age'; that in different ways they embody a new spirit which – and this is inviting misunderstanding, certainly – Nietzsche sees most purely and definitively embodied in Socrates.

Nietzsche's Socrates, then, is not so much the source of Socratism as its personification. Socratism is logically prior to Socrates and indeed *chronologically* prior as well. For while 'we may recognize in Socrates the opponent of Dionysus' (§12), we must also 'assume an anti-Dionysiac tendency operating even earlier than Socrates, which merely receives in him an unprecedentedly magnificent expression' (§ 14). This is not some pseudo-intellectual verbiage concocted for the occasion. One may see it as a tacit admission that the choice of Socrates as archetype of 'rationalism' leaves something to be desired. Nevertheless, for better or worse, it reflects one of the fundamental modes of thought in Nietzsche's book.

The relation between Nietzsche's archetypal Socrates and his Euripides is similar to that between the two archetypes, Homer and Archilochus, in another way. Once again Nietzsche's formula trades on ancient testimony to a link between the two. There was 'a story current in Athens that Socrates used to help Euripides with his plays'; Aristophanes is on record as associating the two in a tone 'half indignant, half contemptuous'; the Delphic oracle 'designated Socrates the wisest of men' and put Euripides second. These and other anecdotes (of variable authority) are accumulated in § 13 – and, one would think, for two quite separate reasons. On a stylistic level, they offer immediacy, concreteness, *vraisemblance*, in support of the concreteness inherent in Nietzsche's personificatory mode itself. In addition they give that mode the sanction of antiquity.

Nietzsche, of course, is no historicist: he is not interested in whether the Athenians would have found his concept of 'Socratism' acceptable any more than whether they would have comprehended his post-Schopenhauerian metaphysic. Nor is he a 'scientific' historian: he is not interested in whether the anecdotes quoted are factually true – in whether, for instance, Socrates actually *did* help Euripides with his plays. He does not (one presumes) believe that Socrates did any such thing. Nevertheless, the story that he did is a particularly 'eloquent expression' of the 'insight' with which he *is* concerned, namely that 'in tendency Socrates and Euripides were closely related'. It is not a factual expression of that insight, but an *appropriate* expression, and as such an instance, however humble, of an important form of Greek creativity. 'Appropriate expression' is something we can see, on a higher or a lower level, in all periods of Greek culture. We see it in the idealizing tendencies of earlier statuary; in the stylized dialogue of tragedy; in the willingness of Thucydides to represent in his speeches not what the historical personages in his history actually did say, but what they 'should' have said;[59] and in a very naïve form in the ancient biographies, like the lives of Pindar which inform us that at a tender age the future poet awoke from a sleep out of doors to find that bees had built a honeycomb in his mouth (honey being a symbol of poetic inspiration).[60]

The anecdotes about Socrates and Euripides clearly belong, in the main, to the naïve biographical. They are, nevertheless, still Hellenic in spirit and not at all 'Socratic'. As such, they provide appropriate expressive immediacy in support of Nietzsche's archetypes. But if this is their function, they have an unfortunate side-effect as well: they divert attention from his real concern of the moment and dissipate it on a series of trivia. Specifically, they serve to conceal the fact that underlying the whole discussion of 'Socratism' in Euripides is an important proposition (to which we shall turn in due course): that, irrespective of any possible connection with Socrates, Euripides and rationalism are connected as, for instance, Sophocles and rationalism are not.

If Nietzsche's interest in Greece is not, on the whole, literary-historical, he is still concerned to ask one question of paramount importance to any literary historian: what is the overall shape of Greek literature? By way of answer, he offers a diagrammatic map of Greek literature: first the great genres, epic, lyric, then – delaying an incipient rationalism (§ 23) – tragedy, whose greatness is overtaken by the pervasive triumph of the rationalistic spirit; under the pressure of the new spirit, Greek literature produces a last, eccentric achievement on the grand scale in the shape of Plato (§ 14); after Plato the new rationalistic age yields no literature comparable with its earlier works either in quality or in kind. Earlier German philhellenes, from Winckelmann to Hölderlin, had located the centre of Greek achievement in the poetry or philosophy or sculpture of the fifth and fourth centuries. For Nietzsche the great age is the age of *religious* depth (although he generally eschews the word), the age that begins in the later sixth century 'with its birth of tragedy, its mysteries, its Pythagoras and Heraclitus' (§ 11) and terminates at that indefinable (§ 14) point in the fifth century where even tragedy is unable to withstand the impact of the new rationalistic spirit. If there is any one trait which is symptomatic of the greatness of the age, it is the wholehearted acceptance of traditional myth (§§ 10, 23 – not that Pythagoras or Heraclitus are actually in any sense upholders of the inherited mythology). Conversely, the degeneracy of the post-classical, Hellenistic age is summed up by its entire lack of mythic feeling. Now the traditional mythology is either bypassed, as in the New Comedy of Menander, or treated as mere fodder for secular literature, as in the famous Alexandrian poets.

Nietzsche's low valuation of the third century is complementary to his high valuation of the sixth. It has not been fashionable in all ages to make that low valuation plain, yet there can be no doubt that, unless we are to reject such literary-cultural valuations altogether, he is right. The ultimate importance of Sophocles lies in his representing a classic articulation of the human spirit, something irreplaceable. The ultimate importance of Menander or the Alexandrian Callimachus is that by their technical innovations and refinements they help to determine the future character of achievements greater than they themselves are capable of producing. Menander helps to make Shakespeare possible; Callimachus does the same for Virgil. The limited originality of the Hellenistic poet is subsumed within a tradition he serves to maintain and develop.

For Nietzsche the decline in Greek literature is identified with, or summed up by, the decline of poetry, which for him begins not in the fourth century, the century of prose, let alone in the Alexandrian third, but in the high-classical fifth. Once again, unless one refuses to speak of trends and epochs at all, it is hard not to agree. What is surprising is that he should see the decline so exclusively in terms of the rise of rationalism, when in fact that phenomenon (whose existence is not in doubt) was only one facet of a still more momentous change – and a change of direct relevance to himself as philhellene and as Wagnerian.

If Eliot was justified in applying 'dissociation of sensibility' as a label to the seventeenth century A.D., it is applicable on a much greater scale to the fifth century B.C. For it is in that century, above all at Athens, that the cultural unity so revered by the alienated artists and thinkers of modern Europe – the unity embodied in traditional *mousikē* and hinted at by the very breadth of meaning of that word – is decisively fragmented. Aeschylus is not only a poet; he is also musical composer – and, as we have seen, there is not, as yet, any fully autonomous entity called 'music'. Aeschylus is also a thinker. A modern distinction like Eliot's between 'thought' and the 'emotional equivalent of thought' is itself a symptom of dissociation. Aeschylus 'thinks', sometimes in directly reasoned forms (though not necessarily forms covered by the attenuated Aristotelian concept of dramatic *dianoia*), sometimes in images and myths. By this we do not mean that when Aeschylus thinks in myth, he employs some special kind of 'mythical thought'. As G. S. Kirk has recently emphasized, there is no cogent reason for accepting the existence of an entity, 'mythical thought', which is distinguishable from ordinary thought.[61] We mean that in the earlier Greek world to which Aeschylus belongs, myth and intellectual endeavour – contrary to one of Nietzsche's assumptions – are not exclusive categories, and that Aeschylean tragedy offers a particularly striking illustration of their compatibility.

If we now ask, 'what kind of thinker was Aeschylus?', one possible answer is given in the title of a much-admired book by Karl Reinhardt, *Aischylos als Regisseur und Theologe*: producer of plays and also 'theologian'. Traditional Greek religion, by comparison with the world-religions of the present day, was unsystematic. Among its other qualities, positive and negative, it had no institutionalized theologians. Its theological spokesmen were poets like

Aeschylus, who did his theological thinking not in learned disputations intended for a dozen like minds behind closed doors, but in poetic discourse at a public festival before a random congregation of the citizen-body of the state.

By the mid-fourth century, a hundred years after Aeschylus' death, the erstwhile unity has made way for specialisms. With its virtuoso effects, music has now gained its autonomy, and the musico-poetic complex of dramatic choral lyric is a thing of the past. Abstract thought, too, has become a specialized activity; or rather, the process of specialization has *made* thought abstract. The poet Pindar, articulating the significance of the old tradition, again and again associates poetry with wisdom, *sophia*. By the time of Plato and Aristotle the word, and the claim it represents, has been appropriated and incorporated in the name of their own new specialism, *philosophia*. For Plato this is part of an ongoing 'argument between poetry and philosophy',[62] which has evidently reached its last stage. For Aristotle that argument is settled to poetry's detriment and almost forgotten. In his *Poetics* (*Ch.* 9) poetry is magnanimously pronounced 'more philosophical than history', it being taken as read that it is intellectually less significant than philosophy itself. As for that theological mode of 'thought' which the tragedians so ostentatiously pursued through their gods and heroes, Aristotle (in whose works 'thought' has travelled a long way from such things) forgets even to identify it as a characteristic of the genre.

From the fourth century, philosophy takes over poetry's intellectual-spiritual function. Its public function is taken over as well – not by philosophy (which belongs in the coterie world of the 'school'), but by another new specialism, *oratory*: public speaking as an art, with an idiom tinged by the art-speech of poetry, but unmediated by myth. Aeschylus' *Eumenides* is concerned with 'politics', matters of public concern to the Athenian *polis*, but not always directly and never exclusively, as is Demosthenes' *De Corona*. The two works are, of course, in no obvious sense competitors. Nevertheless, the rise of oratory undermines poetry's external status as surely as philosophy takes away its inner dignity.

The decline of Greek poetry is to be related also to the intellectual vulnerability of religion. This is perhaps to be inferred from Nietzsche's account, although he nowhere says it in so many words. In the new age, an unsystematic complex of rituals, myths and beliefs could no longer provide inspiration, but would rather provoke attack; yet religion could neither appropriate rational thought not impede its development. Even the silencing of Socrates in 399 (which was in any case untypical) in no way hindered Plato or his successors from developing their own systems without regard to traditional beliefs. It became impossible for serious minds to take the religion seriously; and the same was bound to be true of myth, the idiom in which traditional religion was cast, and of poetry, whose chief forms were mythic through and through. In Cicero's words, 'the Greeks grew more sceptical', a simple formula but a just one.[63] Euripides is the last Greek writer of intellectual stature to use the traditional material, however sceptically and untraditionally. After Euripides, the finest minds gravitate towards philosophy. Needless to say, mythic religion, like mythic poetry, continues for centuries on a lower, semi-creative, level. 'Gods withdraw, but their rituals live on, and no one...notices that they have ceased to mean anything' – the comment is from E. R. Dodds' *The Greeks and the Irrational*, the book that offers the best modern commentary on this aspect (as on several other aspects) of Nietzsche's Greece.[64]

Nietzsche's view of 'Socratism', then, is somewhat distorted. The rise of rationalism is not an isolated phenomenon – or, if it comes to that, a sudden one – as his concentration on the archetypal individual Socrates is bound to imply. There was no overnight invention of rationalism in democratic Athens or elsewhere, but rather the progressive dissociation of rational consciousness from other creative or cognitive faculties with which it was formerly united, and its elevation above them all.

More generally, however, Nietzsche's outline is open to criticism on quite different grounds. It is hazardous to put so much stress on a period – the later sixth century – about which we actually know extraordinarily little. It is also questionable to cast the whole schema, as Nietzsche does, in a rigid teleological mould. Lyric poetry, for instance, is almost ignored except as a stage on the way to tragedy. This means that Nietzsche can barely accommodate either Pindar or (at the opposite extreme) the low lyric that links Archilochus with Aristophanes. Aristophanic Old Comedy itself is not really catered for either, despite Nietzsche's evident approval of both author (§ 13) and genre (§ 7). At first sight, teleological assumptions might also seem to have determined his attitude to the Platonic dialogue: the grudging tolerance of an 'eccentric' art-form which fails to fit in with his preconceptions. Yet in this instance he is surely right to refuse to see Plato – whose gifts he recognizes (§§ 13–14), as he does those of Euripides (§ 11) – as the logical development of traditional Hellas. Plato's achievement, however one values it, does not lie in fulfilling the potential of any tradition or traditions of earlier prose or earlier verse. The Platonic dialogue is indeed a strange hybrid, and it is revealing that (unless with Nietzsche, § 14, we see it as the ancestor of the novel) it had no progeny, except for pale imitations of itself. Plato's real successors, and above all Aristotle, may have tried their hand at writing dialogues, but they achieved their lasting distinction in a plainer medium, from which the art-element was suppressed. Post-Platonic philosophy is not literature, but thought; the disjunction is complete.

Just as Nietzsche minimizes the rôle of rationality in Presocratic Greece, so he exaggerates the inspirational aspect of Greek art. The Greek artist, it appears, is propelled only by 'dream' or 'ecstasy' – Apolline *Traum* or Dionysiac *Rausch* – and creates his masterpieces without reference to that less spectacular complex of expectations and precedents that we call 'tradition'. This emphasis is false, and has the unfortunate corollary of representing Greek art as more individualistic than it actually was. At this point Nietzsche's propensity for archetypes takes on a further significance. Homer, Archilochus and the rest – Greek literature is identified with its great creators, the forest with its tallest trees. It is as if Nietzsche had overlooked the lesson of his beloved *Meistersinger*, which the young impetuous Walther learns from the mature Hans Sachs: the masters, humble craftsmen though they seem, deserve our respect as the custodians of that purity and coherence without which art cannot long survive.

For all its weak points, Nietzsche's candidly evaluative elucidation of the stages of Greek literature has attained something of a classic status. Unlike much else in *BT* it gives no sign of having been formulated in a modern perspective. There is a certain irony in the fact that by taking his eyes off Greece and attending to Wagner on this occasion, Nietzsche might have seen his way to a more balanced interpretation.

MORES AND RELIGION

It is in the area of Greek religion, especially religious attitudes to life, that Nietzsche's reinterpretation of Greece has had the greatest impact on classical studies. Although he has been no more scholarly here than elsewhere, the penetration of his ideas and the forcefulness of their expression have earned the respect of many subsequent scholars – and won, among other rewards, the tribute from Eduard Fraenkel quoted above.[65] Because of the pervasive relevance of religion to Greek life and culture, there is no way in which a book as wide-ranging as Nietzsche's could have bypassed the subject; it is nevertheless remarkable that he devotes as much space to Greek religion as to any other aspect of Greece, tragedy included. Above all, much of the discussion of tragedy itself is vitally concerned with religion as well; witness the proliferation in this context of words like 'metaphysical' and 'mystical' – let alone 'Dionysiac' and 'Apolline'. This is the more striking because of his reluctance to say in so many words that religion is one of his primary concerns, or even that it has a special importance in Greek culture at all.

On the fringes of religion proper, in the area of *mores* or attitudes to life,

Nietzsche's perceptivity is at once apparent. There is the remarkable and (at the time) very unfashionable characterization of the Dionysiac satyr as 'symbol of the sexual omnipotence of nature which the Greeks used to contemplate with reverent wonder' (§8). However problematic *vis-à-vis* the frivolous satyr, the delineation of the attitude and its association with the worship of Dionysus are entirely justified. The phallic god, as fertility god, is (as Nietzsche says) intimately connected with the celebration of all natural sexuality – and however riotous the expression of the celebration, its cultic terms presuppose 'reverence'. It is symptomatic that the openness of sexual expression now felt to be so characteristic of Greek visual art should be first attested in vases representing Dionysus or Dionysiac scenes dating from the archaic period.[66] Nietzsche's divinatory sense here compares favourably with the prudish disbelief shown by Wilamowitz.[67]

The dream-experience of the ancient Greeks provides Nietzsche with the opportunity for a more questionable exercise of his powers of intuition: 'we can hardly refrain from assuming even for their dreams...a certain logic of line and contour, colours and groups, a certain pictorial sequence reminding us of their finest bas-reliefs, whose perfection...' (§2). It is indeed possible that the Greeks dreamed with a visual precision beyond our own normal experience: so much might be inferred from the argument of Dodds that the character of dreams may be in part culturally determined, in the light of the fact, which Dodds discusses at the same time, that Greek dreams were characteristically 'seen', and not 'had'.[68] But even that inference is speculative, and for his further claims Nietzsche has virtually to invent the evidence to suit his thesis. This is in marked contrast with his handling of Greek myth, where a great quantity of evidence could be (but as usual is not) amassed to support his interpretation of it as a metaphysical 'condensation of phenomena' whereby the social group 'is able to press upon its experiences the stamp of the eternal'. Myth in this, its true state is something to which the group 'feels impelled to relate all its experiences..., indeed to understand them only in this relation', and without which 'every culture loses its healthy natural creativity' (§23). This fine statement in one way anticipates, in another might be used to complement, the various interpretations of mythology, such as that associated with Lévi-Strauss, which stress its deep cultural significance. Nietzsche's emphasis is on its metaphysical aspect, to which, in his view, the 'depths' must be referred.

In the area where religious beliefs and attitudes to life in general are hardest to separate, Nietzsche offers one of his greatest insights by indicating the crucial place in archaic and early classical Greek culture of what he calls 'pessimism'. Even here, we must admit, he is liable to indulge his own inventive powers at the expense of his nominal subject. There is, for instance, no evidence whatsoever that in their pessimistic travels the Greeks were ever (as he alleges in §7) close to a 'Buddhistic negation of the will' either as a result of mystical experience or for any other reason. His understanding of their attested attitudes, however, is of a different order altogether. The pessimistic outlook – one could almost call it an ideology – is partly articulated for us by the writers of the time and partly to be inferred from their works and other relics of their age. One presupposition is that there is a cosmos, but not an anthropocentric cosmos; men have a very subordinate rôle within it. Another is most easily expressible in terms of the Greek gods and the nature of their contact with our world. Those deities, Hugh Lloyd-Jones has written, are 'not transcendent, but immanent'; they do not 'interfere from outside with the course of nature, but govern the inanimate world through natural processes and the animate through human passions'.[69] Those processes and passions are man's masters, and define his limitations. If he disregards those limitations, he is in effect seeking to transcend the whole human condition, which is – as Nietzsche says of Prometheus (§9) – to attempt a kind of 'sacrilege'. In the most extreme form of this 'sacrilege' he is, in one of Pindar's phrases, trying to live the life of an immortal god.[70] The willingness to live within the inherent limitations of life and the need *both* to experience them as limitations *and* in some sense (rapturous and horrific) to transcend them – it is this that Nietzsche symbolizes so memorably through his Apollo and Dionysus. In terms of this Dionysiac–Apolline dialectic he defines 'pessimism' ('pessimism of strength', as he calls it in the *Self-Criticism*) in its peculiar Greek shape.

The Greek *Weltanschauung* thus adumbrated was not, and could not have been, the invention of the common man or an invention on his behalf. It is too sophisticated, but, above all, it is too *aristocratic*. It presupposes an aristocratic freedom of action, unimpaired by the petty constraints of poverty, labour and all the restrictions that have traditionally distinguished lower from higher social strata. The *Weltanschauung* was articulated by writers – from Homer to the fifth century – working in an essentially aristocratic tradition populated with heroes, kings, demigods, who possess precisely that freedom of action. That high status, then, is the precondition of their capacity to act on the plane where the deeper, *existential* limitations on human action become painfully visible. The *Weltanschauung* will be transmitted to the common man in various forms in public recitations of Homer and the public performances of tragedy; it is his heritage, and its content is allusively related to the regular rituals in which ordinary Greek piety expresses itself; it is aesthetically familiar, but for all that its ethos is remote from his world. It offers, for instance, no analogue to the Christian message of humility and hope, which is of immediate practical concern to the least elevated of men.

The aristocratic, heroic presupposition of the Greek outlook Nietzsche takes over and reinforces in the strongest possible way. For him the common man barely exists except as a member of the anonymous Dionysiac proto-chorus (in which, Nietzsche insists, the pessimistic outlook is experienced in special terms) – and even here the chorister is seen to be invested with suspiciously un-common preoccupations. 'With this chorus', he tells us in §7, 'the profound Hellene, uniquely susceptible to the tenderest and deepest suffering, comforts himself, having looked boldly right into the terrible destructiveness of so-called world history as well as the cruelty of nature'. The picture has a marvellous intensity – but which Hellene does it portray? Hardly the common man of action, the veteran of Marathon, let us say, depicted by Aristophanes as a charcoal-burner worried by law-suits.[71] Nor even a more sophisticated man of action such as Nietzsche's favourite, the dithyramb-leader Archilochus, with his 'soldierly' background and his 'drunken outbursts of desire' (§5). Up to a point the 'profound Hellene' might recall a figure like Aeschylus, whose *Persians* serves to show that he had at least looked into the destructiveness of the first (and truly world-historical) East–West conflict. Yet the suffering that Nietzsche portrays and the heightened response it produces – these surely point elsewhere, not to the tragic authors, but to their suffering heroes. The 'profound Hellene' has the lineaments of a Prometheus or, above all perhaps, an Oedipus. Greek literary history, on Nietzsche's interpretation, was equated with its greatest individual figures; and now the Greek people in turn are summed up in terms of their mythico-theatrical ideal. The partiality of his view of Greece – even at its most impressive (perhaps *especially* at its most impressive) – is nowhere more evident.

In propounding his view of the Greek outlook, Nietzsche was committed to mounting a major attack on the prevalent notion (beloved of Winckelmann and Weimar classicism) that the Greeks were a nation of serene optimists. This attack is hard to dissociate from his challenge to another favourite idea of the age, that *reason* was the hallmark of the Greek interpretation of life. In the context of ancient Greece, his hostility to reason is widely supposed to be the corollary of the emphasis he places on Dionysiac 'irrationality'. This is not the whole truth. Against rationalism is arrayed not only the Dionysiac, but also the Apolline. In Nietzsche's book 'Apolline' Olympianism is of course more *orderly* than its Dionysiac antipode, but not, strictly speaking, any more *rational*. This can be inferred simply from his opening point (§1) that the most elementary exemplification of the Dionysiac is intoxication, whereas the equivalent in the Apolline sphere is the dream: for Nietzsche, as for Freud after him, the dream is not a symbol of the rational mind at work. It is Nietzsche's view of Greek pessimism itself that involves a particular stress on Dionysus. For in his eyes the Apolline and the Socratic are both sources of optimism. The difference is that the Apolline offers an 'exuberant' (§3), 'higher' (§9), optimism, the Socratic only the optimism of 'cool' (§14) rationality; and that the Dionysiac regularly expresses itself in Apolline form, making its presence felt in the context of, for instance, the Olympian mythology formerly associated with the Homeric epic (§10). Even here, then, the Dionysiac and the Apolline in effect stand together. They are the contributors to, and defenders of, the traditional ideology in all its various forms, whereas Socratism is its enemy.

The depiction of the Greeks as a nation of serene, rational optimists is no longer fashionable, and for this Nietzsche must take considerable credit.[72] In his terms the old interpretation was equivalent to making the Greeks essentially Socratic or, at best, essentially Apolline, but Apolline without any Dionysiac background. His counter-argument involves several distinct steps:

(i) redefining Socratic rationalism as an eccentricity;
(ii) restricting the operations of rationalism to the fifth century and later;
(iii) separating it from the Apolline;
(iv) insisting that behind the Apolline necessarily stands the Dionysiac.

Each of these steps is radical enough; the last is the most radical of them all; it is also the most explicitly presented and the hardest to interpret. In what sense is the Dionysiac *behind* the Apolline? – is it a historical sense? We have faced such a question before, in connection with the 'visionary' stages of proto-tragedy, where Nietzsche's argument requires that the Dionysiac vision comes before the Apolline. Here, at least, the 'behind' would seem, *prima facie*, to be historical. From the final paragraph of §4 one gathers that there was a Titanic 'bronze age' (meaning a 'pessimistic' Dionysiac culture alive to the true reality of life), antedating the Homeric–Apolline culture that overlaid it. Wilamowitz, for one, strenuously denied the evidence for any such pre-Homeric culture,[73] and there is no doubt that Nietzsche's theory was essentially speculation. For us, a hundred years later, the Bronze Age of Greece – the Mycenaean age and the pre-Greek Minoan age before it – has an archaeologically established reality which could not then be dreamed of; and, as we have seen, there are actually good grounds for ascribing to that Bronze Age Dionysiac worship or something very like it. This is not to suggest that we have sufficient grounds for supposing the Mycenaeans to have been 'pessimists'. Other considerations apart, something more than archaeological data is needed to establish the spirit of a culture, except on a very restricted scale.[74]

And yet, once again, Nietzsche's argument is not what it seems. The actual mood of pre-Homeric Greece is not quite beside the point, but it is hardly the nub of the matter. The core of Nietzsche's argument is *not* that a pessimistic Dionysiac culture, receptive to the horror of reality, preceded the artistic culture of Homeric Greece. He *does* think this, and he goes out of his way to reaffirm it in a letter to Rohde during the summer of 1872.[75] But he thinks it in conformity with a more elemental proposition: that there is a causal link between horror and Apolline art. Such a link, irrespective of any large-scale historical embodiment, must in the first instance involve a *psychological* mechanism, one that operates, if anywhere, on or for the individual artist. It is in this sense that the Dionysiac stands 'behind' the Apolline. The depth psychology involved here (for it is clearly that, and something more than a mere 'il faut souffrir pour être belle') obviously anticipates the Freudian view of art as therapy, although Nietzsche's principle is more flattering to the artist. What concerns us immediately, however, is that as with the origin of tragedy, Nietzsche has conceptualized the essentially an-historical in historical terms. This peculiar use, or abuse, of history is one of the predominant features of the whole book.

The Birth of Tragedy embodies what Lloyd-Jones has characterized as 'unprecedented insights' into Greek religion.[76] If we ask, *what kind* of insights, we must answer: large insights into the spirit and psychology of the religion, not insights into particular details. In the first instance Nietzsche's achievement was simply – simply said, but in a culture only used to monotheistic moral absolutism, not so simply done – to take Greek religion seriously, both Olympian religion and its counterkind: to make them credible, even attractive. Lloyd-Jones, referring on another occasion to his insights, has commented: 'in the field of Greek religion...a turning point was marked by the publication...of Nietzsche's *BT*...The importance of the numinous, the daemonic, the irrational side of Greek religion became recognized.'[77] The allusion, of course, is primarily to Nietzsche's representation of the Dionysiac, and in this area one might initially sum up his contribution to the understanding of 'the daemonic' by noting that whereas Dionysus had traditionally been defined with particular reference to the inoffensive celebration of the wine-harvest, *his* Dionysus is rightly defined in terms of orgiasm.[78] At the same time, we should remember that Nietzsche's Olympians (like 'the Apolline' in general) are in essence no more 'rational' than his Dionysus, and not overlook the fact that his insights also bear on them. It would be hard to find a more telling description of Olympian religion from a modern vantage-point than Nietzsche offers in § 3:

Anyone contemplating these Olympians with another religion in his heart, searching [among them] for moral elevation, even for sanctity, for disincarnate spirituality, for loving glances of compassion, will soon be forced to turn his back on them, discouraged and disappointed. For there is nothing here that suggests asceticism, spirituality, or duty. We hear nothing but the accents of an exuberant, triumphant existence, in which all things, good or evil, are deified. And so the spectator may stand quite bewildered before this fantastic excess of life...

The be-all and end-all of Nietzsche's interpretation of Greek religion is of course the Apolline and the Dionysiac. One facet of this antithesis is a contrast of central importance to the history of religious practice in the archaic period. In the standard modern survey of Greek religion Martin Nilsson presents the contrast in the following terms:[79]

The mystical and ecstatic current which runs through the archaic age and brings new forms of religion to the fore was given a fundamental and outstanding treatment by Erwin Rohde in his great work *Psyche*. Beside this current there runs another, which has received far too little consideration. Its aim is to gain the favour of the gods through the exact observance of religious rules and commandments. From the interplay of these two currents Greek religion was further developed and enlarged, with the latter performing the great task of restraining the excesses of the former. One current manifests itself in Hesiod and Delphic Apollo, the other in Dionysus and the miracle-workers who appear in the archaic age.

The contrast – Nilsson calls it 'ecstasy' *versus* 'legalism' – is familiar to any reader of *BT* §§ 1–4. Nietzsche says nothing about 'gaining the favour of the gods' or Hesiod or the 'miracle-workers' of the archaic age, but the rest of Nilsson's argument is there: on the one side, Dionysiac 'excess'; on the other, 'the Delphic god' who exacts '*measure* of his disciples' (§ 4) and copes with Dionysus by 'taking the destructive weapons from the hands of his powerful antagonist' in a 'reconciliation' which constitutes 'the most important moment in the history of Greek cult' (§ 2). It must be emphasized that Nietzsche's Dionysus and Apollo are not purely religious entities; that his depiction of their religious qualities is in some respects brief, not to say perfunctory; and that *BT* does not purport to be a book about religion, Greek or any other. Nevertheless, it is extraordinary that the long shadow of Wilamowitzian orthodoxy should still so inhibit Nilsson from mentioning the name of Rohde's friend and precursor who had in fact made the contrast that (as it happens) it was not Rohde's concern to make.

As for Nietzsche's other insights, there is his recognition – not spelled out, but presupposed throughout – of the dynamic qualities of Greek religion; specifically, that the religion provided its believers with a stimulus and a source of cultural energy. This notion compares favourably *both* with the older supposition that Greek gods, like the divine personages of most Hellenistic and Roman poetry, were essentially an elegant apparatus, *and* with the widespread twentieth-century view of the religion as a colourful but unenlightened ritual complex with a few beliefs thrown in. Then there is the historical aspect, so far as it goes, of his intuition into the primacy of the Dionysiac over the classical Olympians. Here one might properly lay stress not so much on Nietzsche's airy ideas about the Bronze Age, as on his parallel conviction that the attraction felt by the Greeks of the archaic age for the 'ecstatic and mystical current' presupposed an affinity, felt if not expressed, with an older type of worship. This was one of the lessons which Rohde was to restate, with a scholarly amplitude, in his *Psyche*.[80]

However impressive we may find Nietzsche's view of Greek religion, we can hardly overlook its selectivity. Above all, his is a heavily metaphysical, existential interpretation of the religion at the expense of its socio-political dimension: an interpretation in line with his conception of the 'profound Hellene' as the Greek norm. Certainly no sociologist of ancient Greece is likely to find a search for its inner dynamic in the area of metaphysics very congenial. But Nietzsche is extremely selective in other ways besides. The innocent reader of the Nietzschean account of Greek belief in the archaic age would not suspect the importance of religious pollution as an issue; yet this was one of the main preoccupations of the period. He would even come away from Nietzsche's book without realizing the huge part played in Greek religion by ritual. It is not that Nietzsche needed to have discussed such matters at length; it is rather that his tone creates a distorting impression.

DIONYSUS AND APOLLO

Of all the distortions embodied in Nietzsche's version of Greek religion, the most important and the most complicated is his representation of Dionysus and Apollo. As the basis of his theory of tragedy (and much else), it is a uniquely productive distortion; nevertheless, it is also one version of a common error. Greek religion involves a variety of deities: not simply the well-known Olympians and Dionysus, but also a host of lesser, or less official, figures, down to the satyrs and the Muses who make their due appearance in Nietzsche's book. In the classical period each divinity had not only a function or functions, but also identifiable characteristics. The major deities had a variety of both. For instance, the goddess Athene in classical times was patron goddess of Athens; also associated with handicraft (especially weaving and spinning); a warrior; a virgin; and associated with the olive, the snake and the owl. Such a set of multifarious aspects becomes comprehensible when we look at the development of Greek religious traditions in a long perspective from pre-Hellenic to post-classical times, and see a considerable amount of shifting and exchanging of attributes, appellations, myths and cult-sites between one deity and another. It has, for instance, been conjectured that Athene is a composite produced by the amalgamation of two pre-historic deities, a martial maiden-goddess and an Acropolis deity of the mountain-mother type, her various aspects being explained with reference to one or other source.[81]

This does not mean that Athene was an incredible or incoherent figure to the Greek worshipper or to the Greek artist whose medium was myth. To generations of Athenians, to the epic poets, to Aeschylus, she was one of the prime unquestioned facts on the theological horizon. What it does mean is that modern attempts to attach a single significance to each deity are unpromising. It is true that with no powerful priestly caste, no church, no bible, no set theology, Greek religion and its gods were always subject to change. They were in the hands of their worshippers, including especially the poets and others who perpetuated their representation. It is possible that those artists, those mythological interpreters and even creators, should have tended to impose a felt coherence where in origin there was none, and this may indeed have happened in the case of Nietzsche's two deities. However, so long as the religion flourished, it did not happen on such a scale as to reshape the inherited composite entirely.

The conclusion to be drawn is that attempts to pin the Greek gods down tend at best to be partial, at worst illusory; even a divinity as seemingly straightforward as Aphrodite is actually not only a love-goddess, but a deity associated in various parts of the Greek world with war and with the sea.[82] Such attempts were, nevertheless, extremely popular in the nineteenth century, both with scholars and cultivated laymen. With his Apollo and Dionysus Nietzsche was undoubtedly influenced by the unstated princple: a Greek god's various aspects are ultimately related – all we need is the key to the code. In §1, for instance, it is apparently a *donnée* that Apollo's soothsaying faculty must be related somehow to the god's ethic of restraint, however elusive the relationship may prove to be.

But if Nietzsche was simply interpreting given aspects, he would be doing no more and no less than many others have done. He does more. He 'visionalizes' aspects (to use Else's expression again), he reinterprets them, he even invents them. The end of the process is two new composites which carry the Greek gods' names as symbols without any consistent historical justification. And Nietzsche himself, in admittedly fuzzy language, indicates to his reader that this, or something like this, is the case:

> These names [Apolline and Dionysiac] we *borrow* from the Greeks, who intimate the profound mysteries of their vision of art to the discerning mind not through concepts, but through the arrestingly clear figures of their gods (§1, our italics).

> We see the glorious Olympian figures of the gods...We must not be misled by the fact that Apollo stands side by side with the others as an individual deity, without any claim to priority of rank. For the same impulse that embodies itself in Apollo gave birth to this entire Olympian world, and *in this sense Apollo is its father* (§ 3, our italics).

We would seem to have come back to the formula used by Wilamowitz in his old age: 'Apolline and Dionysiac are aesthetic abstractions like naïve and sentimental poetry in Schiller, and the old gods only supplied sonorous names for the contrast.'[83]

If Nietzsche himself pronounced his Apollo and Dionysus supra-Greek, where is the problem – for Wilamowitz or for us? The answer is easily given, but very complicated to substantiate. What Nietzsche has done is take the Greek Apollo and Dionysus, extend their significance, raise it onto a symbolic plane, and then use his symbols as quasi-historical verities like the 'real' Greek gods themselves.

Greek deities, as we have noted, regularly have a composite character, reflecting a complex origin. The composite, therefore, alters with time. Furthermore, it alters with place. Classical Greece, in the age of Homer or the age of Aeschylus, was anything but a coherent nation with a unified national culture in the modern sense, although very much a nation in one sense. The autonomous city-states of which the nation consisted were linked in their totality by a sense of Hellenism that depended ultimately on possession of a common language and shared cultural traditions and achievements, including religion. But neither language nor cultural practices were homogeneous: there were clearly marked dialectical forms, and the favoured religious practices, deities, myths also varied from one community to another. There were unifying factors, among them the elevated literary-mythical tradition which had, since Homer, a pan-Hellenic quality; as against this, the local, more popular, traditions would tend towards fragmentation. One should not overstate the degree of local variation; it *is* usually legitimate to generalize about Dionysus or Apollo. At the same time it may be necessary to ask, *which* Dionysus and *which* Apollo? This is not among the questions that Nietzsche himself is concerned to ask.

Dionysus and Apollo were not simply two of the many Greek deities. They were two very special gods, and they did have a distinctive relationship of a largely antipodal kind. Apollo (to begin at the easier end of the relationship)[84] was god of, *inter alia*, medicine and music (especially the lyre). As Apollo *apotropaios* he was an averter of evil, notably disease; and he had a specific association with flocks and herds, this being perhaps a relic of a once central rôle as protector of the community. In the classical age the chief of his many shrines and the centre of his most important functions was at Delphi. Here was the site of his great oracle, where the priestess, in a state of religious ecstasy, mediated his prophecies. Here too advice was given on ritual matters, especially those involving purification – and in this rôle as Apollo *katharsios* the god was often called upon to assist those polluted by homicide (as happens with Aeschylus' Orestes). Delphi took a particular interest in two political matters: codification of laws and schemes of colonization. And if that made Apollo literally a god of law and order, he could also claim that title in the sphere of morality, where he prescribed self-restraint (*mēden agan*) and deference to authority (*to kratoun phobou*). Until the present century he was widely thought of as sun-god and god of light. Certainly he was equated with the sun by poets from the fifth century onwards, and in Aeschylus' *Prometheus*, for instance, his epithet *Phoibos* is used as if it meant 'bright', of the sun's rays; but modern scholarship can find no basis for the tradition much earlier than this.[85]

This list of functions is not exhaustive. There is also the well-known connection with archery and, less well-known, a destructive potentiality. Apollo assumes this dark rôle on his very first appearance in Greek literature, 'coming down like night' to send a plague.[86] As well as warding off evil, he can produce it. Nevertheless, the god's main activities – medicine, law, and the rest – are positive and, what is more, sufficiently coherent to tempt even cautious scholars of our own day to essay generalizations about his character, as Nietzsche did before them. W. K. C. Guthrie, for instance, offers one in the following terms: 'Apollo...is the very embodiment of the Hellenic spirit. Everything that marks off the Greek outlook from that of other peoples, and in particular from the barbarians who surrounded them – beauty of every sort, whether of art, music, poetry or youth, sanity and moderation – all are summed up in Apollo.'[87] There is a striking correspondence here – to leave Nietzsche and his Apollo to one side for a moment – with Winckelmann's view of the serenity that was Greece, summed up, *inter alia*, in his perception of the Belvedere Apollo. 'Yet', Guthrie goes on, 'there seems little doubt that in origin [Apollo] is not Hellenic.' The name 'Apollo' itself does not look particularly Greek, and ancient myths specifically asserted his foreignness. Whether he was from the 'Hyperborean' north or Asia Minor to the East has been a matter of some controversy. Years after the polemics about *BT* had died down, Wilamowitz was to argue persuasively that his origin was in Asia.[88]

Nietzsche's depiction of Apollo comes in bits: there is no single, comprehensive exposition. It is not until §4 that Apollo is presented to us as an ethical deity, and not until §21 that his political aspect is explicitly noticed. Some other functions – the protection of flocks, for instance – are never mentioned at all, because Nietzsche has no occasion to mention them. The fullest description comes in §1 and is worth quoting at length:

This joyous necessity of the dream experience has been embodied by the Greeks in their Apollo: Apollo, the god of all the energies embodied in the visual arts, is at the same time the soothsaying god. The god of light, 'the shining one' according to the etymological root [of his epithet *Phoibos*], he is also ruler over the beautiful illusion of the inner world of fantasy. The higher truth, the perfection of these states in contrast to the incompletely intelligible everyday world, together with the deep consciousness of nature's healing and helping in sleep and dreams, is at the same time the symbolic analogue of the soothsaying faculty and in general of the arts which make life possible and worth living. But we must also include in our image of Apollo...that measured restraint, that freedom from the wilder emotions, that calm of the sculptor god. His eye must be 'sunlike' as befits his origin; even when it is angry and distempered, it is still hallowed by beautiful illusion. And so, in one sense, we might apply to Apollo the words of Schopenhauer when he speaks of the man wrapped in the veil of *māyā*...: 'Just as in a howling stormy sea, which is unbounded in all directions and lifting and dropping mountainous waves, a sailor sits in a boat and trusts in his frail bark: so in the midst of a world of torments the individual human being sits quietly, supported by and trusting in the *principium individuationis* [principle of individuation].' In fact, we might say of Apollo that in him the unshaken faith in this *principium* and the calm repose of the man wrapped up in it receive their most sublime expression; and we might call Apollo himself the glorious divine image of the *principium individuationis*, through whose gestures and glances all the joy and wisdom of 'illusion', together with its beauty, speak to us.

The family resemblance of Nietzsche's 'restrained' and 'beautiful' Apollo to the Apollo of modern scholarship is obvious. The differences are obvious as well. In good nineteenth-century fashion Nietzsche makes great play with 'brightness'. Other consequential changes, however, are his own innovations. He refers to Apollo's prophetic role, but not to its well-attested ecstatic character. For the time being he ignores music. From §2 we gather that there is 'Apolline music' of a strongly rhythmic character and associated with the lyre, but the god's traditional association with music is not something that he is eager to emphasize. Medicine is alluded to in the shape of 'healing'. It will become evident later on (for instance in §9) that Nietzsche has in mind a more profound, *metaphysical* type of healing than the Greek Apollo was used to providing. The legal-political ethic of self-restraint and deference to convention (defined more explicitly in §§4 and 21) is also infused with a metaphysical meaning, and it emerges from the process as the Schopenhauerian principle of individuation. Finally, three new aspects are added. Nietzsche's Apollo is god of dreams, god of appearance and 'illusion', god of visual art, and these three related functions are subsequently combined in terms of an Apolline 'world of visual imagery' (*Bilderwelt*). The three functions represent Nietzsche's extension in its most extreme form. There is no ancient authority for them, in any ordinary sense of the word:[89] he has invented them. They have, however, one feature in common with his more moderate innovations: they sharpen the antithesis with Dionysus.

The Greek Dionysus' salient characteristics are less easily presented than Apollo's. The principal cause of difficulty is a divergence in the god's personality. In some parts of the Greek world – and once perhaps in all parts – Dionysus seems to have been a wild god; but in classical Athens, where most of our information comes from and where tragedy arose, he presents a much tamer appearance. In origin he was regarded by the classical Greeks as a foreign intruder from Phrygia or Thrace to the north-east. He is hardly mentioned in Homer, a fact which used to be taken to mean that his worship was first introduced to Greece during the epic age – that is, at some time early in the first millennium B.C. As we have seen, recent research has shown that ritual of a Dionysiac type can actually be traced back to the Mycenaean age of the second millennium. Furthermore, the god's name itself has been identified on a Mycenaean tablet in the Linear B syllabary, making it clear beyond reasonable doubt that his cult existed in the Greek world at that time.[90] To complete the picture, Oswald Szemerényi has recently given *Dionusos* (the Greek word of which 'Dionysus' is a Latinized form) a very plausible Indo-European etymology, to mean 'son of Zeus', in conformity with a common ancient tradition about the two gods' relationship.[91] Unlike the 'Hellenic' Apollo, then, the 'foreign' Dionysus has a secure place in pre-Homeric Greece.[92]

The natural way of reconciling ancient tradition and modern knowledge is to say that Dionysus was not introduced, but *re*-introduced, in the early first millennium; although whether we should take the tradition of his arrival as handed down in Euripides' *Bacchae* to be based on the introduction (as Webster seems to have supposed),[93] or the reintroduction, or a mixture of both, is not easy to say. At all events, it is likely that the suppression of Dionysus from the early epic was not due to ignorance of a new phenomenon, but to a quite different factor: the 'mad' god (as he appears on his literary debut in the *Iliad*) was a predominantly *popular* god, as indeed he remained into the early classical period, and he was suppressed because he was alien to the aristocratic world of the Homeric hero.[94]

In his wild aspect,[95] Dionysus was very much as depicted in the *Bacchae*. His festivals were essentially orgiastic and, in the most literal sense, *enthusiastic*. The worshippers were possessed. They were brought to a state of ecstasy, in which they partook of communion with the god: the god was *in* them, *en theos*. Ecstasy was induced perhaps by intoxication, certainly by music ('flute' and percussion) and dance of the type attested in various periods and various cultures, most recently among the dancing Dervishes in the Islamic world. The communion ritual looked to an epiphany of the god in animal form, especially the form of a bull. It involved the use of masks and centred on an act of *sparagmos* and *ōmophagia*, the dismembering and swallowing raw of an animal body – a sacramental meal to symbolize, or rather to permit, the union of the worshipper with the divine. Essentially, then, the Dionysiac *orgia* (not pleasure-seeking 'orgies' in the modern sense) were mystical in character, but this was mysticism achieved by a group, never by an individual. The worship was necessarily that of a mass of people who, being possessed by the god, forfeited their own individual personalities. Frequently, though not invariably, the mass was a mass of women, the famous maenads.

In this wild form the cult of Dionysus was still sufficiently accessible to a classical fifth-century audience to provide material for drama and paintings,[96] although to the Athenian of that time such behaviour was chiefly associated with the so-called 'Corybantic' worship.[97] His Dionysus, most familiar to him from various rural festivals, was a fertility god, a god whose concern for vegetation gave him a specific association not only with the vine and its harvest, but also with ivy, corn, figs and fruit in general. The connection with wine – once accorded an exaggerated significance because of its central place in the Romanized portrait of 'jolly Bacchus' – was real enough, and already attested in the eighth century,[98] but essentially the god's concern was for all natural life. He was son of Semele, originally an earth goddess.[99] The phallus, symbol of fertility, was carried in his processions; and his attendants, the satyrs and Sileni, were regularly represented as phallic, although the god himself was not.

The differences between the god's two faces cannot be ignored. The Dionysiac worship of the *Bacchae* is wild and orgiastic. The annual festivals of the Attic Dionysus, held in winter and spring, were spirited enough, and often the occasion for exuberance and phallic obscenity, but there is little trace of orgiastic ritual.[100] It is often suggested that the wilder Dionysus was the older, and that though he was still alive in artistic contexts like the *Bacchae*, in the actual cult practice of classical Athens the god was largely domesticated. This is certainly one way of explaining the evidence, although it may be that as far back as we can know, the god had always had his two aspects. After all, these are not irreconcilable, even at their extremes. The god, as Plutarch put it in the first century A.D., is lord of 'the whole wet element in nature': sap and semen, blood and wine.[101] There is, again, a characteristic connection between fertility religion and religious 'enthusiasm', and the Mycenaean ancestor of historical Dionysiac worship was apparently both.[102] Thus, without excluding the possibility of additional development before or after Homer, we can continue to see Dionysus as one.

The co-presence of his two aspects necessarily invests Dionysus with a further characteristic. On one side he is a creator, bringing fertility; on the other, a destroyer, as he is with Pentheus in the *Bacchae*, who is lured to a gruesome death at the hands of his own mother. The paradox is stated by Euripides' Dionysus himself: he is 'most terrible, and most gentle, to mankind'.[103] The 'gentle', creative, aspect was particularly in evidence at Athens, not simply in the modest agricultural festivals, but also, since the efforts of Pisistratus in the sixth century, on a grander scale. B. C. Dietrich sums up these developments in the context of the god's earlier history: 'The Athenian Pisistratus is a shining example of the contribution made by the tyrants to the religious harmony within the *polis*, and especially to the survival of the age-old chthonic cults...[namely by] the introduction into Athens of the cult of Dionysus Eleuthereus in whose honour the dramatic festivals came into being. The cult of Dionysus, in fact, in sixth-century Athens became respectable and was observed by all classes in society. The god of the lower orders, as it were, concerned with fertility, orgiastic and mystic rites, had been known to the Homeric poets but was neglected by them. Much of his myth reflected the vigour with which the nobility [i.e. such as Pentheus in the *Bacchae*] had resisted the introduction of Dionysiac cult. However, it was the achievement of Pisistratus and his successors that a reconciliation came about between the religious cult of the lower classes and the city gods, the gods of the aristocracy. Dionysus' ascent to the ranks of the Olympians during this period can be judged by the god's becoming the favourite subject of Attic vase painters, and by the temple which was built to Dionysus in Athens in the last years of the sixth century.'[104]

It will have become apparent that Nietzsche's Dionysus is appreciably closer to the 'real' Dionysus than was the case with his Apollo – and it would be so even if he had not divined the essential sequence whereby pre-Homeric Dionysiac worship was suppressed in Homeric Greece and reintroduced after that (§§ 2–4). Where he deserves credit, above all, is for the vigorous depiction of Dionysiac orgiasm, and its psychological attractions, in §§ 1–2. Much of the imagery in § 1 (beasts of prey at peace, earth yielding milk and honey) is taken from the *Bacchae*,[105] and the data about Greek ritual practices that the account relies on had been available in matter-of-fact compilations for a generation and more,[106] but the vision and the cogency of the portrayal are all Nietzsche. Once again, however, the picture is not without its idiosyncrasies. There is, first of all, one striking omission, the important place of women in the orgiastic cult: Nietzsche has given us his *Bacchae* without the maenads. More important, in his very proper emphasis on Dionysus' orgiastic aspect, he has greatly understated the importance of the god's connection with fertility. There are passing references to the 'earth freely proferring her gifts' (§ 1) and the 'sexual omnipotence of nature' (§ 8), but no adequate impression is created. There is a good deal about wine, but, questionably enough,[107] Nietzsche associates wine exclusively with the *orgia*.

One consequence of this one-sidedness is that Nietzsche fails to convey the paradoxical yet characteristic combination of terror and gentleness. In § 10 he acknowledges that 'Dionysus possesses the dual nature of a cruel, depraved demon and a mild, gentle ruler', but on the whole his Dionysus is not *gently* creative at all. What Nietzsche does convey, and most powerfully, is his own version of the paradox inherent in Dionysiac possession itself – albeit a version that is once again imbued with his own metaphysical coloration:

> Schopenhauer has depicted for us the tremendous *terror* which seizes man when he suddenly fails to make sense of the cognitive forms of phenomena because the principle of sufficient reason, in some one of its manifestations, seems to suffer an exception. If to this terror we add the blissful ecstasy that wells from the innermost depths of man, indeed of nature, at this collapse of the *principium individuationis*, we get a glimpse into the nature of the *Dionysiac*, which is brought home to us most intimately by the analogy of intoxication (§ 1).

This paradoxical combination of horror and rapture has more than a passing similarity with that tense co-existence of opposed feelings – the primitive hunter's feelings of preserving life by inflicting death – from which Walter Burkert in his remarkable *Homo Necans* (1972) infers the original motivation for the ritual of sacrifice. And though the scope of Nietzsche's Dionysus far exceeds any ritual manifestations, there is a further affinity in respect of the postulated association of violence and creative effect. 'The Dionysiac', Nietzsche tells us in § 24, 'with its primordial joy experienced even in pain, is the common source of music and tragic myth.' For Burkert too creativity – in the first instance, rituals and myths – is induced by a primordial violence.

To Wilamowitz the mere idea of deriving anything creative from the Dionysiac *ecstasis* was unacceptable. The art-forms associated with Dionysus – drama and the rest – must (he insisted) be related not to that 'alien' aspect of Greek religion, but to the more visibly beneficent seasonal rituals of the countryside. The mystical-orgiastic Dionysus was depraved and absurd and as such essentially un-Greek.[108] And the particular directness with which Nietzsche linked the irrational 'dissonance' (§ 24) of Dionysiac worship with creativity, and Hellenic creativity at that, was too Nietzschean not only for Wilamowitz, but for most of his less prejudiced successors as well. On this sensitive point – perhaps the most disturbing feature of Nietzsche's challenge to the 'sweetness and light' view of Greece – the only scholar of any standing who has been willing to affirm the link in anything like his terms is W. F. Otto, in whose *Dionysos: Mythos und Kultus* (1933), Dionysus does indeed embody 'creative madness' as the irrational ground of the world. But that which is disturbing is not to be rejected on that account alone. It might be easy enough to tone down the implications of the Nietzschean principle by noting that mystical-ecstatic experience covers a whole spectrum from the homicidal communion of the *Bacchae* to the state of mind responsible for the last hundred verses of Dante's *Paradiso*. Better to accept that 'creative' and 'destructive' impulses – in ancient Greece or in general – do not come conveniently separate; and that Nietzsche's principle represents a fundamental insight, restated by Burkert in different terms, into this fact.

The most blatant divergence of the Nietzschean Dionysus from his Greek ancestor is set out in the opening paragraph of § 1. Apollo and Dionysus, we are told, are the two art-deities of ancient Greece: sculpture is the Apolline art and music the Dionysiac. This bland assertion is equally unhistorical on both sides, for Dionysus was no more a god of music than Apollo was god of the visual arts. Dionysus, like Apollo, was indeed an 'art-deity', but Apollo was the *only* god of music. Music – one special kind of music – was associated with Dionysus too, but he was no more god *of* music than Athene, one of whose symbols was the olive, was a fertility deity like Demeter. Dionysus' association with art in classical times went no further than his connection with the dithyramb and his patronage of drama and the dramatic festivals.[109]

Clearly, then, Dionysus is not a god of music. More problematic are certain of the mystical interests that Nietzsche ascribes to him, such as his association with 'the eternal life beyond all phenomena' (§ 16). Was the cult of Dionysus in the archaic age really associated with 'eternal life'? It is widely supposed that belief in some form of immortality was a feature of the 'original' (i.e. Thraco-Phrygian) cult, and again that from the seventh or sixth centuries it was also a feature of what the handbooks on Greek religion call 'Orphism'. As far as *BT* is concerned, the question about 'eternal life' belongs to a wider problem. Nietzsche does not distinguish between the 'regular' cult of Dionysus and Orphism (or his interpretation of Orphism); the problem is to decide whether 'the Orphics' in fact reflected authentic Dionysiac lore.

The name Orphism refers to an obscure mystical movement, whose coherence, importance and even existence have been very variously estimated.[110] The movement – according to the most popular assessment of the evidence – begins about 600 B.C., claiming Orpheus as its founder and Dionysus among its deities. It is strongly marked by asceticism, a belief in metempsychosis, and an elaborate anthropogony. Modifying and systematizing various pre-existing myths (including a large element of 'orthodox' Olympian mythology), the Orphics began their history of mankind with primeval Chronus (Time), and eventually reached the infant Dionysus, heir presumptive of Zeus. The giant Titans, sons of Gaea (Earth) and representing an earlier generation than Zeus, murdered Dionysus out of jealousy, dismembered him and ate his whole body, all except the heart, from which a new Dionysus was born. The murderers were duly punished. They were burned up by Zeus' lightning, and from their soot men came into being. The Titans are thus the originators of Dionysus' sufferings, while man inherits their criminal nature and has, at the same time, an affinity with the god whose body the Titans had fed on.[111] For the latter part of the sixth century, by which time these ideas will have become more or less established, there are supposed to have been two active centres of the Orphic movement. One, probably in some way associated with Pythagoras, was in south Italy; the other was in Athens, where Onomacritus, its leading representative, is alleged to have versified Orphic doctrines[112] and for a time enjoyed the rôle of soothsayer at the court of Pisistratus, founder of the tragic festival.

In *BT* there is no reference to the Orphics by name,[113] although when Nietzsche lauds the 'sixth century with its birth of tragedy, its mysteries, its Pythagoras and Heraclitus' (§ 11), they are very much there in spirit. Their spirit, furthermore, pervades large areas of the book; for Nietzsche has tacitly conflated the Orphic and the 'real' Dionysus and has thus invested the Dionysiac with what we only know (or presume we know) as Orphic characteristics. Above all, it is from the Orphics that he derives his frequent talk of 'mysteries'. It may indeed be an overstatement to say, as simply as Otto Kern once did, that 'the Dionysus of the Mysteries belongs to the Orphics',[114] for there is no doubt that the authentic Dionysiac *orgia* must have been 'mysteries' in their own right.[115] Nevertheless, any 'Dionysiac mysteries' of the sixth century – which, by implication, is where Nietzsche locates them – are likely to have belonged to an Orphic context; and the Orphic provenance of his mysteries is unmistakably shown by the *doctrinal* aspect he ascribes to them. 'The mystery cults', writes Dodds, 'offered their adepts a supposedly potent kind of *knowledge*, from which the profane were excluded';[116] and though, once again, traditional Dionysiac *orgia* (with which Dodds' comment is in fact concerned) would presumably have involved such knowledge, the mystery knowledge we connect with the early period is specifically Orphic.

Dionysiac 'wisdom', Dionysiac 'truth', Dionysiac 'knowledge' – such collocations represent one of the leading themes of the book, and it is from Orphism (with a little help from the semi-Dionysiac 'wise Silenus' of § 3) that Nietzsche derives the theme. 'The mystery doctrine of tragedy' is defined in § 10 as 'the fundamental knowledge of the oneness of everything existent, the conception of individuation as the primal cause of evil, and of art as the joyous hope that the spell of individuation may be broken in augury of a restored oneness'. Part of this 'doctrine' goes back to Schopenhauer. Its basis, however, is 'the problem of the one and the many' – a problem which obsessed Greek religious and philosophical thinkers of the sixth century – as represented in the Orphic anthropogonical myth[117] recounted above, and which Nietzsche himself recounts in slightly different terms in the same section. The dismemberment of our ancestor Dionysus by the Titans (he tells us) symbolizes 'the state of individuation', which is to be regarded as 'the origin and primal cause of all suffering'. In that myth too is Nietzsche's 'augury of a restored oneness' in the shape of the new Dionysus, for 'the hope of the initiates looked toward a rebirth of Dionysus, which we must now dimly conceive as the end of individuation.' This in fact is what he means by 'eternal life beyond all phenomena', which, as far as the individual is concerned, is a good deal less than the personal immortality promised by the Orphics. However, having failed to inform us that he is drawing on Orphic material in the first place, Nietzsche says nothing when he diverges from it either. There is another instance of such opportunism in connection with the mysteries. His initiates are of course envisaged as participants in mysteries with a *dramatic* element; 'secret celebrations of dramatic mysteries' is a phrase he uses in § 10. To see the dithyramb as proto-dramatic is one thing; to envisage actual ritual drama at Orphic mysteries is quite another. In default of any good reason for associating the Orphics with such performances, Nietzsche's thoughts turn (as we have seen) to the famous *drōmena* at Eleusis – the ritual drama of Demeter and Persephone.[118] Without comment, as usual, he has transferred the idea of such *drōmena* to the Orphized 'mysteries of Dionysus', and then, we are left to conclude, equated the new composite with the supposed 'satyric dithyramb' of the Aristotelian tradition.

Nietzsche, then, has borrowed, for his own purposes, the Orphic mysteries (or an enlarged version of them) and the Orphic Dionysus-myth. With that myth also come the Titans who bulk so large in his vision of the pre-Homeric age as expounded in §§ 3–4. But the really important borrowing is the 'mystery doctrine', from which hardly any aspect of his Dionysus is entirely free. The god's worshipper in § 1 is an 'orthodox' Dionysiac in his song and dance – but, like a good Orphic, feels a sense of *oneness* with his neighbour, as if experiencing 'the mysterious primordial unity' itself. Even that 'symbol of the sexual omnipotence of nature', the Dionysiac satyr of § 8, is a source of *wisdom*, duly interpreted in terms of the 'eternal life' which abides through the perpetual destruction of our phenomenal world. The wise Silenus, the proto-dramatic satyr, and the Orphic mystic have at this point achieved a bizarre identification.

From Apollo and Dionysus as single figures we turn to their relationship. Nietzsche's two gods make what it is fashionable to call a binary opposition. Contrary to a widespread belief, that opposition has a basis in Greek ideology and cult. We have spoken of the wilder and gentler aspects of Dionysus. At the one extreme, we have the 'original' barbaric licentiousness – 'that horrible mixture of sensuality and cruelty which has always seemed to me to be the real "witches' brew"' (§ 2); at the other, the 'creative' festivals whose institutionalization in sixth-century Pisistratean Athens helped to make drama as we know it possible. The remarkable fact is that insofar as Dionysus' gentler aspect appears to have been the later, and accordingly a process of domestication is to be assumed for the archaic period, the process was associated with Apollo and formalized in ritual terms by him. The association was so close, however, that it engendered a further process of syncretism between the two deities, as a result of which 'the characters of the two gods seem to have become thoroughly mingled by the fifth century'.[119] In the beginning convergence was strictly limited. The essence of this phase was a ceremonial juxtaposition of cults at Apollo's centre, Delphi. After an account of the 'feverish excitment' of spontaneous Dionysiac worship as it spread like a epidemic over Greece, Nietzsche himself refers to this 'reconciliation' in vivid terms (§ 2): 'the Delphic god, by a seasonably effected reconciliation, now contented himself with taking the destructive weapons away from his powerful antagonist...the boundary lines to be observed henceforth by each were sharply defined, and there was to be a periodical exchange of gifts of esteem.'

Nilsson describes the same phase of the relationship in a very similar spirit, but more detail: 'No other religious movement took so powerful a hold upon men's minds as the Dionysiac ecstasy. It was something new, something in conflict with ancestral custom. That Apollo managed to bring the ecstasy under control by the force of legalism, to fit it into ancestral custom and himself to derive new vigour from it, is the strongest proof of his power ...It was Apollo who overcame the epidemic, not by working against and suppressing it, but by recognizing and regulating it. A regulated ecstasy has lost its germ of danger. This is what Apolline institutionalism managed to accomplish, and the fact is sufficient testimony of the extent to which it had become engrained in the people. A red-figured vase-painting from the end of the fifth century shows Apollo and Dionysus extending hands to each other before the *omphalos* [the 'navel' stone, regarded as the centre of the earth] at Delphi, surrounded by the train of Dionysus, satyrs and maenads. The sculptures on the gable-ends of the temple of Apollo at Delphi tell the same story. On the eastern pediment stood Apollo, surrounded by the Muses; on the western, Dionysus, surrounded by the Thyiades [maenads]. These groups confirm the information given by Plutarch as to the connection between the cults of Apollo and Dionysus at Delphi. During the three winter months the paean of Apollo was silent and the dithyramb of Dionysus was sung instead. Apollo returned with the spring...Still more important for our understanding of Apollo's influence upon the Dionysiac cult are the accounts of the kind of orgies celebrated at Delphi, or rather on the peaks of Parnassus. In the midst of winter the Thyiades roamed about among mountains and snow, swinging their *thyrsi* [wands][120] and torches in orgiastic frenzy. But these Thyiades were not a band of ecstatic women which could be joined by anyone who was seized by the spirit. They were a body specially elected for this cult...this restriction of the orgies to official communities of maenads was the means by which Apollo curbed the ecstasy and brought the cult of Dionysus into line with ancestral custom.'[121] This institutionalization is what Nietzsche is referring to in §2 when he depicts Dionysiac excess becoming for the first time 'an artistic phenomenon'. Up to this point his account of the relationship between the two deities is historically grounded and, despite its personal idiom, in line with – indeed, in the van of – later scholarship.

In the matter of the Dionysiac–Apolline relationship, Nietzsche's departure from historicity may be said to begin with his conflation of 'orthodox' religion with Orphism. For in addition to his other borrowings from this source, it is Orphism that enables him to extend the relationship onto a *theological* level which we have no reason to believe the Delphic 'reconciliation' implied. The special interest of the Orphics in the two gods is represented in mytho-dramatic form in a lost play by Aeschylus, the *Bassarids*, in which Orpheus is portrayed as a devotee of the sun (identified with Apollo) to the anger of Dionysus who sends his maenads (the Bassarids of the title) to murder him.[122] The preference for Apollo shown here seems to have been characteristic of the movement and implies the desire to impose some kind of ritual purism on the tradition of Dionysiac communion in which the Orphics found a mystical intimation of 'eternal life'.[123] The murder of Dionysus by the Titans in the Orphic creation myth has a different but related significance. Dodds expounds it as follows: 'The Titan myth neatly explained to the Greek puritan why he felt himself to be at once a god and a criminal; the "Apolline" sentiment of remoteness from the divine and the "Dionysiac" sentiment of identity with it were both of them accounted for and both of them justified.'[124] That Dodds should, without comment, be using Nietzschean terms of reference in this Orphic context is testimony to the continuity between the two.

Nietzsche's Dionysus and Apollo start as historical Greek gods and finish as entities with a supra-historical – or at least 'world-historical' – character; at a certain point they take on an 'artistic' life of their own. If the first stage in the process is their assimilation to Orphism, the next, essential stage is their conversion into archetypes like Homer and Archilochus and, above all, Socrates. They become a formula for the Greek gods as a whole: all of Greek religion is subsumed under one or other of these two, or ignored. Apollo (as Nietzsche indicates) is made into *the* representative Olympian, and Dionysus into the representative of the rest. This is the underlying significance of Nietzsche's equation between his Dionysus and the Orphic Dionysus, between mythology with a literal Dionysiac content and any 'dark' mythology, between satyrs and Sileni. And here, too, lies the explanation for his regarding the Silenus–Midas story as Dionysiac, despite the fact that if it was as old as he wants it to be (pre-Homeric), it would comfortably predate Silenus' known association with Dionysus proper.[125]

The author of *BT* is more concerned to present his own construct than to discuss it, and he has nothing explicit to say in answer to the question, why (within the terms of Greek religion) *these two* gods should be invested with archetypal significance. One reason is that contrast between legalism and ecstasy which we have seen Nilsson identify as a central fact of the archaic age, and which he defines precisely, though not exclusively, in terms of these two deities: 'one current manifests itself in Hesiod and Delphic Apollo, the other in Dionysus and the miracle workers...'[126] Above all, however, the plausibility of Nietzsche's choice depends on a larger contrast, one which was expounded by Plato and is generally regarded as a basic fact of Greek religion. This is the contrast between Olympian (or 'uranian') religion, the religion of heaven, and chthonic religion, the religion of the earth.[127]

For Nietzsche's 'Apolline', then, read *Olympian*, and for his 'Dionysiac' read *chthonic*. Underworld deities, like Pluto, are chthonic, as are the mysteries – whether those of Demeter or Dionysus or their Mycenaean ancestral forms. Homer's gods, and the religious practices and beliefs adhered to almost everywhere by the heroes of Homeric epic, epitomize religion of the Olympian kind.[128] Guthrie comments on the two types: 'the one [Olympian]...seems specially suited to a race of roving warriors, the other [chthonic], having its roots in the fecundity of animals and plants, finds a more natural origin in a settled and humble people who wrested their livelihood from the land by hunting, stock-raising or agriculture' – and he adds by way of internal characterization: 'The Homeric Olympian religion shows us a society of gods with clear-cut characters and strong personalities, gods with whom man's relations are purely external, maintained by sacrifice and prayer in a spirit of bargaining or seeking for favours.... In the chthonic cults the religious atmosphere is entirely different. They are mystical, exciting, intoxicating...they contain, either latent or expressed, the promise of immortality.'[129]

So far, the chthonic–Olympian distinction would seem to correspond to the Dionysiac–Apolline, as Nietzsche conceives of it, pretty well. However, discrepancies soon appear. One is implicit in Guthrie's talk of 'warriors' and 'humble people': there is a *social* dimension to the antithesis. On the one side, there is 'folk religion...dominating rural life', and on the other, 'the religion of the gods of epic poetry, which, as it were, reflect the aristocratic society magnified to divine proportions'.[130] As far as the real Dionysus and the real Apollo are concerned, there is no discrepancy. We have ourselves already commented on the popular status of Dionysus when we accounted for his absence from Homer and for Pisistratus' patronage of his worship;[131] and the historic Apollo, for his part, can reasonably be associated with the other 'aristocratic' members of the Homeric pantheon. Nietzsche's two gods, however, are different. He says nothing that could allow them any such affiliations. They are classless, and this is because they are entities that exist beyond the realm of socio-political stratification and (so far as possible) beyond socio-political significance of any kind. This is not simply an inference from Nietzsche's silence; he is obliged at one point to make it explicit. Dionysiac worship, he tells us, is essentially communal. It presupposes a *mass* of worshippers 'whose civic past and social status have been totally forgotten' (§§1, 8). From this it might be concluded that the tragic chorus which is the direct descendant of that mass 'represents the people' as against the aristocratic heroes of the drama proper (§7). Nietzsche rejects the idea indignantly: 'the whole opposition of prince and people – indeed the whole socio-political sphere – is excluded from those purely religious origins of tragedy' (§7).

Insistent on separating the 'purely religious' from the mere socio-political, Nietzsche misinterprets the Homeric suppression of Dionysus and ignores the predominant femininity of Dionysiac worship.[132] (The two points are connected, as is suggested by J.-P. Vernant's definition of Dionysiac worship as essentially 'une expérience religieuse inverse du culte officiel' – which helps to explain its appeal to women, who were excluded from political life.)[133] For Nietzsche the 'purely religious' does at least include the psychological. The inner needs which prompted the early Greeks to espouse Apollo and then eventually Dionysus are treated at some length in the first four sections of his book. Even here, however, lack of interest in social realities limits his thinking. Dodds explains: 'Dionysus was in the archaic age as much of a social necessity as Apollo; each ministered in his own way to the anxieties characteristic of a guilt-culture. Apollo promised security: "Understand your station as man; do as the Father tells you; and you will be safe tomorrow." Dionysus offered freedom: "Forget the difference, and you will find the identity; join the *thiasos*, and you will be happy today."... And his joys were accessible to all, including even slaves, as well as those freemen who were shut out from the old gentile cults. Apollo moved only in the best society, from the days when he was Hector's patron to the days when he canonized aristocratic athletes; but Dionysus was at all periods *dēmotikos*, a god of the people...Dionysus...is *Lusios*, "the Liberator" – the god who enables you for a short time to *stop being yourself*, and thereby sets you free. That was, I think, the main secret of his appeal to the archaic age: not only because life in that age was often a thing to escape from, but more specifically because the individual, as the modern world knows him, began in that age to emerge for the first time from the old solidarity of the family, and found the unfamiliar burden of individual responsibility hard to bear. Dionysus could lift it from him.'[134] In a 'purely religious' perspective such as Nietzsche has fashioned, these insights could never be entertained.

Nietzsche's tacit equation of Dionysus with the chthonians and Apollo with the Olympians raises other difficulties.[135] Two main features characterize the chthonic group as a whole: there is the connection with fertility, and there is also an association with *death*. In some cases – as with the classical Demeter, corn-goddess and mother-in-law of the death-god – the two functions exist side by side. In others – as with the death-god Pluto himself – the *under*world association is dominant. Dionysus, however, does not seem to belong to either category. The Bacchic god of the proto-tragic period may have been a very destructive god, but neither in his Greek, nor in his Nietzschean guise does he have any clear links with death – certainly not more than Apollo who, untidily enough, does have such a connection in his capacity as purifier from blood-guilt.[136] So far as traditional ritual is concerned, Dionysus' claim to any infernal powers seems to rest on the evidence of the Anthesteria, the Athenian All Souls' Festival, over which he presided. However, it was the last day of the festival that was the *Allerseelenfest* proper, and there seems to be a balance of argument against assuming an organic connection between that part of the celebration and the rest.[137]

If we discount the Anthesteria, we are left only with enigmatic titbits like a Heraclitean saying that 'Hades and Dionysus are the same' (which is open to a variety of interpretations),[138] and considerable evidence, largely pictorial, that Dionysus was acquiring an underworld aspect in some quarters from about 500 B.C.[139] We have, for instance, a vase of *c.* 460 on which the god is represented with the cornucopia of Pluto, lord of the underworld.[140] It may be argued that this eventual connection with death implies some interest in the subject at an earlier period, and that only on this basis could one explain why a non-Dionysiac cult of souls should have been attached to a separate, Dionysiac festival in the first place. It is also worth noting that Dionysus' Mycenaean source is now supposed to have been 'male companion' to a 'goddess of nature' of the same type as (but less differentiated than) the classical Demeter; and as such the proto-Dionysus would indeed have had the requisite concern not only with vegetation, but with 'the whole world-process of decay, death, renewal'.[141] But the fact remains that if Dionysus is to stand as archetype for the chthonians of historic Greece, he must subsume Demeter, let alone Pluto – which is grotesque.

Apollo, too, is more than a typical Olympian. Dietrich, restating Nilsson's account of 'the major elements' within 'the religious structure of the archaic *polis*', distinguishes four. There was 'the ecstatic Dionysiac, the legalistic Apolline elements [*sc.* 'that aspect of Apollo which, in connection chiefly with his oracular seat at Delphi, came to represent enlightenment and reason to the Greeks'], and the more localized mystery cults [*sc.* 'the vegetation and mystery rites of the agrarian Demeter']. These various religious streams, including the prophetic and ecstatic Apolline cult, were essentially in contrast with the cult of the Olympian city gods.'[142] One phrase in Dietrich's last sentence is particularly important: 'the prophetic and ecstatic Apolline cult'. If this plays no part in Nietzsche's portrayal of Apollo, it is because he insists on presenting his antithesis in the strongest possible terms. It has often been pointed out that the Delphic ecstasy has little in common with the Dionysiac: the one was purely prophetic, with the function of obtaining knowledge, and was experienced individually without *orgia*; the other was not prophetic but concerned with communion, and was experienced orgiastically *en masse*. But these distinctions are of no use to Nietzsche: his Apollo is serene, and ecstasty of any kind would spoil that serenity. In *Psyche* Rohde was still enough of a Nietzschean to argue that the ecstatic element at Delphi was unoriginal and the direct result of Dionysus' presence there.[143] That view has received some support,[144] but it has been more widely and more plausibly supposed that the ecstatic element is not only original, but a factor that helped to bring the otherwise antipodal deities together in the first place.[145]

In terms of Greek realities, then, Nietzsche's antithesis is too rigid; and when we look closely at the actual properties of the two gods, we can find other signs of overlap that tell against it. *Apolline lyre* versus *Dionysiac 'flute'*, for instance, is not a formula that can be universally upheld, even for the archaic age: as early as the seventh century (witness the poet Alcman) Apollo himself could be depicted as a performer on the *aulos*.[146] Moreover, various of the most striking points of contrast dwelt on in *BT* – dreams *versus* intoxication, illusion *versus* truth, sculpture *versus* music – are not, as we have seen, derived from Greece at all. Nevertheless, in spite of all these objections, the antithesis can still stand: it has a general validity and (in Nietzsche's favour) a greater validity for the archaic period, when tragedy was born, than for the fifth century, when the two deities and their attributes seem to have been subject to a certain convergence.[147] That process was to reach its climax centuries later in the shape of a thoroughgoing syncretism summed up by the comment of Dio Chrysostom (*c.* A.D. 100): 'some tell us that Apollo, the sun, and Dionysus are one and the same'.[148]

Moreover – in Nietzsche's favour too – there is a depiction of Dionysus and Apollo by Dio's contemporary, Plutarch. In place of Dio's syncretism, Plutarch offers a characterization of opposites which looks back to traditional artistic representations of the two gods, their music and their joint cult at Delphi, and forward to Nietzsche's own version of the antithesis:

> Dionysus with his orgies and dithyrambs is the lord of winter, while the pure and stainless Apollo, to whom the regulated and chaste music of the paean is sung, reigns over the summer months...In paintings and sculpture the artists represent Apollo as ever ageless and young, but Dionysus they depict in many guises and forms; and in general they attribute to Apollo a uniformity, orderliness and unadulterated seriousness, but to Dionysus a certain variability combining playfulness, wantonness, seriousness and frenzy.[149]

It is true that Plutarch's antithesis does not go as far as Nietzsche's, and that the Greeks of his day are notoriously given to speculative interpretations of earlier religious traditions. Nevertheless, Plutarch does give us an opposition, and one that is very much in line with Nietzsche's. Plutarch's appeal to the musical side of the opposition is particularly worth noting. For even if the religious habitats of the 'flute' and lyre did overlap, the characteristic moods and effects of Dionysiac and Apolline music (as Plutarch indicates) did not.[150]

Music, then, provides an important piece of evidence for Nietzsche's antithesis. The irony is that Nietzsche himself is unable to do much with it. He has made Dionysus into the god of music, and committed himself to portraying the Dionysiac music of the primitive dithyramb as, somehow, representative and even typical of classical Greek music as a whole. He is therefore unwilling to lay any stress on the continuing existence of 'regulated and chaste' music in the classical age, although he does oppose it to the dithyramb in the context of earlier Greece (§2).

What Nietzsche did not say, let us say for him. There is a large opposition between Greek music in general, which was 'orderly', and the untypical music of the early dithyramb. Apollo, not Dionysus, was the Greek god of music, and the 'chaste' tones of Apollo were and remained the Hellenic archetype as against the 'foreign' Dionysiac. From the fourth century, or possibly from the fifth, a specific contrast of the kind employed by Plutarch was recognized between the untypical dithyrambic music and music associated with Apollo. This contrast was perceptible in the 'ethical' opposition between moderation and excitement, in the 'modal' opposition between Dorian and Phrygian, and (by and large) in the instrumental opposition between lyre and 'flute'.[151] In part, these propositions vindicate the historicity of Nietzsche's antithesis; in part, they demonstrate its autonomy from the realities of historical Greece.

THE PHASES OF GREEK CULTURE

Nietzsche's Dionysus and Apollo, then, are Greek to begin with, and archetypes – in some ways very un-Greek archetypes – in the end. If he had been concerned only to apply these hybrids to the modern world, or to art or life as a whole, but *not* to the Greek world in particular, his antithesis would have been at once less problematic and less engaging. As it is, he has produced a construct whose positive and negative features are hard to separate.

With the aid of the two archetypes, Nietzsche offers a dialectical interpretation of Greek culture. On his reading, that culture and its history is the paradigm for all cultures and their histories, and the Greek paradigm is incomprehensible if seen in terms of any single principle – until, that is, the rise of Socratism, which has only to appear to sweep all before it. Nietzsche gives us five successive historical phases (§§2–4):

(i) The pre-Hellenic age (Dionysiac)
(ii) The Homeric age (Apolline)
(iii) The (early) lyric age (Dionysiac)
(iv) The 'Dorian' reassertion of the Apolline
(v) The tragic age (Dionysiac–Apolline).

He then adds (§§11–14, 17):

(vi) The Socratic–Alexandrian age.

This schema has the advantage of investing a mass of detail with a clear significance and the disadvantage of over-simplification. It points with particular vividness to the break represented by the last, 'Socratic', age, but at the cost of ignoring 'Socratic' elements in the earlier phases: it fails to distinguish between the rationality that is an element in traditional Greek culture and the victorious rational*ism* that is not. Among its more dubious aspects is the elusiveness of the 'Dionysiac' in phases (i), (iii) and (v). In (i) it is literal, referring to religion of a putatively Dionysiac type. In (iii) and (v) its status is variable: besides religion, only a single lyric genre (the dithyramb) and tragic drama in its presumed origin have a literal Dionysiac connection. The difficulty arises from Nietzsche's reapplication of his archetypes to the culture from which they derive.

The most serious defect, however, lies not in what Nietzsche does, but in what he ignores. His schema is essentially two-dimensional in a multi-dimensional world. He is responsive to time. He is responsive – overwhelmingly – to mood. He hardly responds at all to *place*, to *politics*, to *society*[152] – and, above all, not to their variety. He treats Greece as a single entity defined by its leading representatives, not as a multifarious collection of small states, each with its own propensities and peculiarities.

The deficiency is particularly visible in Nietzsche's representation of his fifth phase as a 'tragic' age. The unstated justification for this is simply that the greatest single achievement of the age, in his view, is tragedy. That is reasonable. But while tragedy was being born *in Attica*, Presocratic philosophy was in process of development largely *in Ionia* – and that portentous movement contained not just the 'pessimism' of Heraclitus, but all the seeds of 'optimistic' rationalism too. To give tragedy pride of place also involves an implied claim for its influence on the age, a claim which Nietzsche makes explicit in §21: 'It is the people of the tragic mysteries that fights the battles against the Persians; and the people that fought these wars in turn needs tragedy as a necessary potion to recover.' For tragedy at that time was 'the tremendous power that stimulated, purified and discharged the whole life of the people'. There was, no doubt, a new *élan* and pride in Athens during, or at least after, the great struggles against the Persians in which the city took a leading part; and doubtless those qualities were to an extent stimulated by the ascendant Attic art-form and its marvellous depth and power. But the influence exerted by Attic tragedy at the time of the Persian wars must have been purely parochial: its prestige outside Athens came only with Athens' subsequent rise to political power within the Greek city-states. It was, says Nietzsche, 'the people of the tragic mysteries' who fought the Persians and then needed tragedy to recover. But the Persians were opposed by other Greeks besides, including the allegedly ultra-Apolline Spartans (§4), who, without benefit of regular doses of 'tragic mysteries', nevertheless performed on the field of battle with equal distinction and recovered with no less ease. It is not for tendentious propositions such as these that one feels able to praise Nietzsche's book as a major contribution to the appreciation of ancient Greece, but for its insights into the religious outlook before Socrates and, as we shall see, its elucidation of the spirit of tragedy.

7

Mode and originality

THE MIXED MODE OF *THE BIRTH OF TRAGEDY*

'Scholarship, art and philosophy', Nietzsche had written in 1871, 'are now growing together inside me so much that I'll be giving birth to centaurs one day.'[1] It is not some incidental flaw or quirk but the essential condition of *BT* that it is, as Nietzsche had predicted, a hybrid: a work of mixed mode between literature and 'science', between art and thought. It was this hybridity that prompted Rohde to call it a 'didactic poem' (*Lehrgedicht*) and Cosima Wagner to explain that she felt obliged to 'read it as a poem', even though it dealt with 'the most profound problems' – and finally Nietzsche himself to disown the book in his *Self-Criticism* of 1886 as neither one thing nor the other: 'What spoke here...was something like a mystical, almost maenadic soul...that stammered with difficulty...as if in a strange tongue ...It should have *sung*, not spoken, this new soul. What I had to say then – what a pity that I did not dare to say it as a poet: perhaps I had the ability. Or at least as a philologist: even today practically everything in this field remains to be unearthed and discovered by philologists!'[2] Here as elsewhere, however, Nietzsche's afterthoughts are not to be taken as definitive. We must define the hybridity more closely.

Although Nietzsche does not write as a philologist, he remains unmistakably a Hellenist. Despite his intense admiration for Schopenhauer and Wagner, and notwithstanding his own testimony to the stature or representative importance of the 'entire Aryan community' (§9), of Buddhism (§§18, 21), of Shakespeare (§2), of Rome (§21), he assumes that, within man's entire cultural experience, Greece (in its creative rise or its Socratic fall) comes first, 'that the Greeks, as charioteers, hold in their hands the reins of our own and every other culture' (§15). This unargued assumption – for assertion, however majestic, does not constitute an argument – Nietzsche shares with a hundred years of German Hellenism before him. From the time of Winckelmann, however, the quest for Greece is generally pursued in the spirit of historical method. Nietzsche's tendency is in a different direction. His treatment of Greece reveals a gift akin to that imaginative, empathetic (in England one would say Keatsian) faculty which, since the Romantics, has been regarded as a necessary constituent of the 'poetic character'. So striking is his rapport with the Greece he portrays that many commentators have assumed some special affinity, concluding that 'Nietzsche considered Greek literature, Greek life, and Greek thought from the unreal and unphilological standpoint of a Greek born out of time'.[3] This may be taking the point too far. Apart from anything else, one wonders how any reversion of this kind could be compatible with such a sophisticated modern intelligence; and remembering the mood of 'reckless estrangement from philology' in which Nietzsche set to work on the book,[4] one might do better to think of some self-induced state, like that of the self-conscious dreamer delineated in §1: 'It is a dream – I want to go on dreaming it!'

Nevertheless, of Nietzsche's special empathy with Greece there can be no doubt. It is not so much that he writes *like* the Greeks – that his writing recalls theirs in the way that, say, Milton's recalls Virgil's. It is rather that he writes as if he had spent some formative part of his life in their company. On a few occasions he seems to be thinking in Greek, not German.[5] More generally, Greek writers and thinkers are made to seem as close as if they were his own acquaintances, and, above all, Greek religion as vivid as if it were alive and tenable and perhaps even true.

Nietzsche's empathetic treatment of Greece is one of the artistic manifestations of his hybrid. Another is his archetypes. His Homer and Archilochus, as we have seen, embody and symbolize whole movements; his Socrates is a *personification* of Socratism; his Dionysus and Apollo, sovereign over the whole territory of Greek religion, have a comparable status. To Wilamowitz these symbols (or rather the two, Dionysus and Apollo, that he identified as such) were mere 'aesthetic abstractions'.[6] The tag is inapposite, however, if only because all the archetypes are grounded in ancient reality, and that grounding ensures their concreteness. In this connection it is worth glancing back to their evolution in Nietzsche's thinking. He decided on them, we recall, fairly late. In his own unpublished philological work before 1870, for instance, there is an obvious concern with tragedy and Orphism, but very little with Dionysus; with Homer, but not with Apollo; with the philosopher Democritus, but not with Socrates.[7]

The last pair is of particular interest. Democritus, contemporary with Socrates (although outliving him by a generation or more), was the object of extensive researches on Nietzsche's part in his Leipzig years. In one representative discussion among a series of notes dated to late 1867 or early 1868 he presents Democritus as a major figure in the development of Greek 'science':

He is a confident rationalist...He is the first Greek to achieve the *scientific character*, which implies the aspiration to account for a profusion of phenomena in a uniform way without dragging in a *deus ex machina* at difficult moments...Democritus himself perceived this as a new principle of life; he valued scientific inquiry above the kingship of Persia. In the scientific life he thought he had found the ultimate in all happiness. From this stand-point he rejected the life of the masses and of the earlier philosophers. The pain and sorrow of men he ascribed to their unscientific life, above all to their fear of the gods.[8]

In this instance it is clear not only that Nietzsche's invention of the archetype comes after his interest in the topics which were to attract the archetypal name, but that attributes he once ascribed to Democritus are later transferred to Socrates.

There is, let it be said, a clear similarity between certain of the attitudes of the two philosophers and no easy way to assign historical priority between them. But we have no reason to suppose that Nietzsche's motive for the transference implies some change of mind on the question of priority. *BT* gives no hint of an interest in that scholarly issue, and indeed contains no reference to Democritus whatsoever. Nietzsche's motive is surely quite different. Socrates – to Nietzsche and to the world at large – is not a shadowy figure like Democritus, a name in a handbook, but a solid, complex *persona*, presented live to us in the contemporary satire of Aristophanes' *Clouds* and the later hagiographies of Plato and Xenophon. Socrates is a known, Democritus an unknown. The transference of abstract data to a known personality allows them to be invested with an intimate vividness, a force of description and characterization, which is not just an incidental diversion for Nietzsche's readers, but a necessary instrument of his empathetic–imaginative faculty itself. In this his Socrates is no different from his other archetypal figures. The archetypes are in a sense, therefore, irreducible; they are not like the entities of scholarship; not abstracted truths, or falsehoods, about tragedy or psychology or metaphysics. Among other things, *BT* is (as Else says) 'visionalization'; and the archetypes are required to generate the intensity of the vision. At the same time, an entity like the Nietzschean Socrates still retains enough semblance of historical-scholarly reality to suggest that Nietzsche wants it both ways. He would like his archetypes, and his book as a whole, to be allowed the imaginative freedom of poetry *and* to be rewarded with the earnest attention accorded to scholarship.

If it is accepted that the archetypes have an artistic aspect, that they are to be credited with a literary status, we are entitled to ask what kind of literature they recall. Particularly with Dionysus and Apollo in mind, there is a strong temptation to think first of myth. This might have the advantage of suggesting why Nietzsche cannot, even if he wished, advertise the status of his entities in any self-conscious way: myth, as he is himself well aware (§23), is only genuine if felt as genuine, and the author is the last person to want an illusion of authenticity destroyed. (In the same spirit he says of metaphor in §8 that 'for a poet' it is 'not a rhetorical figure, but a concrete image that he sees in place of a concept'.) On the other hand, myth does not seem a very convincing label to attach to Nietzsche's Socrates, or his Homer and Archilochus, nor does myth have much to do with some of the centaur's other characteristics. There is, for instance, a marked tendency in all parts of the book towards schematism and schematic correlations. The book begins with two sets: Dionysus, intoxication, music, lyric poetry *versus* Apollo, dream, visual art, epic poetry. In §9 we are offered two quite different sets: Aryan, active, masculine, sacrilege, Prometheus *versus* Semitic, passive, feminine, sin, Eve. By §15 our opening pair has been expanded into a triad based on the key terms, Dionysus, Apollo, Socrates, which receives an extensive elaboration in §18. The first sequence now is: tragic, Buddhistic, belief (Nietzsche calls it *metaphysischer Trost*, 'metaphysical consolation'); the second, artistic, Hellenic, beauty; and the third, Socratic (i.e. scientific), Alexandrian, knowledge. In §21 Nietzsche adds India to the Dionysiac list, Greece to the Apolline, Rome to the Socratic. From §19, meanwhile, we learn that history has been obliging enough to dispose itself in symmetrical patterns (for modern culture is re-enacting the stages of Greek culture in reverse order). Finally the later sections of the book, especially §22, insist on the qualitative opposition between true music-dramatic tragedy, with its proper form and content and its 'aesthetic' audience, and opera, with its degenerate attributes and inferior, 'critical' public. Such sets and correlations (and there are many others) recall perhaps the schematism of medieval art, or else the formality of a technical treatise – a nice poise, then, between 'science' and art – but hardly myth.

Nietzsche's centaur is the product of his early yearning for wholeness. That yearning had been explicit before he began to translate it into a personal aspiration realizable, however eccentrically, in his own work. As late as his lecture on 'Greek Music Drama' (1870), he was voicing a public lament over the inability of citizens of the modern world to respond to life as 'whole beings', above all in the sphere of art, and suggesting that if we could recreate the supreme instance of such a response – the interplay of author, actors and audience in the 'total art' of Greek drama – the recreation 'would have an absolutely shattering effect on us, because it would reveal to us the artistic human being in his perfection and harmony'.[9] The aching distance felt to exist here between the Greece that was and the world that is evokes the nostalgia of the earlier German Hellenists rather than anything in *BT*. In the short time, it seems, between the composition of the lecture and the book, Nietzsche has found – or has persuaded himself that he has found – his faith in Wagner strong enough to proclaim the recreation of 'total art' as a reality. Moreover, his consciousness that through his proclamation he is himself, for the first time, achieving something 'whole' ensures that there is no longer any nostalgia in his evocation of the Greek past.

The need that Nietzsche's centaur fulfilled in his philosophizing was a very deep one which its creator never lost. This is not contradicted by his later repudiation of the book. The objections to it in the *Self-Criticism* are essentially objections to its particular hybridity, not to hybrids as such; for his later works, though mostly very different in idiom from *BT*, are no closer to orthodox expository and argumentative prose. Looking back from that period of maturity to *BT* and then to Nietzsche's activities before its genesis, we can see a continuity in terms of a search for an idiom as much as in the evolution of ideas. The importance of Schopenhauer here is very great. From this source Nietzsche inherited not just a philosophy, but a conception of literary prose; and Schopenhauer's influence on his philosophy would not have been so great without the conjunction. To the younger Nietzsche Schopenhauer did indeed seem to occupy a *via media* between philosophical ratiocination and artistic expression. There is a revealing note from 1868: 'in opposition to Kant, Schopenhauer is the poet; in opposition to Goethe, he is the philosopher'.[10] The characterization actually says as much about the pupil's devotion to his master as about the latter's true distinction. Schopenhauer is not the only German thinker who may be set 'in opposition to Kant' in the given sense. On the contrary, he belongs to an identifiable German tradition of literary-philosophical prose which goes back to Herder, Lichtenberg and Schiller and encompasses, *en route*, endeavours as different as Goethe's science and Schelling's metaphysics. That tradition as a whole must have played a supportive role to Schopenhauer's special example in encouraging Nietzsche to follow his literary inclinations. Wagner's prose too, with its strange mixture of heady 'poetic' colour and abstract concepts, seems to have exercised some influence on Nietzsche's style; in his post-Wagnerian period, this was, no doubt, a contributing factor to his distaste for the book and its idiom.

Nevertheless, having looked to these precedents, we must look back to Nietzsche himself. The centaur, with all its eccentricities, is not engendered by precedents. It is engendered by Nietzsche's inability to specialize or, more precisely, by his refusal to accept the Western tradition of specialized and compartmentalized rational thought and the kinds of limitation associated with that tradition and appropriate to it. The mode of the book is explained by its content and, in particular, by the disjunction, as Nietzsche sees it, of art and thought brought about by Socratism. After a fleeting glimpse, afforded by the Platonic dialogue, into the possibility of a new *artistic* philosophy, the logical-analytical and the expressive-imaginative are forced into separate compartments. The dilemma thus created is one from which Nietzsche is no more free than any other post-Socratic, but one to which he is peculiarly sensitive. Accordingly, he shares the dilemma *and* repudiates it. He writes a scenario of life after the Fall *and* defends his scenario – but not by discursive thought, but by a kind of art-thought invented *ad hoc*. The 'artistic Socrates', tantalizingly alluded to as a theoretical possibility in §§ 14–15, is the archetype of what Nietzsche himself aspires to be.

The 'artistic Socrates', however, is not as yet more than a possibility. If Nietzsche is rejecting logical-analytical Socratism, he is reverting not to its artistic equivalent, nor yet to the German literary-philosophical tradition, but, symbolically at least, to the *Pre*socratics – as he was to do, quite literally, in the months after the publication of *BT*. Rohde's private suggestion that his friend's book should be regarded as a 'didactic poem' has a nice relevance here. By way of giving that genre some definition, Rohde added as earlier instances the names of the Presocratics, Xenophanes and Empedocles.[11] These two belonged to the sixth and earlier fifth centuries respectively and both, according to the prelapsarian, unspecialized fashion of their time, philosophized in verse. There is a pleasing irony – which was not, presumably, in Rohde's mind – in the fact that it was Empedocles whose writings Aristotle in the opening section of his *Poetics* chose to illustrate the category of mere verse as against true poetry. Homer, says Aristotle, writes poetry (and so belongs, as we would say, to literature), where Empedocles writes scientific verse. This is not the place to assess Aristotle's criteria for such a judgement (they are primarily mimetic), although it is of interest that by using the same criteria he should apparently be able to claim 'Socratic dialogues' as instances of literary prose. The point is that to this seminal aesthetician and colossus of post-lapsarian logical analysis, mixed modes – Platonic, Empedoclean, or any other – are bound to be of no particular significance.

The idea that the artistic Socrates has a special meaning for Nietzsche is not in itself new. Walter Kaufmann, for instance, writes: 'In the picture of the "theoretical man" who dedicates his life to the pursuit of truth, Nietzsche pays homage to the "dignity" of Socrates. At the same time his own features mingle with those of his ideal (§ 15). Socrates is the antithesis of tragedy, but Nietzsche asks "whether the birth of an 'artistic Socrates' is altogether a contradiction in terms" (§ 14), and nobody has ever found a better characterization of Nietzsche himself. At the end of section 15 we find another self-portrait: "the *Socrates who practises music*" [*der musiktreibende Sokrates*].'[12] Kaufmann, however, has not understood the point. Nietzsche's Socrates practises *Musik*, which in the context is not 'music', but *mousikē* in its wider Greek sense of 'poetry' or 'art'.[13] The 'Socrates who practises *mousikē*' has nothing directly to do with the Nietzsche who esteems and composes music, but once again with the Nietzsche who devises a new kind of conceptual art in *BT* itself. The paradox, Socratic *mousikē*, points to a mode of artistic discourse for which *BT* is the original, perhaps imperfect, prototype.

In this connection the genesis of Nietzsche's Socrates is of renewed interest. Socrates, whether the historical or the Nietzschean Socrates, is essentially an inartistic, non-literary figure. Unlike his pupil, Plato, he is an oral teacher and not a writer of any kind – except for those special, belated compositions on which the paradox in question is based. But as we have noted, before Nietzsche selected Socrates as his archetype of rationalism, his Greek rationalist was *Democritus*,[14] who, unlike Socrates, is very much a writer – and a writer of artistic prose at that. In his notes on Democritus in 1867 and early 1868, Nietzsche repeatedly draws attention to his combination of qualities, 'lust for knowledge – lucidity – poetic charge' (*Wissenstrieb – Klarheit – dichterischer Schwung*)[15] – which not only reads like shorthand for Socratism plus art, but is not so far from the triad Socratic–Apolline–Dionysiac itself. Two years later, however, when that triad is in process of evolution, such versatility can only represent a most unwelcome ambivalence. *BT* presupposes a cultural dilemma: art and thought are, but should not be, disjunct – hence the need for the centaur, the difficulty of achieving it, the aptness of the paradox of the 'artistic Socrates'. But if art and thought can so readily coexist as the case of Democritus might suggest, there is no dilemma, no paradox, no occasion for a paradox, and the painfully achieved mixed mode of *BT* itself is mocked.

On Nietzsche's behalf one could easily argue that Democritus is untypical, being perhaps a transitional figure who retains something of the wholeness of the old while embracing the single-mindedness of the new; or else that the Greek analogy, in which such a conjunction *is* possible, is inexact for modern purposes. But neither of these arguments is open to Nietzsche himself. He is committed to archetypes, and their essence is that they be representative. He is also committed to a reverential view of Greece and a schematic notion of cultural history whereby the Greek analogy provides the key to the interpretation of modern developments. The versatile philosopher who was the object of his earlier researches is therefore something of a nuisance, an obstacle to the coherence of his new endeavour. For this reason as much as any other, Democritus, Socrates' contemporary and fellow-rationalist must be tacitly reinterpreted as a pre-rationalist Presocratic – a late specimen of 'the whole man' in a changing world – and removed from the scene for the monolithic rationalizer Socrates to take his place.

The artistic Socrates, then, is code for Nietzsche himself; but there is more to the code than this. If Nietzsche is, or would like to be, an improved version of the great rationalist, who or what is Wagner? – that 'great artist to whom [*BT*] addressed itself as in a dialogue', as Nietzsche puts it in the *Self-Criticism* (§ 2). In Nietzsche's circle, where that dialogue arose, Wagner was Aeschylus. 'The great Aeschylus', Cosima could write to Nietzsche without further explanation, 'you will find at Tribschen'.[16] The inartistic Socrates is the enemy of tragedy (§ 14) and tragedy is epitomized by Aeschylus; the artistic Socrates, conversely, will be the supporter and spokesman for tragedy, as Nietzsche–Socrates is the supporter and spokesman for Wagner–Aeschylus. And if this is the relationship of Nietzsche to Wagner, there is also a relationship between their works. Wagner's *Gesamtkunstwerk* represents an attempt to reconstitute the 'total art' of Aeschylean Greece, while the hybrid *BT* is a parallel attempt on a more intellectual level. It is Nietzsche's conceptualized equivalent of Wagnerian art – and in using that phrase we echo the terms in which Nietzsche characterizes the relation of his predecessors, Schopenhauer and Kant, to Dionysiac 'philosophy'. Those great thinkers, he proclaims, used rationality to demonstrate the limits of rationality (§ 18); their achievement is Dionysiac wisdom in a conceptualized form (*die in Begriffe gefasste dionysische Weisheit*, § 19). That achievement realizes the true aim of rational thought, its conversion into art (§ 15).

Now that we are thinking biographically, we can hardly overlook the parallel with Nietzsche's own earlier career. He chooses the path of 'cold logic' as a remedy for his inner conflicts, but inexorably, as it seems, that path takes him to the limits of logic and across into art. The conflict between the archetypes is, at this point at least, his own inner conflicts writ large; the personal significance of the book which he stresses in the *Self-Criticism* (§ 1–2) is nowhere more pressing.

Nietzsche's identification with the artistic Socrates also sheds light on his antagonism towards Plato, who, though rejecting art, 'was nevertheless constrained by sheer artistic necessity to create an art-form', albeit one which in its eccentricity mixed 'all extant styles and forms, hovering midway between narrative, lyric and drama, between prose and poetry' (§ 14). The constraint to create and the hybridity of the work created are, for Nietzsche, irritatingly close to his own condition – irritatingly, because Plato was presiding over the dissolution of that old order which Nietzsche is now straining to recall. To interpret *BT* as an autobiographical document helps to explain how Nietzsche can be quite so personally involved with Plato and other figures from the past. It also allows us to treat philosophy as he himself in his later years gives us every encouragement to treat it, for one of the tenets of his mature thought is the 'idea of reducing philosophical systems to the status of personal records'.[17] Few of Nietzsche's readers would wish to take the reductivist, autobiographical interpretation of his book so far as to lose sight of its status as a comment on the objective realities of past and present. It is very much to the point, however, that to invoke objectivity at all is something which Nietzsche himself will feel increasingly unable to do. In *BT* §5 he attacks Schopenhauer's use of the opposition between subjective and objective in aesthetics, which is to be merely the first of a long series of philosophical manoeuvres that culminate in an attempt to unseat the notion of objective reality altogether:

Subject, object, attribute – these distinctions are fabricated and are now imposed as a schematism upon all the apparent facts...It is only after the model of the subject that we have invented the reality of things...Man projects his drive to truth, his 'goal' in a certain sense, outside himself as a world that has being, as a metaphysical world, as a 'thing-in-itself', as a world already in existence. His needs as creator invent the world upon which he works.[18]

That is the Nietzsche of the 1880s talking; the young author of *BT* who can invoke 'the unvarnished expression of the truth' (§ 8) – albeit the truth of poetry not science – has not yet reached this stage. A movement away from 'the reality of things' is nevertheless latent in the mode of the book. In his shift from 'objective' scholarship to artistic centaur, Nietzsche has begun to erode the barrier between the object and himself, the supposedly disinterested subject. That barrier is nowhere so undermined as by his autobiographical projections.

CENTRIPETAL IMAGES

Nietzsche's search for an appropriate idiom for *BT* produces some remarkable effects. Among these is a peculiar kind of sustained intensity, an insistent cohesiveness, as a result of which the great variety of separate topics that Nietzsche deals with give one a feeling of being related, even though it is not easy to say in what their relatedness consists. One of the chief sources of this effect is imagery: metaphor and simile. Imagery, of course, abounds in *BT*, and some of it straightforwardly supports the variety and heterogeneity of the book. It is, so to speak, centrifugal. When, for example, Nietzsche describes the New Comedy of Menander as 'a game of chess' (§ 11), he introduces an idea extraneous to the topics under discussion or about to be discussed. Not only are we required to direct our thoughts to tragedy and Wagner, myth and Socrates – and to such lesser topics as New Comedy as well; we also have to think, however perfunctorily, about chess; and chess has no necessary connection or relevant association with any of these topics.

In any piece of writing, of course, introduction of extraneous material is generally a corollary of using imagery at all, and if imagery ever appears without that corollary, this is usually because the image in question belongs to a theme or leitmotif which has acquired topical status in its own right. In Aeschylus' *Seven Against Thebes* there is a recurrent image of a ship in a storm. Ships and storms have in themselves no connection with the fortunes of the house of Oedipus which form the subject of the play, but once established, the nautical theme is as proximate to the centre of the drama as patriotism, devices on shields, the curse of Oedipus, or any of the play's 'literal' concerns. In the same writer's *Oresteia* there is a legal theme that runs through the whole trilogy, beginning in the *Agamemnon* with the chorus' description of Menelaus as a 'claimant at law' against Priam.[19] This time, however, there is an important difference. Law and legality have an organic connection with the matters presented in the trilogy, and the conclusion of the legal theme is in fact the actual trial of Orestes at the climax of the final play. There is, then, an interplay here between imagery and the 'proper' content of the drama, and in its relation to the content of the work as a whole the legal imagery is centripetal in tendency.

What Nietzsche offers us is different from either of these Aeschylean patterns, but appreciably closer to the second. His imagery is not thematic in any ordinary sense, but much of it is intensely centripetal: he presents a long string of isolated images, a surprising number of which are drawn directly from the underlying concerns of his book, and in many cases directly from the immediate concern of the moment. In § 2, for instance, he tells us how Apollo, as the dominant force in the Greece of the Homeric period, nullified the threat posed to the Greeks by 'the feverish excitements' of Dionysiac worship among their barbarian neighbours. Nietzsche, however, does not say 'nullified...'; he says, 'held out the Gorgon's head to...' – that is, turned to stone:

For some time, however, the Greeks were apparently perfectly insulated and protected against the feverish excitements of these festivals, though knowledge of them came to Greece on all the routes of land and sea; for the figure of Apollo, rising full of pride, held out the Gorgon's head to this grotesquely uncouth Dionysiac power...

It is appropriate that *Apollo* should turn the uncouth power to *stone*, because the Nietzschean Apollo is associated with stone in his capacity as god of sculpture. And it is, of course, especially appropriate that he should be made to do the turning-to-stone in the terminology of Greek myth ('Gorgon's head'), to which he himself belongs. But there is no logic to this appropriateness, except for the logic of metalepsis.* The standing of the image itself (which has no particular distinction) is not affected. What is affected and enhanced – enhanced by the cumulative force of many such instances – is the homogeneity and vitality of Nietzsche's work as a whole.

Compared with the deployment of images in a leitmotif, which has become something of a commonplace to the modern literary critic, this metaleptic use is unfamiliar[20] and it deserves a generous measure of exemplification. The following are cases parallel to the 'Gorgon's head'. (The italics are ours throughout.)

§3, the Olympian gods justify life by living it themselves, and so –

existence under the *bright sunshine* of such gods is regarded as desirable in itself, and the real pain of Homeric men is caused by parting from it.

The Olympians are Apolline deities and Apollo – for Nietzsche – is the sun-god.

§4, the Apolline and the Dionysiac achieve at last their highest form of reconciliation:

the sublime and celebrated art of Attic tragedy...presents itself as the common goal of both these tendencies, whose mysterious union, after many long precursory struggles, found glorious consummation in this child – at once *Antigone and Cassandra.*

Tragedy is metaphorically equated with two tragic characters. (The metaphor, incidentally, has not been understood. Wilamowitz commented: 'Whoever explains these last words, to which Mephistopheles' remark about the witch's arithmetic is applicable, will receive a suitable reward from me.'[21] Nietzsche is thinking ahead to tragedy's painful death, which he expounds in §11. By 'Antigone' he means that tragedy was to die in a noble cause, by 'Cassandra' that at its death tragedy would be offering the most profound truths, but was doomed not to be believed.)

* 'Metalepsis: metonymy, especially of a double, complicated, or indirect kind' (*Chambers's Twentieth Century Dictionary*).

§5, on the lyric poet:

he who, according to the experience of all ages, is continually saying 'I' and running through the entire *chromatic scale* of his passions and desires.

Lyric poetry is essentially a Dionysiac art, music is the Dionysiac art *par excellence*, and *Greek* lyric poetry was literally musical anyway. The allusion to the 'chromatic' aspect of music has a particular point, for it evokes Wagner.

§10, the original hero of Greek tragedy was Dionysus, and furthermore –

it may be claimed with equal confidence that, until Euripides, Dionysus never ceased to be the tragic hero; that all the celebrated figures of the Greek stage – Prometheus, Oedipus, etc. – are mere *masks* for this original hero, Dionysus.

'Masks' recalls one of the permanent conventions of 'the Greek stage'. The tragic masks are what the tragic heroes wore. The metaphor and the metalepsis are echoed in §12, where Euripides is described as a mask for Socrates.

§10, Dionysiac music revived Greek myth:

What power was it that transformed the myth into a vehicle of Dionysiac wisdom? It is the *Heraclean* power of music: having reached its highest manifestation in tragedy, it can invest myths with a new and most profound significance.

Heracles, besides being a proverbial strong man, is one of the celebrated suffering mythical heroes of Greek music drama itself (Sophocles' *Trachiniae*, Euripides' *Heracles*).

§10, on the same:

Through tragedy the myth attains its most profound content, its most expressive form; it rises once more *like a wounded hero*.

The tragic Heracles (or whoever) again.

§11, on the death of tragedy:

Greek tragedy met an end different from that of her older sister-arts: she *died* by *suicide*...

i.e. like a tragic hero

...in consequence of an irreconcilable *conflict*...

i.e. as in a tragedy

she died *tragically*, while all the others passed away calmly and beautifully at a ripe old age.

Metalepsis could hardly be simpler.

§11, on the same:

Just as Greek sailors in the time of Tiberius once heard on a lonely island the soul-shaking cry, 'Great Pan is dead', so the Hellenic world was now pierced by the grievous lament: 'Tragedy is dead! Poetry itself has perished with her!'

Sailors, islands and Tiberius represent, by Nietzschean standards, an extreme digression, but *Pan* is something else. As fertility spirit and half-goat, he is a figure comparable to Dionysus' satyrs and, like the Sileni, was eventually drawn into the Dionysiac mythological circle himself.[22] He can therefore claim an association – albeit at two metaleptic removes – with Tragedy herself.

§12, Euripides recanted too late:

Dionysus had already been scared from the tragic stage by a *demonic* power speaking through Euripides. Even Euripides was, in a sense, only a mask: the *deity* that spoke through him was neither Dionysus nor Apollo, but an altogether newborn *daemon*, called Socrates.

'Daemon' and 'demonic' inevitably recall the *daimonion*, the name given by Plato and others to Socrates' famous 'daemonic' voice,[23] which Nietzsche himself discusses in §13.

§12, Socrates as enemy of Dionysus:

He is the new *Orpheus* who rose against Dionysus, and although he is destined to be *torn to pieces by the maenads* of the Athenian court...

The imagery is drawn from the Orpheus–Dionysus myth which we recounted in connection with Orphism and Aeschylus' *Bassarids*.[24]

§21, on the sufferings of the tragic hero:

he, *like a powerful Titan, takes the whole* Dionysiac *world on his back* and thus relieves us of this burden.

The 'Titan' in question is obviously Atlas who, according to late Greek sources, was the Titans' leader in the mythical struggle against Zeus.[25] Titanic mythology, we remember, was Nietzsche's favourite example of Dionysiac 'pessimism' before Homer (§§3–4).

This list, which does not pretend to be exhaustive, exemplifies the type in its pure form. There are some instances where there is a centripetal evocation, but not one that is felicitously brought to mind at the particular time. At such a moment, then, there is a minor clash between the interests of the immediate context and those of the book as a whole (which are served by *any* intensification of its homogeneity).

§3, on the triumphant exuberance of Homeric man:

the spectator may stand quite bewildered before this fantastic excess of life, asking himself by virtue of what magic *potion* these high-spirited men could have found life so enjoyable...

Homeric man is Apolline man, but 'magic potion' (*Zaubertrank*) evokes alcohol or drugs and therefore suggests Dionysiac release from the phenomenal world rather than Apolline glorification of it.

§9, Sophocles gives the dark truths embodied in the Oedipus myth a lighter, Apolline treatment:

'The edge of wisdom turns against the wise: wisdom is a crime against nature': such horrible sentences are proclaimed to us by the myth; but the Hellenic poet *touches* the sublime and terrible *Memnon's column* of myth *like a sunbeam*, so that it suddenly begins to sound – in Sophoclean *melodies*.

'Memnon's column' was a colossal statue near Thebes in ancient Egypt which is said to have emitted a sound resembling a breaking chord when struck by the sun's first rays each morning. The image is ingenious, but in point of propriety it has got somewhat out of hand. It may be all right for a tragedian in his Apolline capacity to be a sunbeam, but myth is too Dionysiac to be architectural-sculptural ('Memnon's column'), while the product of Apolline genius is not Dionysiac enough to be musical ('melodies'). This is more than a quibble: it is Nietzsche, after all, who has used correlations so insistently that we have come to expect them.

§12, Euripides, having helped to destroy tragedy, is sorry, but –

the most magnificent *temple lies in ruins*. What use is the lamentation of the destroyer to us, or his confession that it was the *most beautiful of all temples*?

An infelicity comparable to 'Memnon's column'. Tragedy is ultimately the triumph of the Dionysiac, as Nietzsche insists in §21. It is not, therefore, to be thought of in plastic terms, even if Nietzsche does recur to the same image in the very last sentence of the book (where tragedy is 'the temple of both deities', §25) and also produces something of the kind for the 'ineffably sublime and sacred' – and Dionysiac[26] – music of Palestrina in §19: 'the *vaulted structure* of Palestrina harmonies...' Having established his centripetal mode, Nietzsche might have been expected to confine himself to musical imagery for tragedy, as he does, unobtrusively enough, in the passage from §21 just alluded to:

In the total effect of tragedy, the Dionysiac predominates once again. Tragedy closes with a *sound* which could never come from the realm of Apolline art.

At the opposite end of the spectrum to such subdued effects, there are instances – in general very successful ones – where centripetal imagery is employed on a larger, more extended scale. There is a simple case in §24, where Nietzsche depicts Wagner's impending renewal of 'the German spirit' in terms taken directly from Wagnerian saga and the Siegfried myth in particular:

We were comforted by indications that in some inaccessible abyss the German spirit still rests and dreams, undestroyed, in glorious health, profundity, and Dionysiac strength, like a knight sunk in slumber...Some day, it will find itself awake in all the morning freshness following a tremendous sleep: then it will kill dragons, destroy vicious dwarfs, wake Brünnhilde – and even Wotan's spear will not be able to stop its course!

The 'exhaustion' of contemporary culture and Nietzsche's hopes for the future prompt another instance in §20:

In vain we look for a single vigorously developed root, for a spot of fertile and healthy soil: everywhere there is dust and sand...But how suddenly the desert of our exhausted culture...is changed, once touched by the Dionysiac magic! A tempest seizes everything that has outlived itself, everything that is decayed, broken and withered, and, whirling, shrouds it in a cloud of red dust to carry it into the air like a vulture.

Dionysus – meaning Wagner's music drama – will destroy the exhausted culture and bring back natural 'fertility' (the imagery is clearly a source for Eliot's *Waste Land*), because Dionysus is literally a fertility-god. The sudden mention of a vulture (*Geier*) appears, by contrast, to be totally extraneous, but it too points inward. Geyer (in old spelling) was Wagner's boyhood surname, and it was the name of his stepfather who was in all probability his real father. Nietzsche had apparently been told as much when staying at Tribschen in the winter of 1869–70.[27] At that time he was also involved in helping Wagner with the publication of his autobiography, *Mein Leben*. In the explicit narrative of that work Wagner did not represent himself as Geyer's son, but he took special pains to have a vulture engraved as a decorative emblem for the work. The *Geier* was to be his secret symbol of the ancestry that he preferred not to publicize directly. In a letter to Nietzsche in January 1870 he wrote: 'The crest turned out very well...However, I still have the same misgivings as regards the *vulture* [*Geier*], which will unquestionably be taken for an eagle [*Adler*] at first glance...It is of the greatest importance, on account of the associations, that the vulture should be instantly recognizable...'[28] If Wagner could use the *Geier* as his symbol, so could Nietzsche. The Dionysiac vulture, by that simple code, is Wagner himself: the autobiographical resonances and the centripetal mode of the book have converged.

A finer instance than either of the last two comes in §3, where Nietzsche proposes

> to *level* the artistic *structure* of Apolline culture, as it were, *stone by stone*, till the *foundations on which it rests* become *visible*. First of all we see the glorious Olympian *figures* of the gods, *standing on the gables of this structure*. Their deeds, *pictured in brilliant reliefs, adorn its friezes*. We must not be misled by the fact that Apollo *stands side by side* with the others...

Apolline culture – meaning the culture that expresses itself through 'individuation', form, bright and beautiful illusion, and, in general, 'serenity' – is depicted as plastic-architectural Apolline art. *This* is the instance that shows why the idea of tragedy as a temple is out of place. The terms of the image seem so natural that one's inclination is to respond to it not as to an analogy at all, but as to an example. The relationship between Apollinity and its various properties is persuasively conveyed, and in its persuasive force the imagery is made to operate almost as a demonstrative argument.

Finally, from §5, the famous characterization of man the artist as himself the 'artistic' creation of a higher power:

> For to our humiliation and exaltation, one thing above all must be clear to us. The entire *comedy of art* is not *performed* for our betterment or education, nor are we the true creators of this *art* world. On the contrary, we may assume that for the real creator we have been *images* and *artistic projections* all along, and that we have our highest dignity in our significance as *works of art* – for only as an *aesthetic phenomenon* [Nietzsche's italics as well as ours] can existence and the world be eternally justified ...Thus all our knowledge of art is basically quite illusory, because as knowing beings we are not one and identical with that being which, as the sole creator and *spectator* of this *comedy of art*, prepares a perpetual *entertainment* for itself. Only insofar as the genius in the act of artistic creation coalesces with this primordial *artist* of the world does he know anything of the eternal essence of art...

The passage has its congeners elsewhere, more theoretically in §24, and more purely imagistically in §1, where the participant in Dionysiac song and dance

> is no longer an artist, he has become a *work of art*: in these paroxysms of intoxication the *artistic* power of all nature reveals itself to the highest gratification of the primordial unity. Here the noblest *clay*, the most costly *marble*, man, is *kneaded* and *cut*, and to the sound of the *chisel strokes* of the Dionysiac world-*artist*...

The overwhelming interest of these passages is their significance for Nietzsche's aesthetics and metaphysics, but here we note the mode of imagery on which they and much of their force depend. We also observe that – except for his momentary status as author of a Dantesque 'comedy'? – the world-artist appears to be an Apolline creator. Even without the 'clay', 'marble' and 'chisel strokes' of §1, the 'images' and 'projections' of §5 would indicate this. Such an impropriety at the very heart of Nietzsche's philosophy is striking, to say the least. In §25, by contrast, the medium of the Dionysiac world-artist is more decorously represented as *music*, with man defined in terms of 'dissonance'.

LITERAL AND PARALITERAL

One instance of centripetal imagery is more momentous and more complex than any yet diagnosed as such: Nietzsche's three great archetypes, Dionysus, Apollo, and Socrates. When Nietzsche tells us that 'Socrates' went to his death calmly (§13), this is the literal Socrates, who literally and legitimately belongs to his discussion of Greek creativity. When, however, Nietzsche perceives a 'power' speaking through Euripides and identifies that power as 'Socrates' (§12), he is giving the name to something that in his judgement bears an essential similarity to this historical Socrates. This is metaphor, and as in the easier examples of centripetal imagery discussed above, the vehicle of the metaphor is drawn from one of the underlying topics of the book; the effect, moreover, is argumentative, as it was in the example of the Apolline temple in §3. Again, when Nietzsche calls the dithyramb Dionysiac, this is literal. When he calls music (other than the music of the dithyramb) Dionysiac, this is metaphor. Apollo's cult-song, the nome – had Nietzsche ever mentioned it – would be literally Apolline; epic is Apolline only metaphorically. The metaphors in each case are centripetal.

Nietzsche's archetypes, however, have some special features. Whereas centripetal images are, as a rule, easily identifiable as images, it is often far from obvious, especially to the non-specialist reader, when (for instance) 'Dionysiac' is being used literally and when not. There are also uses which even the most erudite analyst would have to pronounce indeterminate, such as the ascription of Dionysiac status to lyric poetry, midway (as it seems) between the literally Dionysiac dithyramb and the metaphorically Dionysiac world of music. There are, finally, uses involving a different kind of extension, and not metaphor at all: Dionysiac truth, as opposed to Apolline illusion, for example. The implication is that it would be artifical to pursue the analysis of the archetypes in these terms. While not forgetting the centripetal propensity of the construct as a whole, we would do better to distinguish individual uses of 'Dionysus', 'Apollo' and 'Socrates' as literal and (let us say) paraliteral, a word which is meant to evoke that aura of literal grounding which the three terms never quite lose, even in their most abstract applications. Dionysus' claim to the dithyramb is literal; his claim to lyric as a whole, paraliteral; his claim to music and 'pessimism' and the ground of being, paraliteral to a much greater degree.

By 'literal grounding', we mean the relation of Nietzsche's terms to their – Greek – sources. As literal entities, his Dionysus, Apollo, and Socrates obviously derive directly from historical Greek reality, or ancient testimony to it. In their first paraliteral stage, this is still partly true. Nietzsche's representation of Silenus as Dionysiac depends on ancient authority, although not as ancient as it would have to be for the representation to count as literal. The idea of Apollo as the bright sun-god is Greek, but probably no earlier than the fifth century. It is Orphic sources, but not strictly relevant sources, that provide Nietzsche with a certain justification for making Dionysus the god of primordial 'oneness'. And even the equation of Socrates and Greek rationalism has a certain Greek basis, in that eye-witnesses of the great rationalist himself had already taken to representing him as the typical Greek intellectual that we love to hate (Aristophanes' *Clouds*) as well as the model Greek thinker (Plato, *passim*) – in either case freely attributing to their Socrates doctrines or attitudes which we have every reason to believe the historical Socrates never held.[29] At the paraliteral extreme, by contrast, there is no discernible connection between the construct and historical reality at all. Dionysiac ground of being and Apolline illusion, for instance: however suggestive this addition to the antithetical properties of the two archetypes, it is hard to see any Greek basis for it.

We are left with a large intermediate area between the extremes, in which there is a Greek basis, but not one of a historically respectable kind. In this area the support that the Greek sources give consists of no more than incidental associations. It is, once again, essentially metaleptic in character. An example we have already met is the association between Dionysus and 'pessimistic' wisdom. This association has no substantial historical authority. In part it presupposes Orphic doctrine. For the rest it depends on the assimilation to the Dionysiac of Silenus, who *is* associated with wisdom and (on the strength of the Midas anecdote that Nietzsche quotes in §3) might be said to be associated with pessimism too.[30] In logical terms, the argument is:

a is associated with *b*;
b is associated with *c*;
therefore *a* is associable with *c* –

but of course the argument never is presented in bare logical terms. So uncommunicative, indeed, is Nietzsche about his procedures that this is one of the very few examples where we can reconstruct the missing link (the *b*) with any certainty. On the basis of such examples, however, together with Nietzsche's general inclination towards metalepsis, we conclude that this is how most of the paraliteral attributes are generated:

RIDDLE: *what is the link between Dionysus and pessimistic wisdom?* ANSWER: *Silenus and the Orphics.*

RIDDLE: *why is Buddhism associated with Dionysus (§§18, 21, 7)?* ANSWER: *because Buddhism is originally Indian, and there was a legend, which attained some popularity after the eastern adventures of Alexander the Great, that Dionysus with his company of ecstatic followers had conquered India itself, and returned home in triumph.*[31] Nietzsche alludes to the legend himself (§20):

> The age of Socratic man is over; put on wreaths of ivy, put the thyrsus into your hand, and do not be surprised when tigers and panthers lie down, fawning, at your feet. Only dare to be tragic men; for you are to be redeemed. You shall join the Dionysiac pageant from India to Greece.

The idea that 'the entire Aryan community of peoples' was Dionysiac, which is implicit in the discussion of Prometheus in §9, presumably relies on the same association. On the basis of nineteenth-century comparative philology, the Aryan (i.e. Indo-Iranian) languages in general, and Sanskrit in particular, were widely, though erroneously, supposed to be closest to the 'primeval' parent tongue – that is, the common source of Sanskrit, Greek, Germanic, etc. That parent language, which is now known as 'Indo-European' (or 'Indo-Germanic'), was, accordingly, often referred to as 'Aryan' itself, and the 'community of peoples' that spoke the language was widely supposed to have originated near or even in India.[32] (Nietzsche's motives, we note, are liable to differ from his pretexts. His motive for Indianizing Dionysus is to accommodate within his schema the Indian – Buddhistic – affinities of Schopenhauerianism.)

RIDDLE: *why is lyric poetry Dionysiac?* ANSWER: *because in a memorable passage of the* Ion, *Plato compares Greek lyric song-composition to Dionysiac ecstasy:*

> just as Corybantic dancers perform when they are not in their right mind, so the lyric poets compose these beautiful songs when they are not in theirs; once involved in melody [*harmonian*] and rhythm, they are in a state of possession and it is then – just as women draw honey and milk from the rivers under Bacchic possession, but not when in their right mind – it is then that the lyric poets have the experience they describe to us.[33]

(Plato has, however, said the same of *epic* poets in the sentence immediately before.)

RIDDLE: *why is music Dionysiac?* ANSWER: *because of a set of incidental associations between tragedy (which is Dionysiac in origin), orgiastic ritual (of a Dionysiac type) and music, which chiefly centre on the word* katharsis. This is the word which Aristotle uses in the *Poetics* for the 'purgative' effect of tragedy (presumably the emotional *release* it provides), and the word he uses in his *Politics* for the effect on listeners – especially on morbid, or as we would say neurotic, listeners – of 'enthusiastic' music, to which category Dionysiac music did or would belong. The whole question of *katharsis* and the relation between the two Aristotelian discussions had recently been aired by the controversy surrounding Bernays' essay on the subject in 1857;[34] Nietzsche himself alludes to the dispute in §22.

RIDDLE: *why is early tragedy Dionysiac? – that is, why is tragedy of the Aeschylean period Dionysiac (as opposed to proto-tragedy, which is literally so)?* ANSWER: *because Aristophanes in the* Frogs *refers to Aeschylus'* mania, *'madness', and at one point calls him 'the Bacchic king',*[35] *and because (very possibly under the influence of those references) there is a later biographical tradition that details his 'Dionysiac' connection.* There is, first, a story that (as the raconteur Athenaeus, *c.* A.D. 200, put it) 'Aeschylus composed his tragedies when drunk', or in Plutarch's words, a century earlier, that all Aeschylus' plays are 'full of Dionysus', i.e. the after-effects of wine.[36] There is also a charming anecdote recorded by the traveller Pausanias in the second century A.D.: 'Aeschylus said that when he was a boy he fell asleep while guarding grapes in a field, and that Dionysus appeared and told him to write tragedy.'[37] As far as historical verisimilitude goes, these anecdotes are on a somewhat lower level than those connecting Euripides and Socrates which Nietzsche cites with such relish in §13.[38] In the light of the foregoing discussion his appeal to that 'evidence' too may be relevant here.

From Dionysus to Apollo. RIDDLE: *why is epic Apolline?* ANSWER: *because the Olympian gods are all judged to be Apolline (§3), and it is they, but not, as we have seen, Dionysus, who bulk so large in the epics of Homer.*[39] (It is also worth mentioning that Greek epic and Apollo's oracles at Delphi used the same metre, the dactylic hexameter.)

RIDDLE: *why are 'the Dorian state' (meaning Sparta) and Doric art regarded as specially Apolline (§4)?* ANSWER: *because according to the conventions of Greek music Apollo's nome was written in the Dorian mode.*[40]

RIDDLE: *why is the Apolline order derived from the Dionysiac? – 'the Dionysiac is seen to be, compared to the Apolline, the eternal and original artistic power that first calls the whole world of phenomena into existence' (§25).* ANSWER: *because Herodotus, expounding the religion of ancient Egypt in the second half of the fifth century* B.C., *says that the god Orus is the son of Osiris and, offering equations for the benefit of his Greek public, explains that 'the Greeks call Orus* Apollo. . .*while Osiris is* Dionysus *in the Greek language.'*[41]

RIDDLE: *what have dreams got to do with Apollo?* POSSIBLE ANSWER: *Phemonoe.* This was a legendary woman, who, according to a variety of late accounts, was daughter of Apollo (Pliny the Elder), the first priestess of Apollo at Delphi (Pausanias, Strabo), and alleged authoress of a book on dreams (Artemidorus).[42] For good measure, and very pertinently, she is also said to have invented the saying 'know thyself' (Antisthenes of Rhodes), and even to have invented epic poetry (Proclus, *Etymologicum Magnum*) – though this last claim probably means no more than that she was the first to use 'epic' metre, the dactylic hexameter, whose original employment was assumed to have been in Apolline oracles.[43]

RIDDLE: *why is Socrates equal in status to the deities Dionysus and Apollo? – 'the deity that spoke through [Euripides] was neither Dionysus nor Apollo, but an altogether newborn daemon called Socrates'* (§ *12*). ANSWER: *for a variety of reasons. First and foremost, because of the implications of Nietzsche's parallel between tragedy and the Platonic dialogue.* Tragedy had as its original hero Dionysus (§ 10); the new dialogue was the medium through which Plato challenged tragedy (§ 14); the Platonic dialogue had as its 'hero' Socrates (§ 14); *therefore*, Socrates is on a par with (as well as hostile to) Dionysus – and if to Dionysus, then to Apollo too. As far as Apollo is concerned, there was also a recurrent theme in the ancient biographies of Plato – including the one, well known to Nietzsche, by Diogenes Laertius – that Plato himself (although not Socrates) was associated with Apollo and even that 'Apollo was somehow Plato's father'.[44] Then there is – one step down – the famous Platonic comparison of Socrates to a *Silenus*;[45] and, for what it may be worth in this connection, the mass of evidence for the hostility of the Platonic Socrates to Dionysiac music and tragedy (there is also fifth-century testimony to Socrates' antipathy to tragedy in Aristophanes' *Frogs*), and his sympathy for Apolline music and the god Apollo himself.[46]

Some or all of these sets of associations helped Nietzsche on his way to the construct as it appears in the book. Two other probable associations should be added, both of them strictly post-classical and both exceptionally trivial, if judged as intellectual grounds for the links one supposes them to have assisted. First, Nietzsche may well have been encouraged in his association of Wagner with Dionysus because – among other reasons – in his salon at Tribschen Wagner had a water-colour of 'Bacchus among the Muses' by the painter Bonaventura Genelli (1798–1868) to which he was specially attached: it was through this painting (as he once told King Ludwig) that he had first really perceived the Greek ideal of beauty.[47] Secondly, the idea of Apollo as god of sculpture may have been adventitiously influenced by the special status for Winckelmann and later aestheticians of one particular statue depicting the god, the Belvedere Apollo.[48] Other elements in the construct, finally, may be taken to have been inferred or reinforced from some part of the construct itself. For instance, once the association between Apollo and epic is established, the relation between Dionysus and lyric becomes that much more plausible. In the same way, Dionysiac 'excess' may have been generated or validated by Apolline restraint (which is a specifiable part of the Greek Apollo's make-up);[49] the Dionysiac status of Wagner by the equivalent status of Wagner's idol, Aeschylus;[50] and the Dionysiac status of the Titans (§§ 3, 4) by the Apolline status of Nietzsche's Olympians (because the Titans were the Olympians' mythological enemies), although the quite separate Orphic association of Dionysus and the Titans is equally important here.[51] Similarly, 'Apolline optimism' is facilitated by 'Dionysiac pessimism'; 'Dorian Apollo', in a geographical or cultural sense, by 'Phrygian Dionysus' (because Phrygia was one of the god's mythical homes and *Dorian* and *Phrygian* are antithetical in Greek music);[52] and 'Apolline individuation' by the Dionysiac 'oneness' of the Orphics and, in a different way, by the epidemic, communal, *mass* anonymity of the Dionysiac (§§ 1, 8) in its social – or anti-social – capacity.[53]

THE ORIGINALITY OF THE DIONYSIAC–APOLLINE ANTITHESIS

Our discussion of the mode of Nietzsche's book has brought us to the question of his sources and, with it, we come to the large question of his originality. One of the most striking features of *BT* is its unorthodoxy. But even with the wholly unorthodox, there is no such thing as absolute originality. Even at its most surprising – in the construct, for instance – *BT* is in fact dependent on a great variety of source-material, most of it derived from those two areas that Nietzsche knows about and cares about: ancient Greece and the modern world of German art and intellect.[54]

To begin with Nietzsche's construct: one third of it, at least, is his own idea. There are no precedents (as opposed to paraliteral pretexts) for raising Socrates to the level of Apollo and Dionysus. There are straightforward precedents for *their* opposition: in Greek cult; in the Orphic reinterpretation; in Greek music; and in the more generalized tradition represented by Plutarch. Among other Greek ideas that have influenced Nietzsche's conception is the insistence of his hero, 'the great Heraclitus' (§ 19), on nature as a relationship between opposites, expressed in such aphorisms as:

Things taken together are whole and not whole; conjunction and disjunction, in tune and out of tune; from all things there is one thing and from one thing there are all.[55]

(Heraclitus' musical imagery is also relevant.) Again, insofar as Nietzsche's antithesis is concerned with original artistic energy *versus* artistic form and verbalization, one might detect some influence from the traditional dichotomy between *phusis* and *technē*, better known under the Latin names, *natura* (or *ingenium*, 'nature') and *ars* ('art'), or in its Shakespearean guise:

The poet's eye, in a fine frenzy rolling,
Doth glance from heaven to earth, from earth to heaven,
And as imagination bodies forth
The forms of things unknown, the poet's pen
Turns them to shapes, and gives to airy nothing
A local habitation and a name.[56]

The opposition between, on the one hand, 'things unknown' and 'airy nothing' and, on the other, 'shapes', 'habitation' and 'name' is to the point.

So much for the Greek precedents. On the modern, German side we can distinguish three fairly recent traditions which underlie Nietzsche's antithesis, involving respectively Apollo, Dionysus, and the antithetical habit itself. That habit is in no way peculiar to German thought, but notoriously characteristic of it, not least in the area bounded by psychology, aesthetics and metaphysics, in which Nietzsche's thinking is done. For our purposes, major representatives of the tradition would include the two alluded to in the titles of Schiller's treatise *On Naïve and Sentimental Poetry* (*Über naïve und sentimentalische Dichtung*, 1800) and Schopenhauer's central work *The World as Will and Idea* (*Die Welt als Wille und Vorstellung*, first edition 1819). Both of these pairs can claim to be not only precursors, but formative influences on Nietzsche's. Schopenhauer's antithesis is especially important, along with the further oppositions that it subsumes – reality and illusion, unity and individuation – these being ultimately derived from Plato, though for the heterodox professor of Greek reinforced rather by Heraclitus.[57] Among other pairs we must single out Hölderlin's *Apolline* and *Junonian*. In a letter of 1801 that poet, to whom Nietzsche was to feel so close in his youth, represents Greek culture as a harmonious synthesis of the Apolline 'fire from heaven' (which he takes to be the primary element in the Greek character) and what he calls 'occidental Junonian sobriety' (*die abendländische Junonische Nüchternheit*). It was, Hölderlin believes, the Greeks' excessive cultivation of their Junonian faculty that led to the destruction of true Hellenic balance.[58] A similarity with Nietzsche's schema is apparent – not so much with his Dionysiac *versus*

Apolline, as with his Dionysiac–Apolline *versus* Socratic – and it is possible that he knew of the letter in question.[59]

The Apollo tradition itself can be dealt with very briefly. Hölderlin's Apollo, though not entirely typical of the German Apollo in respect of its implied properties, is abundantly typical in another way: the name is felt to symbolize the truest essence of Greece, even if its precise signification varies according to the particular notion of Greece adhered to. This reverent attitude towards the name can be traced back to Winckelmann's belief that the Belvedere Apollo represented the highest ideal of classical antiquity.[60] By the time Nietzsche was writing *BT*, the name had passed into academic currency as a symbol of that vision of 'Greek serenity' which he was determined to undermine.[61]

The Dionysus tradition is more complicated. During the hundred years that lead up to *BT*, Dionysus (often called Bacchus) becomes an interest and even an obsession among a wide variety of German thinkers, usually as a symbol of sensuality, creativity or natural abundance. The line can be traced through Hölderlin and Novalis to Heine, through Hamann and Herder to Schelling (who expends hundreds of pages on a 'Dionysiological' theory of the evolution of the human spirit in various treatises published between 1813 and 1858), along with a good many lesser writers, artistic and semi-scholarly, *en route*.[62] In this tradition Dionysus is frequently an isolated figure, although Hölderlin in his mature poetry achieves an intuitive synthesis between the Greek god and Christ, which Heine subseqently converts into an antithesis. We have here an anticipation of the formula that will come to occupy Nietzsche in his last phase.[63]

As far as the early Nietzsche is concerned, however, the first really significant use of Dionysus is the point at which the three traditions may be said to meet. This point is reached by Schelling.[64] In the course of a discussion of Dionysus in his posthumously published work, the *Philosophy of Revelation* (*Philosophie der Offenbarung*, III, 1858), Schelling contrasts two types of artistic power, one 'blind, creative' and 'unrestrained', aspiring towards 'an infinite content', the other 'reflective' and 'sober', aspiring towards 'form'. The antithesis with Apollo then abruptly appears:

> not only in God, but even in men – to the extent that they have been blessed with the slightest glimmer of creative power – the same relationship is to be found...: a blind creative power, by its very nature unrestrained, opposed by a reflective, and thus in reality a negative power, residing in the same subject, which restrains and forms this blind power...To be intoxicated and sober, not at different times, but simultaneously – this is the secret of true poetry. It is this which distinguishes

Apolline inspiration from the merely Dionysiac. An infinite content, and thus a content which actually resists form and appears to destroy all form – to depict such an infinite content in its most complete, that is, in its most finite form, is the highest calling of art.[65]

One's first impression of this Schelling passage is of how Nietzschean it is, and not merely because the context concerns art. A closer inspection reveals the differences. The opposition between 'creative' and 'negative' is not compatible with Nietzsche's antithesis: his Dionysiac and Apolline are both equally 'creative', and it is only his 'Socratic' impulse that could be called negative (§13). Moreover, although it is obviously intoxication that is being labelled 'merely Dionysiac' (*bloss dionysisch*), the context does not make it entirely clear whether it is the negative, formalizing power on its own that Schelling associates with 'Apolline inspiration', or rather the synthesis of the two powers. A synthesis, however, is suggested both by the run of the passage and by Schelling's view of Apollo (expressed elsewhere) as an entity which subsumes and is superior to 'the merely Dionysiac'.[66] Schelling's Apollo therefore seems to be closer to Hölderlin's than to Nietzsche's, while his 'negative power' remains without a name. As for Schelling's nomenclature itself, the choice of 'Dionysus' merely follows his dominant mythological preoccupation, while his employment of 'Apollo' no doubt reflects knowledge of the ancient antithesis in its Plutarchan guise. (Like so many German thinkers of his day, Schelling was steeped in Greek ideas – in his case, mythological ideas – and as a young man in 1815 he composed a treatise *On the Deities of Samothrace*.) How far Schelling's discussion anticipates Nietzsche is one question; whether Nietzsche knew of it is another. It is much less likely that the Nietzsche of 1871 had encountered Schelling's antithesis than Hölderlin's.[67]

As far as direct influence goes, Nietzsche had a more significant precursor in a personal acquaintance at Basle and former professor at the University there, Johann Jakob Bachofen, lawyer, social philosopher and theoretician of religious symbolism. The point can be made by setting part of Nietzsche's account of Dionysus in §1 –

> Now the slave is a free man; now all the rigid, hostile barriers that necessity, caprice or 'impudent convention' have fixed between man and man are broken. Now, with the gospel of universal harmony, each one feels himself not only united, reconciled and fused with his neighbour, but as one with him –

alongside Bachofen's representation of the god as 'the promoter of freedom' *vis-à-vis* the state:

> If the political, civil viewpoint everywhere erects barriers, separates peoples and individuals, and expands the principle of individuality to the most complete egotism,

Dionysus, on the other hand, leads everything back to unity, to peace, and to the *philia* of primal life. Slaves as well as free men take part in all mysteries, and all barriers fall before the god of material lust, barriers which political life would raise in time to ever greater heights.[68]

That passage comes from Bachofen's *Discourse on the Tomb Symbolism of the Ancients* (1859). In his most celebrated work, *Mother Right* (*Das Mutterrecht*, 1861), an exposition of matriarchy and patriarchy in the history of antiquity provides the context for a discussion of Dionysus in antithesis with Apollo:

This is the Dionysiac stage of father right, the stage of the god who is celebrated both as the fully developed solar power and as the founder of paternity... Wholly different and far purer is the third stage of solar development, the Apolline stage. The phallic sun, forever fluctuating between rising and setting, coming into being and passing away, is transformed into the immutable source of light... Dionysus merely raised paternity over the mother; Apollo frees himself from any bond with women...

We see paternity falling back from Apolline purity to Dionysiac materiality, so preparing the way for a new victory of the feminine principle, for a new flowering of the mother cults. Although the intimate union which the two luminous powers concluded in Delphi seemed calculated to purify Dionysus' phallic exuberance through Apollo's immutable repose and clarity, and to lift it above itself, the consequence was the exact opposite: the greater sensuous appeal of the fecundating god outweighed his companion's more spiritual beauty... Instead of the Apolline age, it was a Dionysiac age that dawned... Dionysus assimilated all other cults, and finally became the focus of a universal religion which dominated the ancient world.[69]

Once again, we can see an anticipation of Nietzsche, partly in the tone and semi-concrete idiom, partly in notions like that of Apollo's 'immutable repose and clarity'. Bachofen's depiction of the 'universal religion', too, is very reminiscent of Nietzsche's 'secret cult which gradually covered the earth' (§12) – although where Nietzsche is referring to Christianity,[70] Bachofen is alluding to the triumph of syncretistic mystery religion in the Greco-Roman world. But again, fundamental differences are obvious. The social theorist's concern with male and female imbues the two symbols with associations quite alien to those that Nietzsche sets up in his book; and Bachofen's notion of Apollo and Dionysus as both 'solar' powers, but differentiated in terms of Apolline 'spirituality' and Dionysiac 'materiality', is also out of line with *BT*. In his early years at Basle, Nietzsche was on good terms with Bachofen and occasionally visited his house.[71] On those occasions, no doubt, subjects of common intellectual interest would have been aired. It is on record that Nietzsche borrowed Bachofen's *Tomb Symbolism* from the Basle University Library during the composition of *BT* – but in June 1871, after most of the book was already written.[72] All in all, we may conclude that contact with Bachofen must have encouraged Nietzsche to use the antithetical terms, to give them a large signification, and perhaps to invest them with certain of their properties; but, for the rest, we seem to have two independent developments of ancient tradition.

For all these precedents, Nietzsche's construct is new in many aspects – and as a whole. In his hands the antithesis is greatly extended, particularized and elaborated. There remains one outstanding question: Wagner's influence. Wagner, we know, was interested in Dionysus. In June 1870, doubtless in that room where Genelli's picture of 'Bacchus among the Muses' was hanging, Nietzsche read out the earlier of his two Basle lectures, 'Greek Music Drama',[73] and, it appears, a discussion arose (Rohde was also present) in which 'Dionysus' and 'Apollo' may have played a part.[74] In those Basle lectures, we recall, the antithesis was not explicit, whereas in Nietzsche's next draft ('The Dionysiac Philosophy'), composed later that summer, it is amply present.[75] At the end of the year Nietzsche sent a slightly modified version of the draft to Cosima Wagner under the title 'The Birth of Tragic Thought', and on the title page he wrote 'From June of the year 1870',[76] thus paying tribute to the inspiring effect of that particular stay at Tribschen. The Genelli painting no doubt contributed its quota of inspiration. Nietzsche liked his thinking to be sanctioned by coincidences. 'Bacchus among the Muses' had a superfical relevance to his preoccupations, and we find the picture fondly alluded to in a letter to Rohde, and by Rohde himself in his *Pseudo-Philology*.[77] Early in 1871 – still several months before the final version of *BT* – Wagner himself publicly employed the antithesis for the first time. His essay *The Destiny of Opera* invokes, in an off-hand way, the 'compromise of the Apolline with the Dionysiac element' as a formative fact of tragic drama.[78]

The inference to be drawn from these circumstances is that Wagner took the antithesis from Nietzsche, but that Nietzsche himself had already derived or reinforced, his interest in it from the association in his own mind between his musical idol and Dionysus. Some students of the question, it must be said, have reached different conclusions, namely that the borrowing was all one way, that Nietzsche owed the antithesis in its entirety to Wagner, to Wagner's picture, to Wagner's thoughts and ideas as represented in the June conversation.[79] That cannot be. In the first place, there is no evidence for any awareness of the antithesis on Wagner's part prior to that meeting. As long ago as 1849 in his treatise *Art and Revolution* he had, as it happens, produced a panegyric on Apollo in the god's now conventional capacity as 'the Grecian spirit in its fullest expression' and had, *en passant*, alluded to 'the tragic poet inspired by Dionysus',[80] but there is no antithesis in Wagner's mind here – except for a quite irrelevant one between Apollo and *Jesus* –[81] nor, indeed, is any relationship implied between the two deities at all.

Nor is Genelli's masterpiece concerned with an antithesis – on the contrary. The painting portrays only the one deity, Dionysus, in company with Apollo's companions, the Muses.[82] Such a conjunction certainly implies a relationship with Apollo, a relationship not of opposition, but of *identification*: Dionysus is, so to speak, Apollinized. The interest shown by Genelli in this Apolline Dionysus can be traced back to earlier traditions of Renaissance and neo-classical art.[83] There is, for instance, a painting by Poussin from the seventeenth century entitled *Liber Pater qui et Apollo est* – 'Father Bacchus who is also Apollo' – that title being taken from a late Latin discussion of the gods by Macrobius (*c.* A.D. 400).[84] Genelli's own picture belongs to the same tradition: not, that is, the antithetical tradition of Plutarch and early Greek music and cult, but the contrary syncretistic movement which begins in the fifth century B.C. but only reaches its climax centuries later.[85] Whenever it was that the Dionysus–Apollo polarity first fully impinged on Nietzsche, that impact is hardly likely to have been caused by a picture that fails to convey any polarization at all.

But in any case it is quite certain that Nietzsche did not derive the antithesis from Wagner or anything done, said, or owned by Wagner or in any way associated with him. He knew it, and was interested in it, already, as his notes and lectures before the June 1870 meeting make clear. The antithesis is employed in his lectures on Sophocles' *Oedipus Rex*, which must have been composed in the spring of that year, and in his notes from the winter of 1869–70.[86] In fact it can be traced back still further. Early in 1869 – after he had met Wagner once in Leipzig, but before he had ever been to Tribschen – he included in his notes for the forthcoming lectures on Greek lyric poetry a disproportionately long account of the Dionysiac dithyramb, in the course of which comes the following comment: 'essence of Dionysus in change and mutation (Apollo everything ordered and permanent).'[87] And earlier still, in the winter of 1867–8, before he was even particularly interested in Wagner, his notes for a planned paper on the chronology of the early Greek epics contain what are, in that context, totally unexpected comments on 'Dionysiac pessimism' and the alternating Dionysus–Apollo choruses at Delphi.[88]

Our conclusion is that Nietzsche derived from Wagner neither his knowledge of the antithesis nor his interest in it, but that Wagner's own Dionysiac connections (via Genelli) served to reinforce and glamorize that interest. As for the conversation in Tribschen, one can only (at most) conjecture that after Nietzsche – aided, no doubt, by Rohde – had taken up the subject, enthusiasm for the formula on Wagner's side acted as the further stimulus that induced Nietzsche thenceforth to commit himself to its fullest possible elaboration. In this sense, but only in this sense, the June meeting and Wagner's contribution in general will have been formative. Wagner's monomania is well known. In his whole life there seem to have been hardly any occasions when he was capable of disinterested co-operation. This is one of them.

THE ORIGINALITY OF THE BOOK AS A WHOLE

As we turn to the wider question of the overall originality of *BT*, we shall find it useful to think of Wagner's influence as representative, in that it shows itself, above all, in validating a course already marked out. Nietzsche is not a writer one can hope to 'explain' in terms of his influences or sources. He was widely read in the literatures of modern Germany and ancient Greece. There are some earlier writers such as Hölderlin, whom he knew well and with whom he shows marked affinities. There are the three major influences – Schopenhauer, Wagner, and his Greek background. But above all he was a thinker with a sense of direction: one who knew which way his ideas were to go and who, to a large extent, used his 'influences', especially literary ones, to get there. This awareness of his path as his *own* path led not only to the sense of mission that is rightly part of his popular image, but also to a highly ambivalent attitude towards books and reading, even though from childhood he was very much a writer himself. He owned a sizable library,[89] but even before his eyesight deteriorated in the 1870s, he was anything but a model of the disciplined reader. In his Leipzig days he had written to a friend: 'Our whole mode of working is quite horrible. The hundred books on the table in front of me are so many tongs that pinch out the nerve of independent thought.'[90] In 1882 the same resentful impatience produces the rhetorical question, 'What good is a book that does not even carry us beyond all books?', and in 1888 it leads to the caustic reflection that 'scholars who at bottom do little nowadays except thumb books – philologists, at a conservative estimate, about two hundred a day – ultimately lose their capacity to think for themselves.'[91] There is an element of rhetoric in such pronouncements, and neither they nor any other assertions of Nietzsche's independence prevent us from looking into his debts to others, but we should bear them in mind while we do.

Nietzsche being the kind of reader that he was, it is ironic that those who discuss his sources tend to come up with long lists of possibles and probables, to have assimilated which he would have had to spend a whole lifetime of mole-like reading.[92] As far as his Greek background is concerned, we have already gone into sufficient detail. *BT* depends on a wide variety of ancient material ranging from the Orphics to Aristophanes – from whom, we recall, he derives the notion of the death of tragedy and the sinister significance of the new rationalism.[93] As a safeguard against making too much of his classical background, it is salutary to note that in the course of some reflections on antiquity in his late work, *Twilight of the Idols* (1888), he denied that one can 'learn' from the Greeks as one can from the Romans and claimed that in any case 'at bottom it is a very small number of ancient books that counts in my life.'[94] The point about Romans *versus* Greeks, however, chiefly concerns models for his later 'epigrammatic' prose style, while the proper comment on the 'small number of ancient books' has been made by Lloyd-Jones: 'The truth is that in building his philosophy Nietzsche used not so much the doctrines of any individual ancient thinkers, not even that of Heraclitus, whose thought seems to provide several striking parallels, as the religious and ethical attitude held generally in Greece down to the fifth century, and expressed, with variations, by many Greek poets, historians and thinkers.'[95] For 'used' read 'made his own'.

We have also said enough in passing about Nietzsche's debts to classical scholarship. Ernst Howald once wrote that Nietzsche owed a good deal to antiquity, nothing to philology[96] – but this hardly applies to *BT*. The debts there, however, mostly involve a straightforward use of respectable nineteenth-century scholarship, from Lobeck on Dionysus to Bernays on *katharsis*.[97] These are, in other words, plain sources rather than influences. When Nietzsche diverges from them, equally, it is not because he has outgrown their influence any more than it is because of new material that he has unearthed (although he had reinterpreted some of the relevant material during his researches at Leipzig). They were never influences in the first place, and it is his wider perspectives that determine any divergence.

It is possible to make out a case for one or two rather more significant contributions to Nietzsche's book from somewhat less conventional philologists. In the first place, there is Georg Friedrich Creuzer, whose four-volume *Symbolism and Mythology of the Ancient Nations, Especially the Greeks* (1819–23) initiated a controversy in some ways like the one destined to encompass *BT* itself through an attempt to find symbols of ancient oriental theosophy in the myths and mysteries of classical Greece – with Dionysus well to the forefront of the speculations.[98] Another instance involves a book by Anselm Feuerbach (brother of the philosopher), *The Vatican Apollo* (1833), a critique of Winckelmann's interpretation of Greek art as typified by his view of the Belvedere Apollo, and very possibly the inspiration behind Nietzsche's association between Apollo and the plastic arts, if nothing more.[99] But these are only small-scale exceptions to the general rule: Nietzsche used, but was not appreciably affected by, the work of his fellow-scholars.

If any classical scholar was to have exerted any real influence on *BT*, it would have been Rohde. While Rohde himself in his later work shows the marks of Nietzsche's influence,[100] one influence does not preclude another, and a claim that Rohde *did* have an impact on Nietzsche's thinking was made, as we recall, by Wilamowitz in his memoirs: 'Nietzsche had learnt something about Dionysus from Erwin Rohde; for it is one of the chief merits of this eminent scholar to have recognized that with the alien god there came in a new form of religious feeling and action alien to the old worship of the Hellenes.'[101] In support of this claim a letter from Rohde to Nietzsche of April 1871 has been adduced. After remarking on his interest in Pythagoras, Rohde comments on the need for a satisfactory book on Greek mysticism and adds: 'How I hate this wretched Göttingen dictum[102] about the "serenity of the true Greece"! Dionysus had as profound an influence as Göttingen's enlightened Apollo, which this wretched race of professors see at every turn. Between Homer and Aeschylus lies a period of profound mystical agitation and a growing inner profundity of which only a few traces survived the superficial clarity of the Alexandrian period.'[103]

These remarks, so obviously in line with Nietzsche's own thinking, prompted Rohde's biographer Crusius to suggest that Rohde had 'met the author of *BT* half-way'.[104] This is not impossible, but the date of the letter makes it seem very likely that Rohde was in fact rather following his friend's lead. By mid-1871 Nietzsche had been immersed in just these topics for a year and a half, as Rohde well knew; hence, of course, the off-hand way in which the comments are introduced. There is every reason to suppose that Rohde's interest was genuine – that, in other words, the interest that came to fruition two decades later in *Psyche* was already active – but no reason to think that his interest came before Nietzsche's or influenced it. A year earlier, in the summer of 1870, Rohde had set down in a notebook a series of thoughts on some rather different matters: tragedy, the Socratic antagonism to instinct, and the correlation between this antagonism and the death of tragedy.[105] These questions, though no less central to Nietzsche's work, are by comparison remote from Rohde's, so that here it is even more likely that it was Nietzsche's thoughts he was pursuing.[106] All in all, despite the two friends' great rapport during these years, one is inclined to accept Rohde's own estimate: 'like all his friends, actually, except for Wagner, I had no real influence at all on Nietzsche's development'.[107]

Wagner himself, as we have seen, had a formative effect on Nietzsche's elaboration of the construct. More than that: without him *BT* would never have been written at all. Though never going against his own inclinations for Wagner's sake, Nietzsche wrote a book which (to repeat our earlier conclusion) was indebted to Wagner in two distinct ways: its material had a 'Wagnerian connection' from the outset, while the decision to base a book on that material was prompted by Wagner's personal encouragement. In fact, as Nietzsche himself put it, *BT* was his whole Tribschen world, petrified.[108] Wagner's impact, furthermore, was not only a matter of inspiration of this kind. His ideas have left their mark on Nietzsche's book as well, and never more obviously than when Nietzsche is pointing to his friend as the new Aeschylus, the leading cultural force of the day, and, above all, the long-awaited redeemer of the German spirit. The ideological-historical perspective here – also visible in the accounts of opera in §19 and 'Aryan' *versus* 'Semitic' mythology in §9 – certainly bears the stamp of Wagner's influence; and Nietzsche will soon reject it when he turns his back on Bayreuth.

Among other indications of influence, less crude but no less real, is Nietzsche's high estimate of Aeschylus himself. In 1847 Wagner read the *Oresteia* in translation, and proudly proclaimed that his vision of the possibilities of drama had been deeply affected by the experience.[109] If 'the stage of Aeschylus and Sophocles' represented 'the brief time span of the flowering of Athenian art',[110] it was, nevertheless, specifically Aeschylus that Wagner looked to as the original *Gesamtkünstler*. In 1849 Wagner praised his *Prometheus* as the 'deepest of all tragedies', and Aeschylus' work as a whole prompted him to jot down a note: 'Birth from music: Aeschylus. Decadence – Euripides'.[111] Here in embryo is Nietzsche's relative valuation of the two tragedians and, for good measure, an idea for his eventual title. It is likely that by 'music' Wagner simply had in mind the prominence of the lyric component in Aeschylean drama as against its reduced importance in Euripides, but whatever the note means, it is certainly possible that Nietzsche knew of it.[112] He knew far more than Wagner about Aeschylus and Euripides, and he was more attuned to the archaic and early classical than to the 'Socratic' world of Euripides anyway. Wagner, moreover, had his own reasons for admiring Aeschylus, which were not Nietzsche's.[113] But without that admiration on Wagner's side, Nietzsche would hardly have thought of using 'Aeschylean tragedy' (§15) and 'Aeschylean man' (§19) as formulae for human achievement at its highest.

If Wagner induced Nietzsche to think about Aeschylus, this was as corollary of a more straightforward manifestation of his influence: he interested Nietzsche in drama. As our earlier discussions have shown,[114] Nietzsche had his own interest in tragedy, as, of course, in music – Wagner, one might say, refocused those interests – but *drama*, as a cultural form, only concerned him so long as he was under the Master's spell. The ideal of a cultural cure for human ills, which informs his interpretation of Greece (§21) as well as his hopes for the future, is equally one that he derived from Wagner. The Bayreuth ideal has been described as academic, but it had its ideological aspect and aspired to be realized in terms of concrete reform. The introspective student and the anti-worldly Schopenhauerian that Nietzsche had been would never have had any reason to look to practical cultural projects with such enthusiasm – no more would the wandering free-thinker that he later came to be.

And yet, important though Wagner was for the making of Nietzsche's book, that importance remains primarily a matter of inspiration, then of redirection, and only to a limited extent of actual borrowings. Even the 'Wagnerian' interpretation of Greek tragedy through the perspective of *Tristan* and the *Ring* (unlike the complementary promotion of Wagner as the spirit of Hellas reborn) is Nietzsche's idea, not Wagner's. Furthermore, much of the common ground between the Nietzsche of *BT* and the Wagner of the early 1870s is the result of coincidence between the two men's independent interests. In a typical passage from the 1870 essay *Beethoven*, for instance, we find a discussion of the 'beauty', the 'illusion', the 'aesthetic will-free contemplation' associated with plastic art, and (after a quotation from *Faust*) an insistence on the illegitimacy of associating those principles with music.[115] These ideas, of course, are eminently characteristic of *BT*, but only because Nietzsche's book, like Wagner's essay, presupposes Schopenhauer, from whom the ideas derive. Nietzsche is in no way indebted to Wagner for them – even though *Beethoven* may have encouraged Nietzsche to think himself back into a Schopenhauerian perspective from which he had lately been somewhat distanced.[116]

Wagner's influence has been exaggerated. There is in fact a tradition still current among Wagnerians that Nietzsche was a peculiarly unoriginal figure *tout court* and that, in particular, *BT* is little more than (in Ernest Newman's phrase) 'Wagner literature'.[117] The tradition goes back to Wagner himself and his embittered attitude towards Nietzsche after their estrangement. Wagner was not used to losing admirers and Nietzsche's intellectual emancipation was intolerable to him. One of his characteristic responses to the subject of Nietzsche and his work was to deny the apostate's capacity for independent thought altogether. Of *The Gay Science* he said to Cosima: 'everything in the book that is worth anything is borrowed from Schopenhauer', while four days before his death he assured his devoted conductor Hermann Levi that Nietzsche had no thoughts of his own, no drop of his own blood in him.[118] As far as *BT* is concerned, it might seem tempting to take those later rancorous comments at face value – making Wagner himself a principal donor of the book's life-blood. After all, not only is there the obvious debt to Wagner in the book; Nietzsche himself at the time went out of his way to point to it. In the 'Preface to Richard Wagner' he defers to 'the illustrious pioneer on my path'; in the letter sent to Wagner with his advance copy of the book (January 1872) he writes, 'if I myself think that in essence I am right, then that only means that *you* with *your* art must be eternally right'; and in an earlier letter (November 1870), 'How much it has meant to me to get to know your philosophy of music – which is to say, *the* philosophy of music – I could show you by an essay I wrote in the summer called "The Dionysiac Philosophy".'[119]

All of these communications, however, are addressed to the Master and meant for him to read. A few days before the 1870 letter Nietzsche had written to another friend, an ardent Schopenhauerian, with the same modest tone, but a different ascription of credit: 'This summer I wrote an essay on "The Dionysiac Philosophy", dealing with an aspect of Greek antiquity, to which, thanks to our philosopher, we can now get closer.'[120] 'Our philosopher' is of course Schopenhauer himself, to whom Nietzsche by this time was far from owing full allegiance. The modesty, in other words, is largely deference *ad hominem*, and so it is in Nietzsche's letters to Wagner. The most extreme example of all is to be found in a rejected draft of the January 1872 letter to the Master. '*You* with *your* art must be eternally right' is what he eventually wrote. His first thought had been to tell Wagner: 'everything I have to say here about the birth of Greek tragedy would have been said more beautifully, clearly, and convincingly by you'.[121]

Wagner himself, though no doubt suitably gratified, might have been a little surprised at such a tribute, for contrary to his public statements on the subject in later life, he was repeatedly impressed by Nietzsche's originality and independence of mind. On learning the contents of the two Basle lectures in February 1870, Wagner told Nietzsche his views were 'new' and 'incredible' and that he was 'terrified by the boldness' with which the young professor had launched them; while on receiving those ideas in their final form two years later, he wrote: 'You are now publishing a book which has no equal. Every influence that might have been brought to bear on you has been nullified by the entire character of this work.'[122] By July 1872 Wagner, in private conversation with Cosima, could speak of Nietzsche in the same breath as Kant.[123] It is in accordance with this view of his 'disciple' that even before the appearance of the book, the Master should have been prepared, as we have seen, to learn and borrow from Nietzsche himself.[124] This was a point which did not escape the critical eye of Rohde. In May 1871 he wrote to Nietzsche about Wagner's essay *The Destiny of Opera*: 'I have read the essay on opera attentively. It often occurred to me, dear friend, that I could hear you in the prompter's box when Greek drama was under discussion.'[125] A few months earlier Wagner had said as much to Cosima: Nietzsche had 'enlarged his perception.'[126]

If there were still any doubt about the essential independence of Nietzsche's ideas, it would only be necessary to think back to his early essays and notes and recall how much of what was later to become part of *BT* – ideas, facts, key-words, associations – was already in his mind in 1868 when his attachment to Wagner was only beginning. If this was the case with the Dionysiac–Apolline antithesis, it was equally so with the large areas of tragedy, aesthetics and music,[127] in which, moreover, there is an unmistakable continuity with his ideas from a still earlier period. Above all, there is the school essay on Sophocles' *Oedipus Rex* (1864), in which he offers an explicit association between Greek tragedy and Wagner; while his notebooks of 1862–3 reveal an interest in the 'demonic' power of music and its metaphysical significance.[128] In such early formulations we find not only an incipient interest in the relation between the old and the new music drama, but an anticipation of the neo-Schopenhauerian cosmology of music embodied in *BT* ten years later.[129]

As a direct source of ideas, Schopenhauer himself is more important than Wagner, and far and away the most important modern influence on Nietzsche's book. His metaphysics of music, his notion of 'the will', his pessimism (a philosophical version of the Romantics' *Weltschmerz*) – all of these, with or without modification, are vitally present. Nietzsche may insist on contradicting some of his tenets (as well as offering much that has no direct connection with him at all), but it is still Schopenhauer that he is contradicting. When Nietzsche rejects a Buddhistic-pessimistic negation of the will (§7) in favour of the Greek 'pessimism of strength' (as he labels it in the *Self-Criticism*), or when he denies the meaning of an opposition between 'objective' and 'subjective' art (§5), he is conducting a straightforward dialectical argument with the philosophy of which he was so recently a wholehearted partisan. Schopenhauer's is by no means an isolated influence. In tone and in content Nietzsche's book presupposes the cultural and spiritual aspirations of German Romanticism and its roots in the *Sturm und Drang*. His aesthetic theories, as we shall see, belong as firmly to that German context as does his Dionysiac–Apolline antithesis. But it is a German context of which Schopenhauer remains, for him, the crowning representative.

Specific debts and innovations aside, much of Nietzsche's book is a remarkable reinterpretation of commonplaces. Its originality is not like the originality of a work of scholarship; it does not unearth new data or submit old data to a newly systematic re-examination. Rather, in its use of Greek material in particular, it recalls an artist's use of public property – say, Shakespeare's use of Plutarch: a comparison which, if it is gratuitously flattering to Nietzsche as artist, at least serves to remind us that *BT* is to be judged as much by quasi-artistic criteria as by those appropriate to classical scholarship and 'science'. Just how public much of the property of *BT* actually was, not only for Nietzsche's post-Romantic Germany, but for pre-Romantic Europe a century before, we can gauge from a glance at a work which few Germans of Nietzsche's generation would ever have heard of, the *Dissertation on the Rise, Union, and Power, the Progressions, Separations, and Corruptions, of Poetry and Music* by the Englishman John Brown, which was published, more than eighty years before Nietzsche's birth, in 1763. Quotation can be left to speak for itself:

[The Greeks'] earliest religious rites were performed or accompanied by dance and song. The orgys of Bacchus, celebrated in this manner, were famed through all the ages of antiquity (p. 59).

...the effects of the two arts [*sc.* Greek 'melody' and 'sculpture'] being by no means parallel, but rather contrary to each other (p. 76).

From an union of these two kinds [*sc.* Greek lyric and epic] a certain rude outline of tragedy arose (p. 105).

It appears, therefore, that tragedy had a much earlier and deeper foundation in ancient Greece than the accidental adventure of Thespis and his rout: that it arose from Nature, and an unforced union and progression of melody, dance, and song (p. 108).

The modern poetry and music of Europe [are] the casual offspring of the corrupted Roman arts, which were themselves no more than partial imitations of the Greek in their state of separation and weakness (p. 195).

the art [*sc.* poetry] which in ancient Greece had been the genuine effect of natural enthusiasm and, aided by a native and correspondent melody, had been delivered to the people by the enraptured bard, could now be studied and attained only by the sequestered few (p. 196).

...the separation [i.e. in contemporary Europe] of music and poetry from their important ends, and from each other...(p. 199).

...all the...unnatural and distorted...features of the modern opera...[whose] ...absurdities...[include]...the recitative...(pp. 203f.).

The established separation of the poet's from the musician's art [*sc.* in the modern opera]...produced an improper poetry; so the separation of the musician's from the poet's character was productive of improper and unaffecting music (p. 205).

. . . the whole farrago of the modern opera . . . a mere musical entertainment, . . . the tragic action commonly forgot (p. 206).

It remains now to consider the circumstances in which, and the means by which, 'tis possible that the arts of poetry and music may again be powerfully and effectually united (p. 221).

the tragic poem can never again be powerfully united with music (p. 225), [but it is possible to envisage] another . . . kind of reform in which many of the subjects of [the two dramatic forms (p. 232)] the opera and the oratorio may be exhibited in full union with the powers of music (p. 234).

Quite apart from various other differences, large and small (including the very different estimates of the prospects for musical tragedy), in one way Brown's dissertation differs blatantly from *BT*. Through all his learned discussions of poetry, music and song in diverse ages and cultures from ancient China and medieval Wales to the supposedly disadvantaged Europe of his own day, there is no mention of Germany – not in connection with music (where Bach was still an undiscovered composer and Mozart now beginning his career as a child prodigy), nor in any other sphere. For Brown, Handel is evidently an honorary Englishman:[130] Germany has not yet impinged on the consciousness of educated Europe. But if Nietzsche's book, by comparison with Brown's, richly evokes the cultural rise of Germany in the hundred years that separate their composition, Brown's, conversely, serves to remind us that the ideas and interests of the nineteenth-century German intellectual rest on wider European foundations.

8

Tragedy, Music and Aesthetics

THE BIRTH OF TRAGEDY AND ARISTOTLE'S *POETICS*

The Birth of Tragedy represents Nietzsche's most sustained attempt at a theory of art. Apart from the late essay, *The Wagner Case*, and its companion piece, *Nietzsche Contra Wagner*, it is his only book in which art occupies a central place, even though musical and literary criticism and aesthetic speculations abound in all his writings. Those who discuss Nietzsche's views on art often treat his books as if they were separate chapters of one continuous work. The coherence of this *œuvre* is sometimes strongly affirmed, sometimes denied, but the whole sequence is taken to be a single work in the sense that excerpts from different parts of it may be played together, like cards from a single pack, without further ado. Allowance is usually made for Nietzsche's revaluation of Wagner, which is too obvious a reversal to be ignored; this apart, the question of development or changes of mind is hardly raised.

This procedure is unacceptable. Whatever may be said of Nietzsche's thought as a whole, the fact is that, despite continuities, his view of art does develop and change, and nowhere is the development more marked than between *BT* and the work of the later 1870s and 1880s. That development proceeds in conjunction with the revaluation of Wagner, but is not restricted to it. In opposition to the thesis put forward in *BT*, the later Nietzsche will espouse the ideals of classicism, partly with reference to French culture; he will express hostility to the theatre; he will be able to see convention as 'the condition of great art, not an obstacle to it' and art itself as 'the cult of the untrue'[1] – and insofar as these two propositions are relatable to his earlier conception of art, it can only be to his conception of *Apolline* art. A further important change, implicit in this last pair of instances, will be the tendency to equate all forms of art at the expense of those distinctions to which *BT* is devoted. In this development tragedy must forfeit much of its special status – and so too will music, which, as far as the post-Wagnerian Nietzsche is concerned, is no longer 'a universal language for all time'[2] or a language with a unique, metaphysical power. The knowledge that his ideas do develop should make us wary of using his later philosophy to interpret *BT*.

The later comments on tragedy are not nearly so numerous as those on music. It is striking that a considerable number of them show Nietzsche still doing what so many other German theorists of tragedy have done: defining his own position with reference to Aristotle's *Poetics*. For instance, we find him protesting against Aristotle's emphasis on tragedy as action (*praxis*) and – repeatedly – against the Aristotelian concept of *katharsis*. The precise terms of his objections to *katharsis* vary, but there is one fundamental ground of complaint: the notion fails to do justice to tragedy's life-enhancing force[3] – on which point the later Nietzsche is more or less at one with the author of *BT*. His alternative to *praxis* is the Greek loan-word *pathos*. In the *Poetics* this word refers to a 'scene of suffering'; in ordinary Greek it means 'misfortune' or 'experience' or 'emotion'; and emotion, especially intensity of emotion, is what it signifies in German.[4] Nietzsche's implicit alternative to action, it would seem, is something approaching *Stimmung*, 'mood' or 'impression', and in such an elevation of mood above action we have a very German propensity. We can see it manifested in the curiously undramatic quality of a good deal of German drama (and even the native equivalent for 'tragedy' – *Trauerspiel*, 'mourning-play' – emphasises mood). We shall see it also in certain aspects of Nietzsche's first book.

The relationship with Aristotle provides some of the continuity between the different phases of Nietzsche's thinking about tragedy. It also, perhaps unexpectedly, offers a good access to the theoretical content of *BT*. For a start, Nietzsche's book and the *Poetics* have more in common than is generally realized – and when we say this, we are not referring to Aristotelian influence on Nietzsche. The literary-historical basis of his disquisitions on the origin of tragedy is, we recall, essentially neo-Aristotelian. But his concern with the origin of the genre is not, ultimately, a historical one, and to this extent the Aristotelian provenance of his dithyramb and his satyrs is a minor matter.

More to the point: the treatises share an academic stance. In §15 Nietzsche turns away from antiquity to the cultural conformations of his own day:

> we stand aside a little while, contemplative men to whom it has been granted to be witnesses of these tremendous struggles and transitions. Alas, it is the magic of these struggles that those who behold them must also join in and fight.

There is a *Kulturkampf* in progress between effete Socratism and the new Dionysiac movement spearheaded by Wagner, and Nietzsche is unreservedly committed to Wagner's side. For all that, he can still feel himself to be a 'contemplative man', a man who *has* – alas – to join in, but would prefer to 'stand aside', to interpret, to judge.

It is a commonplace to see in the author of the *Poetics* an armchair critic, a philosopher in his study, a theoretician of tragic drama so detached from the live art of his day that for him the *opsis*, the theatrical side of an essentially theatrical form, is its least important aspect, and reading a play is almost as good as seeing it (*Poetics*, Ch. 14). Aristotle is also – as we would add – so far removed from the now imperilled religious presuppositions of Greek culture that he can forget to mention them in his discussion of the dramatic form that most intimately involves them.[5] In common with most other German theorists of tragedy, Nietzsche is not detached in the way that Aristotle is detached, but like Aristotle he has an intellectual's stance and an intellectual's point of departure. Above all, he is not a man of the theatre: he starts not from the practising artist Wagner, but from Schopenhauer. Aristotle's most immediate dependence is on Plato: the essential Aristotelian concept of *mimēsis* – art as 'imitation' – is Platonic, while his theory of *katharsis* is one of a series of manoeuvres, contra Plato, designed to reinterpret tragic drama as a respectable entertainment. Similarly, Nietzsche takes over from a philosophical predecessor conceptual building-blocks like the will, 'pessimism', and the special status of music – and uses them to support his own, un-Schopenhauerian vindication of art.

The two philosophers have other things in common. They share a special interest in Sophocles' *Oedipus Rex*,[6] although hardly for the same reasons. They agree that the effect of tragedy is to some extent therapeutic – even if, once again, Nietzsche's notion of the tragic art as 'the quintessence of every prophylactic power of healing' (§21) is rather different from the idea of an emotional safety-valve which seems to be implicit in his predecessor's doctrine of *katharsis*. More significant is an assumption that underlies the two conceptions of tragic drama: a belief in genres. For both thinkers 'epic poetry' or 'lyric poetry' is an entity with specifiable properties and peculiarities. 'Tragedy', in particular, is not a mere label used by convention to cover a series of individual plays which exist – which, in the schoolman's terminology, have their *haecceitas* – only as individual plays. When Aristotle adverts to *tragōidia* and Nietzsche to *Tragödie*, the genre exists in its own right. In *Poetics*, Chapters 4–5, Aristotle discusses the evolution of the Greek forms of poetry. We gather from his account of the development of tragedy that at one stage tragedy was 'satyric', that at a later stage Aeschylus curtailed the rôle of the chorus, and so on. We do not gather, however, that a tragedian – Aeschylus or any other – introduced a new feature which became a regular part of tragedy thereafter, but rather that various successive stages of tragedy had always existed as possibilities and were waiting in some pre-natal, pre-conceptional state to be realized in practice. Hence (*Poetics*, Ch. 4):

tragedy gradually grew to maturity as people developed the capacities that materialized in it, and after many changes it stopped, once it had attained its full growth.

The quasi-biological tone of Aristotle's 'grow to maturity' (*auxanesthai*) and 'growth' (*phusis*) associates itself with his teleological preconceptions. Nietzsche's terms of reference are remarkably similar, though in his case teleology is tacitly informed by the Darwinian model of evolution:[7]

...the sublime and celebrated art of Attic tragedy...presents itself as the common goal of [the Dionysiac and the Apolline] tendencies...(§4)

tragedy arose from the tragic chorus (§7)

Greek tragedy...died by suicide, in consequence of an irreconcilable conflict... When a new artistic genre blossomed forth after all..., it was noted with horror that she did indeed bear the features of her mother – but those she had exhibited in her long death-struggle. It was Euripides who fought this death-struggle of tragedy; the later artistic genre is known as New Attic Comedy. In it the degenerate form of tragedy lived on...(§11)

ancient tragedy was diverted from its course by the philosophical desire for knowledge (§17).

One immediate corollary of a conception of autonomous artistic kinds is a belief in their *essential* characteristics. Accordingly, we are assured by Aristotle that horrific optical effects have no place in tragedy, because they induce the *wrong* emotional response (*Poetics*, Ch. 14). In the same vein Nietzsche tells us in *BT* §14 that 'the essence of tragedy' is destroyed by optimistic dialectic. There is no inclination here towards a Crocean (or Wittgensteinian) scepticism about hypostasizing the type, nor any 'common sense' empirical recognition of the fact that even within the corpus of Greek tragedy there is a wide variation from the canonical virtues of the *Oedipus Rex* to the 'happy ending' of Aeschylus' *Oresteia* – let alone the unabated melancholy of Euripides' *Trojan Women* and the melodrama of his *Iphigenia in Tauris*. For Nietzsche as for Aristotle, there is an acceptable tragic norm and more or less unacceptable deviations from it. Individual playwrights can be assessed according to their willingness or capacity to accede to the norm: some tragedians (the theorists agree) are more tragic than others. There is no licence for eccentricity.

The genre, then, has its own existence, independently of the plays that exemplify it and the playwrights who produce the exemplifications. And if each genre has its independent existence and its own essence, the genres collectively are entities open to critical comparison: they can be valued against one another. This is one of the operations conducted at some length in the *Poetics*. In Ch. 4 Aristotle groups the poetic kinds into serious and non-serious, clearly valuing the former (which include epic and tragedy) above the latter (primarily represented by comedy). In Ch. 26 epic and tragedy are subjected to a systematic comparison, at the end of which tragedy is pronounced superior. This evaluative attitude to the genres is something familiar to any reader of Nietzsche's book. He too assigns comparative values and makes no attempt to conceal them. For good measure, his hierarchy is markedly similar to Aristotle's. At the top stands tragedy. Below tragedy – in which order is not, perhaps, clear – come epic and lyric, and below them comedy, which is respectable (§7) but (*ex silentio*) no more than that. At the bottom come the untraditional 'inartistic' arts like opera (§19), farce and ballet (§16) and the novel (§7). One would be justified in inferring a similar place in Aristotle's schema for the Platonic dialogue: it is worth mentioning as an extra, eccentric kind, but one seemingly deserving no further discussion (*Poetics*, Ch. 1). For Aristotle as for Nietzsche it is not enough to say that a work is good *of its kind*, while to judge the kind is a separate matter from judging its particular examples. When Aristotle and Nietzsche value tragedy above epic, an empiricist may say that they are really valuing the *Oedipus Rex* above the *Iliad* and generalizing their verdict – but this is certainly not what either Aristotle or Nietzsche think they are doing.

The degree of coincidence between the two theorists is surprising only because their differences are so many and – in part – so obvious. An index of the distance between them is provided by Aristotle's analysis of the departments (*merē*) of tragedy in *Poetics*, Ch. 6. Aristotle parcels tragedy into six lots which he arranges in descending order of importance from *muthos* ('plot' or 'myth') at the top, down to *opsis* (the visual dimension) at the bottom. In full the list runs: *muthos*; *ēthē*, characters or characterization; *dianoia*, 'reason' (i.e. rational thought, especially as vested in the characters); *lexis*, verbal expression (specifically that of the spoken parts of the play); *melopoiia*, 'song-composition' (i.e. the melody and words of the lyrics); *opsis*. That is Aristotle's order. If we look at *BT* we find a quite different ordering. At the head of Nietsche's card comes music, as 'the essence of tragedy' (§14). The second place is occupied perhaps (Nietzsche is not explicit here) by *muthos*, albeit in the sense of heroic-metaphysical myth (§23), rather than 'plot', the abstracted structure of events interrelated by probability or necessity, which is what Aristotle means by the word (Chs 6–10).

As far as actual 'plots' are concerned, Nietzsche's active interest is largely restricted to what Aristotle classifies as one particular feature of the tragic plot-structure, *peripeteia* or 'reversal', which for Aristotle is an important and impressive feature, but not a necessary one (Ch. 10). In Nietzsche's scheme of things the reversal assumes a new significance as the 'annihilation' (*Vernichtung*) of the individual hero (§16) – it being premised here that the essential movement of tragedy is in this cataclysmic direction, notwithstanding the fact that in Greek tragedy, at least, the overt movement is frequently the other way, as Aristotle for one was well aware (Ch. 13).

Nietzsche's valuation of plot and even myth below music has further implications. The emphasis on plot in the *Poetics* is above all an emphasis on *praxis*, action. In Chapter 6 tragedy is defined as an 'imitation of action', and without action, Aristotle tells us, there would be no tragedy – that is, no drama – at all. For *praxis*, as we have pointed out, the German tendency is to offer us something like *Stimmung*, the mood or atmosphere of the drama and the impression it makes on its audience; and of all the possible means of creating moods and conveying impressions, music, at least in its modern form, is incomparable. Nietzsche does not discount the drama and its action. But music, in his theory, epitomizes the Dionysiac; dramatic action, with all its individuated particularities, belongs to the Apolline; and tragedy consists of a marriage between the two principles from which the Dionysiac must in the end emerge as the dominant partner (§21): the conception of tragedy as mood, not action, is implicit.

Nietzsche's interest in what Aristotle calls *ēthē* is again heavily concentrated, this time on the person of 'the tragic hero', the victim of the annihilation. The victim's individual moral qualities and the other facets of dramatic characterization are not high up among Nietzsche's priorities (§§10, 17). The visual aspect of tragedy too is alluded to (§8) without animation (here at least the theoreticians are at one), as is the verbal (§§9, 11–12, 17). One last difference is that Nietzsche does not share Aristotle's respect for the ratiocinatory element, *dianoia*. Dionysiac 'wisdom' (§22) or 'mystery doctrine' (§10) may be a *sine qua non* of true tragedy, but Nietzsche leaves us in no doubt that in its every guise – 'debates and conclusions', 'philosophizing', 'cool, paradoxical thoughts' – the dialectical spirit is something alien and Euripidean (§§10–12).

The valuation of Euripides provides one of the more obvious differences between the theorists. They may agree that one tragedian is more tragic than another, but Aristotle's candidate for the most tragic of all is Euripides himself. The Aristotelian formula reveals reservations about the apostate,[8] but it is even more telling for that: 'and Euripides, even if he manages everything else badly, is certainly the most tragic [*tragikōtatos*] of the poets'.[9] For Nietzsche 'the tragic' is epitomized by Sophocles and, above all, by Aeschylus, and it is Euripides who 'combated and vanquished Aeschylean tragedy' (§12).

Aristotle commends Euripidean drama for producing the right effect. Euripides is 'the most tragic', because he is the best at evoking in an audience that particular combinatory response which Aristotle interprets as 'pity and fear' and regards as proper to tragic drama (Chs 6, 13). Such a concern with the effect of art on its audience is characteristic of the *Poetics*. Insofar as Aristotle is not preoccupied with the qualities and the constitution of the work of art *per se*, it is his chief interest. The effects of art, therefore, bulk rather larger in his treatise than the relation of art to life (where his thinking is largely summed up by the single recurring word *mimēsis*), and much larger than the relation of art to its author.[10] Here is another differentia. Between the art theory of the fourth century B.C. and that of the nineteenth century A.D. comes the Romantic discovery of the creative artist. When Aristotle constructs his famous definition of tragedy (Ch. 6), he makes no reference to the artist at all:

> tragedy is a *mimēsis* of an action that is serious and complete...in heightened language...in dramatic, not narrative form, which by rousing pity and fear effects the *katharsis* of such emotions.

When Wordsworth offers his definition of poetry to the changed world of 1800, the artist is given his due place, and more – the whole definition is pitched in terms of his creative process: 'poetry is the spontaneous overflow of powerful feelings: it takes its origin from emotion recollected in tranquillity'.[11]

Though far from agreeing with any Romantic on the precise interpretation of the poetic sensibility, Nietzsche is very much a Romantic in his stress on its importance. For Aristotle the poet may indeed require special gifts (the *Poetics* contains two passing references to poetic 'genius'),[12] but in essence he is simply a man who, with or without benefit of tips from the theorist, constructs the poems which are the object of the theorist's lucubrations. In Nietzsche's book creativity receives ampler attention and much of the discussion of art is pitched in terms of the artistic process and the artist himself. Music is an 'expression of the Dionysiac capacity of a people' (§25). Opera is 'the offspring of theoretical man...not the artist' (§19). The visual artist and the epic poet are 'absorbed in the pure contemplation of images', whereas the creator of Dionysiac music is 'pure primordial pain and its primordial re-echoing' (§5). As for the proto-tragedian, 'we may perhaps picture him sinking down in his Dionysiac intoxication and mystical self-abnegation, alone and apart from the singing revellers...' (§2). The creative character of specific artists is reconstructed too. In §12 we are invited to see Euripides as 'the actor whose heart beats, whose hair stands on end'. Archilochus, on the other hand, is 'a world-genius expressing his primordial pain symbolically in the symbol of the man Archilochus' and again, 'a drunken reveller sunk down in slumber' (§5). The similarity between the Archilochian snapshots and those of the composer and the proto-tragedian serves to show that all of these reconstructions are equally typical.

In a certain sense Nietzsche's whole discussion of art is concerned with the artistic process. The Dionysiac and the Apolline are his ultimate artistic categories and they are identified, in the first instance, not with artistic products, but with the two proto-creative processes or states, intoxication (or ecstasy) and dream. More precisely, ecstasy (*Rausch*) and dream (*Traum*) are offered to us in §1 as models or analogies of art, but as the book proceeds, the impression is irresistibly created that they also designate the means or even the precondition of art: without entering a state akin to ecstasy or dreaming, the artist cannot create. However, 'Dionysiac' and 'Apolline' do not simply refer to process in lieu of product (as with Wordsworth's equation of poetry with emotion): they presuppose a correlation between the two. A process that involves 'contemplation of images' can only result in epic poetry, visual art, or some other Apolline form, whereas true music must be associated with some kind of 'self-abnegation'. It might be said that in his sober way Aristotle presupposes a comparable correlation – between a largely rational process (reducible to theoretical formulation) and a rationally accessible product (inducible by it). But this is not the same. Aristotle appears to assume one homogeneous rational process, almost irrespective of the character of the product.[13] In Nietzsche's view of art, the degree of correlation is such that a particular process guarantees a product of a particular type.

It is open to us to say that Nietzsche's Dionysus and Apollo – and for that matter his Socrates as well – refer us both to art (or aesthetics) and to psychology. Nietzsche himself makes no such distinction. In consecutive sentences at the beginning of §12 he refers to tragedy as 'the expression of the Apolline and Dionysiac artistic *instincts*' (*Kunsttriebe*) and to 'that original and all-powerful Dionysiac *element*' (*jenes...dionysische Element*) within tragedy. The idea of generative process, therefore, is always implicit in the terms of Nietzsche's construct, but we cannot predict how far that idea will be in the foreground. Sometimes we may not even feel able to answer that question with hindsight. When Nietzsche mounts his attack on Euripides for creating art in full consciousness, is he really criticizing the man for thinking too much or his plays for being too cerebral?

Like most of Nietzsche's manoeuvres, the correlation of process and product carries with it evaluative implications. The Dionysiac and the

Apolline processes are conducive to the production of true art; the Socratic process is not. It is left to the reader to infer that for the production of art that is not merely true in kind, but also successful in its particularity, something more is required. We have seen that Nietzsche overstates the inspirational aspect of Greek art at the expense of tradition.[14] On a wider canvas, he is prepared to acclaim instinctive modes of creativity without due qualification. However, we should beware of oversimplifying his construct. Dionysus and Apollo represent something more than a mechanism for affirming the instinctive background of art. They also propose a connection between art and *suffering*. The artist must in some form or other honour Keats' goddess, Melancholy: 'his soul shall taste the sadness of her might'. The Apolline artist creates by sublimating the suffering of the world, his Dionysiac counterpart by self-negating participation in it. It is no accident that one of Nietzsche's most scathing comments on the Socratic art of the opera concerns its subversion of this nexus. Opera, he suggests (§19), holds to an ideal of an attainable paradise, symbolized by its representation of 'the artistic and good man' who 'sings and recites verses under the influence of passion'. With opera (Nietzsche continues) we dream ourselves back into an imaginary time 'when passion was enough to generate songs and poems; as if emotion had ever been able to create anything artistic. The premise of opera is a false belief concerning the artistic process.'

In the course of his retrospective comments on his first book in *Ecce Homo*, Nietzsche writes:

> How I had thus found the concept of 'the tragic' I have explained...in *Twilight of the Idols:* 'Saying Yes to life even in its strangest and hardest problems...this is what I understood as the bridge to the psychology of the tragic poet. Not in order to purge oneself of a dangerously strong feeling by its vehement discharge – Aristotle misunderstood it that way – but in order to be oneself the eternal joy of becoming...'[15]

Looking back at *BT*, Nietzsche reproduces one of its remarkable features. In the progression from 'the tragic' and 'the psychology of the tragic poet' to the talk of *katharsis* and 'purging oneself', he reveals his commitment to a yet more extensive correlation: between creative process, the artistic product, *and its effect;* between author, work, *and audience.* In *BT* the music drama of Wagner (or Aeschylus) is engendered by the Dionysiac–Apolline process; duly consists of Dionysiac–Apolline elements; *and* exercises the appropriate, combinatory effect. The expressions 'Dionysiac' and 'Apolline' themselves are as applicable to the spectator's activity as to the artist's. Thus the spectator of 'musical tragedy' is 'receptive in his Dionysiac state' (§21) and also subject to 'the excitation of the Apolline emotions to their highest pitch' (§22). The complete set of correlatives is very evident in the case of Euripidean drama. *One*, Euripides 'lays his plan as Socratic thinker'; *two*, his drama eliminates or transforms unreasonable conventions; *three*, it caters for the spectator who is nagged (like Euripides himself) by any uncertainty concerning 'the meaning of this or that person, or the presupposition of this or that conflict' (§12).

An anticipation of these extended correlations is to be found in Plato's *Ion*, a work from which Nietzsche quotes during his discussion of Euripides in §12. In that dialogue Plato represents Socrates as suggesting to Ion, a rhapsode or professional reciter of epic poems, that poets compose in a state of ecstasy, which is communicable to a rhapsode or an actor, who in turn communicates it to his audience:

> It is a divine power that moves you, like the power...of a magnet. This stone not only attracts iron rings, but imbues them with its own power to attract other rings, so that sometimes it forms quite a long chain of bits of iron rings, suspended from one another; and the power to attract in all of them derives from the magnet. So the Muse herself inspires men, and the inspiration passes from them to others, till we have a whole chain of men possessed.[16]

Plato's distaste too extends along the whole chain. Non-rational process, non-rational product, non-rational effect are all as objectionable as in Nietzsche they are praiseworthy. The odd thing is that the appurtenances of the Nietzschean Euripides, to whom the *Ion* is reapplied, are exactly opposite to those associated with the poet by Plato.

Implicit in many of Nietzsche's differences with Aristotle is a fundamental disagreement about the value of art as a whole and tragedy above all. Without rejecting art, like his master Plato, Aristotle very obviously puts a much lower valuation on it than Nietzsche. To put the matter into historical terms, Nietzsche belongs to a movement of European thought committed to the championship of art and its importance for society and the individual (not least the modern alienated individual), in opposition to a tradition of thought represented more recently by utilitarians and positivists and established by Plato and Aristotle themselves. The elevation of art, which in the first instance is part of the history of Romanticism, is epitomized for many English readers by the words of Nietzsche's contemporary, Matthew Arnold, on poetry:

> More and more mankind will discover that we have to turn to poetry to interpret life for us, to console us, to sustain us. Without poetry, our science will appear incomplete; and most of what now passes with us for religion and philosophy will be replaced by poetry.[17]

Nietzsche, like Arnold, must count as one of the more extreme spokesmen of this movement. Using Greek tragedy and Wagner as twin paradigms, he affirms the power of art to penetrate to the deepest, and harshest, secrets of life. It is allowed that *some* philosophy (Kant and Schopenhauer, §§18–19) may reach the same point, but only as it were by some special dispensation. This stance is the reverse of Aristotle's. Where the *Poetics* overlooks the metaphysical content of the greatest (and most intractably metaphysical) Greek art, Nietzsche reclaims the significance of art founded, as Greek tragedy is founded, on religious myth. He talks of Dionysiac *wisdom*, thus giving tragedy back its *sophia*, which Aristotle and the earlier founders of *philosophia* denied it.[18] As far as Nietzsche is concerned, we can learn true philosophy from tragedy – as indeed he himself is learning it. This biographical point is worth emphasizing. Aristotle brings to art a fully developed philosophy, the modified Platonism which has already employed philosphical thought to reject all but philosophical paths to wisdom. Nietzsche, by contrast, learns from responding to art and from contemplating the phenomenon of art; and he duly acknowledges the significance of art in his book.

Wherever we look, we find Nietzsche's terms of reference more flattering to art than Aristotle's. Where Aristotle's tragedian is a craftsman who perhaps needs a touch of 'genius' for certain special purposes, Nietzsche's is a very special human being in contact with the primordial unity of all things. The pity and fear that Aristotelian drama arouses in its sober public is somewhat more modest than the effect of Nietzschean musical tragedy, which 'stimulates, purifies and discharges the whole life of a people' (§21). Tragedy, says Aristotle, is an imitation of life (*mimēsis...biou*, Ch. 6). Nietzsche's conception of mimesis presupposes Schopenhauer, according to whom art in general tells the tale of ordinary reality, but music points us to a world of higher truth. The structure of this theory is preserved in *BT*, with the chief difference that tragedy joins music in representing that higher world. Plato had initiated this particular debate by postulating the two realms, but acknowledging art only as an imitation of the lower. The possibility of seeing some or all art as an intimation of the other, ideal world eventually occurs to the neo-Platonist Plotinus in the third century A.D.,[19] but it was not recognized by Plato himself. In Aristotle the notion of a higher world is in any case abandoned: there is one reality and art imitates it.

Aristotle is preoccupied with tragedy's separate properties, considered in respect of plot, character *et al.* What most concerns Nietzsche, with his loftier valuation of the genre, is its religio-mythic basis and its associated attitude to life. Aristotle's generalizations about tragedy, therefore, often do no more than identify contingent features of Greek plays, where Nietzsche's constant endeavour is to elicit the essence. Aristotle, for instance, moralizes tragedy:

except where unavoidable, its characters must be morally good (*khrēsta*, Ch. 15). We do not have to go outside Greek drama (to *Macbeth* or to *Faust*) to query this doctrine. It may be true that the characters of Greek tragedy usually are 'good', more or less, and therefore that, if the superficial norms of the genre are to be maintained, they ought to be. But this tendency is not essential. In Aeschylus' *Agamemnon*, for instance, *none* of the main characters – Aegisthus, Clytemnestra, Agamemnon himself – could be called edifying. Contrast Nietzsche's favourite complaint against Euripidean character portrayal, its naturalism. Whatever the necessary qualifications which he fails to make, this is a shot at the centre of the target. Naturalism, he argues (§§10, 11, 17) militates against the 'ideal' quality of traditional myth, to which the vitality of tragedy is intimately related. His exposition of the point does Euripides less than justice. Methodologically, nevertheless, the argument stands or falls on a higher level of significance than Aristotle's observation can aspire to.

The most important of all the differentiae between the two theories of tragedy concerns the origin of the genre. The theorists agree, of course, about their satyrs and their dithyramb. They assume, furthermore, that the origin is more than a historical *datum*, that it continues to matter afterwards, that without a knowledge of it our understanding of tragedy is necessarily incomplete. Having reified the genre, they think of it as an entity whose development is implicit in its form and its other properties. In opposition to 'objective' analysts of our own time, both would agree with Herder that 'origins show the nature of a thing'.[20] But Nietzsche goes further. We have already seen that his interest in literary developments is not an interest in literary history and reflects instead a concern with aesthetic or psychological principles[21] (as, of course, does his emphasis on the creative process). The next step is to set up – as so often in *BT* – an exact correlation: a correspondence between the origin and the essential 'nature of a thing' that is more than an incidental link between diachrony and synchrony.

Greek tragedy, as Nietzsche sees it, represents life truly. According to the Aristotelian tradition which he follows, tragedy also developed from the satyr chorus. *Therefore* – for Nietzsche the logic is irresistible – the satyr chorus must have had the capacity to do what tragedy is seen to do. His reinterpretation of the satyr[22] duly gives the chorus this capacity. The satyr becomes 'the archetype of man...who proclaims wisdom from the very heart of nature' (§8), and the satyr chorus accordingly is said to 'represent existence more truthfully, really, and completely than civilized man' (§8): the chain is complete. A little earlier (§7), Nietzsche considers alternative interpretations of the tragic chorus, among them Schlegel's formula, 'the ideal spectator'. Dismissing this brusquely as 'crude' and 'unscientific', he subsequently (§ 8) accepts it in a modified sense. Why, then, is he so scathing at first? Because to countenance the idea as it stands would, *for him*, imply that the rôle of ideal spectator was primal, there from the beginning. It is apparently inconceivable that a type might pass through so many stages as eventually to bear no discernible relation to its earliest form – as if such developments never happen, or else, if they do, we are no longer to regard the new instances of the type as specimens of the same type at all.

Up to a point, it might be argued, Nietzsche's peculiar insistence on origins involves no more than hypothesizing a 'spiritual' origin for a genre, as Aristotle too does. In the *Poetics* we are offered not only the historical pedigree of tragedy out of the dithyramb, but also a spiritual derivation from the epic (Ch. 4). Nietzsche's innovation (the argument would continue) consists in his running the historical and the spiritual together: his satyric dithyramb, unlike Aristotle's equivalent, offers *both* genealogical credentials *and* the appropriate spirit. But Nietzsche is doing more than this. A final step takes him clear of anything that Aristotle or most critics or aestheticians have ever thought of doing. He defines tragedy with reference to its origin and formulates its characteristics *in terms of* that origin. Aristotle certainly wishes to identify the origin and he regards his findings as relevant to the understanding of the genre. But when it comes to discussing actual tragedies or tragedy as such, he formulates his subject quite differently. He conducts the discussion in terms of plot and the other *merē*, or aspects of them, such as the plot-patterns involving 'reversal', or concepts, like *mimēsis*, with a wider aesthetic significance. Having once associated tragedy with the dithyramb early on in his treatise (Ch. 4), he makes no subsequent allusion to the association and proposes nothing that in any way depends on it. Contrast *BT*. Nietzsche locates the origin of tragedy in the interaction between the Dionysiac and the Apolline, and from first to last he formulates his thoughts about classical tragedy and tragedians, particular tragedies and tragedy as a whole, in terms of that same interaction: 'a form of art equally Dionysiac and Apolline – Attic tragedy' (§1); 'the language of Sophocles' heroes amazes us with its Apolline precision and lucidity' (§9); 'the Prometheus of Aeschylus is a Dionysiac mask' (§9); 'in the total effect of tragedy, the Dionysiac predominates once again' (§21).

As we have seen, Nietzsche's 'Dionysiac' and 'Apolline' are not literally applicable to the wide areas to which he applies them. To a large extent, we decided, they are not literal, but paraliteral. How, then, are we to regard them now in their transference from the origin of tragedy to its essence? Aristotle's categories – plot, character, reversal – are straightforward. They epitomize the analytical tradition which since his time has been predominant in Western thought. With these categories Aristotle is making the same attempt as most subsequent theorists have made: to reduce a whole to its parts, especially some of its more manageable parts. Nietzsche is after something quite different. His categories are not reductive. Their applicability to discrete parts of the drama is limited: the 'Dionysiac chorus', the 'Apolline part of tragedy, the dialogue' (§§8–9). Overall they have a Protean subtlety which makes it misleading to think of them as analytical in the usual sense. The tragic chorus is Dionysiac, Prometheus is a Dionysiac mask, the final effect of tragedy is predominantly Dionysiac. Categories of this kind can hardly be said to make tragedy more manageable. If anything, they make it more surprising, more mysterious.

If Nietzsche's terms are paraliteral in their application to the Greek world in general, they are specifically metaphorical in their re-application from the origin of tragedy to its essence, from the diachronic axis to the synchronic. The construct, accordingly, has something of the unsimplified immediacy of metaphor as opposed to the simplification and distance of ordinary analytical description. And because its terms are drawn directly from one of the book's central topics, the origin of Greek tragedy, we are entitled to regard it as another instance of centripetal imagery, the largest and most momentous instance of that 'poetic' peculiarity of the book, and the instance that shows just how important the peculiarity really is.

Nietzsche uses terms associated (more or less) with the origin of Greek tragedy as metaphor for its essence. The result is that the terms are akin in idiom to their new subject. Not only do they possess a suitably high, poetic tone for tragedy; they evoke its distinctive atmosphere. To an extraordinary degree, therefore, his primary categories offer an equivalent for their subject. The idea that a theory of art may in some sense match the art it treates is not without precedent. One thinks of Pope's compliment to 'Longinus', *On the Sublime* –

> Whose own example strengthens all his laws,
> And is himself the great Sublime he draws.[23]

But it is hard to think of a theory that embodies an equivalence on Nietzsche's scale. *BT* does not exclude the reductive categories of traditional analysis. Nietzsche cannot dispense with Aristotle's 'plot' and 'character' any more than he can do without the elementary analytical distinctions between music and tragedy, Greece and Germany, one thing and anything else. For the purposes of his tragic theory, such constants provide the literal context within which every metaphor must operate.

MUSIC AND 'MUSICAL TRAGEDY'

The word 'tragedy' (*Tragödie*) that occupies pride of place in the title of Nietzsche's book is a signpost pointing in more than one direction. It directs us to Aeschylus and Sophocles; to *Tristan* and *Lohengrin;* and to an attitude or experience often referred to as 'the tragic' (*das Tragische*), which may be identified most easily in a theatrical context, although not only there. While the first two paths lead to aesthetic and critical questions of a more or less circumscribed character, the last takes us into the heart of Nietzsche's philosophy of life. And in case this profusion of pointers is not enough, the theatrical contexts under review are widened, rather tentatively, to include the Shakespearean, among others; while all of Nietzsche's paths have the habit of suddenly bringing us face to face with the problem of modern culture. We begin with Wagner and his music drama and – as a necessary prelude to the discussion of tragedy itself – Nietzsche's ideas on music as a whole.

We have established that the Wagnerian part of Nietzsche's book is organic to it.[24] His ideas about music, similarly, are not to be spurned, as they often are, as an otiose adjunct to a discussion of tragedy which is, or should have been, his real concern. This is not to say that his views on music are as impressive as those on tragedy – at least not in this book. His reflections on Wagner have prompted one of the composer's critics to refer to him as 'the greatest name in Wagnerian studies',[25] but such a verdict only makes sense if we take into account the whole series of dicta from *BT* to 1888 – those *contra* Wagner as well as those *pro*.

The thoughts about music in *BT* centre on three topics: the philosophy of music with particular reference to the relation between music and words; Wagner's own 'musical tragedy' (as Nietzsche calls it from §21 onwards); and opera. The rest is slight indeed: a comment in §6 on the melodic power of the anthology of German folk-songs, *Des Knaben Wunderhorn*, and a couple of complimentary sentences in §19 on Palestrina, Bach and Beethoven, which, though notable for the vividness of their formulation, serve chiefly to show how totally Nietzsche accepts Wagner's perspective of European music as a drama in which his own *œuvre* provides the inevitable and irresistible last act.

In the account of opera in §19 Nietzsche outdoes Wagner himself in his distaste for 'this thoroughly externalized' form. Wagner always took care to distance himself from the operatic tradition to which he owed so much,[26] but in such treatises as *Opera and Drama* (1850–1) he pays a qualified tribute to Mozart and Gluck, Rossini and Weber. He opposes opera to his own *Zukunftsmusik*, but the opposition is not as rigid as Nietzsche makes it.

Rehearsing the well established traditions about the scholarly origins of opera in sixteenth-century Florence, Nietzsche damns it as an 'unnatural' composite generated by 'extra-artistic impulses'. Its premise is 'a false belief concerning the artistic process'. It is 'based on the same principles as our Alexandrian culture'. This assault cannot be said to reveal any sympathetic understanding of its object, either as a cultural phenomenon or as a form with its own dynamic and technique. On the technical side, Nietzsche concentrates on the recitative, which (as he allusively reminds us) the Florentines devised as equivalent to the melodized speech in which they erroneously supposed the dialogue of Greek tragedy had been delivered. There was a widespread Renaissance tradition to this effect. As the librettist Ottavio Rinuccini puts it in his dedication of the first publicly performed opera, *Euridice*, to the Queen of France in 1600: 'It is generally imagined that the tragedies of the ancient Greeks and Romans were entirely sung; but this noble kind of singing had not till now been revived...'.[27] In Nietzsche's scornful version any idea of nobility is lost without trace: 'the inventors of the recitative..., together with their age, believed...that the mystery of ancient music had been solved by this *stilo rappresentativo*, in which, so they thought, was to be found the only explanation of the enormous influence of an Orpheus, an Amphion, and even of Greek tragedy.' Being an experiment based on theory not inspiration, the development is dismissed out of hand.

As so often with Nietzsche, there is no question of judging something purely by its fruits: it has to be assessed according to its provenance. In fact, his exposition of opera virtually ignores its mature achievements altogether. Instead, he lays stress not only on its scholarly origins, but also on its early association with the sophisticated tradition of pastoral, which is characterized by the idealization of pristine rural simplicity. Here his remarks on the 'yearning for the idyllic' gain added force from the contrast with the discussion of man's true rustic archetype, the satyr, in § 8. There is a felicitous characterization of the operatic hero as the 'eternally virtuous..., eternally piping or singing shepherd, who must always eventually rediscover himself as such, should he ever at any time have really lost himself'. The more general assertion that opera caters for a 'comfortable delight in an idyllic reality' also has a persuasive force – until we detach ourselves from Nietzsche's rhetoric sufficiently to recall the bitter-sweet quality of, say, *Così fan tutte*, and at this point think back, perhaps, to the comparable mood of the 'pale primroses that die unmarried' in the Shakespearean pastoral world.[28] Both in its narrow and its broader sense, 'the idyll' is capable of more than Nietzsche is prepared to see.

We may also agree with Nietzsche that the invention of a mock-classical genre by a coterie 'in the very age that had produced the ineffably sublime and sacred music of Palestrina' is not in itself a sign of progress – and again add a rider. A work such as Verdi's *Otello* would seem to satisfy Nietzsche's criteria of construction and ethos, yet it was written as opera by an operatic composer. It is no objection that the best instances of this kind were as yet unknown (*Otello* itself was first performed in 1887). The mere fact of the development of such a piece from within the conventional operatic tradition belies Nietzsche's presumption that opera is inherently idyllic – and, more generally, serves to remind us how hard it is to believe that a genre which develops can ever be inherently anything. But if, with this theoretical problem in mind, we detach the operatic form from its 'inherent' origins, another of Nietzsche's objections to the genre begins to look distinctly suspect. In §19 we are asked to see the traditional operatic sequences of aria and recitative as 'utterly unnatural', whereas in §8 the alternation of lyric and dialogue in Greek tragedy is expounded with unqualified respect. If we discount the historical rationales of the two patterns (to which spectators and participants in most generations will have been blissfully indifferent), it is surely gratuitous to maintain that either is any less arbitrary and conventional than the other.

The Birth of Tragedy takes over Schopenhauer's postulate that behind ordinary reality lies an ultimate ground of being, the *Urgrund*, and that whereas other arts, including those based on the word, reproduce ordinary phenomena, music uniquely reflects the ground itself. The problem of the relation between music and word in any work of art that combines the two is implicit in this theory. Nietzsche had first thought about the problem in his *Germania* days.[29] The sense of urgency that he shows when returning to it now derives from Wagner's search for a Schopenhauerian vindication of his own music drama. By 1871, we recall, Wagner had modified his earlier ideal of equality between music and word in favour of the belief that 'the union of music and poetry must always end in...a subordination of the latter'. He proceeded to distinguish three elements in a hierarchy: music first, dramatic stage action (apparently) second, and the verbal element a clear third.[30] Nietzsche offers a compromise between his two guides. With Wagner he agrees that the word has a significant, albeit ultimately subsidiary role in such a combination. With Schopenhauer he sees essentially two, rather than three, elements in the artistic whole and relates those two directly to the metaphysical model of a two-tier reality. The compromise, however, is not presented as such: Nietzsche is prepared to differ publicly with Schopenhauer (as in §5), but not with Wagner.

Nietzsche's formula, cast in the mould of his new construct, is simple:

music is Dionysiac, the word – and 'the drama' – Apolline. It follows from the definition of Dionysus and Apollo with reference to the *Urgrund* and phenomena respectively that music with its metaphysical significance comes first. Any composition that gives the word priority or that gives music the rôle of mediating phenomena is Socratic: the first vice is ascribed to opera in §19, the second to the New Dithyramb (which imitates phenomena 'in the manner of a tone-painting') in §17 and to opera again, by virtue of its *stilo rappresentativo*, in §19.

Apolline art – epic poetry, painting, sculpture – is, of course, allowed to represent phenomena, and one might be forgiven for wondering why music too should not be given the right to do what, on Nietzsche's own showing, it evidently can do. At this point his theory is incoherent. For there is also, as he tells us in §2, a category of Apolline music, limited in scope but apparently legitimate. Its diffusion, however, is not defined. His explicit comments on the matter are confined to the music of the ancient lyre, which (as we gather from the exposition in §2) was characterized by rhythmic regularity and emotional restraint. If these are the criteria, it might be thought that (for instance) much of the baroque of the seventeenth and eighteenth centuries would qualify, although in §19 he appears to associate 'the arithmetical counting-board of fugue and contrapuntal dialectic' (shades of Beckmesser?) with Socratism. The question is further complicated by his naming Bach as the starting point for the rise of Dionysiac music in modern times (its 'vast solar orbit from Bach to Beethoven, from Beethoven to Wagner', §19). Apolline music evidently exists, but Nietzsche is not eager to discuss it.

Nietzsche attempts to support his theory in a number of ways. He offers discussion on the metaphysical level, much of it (§§5–6, 16) unashamedly Schopenhauerian in vocabulary, and hardly calculated to impress the uncommitted reader. More worldly but no more persuasive is an appeal in §5 to a piece of anecdotal evidence emanating from Schiller:

> Schiller has shed some light on the poetic process...He confessed that before the act of creation he did not have before him any series of images in a causal arrangement, but rather a *musical mood*. ('With me the perception has at first no clear and definite object; this is formed later. A certain musical mood comes first, and the poetic idea only after that.')

Quite apart from the problem whether we should ever take any such autobiographical statements at face value, it is an open question whether Schiller can have meant a literally 'musical' mood. Even if he did, it is not obvious why we should generalize from Schiller to poets (that is, lyric poets) as a whole, especially as this particular poet – the self-conscious father of the theory of naïve and sentimental poetry – was actually a Socratic artist if ever there was one. And even if we do, the most we could thereby establish would be the psychological priority of the 'musical' element. Its ontological primacy – notwithstanding Nietzsche's assumptions about the link – would still need to be demonstrated.

More substantial is Nietzsche's justification of the theory in the context of music itself. In §6 he presents folk-song as the simplest paradigm of a pattern which we are to see on a grander scale elsewhere:

> *melody is...primary and universal*, and so may admit of different objectifications in different texts...Melody generates the poem out of itself, over and over again: this is what the *strophic form of the folk-song* signifies.

That is to say, there is a widespread type of song in which a given musical sequence is repeated several times with different words. The type is represented in the anonymous, relatively unsophisticated compositions from early modern Europe to which Nietzsche refers under the heading 'folk-song'. It is also common in early Greek lyric. Whether in any or all such cases the music (or 'melody') actually was composed first may be doubted. In the case of Greek verse, there is Plato's pronouncement that 'melody and rhythm should follow the word',[31] and many would take this to be valid both for Greek lyric and its modern 'folk-song' equivalent. Nietzsche's argument is ingenious, but all it shows for certain is that music is translatable into more than a single set of words or 'images'; the point is supported by the citation (later in §6) of the Beethoven symphony that impels its listeners (like Helen Schlegel in Forster's *Howards End*) to describe the music pictorially, but in so many different ways.

This, at all events, is Nietzsche's paradigm, and during the second half of the book he develops it. In a rather unsystematic argument begun in §§16–17, but only finally spelled out in §25, he insists that just as the *Urgrund* is the source of the world of phenomena, so Dionysiac music engenders Apolline 'imagery' including, above all, tragic myth: music expresses truth on a universal scale and engenders the myth as its highest concrete instance. Contrary to appearances, this is not another example of Nietzsche abandoning direct experience in favour of metaphysics. In §§21, 22 and 24 he expounds the co-existence of opposite impressions to which the eyewitness of 'musical tragedy' is subject. The spectator sees the particular instance, the dramatized myth, and belies that vision by insight into a truth operating on a deeper, more universal level. Both impressions are strong, but the second – the 'musical' or Dionysiac – is the stronger. In accordance with Nietzsche's habitual correlation of effect with origin, we may take this as his experiential argument in favour of the primacy of 'music' over 'tragic myth'.

It is one major weakness of Nietzsche's treatment of music that it should be so closely associated with a particular metaphysic. Two others call for mention. In the first place, he generalizes about music on far too narrow a base. Music in *BT* means music in the modern Western tonal tradition, and even where an instance of a fundamentally different kind is available and relevant to him – as with the modal music of ancient Greece – he fails to point to the difference. His generalization proceeds without any reference to cultural limitations or the variety of known musical experience. It is of course true that the development of musical archaeology and anthropology and the invention of the gramophone and tape recorder have given the modern theorist an awareness of variety in time and place which in Nietzsche's time could not have been foreseen. It is also true that our century, by contrast with his, is aware not only of the orderly structures of European baroque (or Bach or Beethoven or even Wagner), but (on the one hand) the cerebral abstractions of atonal and electronic music and (on the other) the ecstatic qualities of jazz. In this enlarged context, distinctions between Apolline, Dionysiac and Socratic would seem to take on a new meaning.

Moreover, it is obvious that Nietzsche is bent on minimizing whatever variety is available to him. His conception of music excludes Mozart and Chopin, let alone Johann Strauss. In the final analysis, his notion of music as a Dionysiac art is derived from Wagner's rebellion against classical 'form', not least Wagner's use of chromaticism to disrupt the predictable hierarchy of tones that was essential to traditional tonality. A vignette on the title page of Nietzsche's book – Prometheus, 'the Titanic artist' (§9), breaking his bonds – aptly symbolizes this particular endeavour. It is as if Nietzsche were acting on the satirist's principle that the extreme may be taken to represent the type. As we have seen, he makes the music of the dithyramb somehow typical of Greek music in general,[32] and in the same way he now sets up Wagner as typical of music as a whole. Within a few years Nietzsche himself will acknowledge, with tacit reference to Wagner, how questionable it is to theorize about the Babel of musical languages on the basis of a single dialect, let alone a mere idiolect:

> Music is not in fact a universal language for all time, as is so often said in its praise, but corresponds exactly to a particular period and emotional temperature which involves a quite definite, individual culture, determined by time and place, as its inner law. The music of Palestrina would be quite unintelligible to a Greek; and again, what would the music of Rossini convey to Palestrina? It may be that our most modern German music, however much it may dominate the scene and enjoy its domination, will very soon cease to be understood.[33]

The most radical objection to Nietzsche's theory is already latent in our discussion. He categorizes music as the Dionysiac art, but allows us to see that there is also a category of Apolline music. Furthermore, it is implicit in his presentation that Wagner is the destroyer of pre-existing form, the creative violator of convention. What is that 'form' and that 'convention' if not, in Nietzsche's terms, an Apolline element? And does Wagnerian music itself have no formal aspect, no structure, no conventions? It could only do so if it were totally original, which (as the truism goes) is the same as totally meaningless. As Walther learns from Hans Sachs, all music must have a formal, conventional aspect. We, like the master-singers, may find it hard to recognize in the latest product of the avant-garde, but it must always be there. At the very least, music shows 'a natural formality in the resolution of a dissonance and in the consonance of a chord' and 'an arithmetical regularity...in the sounding of a single tone, whose resonances can be described in whole-number ratios'.[34] Rhythm too presupposes some 'underlying regularity'.[35] In short, any acoustic pattern is Apolline, and it is inconceivable that music could ever lack that and still make a psychological impact of any interest. Nietzsche deals in psychological impacts, but not in their acoustic bases. Had he dealt in both, he would surely have found music's Apolline element hard to ignore.

The point can be restated. Nietzsche is making yet another correlation, but an exceptionally confusing correlation, between Dionysiac effect and Dionysiac form, or rather formlessness. If we take up the twentieth-century examples again, the difference between the two is unmistakable. Within contemporary musical experience both 'serious' music and jazz exhibit a wide range of expression that includes, at one extreme, 'free form', irregular rhythm, unscripted improvisation, instant collaboration between performing musicians and audience. Such music is as formless as it would be possible to imagine and in that sense, perhaps, Dionysiac. But music that is 'rapturous' or emotionally 'shattering', or that has any of the other qualities which Nietzsche predicates of the Dionysiac *effect*, tends to occupy some quite different part of the musical spectrum. It is little favoured by 'serious' twentieth-century composers, except for conservatives in the *Wagnerian* tradition such as Richard Strauss, and is certainly not associated with the formless avant-garde. In jazz too ecstatic effect is associated with one phase of the music (the 'swing era' of the late thirties and early forties), formlessness with another (the experimental sixties); ecstatic effects in jazz, moreover, have generally been achieved by an intense exploitation of regular (albeit un-European) rhythms.

The conclusion to be drawn from these separate arguments is that if we accept Nietzsche's terms and the logic of his own definitions, we must accept that music, however Dionysiac in effect, always embodies an Apolline element. This is no less true of Wagner, Nietzsche's paradigm, than of any other possible instance – and we can say what Nietzsche could not, that by comparison with the formless excesses of the present century, the formal qualities of the music of *Tristan* are obvious. Music, then, cannot strictly be a Dionysiac art, but must be, at most, a combination of the Dionysiac and the Apolline.[36]

We can go further. Music is Nietzsche's sole example of the pure Dionysiac in art, and if music is not in fact purely Dionysiac, no art can be. If he had admitted this, he could have cleared up a large area of confusion in his book. At certain points he tells us that in its undiluted or unmediated state the Dionysiac cannot be borne. In §2, speaking of the Near-Eastern orgiastic festivals, he shudders at the thought of 'that horrible mixture of sensuality and cruelty which has always seemed to me to be the real "witches' brew"', and in §21 he speculates about the effect of overexposure to Dionysiac music, and suggests that no human being 'could apprehend the third act of *Tristan und Isolde* without any aid of word and image, purely as a tremendous symphonic movement, and not expire in a spasmodic unharnessing of all the wings of the soul'. Even in the creative form of music, then, Dionysus pure and simple is unbearable – let alone in his destructive physical manifestations: this is one of the ways in which the Dionysus of *BT* differs from Nietzsche's later conception of him.[37]

The discussion in §2, however, makes it clear that in the Greeks' orgiastic festivals Nietzsche detects an ethos different from that of their barbaric counterparts. The Greek festivals lacked the unredeemed cruelty; they showed refinement; 'with them...the destruction of the *principium individuationis* becomes for the first time an artistic phenomenon'. Similarly, while we are assured in §1 and periodically reassured that music is 'the Dionysiac art', it is apparent that Nietzsche knows not a single instance of wordless Dionysiac music – Greek *aulos*, Bach, Beethoven, Wagner or whatever – which actually is unbearable at all.

The meaning of these contradictions is now clear. It is not that the Dionysus of *BT* comes in two guises, one wild, the other not so wild – even if that happens to chime in with the nature of the original Greek god. It is that the Nietzschean Dionysus *by himself* is always unbearably wild and unacceptably destructive. He is (Nietzsche will argue) necessary for cultural vitality – even for the vitality of Apolline art which takes its formal character from the reaction against the Dionysiac – but *all* creativity requires Apollo's mediation. The Greek Dionysia then, with their aesthetic quality, were not and could not have been purely Dionysiac, but show the influence of Apollo; and this, as we saw when discussing the Greek cults,[38] is both literally true and recognized by Nietzsche himself: 'the destruction of the *principium individuationis* becomes for the first time an artistic phenomenon' after, and only after, the 'reconciliation' between the two deities. We may likewise suppose that the mystical ecstasies of §7 and the simple intoxication of §1 are mediated states too – unless their self-negating properties make them literally destructive of life.

The Dionysiac is necessary, but must always be mediated through the Apolline – that should have been Nietzsche's formula. We might almost say, it *is* his formula. Not only is it, as we see, implicit in his own account of Dionysiac religion in Greece. Once, belatedly, he all but spells it out (§25):

> Of this foundation of existence – the Dionysiac ground of the world – not one whit more may enter the consciousness of the human individual than can be overcome again by this Apolline power of transfiguration. Where the Dionysiac powers rise up as impetuously as we experience them now, Apollo too must already have descended among us...

Even here, though, Nietzsche cannot quite bring himself to say outright that no art can ever be Dionysiac *tout court*.[39] What is it that prevents him? The answer must surely be: the assumption about the special metaphysical status of music which he derives from Schopenhauer and whose 'eternal truth' had been confirmed by Wagner in his recent essay on Beethoven (§16). In this important instance, then, Nietzsche's Schopenhauerian-Wagnerian loyalties and the logic of his own position are at odds, and he opts, tamely, for the former.

The central question arises: *why music?* Why does music stand so high in Nietzsche's vision of life? We have supplied one reason: because Schopenhauer put it there and Wagner's authority confirmed it. There are other reasons. The conviction, born of his own responses, that music has a unique character and potency, is one that Nietzsche carries with him throughout his life. In late 1871 he writes: 'If only a few hundred people of the next generation get what I get out of music, then I anticipate an utterly new culture. There are times when everything that is left over and cannot be grasped in terms of musical relations actually fills me with disgust and horror'.[40] And in a note from the 1880s: 'Compared with music all communication by words is shameless'.[41] Music in contra-distinction to the word: this may seem a strange faith for one of the masters of German prose, but he will never lose it. It is symbolically appropriate that during his eleven years of madness his last creative activity will be extemporization at the piano – long after his interest in verbal discourse and his capacity for it has dried up.[42]

There are also factors of a less personal kind, such as the cultural status of *mousikē* in the ancient Greek world and the interest shown in it by Greek thinkers from Pythagoras onwards. Equally important is the actual stature and magnificence of German music in its development 'from Bach to Beethoven, from Beethoven to Wagner', and its peculiar place in German thought, especially thought concerning German culture itself. It would be hard to find a criterion by which to judge whether a culture is 'musical', but there is no doubt that this is how, long before Nietzsche, certain sections of the German intelligentsia had decided to interpret the culture of their nation. This self-understanding is attested in document after document. We find it in Schopenhauer. Before him we find it in the *Athenäum-Fragmente* of Novalis and in Hölderlin's *Hyperion*. What is involved is not merely a particular interpretation of Germany, but the equally particular conception of music as a spiritual phenomenon with a unique position not only in aesthetics but, above all, on an existential scale of values; and while such an evaluation may reach its high point in the nineteenth century, it goes back at least to Luther: 'next to theology there is no art equal to music...the prophets practised no other art, neither geometry, nor arithmetic, nor astronomy, as if they believed music and divinity nearly allied'.[43]

This conception comes to Nietzsche, therefore, not only direct from his prime source, Schopenhauer, but diffused through a wider tradition. It is also reinforced in a special way by Wagner. 'How necessary and close', Nietzsche remarks in §23, 'the fundamental connections are between art and the people, myth and custom, tragedy and the state.' These links had existed once in Greece; they might now (Nietzsche believes) be bewitched back into existence under Wagner's spell. Drama, as Schiller had seen, is the most social of the arts,[44] and it is as a musical dramatist, above all, that Wagner seems to promise the desired interaction between the artist and the people as a whole; his plans for Bayreuth, moreover, specifically encompass the vision of a new – artistically and spiritually renewed – society.

It is true that many of the more sober theorists of Nietzsche's day were content to equate music with 'exciting pleasure in beautiful forms', to use one of his own disparaging phrases (§16); the endeavour is summed up in the title of an influential book by Wagner's *bête noire*, Eduard Hanslick: *The Beautiful in Music* (first edition, 1854). But in the German philosophical tradition to which Nietzsche belongs, the function of music transcends this by far. Music becomes a full alternative world, a world of bloodless conquest. For Schopenhauer, of course, 'alternative world' has an all but literal meaning. Music, he believes, can take us beyond the travail of space and time and the rule of causality, beyond the tyranny of the particular, beyond the restrictions and strife of what Wordsworth once called the world of 'common indication'.[45] There is an echo of this theory in Nietzsche's refusal to acknowledge the propriety of Apolline music. As Wagner's admirer, he seeks to identify all music with music of the inward, 'spiritual', Dionysiac variety. As Schopenhauer's disciple, he sees an Apolline, this-worldly use of music as a betrayal of its true capacities.

Nietzsche's comments on Wagner himself do not differ in kind from his observations on pre-Wagnerian opera. His overriding concern is the cultural or spiritual impact of Wagnerian music drama, not the quality of particular specimens of Wagner's work. It is not that Nietzsche has no preferences in the matter, or no interest in the details of form and structure on which the preferences might depend.[46] In *BT*, however, there is barely a word about the formal or structural properties of any Wagnerian work. As if mindful of his principle that form is irreducibly Apolline and eager to convince us that Wagner is all Dionysiac effect and not even discussibly formless, Nietzsche selects an example of the required effect – *Tristan*, Act III – and centres his account on that (§§21–22). His description is vivid, and its potency is not negated by our realization that it is partly the product of the same empathy that he shows in recreating the ethos of ancient Greece. Nietzsche had known the piano score of *Tristan* for a decade; he had heard its famous prelude in performance; in his presence Wagner will have played through the score on the piano and discussed its dramatic realization; but at the time of writing the book, Nietzsche had seen neither this nor any other of Wagner's works performed on stage except for *Meistersinger*.[47]

The effect that Nietzsche is striving to articulate is the cumulative effect of the whole work: 'In the total effect of tragedy the Dionysiac predominates once again' (§21). He may allude to the unfolding of the drama; he may give us fleeting glimpses of 'the jubilation of the horn', 'the rejoicing Kurwenal', 'the hero wounded, yet not dying' (§21); but it is total effects that he focuses on. Even the glimpses are of representative, not distinctive moments: others would have done as well. Here Nietzsche's antipathy to reductive analysis receives its most extreme expression. In so far as he can be said to be isolating any determinable aspect of the work itself, as opposed to the responses of its hypothetical auditor, it is its mood or ethos as viewed in a cosmic perspective. His coin is the shattering evocation of universality induced by the Dionysiac music and the 'glorious illusion' of the Apolline (§21) – the seductive particularity of the words, myth, and dramatic action that makes that evocation bearable. Music invests the drama with a supreme vividness, but still 'the Dionysiac predominates once again'. The climax of Nietzsche's depiction comes with a sustained and penetrating account of the 'co-existence of opposite feelings' in §22, which is later summed up as 'the experience of having to see and yearning for something beyond sight' (§24).

The picture is unsurpassed. Its colours are bold and, in the representation of the opposed feelings, the line is convincingly precise. And yet what is it a picture *of*? An experience, a complex response – to what? In this aspect the picture is so undefined, so generalized, that if the reader of §22 pauses to take his bearings, he must reflect that it is not even clear now whether this account of a 'true musical tragedy' is actually concerned with *Tristan*, Act III or Wagner at all, rather than tragedy as such.

Nietzsche's discussions of Wagner after their breach – for instance in *The Wagner Case* – will still put mood and ethos in the foreground, but they will be more particularized, more pointedly descriptive. And of course his descriptions will be generally hostile: while he never varies in his estimate of Wagner's stature and archetypal significance, his estimate of the merit of the archetype is quite different. Once he has become sceptical about Schopenhauerian metaphysics, he will never again have an elaborated theory of music to lean on for his descriptive purposes;[48] but once he has returned to a critical view of Wagner, he will feel free to reapply to him characterizations which in *BT* he reserves for representatives of decadence. Wagner, therefore, will be depicted as one who deals in 'literature' not life, an actor and a showman, neurotic, modern, unnatural and essentially false – like opera (§19), the New Dithyramb (§17), Euripides (§§10, 12).[49] For good measure Nietzsche will reinterpret Wagner's rebellion against form as a questionable flight from good order. On Wagner's 'infinite melody' he writes:

> it strives to break and sometimes even to despise all mathematical equilibrium of time and force...He dreads petrifaction, crystallization, the development of music into the architectural.[50]

He comes to see that Wagner's 'endlessly varied leitmotivic repetitions without any real "development"' had in effect 'replaced the clear contrastive dialectic of a Mozart, Beethoven, or even Chopin with a kind of rhetoric'.[51] Above all, he will insist on dissociating the effect of Wagnerian music drama from the tonic quality he sees in true tragedy. In a late note he relates tragedy to the strong man and his 'preference for terrifying things'. The same preference is said to be characteristic of Wagner – only 'the art of terrifying, in so far as it excites the nerves, can be esteemed by the weak and exhausted as a stimulant: that, for example, is the reason why Wagnerian art is esteemed today'.[52]

The later Nietzsche's antipathy to Wagner is not as one-sided as his earlier admiration. For the point needs making that the designation of Wagner as 'decadent' is, in Nietzsche's later parlance, not exclusively pejorative. On the contrary: in *The Wagner Case* and elsewhere the 'spirit of decadence' is presented as a historically necessary and even welcome preliminary to Europe's cultural rebirth, and Wagner acknowledged as one of its most powerful manifestations.

In *BT* there are no comparable qualifications. The passages dealing with the characteristic effect of Wagner's music (scattered over §§21–24) are certainly forceful and assured. This cannot be said of the discussion of Wagner's individual works, which largely consists of an endlessly repeated, but never fully explicit, assertion about their generic affiliation. Nietzsche represents Wagnerian opera as tragedy on a par with the work of the Greek tragedians. He nowhere argues for the right to do this: he seems to assume that Wagner's Aeschylean pretensions together with the impact of a work like *Tristan* guarantee it. Yet on the face of it, the drama that Wagner created is melodrama, 'near tragedy', as George Steiner calls it, 'four acts of tragic violence and guilt followed by a fifth act of redemption and innocence regained' – with redemption through love the arch-Wagnerian theme.[53] Such drama, Steiner claims, cannot be truly tragic, and the claim is precisely in line with the idea of the tragic which Nietzsche himself has helped to develop. If Wagner was to have been successfully portrayed as an Aeschylus, Nietzsche would have been obliged to argue a special case, or else modify his own conception of tragedy. Whatever service the portrayal of Wagner as tragedian may render to the theory of the tragic, it is not apparent that as it stands it sheds much light on him.

GREEK TRAGEDY AND GREEK TRAGEDIANS

In his critique of opera in §19 Nietzsche makes no mention of any composer or any operatic work by name. His book is a celebration of Wagner, and yet apart from an isolated reference to *Lohengrin* (§22) and a comment on the rebirth of German myth which presumably alludes to the *Ring* (§23), the only Wagnerian work to be discussed is *Tristan* (§§21–22) – and there the discussion is so selective and at the same time so generalized that it is not even clear at what point Nietzsche has turned away from Wagner's erotic masterpiece to 'musical tragedy' as a whole. His focus is wide and the nature of his argument is not calculated to make it any narrower.

It is essentially the same with Greek tragedy. Nietzsche is interested in tragedies and tragedians, but more interested in the tragic. Even so, he is not disposed to sacrifice concrete particularity in a quest for universals, as a thinker in the tradition of abstract analysis probably would be. If he is bent on defining the tragic, the only definition that will satisfy him is a definition in terms of individual experience. The tragic is not a commodity directly accessible to sense perception, yet for Nietzsche it is as if it has an inner pattern, an 'inscape', to borrow Hopkins' expression, which must be felt, lived through, to be known. Merely Socratic knowledge of it is not possible, or not enough.

Between the formal establishment of the Athenian tragic festival in or around 534 B.C. and the death of Sophocles in 406, over a thousand different tragedies (not counting satyr plays) were written and performed, some as connected trilogies, most as single, self-contained dramas. Various of the playwrights who were active over this period have left us names and fragments of their work. From only three of them – Aeschylus, Sophocles, Euripides – do we have whole dramas.[54] Between them, these three wrote over two hundred tragedies, of which we have (besides many fragments) thirty-two more or less intact: eighteen ascribed to Euripides, seven to Sophocles, and another seven to Aeschylus, three of which – *Agamemnon*, *Libation Bearers*, and *Eumenides* – constitute our sole surviving instance of a connected trilogy, the *Oresteia*. In §8 Nietzsche alludes to Euripides' *Alcestis* and on a few other occasions to mythological characters whose exploits or fates are particularly associated with Greek tragic contexts: Orestes in §3, Antigone and Cassandra in §4, Heracles in §19. None of these references, however, involves any comment on actual plays. The only plays commented on are: Sophocles' *Oedipus Rex* (§9), Aeschylus' *Prometheus* (§9 and, briefly, §10), Sophocles' *Oedipus at Colonus* (§9 and, briefly, §17), and Euripides' *Bacchae* (§12). For the rest Nietzsche relies on generalization, formulated largely in terms of his theory about the origin of tragedy or the construct associated with it – or the analogy he posits between Greek drama and Wagner.

Nietzsche's views on the three tragedians, his conception of Greece and his interpretation of the tragic are closely interwoven. Aeschylus, he believes, represents Greek tragedy's highest form (although Sophocles, with certain reservations, is comparable), just as the Greece of the late sixth and earlier fifth centuries – the period that centres on the Persian wars – represents the highest form of achieved life; and Aeschylean tragedy both epitomizes and supports life in that form. Early tragedy on his view is characterized by what in the *Self-Criticism* he calls a 'pessimism of strength': *pessimism*, because (unlike Socratism) it sees the riddle of life as insoluble; *strength*, because (unlike Buddhism and Schopenhauer) it associates that pessimistic vision not with a desire for passivity or escape, but rather with action and acceptance, even – or *especially* – acceptance of the darkest and hardest truths about life.

This complex attitude, which Nietzsche will subsequently subsume under his own phrase *amor fati*, is what enabled the Greeks to 'live resolutely in wholeness and fullness' (§18). It is this attitude, he argues, that Winckelmann and others misinterpreted as what he would call an untroubled condition of Apolline serenity. By the same token earlier aesthetics had made the Apolline qualities of serenity, beauty and harmony the key to Greek art and therefore art in general. This, Nietzsche insists, does not work for tragedy. Its essence is a dialectic: between beauty and truth, between serenity and suffering, between all the Apolline qualities of individuation, limitation and form and the destruction of everything individual in the Dionysiac – just as the tragic hero is destroyed by his transgression, intended or unintended, beyond the permissible limits of individual existence. In tragedy we glimpse the dark Dionysiac truths of life, we are confronted with Dionysiac experience in the shape of painful mythology and the annihilation of the hero – but the confrontation is experienced in Apolline terms (and therefore creatively) through the formality of art and the concrete specificity of myth. Nevertheless, tragedy began in the realm of the Dionysiac and through music and dark myth its basis remains Dionysiac.

It is true (Nietzsche continues) that even at its peak Greek tragedy offers a certain kind of higher optimism, as Aeschylus does with his concern for cosmic justice (§9). But this is a legitimate Apolline concern which is pursued in reaction to the Dionysiac truth, yet without damage to tragedy's Dionysiac basis. It is the Euripidean *rationalistic* version of optimism that is so damaging (§§10–14). Euripides' rationalism induces him to subvert the traditional Dionysiac basis of the genre, so that he tampers with the music and the myth. His penchant for naturalism, Nietzsche believes, is closely related; this too is untraditional and subversive. In Euripides' hands tragic language and formal stylization of all kinds are assimilated to quotidian reality, and so trivialized: the tragic heroes are no longer suffering heroes in lieu of the suffering god himself, but recognizable men and women. Furthermore, having abandoned tradition, his drama has to develop new and questionable sources of interest – elaborate argument and emotional excitement, rhetoric and pathos, 'freezing and burning' – the whole culminating in 'the great rhetorical–lyrical scenes in which the passion and dialectic of the protagonist swelled to a broad and powerful current' (§12). The formal hallmarks of Euripidean drama are the expository prologue, which is designed, like an epic narrative, to give the spectator an untroubled enjoyment of the drama, and the *deus ex machina* at the end, whose function is parallel ('to reassure the public about the future in store for his heroes'): 'between this epic preview and epic prospect lies the dramatic–lyric present, the "drama" proper' (§12).

Nietzsche's is very much a black and white assessment: Euripides all wrong, earlier tragedy all right. It is largely unqualified by reference to the range of extant plays and entirely heedless of the possible range of the lost ones. As such, it is bound to be in some degree a satirist's portrait, a caricature whose shape, as we have seen, is partly modelled on the ideas of that earlier master of satire, Aristophanes.[55] And yet, at the same time, it constitutes a schema of great suggestive power, and like the large interpretation of Greek literary history of which it forms the centrepiece, it has played its part in shaping subsequent interpretations of Greek tragedy.

On the white side of the caricature stand a largely undifferentiated Aeschylus and Sophocles. Sophocles is said to exhibit a certain 'perplexity' about the role of the chorus, which leads him to modify its activities and align it with the actors (§14); and it appears that he initiates realism in character portrayal, although within the limits suggested by the myth in question (§17). In both these respects, the contrast is with Aeschylus, but these apart, there is no obvious differentia between the two playwrights. In §9 Nietzsche opposes 'the glory of activity which illuminates Aeschylus' *Prometheus*' with the Sophoclean 'glory of passivity', but the latter is apparently confined to *Oedipus at Colonus* and there is, for once, no suggestion that the contrast is representative on a larger scale.

Apart from the discussion of the *Prometheus*, Nietzsche's interpretation of Aeschylus is largely implicit in his generalized account of Greek tragedy as a whole or else inferential in the criticisms of the subversive Euripides. Much is left unsaid as a result. One particular omission is revealing. Nietzsche does not find time to consider how far the connected trilogy pattern represented in the *Oresteia* (and apparently characteristic of Aeschylus and only of Aeschylus)[56] enacts the Dionysiac–Apolline dialectic. Certainly the Oresteian imposition of order on an unintelligible chaos of blood and revenge invites a discussion in these terms, and the conflict between the chthonic Erinyes (behind Clytemnestra) and Apollo (behind Orestes) offers the possibility of a paraliteralism that one would have thought Nietzsche could hardly resist. But he says nothing. If we turn to his treatment of Sophocles, we can perhaps see why. In §9 he discusses 'the most sorrowful figure of the Greek stage, the unfortunate Oedipus', who is presented by Sophocles as 'the noble human being who in spite of his wisdom is destined to error and misery [i.e. in *Oedipus Rex*], but who eventually [i.e. in *Oedipus at Colonus*], through his tremendous suffering, spreads a magical power of blessing that remains effective even beyond his decease'. Oedipus, that is, is to be buried on Attic soil and his spirit will thereafter become a protection to Athens. In §17 Nietzsche adds:

> In the old tragedy one could sense at the end that metaphysical consolation without which the delight in tragedy cannot be explained at all. The tones of reconciliation from another world sound purest, perhaps, in the *Oedipus at Colonus*.

But why this play? And why this playwright? 'Reconciliation from another world' is surely what Aeschylus offers us at the end of the *Oresteia* and, according to a widespread view, at the end of his trilogies in general. The Aeschylean trilogy, as one writer puts it, 'both destroys and constructs the universe';[57] and even Nietzsche's favourite, the *Prometheus*, is generally assumed to belong to such a larger, constructive whole.[58] Sophocles, by contrast, operates habitually with the single play (the two Oedipus tragedies are single plays and probably written as much as twenty years apart), and his single plays as we know them are not predominantly of this pattern at all. *Oedipus at Colonus* is in fact the only one of his extant works which could be so described – excepting, that is, the *Philoctetes*, whose resolution depends on a *deus ex machina* under Euripidean influence. The fact is that extant Sophocles is appreciably darker than extant Aeschylus, nor is there any particular reason to suppose that our samples are unrepresentative. In its relentless intensity, furthermore, the Sophoclean dark mode provides the purest examples not of 'reconciliation', but of those destructive patterns to which Nietzsche himself gives pride of place in his definition of the tragic.

We have nothing of Aeschylus that is as total in its 'annihilation of the individual' as *Oedipus Rex*. Nor (to take an instance Nietzsche ignores) do we have anything in Aeschylus that exudes 'the ugly and the disharmonic' (§24) on the scale of Sophocles' *Trachiniae*, where the traditional apotheosis of its hero, Heracles, has been suppressed, and we are left with his son agreeing to marry Heracles' concubine, thanks to whom the hero has met a peculiarly hideous death. But as Nietzsche would wish, this pessimism is not a pessimism of weakness. Hyllus will marry Iole, repugnant though it is, and the closing verses of the play refer us to 'strange deaths and unheard-of sufferings' –

koủden toutōn ho ti mē Zeus
and each one of these things Zeus.

Into this final, verbless sentence – Zeus has caused it all or simply *is* it all – the whole strength of the traditional religious outlook is compressed. The last word is *Zeus:* the keynote is therefore acceptance.

> Saying Yes to life even in its strangest and hardest problems; the will to life rejoicing over its own inexhaustibility even in the very sacrifice of its highest types – this is what I called Dionysiac, this is what I understood as the bridge to the psychology of the tragic poet.[59]

However misleading some of Nietzsche's late glosses on his first book, this one is a fair summary (apart, perhaps, from the use of 'Dionysiac') – and it sums up the *praxis* of *Trachiniae* and *Oedipus Rex* no less than the theoretical position of *BT*. The Greek religious pessimism that Nietzsche understands so well receives its finest expression in tragedy, and not in Aeschylus, but in Sophocles.[60] There is a 'yes to life' in both poets, but in Aeschylus the 'strangest and hardest problems' are associated with a constructive vision which Sophocles gives no consistent sign of possessing, and which serves to temper the strangeness and hardness of the problems concerned. The procession at the end of the *Eumenides* proclaims peace (*spondai*). It is presented as a peace sanctioned and determined by Zeus and Fate, but also, explicitly, as peace on earth, a better future for man. This is not metaphysical consolation in the sense that *Trachiniae* offers it or even in the sense that *Oedipus at Colonus* offers it. For if the latter play at last sees Oedipus released from his earthly sorrows and thereby bringing divine protection to the land, it also sees him invoking the fateful curse on his two sons, and the focus of interest at the close of the play is in fact Antigone's all too justified apprehensions about the future.

If we may legitimately generalize from the *Eumenides*, Aeschylus' reconciliatory tones include an extra positive note. His Nietzschean-tragic pessimism is less pure. His principle of divine power working through human suffering to create order out of chaos is not what Nietzsche dismisses as 'an earthly resolution of the tragic dissonance' (§17), but it is closer to such optimism (if that is the word) than anything Sophocles has to offer. Of Aeschylus' extant works, the *Prometheus* (unlike the trilogy to which it is presumed to belong) is the most pessimistic in Nietzsche's sense –[61] and this is the only one of his plays that Nietzsche invokes in detail.

If Aeschylus is not, after all, the model of Nietzschean pessimism, why must he be presented as if he were? The answer, in a word, is Wagner. Nietzsche's commitment to the Master and the Bayreuth ideal leaves him no choice. It is Aeschylean, not Sophoclean, drama that Wagner aspires to emulate. His admiration for Aeschylus, however, is based on several grounds which, though entirely reasonable in themselves, have very little to do with the Nietzschean-tragic at all. There is the grand sweep of the connected trilogy (which is imitated in the *Ring*) and the playwright-composer's total involvement in performance, in accordance with Greek tradition, as producer and actor. There is the political rôle of the drama: it is Aeschylus who mythologizes the Persian wars and Aeschylus who is called upon in Aristophanes' *Frogs* to save the community in its hour of need. And there is, of course, the musical element in Aeschylus' plays; it is true (as Nietzsche says) that the choral component in Sophocles is somewhat reduced in scope.

This last point supplies Nietzsche with his pretext for choosing Aeschylus. Although he briefly and belatedly associates tragedy with politics (§§21, 23), its association with music matters far more to him – and, of course, not only for reasons of loyalty to Wagner. His belief that tragedy arose from music is supported by the Wagnerian analogue, but not dependent on it, and his theory about the Dionysiac element in the two arts is equally his own. If, therefore, tragedy and music are so intimately related, and if Aeschylus is not merely chronologically closer to the supposed musical origin, but a more obviously musical (lyrical) dramatist in any case, Aeschylus, on this count, must be the paradigm. Nietzsche is thus faced with a contradiction. His argument about the link between tragedy and music seems to be substantiated most satisfactorily by Aeschylus, but his conception of the tragic by Sophocles. Nevertheless, he cannot admit any difficulty. Loyalty to Wagner prevents it, and that same loyalty makes it inevitable that he should look to the earlier tragedian for a way of cutting the knot. Aeschylus accordingly becomes the paradigm, and Nietzsche seeks to evade the contradiction by concentrating on the Aeschylean play most amenable to his special purpose.

And yet there is another aspect of Sophocles' tragedy that should have made him more congenial than his predecessor. If Aeschylus has the right kind of chorus, Sophocles unquestionably has the right kind of hero. Nietzsche's conception of the tragic presupposes the suffering and destruction of a single, great individual. The spectator of tragedy 'feels the actions of the hero to be justified, and yet is even more uplifted when those actions annihilate their agent' (§22); in the central hero he – or his Greek predecessors – is seeing an image of Dionysus himself (§10). As John Jones has pointed out, the central hero has no canonical status either in ancient theory or – a separate and more important matter – in ancient practice.[62] Aeschylus' *Agamemnon*, Sophocles' *Antigone*, Euripides' *Trojan Women*: these and many other plays are distorted if we insist on forcing them rigidly into what is very much a Shakespearean-Romantic frame of reference. At the same time, many tragedies conform to the type more or less (for which reason alone Jones' argument is overstated),[63] and it is Sophocles rather than Aeschylus who best exemplifies it. Bernard Knox goes so far as to suggest that 'the presentation of the tragic dilemma in the figure of a single dominating character seems...to be an invention of Sophocles'.[64] The two Oedipus plays, Nietzsche's Sophoclean witnesses, centre on a single character. So too does his Aeschylean instance, the *Prometheus*. That play, Knox argues, may well be the latest of Aeschylus' extant tragedies (which is a widespread view) and written under Sophoclean influence.[65] Others have supposed that the play is not by Aeschylus at all;[66] it is, at all events, his sole extant example of the type. Sophocles, by contrast, leans towards it even in his reconciliatory mood (*Oedipus at Colonus* and *Philoctetes*); and in *Oedipus Rex* he produces its classic realization. Here, in particular, we find the Nietzschean pattern, the hero's suffering and his annihilation.

If Nietzsche's obligations towards Aeschylus inhibit him from developing his formula for tragedy on its natural Sophoclean ground, the formula does not lose its value. Annihilation, *but also* metaphysical consolation: this is a successful crystallization of earlier tragedy in general and Sophocles in particular, and it plays a central part in Nietzsche's statement of the tragic. It serves also to sum up what he misses in Euripides. From the *Medea* to the *Bacchae*, there is plenty of annihilation in Euripides, despite his fondness for using the *deux ex machina*. But metaphysical consolation is certainly not the note he strikes.

Nietzsche is not renowned for his fairness, and his critique of Euripides is in many ways grossly unfair. The portrait, nevertheless, has its impressive aspects. In itself it is not dissimilar to the later portrayal of Wagner: 'genius', 'richly endowed', especially with 'an extraordinary fund of critical talent' (§11) – but a degenerate genius, one whose peculiar greatness threatens the stability of its own medium and one which in its peculiarity symptomatizes the disruption of a whole cultural equilibrium. It is not the scale of Euripides' abilities that Nietzsche casts doubt on – and this part of his assessment is reiterated in later years[67] – but rather their character.

Where Nietzsche's treatment of Euripides is consistently right is in raising the right issues: and if we allow for the extreme and generalized tone of his presentation, we will not find his answers wholly unacceptable either. Nietzsche's denunciation of the destroyer of traditional myth, for instance, receives its scholarly confirmation in D. W. Lucas' summary:

In Euripides' plays...there appears a loss of confidence in the innate significance of the old stories and a readiness to give them an unnatural twist in order that they may fulfil momentarily a new purpose. Jason and Medea, selfish male and passionate woman, belong only intermittently to the heroic world;...in the *Electra* an invented character, Electra's peasant husband, takes a leading part, and Apollo's dubious oracle is flatly rejected... In his later years Euripides used myth almost for pure entertainment in his numerous plays of intrigue, [in which he concentrated on]...dramatic excitement...and diverted his audience with brilliant scenes of recognition, cunningly planned escapes, and salvation snatched from catastrophe. *Iphigeneia in Tauris*, *Helen* and *Ion* belong to this class and so did many lost plays. They end in unalloyed happiness, and in the *Andromeda* this was accompanied by the wish-fulfilments of triumphant love. Such things must have seemed to many a profanation of myth; really they showed a new kind of sensibility.[68]

It is not at all clear that the 'profanation' and the 'new kind of sensibility' are incompatible. The further we go towards identifying them, the closer we come to Nietzsche's position.

Tragic myth relates men, usually in a heroic setting, and gods; and if Euripides is uncomfortable with the heroic end of the relationship, he is equally so with the divine. In antiquity he had the reputation of an atheist, while Nietzsche, of course, presents him as implacably hostile to the one deity, Dionysus. Such interpretations are crude, to say the least, and Nietzsche hardly improves his case by taking his paraliteralisms so literally as to be willing to subscribe to the gratuitous and naïve 'recantation' theory of the *Bacchae* (§12):

> To excise this original and all-powerful Dionysiac element from tragedy, and to reconstruct tragedy purely on the basis of an un-Dionysiac art, morality and world view – this is Euripides' tendency...In the evening of his life, Euripides himself propounded to his contemporaries...the question of the value and significance of this tendency by means of a myth. Is the Dionysiac entitled to exist at all? Should it not be forcibly uprooted from Greek soil? Certainly, the poet tells us, if only it were possible: but the god Dionysus is too powerful; his most intelligent adversary – like Pentheus in the *Bacchae* – is unwittingly enchanted by him, and in this enchantment runs to meet his fate...This is what we are told by a poet who opposed Dionysus with heroic valour throughout a long life – and who finally ended his career with a glorification of his adversary...

A comparison of the *Bacchae* with *Hippolytus*, written twenty years earlier (428 B.C.), suffices to show that Euripides had been willing to defer to the power of the irrational-divine well before the 'evening of his life'.

Dramatists' beliefs are, in any case, not so simply inferred from their dramas as Nietzsche appears to suppose: the correlation he posits between the author and his product is peculiarly deceptive here. What one can say about Euripides and the divine is that he has a habit of bringing the gods into disrepute (plays as different as *Ion*, *Trojan Women*, and *Heracles* come to mind), and sometimes confronts his audience with the thought that if the gods are disreputable, they may as well not exist.[69] It does not, however, seem to follow from this that Euripides is an 'optimist', as Nietzsche calls him and as Socrates assuredly was. He sounds much more of a pessimist like Nietzsche himself – with the important proviso that the affirmation, the pessimism of *strength*, is not apparent. Certainly, if we discount the melodramas, Euripides' plays are as gloom-ridden as one could imagine. The numerous debates between his characters usually achieve nothing, except to demonstrate the futility of debate, and his *deus ex machina* by its very arbitrariness is liable to make life seem less, not more, soluble: *Medea* serves to illustrate both points. Euripides, then, is appreciably less of an 'optimist' than Aeschylus – but (we can add in Nietzsche's defence) Aeschylus offers 'higher' optimism within the terms of traditional religion, where Euripides, assuredly, finds no consolation.

If Euripides is not an optimist, is he at least a rationalist? Is he (in the first place) more of a rational, 'critical' artist than his predecessors? 'The philosopher of the stage', as Sextus Empiricus (*c.* A.D. 200) called him,[70] is certainly a cerebral writer, the prototype of the Western intellectual. He thinks and he makes his audience think – about the gods, about women, about war. He even draws attention to earlier tragedians' technical inadequacies: the satire in his *Electra* on the recognition scene in Aeschylus' *Libation Bearers* is a celebrated case in point. It is as if he wished to induce his audience to think not only about the content of his plays, but their dramaturgy too. But none of this makes him more of a 'critical' artist than Aeschylus, who implicitly criticized the dramaturgical resources of the tragedy of his day by inventing the second actor, or Sophocles, who did the same when he added the third – or Wagner, with his many formal and theatrical innovations. And (unlike the German dramatists of Nietzsche's age) all the Greek tragedians could not but be technically alert, if only because, as producers of their own plays, they were bound to be mindful of dramatic effects and audience reactions when writing. This is simply one facet of the 'wholeness' of their artistic milieu. If Euripides is a critic on this account, Aeschylus and Sophocles are critics as well. So too is Wagner; and in the context of Wagner's theatrical expertise and the unabating consciousness revealed in his innumerable prose treatises, Nietzsche's characterization of Euripides as a Socratic on the strength of his 'critical' interest in drama is not the least remarkable of the acrobatic feats in the book.

In what sense, if any, *can* Euripides be called a rationalist? The question was once posed in a celebrated essay by E. R. Dodds.[71] In direct opposition to the thesis of *BT* (although Nietzsche is not mentioned by name), Dodds dissociated Euripides from Socrates and pronounced him an 'irrationalist'. He defined rationalism in terms of three beliefs, none of which could be ascribed to Euripides: 'reason as the instrument of truth – as the essential character of reality – as the means to personal redemption'. In support of his case he produced an array of citations, from the inability of Medea's reason to keep her from what she herself calls a 'foul murder', to Cadmus' plea in the *Bacchae* that gods in their wrath ought not to be like men. That 'ought', however, and Medea's inner conflict suggest a conclusion which Dodds fails to draw: Euripides may not comply with Dodds' formulae for rationalism, but he would dearly like to. Furthermore, in those formulae the connection between rationalism and optimism is quite clear.

Up to a point, then, Nietzsche is right to associate Euripides with rationalism and, after all, with optimism and even with Socrates. Faced with the painful complexities of life and a traditional religious view of them, Sophocles accepts that view; Aeschylus, before him, offers a positive interpretation of it; Euripides laments the pain and exposes his discontent with the traditions. He appears to want a different world. It would be a world, perhaps, without the conflicts he diagnoses so well: conflict inside a single individual, sterile argument between two opposing individuals, collisions between the living and the forces seemingly larger than life, and, not least, the conflicts of war. That last expression of the Greek agonistic spirit (which is how Nietzsche himself elsewhere sees it)[72] is given its exemplary Hellenic treatment in the *Iliad:* war is destructive, but also heroic and glorious; poignant, but also a presupposition of life. The disillusionment with war in a play like *Trojan Women* is as untraditional as any of Euripides' other stances. He wants a rational world; he is, therefore, Socratic in aspiration. This is not Nietzsche's thesis, but his argument, at least as much as Dodds', leads one to it.

Concerned, as his predecessors had been, with the human condition, but dissatisfied with traditional explanations, Euripides looks inside the human psyche for illumination. He replaces theology with psychology, shifting the emphasis from the conditioning to its human object, sometimes (as in *Bacchae* and *Hippolytus*) even converting the gods who had once defined the condition into personifications of internal drives. In his hands tragic characters become more human, more individual, more naturalistic. 'People as they are, not as they should be', reports Aristotle; 'ruthless realism and psychological insight', writes one critic; the discovery of 'inwardness', suggests another.[73] Wilamowitz, in one of the more impressive moments of his tirade against *BT*, alluded to the 'disjunction between desire and fulfilment' embodied in Euripidean characters.[74] In this sphere Nietzsche is at his most prejudiced. It is not that there are no grounds for his critique; but he distorts them so singlemindedly that one wonders how Euripides can possibly deserve the title of 'genius' which he is ready to award him:

> The mirror in which formerly only grand and bold traits were represented now showed the painful fidelity that conscientiously reproduces even the botched outlines of nature (§11).

It is ironic that the admirer of Hellenic man should speak so disparagingly of that man's 'nature'; ironic too that he should himself be in process of developing a psychological penetration not unlike Euripides' own.

Perhaps Nietzsche's worst failing is that he makes this varied and, in some ways, inscrutable dramatist into a monolith. Apart from anything else, Euripides is an uneven writer whose work has some indefensible characteristics. One thinks of the tediously insistent emotive-operatic repetitions of single words in his lyrics[75] – or the self-sufficient rhetorical debates in which the presentation of a case exceeds the character and even the action, like the notorious argument between Theseus and the Theban herald on the merits of alternative political systems in *Suppliants*. It is not to Nietzsche's credit that he puts creative, albeit hazardous, innovations like naturalism, or even melodrama, no higher than lapses like these.

The measure of Nietzsche's unfairness to Euripides is his assertion that Euripides killed tragedy. The repeated subversion of traditional norms by a revolutionary genius undoubtedly made it hard for his successors to revert to tradition or (for want of his genius) to take his innovations much further, but Euripides is a symptom of crisis, rather than its cause. There were, as we have seen, much larger forces at work.[76] Nor is Euripides alone as a subverter of traditional proprieties: the 'traditionalist' Aristophanes is another for whom the old generic norms have clearly lost some of their significance.[77] Nietzsche grants that Euripides is not the inventor of his 'Socratic' spirit, but still apportions too much blame to him.

One likely reason for this excessive antagonism is that Euripides, like the New Dithyramb,[78] reminds Nietzsche uncomfortably of Wagner – that is, of some of those aspects of Wagner's personality and art which for the moment he contrives to ignore. Not only does Euripides reflect the New Dithyrambic victory of music over word of which 'operatic' repetitions are a symptom. He is also, like Wagner, a 'critic' and conscious innovator on a large scale, and worst of all, he even anticipates Wagner's quintessential mode. For as surely as Euripides' romantic melodrama is the spiritual ancestor of grand opera, *Tristan* itself is directly prefigured by the neurotic love-death configuration of a work like *Hippolytus*. This unacknowledged affinity might have served to evoke others, not all of them unwelcome – Racine's Euripidean *Phèdre*, Shakespeare's *Antony and Cleopatra* – but the association with Euripides cannot be countenanced, and Wagner must be protected from it.

It is perhaps to the point that if Nietzsche shows no sympathy with Euripides, he nevertheless pays him the compliment of empathy. Where Aeschylus and Sophocles remain shadowy figures, Euripides is made real. He sits in the theatre and thinks (§11); he is a 'passionate actor' (§12); in the 'evening of his life' he recants (§12). Accurately or not, Nietzsche 'goes into' him, in fact he psychologizes him – and thereby, without any such intention, vindicates one of Euripides' own supreme innovations.

Nietzsche is not interested in giving an exhaustive account of the incidentals of Greek tragedy, but in locating its essence. A major rôle in locating that essence is played by Wagner. On the face of it, Wagner's presence in *BT* is not overwhelming; it seems representative that the first and the last sections (§§1 and 25) should be about tragedy and aesthetics, and not modern music at all. Wagner, nevertheless, has a central importance, because of his influence on Nietzsche's tragic and aesthetic theories themselves. Tragedy is an art in which the Dionysiac is predominant; Wagner is one model of Dionysiac art;

and in particular the live *effect* of Wagnerian music drama serves as the pattern for the effect of 'musical tragedy' as a whole. The relationship, therefore, between Nietzsche's responses to tragedy and to Wagner is two-way. He has reinterpreted Wagner to align him with Aeschylus and Sophocles; and he has projected his experience of Wagner onto Greek tragedy.

The heart of Nietzsche's analogy between tragedy and Wagner is his supposition that Wagner can recreate the kind of impact that the Greek dramatists had on their audiences. The impact of Wagner's music on Nietzsche himself is not in doubt:

> every tissue, every nerve vibrates in me and it is a long time since I had such an enduring feeling of rapture...[79]

Nor is there any question about the potent effect of Greek tragedy in its theatrical context: a drama that moved audiences to tears and induced miscarriages in pregnant women[80] was certainly no less stirring than *Meistersinger* or *Tristan*. Further than this, Nietzsche's recreation of tragedy's effect by analogy is inevitably speculative; but this is not to deny his right to speculate. Any criticism of his attempt should be set against the impossibility of recreating the original experience *as an experience* by means of cumulative scholarship alone.

There is no virtue, however, in overlooking the distortions which the Wagnerian perspective on tragedy produces. The grossest of these arise from the discrepancy, which Nietzsche refuses to admit, between the dominance of music in Wagner and the dominance of the word in tragedy. Nietzsche's treatment of music in the mature Greek drama is no more acceptable than his treatment of the music of its putative ancestral form, or of Greek music as a whole. In §17 he makes a half-hearted attempt to represent the effect of tragic music as comparable to Wagner's, though elsewhere he tends to ascribe a Wagnerian capability rather to the dithyramb. The musical element of tragedy, however, is in any case credited with a special importance as a result of a loose identification (as in §14) with the chorus. This is specious. The choral portions of tragedy *are* important, but as far as we can tell, their importance in Aeschylus or Sophocles (as opposed to the proto-drama) is heavily dependent on their verbal component. There is no more reason here than elsewhere to doubt the truth of Plato's dictum that music follows the word.[81] Although disdained by Nietzsche (§19), the principle is confirmed by all the observable facts of Greek tragedy as we have it – until we reach the lyrics of Euripides...

Nietzsche does not devote too much of his energies to this facet of his argument; he spends rather more on a covert, and still more surprising, equation between Wagner's music and the *mythic* patterns of Greek drama. Only the tragedians' characteristic use of the chorus to explicate those patterns gives the equation any plausibility, but after a time Nietzsche seems to look upon it as an established fact: the unexplained shift from music in §21 to tragedy in §22 is the most obvious sign of this. Erich Podach has argued that *BT* embodies a tension between Nietzsche's aims and Wagner's,[82] and such complications as follow from Nietzsche's attempt to assimilate two different genres might seem to justify this idea. The complications, however, are partly of Nietzsche's own making, and in any case Wagner's rôle deserves a more positive evaluation. Without Wagner there would have been no occasion for *BT* or for any elaborated tragic theory at all. Without any 'tension' there would have been no impetus for Nietzsche to develop his own ideas. Wagner's is a creative presence, not a mere distraction or disruption. It is not as if Nietzsche says much about the aspects of tragedy which actually interested Wagner himself – cultural context, dramaturgy, theatrical properties and techniques. It is characteristic of Nietzsche, but hardly of Wagner, that the discussion of the effect of Greek tragedy should be pursued virtually without reference to a theatrical context, ancient or modern: the Wagner whose presence is felt in *BT* is a Nietzscheanized Wagner. Nevertheless, it is his blood that Nietzsche has used to make the ghosts of Greek tragedy talk; and they have seldom been made to talk more arrestingly.

Nietzsche's detailed observations on tragedy are generally part and parcel of the quest for its essence. Accordingly, they are mediated through the construct, which for him embodies the determinants of that essence. This is apparent in his discussion of the metaphysical depth of the chorus (first alluded to in §7); in the thesis that until Euripides the suffering hero is a surrogate Dionysus (§10); in the dictum that heroes 'talk more superficially than they act' (§17) and in the closely related passage on Sophocles in §9:

> The language of Sophocles' heroes amazes us by its Apolline precision and lucidity, so that we immediately have the feeling that we are looking into the innermost ground of their being, with some astonishment that the way to this ground should be so short. But...suppose we penetrate into the myth that projects itself in these lucid reflections: then we suddenly experience...the effects of a glance into the innermost terrors of nature.

In such passages the peculiar impressiveness of Nietzsche's construct shows up well. Above all, when he invokes his 'Apolline precision' or tells us that 'until Euripides, Dionysus never ceased to be the tragic hero', he recreates the god-heavy world of Greek tragedy in the act of discussing it.

The force of that recreation in its turn depends on Nietzsche's feeling for Greek religion. Greek tragedy is not a religious entity in the exclusive sense that medieval mystery plays are, but compared with Ibsen – or with Shakespeare – its religious character is unmistakable. Through his construct Nietzsche affirms the generic religious ground and the 'theological' significance of tragedy. At the same time, however, the generic basis of his categories helps to ensure his inattention to individual plays. Attic tragedy preserves the religious outlook of archaic Greece as a condition of its being. It is a *donnée* and, as such, it cannot also be a point of differentiation between one tragedy and another. It does not, therefore, afford Nietzsche any criterion for evaluating single plays. It cannot, in itself, even distinguish *Prometheus* from *Oedipus Rex:* those plays are simply two versions of the imposition of Apolline order on Dionysiac horror. Like the classicism of classical music or the grandeur of grand opera, the religious basis of tragedy is a precondition of its status, but not a guarantee of its particular effectiveness. And Nietzsche's construct, by directing us to that basis, directs us to tradition, not individual design; to art as phenomenon and symptom, not art as achieved success. His terms – the Socratic, as well as the Dionysiac–Apolline – are so unconcerned with the individual work that we cannot even gauge from them whether the best Socratic art (say, Euripides' *Hippolytus*) has in itself more to offer the world than a competent 'Apolline' temple statue of the sixth century B.C. In such matters the 'in itself' is remote from Nietzsche's interests.

If Nietzsche gives tragedy back its religious ground, it cannot be said that he gives it back its wholeness. Not only does its theatrical aspect mean little to him. Even within the religious basis, his concentration on the metaphysical at the expense of the socio-political leads to a further narrowing; and for all his insistence on the corporate nature of Dionysiac worship, even the metaphysical itself is seen in individual existential terms. In all this he reflects the predispositions of the German intellectual ethos of his age. The result is a marked emphasis on the kind of tragedy which, like *Prometheus* and *Oedipus Rex*, not only centres on a suffering heroic individual, but exposes him to the full force of the cosmos. Such plays satisfy all of Nietzsche's requirements, unlike, for instance, those that present the sufferings associated with the human configurations and conflicts of saga: *Seven Against Thebes*, *Antigone*, even the *Oresteia*. Not for the last time, we see Nietzsche faced with a discrepancy between tragedy and his notion of the tragic, and determined to concentrate his attention on the latter.

TRAGEDY AND THE TRAGIC

The essence of Nietzsche's interpretation of the tragic is the dialectic between the Apolline and the Dionysiac, but a presupposition of this dialectic is the protean nature of its constituents. For better or worse, the Apolline and the Dionysiac are not translatable into constant analytical equivalents: the embodiment of each varies according to the embodiment of the other. At times the variation can be alarming. In his discussion of *Prometheus* and *Oedipus Rex* in §9, Nietzsche identifies the poetic conception with the Apolline, myth with the Dionysiac, whereas in the origin of the genre the Apolline is words, dialogue, actors and drama as against the Dionysiac sphere of music, lyrics and chorus. But in §21 he opposes Dionysiac music to protective – and therefore Apolline – myth. From §9 we gather that tragedy consists of a Dionysiac basis and an Apolline surface; from §10, that its 'mystery doctrine' is Dionysiac, as opposed to its Apolline form. To judge from §22 and §24 it would seem that the tragic hero is Apolline, but his annihilation Dionysiac; and yet at the end of §9 Prometheus is described as a Dionysiac figure in a formula echoed in §21.

These apparent contraditions are resolved as soon as we perceive what Nietzsche prefers not to say: that the *pure* Dionysiac never exists in art, and that therefore the dialectic between Dionysiac and Apolline is visible in all forms and all aspects of art. Wherever we look, we see both tendencies, but in varying degrees. Tragic myth is neither Dionysiac nor Apolline, but both, as Nietzsche in fact makes clear in §22. Even music, as we have seen, must be regarded as both. The choral component of tragedy, as a combination of music and word, is in any case both. But by comparison with tragedy, music is Dionysiac. By comparison with sculpture, tragedy is Dionysiac. Within tragedy the choral part is Dionysiac by comparison with the dialogue, and the music of the choral part by comparison with the words. The suffering hero is Dionysiac by comparison with other characters; his annihilation is Dionysiac by comparison with his dramatic *persona*. He too is both Dionysiac and Apolline; this is shown in §10. Nietzsche is certainly open to criticism for failing to explicate his own theory more fully (scorn of expatiation is a persistent trait of his philosophizing), but the theory itself is readily explicable.

Of the various manifestations of the construct, the most important for Nietzsche's conception of the tragic is the hero's suffering and destruction. The hero belongs to the physical, the ephemeral; his destruction to the metaphysical, the eternal; and his status is defined by contrast with the chorus, whose concern with the eternal, explicit in their gnomic comments and implicit in their dramatic permanence, gives them a special rôle. An important corollary is that the ephemeral Apolline is *unreal* compared with the permanent Dionysiac; that is, we perceive it as such, we respond to the

Dionysiac on a deeper level. Nietzsche's aesthetic here runs parallel to his interpretation of the Greek Olympians as psychologically superficial, which Wilamowitz for one found hard to comprehend; but with the concept of depth psychology now a commonplace and with the recognition among competent scholars that by contrast with his Olympian counterparts Dionysus represents (in Dodds' phrase) 'the elemental in one's own nature', the peculiar vividness of Nietzsche's construct is especially telling here.[83]

In one sense the Dionysiac–Apolline dialectic represents an answer – and a quite original answer – to a question which had occurred to Plato and which clearly concerns Aristotle: why do we get pleasure from tragedy?[84] The question is one that has been raised repeatedly in modern times, where the wider experience of literature than a fourth-century theorist could envisage has informed the discussion with a double awareness: that tragedy has an effect which, if not confined to it, is peculiarly characteristic of it; and that the effect is associated with tragedy as a whole, not only Greek *tragōidia:* Shakespeare as well as Sophocles. Aristotle's answer to the question seems to be summed up in the formula that tragedy 'produces the pleasure that springs from pity and fear'. In the course of the *Poetics*, however, he also tells us that the human species enjoys miniature versions of unpleasant things, and that serious poetry helps us to learn about patterns of action in life. The pleasure in miniatures apparently depends on the pleasure in learning,[85] but still no coherent answer to the question emerges.[86] Nietzsche's answer is coherent and impressive. Tragedy, he argues, presents us with the destruction of individuals in a way which is exalting, because it gives us a glimpse of the underlying deeper power of life ('"we believe in eternal life", exclaims tragedy', §16), in which we have a share, but which is only glimpsed when individuality is transcended.

The glimpse of the eternal is what Nietzsche elsewhere calls 'metaphysical consolation...from another world' (§17). As a product of the Dionysiac, this part of the tragic effect is closely associated with the embodiment of Dionysiac wisdom, the chorus (§7); and in the context of the opposition between chorus and hero, the formula 'from another world' has a unique value. It conveys with a superb rightness the impression of cosmic insight we are offered by (for instance) the first stasimon of Sophocles' *Antigone*. Creon, newly king of Thebes, has issued his edict that the body of the exiled Polynices be left unburied, and an unknown hand (Antigone's) has defied the edict. After Creon's expressions of anger and his talk of treachery and punishment, the chorus sings. This chorus consists of Theban elders, loyal supporters of their king, and during the action before and after this song, their spoken comments, respectful or reserved, reveal those elder-ly traits of which Eliot's first hero *manqué*, Prufrock, supplies a suitably ironic modern version:

> No! I am not Prince Hamlet, nor was meant to be;
> Am an attendant lord, one that will do
> To swell a progress, start a scene or two,
> Advise the prince; no doubt, an easy tool,
> Deferential, glad to be of use,
> Politic, cautious, and meticulous;
> Full of high sentence, but a bit obtuse.

Such is the chorus as a speaking individual, or group of individuals, within the individuated world of the drama proper. When they sing, and in this song in particular, they are something else. *Polla ta deina*, they begin, 'wonders' (or 'terrors') 'are many, and none more so than man', and with these words they launch the famous ode that traverses man's achievements, then his mortal limitations, and eventually comes to rest on the matters of the moment: the law of the land and the justice of heaven.[87] In point of fact, no Theban elders would ever have had thoughts like these or in this order or expressed in such terms; and the popular notion that here and there the elders say (or sing) more than they know 'by dramatic irony' is no more adequate than the idea that such lyrics are what they are 'only' by convention. The words have a deeper or higher wisdom altogether. They seem to have been transmitted from a great and mysterious distance and to be coming gradually closer, but only at the end of their journey is their contact with everyday meaning fully established. The elders' veneer of characterization is not abandoned in this song, but it is shown to be no more than a veneer. We are thus given precisely that sense of double perspective which Nietzsche points to in the later sections of *BT* (although he does not himself discuss the chorus in these terms): the impact of the deeper, lyric chorus serves to undermine its 'real' worldly status and, by extension, the status of the characters in their 'real' world too.

Nietzsche's answer to Plato's question is pitched in terms of the special recreative experience which the spectator or auditor of musical tragedy is privileged to have. In §22 he tells us that the Greek audience responded 'aesthetically' to tragedy and that now, 'with the rebirth of tragedy, the aesthetic listener [*der ästhetische Zuhörer*] is reborn too'; in §24 we hear also of 'the aesthetic spectator' (*der ästhetische Zuschauer*). The aesthetic response, we gather, is distinct from three others, past or present: an intellectual or critical response, which (for instance) prevents myth from being taken seriously (§§22–23); a moral response, where 'the sacrifice of the hero' is seen to be 'in the interest of a moral vision of the universe'; and the Aristotelian 'pathological response', where we feel as involved in the action as if we were participants ourselves,[88] and where 'the serious events are supposed to prompt pity and fear to discharge themselves in a way that relieves us' (§22).

In the light of Nietzsche's understanding of the tragic experience, there is nothing surprising in his rejection of these alternatives. What is surprising is that he should associate the right response with the word 'aesthetic', a word strongly evocative of the ideal of distant, dispassionate, painless contemplation of art which is associated with Kant and, in his wake, with Schopenhauer. In §6 Nietzsche uses the word with direct reference to this ideal in its Schopenhauerian version:

> 'As what does music appear in the mirror of images and concepts?' It *appears as* will, taking the term in Schopenhauer's sense, i.e. as the opposite of the aesthetic, purely contemplative, and passive frame of mind.

But it is perverse of Nietzsche himself to use the word as he does, because *his* 'aesthetic response' is not intended to be purely contemplative and passive at all. In an ironic discussion of Schlegel's 'ideal spectator' in §7 he does indeed purport to accept the contemplative ideal:

> We had believed in an aesthetic public and considered the individual spectator the better qualified the more he was capable of viewing a work of art as art, that is, aesthetically. But now Schlegel tells us that the perfect, ideal spectator does not allow the world of the drama to act on him aesthetically at all, but rather physically and empirically. Oh, these Greeks! we sighed; they upset all our aesthetics!

The implication, one might suppose, is that Nietzsche too equates the perfect response with disinterested contemplation, that he, at one with the Kantian tradition, opposes the aesthetic to voluntary energy and active involvement. But what he now does is to redefine the perfect response in a way that undercuts such equations and oppositions, while at the same time retaining for it the denomination 'aesthetic'.[89] The redefined response is the 'coexistence of opposite feelings', Apolline and Dionysiac: on the Apolline side, will-less contemplation; on the Dionysiac, an enhanced involvement, which in its own way reflects the relation between the Dionysiac and the will.

To the aesthetic spectator (Nietzsche tells us in §22) the inner content of the dramatic action, its motives, its passions become 'sensuously visible...like a multitude of vividly moving lines and figures'. But –

> while he thus becomes conscious of the highest exaltation of his instincts for clarity and transfiguration, he nevertheless feels...that this long series of Apolline artistic effects still does *not* generate that blissful dwelling in will-less contemplation which the sculptor and the epic poet, those strictly Apolline artists, induce in him by their

artistic productions...He beholds the transfigured world of the stage and yet denies it. He sees the tragic hero before him in epic clarity and beauty and yet rejoices at his annihilation. He comprehends the events of the scene to their core, and yet delights in fleeing into the incomprehensible. He feels the actions of the hero to be justified and yet is even more uplifted when those actions annihilate their agent. He shudders at the sufferings which are to befall the hero, and yet divines in them a higher, much more overpowering joy. He sees more, and sees it more profoundly, than ever, and yet wishes he was blind.

It is implicit in this exposition that the Dionysiac spectator is personally, emotionally, totally involved in Dionysiac art (or the Dionysiac component of art). That premise helps to explain why an unmediated Dionysiac artistic experience would be a totally shattering one (§21). It also sheds light on Nietzsche's depiction of the empathetic stage of proto-tragedy (§8):

to begin to act as if one had actually entered into another body, another character. This process stands at the beginning of the development of drama. Here we have something different from the epic reciter who does not become fused with his images, but like a painter sees them *outside himself* with his contemplative eye. Here we have a surrender of individuality...

In so far as Nietzsche attempts to reconcile any of this with the Schopenhauerian opposition between the will and the aesthetic, it is largely in the elaborate argument in §5. There he suggests that the proto-tragic artist (the lyric poet), is, *qua* artist, necessarily released from his individual will and instead becomes a medium for the 'world-artist' – which (as §24 shows) is the universal will under another name. Since Nietzsche also regards the activities of spectator and tragic poet as parallel (§24), it follows that the aesthetic spectator's empathy is in this sense free from the burden of the will too.

Our endeavour to understand what Nietzsche means by 'aesthetic' is not assisted by an oscillation about Aristotle's pity and fear. Nietzsche does not deny that tragedy does or can evoke these emotions, but he seems unable to decide whether that evocation is relevant to his conception of the tragic and the aesthetic response. In §22 and again in §24 he is dismissive:

If you want to explain tragic myth, the first requirement is to seek the pleasure that is peculiar to it in the purely aesthetic sphere, without transgressing into the region of pity, fear, or the morally sublime (§24).

Elsewhere he is not so sure. For a start, the discussion of *Tristan* in §21 seems to invest pity with a specific rôle:

the Apolline wrests us away from Dionysiac universality and lets us find delight in individuals; it attaches our pity to them –

so that, as Nietzsche puts it, the pity

> saves us in a way from the primordial suffering of the world, just as the symbolic image of the myth saves us from the immediate perception of the highest world-idea, just as thought and word save us from the uninhibited effusion of the unconscious will.

The two quotations just given reveal more complications still. Not content with appealing to pity, Nietzsche explicitly attaches it to the Apolline, and in case there was any doubt he makes the point again, this time referring to pity under the heading of 'sympathetic emotion' (*sympathische Erregung*):

> With the immense impact of image, concept, ethical teaching and sympathetic emotion, the Apolline...blinds [the spectator] to the universality of the Dionysiac process...(§21).

Fear too is associated with the aesthetic spectator's Apolline response. The 'shudders' he is said to experience at the impending fate of the heroic individual (§22) can only be Apolline shudders, just as the terror felt by civilized man at a sudden collapse of causal laws (§1) must be Apolline terror. Pity and fear, then, belong to the Apolline, which we had taken to be the sphere of the aesthetic in the Kantian–Schopenhauerian sense of disinterested contemplation.

It is clearer than ever that Nietzsche's argument is not assisted by his determination to retain the key-word 'aesthetic', although his uncertainties about pity and fear indicate that even without the word this whole area of his theory would be in a confused state. His problem is partly the problem of audience identification. He, like most other students of drama before Brecht, accepts as a fact of life the principle that audiences are apt to identify with dramatic characters. He must, therefore, find some place for it in his theory of the essence of tragedy, as he has already done in his account of its origin, where empathetic identification is ascribed to the chorus of proto-spectators (§8). But (more confusion) that identification is a property of the Dionysiac and its oneness, whereas the aesthetic spectator's sympathetic pity and his shudders are Apolline responses. Between Nietzsche's vivid depictions there is an incoherence which he makes no attempt to defend or resolve.

Nietzsche's theory of tragedy (it is clear) is as unmethodical as the historical parts of his book. For all that, it has had a great influence on later discussions of tragedy – not only, or even primarily, Greek tragedy – and, with its immediacy and force, deservedly so. If it has not always been accorded the classic status it deserves, the reason is partly the limitations of method just noted, partly misunderstanding, partly discomfort about the assumed equivalence between tragedy and Wagner.

The fullest definition of the rhythms of Greek tragedy, as opposed to those of the responsive spectator, comes in §9. There Nietzsche outlines a pattern of heroic self-assertion leading to heroic self-destruction in what is (whether the heroes recognize it or not) a universal cause. One might well have exemplified this pattern from *Oedipus Rex*, although Nietzsche chooses *Prometheus*. The Promethean individual violates norms, he attempts to transcend the limitations of the individual, he therefore forfeits the secure status of an individual and suffers accordingly. By this fate he illuminates the meaning of suffering as well as the meaning of individuality. 'Active sin' is the Promethean virtue, and in that paradox resides

> the ethical basis for pessimistic tragedy: the justification of human evil, meaning both human guilt and the human suffering it entails... In the heroic effort of the individual to attain universality, in the attempt to transcend the curse of individuation and to become the *one* world-being, he suffers in his own person the primordial contradiction that is concealed in things, which means that he commits sacrilege and suffers (§9).

The 'titanically striving individual' must *ipso facto* 'commit sacrilege' (§9), and thereby (Nietzsche adds in §21) he provides us, the aesthetic spectators, with our vicarious experience of Dionysiac wisdom:

> the tragic hero..., like a powerful Titan, takes the whole Dionysiac world upon his back and thus relieves us of this burden. At the same time... [we are reminded of]...a higher pleasure for which the struggling hero prepares himself, with forebodings, by means of his destruction, not his triumphs.

Nietzsche does not underline the importance of self-assertion to his conception of the tragic, perhaps because, unlike self-destruction, it has rather little to do with *Tristan* (his long discussion of which immediately follows the last quotation). Even so, the whole nexus of ideas – self-assertion, self-destruction, and the 'justification of human evil' – has found its way into most subsequent discussions of the tragic. It tends, however, to be praised but misinterpreted, or else rejected but tacitly taken over in some modified form; whether this is because of Nietzsche's failure to expound his theory fully in all its aspects, or simply because of the disconcerting character of the book as a whole, is not easy to say. One spectacular instance from the English-speaking world is worth particular attention, providing as it does an admirable commentary on Nietzsche's theory and yet a graphic illustration of the misunderstandings it is liable to produce.

The *Proceedings of the Aristotelian Society* for 1960 included a notable essay on tragedy by A. M. Quinton, in the course of which he attempted both to elucidate the concept of tragedy and to show 'how it is that [this] concept...suggests a metaphysical view of the world.'[90] Although not cast in Nietzschean language, this at once sounds a highly Nietzschean undertaking, and so it comes as no surprise to find *BT* commended (with suitable reservations) in both connections and employed as the chief guide to tragedy's metaphysical import. The commendation, however, is problematic. At the very beginning of the exposition of Nietzsche's theory a symptomatic error greets us. 'Tragedy', Quinton explains, 'is the master-art...in which the Apollonian individuality of the hero is destroyed by the wild, depersonalized forces of the Dionysian abyss',[91] which is true (although *supra*-personal would be better than *de*personal*ized*), but (Quinton goes on) – 'It is as if the conflicting elements in tragedy were the fixity of the intellect on the one hand and the unformed creativeness of the emotions or the unconscious on the other' – which is false, because the Apolline is not equivalent to 'the intellect', nor does it symbolize consciousness, nor (as we have seen) is it even opposed to 'the emotions'; these are the properties not of Apollinity, but of Socratism.[92] Quinton continues: 'as if, that is to say, the two sides to the conflict were both somehow contained in man. The tragic hero is not destroyed by impersonal forces quite external to humanity but by the more vital features of humanity.' This is more to the point, in so far as it presupposes Nietzsche's interpretation of the literal Greek gods as immanent forces and his construction of the paraliteral Dionysiac and Apolline in the same terms. Nietzsche's 'profound Hellene', however, has 'looked boldly...into...the cruelty of nature' (§7), and in his discussion of *Oedipus* and *Prometheus* in §9 as well as in his metaphysical expositions throughout the book, Nietzsche insists that this destructive 'nature' is (whatever else it is) a supra-human force.

Quinton, in fact, for all his interest in the metaphysical, is attempting to make Nietzsche's theory much more *humanistic* than it really is. This becomes unmistakable as he paraphrases Nietzsche's view of the tragic:

> The values that men create are somehow more than the men who create them and can survive the destruction of their creators. In tragedy this destruction is represented and here above all the valuable qualities of men are most strikingly revealed. The necessary impressiveness of the tragic hero is provoked to its fullest expression in the face of imminent destruction and stands all the more noticeably against the background of disaster.[93]

At which point Quinton suddenly appeals to a celebrated discussion of the tragic offered by F. R. Leavis in *The Common Pursuit:*

> Dr Leavis, although he disowns Nietzsche ('the Nietzschean witness had better be dispensed with; at the best it introduces a disturbing vibration'), admirably states this side of Nietzsche's doctrine. 'The sense of heightened life that goes with the

> tragic experience is conditioned by a transcending of the ego – an escape from all attitudes of self-assertion. 'Escape', perhaps, is not altogether a good word, since it might suggest something negative and irresponsible...Actually the experience is constructive or creative, and involves recognising positive value as in some way defined and vindicated by death. It is as if we were challenged at the profoundest level with the question 'In what does the significance of life reside?' and found ourselves contemplating, for answer, a view of life, and of the things giving it value, that makes the valued appear unquestionably more important than the valuer, so that significance lies, clearly and inescapably, in the willing adhesion of the individual self to something more important than itself.

Quinton resumes his own voice to expound a version of this doctrine. In it he finds an emphasis on 'the contingency of value...in the sense...that the achievement and maintenance of value in the world can only be brought about by the efforts of men', which he contrasts with 'the kind of optimism represented by Hegel, which asserts the necessity [i.e. the ultimate, guaranteed stability] of value, and the kind of pessimism represented by Schopenhauer which asserts its impossibility'.[94]

We shall be returning to the tragic theories of Hegel and Schopenhauer in the next chapter. What concerns us here is Quinton's exposition of Nietzsche and of a theory supposedly founded on Nietzsche's – and he is quite explicit that his concern is 'this Nietzschean point of view, midway between the extremes of Hegel and Schopenhauer'.[95] The fact is that Nietzsche's position, despite some agreement, differs from – and is (to use Leavis' word) more 'disturbing' than – either Quinton's or Leavis' (nor, incidentally, is it apparent that Quinton is entirely in agreement with Leavis either). Nietzsche would agree that 'the impressiveness of the tragic hero...stands out all the more noticeably against the background of disaster' (Quinton), but this is subsidiary to his claim that the hero's destruction reveals the impressiveness of *life* – not the hero's life, but life itself: 'the will to life rejoicing over *its own* inexhaustibility even in the very sacrifice of its highest types.'[96] Leavis (it would appear from Quinton's account) is rather more Nietzschean, and not only because of some quasi-Dionysiac vocabulary ('heightened life', 'transcending of the ego'). There is a specific coincidence on one point: 'significance lies...in this willing adhesion of the individual self to something more important than itself'. At the same time, it seems that Leavis, like Quinton, thinks that 'value' is created by the individual in his life, but most fully vindicated by his death. Nietzsche (in these terms) thinks that the highest value is created in the destructive process itself. What is vindicated here is nothing but the destruction. That is the value affirmed and our joy is the joy of seeing in the tragic image our own destruction made creative, because subsumed into a higher creativity: tragedy is 'the justification of...human suffering' (§9).

If we turn to Leavis himself, we find further distortions of Nietzsche, but considerably more for the student of tragedy than we do in Quinton. In the first place Leavis – it would seem, unwittingly – offers some valuable glosses to Nietzsche's theory of the aesthetic response: 'we have contemplated a painful action involving death and the destruction of the good, admirable and sympathetic, and yet instead of being depressed we enjoy a sense of enhanced vitality.'[97] A little later, Leavis adduces some comments by his *Scrutiny* colleague D. W. Harding with which (unwittingly again) he further illuminates the 'coexistence of opposite feelings' and the doctrine of 'pessimism of strength'. It now becomes clear that Leavis does *not* characterize the meaning of the tragic, as Quinton does, specifically in terms of 'the value of what was destroyed...[being] brought into sight only by the destruction', but rather in terms of the combination of this sense of waste with a sense of the 'immortality of the possibilities of life'.[98] These are quotations from an essay by Harding on the First World War poet Isaac Rosenberg. They represent Harding's estimate of Rosenberg's remarkable capacity to 'respond to both facts without allowing either to neutralize the other', which Harding relates to the poet's ability to accept suffering: 'Here as in all the war poems his suffering and discomfort are unusually *direct;* there is no secondary distress arising from the sense that these things *ought not* to be. He was given up to realising fully what *was.*'[99]

The Nietzschean quality of these formulations speaks for itself, although Leavis makes no comment on it. And though Leavis quotes them in furtherance of his own position on the tragic, it is difficult to relate them in their entirety to his own remarks (repeated by Quinton) about 'value as in some way defined and vindicated by death'. From our point of view, we might say that Harding is the most Nietzschean of the expositors under discussion and Quinton the least, with Leavis somewhere in the middle. At all events, Leavis' exploration, still more than Quinton's, takes place on what is unmistakably Nietzschean ground, so that it is a little disconcerting to find him spurning Nietzsche himself quite so summarily. Further inspection of his own discussion, however, suffices to show that Quinton has no monopoly of misinterpretations of *BT*.

Leavis prefaces his definition of the tragic with some explanatory generalities:

> To postulate a 'tragic experience' or 'tragic effect' and then seek to define it is to lay oneself open to the suspicion of proposing a solemn and time-honoured academic game. Yet the critical contemplation of the profoundest things in literature does lead to the idea of such an experience...It need hardly be said...that what we are concerned with will not be found in all tragedies, or in most[100] –

a frank if rather helpless statement of a point which Nietzsche ignores. Leavis proceeds first to define the effect negatively: Aristotle's *katharsis* is rejected as unhelpful, as is a neo-Senecan 'indulgence in the dramatization of one's nobly-suffering self'.[101] Then, more positively, he invokes

> a kind of profound impersonality in which experience matters, not because it is mine – because it is to me it belongs or happens, or because it subserves or issues in purpose or will, but because it is what it is, the 'mine' mattering only in so far as the individual sentience is the indispensable focus of experience –

the whole constituting a 'transcendence of ordinary experience'.[102]

Not only is this Nietzschean territory. These are Nietzschean conclusions, on the positive side and on the negative, and Leavis seems to know it: 'We might further invoke as obviously relevant Nietzsche's insistence on the Dionysiac. But' – the 'but' cited by Quinton – 'perhaps after all the Nietzschean witness had better be dispensed with; at the best it introduces a disturbing vibration.' In their context these words invite the reflection that if Leavis has actually encountered *BT* at first hand, he has not read it properly. Nietzsche's 'insistence on the Dionysiac' is generally associated with an insistence on the Apolline and on the necessity of their co-presence – a point which would have been aptly made *apropos* Harding on Rosenberg. The lukewarm tone in any case comes oddly from the critic who elsewhere in the same book very properly calls the genius of T. S. Eliot 'a disturbing force and *therefore* capable of ministering to life'.[103]

Leavis now adds a comment not quoted in Quinton's exposition:

> The Nietzschean context is uncongenial to the present purpose, and a glance at it prompts the remark that the tragic calm (if 'calm' is the word), while not the product of any laxative catharsis, is not in the least the calm of the tensed and self-approving will –

a comment revealing the same, more or less Nietzschean, attitude to the tragic that characterizes Leavis' essay as a whole and, at the same time, a fundamental ignorance about Nietzsche's attitude to the individual will. There is no 'self-approving' will in Nietzsche's theory. The Apolline component of the tragic experience is 'will-less' (§22), the Dionysiac involves not self-approval, but 'self-annihilation' (§21). When, therefore, Leavis goes on to observe that 'the sense of heightened life that goes with the tragic experience is conditioned by a transcending of the ego', Quinton is right: Leavis has – unwittingly – stated this aspect of Nietzsche's argument admirably.

In the course of his discussion Leavis introduces another set of issues of some importance to *BT*, although in this instance he makes no reference to Nietzsche at all. Speaking of that 'profound impersonality in which experience matters...because it is what it is', he comments: 'The attainment in literature of this level, and of organization at this level, would seem to involve the poetic use of language.'[104] He then adduces points tending in the same direction made by Yeats, a great admirer of *BT*[105] (though Leavis makes no mention of the fact). For Yeats 'modern naturalistic speech... precludes beauty and significance'. He sees that 'you cannot...be passionate in educated modern speech'; that 'poetry, with attendant non-naturalistic conventions..., is necessary in order to provide the distance and the frame without which there can be no intensity of the right kind'; and that 'tragedy must always be...a breaking of the dykes that separate man from man'.[106] The associative logic of this sequence is revealing. The 'conventions' alluded to are Apolline, the 'breaking of the dykes' (Yeats' own phrase) is Dionysiac, and the two are felt to belong together and against naturalism.

If the discussion were to proceed with direct reference to *BT*, one other justification for the 'non-naturalistic conventions' of tragic verse would need to be spelled out. George Steiner makes the point in very general terms: 'There is nothing democratic in the vision of tragedy. The royal and heroic characters whom the gods honour with their vengeance are set higher than we are in the chain of being, and their style of utterance must reflect this elevation.'[107] In Greek tragedy, as a matter of fact, the language of the not-so-heroic chorus is even more elevated than that of the heroic characters, and it is in the chorus as well as in the heroic dialogue that the non-naturalistic, Apolline conventions of Greek tragedy are embodied. Nevertheless, Steiner's point tends to bear out Nietzsche's approval of the conventions and his disapproval of Euripides for undermining them (§11). Together with Leavis' argument, furthermore, it serves to point up the significance of a remark by Goethe which Nietzsche quotes in §22.

Explaining to Schiller his failure to write 'a true tragedy', Goethe puts it down to the 'lively pathological interest' which he shares with his age, and without which (he says) no modern drama can be written, but which he personally finds unendurable.[108] In antiquity (Goethe suggests) even subjects involving the most intense emotion (*das höchste Pathetische*) were treated in the spirit of an 'aesthetic game' (*ästhetisches Spiel*). With us, however, art of such intensity can only be achieved by compounding the 'aesthetic game' with naturalistic 'truth' (*Naturwahrheit*); that is, by some use of what Nietzsche calls 'the botched outlines of nature' (§11). Those random and (in every sense) inaesthetic vagaries of ordinary life demand, in their turn, the 'pathological' involvement on the part of author and audience which Goethe regards as part and parcel of modern tragedy, but Nietzsche as illegitimate in any age.

Appeal to the 'undemocratic' vision of tragedy in conjunction with the 'distance' required for the supra-normal experience of tragic 'intensity' amplifies and enforces Nietzsche's association of naturalism and pathological response which he learns from Goethe. One other relevant association Nietzsche himself fails to acknowledge. Leavis, however, with his characteristic awareness of creative language, calls attention to it: supra-normal experience can only be 'realized' – induced, conveyed, as opposed to merely stated – through a supra-normal idiom. Hence, above all, the need for stylized language. The special value of music might be argued on similar grounds.

The effect, then, of these parallel discussions of the tragic is to vindicate the coherence of Nietzsche's position. Pessimism of strength, aesthetic response, high actors and stylization of idiom belong together. Music too would seem to belong here, and so does the metaphysical pretension of the genre. Leavis' 'transcendence of ordinary experience' and Quinton's discussion of 'value' in their own ways reach out to the realm of metaphysics, while Steiner's remarks about the 'chain of being' point the same way too. Nietzsche's emphasis on myth completes the argument. Poetic language and metaphysical implication between them enclose the mythic mode. That is, the natural (and not merely historic) affinities of poetry with myth, and myth with metaphysics, go a long way to validating tragedy's association with mythology.

One of Nietzsche's credos, however, does not yet follow: the necessity of dramatic form. The problem is implicit in Leavis' parallel between his own account of the tragic effect and Harding's discussion of Isaac Rosenberg. Can lyric poetry produce the tragic *effect*? Or merely the tragic attitude (*das Tragische*)? How far can the effect on an audience be said to follow from the representation of the attitude? Can even the epic serve as vehicle? The *Iliad* is a case in point.[109] The sacrifice of Patroclus to Hector and then Hector to Achilles in a sense anticipates the rhythms of fifth-century tragedy; and certainly from its menacing divine ground the poem derives a full measure of 'incurable sufferings'.[110]

The comments on Homer in *BT* conveniently avoid discussion of this aspect of the *Iliad*. Nietzsche concentrates on Homeric man's customary – and undeniable – enjoyment of life and the principle that epic is the sphere of beauty. If it is allowed that tragic elements can exist within the epic form, one of Nietzsche's underlying assumptions is put at risk. Certainly, by virtue of being drama, tragedy is bound to make an impact that differs from those of other forms. But other forms *can* contain 'the tragic' and, in its denial of this, *BT* is simply too schematic.

Nietzsche is asserting the identity of the medium and the message. Here an analyst like Aristotle is more discriminating. In the *Poetics* genre and effect – tragedy and *katharsis* – are correlated, but not genre and outlook, except in so far as some genres are held to be more 'serious' (*spoudaios*) than others.

Nietzsche's is a very difficult position to argue, and there are signs that he senses its insecurity. In lyric poetry (he writes in §16)

> music strives to express its essence in Apolline images. If now we reflect that at its highest stage music must also seek its highest objectification in imagery, we must accept the possibility that it also knows how to find the symbolic expression for its unique Dionysiac wisdom. And where shall we look for this expression if not in tragedy and in the conception of the tragic in general [*und überhaupt im Begriff des Tragischen*]?

With this last phrase Nietzsche almost, but not quite, takes a crucial step that would mean abandoning his attempt to define Greek *tragōidia* and concentrating on the attempt to define 'the tragic' instead. In this connection the treatment of Sophocles' *Oedipus Rex* in §9 is revealing. From his discussion it appears that he locates the tragic as much in the pre-dramatic myth as in the drama itself. It is certainly the myth that provokes his most striking single comment:

> Oedipus, the murderer of his father, the husband of his mother, the solver of the riddle of the Sphinx! What does this mysterious triad of fateful deeds tell us?...that wisdom, and particularly Dionysiac wisdom, is an unnatural abomination; that he who by means of his knowledge plunges nature into the abyss of destruction must also suffer the dissolution of nature in his own person.

Tragic wisdom indeed, but, as Nietzsche himself insists, wisdom that precedes its incorporation into tragic drama. Tragic myth is to some extent autonomous of tragedy itself, so that he can even speak of 'tragic myth, too, in so far as it belongs to art at all...' (§24). In the end, therefore, the unconvincing dictum that tragic myth arises from music (first explicit in §16) seems as much an anxious attempt to attach this awkward source of tragic wisdom to his system as a principle born out of evidence or conviction.

For all its shortcomings, Nietzsche's theory has justly taken its place among the major ideas of modern criticism and aesthetics, and might be expected to take a still larger place once the numerous occasions for misunderstanding have been removed. At the same time, the impact of his account of the tragic (like the very different impact of tragedy itself) is not conveyed by distilled versions. Nietzsche's theory cannot be detached from his metaphysics and his unprosaic prose without distortion and loss of force. No 'pure' theory of tragedy can be abstracted from the book. For every reader there comes a point where *BT* ceases to be acceptable as a theoretical statement – *not*, however, because Nietzsche's idiom and his categories are (as Leavis said) 'disturbing', but because they are, as Nietzsche wished them to be, too 'artistic' to be easily transferable. The value of the perspective into which he puts tragedy is inseparable from the disturbing qualities of his book.

AESTHETICS AND METAPHYSICS

The young classical scholar writes a book about tragedy that looks outwards beyond the tragedies of his beloved Greeks. Its further target, however, is not later drama, but a philosophy of life. Though he makes a determined attempt to see tragic form as a criterion of the tragic outlook, the two are separable, and it is ultimately the outlook, not the form, that concerns him. This is not in the end a genre study; and it is a symptom of this fact, as much as a mark of his Hellenocentricity, that he should have devised a construct so inescapably Greek that detailed discussion of other drama in its terms seems, to say the least, unreal. In colouring as well as intensity, his categories belong to the world of Greek tragedy. Where other drama, including Wagner's music drama, is in question, the colouring is distractingly alien ('Dionysiac', writes Leavis with Shakespeare in mind, 'carries unacceptable suggestions of the Dark Gods').[111] As far as Greek tragedy itself is concerned, the mythical quality of Nietzsche's construct also represents an ingenious solution to the notorious historicist dilemma: are works of the past to be discussed only in the categories of their time, the timeless only in terms of the outmoded? But Nietzsche's categories have no temporal connection with the world of Shakespeare or with any tragic world except the Greek.

His thoughts on other drama, all in all, are perfunctory. The notes of 1869 to 1871 show that he had ideas about a variety of modern playwrights, but many of them are clearly tentative and most have been excluded from the book.[112] Outside Greece – and Wagner – his model of tragedy, insofar as he has one, is Shakespeare, whose work is invoked with the utmost respect (§§2, 7, 17, 22), although only *Hamlet* is mentioned by name (§§7, 17). If Shakespearean tragedy is any kind of model for Nietzsche, it presents, of course, obvious and embarrassing differences from the Greek. Shakespeare's drama has no music, except incidentally, and certainly no musical origin. It has no chorus, and therefore no metaphysical foil to the earth-bound hero. It presupposes the existence both of Christianity and of Greco-Roman literary mythology, but it has no comparable mytho-religious basis. It is a sign of the remoteness of Nietzsche's mythic apparatus from Shakespeare that only once are the two directly associated, and even then in a very restricted way: Nietzsche compares the Dionysiac state of knowledge and lethargy with

Hamlet's own (§7), but offers no discussion of the play itself in these terms. In his 1870 lecture on 'Greek Music Drama', while still evolving his theory, he notes at one point that Shakespearean tragedy is a descendant of New Comedy, and at another that English tragedy (which must mean Shakespeare) is more Dionysiac than the Greek; while in his notes of the same period Shakespeare is seen now as the 'artistic Socrates', now as an 'utterly Dionysiac' successor to Sophocles.[113] In *BT* Nietzsche copes with such contradictions by the expedient of silence. Hamlet, he remarks in §17, 'talks more superficially than he acts'. The dictum, which prefigures Eliot's famous allegation that the play lacks an adequate 'objective correlative', is certainly not without point (and a decade later Nietzsche will develop it in a deeply perceptive note on *Julius Caesar*).[114] But it is offered without reference to Apollo and Dionysus, and it could be argued without any reference to that part of his elaborate theory at all.

Outside Shakespeare there is remarkably little. Nietzsche's thoughts on seventeenth-century French tragedy are confined to an unstated implication of a single sentence in §23 referring to the former superiority of French culture. At this period of his life he was no expert on anything French,[115] and he was in any case under the influence of the classicist reaction against French culture initiated by Winckelmann, Herder and Lessing, as well as Wagner's peculiar disdain for most things Gallic. Nor is he much more expansive on the drama of his own countrymen. Goethe's reluctance to 'elaborate a tragic situation' receives the briefest of allusions in §22, and Nietzsche forbears even to tell us whether he regards it as a legitimate Apolline manoeuvre on Goethe's part, or a sign of some deficiency in his make-up, or the result of what Erich Heller has called 'a violent clash between the nature of Goethe's genius and his historical situation'.[116] We might have anticipated some discussion of *Faust*, but (apart from numerous quotations of well-known passages) Nietzsche's interest in the play turns out to be of the same restricted kind as his interest in *Hamlet*. The discussion of 'Faust, the modern cultured man' in §18 shows that for Nietzsche what matters here is the grand image of the emancipated individual, especially the individual who has acquired too much knowledge for his own good. Even more than Hamlet, Faust attracts him as antipode to Socrates. Faust as tragic man, not *Faust* as tragic drama: once again Nietzsche's thoughts are directed beyond the genre. This perspective, at least, is in no way original: preoccupation with the Faustian ideology at the expense of Goethe's actual play is one of the *idées reçues* of Nietzsche's century.

Nietzsche's interest in Schiller is no less selective. Despite evident respect for Schiller as 'heroic' fighter for culture (§20), as aesthetician (§§3, 7–8, 19) and as *bona fide* poet (§5), Nietzsche shows no inclination to comment on his dramatic work, not even his central hero-drama, *Wallenstein*. All we are offered is an aside about 'the attempt to use the theatre as an institution for the moral education of the people, which was still taken seriously in Schiller's time' (§22).

In his notes of 1871 Nietzsche shows much more enthusiasm, but his book (supported by references in his later writings) leaves us to infer that Schiller's concern with Kantian ethics makes him into the boring moralizer among the world's dramatists; or that Schiller's interest in the definition of true beauty and his place in the neo-Euripidean drama of intrigue and rhetorical self-assertion combine to make him recalcitrant to Nietzsche's purpose, and so best passed over in silence.[117]

The large focus of *BT* involves Nietzsche in formulations concerning the theory of art as a whole. Yet here too, except for the selective discussion of music, little of a specific nature is said. Tragedy and music apart, he offers us a series of generalizations inferred (or divined) from unspecificed instances and not tested against others. The visual arts are Apolline. Since he has fettered himself by his rigid correlation between attitude, form, and effect, epic is Apolline too. In the light of our conclusion that 'Dionysiac art' can never mean *pure* Dionysiac art, but only 'more Dionysiac than...', we might consider the hypothesis that the same holds for the arts assigned to the opposite camp. Is epic poetry not perhaps less Apolline than sculpture? Nietzsche declines to admit the question; he simply contrasts epic with music, with lyric and with tragedy. On lyric itself he is hardly more illuminating. We have pointed out how unsatisfactory his discussion of Greek lyric poetry is.[118] It is even worse to equate Greek lyric poetry (that is, song) with the indeterminate modern category of 'lyric' verse, as he does in the case of Schiller (§5), notwithstanding his caveat immediately afterwards that the Greeks 'took for granted the union, indeed the identity, of the lyric poet with the musician. Compared with this, our modern lyric poetry seems like the statue of a god without a head.' Above all, he has no ready explanation for the very obvious fact that despite its Dionysiac background, lyric has no such characteristic connection as tragedy does with pessimism (strong or otherwise) or metaphysical truth.

Of the other literary or semi-literary genres, folk-song earns a few complimentary words in §6, partly in deference to the special significance it had for Schopenhauer.[119] There are the scattered comments on Greek comedy (§§11, 13, 14, 17), good (Aristophanes) or bad (New Comedy), together with a much more striking, but unexplored, Schopenhauerian interpretation of 'the comic' as 'the artistic discharge of the nausea of absurdity' (§7). There are scattered observations on the novel, which is associated with 'waxwork cabinets' because of its characteristic naturalism (§7) and dismissed as 'an infinitely enhanced Aesopian fable' (§14); the Nietzsche who will admire novelists as different as Stendhal, Keller and Dostoevsky[120] is not yet in sight. The rest of the picture is made up of innumerable generalizations about 'the artist' and his creative processes. To a very large extent, then, the aesthetic is based on Greek tragedy and Wagner, treated more or less as a single entity, in opposition to an undifferentiated Apolline. Whole generic areas are almost ignored, as are whole periods. Very little is said about the large span between Alexandria and the nineteenth century, and practically nothing about the Middle Ages.

Nietzsche's aesthetic theory is closely associated with his cultural hopes, but his treatment of culture is still more selective and generalized than his exposition of aesthetics. He wants a 'tragic culture', and he portrays such a culture as one in which both the Dionysiac and the political (Apolline) instincts are strong and balanced: a culture poised between the Buddhist yearning for *nirvana*, which is the logical outcome of unmediated Dionysiac experience, and the 'extreme secularization' of the Roman empire (§21). In human experience, such a culture has been realized only in Aeschylean Athens, where it was associated with Aeschylean drama (§21). A renewed tragic culture is in prospect now (for Aeschylus read Wagner, §§20–24), but as to its content Nietzsche is not specific. We hear nothing about its economic or political aspects, although even without the benefit of his later writings, we could infer from *obiter dicta* on the masses in §7, 'civic mediocrity' in §11 and socialism in §19 that it is unlikely to be democratic, let alone egalitarian. We hear nothing of its social patterns or attitudes. It is defined spiritually. It is the kind of culture in which myth is taken seriously – although there is no real sign that this artistic Socrates actually favours a religious context for the new mythology, which alone would ensure its seriousness: the sections (§§23–24) that look forward to the 'rebirth of German myth' say nothing about the specific system of beliefs, let alone the cult practices, that would be necessary to sustain such a revival. It is a culture in which

> wisdom takes the place of science as the highest end – wisdom which...turns with unmoved eyes to a comprehensive view of the world, and seeks to grasp, with sympathetic feelings of love, eternal suffering as its own (§18).

Men of such wisdom will have 'a heroic penchant for the immoderate'; they will 'live resolutely in wholeness and fullness'; they will need tragedy for their metaphysical solace (§18).

For all this talk of 'wholeness', Nietzsche is not seriously concerned to envisage a whole *society*. He envisages the whole *man*, but he shows insufficient interest in the social patterns which would facilitate and sustain his wholeness. The excessive individualism of his interpretation of Greek art[121] is matched by the nature of his concern for the creative individual and the social needs of his creative individuality at the expense of society's other members or functions. It is revealing that Nietzschean man, reacting to the horror of existence, is only allowed three ways out: religion, art, and science (§18). Anything else is bound to be merely one of 'the more vulgar and almost more powerful illusions which the will always has at hand'. This is a remarkably narrow view of culture, even in its creative aspects. There is no place in Nietzsche's view of salvation for 'the holiness of the heart's affections', for good works, for the sustaining power of kinship and other personal relationships. His concentration on the three higher illusions and his particular obsession with the high standing of the third, the Socratic, also takes little account of the massive developments under way in contemporary Germany, as elsewhere, which were rapidly turning higher culture into a fetish of the leisured classes. Many of the representatives of the new industrial-mercantile society would have agreed with Nietzsche that Socratic knowledge was the goal of modern man – but only when they were home from work and free to summon up a veneration for learning, quite unrelated to Nietzsche's despair at the insufficiency of the whole Socratic ideal.

Nietzsche is, of course, aware of the different forms that Socratism can take; he recognizes its extension to 'machines and crucibles' (§17); he recognizes too that the three higher illusions 'are actually designed only for the more nobly formed natures' (§18). Nevertheless, his habit is to equate Germany with those natures only, German culture with *their* ideals. Here is the same heady over-emphasis on high culture that we have seen in his interpretation of Greece and in the hopes he places in Wagner.[122] What above all he refuses to recognize is the complex status of high culture within the society that gives rise to it. With his uncompromising stress on the individual artist or thinker, he treats art and thought as essentially independent of society in origin, and yet gives them a pre-eminent social rôle as creators of the new man. While insisting on the close links between art and the state (§23), he belies the links by his own exposition. While deploring the isolation of the creative individual in the modern world (§§20, 22), he builds his cultural ideal on the dichotomy between such an individual and his society which is a symptom of that isolation. In so far as *BT* offers an implied justification for the dichotomy, it is through the association of culture, especially art, and the supra-human (and therefore supra-social) sphere of metaphysics. Nietzsche does not, like Wagner, confront culture through the theatre, but through the existential problem: what is life – the life, ultimately, of the individual – *for*?

Nietzsche's view of culture has other problematic aspects. There are fundamental uncertainties in it. One is associated with the ideal of an 'artistic Socrates'. *How* ideal is it? Would the achievement of an artistic Socrates be merely an acceptable compromise in an imperfect world – or is it a good *per se?* Another, more serious, uncertainty concerns Nietzsche's nominal approval of a 'tragic culture'.[123] There are some indications in the book that in the last resort he would actually prefer an Apolline culture, presumably of the type associated with the Greek Olympians: 'an exuberant, triumphant existence in which all things, good or evil, are deified' (§3). A eulogy of Greece from his later years well illustrates the attractiveness and the spiritual dignity of the Apolline, although the name is not used:

> Oh, those Greeks! They knew how to live. What is required for that is to stop courageously at the surface, the fold, the skin, to adore appearance, to believe in forms, tones, words, the whole Olympus of appearance. Those Greeks were superficial – *out of profundity*.[124]

In §19 he interprets the modern world as experiencing the stages of Greek culture in reverse, which would imply that the new tragic age to be inaugurated by Wagner will be followed by an Apolline age beyond it. Is this perhaps what he is looking forward to in a curious passage in §25?

> Where the Dionysiac powers rise up as impetuously as we experience them now, Apollo, too, must already have descended among us, wrapped in a cloud; and the next generation will probably behold the most luscious effects of his beauty.

In the light of these passages, is it only a coincidence that Nietzsche's world-artist should be unmistakably an Apolline artist?[125]

This difficulty will never be resolved. Throughout Nietzsche's later writings there is a contradiction between grave exhortations to tragic courage and praises of light-heartedness, between an affirmation of the dark ground of all existence and an injunction to 'stop at the surface'. As in *BT*, the tragic affirmation predominates, but the conflict is always there.

The problems associated with Nietzsche's construct do not end here. If culture is at present Socratic, but is to become Dionysiac (or at least Dionysiac–Apolline) and then presumably Apolline, what does this imply about the relations between the three categories? One particular grey area involves the Apolline and the Socratic: what is their relation? We have pointed out that before Nietzsche had identified Socrates as the archetype of rationalism, his Greek rationalist had been the 'artistic' philosopher

Democritus.[126] It would seem to be implied that Nietzsche had once assumed a closer connection between rationalism and art than appears in *BT*, from which it would follow that the categories of the Apolline and Socratic are genetically related. The supposition is both confirmed and challenged by a passage in the 1870 lecture on 'Socrates and Tragedy': 'In Socrates was embodied one side of Hellenism, that *Apolline clarity*...like a pure, piercing ray of light he appears, as herald and harbinger of *science*...But science and art are mutually exclusive.'[127] The conclusion to which *BT* itself leads is that the Socratic is a plainer offshoot of the Apolline and results from a total rejection of the Dionysiac. This is the lesson of Euripides, who aspired to reconstruct tragedy as a purely Apolline art (§§10, 12), and of Plato (§14), and apparently of Rome (§21). For reasons that are not apparent, the rigid Apollinity of Sparta (§4) and Egypt (§9) produces no such outcome. Nevertheless, wherever it does appear, Socratic rationalism is to be taken as the product of the divorce of the Apolline from the Dionysiac (and in that sense a denial of nature and art alike), so that Nietzsche's whole theory is seen, after all, to have a polar, not a triadic, basis.[128]

The relation between Dionysiac and Apolline would of course be clearer if Nietzsche had found it possible to admit the Apolline component in all so-called Dionysiac art. There is, presumably, a fundamental distinction between modes of art, where the pure Dionysiac has no place, and modes of life, where a pure Dionysiac condition can be found. The Dionysiac *tout court* is to be found in the destructive indulgencies of barbaric sensuality (§2) and, more respectably, in mystical ecstasies and those ascetic dispositions that follow the withdrawal from the ecstatic state (§§7, 21). Nietzsche's contrast between these Dionysiac modes of life and their Apolline opposites is unambiguous, and it has commended itself to eminent anthropologists.[129] The contrast between the purely and the partly Dionysiac culture (in existential terms, the contrast between negation of life and tragic pessimism) is not presented with equal precision.

Associated with Nietzsche's over-insistence on the Dionysiac character of Dionysiac–Apolline art is a striking confusion about the relation between Buddhism and the tragic. In §7 Nietzsche seems quite clear about the difference: the 'profound Hellene', who is 'in danger of longing for a Buddhistic negation of the will', consoles himself *instead* with the tragic chorus. Similarly in §21 the Greeks are said to have found a *via media* between the extremes of India and Rome. In §18, however, Nietzsche offers us three equations: Socratic = Alexandrian, artistic = Hellenic, *and* tragic = Buddhistic.[130] How is the contradiction to be explained? At first sight it might seem that Nietzsche has slipped back into Schopenhauerian habits. For

Schopenhauer, negation of the will is the highest calling, and tragedy is seen as a means to that end; *Buddhistic* and *tragic*, accordingly, are aligned, whereas in *BT* (this is the hallmark of Nietzsche's independence) they are opposed. The real answer is rather that Nietzsche's concern to assert the dominance of the Dionysiac within tragedy once again gets the better of his interest in the Dionysiac–Apolline dialectic. The distinction between the purely and the partly Dionysiac disappears altogether, and he allows the spurious equation to tempt him into another schematic pattern to add to the series, Socrates/science, Apollo/art, Dionysus/religion.

The last association is problematic as well. To align religion, especially mystical religion, with Dionysus, raises the question of the status of Christianity. In *BT* Nietzsche clearly regards the religion of his own culture as some kind of Dionysiac phenomenon.[131] He does not say so overtly, because the admission would give Christianity a dignity he is reluctant to allow it. The problem in his terms is presumably that Christian religion, while Dionysiac in some ways, is Socratic in others. It is mystical – and also concerned with moral justification; ascetic and will-negating – but also interested in the etablishment of a kingdom of heaven *on earth*. If Christianity's practical-ethical side is to be classified under any of his three headings, it can only be associated with the Socratic. (In later years Nietzsche will argue the paradox that Christianity is actually created, but then eventually destroyed, by this Socratic-scientific attitude.) But this conclusion would obviously imply the compatibility of the Socratic with the Dionysiac, and for Nietzsche the two are incompatible. No solution to the problem is proposed, and even evasion is difficult. He can avoid discussion of Christianity, but he cannot avoid expounding the Dionysiac, and there an evocation of the religion of his youth is always likely to appear. Even in the images with which (under Bachofen's influence)[132] he depicts the Dionysiac state in § 1, there are clear echoes of Christian feeling:

> Transform Beethoven's 'Hymn to Joy' into a painting; let your imagination conceive the multitudes bowing to the dust, awestruck – then you will get near to the Dionysiac. Now the slave is a free man; now all the rigid, hostile barriers which necessity, caprice, or 'impudent convention' have fixed between man and man are broken. Now, with the gospel of universal harmony, each one feels himself not only united, reconciled and fused with his neighbour, but as one with him...

After which, instead of the rhetoric about 'the veil of maya' which Nietzsche actually offers us, we fully expect to find

> There is neither Jew nor Greek, there is neither bond nor free, there is neither male nor female: for ye are all one in Christ Jesus.[133]

There is no gap in *BT* between aesthetics and psychology; nor is there any between aesthetics and metaphysics. The polarity at the basis of Nietzsche's theory consists of two entities with a complex significance that covers all three fields. On the psychological level, the Dionysiac and the Apolline are creative human impulses, *Triebe*, under which are subsumed modes of perceiving, experiencing, expressing and responding to reality. On the aesthetic level, the two terms refer to any artistic or cultural tendencies or manifestations which are the outcome of those impulses. On the metaphysical level, they denote the conditions of existence apprehended through the operation of the impulses or the impulses themselves as universal principles belonging to the timeless cosmos. As psychological and aesthetic realities, Dionysiac and Apolline are parallel, even if the Dionysiac is more powerful, once its effects are felt. On the metaphysical level they are not parallel at all. Ontologically, the Dionysiac is primary and the Apolline, as creation and individuated reflex of the Dionysiac (§25), is secondary – even if mundane existence almost submerges the Dionysiac and allows the everyday experience of particularity and distinctions to proceed unchallenged (§1).[134]

The connection between Nietzsche's aesthetics and his metaphysics deserves a special emphasis. It is not just that art has a very privileged position within his metaphysical theory (as it does in Schopenhauer's): it is also that his aesthetics is thoroughly metaphysical itself. On hearing the rumour that the Louvre had been destroyed in the summer of 1871, Nietzsche writes to a friend:

> the whole academic, philosophical, artistic world seemed an absurdity, if a single day could wipe out the most glorious works of art, even whole periods of art; I clung with earnest conviction to the metaphysical value of art, which cannot exist for the sake of poor human beings, but has higher missions to fulfill.[135]

The 'earnest conviction' is written into the book. It is proclaimed in the preface to Wagner, where Nietzsche tells us that 'art represents the highest task and the true metaphysical activity of this life'. It underlies the principle that tragedy provides its audience with 'metaphysical consolation', and the enigmatic notion that 'the genius in the act of artistic creation coalesces with the primordial artist [*Urkünstler*] of the world' (§5). It also helps to explain why Nietzsche should have chosen the names of deities for his two art-impulses; the pervasive presence of Apollo and Dionysus in the book means that the metaphysical status of art is conveyed from first to last.

Nietzsche's relative assessments of artistic media and literary genres depend on their varying metaphysical capacities: that is, their capacity to confront mankind with the dark truth about life. However problematic the concept of truth will become in Nietzsche's later philosophy, here it seems straightforward enough – in philosophical terms, if not in fact: truth is destructive, but apparently attainable. *BT* takes for its premise the senselessness of existence, where 'sense' is defined with respect to the individual's hopes and needs. The full impact of this terrible lesson cannot be borne, but must be mediated through art. The most Dionysiac of the arts reveal the truth: music, with its wordless intimations of supra-individual existence, and tragedy, in which the truth is symbolized more explicitly. And in case we should think there is some significant difference between these two arts, Nietzsche offers us a paradoxical equation: music 'in its highest form' *is* tragedy (§16). The paradox, however, is only apparent. For Nietzsche, music is at its most effective in drama, and tragedy is 'musical tragedy' anyway. The assimilation of music and tragedy is the assimilation of Wagner and Aeschylus in another guise.

In the Apolline – that is, the *more* Apolline – arts, the truth is not revealed, but creatively concealed; in Socratic art, it is simply evaded. The highest arts, then, are highest because they express the truth most fully and directly. The contrast with Freudian theories here is revealing. Like Freud a generation later, Nietzsche psychologizes art, and the concepts of the unconscious mind, repressed experience and sublimation are all implicit in *BT*. For the Freudian, however, once the menacing truths that engender the sublimation have been laid bare by psychology, they lose their menace. They have no deeper reverberations. There is no higher dimension of being for sublimation to mediate, and no higher dignity to accrue to art and the artist in their turn.

If, on our showing, all art, even music, has an Apolline element, it follows that all art has an element of illusion. It is Apollo 'through whose gestures and eyes all the joy and wisdom of illusion, together with its beauty, speak to us'(§1) – and illusion is the artistic mediation of truth by another name. Here Nietzsche's theory looks back to Schopenhauer and beyond him to Plato. For Plato too art is illusion, but with the great difference that the truth which art serves to obscure is a glorious, more perfect order of existence altogether. In Nietzsche's universe order is the illusion which art, above all else, creates: life itself has none. And yet such illusion is not to be disparaged, as Plato disparaged it. It is a necessary life-sustaining protection, and Apolline art is its highest form. It is not, however, its only form: 'By means of an illusion spread over things, the insatiable will always finds a way to detain its creatures in life and compel them to keep living' (§18). This may come about (Nietzsche explains) through art, through science ('the Socratic love of knowledge'), or through mystical religion ('the metaphysical consolation that beneath the whirl of phenomena eternal life flows on indestructibly').

The Apolline solution, then, the Socratic, and even the Dionysiac are all illusory. But art remains the definitive form of illusion. If even religion and science are illusions, it is because they too are ultimately forms of art. In § 15 Nietzsche poses the question: what will become of human creativity in the years ahead?

Will the net of art that is spread over existence, albeit under the name of religion or science, be woven even more tightly and finely...?

At this point it becomes clearer than ever how totally art-centred this view of life is. The elaborate tripartite schema – Dionysiac, Apolline, Socratic – and even the Dionysiac–Apolline diptych fold up to form a new, simpler, but telling nexus of thoughts: art as illusion, art as protection. Henceforth, this nexus will be a constant in Nietzsche's thinking:

Truth is ugly. We have *art* lest we *perish of the truth.*[136]

The words come from his last active year, 1888, but the sentiment is essentially that of his first book.

At the grim news from Paris Nietzsche thinks of art's 'higher missions' (*höhere Missionen*). In his preface he speaks of art's 'highest task' (*höchste Aufgabe*). To see art as protection is to ascribe a purpose to it, a high metaphysical purpose; and here the familiar antithesis reappears. In contrast, then, to his later inclination to bring all art under a single heading, in *BT* he distinguishes between the purposes of art that is – predominantly – Dionysiac and art that is Apolline. All art (including science and religion) is in part protective illusion, but Apolline art is nothing but that. Its purpose is to 'overcome the suffering of the individual by the radiant glorification of the *eternity of the phenomenon:* here beauty triumphs over the suffering inherent in life; pain is, as it were, obliterated from the features of nature by means of lies' (§ 16). The arts of music and tragedy, on the other hand, affirm that pain, but by virtue of their Apolline component (as we, in lieu of Nietzsche, insist) do so without destroying their individual auditors in the process. And by their affirmation of the ultimate condition of existence, they provide the blood of life for the culture to which they belong. Without the Dionysiac, civilization would atrophy:

Lest this Apolline tendency congeal the form to Egyptian rigidity and coldness, lest the effort to prescribe to the individual wave its path and realm should annul the motion of the whole lake, the high tide of the Dionysiac destroyed from time to time all those little circles in which the one-sided Apolline 'will' had sought to confine the Hellenic spirit (§ 9).

The fitful apprehension of the truth guarantees human creativity, and here Nietzsche's metaphysical position points back to his cultural programme.

Apprehension of the truth is necessary, but only the Dionysiac instinct can achieve it. In our higher civilization that instinct has been destroyed. It must be revived, and for *this* urgent task, at least, the thinker, though himself a product of the age of destruction, has an unambiguously creative rôle. It now falls to him to become a Dionysiac conceptualist (§ 19) or even an artistic Socrates (§ 15) and assist the process of revival. At a time when art is less appreciated than ever before,

> many a being more nobly and delicately endowed by nature...might have had something to say about the unexpected as well as totally unintelligible effect that a successful performance of *Lohengrin*, for example, had on him – except that perhaps there was no helpful interpreting hand to guide him...(§ 22).

Such 'helpful interpretation' presumably represents one of the ways in which Socratic rationality 'again and again prompts a regeneration of art...and its own infinity also guarantees the infinity of art' (§ 15). In the absence of this function Socratism is 'inartistic and life-consuming' (§ 24), opposing the instincts from which the Dionysiac could be reborn, trivializing the experience of reality, denying the dialectic between creativity and pain. Once the Dionysiac experience has materialized, tragedy has a further task, which (to judge from Nietzsche's silence) is not shared by music in its lower forms. It is tragedy that offers us 'metaphysical consolation' (§§ 7, 18), and, specifically, tragedy that averts the process whereby a glimpse of the painful truth leads to nausea, and nausea to asceticism and the negation of life altogether (§§ 7, 21). Here, if anywhere, the Schopenhauerian–Wagnerian claims for music yield in Nietzsche's mind to his esteem for tragedy.

Art sustains life: life is the purpose of art. Such conclusions raise as many questions as they seem to answer. In the first place, how far is it justifiable to put 'life' and 'art' into such separate compartments? What Nietzsche is doing, one might say, is transposing onto the existential plane the brutal fact of nineteenth-century civilization that life, as lived by most of its members, and art, as experienced by them, were indeed utterly separate things – though this is not an answer. But in any case, if we allow Nietzsche the right to pit art against life in the context of purposes, as he does, we can hardly avoid a further, ultimate question: if life is the purpose of art, is there in his view a purpose to life? To this there is no easy answer. He is either very subtle or equivocal or elliptical. In the first place his metaphysic, like Schopenhauer's, is pessimistic. Where the Greeks in their 'age of mysteries' hit upon the word *kosmos*, 'order', to denominate the universe, and where even the dark Heraclitus discerned that order as a secret reality behind apparent disorder,[137] in Nietzsche's universe, as in Schopenhauer's, the order is apparent and the disorder lies behind it. Yet unlike Schopenhauer's pessimism, *his* purports to be a pessimism of strength, an affirmation of life. His cosmos is one in which existence can fairly be seen as an absurdity (§7) – and yet it is also one in which metaphysical activity takes place with specifiable aims:

This sublime metaphysical illusion [that thought is capable of knowing reality and even correcting it] accompanies science as an instinct and leads it again and again to its limits, at which it must turn into *art* – *which is really the purpose of this mechanism* (§15).

Nietzsche can tell us that 'suffering, primal and eternal' is the 'sole ground of the world' and in the same breath talk of 'redemption' (*Erlösung*): 'the truly existent primordial oneness, eternally suffering and contradictory, also needs the rapturous vision, the pleasurable illusion, for its continuous redemption' (§4). As the creative source of phenomena, the Dionysiac is described as 'eternal and original' (*ewig und ursprünglich*) – and yet Nietzsche can apply the word 'illusion' (*Illusion* is the German word used) even to 'the metaphysical consolation that beneath the whirl of phenomena eternal life flows on indestructibly' (§18). Is it the indestructibility of life that is illusory or merely the consolation? Perhaps truth is not attainable after all. Could there be layers of reality concealed even behind the 'primordial oneness'? Or is it that *BT* in fact puts forward that oneness as ultimate reality, but not as a *stable* reality? Is Nietzsche anticipating his later structuralist experiments, in which 'being' is seen as 'being in relationships'? In Presocratic terms, is there or is there not a true *archē*?

A resolution of these uncertainties is attempted. Words like 'redemption' have inescapable religious overtones, and at various points in the book Nietzsche explicitly invokes the notion of a divine or deified principle, such as the Presocratics would have found tolerably familiar. 'Even the ugly and disharmonic', he writes in §24, 'are part of an artistic game [*ein künstlerisches Spiel*] which the will in the eternal amplitude of its pleasure plays with itself.' And in very Presocratic mood he appeals to 'the dark Heraclitus' who 'compares the world-building force to a child at play, who places stones here and there, builds sandcastles and knocks them down again' (§24). As befits an art-centred philosophy, however, the world-building force is most distinctively represented not as a child, but as an artist: the Dionysiac world-artist (*der dionysische Weltenkünstler*), who yet works in an Apolline medium, and whose finest creation is *us*:

The noblest clay, the most costly marble, man, is kneaded and cut...[under] the chisel strokes of the Dionysiac world-artist (§1).

The entire comedy of art is not performed for our betterment or education, nor are we the true creators of this art world. On the contrary, we may assume that for the real creator we have been images and artistic projections all along, and that we have our highest dignity in our significance as works of art (§5).

...that being which, as the sole creator and spectator of this comedy of art, prepares a perpetual entertainment for itself...(§5).

The striking conjunction 'creator and spectator' (*Schöpfer und Zuschauer*) is to be compared with a comment in §24 about the aesthetic spectator and his experience of 'having to see' and 'yearning for something beyond sight' at one and the same time. Nietzsche invites us to

transfer this phenomenon of the aesthetic spectator into an analogous process in the tragic artist...With the Apolline art sphere he shares the complete pleasure in mere appearance and in seeing, yet at the same time he negates this pleasure and finds a still higher satisfaction in the destruction of the visible world of appearance.

The aesthetic spectator and the tragic artist share the same 'coexistence of feelings' – and they share it with the world-artist himself. Our life is his spectacle. Life therefore has its purpose. It is a means to an end, however dubious that end may seem to us as individuals, and the purpose of art in sustaining life is subordinate to the purpose of life in providing an artistic spectacle for the art-deity. On both levels, art is not merely useful but necessary, in the same way that the proto-artistic phenomenon of the dream is a 'joyous necessity' for the ordinary man (§1).

If we are disposed to inquire further into the identity of the world-artist, we find nothing to fall back on but those ultimate realities of which we have already heard: the universal will, playing its 'artistic game' in the 'eternal amplitude of its pleasure' (§24); and the primordial oneness, which in §4 is said to 'need the rapturous vision, the pleasurable illusion, for its continuous redemption'. The universal will, the primordial oneness and the world-artist are one and the same. He, or it, is presumably Dionysus or the Dionysiac: 'the Dionysiac is seen to be...the eternal and original artistic power that first calls the whole world of phenomena into existence' (§25). Faced with these equations, we must surely feel all the uncertainties flowing back. In *BT* Nietzsche does not in fact ever give the world-artist the name Dionysus or ascribe any definite properties to him at all. He does not attempt to demonstrate his existence by argument or – what is more revealing – to convey it by description. What Nietzsche feels he describes; and the more honest the feeling, the richer the description, whether the topic is the ideal response to music or the world-view of archaic Greece.

His inability to describe the world-artist is a sign that this talk of divinity is hollow. Of the Olympians Nietzsche comments that 'the Greeks had to create these gods from a most profound need' (§3). His unnamed demiurge is hardly less of a hypostatic fiction, engendered by the 'logic' of his own imagery, and thinly concealing the unstable *Urgrund*, which creates art for *its* own 'redemption'. It is through 'the entire world of suffering', Nietzsche writes in §4, that 'the individual is impelled to realize the redeeming vision'. But such redemption can be of little use to the individual himself, who seems after all to be the sole carrier of life. Even 'the genius in the act of artistic creation' will derive little comfort now from the flattering suggestion that to him alone is any knowledge of 'the eternal essence of art' available – in so far as he in his creative act 'coalesces with this primordial world-artist' (§5). The principle that art exists for life and life for the world-artist is nothing but a vicious circle: art for life and life for art.

Nietzsche makes one further attempt at a solution. Into the discussion of the world-artist in §5 he sets a parenthesis:

we may assume that for the real creator we have been merely images and artistic projections all along, and that we have our highest dignity in our significance as works of art – for only as an *aesthetic phenomenon* can existence and the world be eternally *justified* [*nur als* ästhetisches Phänomen *ist das Dasein und die Welt ewig* gerechtfertigt]...

The pronouncement recurs, slightly altered, in §24:

How can the ugly and the disharmonic...stimulate tragic pleasure? Here it becomes necessary to take a bold running start and leap into a metaphysics of art, by repeating the sentence written above, that *only as an aesthetic phenomenon are existence and the world seen to be justified.*

The dictum is striking but far from self-explanatory, and it is hardly clarified by the comment that 'only music, placed beside the world, can give us an idea of what is meant by the justification [*Rechtfertigung*] of the world as an aesthetic phenomenon' (§24) – which tells us something about Nietzsche's desire to give music back its supreme place in the hierarchy of arts, but not much about aesthetic phenomenology.

What does the dictum mean? Nietzsche might be using 'aesthetic' either as he uses it in connection with the proper, complex response to tragedy, or else in the Kantian–Schopenhauerian context of contemplation. 'Only' implies the rejection of an alternative justification, while 'justified' appears to reintroduce some idea of *religious* validation. We would seem to be back to the world-artist, for whom our lives are to provide a spectacle. A retrospective comment in one of Nietzsche's notebooks from 1878 provides some confirmation for this inference:

At that time I believed that the world was intended as a spectacle [*Schauspiel*] from the aesthetic standpoint by its poet-author [*Dichter*], but that as a moral phenomenon it was a *deception*. That is why I came to the conclusion that only as an aesthetic phenomenon could the world be justified.[138]

It does not inspire confidence in Nietzsche's memory of the meaning of his first book that he should have converted his sculptor world-artist into a poet-creator, but, this apart, the comment is unexceptionable. Its most important feature is the claim that 'only' in 'only as an aesthetic phenomenon' implies a contrast with a *moral* justification. This must be so, if tragedy is to be credited with 'the justification of human evil' (§9), and it is perhaps the chief ground – though not adequate ground – for Nietzsche's later interpretation of the book as an anti-Christian tract.[139] His dictum, therefore, does not, as has been suggested, mean that life is only worth living if we accede to 'the illusory delight in individuals effected through Apollo'[140] – although Nietzsche would agree that this does make life appear to be 'worth living'. It means that life as it stands is not defensible by moral criteria and only seems to be so with the introduction of a benevolent deity – or (equally, no doubt) by the Socratic pretence that knowledge and reason can cure all human ills. If life is defensible at all, it can only be defended in the way that one creator might justify his handiwork to another: ethically unedifying, but marvellous to look at. And if one of the created individuals too is to feel it as justified in this sense, it will not be through 'illusory delight' in his individual status: that delight must have already begun to pall the moment he begins to look for such a justification. It will be by seeing himself in a double perspective (like the perspective in which the aesthetic spectator of tragedy sees the hero), *both* as a suffering individual *and* as part of a marvellous work of art. The creative – i.e. Dionysiac – artist (Nietzsche argues) experiences his own version of this double perspective:

> insofar as the genius in the act of artistic creation coalesces with this primordial artist of the world...he is, in a marvellous manner, like the weird image of the fairy tale which can turn its eyes at will and behold itself; he is at once subject and object, at once poet, actor, and spectator (§5).

But the solution still hinges on a world-artist, who now seems less satisfactory than ever: either incredible, or, if credible, then himself surely part of the world that stands in need of justification. The question is not one that Nietzsche will ever settle, but its presence in *BT* serves to relate the book closely to his later thought. Even the imagery recurs. Once God has been pronounced dead, the world-artist as such may no longer be invoked, but the universe will retain its character as 'a work of art, giving birth to itself',[141] and from time to time Nietzsche will be seen to be playing variations on a now familiar theme:

> As an aesthetic phenomenon existence is still *bearable* for us.[142]

In any event, his failure to settle the question – if to leave it unsettled deserves to be called a failure – does not leave us in any doubt that this is one of the issues that count for most in the book. *BT* is a many-sided work, but wherever we look we see that it is not, in the end, a genre study, a work of literary or aesthetic theory. It offers unforgettable insights into tragic drama, but its ultimate concern is with man's tragic condition. If Kierkegaard is the first existentialist and Schopenhauer the first to present aesthetics as an alternative to existence, Nietzsche's book, by identifying aesthetics with the existential, is the first essay in post-Christian existentialism.

Nietzsche's first book does what all his later works will do. It proclaims the necessity to evaluate – works, authors, genres, periods, life itself. This is done in the name of aesthetics; but aesthetics in the Kantian tradition had been taken as the preserve of value-free, disinterested contemplation. Nietzsche's aesthetic inquiries take place on a value-laden, psychological–metaphysical plane. When he asks, 'what is Greek tragedy?', he means 'what is Greek tragedy *for*?' – and when he asks this, he denies the traditional character of aesthetics as well as the traditions of classical scholarship and relativistic historicism. In opposition to all these traditions, his starting point is an urgent appeal to the timeless here and now in keeping with 'the true, that is, metaphysical significance of life' (§23).

Partly out of loyalty to Wagner, partly out of a desire for a total solution, Nietzsche makes a valiant attempt to identify tragedy and the tragic, genre and existence. But in the final analysis genre cannot be decisive for him. His objection to Euripides or to Plato is ultimately determined by their outlook, as he sees it, not by their formal innovations. His attraction to earlier Greek tragedy depends not only on its generic religious-existential ground, but on a pattern – the destruction of a suffering central hero at the hands of cosmic forces – which may arise from the generic ground, but is not a necessary feature of Greek or any other tragedy at all. There will come a point in Nietzsche's life when he will look at the generalized suffering hero and say: 'this is *our* supreme condition: can *we* be like that?' The suffering hero of Greek tragedy, Oedipus or Prometheus, is the original model for Nietzsche's *Übermensch*, the superman,[143] and *BT*, accordingly, the prototype of his whole philosophy.

9

Nietzsche and earlier German theories of tragedy

LESSING

An ironist might observe that the unbroken sequence of German theories of tragedy from Lessing to Brecht and beyond constitutes a body of writing at least as interesting, and possibly more interesting, than the German tragedies which were written during that time. And even though the statement is unfair and an exaggeration, it does reflect a tenacious preoccupation with the theory of drama and the idea of 'the tragic' which has no parallel in any other literature. Nietzsche's own theory must be assessed, as we have tried to assess it, as a contribution to the understanding of tragedy in its own right. At the same time, consideration of the German theoretical tradition to which he belongs provides a necessary perspective. In the first place it helps to explain the extra-literary character of his interest in the tragic stage. The particular existential slant of his theory may be his own, but throughout this long line of theories tragedy is anything but a narrowly literary concern. Correspondingly, the theorists tend tacitly to agree with Nietzsche that detailed technical analyses of an Aristotelian kind are not their business. Nietzsche, once again, may have a special aversion to technicalities, but the German theorists as a whole are not given to them. It may sound paradoxical, but their theories are more philosophically far-ranging than Aristotle's, while his is more detached, more 'aesthetic' in the Kantian sense; but then, the Kantian critical mode of thought is closer to Aristotle than to the speculative theoreticians of the post-Kantian era.

Lessing's observations in *Hamburg Dramaturgy* II (1759), our first case in point, reflect that multiplicity of interests, or rather cares, of which Nietzsche remarked that they squandered Lessing's finest gifts.[1] Dramatic critic and dramatist, cosmopolitan and patriot, theologian and enlightened moralist, savant and popularizer – Lessing pursues all these callings and uses his theorizing about drama in each of them. We may summarize his thinking – to the extent that it is relevant to our historical sketch – under three headings, all of which really point in the same direction:

(i) The theatre is an inculcator of virtues.

(ii) The theatre – or rather the taste for it – is a matter of national culture, and consequently the virtues (that is, a people's sense of values) are at least co-determined by historical and national considerations.

(iii) As a consequence of its didactic intention and its national characteristics, the theatre makes for social harmony, which (alas) is perfectly compatible with its having an anodyne effect.

We may begin with the last point. Lessing's attack on Gottsched and the neo-classical preoccupation with dramas of kingship and political intrigue (*Haupt- und Staatsaktionen*) is a commonplace of German literary history. His insistence that a middle-class public requires middle-class heroes, and that the problems presented on the stage should be of direct concern to its audience, requiring no social transposition, is closely related to his insistence that the *phobos* which Aristotle observes in the spectator of tragedy means 'fear' (*Furcht*) rather than 'terror' (*Schrecken*).[2] Lessing's aspiration is to make tragedy into an intimate and familiar art, and to have the nature of its intimacies determined by the aspirations of the German Enlightenment.

With his didactic purpose, Lessing reminds us of Brecht in our day, but the means he proposes to employ in drama are the opposite of those that Brecht employs. Where Brecht uses alienation, the estranging of the audience from the text or the stage, Lessing proposes familarization. The distance between dramatic action and audience is to be diminished: the audience is to identify emotionally, socially and historically with the characters on stage. The dangers of excessive familiarization, of stage issues becoming trivial, stage techniques becoming boring, stage effects becoming insipid, are obvious enough.

Almost two decades before Herder's *On German Idiom and Art* (*Von deutscher Art und Kunst*, 1772–3) Lessing brings national criteria to bear upon his evaluation of drama. They are formulated less clearly than in Herder, but they amount to the same argument: the stage is part of a national culture; nations have distinct characteristics (Herder's argument is sharpened by the consideration that certain historical epochs as well as certain geographical entities have distinct traits); and English rather than French drama – that is, Shakespeare rather than Corneille or Racine – is the proper exemplar for the new German theatre. Here, at the very beginning of the modern theoretical tradition, there is a political concern which is inimical to the kind of aesthetic detachment one finds in Aristotle. There is nothing in Aristotle that is analogous to Lessing's injunctions about a national theatre: a national absolutism is self-evidently implied in everything he says. No other cultures or dramatic practices were available to Aristotle and it would not have occurred to him to speak of the *Greek* stage. These Aristotelian *données* become Lessing's goals. The traditional national order and hierarchy which Aristotle takes for granted have no equivalent in the world from which Lessing's ideas of the theatre arise. On the contrary: where for Aristotle the drama is only one of many embodiments of the ethos of the city-state, for Lessing the stage is a means, at times the most appropriate means, towards the creation of such an ethos in contemporary Germany. Drama is not so much expression as creation.

This is the one idea for which, in Lessing's scheme of things, paramount importance may be claimed. It is largely unprecedented and immensely influential. This vision of the patriotic and ethos-forming function of literature, especially the stage, will in due course be common to all the literary and philosophical movements of the late eighteenth and early nineteenth centuries in Germany. Politics, economic independence and social emancipation are in different degrees closed to the *Bürgertum*, the German middle classes. Literature and philosophy are to replace them as sources of a prospective political unity and national culture; and among the literary means to this end, drama, being obviously the most public, is the most readily available. It is therefore the ideal of a national enlightenment that informs the various elements of Lessing's theory. The enlightening function of the stage presupposes a particular age and its very particular needs, and it envisages the creation of a particular public. Again these are critical moves which have no equivalent in Aristotle and few if any precedents elsewhere. We meet them later, of course, in Wagner and in the last sections of *BT;* and in our own day they are familiar from the works of socially and politically aware playwrights (Osborne, Wesker, Hochhuth) in the wake of Brecht.

There is very little aggressive nationalism in Lessing's argument; the coarsening of his views into that is left to the next but one generation of romantic philosophers. As often as not the terminology which he chooses is related to universal humanity. The idea of *katharsis* in particular he sentimentalizes into an effect whereby 'man as such' comes to be reconciled to the ways of God. But although Lessing's is the terminology of the brotherhood of mankind, and although he comes to exercise a not inconsiderable piecemeal influence on late eighteenth-century French dramatic theory, especially through Diderot, it is clear that the coherent application of his theories lies within German literature and the German stage. His attempts to come to terms with some of the intractable difficulties created by Aristotle's theory of drama are entirely characteristic of the age in which, and the country for which, he wrote. Among them is the notorious paradox at the root of our enjoyment of tragedy. We have looked at Nietzsche's metaphysical explanation of our pleasure in tragic pain and also the several possible explanations offered by Aristotle:[3] tragedy arouses pity and fear; it is a miniature (and we enjoy miniatures); it teaches us about patterns of action in life. These patterns (we may now add) are sequences of events which Aristotle sees as following one another not randomly, but by 'probability' (*to eikos*) or 'necessity' (*to anankaion*). This pair of terms, expounded in *Poetics*, Chs 7–11, is of central importance to his dramatic theory, and his interest in it is related to his belief in the importance of tragic action and plot.

Lessing's thinking about the tragic paradox presupposes a type of drama with visual conventions different from those of the Attic theatre. It is well known that the Greek tragedians avoided scenes of bloodshed. Agamemnon's murder takes place during Aeschylus' play; his death-cries are heard by chorus and audience; but the murder itself is not seen by either. In general, however, the genre did encompass direct representation of the more monstrous or horrific sides of life, real and imaginary. The corpus of extant plays abounds not only in verbal allusion to violent incidents, but in visible reminders of them. The entry of the blinded Oedipus will not have been a pretty sight, nor that of the Furies in Aeschylus' *Eumenides*, 'black, hideous, with noses snorting and eyes oozing, creatures so disgusting that the priestess who first saw them could no longer stand upright'.[4] In the case of suicide, even killing in full view of the audience was permitted, as in Sophocles' *Ajax*.

In practice, and even, though less obviously, in theory, Lessing does not envisage the presentation of monstrous events at all. He certainly does not countenance it in his or anybody else's contemporary drama, and though he attacks contemporary critics when they try to whittle down the horrors of classical Greek plays, those of Euripides in particular, he himself does not really proceed very differently. Like Goethe in his *Iphigenia*, Lessing looks to an ideal drama in which the horrors are confined to inner anguish and not realized in actual disaster. The difficulty he has to solve is therefore smaller than that faced by the Greeks: the tension between the event represented and our contemplation of the event is reduced. His new aim is not merely to render the not-so-gruesome events necessary or probable, but to render them harmless; that is, he wishes to show them in such a light that they will be seen to justify, if not the ways of God to man, at least the ways of an impersonal Providence to modern humanity. Hence, in Lessing's theory, the emphasis on 'poetic justice' (an emphasis which, as F. L. Lucas observes, can be singularly unpoetic);[5] hence, in Lessing's drama, the lack of any great excitement in the discovery of the truth and in the *peripeteia*. Hence, above all, the interpretation of *hamartia* in the villain not as tragic error but as fundamental moral flaw. How this theory takes the spunk out of drama and ends in the *comédie larmoyante* needs no further demonstration.

KANT AND SCHILLER

A quite different solution to the tragic paradox is implicit in Kantian aesthetics. In the influential work of Kant's teacher, Alexander Baumgarten,[6] the process of liberating art from its purely representational action is set in train. Baumgarten, and after him Kant, sees the work of art as the product of a human activity in its own right, an 'imitation' of the world outside, but not always and not necessarily so in all its details, with 'heterocosmic' laws of its own which are independent of, though they may retrace, the laws of actions and happenings in the world. Kant heightens these ideas of Baumgarten – he increases the hiatus between art and non-artistic experience – by concentrating, in the *Critique of Judgement* (1790), on the 'analogous' or 'independent' nature of art. The link between the finished work of art and ordinary human experience must of course lie in our experience itself: it is provided by the human capacity to contemplate *disinterestedly*. *Interesselos*, 'disinterested', henceforth becomes the cardinal term of Kantian aesthetics and consequently of Schiller's discussions of the functions of drama. Here, then, is that nexus between art and disinterestedness which Nietzsche will half undo by his tacit redefinition of 'aesthetic'. For Kant *interesselos* denotes, above all, the absence of any practical or 'material' use or value, including the uses of a representational artefact. It implies the self-containedness of the work, and the independence of its effects from other effects. It means, at least for the duration of the contemplation, a wholly selfless and even, in a sense, an impersonal response to the work of art.

The idea of *Interesselosigkeit* certainly stands in acute contrast to Lessing's didacticism, even more than to Nietzsche's redefined concept of the aesthetic. Nevertheless, later dramatic theories, and in particular Schiller's theory, succeed in finding a compromise between enlightened moral didacticism and the Kantian emphasis on the disinterestedness of art. Such a compromise is possible because for Kant morality itself is a disinterested activity, an inward matter divorced from its visible results in the life of the individual. Hence art in general (for Kant) and the theatre in particular (for Schiller) are precisely the means by which such a 'disinterested' – that is, moral – state of mind is brought about in the spectator or reader. Art in general is simply the most fitting means by which this may be achieved, and the theatre is the most fitting public means towards this end. In this context the effect of tragedy is taken to be a purely moral factor, through which the good state of mind is attained.

Art is not in fact the only means by which this positive disposition may be brought about. In his *Critique of Judgement* Kant perceives that the contemplation of nature as a pure spectacle leads to the same state of mind. And because nature, in this pre-Romantic argument, yields such a positive state of mind, it follows for Kant, and *a fortiori* for Schiller, that the whole range of artistic activities, which is said to yield the same results, is conceived as a vast analogy to the edifice of nature. In this analogy lies the foundation of all subsequent discussions of the 'natural' character of art. Aristotle had already interpreted the work of art as an 'organic' structure, like a living creature (*Poetics*, Ch. 23), and, as we have seen,[7] he had ascribed to the world of art 'kinds' corresponding to the *genera* of the world of nature. But now every aspect of art is defined as analogous to the natural world. The artist is the creator of the artefact, as God is the creator of the natural world. The structure of the artefact is said to retrace the structure of this or that individual part of the natural universe. And in his essay *On the Marionette Theatre* (1810) Kleist will conclude that it is precisely the artist's task to create an artefact so perfect that it will be indistinguishable from the creations of nature, and so lead man back into the natural paradise from which his sophistication has expelled him.

It is in Schiller's theoretical writings that these idealistic notions of art are related to serious drama. We can summarize his argument by concentrating on his conception of *die schöne Seele*, 'the beautiful soul', a term common in the second half of the eighteenth century, to which he gives a very particular meaning.[8] As a character in a play, *die schöne Seele* has two functions to perform: first, it is the character which most fully *displays* that harmonious and valuable disposition to which Kant had given the name of good will; and secondly, it is a character *conducive to* that positive disposition of mind. As a literary creation, it is regarded as an artefact. But it is an artefact the qualities of which are essentially the qualities of a *natural* creature; hence Schiller's emphasis on the unintellectual, unselfconscious, instinctive or intuitive manner of 'the beautiful soul's' responses to human situations. Because it is so much like a natural creature (the argument runs), our response to it is like our response to nature herself. And thus far the matter is simple enough. The difficulty arises at the point where morality is to be brought in.

Kant is not a romantic philosopher. In particular he rejects the pathetic fallacy: that is, he rejects the view – for instance Wordsworth's view – that the workings of nature are themselves moral. On the contrary: in the realm of nature (he argues) there obtains a blind, mechanical necessity which is totally at odds with morality. It is only when we contemplate nature, as it were from afar, at an 'aesthetic distance', that its workings, which in themselves are blind and necessity-ridden, *look* harmonious and conducive to the positive state of mind. Another way of putting this is to say that in the aesthetic contemplation the natural phenomena appear *as if* they obeyed the same laws as those of morality. Similarly with Schiller's *schöne Seele*: a creature behaving naturally *as if* it obeyed the moral laws. For this creature, therefore, the moral laws are an intuitively accepted mode of behaviour. It is 'perfectly natural' for such a creature to behave morally, since in it nature and morality are not divided.

All this makes *die schöne Seele* an undramatic conception in which no genuine conflict – or as Nietzsche would say, no destruction – is possible. Dramatic conflict is resolved by a choice which is conscious at the same time as it is instinctive – and it is always the morally right choice. However, since a choice for evil is either not envisaged at all (as with Thekla in the last part of Schiller's *Wallenstein* trilogy) or envisaged only tentatively and intermittently (as with Goethe's Iphigenie), the plain dramatic interest of the 'What will she do next?' kind is bound to suffer. The creature is undramatic for the Aristotelian reason that it is simply too good. And we may be glad that Schiller himself, in spite of his theory, attempted to put it into practice only rarely. For all that, it represents his strenuous effort to make the Kantian ideal – the most exciting intellectual stimulus he had encountered – compatible with the prevalent idea of the stage as a moral institution. There is a profound paradox in Schiller's aesthetics and in the ethical aspirations which his aesthetic theory is intended to support: the goal of man's moral and cultural endeavour is to return to his origin and to become again a part of 'nature'. And this paradox will be a part of Nietzsche's heritage.

From about 1793 onwards, Schiller clearly recognizes – his correspondence with Goethe testifies to this – that the kind of cosmic order within which Greek tragedy had its bearings has no meaning for his contemporary world. In the Introduction to *The Bride of Messina* he stresses, and in fact exaggerates, the idea of an independent fate in Greek drama, seeing it as a wholly transcendent non-terrestrial force. But since the contemporary world is governed by no comparable religious order, he proclaims the idea of a *natural* order and hierarchy as a substitute. What is remarkable is that, unlike his successors, he does not postulate this natural order at the expense of a psychological realism. On the contrary, his idea of nature as the equivalent of Greek fate enables him to hit upon a most accurate psychological truth; it is this that informs the *Wallenstein* trilogy.

Wallenstein is not a Greek hero. The self-consciousness of his preoccupation with personal ambition clearly excludes him from Greek drama. What determines his tragic actions is not an Aristotelian mistake but a modern moral flaw. The psychological truth about him is that he feels himself to be imprisoned in an order which is hostile to his ambition; its objective reality as a transcendent order is not at issue in the play. What is at issue is Wallenstein's power-complex, the support he derives from his *belief* in an objective order, and his destruction when that belief is undermined. Schiller describes this transcendent order as emanating from the stars, which is not just realistic historical background, although it is certainly that too. It is the stars and not, say, a curse or fate or providence that are invoked, precisely because stars are, first and foremost, phenomena in nature. Here, therefore, they are representative of that cosmic *and* natural hierarchy which Wallenstein with his ambition is conscious of violating. It is the natural propensities of the stars that are clearly shown forth, and it is Wallenstein's belief in their influence which is the source of the play's psychological realism, its modernity.

At this point we are back again at the Kantian analogy from which Schiller derives so much inspiration – the analogy between the natural universe and the moral. Schiller the theorist is proposing to square the circle by trying to show that the analogy can be established in drama in a positive way; hence the theory of *die schöne Seele*, with its occasional insipidities, its undramatic character. Schiller the dramatist knows better: he knows in particular that it is only negatively, in the violation of the natural law as in the violation of the moral law, that the analogy can be demonstrated on the stage. And the result is the greatest political drama of German and also of modern European literature. The greatness of *Wallenstein* lies in the realistic and political insight which it gives us into what stature in a political leader means, what it can achieve, and what it cannot. There is nothing unlimited or absolute or utopian about Wallenstein's charisma. It is what human greatness always is: it fits into a larger order, is strengthened by it, weakened by it, threatened and ultimately destroyed by it.

Nietzsche is no friend of Schiller the dramatist,[9] but the conception of tragedy realized in *Wallenstein* – the grandeur, the destruction of the individual – captures something of the spirit of Greek tragedy as Nietzsche will see it. What keeps Nietzsche from appreciating this kinship is the Schiller cult. Had the contemporary admiration of Schiller been less ridden with liberal clichés, he might have recognized that the products of Schiller's moral imagination are at least as close to the Greek outlook as the products of Wagner's mythopoeic mind.

SCHELLING

In his postscript to the second part of Aeschylus' Oresteian trilogy, the *Libation Bearers*, Emil Staiger sums up the action of the play, showing how Orestes is impelled by the murder of Agamemnon to his murder of Clytemnestra, his own mother:

The corpse [of the recently slain Agamemnon] in its grave, the shouts of lamentation rising towards Dike and Zeus, the highest judge, the lament heightening into frenzy – all this drives [Orestes]...towards the deed. Face to face with his mother for a last time, he hesitates. Yet at this instant, and to our astonishment, his companion, silent until now, receives the power of speech:

ORESTES: Pylades, what shall I do? Respect my mother and not kill her?
PYLADES: What then becomes of Apollo's words,
His Pythian oracles, and the oath you swore?
Make all men your enemies, but not the gods.

These three verses that Pylades speaks to remind us of the will of the gods are decisive. The mother is killed. But hardly is the deed done when that which has been hidden or forcibly suppressed enters the consciousness [of Orestes]...He returns on stage, still in ecstasy at his triumph, convinced that it is merely a monster of iniquity that he has destroyed. However, the very details which he recalls in order to assure himself of the murdered mother's shameful guilt make us suspect that evil will come. Then he suddenly doubts whether everything has really happened the way he remembers it. His senses are confused, and from the mists there emerges only the knowledge that he has killed his mother. The Furies suddenly appear. He feels their breath. The chorus attempts to calm him. Like a hunted animal he takes to flight.

We are deeply disturbed. The poet has done everything to convince us of the necessity of Orestes' deed. Equally, he now convinces us of its monstrousness, and makes it clear that the Furies are fully justified in pursuing the matricide. Now at this point our modern sensibility immediately resorts to the concept of the tragic as the inescapable inward contradiction, the contradiction on which the very meaning of life is wrecked; what we call tragic is an entirely inescapable guilt or a collision of duties, and this is the meaning of the word which we find confirmed in the fate of Orestes. But we soon recall that the notion of the tragic does not arise before the age of German idealism, especially Schelling's *Letters on Dogmatism and Criticism* of 1795. Lessing as yet knows nothing about it; the idea is alien to the French [neo-classical drama], it is alien to the Spanish dramatists and to Shakespeare. In antiquity above all we must look for no such sequence of ideas. There is not a word about it in Aristotle's explication of Attic tragedy...and anyone who reads the works of Aeschylus, Sophocles and Euripides faithfully and without prejudice must admit that he will almost always look in vain for a fate 'tragic' [in this sense]...[10]

The idea of the tragic predicament (Staiger concludes), with its emphasis on inescapable contradiction and inescapable guilt, is wholly modern; where it occurs in Attic tragedy, it is only by virtue of a chance concatenation of circumstances, peripheral to the main action.

Staiger's discussion is no less illuminating for being in need of qualification. Fifty million Frenchmen can be wrong; and no age or individual has a monopoly of authentic interpretation. The existence or importance of any characteristic of a work of art is not dependent on the capacity of theory – contemporary or otherwise – to identify and articulate it. Nor are neo-classical or Aristotelian theories of Greek tragedy to be taken as authoritative guides *in one way* merely because they may *in other ways* be closer in ethos to Aeschylus and Sophocles than the theories of German idealism. The question of tragic inevitability has a *prima facie* claim on our attention, and like Nietzsche (and Quinton and Leavis) we have judged that the modern conception of the tragic provides an indispensable perspective on Greek tragedy as on Shakespeare (to cast the net no wider). And if it is Nietzsche who provides the classic delineation of the concept, it is the idealist Schelling who articulates the concept in the first place.

Thus Staiger does well to draw our attention to the unexpected context in which 'the tragic' proves to have originated. Schelling's notion is arresting, and yet its moral implications are, as Staiger insists, alien to the Greek world. Nor is this surprising, for Schelling's interpretation of Greek tragedy serves above all as an occasion for the expounding of his own moral views.

Schelling's argument begins[11] with a summary of Chapter 13 of the *Poetics*, where Aristotle examines the suitability of various kinds of plot-structure for tragedy. The plot in each case involves a reversal (*peripeteia*) and, as so often in the *Poetics*, the discussion proceeds with close reference to the two emotions taken to be the requisite effects of tragedy, pity and fear. Four possible structures are considered, the first three of which Aristotle pronounces unsuitable.

First: a good man suffers a reversal and falls from good fortune into misfortune undeservedly. This, Aristotle says, yields neither the effect of pity nor the effect of fear (Schelling uses the word *schrecklich* and not *furchterregend*): it is merely 'repulsive' (*miaron*).

Secondly: Aristotle considers the possibility of a bad man passing from misfortune to good fortune. This situation, he suggests, 'is the most untragic situation possible, for it has none of the requisites: it does not satisfy our human feeling, nor does it arouse pity or fear'.

Thirdly: the reversal from good fortune to bad comes upon a man who is especially wicked – and presumably (though this is not said explicitly) his fall is due to his wickedness. This too, Aristotle says (and Schelling agrees with him), is of no use to the tragedian: 'For though a pattern of this kind would appeal to our human feeling [by which Aristotle seems to mean it would be morally satisfying], it would not induce pity or fear: pity is induced by undeserved misfortune, and fear by the misfortune of someone like us'.

Fourthly: there is, for Aristotle, only one serious possibility left, which is the one he approves: catastrophe overtakes a man who is neither a saint nor a villain, but in between (and better rather than worse); his fall, however, is not due to any vice or crime, but to a mistake (*hamartia*). Oedipus and Thyestes are mentioned by Aristotle as examples of such men, and there then follows his approbation of plots centred on the troubles of a few well-known families as providing the most suitable subject-matter for tragedy.

Aristotle's argument (says Schelling) 'is conceived in and for his age': what can *we* make of it? Appropriating the Aristotelian notion of tragedy, Schelling now falls back on a move which is wholly alien to Aristotle himself and depends on the Kantian distinction between *Verstand* (understanding) and *Vernunft* (reason). What Aristotle is really saying (Schelling claims), if looked at 'from the aspect of reason' (*von der Vernunftseite*), is capable of 'a higher interpretation'. And this *höhere Ansicht* is the wholly non-Aristotelian idea of necessary guilt:

> Thus it is necessary that guilt be incurred by necessity and not, as Aristotle says, by an error, but rather through the will of destiny and an inevitable fate or a revenge of the gods.

We are on the threshold of Hebbel's antinomian dramatic ideology with its insistence on heroes who are 'guilty' yet morally innocent – an argument of immense and (we may think) misplaced sophistication.

For Schelling, then, the tragic hero *par excellence* is

> a mortal who is destined by fate for guilt and crime, even like Oedipus fighting *against* fate, fleeing his guilt, and yet terribly punished for his crime, which was the doing of destiny –

and Schelling continues:

> Are these contradictions not purely destructive, and where are the grounds of that beauty which nevertheless the Greeks reached in their tragedies?

'The beauty of tragedy', he suggests, lies in a peculiar twist: the horror of the misfortune and the punishment are *counterbalanced* by the suggestion (which Schelling discovers in the Greek tragedians) of a very particular *honour* attached to the hero. ('The prisoners', writes Kafka in one of his notes to *The Trial*, 'sing so beautifully.') It is the honour that he, the hero, should be chosen to suffer punishment, that he is worthy of the wrath of the gods, that he has been elected:

> That the guilty [hero], who was defeated by no less than the superior might of destiny, should nevertheless be punished was necessary in order to show the triumph of freedom; it was the acknowledgement of freedom, it was the honour that is freedom's due. The hero had to fight against the decreed fate, for otherwise there would be no conflict at all, no expression of freedom.

Freedom here lies in the necessarily hopeless fight against the transcendent power of the gods:

In respect of that which is subject to necessity

– that is, in his physical being –

the hero had to be defeated. But in order not to allow necessity to overcome without overcoming it in turn, the hero had freely to expiate for this guilt [even though it was] imposed by destiny. [For] it is the highest idea and the highest victory of freedom

– and thus the source of tragedy and beauty –

willingly to bear punishment for an inevitable crime, in order to prove freedom in the very loss of it, and to go under while proclaiming the freedom of the will.

No need to emphasize that there is not a word of any of this either in Aristotle or in Aeschylus, Sophocles or Euripides.

What does it mean, 'to prove freedom in the very loss of it'? It means to see existence through Protestant eyes. The paradox is the Protestant paradox *par excellence* (even if we may also detect it elsewhere, as in Kafka's conception of guilt). It lies at the root of the theologies of Luther and Kierkegaard. Luther's relatively simple formulation of it occurs in his *On the Freedom of a Christian* of 1520: 'The more enslaved the body, the freer the soul.' The paradox is founded on two distinctions which to us seem entirely familiar and closely related: the one between the gods (or God) and the world, the other between the spiritual identity and the physical being of man. The relationship between the two is one of the data of modern cultural history. In the Christian or post-Christian world they belong together. In the world of fifth-century Athens, however, the opposition between human and divine has a significance – and tragedy after tragedy attests it – which the opposition between body and spirit cannot be said to possess.

This is not to say that Aeschylus or Sophocles had *no* conception of spirit in the given sense. It is not to say that we accept the argument of Bruno Snell that in the earliest Greek literature there can be no conception of a psyche because there is no word for it (the Greek word *psukhē* itself at first means 'breath of life' or else 'ghost')[12] – let alone John Jones' claim that a fifth-century Greek had so little sense of identity that he was unable to equate the 'you' of 'what you are doing now' with the 'you' of 'what you might be doing in a different, hypothetical situation'.[13] Snell's view is only meant to apply to Homer, but even for Homer it may be an overstatement. The relation between language and concept is not as tidy as Snell would like:[14] if it was, one wonders how most new concepts would ever arise. Jones' position, which reads like a caricature of Snell's, is itself refuted not only by observation of Greek pronouns, but by Snell's own reminder that something like the 'modern' notion of the individual consciousness is visible at least as early as Heraclitus.[15]

The truth is that the Greeks of the fifth century *did* have a concept of spirit which *was* on occasion opposed to the concept of body, but that their concepts and their opposition had a different weight and tone from their modern counterparts. We may certainly recall the Orphic conception of the immortal soul and Plato's impending development of such notions. We may add Heraclitus and a humble sepulchral inscription on the Athenian soldiers who died in action during the revolt of Potidaea (432 B.C.): 'aether received their souls [*psukhas*], earth their bodies'.[16] Nevertheless, a Christian or Cartesian elaboration of the dichotomy between body and soul, or body and spirit, is alien to the playwrights of the tragic age and to the view of life which they presuppose.

Yet it is from this opposition, in its speciously 'natural' association with the distinction between man and god, that Schelling derives his antithetic interpretations of Greek drama. In addition, the more authentic polarity, man and god, is rendered alien in its turn by Schelling's tacit conversion of the Greek gods' divine immanence into a quasi-Christian transcendence. As he sees it, then, Greek drama is enacted in the existential space between the omnipotent and mysterious ordinance of the transcendent gods and man's situation wholly at the mercy of that ordinance; and again, between the necessity-stricken and wholly unfree physical being of man (the physical being at the mercy of what Kant had called the blind forces of nature) and the triumphant, wholly spiritual and inward 'freedom' of the will and the moral intention, whose workings are entirely independent of a man's material and physical nature. By imposing these antitheses onto the Greek world view, Schelling makes them operative in his interpretation of ancient drama.

The tragic hero of Sophocles' *Oedipus Rex*, to choose Schelling's own example, is hardly the Protestant hero that Schelling makes out. It is not any external fate, but rather his own determination to search out the truth, that brings about his defeat; and what he proclaims as he goes under is not so much the freedom of the will as its irrelevance, not his personal guilt for preordained crimes but his monstrousness as involuntary criminal. Above all, there is no special 'honour' attaching to him as an individual in respect of his 'free' but 'hopeless' endeavour to fight against his fate. The honour that accrues to him is the honour due to his kingship – except in so far as he is publicly respected also for the particular qualities which enabled him to solve the riddle of the Sphinx and so gain the kingship in the first place. But even that respect is accorded to him only until the revelation of the truth and, like his royal status, it precedes the revelation and is not enhanced but imperilled by it: the text runs directly counter to Schelling's argument. That a conscious recognition of his guilt and hence a conscious expiation of it should *create* his honour (as Schelling claims) is unthinkable. His honour is essentially external, and it is doubtful if the blind figure who is patronized by Creon at the end of the play preserves any but the conventional dignity of elevated diction.

The concept of the tragic which is inaugurated by Schelling becomes dominant in the nineteenth century; only Hegel departs from it. Schelling's theological predispositions may not be shared by all those who invoke the concept henceforth, but detaching the concept from the theology will not always be easy: his version of the tragic appeals too strongly to modern prejudices. Its two antitheses – divine and human, spiritual and physical – delimit our modern idea of human individuality. Its salient point is Schelling's exclusive (and characteristically Lutheran) stress on the individual character of the tragic hero, where 'individual' implies an undivided psychic whole which is characterized by its separation from others. Of course this separation can be bridged in social experience. But throughout the German nineteenth century this sort of bridging of self with society, individual with collective, is seen by the philosophical consciousness not as a *donnée*, not as part of the essential nature of the psychic whole or of the human character, but as one of its major and problematic tasks. Not until Marx and then Max Weber is this view radically challenged. Schelling himself sees man as essentially and at his best a solitary being. This is a view peculiarly inapplicable to the organic society whose *Weltanschauung* is represented in the dramas on which he theorizes.

At every point Schelling's ideas evoke their alien theological context. For him the *Eumenides* is concerned with Orestes and his voluntary decision to expiate his crime, which is presented as an *acte gratuit*. What he envisages is something comparable to the Christian idea of expiation: 'Guilt can only be taken from him through genuine expiation' (*wirkliche Sühnung*). This is not a helpful comment on the play at all. What Schelling calls expiation, Aeschylus calls purification, *katharmos*. What Orestes has undergone is not an experience affecting his individual conscience, but a ritual act appertaining to a communal cult, and the play is not even ultimately concerned with the validity of that act, but rather with the cosmic progress from a more to a less primitive dispensation of justice through the resolution of a conflict between two sets of deities. Nothing could be further from an inward act of a consciousness meditating on guilt or innocence, such as Schelling envisages, than the great jury scene in which selected Athenian citizens address themselves to the question whether the killing of Clytemnestra was justifiable homicide. The theme of the play is not the journey of Orestes towards expiation in accordance with divine law, but his vindication according to the law that is now, in this scene, being constituted in Athens. The play, in short, is not concerned with the attainment of a private virtue, but with the attainment of the public weal; not with the spiritual advancement of an individual, but with the advancement of the whole world, human and divine. Its issue is deeply religious, but it cannot be in any sense a 'purely spiritual' issue, because for Attic tragedy there is no such thing as pure spirit.

Nietzsche is one of the heirs to Schelling's discovery of the tragic. How far has *he* succeeded in detaching the concept from its alien modern connotations? It is clear, in the first place, that his rapport with Greek religion and religious ideology is much greater. Compared with Aristotle (we have said), Nietzsche puts religion back into Greek tragedy. It is (we can now see) Schelling who puts it back before Nietzsche – but Schelling's religion is not the right one: Nietzsche's is. One corollary of this is the absence in *BT* of Schelling's preoccupation with responsibility and guilt. There are remarks in §9 on the sin (*Sünde*) and sacrilege (*Frevel*) of Sophocles' Oedipus and Aeschylus' Prometheus, but these comments bear no relation to Schelling's thoughts on the hero's internal state of mind and his 'inescapable guilt'. A decade later Nietzsche will write:

> It is not guilt and its pernicious consequences which interests these poets – Shakespeare as little as Sophocles (in the *Ajax*, *Philoctetes*, *Oedipus*): however easy it might have been in the given instances to make guilt the lever of the play, it was carefully avoided.[17]

The comment does imply that a Greek playwright made a conscious decision *not* to worry about guilt, which seems to presuppose a Schellingian world in which the decision might have gone the other way. This apart, the view taken – which is implicit in *BT* – is clearly distinct from Schelling's.

In one important respect, however, the ideology prescribed by Schelling's interpretation of the tragic continues to act as a limitation on Nietzsche's thinking. For Schelling tragedy centres on a solitary hero; it premises his emergence from the collective. Nietzsche's very different theory presupposes the same nexus of ideas. His hero emerges from the safety of the anonymous chorus, acquires a name and an epic status, asserts his solitary selfhood – and having thereby achieved the status of an individual, he is duly destroyed. His destruction, however, although a literal fact, is also a symbol, a particular instance of the impermanence of the Apolline as a whole. In the fate of an

Oedipus the spectator sees not only the annihilation of one man but 'the destruction of the visible world of mere appearance' (§24). To that extent, it follows that a play like *Oedipus Rex*, in which one central individual is destroyed, must actually be no more exemplary, no more tragic, than a play like *Antigone*, where the destruction is multiple: the sufferings of several individuals together can be no less indicative of the impermanence of the visible world than the fate of one. In the later sections of *BT* we hear a good deal about the destruction of a whole *world* of appearance, but Nietzsche's characteristic stress continues to fall on the negation of the Apolline *individual* and therefore on tragedies with a central suffering hero. Even within his own terms of reference, this stress is in some degree gratuitous. The discrepancy between tragedy (which includes *Antigone*) and his version of the tragic (which tends to exclude it) is wider than it need have been.

Schelling's views on the tragic are not central to his philosophy. We may assume that Nietzsche had encountered versions of them elsewhere, but it is unlikely that he knew them at first hand when writing *BT;* and there is no mention of them even at the end of his philosophical career when, in *Ecce Homo*, he is settling his account with those 'unconscious forgers', the philosophers of German idealism, and mentions Schelling among them.[18] Yet there is no doubt that more than any other modern theorist it is Schelling, with his emphasis on the existential problems of *das Tragische* (as against the dramatic problems of tragedy), who anticipates Nietzsche's views; and that a close kinship exists between Schelling's antinomian attribution of value to the single man in his 'tragic' predicament and Nietzsche's Dionysiac amoralism. In this respect, as in several others, there is nothing 'untimely' about Nietzsche's meditations. What occasions them is the central question of German philosophy in the nineteenth century: how to replace Christianity, what to do after 'the death of God'.

HEGEL

Hegel's theoretical observations on Greek tragedy are no less difficult in the sheer complexity of their formulation than the rest of his philosophical system, but they are very far from being esoteric. We should find little difficulty in agreeing, at the present time especially, that conflict is a constant factor – or even *the* constant factor – in human history; furthermore, that the conflicting agents change, perhaps radically, from age to age. What is true in the sphere of history and of concrete life, Kant had shown to be true also in an important area of intellectual argument: the moment you take up an extreme speculative position on any of the major questions about existence, you are brought face to face with its radical contradiction, a total denial of the validity of the first position. Such contradictory arguments Kant had called *the antinomies.* And since he had regarded them as a matter of misguided reason, rather than as an indication of how the world *is* (or, as we might regard them, as a condition of language), he had then proceeded to show how they should be avoided. Not so Hegel. What he insists on is the universal tendency to contradiction in all statements and, parallel with that, the universal tendency towards conflict in all concrete manifestations of life. For him neither contradiction nor conflict can possibly be avoided. If they are in reason (i.e. in language), they are in the world. All ideas, all situations, contain within themselves an inherent dynamism, which means a tendency to enter into conflict. To regard them as fixed and stable is not merely to regard them falsely, but to deceive oneself: stasis and arrest do not exist. We may note that most of the notorious difficulties in Hegel's use of the German language derive from an effort to overcome the static character of statements and to replace it with a dynamic style which would re-enact the flux of experience. This is what Nietzsche aims at too; his means, however, are quite different.

The tendency in all men towards contradiction and conflict Hegel hypostasizes as 'spirit': *Geist. Geist* is not simply the human mind, but the proneness of the human mind to proceed from one incomplete certainty to the next, from one legal arrangement to the next, from one political constitution to the next, from one philosophical or religious insight to the next, from one power-position to the next, and never, never to rest – or (to put it in Faustian terms) never to assent to the moment of stasis whether it be good or bad. But then the very terms 'good' or 'bad' are here offered not as independent moral criteria but as themselves reflections of the unending dynamic activity of the spirit. The spirit is everything and nothing. It is nothing we can give a fixed form to, nothing that has fixed properties. It is everything, since its agency, its 'striving' (to use a Faustian term once more), is constitutive of all manifestations of life.

But what is it moving towards? The process may be endless, but it must have a direction. The direction it takes throughout the history of mankind is towards itself, says Hegel. This is the sort of statement that an impatient critic like Bertrand Russell will regard as a deliberate mystification. Yet it is consistent enough. For if the spirit is everything, then the direction of its development is towards an ever-increasing intellectual clarification of everything in the world, an ever-increasing elucidation of all that at any given point in time was obscure, unenlightened or unreasonable. It now begins to look as if history is nothing but the totality of the efforts of philosophers towards greater enlightenment, consummated in Hegel's own work – which is the kind of nonsensical statement we are all too ready to attribute to German idealist thinkers. But philosophers in this scheme are only in the vanguard of the process at a certain time, and whether the particular understanding they bring to the world is effective in shaping it, or whether the enlightenment they attain and promulgate remains unheeded, or whether (as often) the rest of the world *in time* catches up with what *they* had been the first to see and understand – all this cannot depend on their efforts alone, but on the outcome of the meeting, the dialectic, between their ideas and the practicabilities of their day and age. The outcome must depend once again on conflict, on the sort of conflict of which Jesus and Socrates are for Hegel the most impressive witnesses and victims.

But if the philosophers are the vanguard of this development, Hegel is far from exaggerating their importance. In his *Philosophy of World History* he is specific enough about their function. He examines the founding of Athenian democracy, the evolution of the Roman legal system, the political, religious and national causes and effects of the Reformation, he discusses Montesquieu's legal and political philosophy, he considers the ideas and results of the French Revolution, and each time he sees each of these historical moments in the light of the self-realization of the human mind. Each time the outcome of the historical event creates conditions in which the rational human mind has disposed of some taboo, some prohibition, which had previously kept it in darkness about some aspect of its own reality. And each time a philosopher had pointed (but no more) in the direction where enlightenment was to be found.

Whatever may be said about this scheme of things, it does not preach a facile optimism. It has nothing to say about material, social or political progress in the humdrum nineteenth-century sense of that word. In fact the ever-increasing enlightenment and spiritual realization it proposes is supremely strenuous and in no sense a comfortable goal. Nor is Hegel guilty of simply identifying any actual state of affairs with the absolute spiritualization towards which history is moving, and when he says that 'whatever is, is reasonable',[19] he is making a statement concerning the capacity of the human mind to encompass all being, not a statement in political conservatism. On the other hand, he does accept the horrors of history as necessary means towards the grand goal; and by making conflict perpetual and fundamental, he implies a certain fatalism which concedes that only certain individuals are chosen to carry this conflict on, and that they too are replaceable by others.

This outline of the historical dimension of Hegel's philosophy is merely intended to show that his designation of tragedy as the highest art form of all has nothing arbitrary about it. It follows directly from his entire conception of history as a conflict, and the world at any point in time as the imperfect realization of that domain of the spirit within which the conflict is enacted. That tragedy is informed by conflict is implicit in Aristotle (*Poetics*, Ch. 14) and is, in any case, a proposition requiring no proof. That tragedy should, furthermore, present important conflicts rather than trivial ones is again in no need of demonstration – even if there are times, such as the present, when we have few commonly accepted criteria to distinguish the trivial from the important. For Hegel the question of what are important human themes is settled by the overall philosophical scheme we have described. Tragedy is central to his scheme of things because, more than any other genre, it is capable of conveying those major moments in the history of mankind which for him make up the history of the spirit. As Hegel's English disciple, A. C. Bradley, puts it: 'The reason why the tragic conflict thus appeals to the spirit is that it is itself a conflict of the spirit. It is a conflict, that is to say, between powers that rule the world of man's will and action – his "ethical substance".'[20]

The form this conflict takes is the famous (or notorious) triadic system: the dialectic of thesis and antithesis, whose conflict produces a new synthesis. In Hegel's aesthetic arguments generally, and his observations on tragedy in particular, the relevant dialectic is between *form* and *content*.

Time and again in Hegel's aesthetic writings we meet the proposition that form turns into content, or content into form. We have of course some idea, for instance in poetry, that a certain formal characteristic – say, a rhythm or a rhyme scheme – adds to the meaning of a poem. Something like this is what Hegel has in mind, though in tragedy the dialectic works most often in the opposite way, from content to form. Here is the premise:

> The general basis for tragic action is provided by that condition of the world [*Weltzustand*] which I...have called the heroic [*den heroischen*].[21]

Greek tragedy, Hegel is saying, is founded and enacted in a certain historical situation, 'the heroic condition of the world', which is apparently a continuum of the period in which the plays were composed and the earlier mythical world to which they refer. It is a condition in which the moral laws – what he calls 'the general moral forces' – appear to men 'in their pristine liveliness' in the shape of the gods. For the spectator of Greek tragedy the gods are the natural embodiment of those moral forces with which he is familar and which inform his daily life. These gods or forces are not fixed images or rigid commandments. They are the living substance from which tragedy is formed, just as they are the living substance by which human actions are determined – and it is a characteristic strength of Hegel's aesthetic arguments, unlike Nietzsche's, that in such ways they keep art and life, tragedy and *Weltzustand*, close together. Now (Hegel suggests) if these moral forces are to be really effective, if they are to be factors in the actual lives of men and, at the same time, factors in the shaping of tragedy which are concretely embodied (*anschaulich*) in it, they must make their appearance simultaneously in two forms, one general, the other particular, and the two are complementary.

The general form in which they appear Hegel calls 'the simple, undivided, or general consciousness'. Here the basis of tragedy is a passive, undifferentiated awareness which men have of their world. This awareness precedes all action and sees in it a break or disruption of the status quo; it is the consciousness of a spectator who is aware of what is happening but cannot or does not himself interfere. Such a consciousness is therefore static. It must view all deeds with fear and apprehension, for all deeds bring with them change and disruption. In tragedy this general consciousness provides the basis – Hegel's phrase is *substantielle Grundlage* – upon which the deeds of heroes are enacted. It is the basic substance or content of the play. And now comes the dialectical trick. In tragedy this basic substance is seen to assume a formal function: in describing 'the simple, undivided, or general consciousness', Hegel has in fact been describing the Greek chorus.[22]

The chorus, then (Hegel is suggesting), is not merely some convenient device for the conveying of relevant information, but the substantial basis in which a given historical morality and ethos are dramatically presented, the substantial basis against which individual heroic actions rise up in sharp outline. This is Hegel's powerful historical sense at its most impressive and its most problematic, and the two are not easy to distinguish. His way of interpreting the chorus suits a play like *Oedipus Rex* admirably. The chorus of elders there does certainly embody the given moral-religious ethos and, as compared with the knowing individual Tiresias or the seemingly knowing individual Oedipus, it offers a very static awareness of the situation. At the same time, Hegel's perspective would tend to obscure the difference between that chorus and the chorus of the *Antigone*, which is only superficially similar: for with its majestic survey of man's achievements and limitations, the *Antigone* chorus offers its 'relevant information' on a higher level altogether.[23] Furthermore, there are plays – Aeschylus' *Eumenides* is one – of which Hegel's formula, as it stands, makes nonsense. In the *Eumenides* the chorus of Furies is itself one of the 'individual' parties to the dramatic conflict and if it represents a 'consciousness', it is a very particular, divided consciousness that it represents.

Like Nietzsche after him, Hegel is unwilling to let a brilliant generalization be spoiled by empirical qualms. Like Nietzsche too, he uses his principle to find an unexpected explanation for two characteristic traits of the tragic chorus, its passivity and its power of survival. (It is questionable generalizations that lead both thinkers to some of their best insights.) And like Nietzsche once again, Hegel sees that the chorus is a necessary formal component of Greek tragedy, and that there is nothing accidental or arbitrary about its qualities. But for Nietzsche these qualities are ultimately explicable in terms of the metaphysical aesthetics of the genre, whereas for Hegel it is the presuppositions of Greek society that show why the qualities are as they are. Conversely, Hegel argues, the attempt to recreate such a chorus in what he calls 'the Romantic age' – an age which lacks those heroic foundations of which he spoke – is a misguided attempt which can only lead to bathos. Substance – the substance of a historical age – turns into form.

If the general guise assumed by Hegel's moral forces in tragedy is the static consciousness embodied in the chorus, the particular guise is the energy embodied in the individuals, the acting characters. Hegel describes this energy as 'the individual emotion [*Pathos*] which drives the acting characters in their state of moral justification [*mit sittlicher Berechtigung*] to oppose others and thus brings them into conflict'.[24] The individual characters will be engaged in actions which will bring them into the harshest possible strife with each other or with the status quo. What Hegel envisages is an absolute conflict, a total collision, of two rights. What could such a 'morally justified', total collision mean?

Aristotle (we recall) favoured the kind of tragedy where a reversal of fortune derives from a mistake, which would tend to mean a single act of blindness. In Schelling the act of blindness is converted into a criminal act, a wrong, which is opposed by an overwhelming right and punished – but a wrong whose punishment brings with it a certain validation; and this validation justifies *a posteriori* not indeed the act but the agent, establishing his character as heroic and, in a desperate sense, *in the right*. What in Aristotle figures as exceptional, in Schelling becomes a necessary disposition of character. And now in Hegel this necessary, constitutive disposition of character is once more raised to the level of a moral law: not merely a maxim governing the action of an individual man, but a general human law. Thus the tragic conflict becomes the conflict of law against law, right *versus* right. Morality – the objective condition of the spirit's working at a given time – is on both sides. There is no blindness or ignorance. There is no crime. The absolute tragic conflict is the conflict of two all but fully informed consciousnesses, two agents who all but fully understand themselves and each other, and who oppose each other by the assertion and counter-assertion of valid but conflicting laws.

But how can two laws be both valid and conflicting? The answer lies in the dynamic nature of human history as Hegel conceives of it. Any moment in history is for him a compromise between forces which are already on their way out and forces which are not yet fully established. If we look at the conflict of rights in spatial terms, we see every part of the world – the natural world as much as the world of men – as a battleground between two conflicting centres of power. Each consciousness, in order to manifest itself in the world, must affect other consciousnesses. Each centre, in order to assert itself, must go outside itself and its own sphere, and so encroaches on another. And the moment this happens, conflict ensues.

The classical example to which Hegel returned again and again is the *Antigone* of Sophocles. Clearly, in few other plays is the heroic substance of the conflicting agents more grandly manifest. The Antigone of Sophocles is not Anouilh's Antigone. She is not an oversexed teenager with a crush on a Gestapo-officer and a grudge against her family for having to be in by 11 p.m. (The abysmal dreariness of a good deal of post-Ibsenite drama is summed up by this adaptation.) Sophocles presents a girl of character. She is spirited – in the old-fashioned sense and in the Hegelian sense too. That is, she is moved by the spirit in her, she is that spirit and very little else. Acknowledging it to be her duty to bury Polynices, her brother, she commits her entire being to the execution of that duty: she is not concerned with the risk to herself, nor with the circumstance that Polynices died in arms against the city. The singleness of her person, the equation between duty and character, allows for no Hamletish wavering in her resolution. The identity between what she is and what she does contrasts with the indecisiveness of her sister Ismene, of whom the main Hegelian thing to say is precisely that she lacks Antigone's spirit, which is the spirit of duty as Antigone cannot help conceiving of it. The law, as Antigone understands and lives it, commands her to do a deed which has been prohibited by her uncle Creon, the new ruler of the city. From first to last Antigone is as clear in her mind about the punishment that will follow the forbidden act as about her duty towards Polynices; and this clarity of mind and purpose is not impaired by that remarkable passage in her last exchange with Creon when (to Aristotle's surprise and Goethe's dismay) she restates her duty with reference to the fact that for an orphan, as she is, brothers, unlike husbands or children, are irreplaceable.[25]

With religiose notions like Schelling's behind them, modern critics of the play have been quick to identify Antigone's stance with the divine, Creon's with the secular – and furthermore to interpret divine and secular in terms of moral sufficiency and insufficiency. The result is a familiar stereotype: Creon, the tyrant, follows the worldly law, the law of power-politics, and Antigone opposes him by following the divine law, the commandment of the gods; and although driven to her death for her opposition, her cause is vindicated in the end by Creon's downfall and admission of error. The stereotype, however, is unacceptable. In the first place, as Hegel saw, *both* characters are concerned with the divine, *both* with the secular. It is not fashionable to make the point,[26] but it is written into the play. Antigone indeed appeals to the 'unwritten laws [*nomima*] of the gods', but Creon too has his deities, 'the gods of the race';[27] and while he seeks to uphold the city by damning its enemy, she upholds the family. As Bernard Knox puts it in an avowedly Hegelian discussion, the two have 'opposing religious attitudes', which are 'extensions of the political: Creon is the champion of the *polis* and its gods, Antigone of the family and those gods invoked at the funeral, the ceremony which emphasizes the family's unity and its exclusiveness. The conflict between two individuals represents the conflict between two different complexes of social and religious loyalties.'[28]

So far, Hegel's reading of the play seems to reveal the value of his socio-historical perspective. But its limitations are also readily apparent. With his doctrine of two conflicting rights, Hegel too is bent on reducing the play to a schema, only his schema is based on the values or propensities of the social group – that is, on lowest common denominators which are one stage further from immediate experience than the values or propensities of the groups's individual members. Both his version of Sophocles' drama and the more fashionable opposite view fail to see that the play is not entirely closed – it does not answer all our questions – or entirely tidy. It is a perfect model of conflict, but it is *not*, after all, a perfect model of two equal but conflicting rights, *not* of an individual wrong revealed and a universal right vindicated.

These are the data:

(i) Antigone and Creon both represent different *legitimate* interests, which are definable in social or socio-religious terms.

(ii) Antigone as a character is noble, although strident (especially in her treatment of Ismene). Creon is obnoxious and arrogant – until his fall, after which his individual character is barely visible beneath the humiliation.

(iii) Notwithstanding the legitimacy of his rule, Creon was wrong – in breach of Greek ethics – to produce his edict proscribing the burial of Polynices' body and to punish Antigone as he did: this is made clear by Tiresias and by Creon's own admissions after the event.

(iv) It is never established whether Antigone (for all the legitimacy of *her* interest) was right to disobey the edict. It does not follow from the viciousness of a law that disobedience of that law is right. 'When you are making laws', notes the orator Demosthenes in the fourth century, 'it is right to examine what sort of laws they are; but once you have made them, you must guard them and obey them'[29] – and the principle, though expounded here in the context of a democracy, is readily applicable to Sophocles' play. Creon is the city's legislator, and, as the chorus intimates, loyalty to the city's legislation is one of the conditions of its survival:

> When man weaves together the laws of the land
> And the justice of heaven that binds his oaths,
> High is his city.[30]

Before Antigone's removal from the scene, various of the play's participants offer evaluations, explicit or implicit, of her action. Creon's is all *parti pris*, Ismene's and Haemon's are not authoritative, the chorus' comments are elusive. After Antigone's disappearance, no evaluative reference whatsoever is made to her action by chorus or by any character. There is no reason to suppose that this is because the evaluation is, as it were, part of the ground-rules of the culture and therefore too obvious to need spelling out: Greek tragedians are only too ready to spell out obvious evaluations, especially after the *dénouements* of their plays. Whether we like it or not, the question is simply left open, and our undivided attention henceforth is given to the fate of Creon.

(v) It is not clear whether our evaluation of Antigone's action is to be governed in any way by the knowledge that there is an inherited curse on her family. All that is clear is that the curse is presented as relevant to the overall action of the drama,[31] as for instance when Antigone, during her last scene in the play, bitterly agrees with the chorus that she is somehow atoning for her ancestors' troubles.[32]

The first of these five points is Hegel's; the second and third are commonly made (and commonly confused) by his opponents; the fifth and especially the fourth are widely ignored. Taken together, as they should be, the five points invalidate any tidy interpretation of the play, Hegelian or otherwise.

Contrary to Hegel's assumptions, then, *Antigone* is not entirely amenable to his purpose. It is not *exactly* a conflict of 'right against right'; in this respect Aeschylus' *Oresteia* (on which he also has something to say) serves him much better. It is revealing to see how Bradley, as a follower of Hegel, tries to exonerate him from any damaging criticism, while implicitly recognizing at least some of the difficulty. Hegel, for instance, writes:

The collision between the two highest moral forces is set forth in a plastic fashion in that supreme and absolute example of tragedy, *Antigone*. In this instance, family love, that which is holy, that which belongs to the inner life and to inner feeling, and which because of this is also called the law of the nether gods, comes into collision with the law of the State. Creon is not a tyrant, but really a moral force; Creon is not in the wrong; he maintains that the law of the State, the authority of government, is to be held in respect, and that punishment follows the infraction of the law. Each of these two sides realizes only one of the moral forces...they both have their own validity...[33]

In other words, Hegel asserts our first point and a tendentious interpretation of our fourth at the expense of the rest. Above all, he specifically denies the third: 'Creon is not in the wrong'. Commenting on Hegel's account of the conflicts in such plays as *Antigone* and *Eumenides*, Bradley writes:

it is most important to observe that Hegel is not discussing at all what we should generally call the moral quality of the acts and persons concerned, or, in the ordinary sense, what it was their duty to do. And in the second place, when he speaks of 'equally justified' powers [i.e. moral forces], what he means, and indeed sometimes says, is that these powers are *in themselves* equally justified. The family and the state, the bond of father and son, the bond of mother and son, the bond of citizenship, these are each and all, one as much as another, powers rightfully claiming human allegiance. It is tragic that observance of one should involve the violation of another. These are Hegel's propositions, and surely they are true. Their truth is quite unaffected by the fact (assuming it is one) that in the circumstances the act combining this observation of one and violation of another was morally right, or by the fact (if so it is) that one such act (say Antigone's) was morally right, and another (say Creon's) was morally wrong. It is sufficient for Hegel's principle that the violation should take place, and that we should feel its weight. We do feel it. We may approve the act of Antigone or Orestes, but in approving it we still feel that it is no light matter to disobey the law or to murder a mother, that (as we might say) there is much justice in the pleas of the Furies and of Creon, and that the *tragic* effect depends upon these facts...[Nevertheless] our everyday moral judgements...are...out of place in a discussion on tragedy.[34]

Bradley attempts to save Hegel's theory by insisting that it is only concerned with Antigone and Creon as representatives of larger moral forces – our first point – anyway. In view of Hegel's readiness to claim that 'Creon is not in the wrong', this is clearly not the whole truth. But even if it were, Bradley would be begging the question. It is precisely Hegel's entitlement to concern himself so largely with our first point that is at issue. How, for instance, can 'moral forces' be entirely dissociated from what Bradley dismisses as 'everyday moral judgements' – if not our judgements, then those of the Greeks? Alternatively, if a complete dissociation is possible, then 'moral forces' can hardly be as important as Hegel has led us to believe.

Bradley, like Hegel, further confuses the issue by equating *Antigone* with the *Oresteia*, where there *is* a moral balance between the two sides. Not only is the parity between Clytemnestra (who murders Agamemnon) and Orestes (who murders Clytemnestra) not matched in the *Antigone*. Disobedience of the law, especially Creon's vicious law, is hardly on a par with murder.

Hegel's theory of tragedy presupposes a great deal of literary interpretation, good or bad. This is true not only of his notion of conflict, but also of his understanding of tragic character. For Hegel Greek tragedy is not about anyone's subjective feelings: the characters may have such feelings, but those feelings are not the centre of interest. In modern drama, he argues, the opposite is the case – which, in Hegelian terms, is to say that modern drama is concerned with essentially trivial issues. In this spirit he discusses the part of Haemon in the *Antigone*. Haemon is Creon's son and betrothed to the heroine. It is (Hegel believes) these relationships, rather than the feelings associated with them, that are crucial in determining his conduct in the play. When facing Creon, for instance, 'he only asserts objective circumstances' (*er machte nur objektive Verhältnisse geltend*),[35] notably the impending ruin of the state if his father persists in his present course of action. What Haemon does not do is fall back on his own feelings for Antigone. There is no 'I love her and she loves me' in his speeches. This is true. Nevertheless, it is reasonable to ask whether Haemon would in fact be acting as he is if he was not under the influence of his passion for Antigone, and certainly the choral ode on 'invincible love' (*erōs*) which immediately follows the debate with Creon assumes that he would not.[36] And we have only to think of Neoptolemus in Sophocles' *Philoctetes* or various of the characters in Euripides' *Hippolytus* or *Andromache*, to see that Hegel's point about subjective feelings may be valid for earlier tragedy by and large, but is not valid for Greek tragedy *tout court*. Elsewhere Hegel has some striking things to say about the modern and problematic character of individual 'romantic' love as a subject for tragedy (and Nietzsche might have done well to ponder them in connection with *Tristan*), but there is still no room for a black and white contrast with Greek drama as a whole.

For Hegel the conflicts of Greek tragedy must be absolute, because their human instruments are heroic – that is, unified – characters, each of whom asserts one of the conflicting rights absolutely. In contradistinction to the heroes of modern tragedy, Hegel defines a 'unified character' as one in whom being and willing are one. The substantial being of such a character – his status, the way he belongs to the social hierarchy of his age and is representative of it – is co-extensive with all his aspirations and acts of volition. He is, to use a favourite expression, not of Hegel's but of later German nineteenth-century authors, *eine geschlossene Persönlichkeit*, 'an embattled personality'; except that the giants and Ahabs of post-Napoleonic Europe exert their personality *against* their socio-political world, whereas the classical character, as Hegel sees him, represents and reinforces his world. This is not true of all the characters of Greek tragedy: it is not, of course, true of an Ismene. But it is an important insight into the dramatic significance of an Antigone.

Hegel's distinction between the leading characters of Greek and modern tragedy is explained most clearly in a comparison of the two relationships of Hamlet and the King, and Orestes and Agamemnon:

> Hamlet too has had a father and a king killed, and his mother has married the murderer. But the death of Agamemnon, which in the Greek poets has a moral justification [i.e. as punishment for the sacrifice of Iphigenia], has for its Shakespearean equivalent what can only be seen as a terrible crime of which Hamlet's mother is innocent, so that her son in his revenge has merely to turn against the fratricidal king in whom he sees nothing he can genuinely honour. The real issue, therefore, is not that the son in his moral revenge is forced to violate morality itself; the real issue is the subjective character of Hamlet, whose noble soul is not made for this kind of energetic action; so that filled with disgust of the world and life, haunted, and vacillating between decisions, attempts, and preparations for the execution of his deed, his soul is wrecked by his own hesitations and the outward development of circumstances.[37]

Here then we have, in contrast with the ancient objectivity and necessity, the subjectivity and chanciness, indeed the arbitrariness, of modern tragedy. Few things in Hegel are more impressive than his recognition, in the midst of the German tradition of inwardness and private feeling, of the essential arbitrariness of that tradition: his recognition that the private is the arbitrary. Modern tragedy for him arises from the disjunction of character and objective moral circumstances, which, more pointedly, he calls 'objective feelings'.

Our conception of tragedy, like Nietzsche's, tends to be individualistic. We are accordingly liable to feel that the tragic hero as Hegel portrays him is too monolithic, too undifferentiated a character to be sufficiently distinct from the world he represents. This kind of hero is in fact dramatized, not by any Greek playwright, but by Nietzsche's near contemporary, Friedrich Hebbel, in whose plays endless pairs of antagonists assert interests so total that their individualities cease to be discernible to the naked eye, and only bathos ensues. Bathos is not very far from Hegel's scenario either. For in order to bring out the absoluteness of the conflict, he does not sufficiently acknowledge the wilfulness – and thus the arbitrariness – embodied even in Antigone, to whom the chorus proclaims, unanswerably:

> your self-willed nature has destroyed you.[38]

At the same time, Hegel understands perfectly well that the conflict is worked out not through abstractions but through living people: men who, unlike Hamlet, are informed by a perfect congruity between their strongest passion and some aspect of the moral law. What is fully conveyed in his strange and sometimes barely readable prose is the way the heroes of older Greek tragedy are pitched between their rôles as pure individuals and representatives of an idea. It is the immense virtue of Hegel's argument that he sharpens our vision for the hierarchic and functional aspect of Antigone's character. Her stubbornness and the arbitrary strength of her feeling – manifest for instance in the way that she spurns Ismene's well-meant attempt to share responsibility for the burial – in no way abrogate from her representing that aspect of the law that is in conflict with Creon's.

Guilt as we understand it, Hegel concludes, is not involved. Our modern conception of guilt, he argues, presupposes a split in the tragic character, a non-congruity between his substantial being and his volition. A hero's capacity for knowing that he is 'in the wrong' and his willingness to be going with one part of his mind against another part (prefigured, as we have seen, in Euripides) are for Hegel signs of a modern fragmentation of consciousness. Since the true tragic hero's consciousness is not thus fragmented, he is not, in our sense, guilty:

Oedipus has killed his father, has married his mother, has produced children in an incestuous bed, and yet it is without knowing and willing these things that he has been involved in the most heinous sin. Our modern, deeper consciousness would claim that since these crimes have their roots neither in his own knowledge nor in his own volition, therefore they may not be recognized as acts of his own self. The plastic Greek...

The term is clear, though difficult to translate: Hegel expresses with it the unitary conception which elsewhere he calls *substantiell* –

The plastic Greek pledges himself to all he has done as an individual, and he does not distinguish between the subjectivity of his self-consciousness and that which is objectively the case... The tragic heroes are equally guilty and innocent. If the idea is accepted that a man is only guilty when he had a choice open to him and decided arbitrarily in favour of what he will do, then the ancient plastic characters are innocent; they act from that character, that emotion, precisely because they are that character, that emotion – here is no indecisiveness and no choice. This is indeed the strength of the great characters: that they do not choose, but that through and through they *are* that which they will and accomplish...

Reality itself (Hegel believes) is the coincidence of intention and execution, the suspension of the breach between willing and doing –

They are that which they are, eternally, and that is their greatness. For weakness in acting consists only in the separation of the subject as such and its content, so that character, will, and purpose do not appear as having grown absolutely into one; and since no firm purpose lives in his soul, providing the substance of his own individuality, providing all his willing with emotional intensity [*Pathos*] and authority, the individual can turn from one thing to another, undecided, and his decisions follow the biddings of arbitrariness.[39]

This is the portrait of the modern hero. He is indeed liable to guilt. Partly of course it is the guilt involved in what he does, how he contravenes the historically determined morality of his day. But Hegel goes beyond, or perhaps rather behind, this notion of guilt. Ultimately it is not a question of what the individual does, but *that* he is an individual, *that* he has emerged from the collective, as no Greek hero has every fully emerged. It is this that puts him in his tragic situation.

Hegel's is the only German theory to stand comparison with Nietzsche's. It has its own limitations. Even on its chosen ground, it raises difficulties, and not only because of misinterpretations of specific plays like *Antigone*. We are no doubt estranged by Hegel's insistence that not only must *all* tragedies embody a conflict between antagonistic forces, but that only when those forces can be identified with the socio-political circumstances of an age can an adequate, serious conflict ensue. We may well protest against the moral consequences of that view, seeing that it diminishes the notion of personal guilt (and with it responsibility) and ultimately suspends it altogether. More generally, Hegel's theory is at least as partial as Nietzsche's. The Hegelian principle of conflict is as poorly served by *Oedipus Rex* as Nietzsche's pessimism of strength is by the *Oresteia*. Its partiality, furthermore, is less persuasive: it is an odd theory that elevates *Antigone* above *Oedipus Rex*. And if Hegel finds it easier than Nietzsche to deal with modern tragedy, he seems ill-equipped to deal with Euripides. Although, like Nietzsche, he takes Greek drama as the exemplar, he has no counterpart to the archetypes – Dionysus, Apollo, Socrates – with which Nietzsche encompasses the whole of Greek tragedy, Euripides included.

All the same, the two theories are not entirely at odds. Up to a point, Hegel's ideas about guilt or the tragic character could be reconciled with *BT*. For though Nietzsche sees tragedy as the destruction of individuals, especially isolated individuals, his theory is not at all concerned with a validation of the self through a pseudo-Christian appeal to the individual conscience. Hegel's principle of conflict, on the other hand, is incompatible with Nietzsche's argument. It ties tragedy to the historical – that is, political – circumstances of its age, as surely as Nietzsche's pessimism of strength proposes a link between tragedy and timeless metaphysics. The only discernible Hegelian influence on Nietzsche's book lies in his use of a *dialectical* (and therefore protean) opposition, Dionysus and Apollo; and it is revealing that Nietzsche should have succeeded in making it entirely supra-historical. Hegel's feeling for the socio-political aspect of tragedy is unique: it is not recaptured in later nineteenth-century theories, and in *BT* least of all. For this reason alone Hegel provides a natural complement to Nietzsche's book.

SCHOPENHAUER

Is it an accident that in his discussion of tragedy[40] Schopenhauer seems to avoid the word *Tragödie*, with its Greek connotations, preferring instead to speak of serious drama in terms of the native German *Trauerspiel*? What the German 'mourning play' involves is a steady, undeviating descent towards catastrophe, without the sudden twist which makes for what Aristotle called *peripeteia:* a progress of events which in its steadiness implies that the tragic issue arises not from accidental misfortune or exceptional design, but from the regular course of life.

The static quality that is implicit in *Trauerspiel* characterizes Schopenhauer's theory of tragedy and the philosophical system of which that theory forms a representative part. Where Hegel is concerned to give a dynamic, historically based account of man's art and man's universe, Schopenhauer's is a purely synoptic perspective. Whatever we may think about other aspects of his philosophy, his disdain for history is surely among the reasons why his discussion of tragedy, by comparison with Hegel's (as with Nietzsche's), strikes us as primitive and unsophisticated.

Schopenhauer puts before us three possible sources of the tragic catastrophe. The first is some exceptional wickedness or criminality, such as is shown by Shakespeare's Richard III, Iago and Shylock, by Franz Moor in Schiller's *The Robbers*, by Phaedra in Euripides' *Hippolytus*, and by Creon in Sophocles' *Antigone*. The second is man's blindness in the face of his future, which Schopenhauer finds exemplified in Sophocles' *Oedipus Rex* and *Trachiniae* (and most ancient tragedies), Shakespeare's *Romeo and Juliet*, Voltaire's *Tancred* and Schiller's *The Bride of Messina*. The third is described as the circumstances of the world and men's relationships with each other, as exemplified in *Hamlet* and *Wallenstein*, in Corneille's *Le Cid* and Goethe's *Faust* and *Clavigo*. With his pessimistic interpretation of existence, Schopenhauer pronounces the third the most important and propitious starting-point for tragedy.

'It is one and the same will', Schopenhauer tells us, 'which lives and appears in all men, but whose appearances fight against each other and devour each other.'[41] Men's conflicts, and therefore all evil and all misfortune in the world, are tantamount to the will's strife with itself, for all individuation is – all individuals are – no more than a dereliction of an original state of unity and totality. This is what makes the world the contingent thing it is, and this is what, within that contingency, makes conflicts the constitutive necessity that they are. All the arts in their different ways, and above all in their different degrees, contribute to an assuagement of this necessity – or rather, not an assuagement but a renunciation of it. And since the world is no more than a battle-ground, the invitation to abandon its conflicts is an invitation to abandon the world itself. The motive (conscious or unconscious) from which drama springs is the desire to pierce through and abandon what, from some world beyond these conflicts, will be seen as a world of mere appearances, mistakes, *maya*.

Like Nietzsche and Aristotle, Schopenhauer arranges the various arts in a hierarchical order. At the bottom of his system he puts those arts which have a practical function, like architecture. Next come sculpture and painting, and then the three branches of literature: lyric poetry (which is 'subjective'), drama ('objective') and epic (in between) – where the distinction between objectivity and subjectivity merely refers to the absence or presence of the author in his work. Epic in this classification means verse epic: as with many of the German thinkers of the century, Hegel and Nietzsche included, the novel is not seriously considered. At the apex of Schopenhauer's system stands music, to which literature is said to be closely related, although not, as in Nietzsche, for any very profound reason. Schopenhauer's reason is simply that these arts have in common two constituents, rhythm and sound, which (he believes) are as important as – and in some ways more important than – the third constituent of literature, meaning.

For Schopenhauer, drama beckons man to leave the world of strife and seek his salvation beyond it. The crypto-Christian quality of such formulae is unmistakable, and Schopenhauer himself alludes to it, albeit in a somewhat disingenuous tone of surprise. In itself, however, the function he ascribes to drama has nothing in common with the traditional Christian glorification of the majesty or mystery of a loving God. Drama, he asserts, has for its main purpose the sustained demonstration of the vanity of all human undertakings. It is this purpose that he concentrates on, to the virtual exclusion of all dramaturgic, historical or linguistic considerations. Like earlier theorists he considers the question why we take pleasure in the dramatic display of pain. His answer is simply that the tragic stage shows us the joy of renouncing a world whose own joys are necessarily evanescent, and finding instead another mode of existence and being (*eine andere Art Daseyn*), a condition of aesthetic contemplation. Up to a point, then, that elusive apothegm in *BT*, 'only as an aesthetic phenomenon...', can be seen as a sophisticated inference from Schopenhauer's scheme – although Nietzsche's understanding of 'aesthetic' is not identical with Schopenhauer's, while in its generality Nietzsche's formula goes beyond the Schopenhauerian view of aesthetic contemplation as merely a stage on the journey towards sainthood, *nirvana*, and silence.

There are two ways in which the theatre can inspire us to renounce the world and all its weal and woe. We, the spectators, either succeed in arriving at an appropriate evaluation of the events on stage ourselves, or find our reaction anticipated by the consciousness of one or other of the main *dramatis personae*, and thereby receive the evaluation in fully articulated form. This latter case, according to Schopenhauer, leads to a more complete communication of the tragic message. And since, in his view, most Greek drama lacks characters who display the requisite kind of consciousness, it follows that even the most esteemed tragedies of the Attic stage tend to fall short of his ideal. For Schopenhauer, in fact, the Greeks are inferior to the moderns, to Shakespeare, Goethe, and even Schiller, some of whose characters *are* consciously dissatisfied with life and, in their dissatisfaction, ready to renounce it. We need think no further than Faust's first lines –

Philosophy have I digested,
The whole of law and medicine;
From each its secrets have I wrested,
Theology, alas, thrown in.
Poor fool, with all this sweated lore,
I stand no wiser than I was before[42] –

or Macbeth's 'out out, brief candle', to gather what kind of hero Schopenhauer has in mind.

This negative appraisal of Greek tragedy occasions one of Schopenhauer's more detailed discussions of particular plays. At the same time, the passage provides a summary of his whole theory:

Our pleasure in *tragedy* belongs not to the faculty of beauty, but to that of sublimity...What gives everything tragic its peculiar elevating force...is the realization that the world and life can never give real satisfaction and hence are not worthy of our affection: this constitutes the tragic spirit – which therefore leads to resignation. I admit that in the tragedy of the ancients this spirit of resignation rarely appears directly and explicitly. Oedipus at Colonus certainly dies resigned and docile; yet he is comforted by revenge on his native land. Iphigenia at Aulis is quite ready to die, yet it is the thought of the welfare of Greece that consoles her and brings about her change of mind. By virtue of this change she readily takes upon herself the death she at first sought by every means to avoid. Cassandra, in the *Agamemnon* of the great Aeschylus, dies willingly – *arkeitō bios* ['enough of life'] – but she too is comforted by the thought of revenge. Heracles in *Trachiniae* yields to necessity and dies composed, but not resigned. Similarly Euripides' Hippolytus..., like almost all the tragic heroes of the ancients, displays submission to inevitable fate and the inflexible will of the gods, but no surrender of the will to live itself...whereas Christian tragedy shows the giving up of the whole will to live, the cheerful abandonment of the world in the consciousness of its worthlessness and vanity. But I am fully of the opinion that the tragedy of the moderns is altogether superior to that of the ancients. Shakespeare is much greater than Sophocles; compared with Goethe's *Iphigenia*, Euripides' play may almost be felt coarse and vulgar. The *Bacchae* of Euripides is a revoltingly botched job in favour of the heathen parsons. Many dramas of antiquity have no tragic tendency at all, like Euripides' *Alcestis* and *Iphigenia in Tauris;* some have unpleasant, or even disgusting themes, like *Antigone* and *Philoctetes*. Almost all show the human race under the dreadful domination of chance and error, but not the resignation these bring about which redeems us from them...Nevertheless, the characteristic tendency and effect of tragedy remains the awakening of that spirit in the spectator, the evocation, if only temporarily, of that frame of mind...he becomes aware, if only obscurely, that it is better to tear his heart away from life, to turn his willing away from it, not to love the world and life. Thus in the depth of his being there arises an awareness that for a different kind of willing there must be a different kind of existence too. For if this were not so,...how would it generally be possible for the presentation of the terrible side of life, brought before our eyes in the most glaring light, to be capable of affecting us beneficially, and of affording us an exalted pleasure? Fear and pity, the stimulation of which Aristotle identifies as the ultimate purpose of tragedy, certainly do not in themselves belong to the agreeable sensations; therefore, they cannot be the end, but only the means...Like the ancients, many of the moderns are content to put the spectator into the mood described above by the objective presentation of human misfortune on a large scale, whereas others exhibit this through a change of mind in the hero himself, which is effected by suffering. The former give, so to speak, only the premises, and leave the conclusion to the spectator; while the latter give the conclusion, or the moral of the fable, as the conversion of the hero's frame of mind...It should be mentioned here that the genuinely tragic effect of the catastrophe, the hero's resignation and spiritual exaltation produced by it, seldom appear so purely motivated and distinctly expressed as in [Bellini's] opera, *Norma*, where it comes in the duet *Qual cor tradisti, qual cor perdesti* [What a heart you betrayed, what a heart you lost].[43]

The shortcomings of Schopenhauer's perspective are as evident in this discussion as the idiosyncrasies of his taste. His search for the spirit of resignation predisposes him against any sensitive response to the complexities of artistic presentation or effect. He has only one criterion, and he applies it to tragedy entirely from the outside: there is no hint that the value of resignation might itself be brought into question by a less biased assessment of the dramas he knows. He exhibits a naïve interest in the individual hero at the expense of the achieved artistic whole, and the crudest kind of preference for explicit assertions of 'the moral' of a play as against more subtle, and often more telling, forms of poetic or dramatic expression. It is symptomatic of a very limited understanding of Greek tragedy that he should neglect the chorus – his most striking comment on which, a little earlier, is that the choral passages in Greek tragedy were written, like the sung portions of Chinese drama, for their sound not their sense. It is equally revealing that he should so esteem Goethe's undramatic *Iphigenia*, with its saintly heroine (modelled partly on a picture of St Agatha which Goethe had seen in Milan)[44] – and Bellini's *Norma*.

Schopenhauer's discussion does contain one set of ideas which point straight to *BT*: those concerned with the tragic effect. In part Nietzsche makes use of them (without acknowledgement), in part he asserts their contrary. At the same time, Schopenhauer's exposition is full of preconceptions, judgements and conclusions which – for all his immense influence on Nietzsche in general – find no echo in Nietzsche's book. Notwithstanding the fact that in *BT* the young professor's overt attitude towards his 'educator' is one of admiration and deference, and that his whole book has been materially influenced by Schopenhauer's central philosophical doctrines, his theory of tragedy is not only vastly more substantial than Schopenhauer's: it is also surprisingly independent of it.

One reason for this is that Schopenhauer is a systematic philosopher, as Nietzsche – by instinct and conviction – is not. Schopenhauer has a core of doctrine, profoundly thought out, to which his philosophical energy is committed and around which, in the course of a long life, he constructs a system, drawing out the various implications of his ideas for all the important aspects of human existence. Some of these aspects interest him more than others. On some he has profound things to say. On others he feels obliged to say something for no other reason than that they are there. Tragedy is one of these. Were it not for the system, and especially the place of aesthetics within it, one wonders if it would occur to him to write about tragedy at all. What is interesting about his account is not anything we learn from it about tragedy itself (which is very little), but the illustration it provides of his own thinking, of the German preoccupation with the tragic – and of Nietzsche's relationship with the body of his philosophy. The Schopenhauerian influence on Nietzsche emanates from the centre of Schopenhauer's system and not from its peripheral expatiations. There is, therefore, less direct resemblance between the two philosophers' theories of tragedy than there is between any other aspect of their thought. Nietzsche's Dionysiac and Apolline presuppose (among much else) Schopenhauer's central opposition between will and idea and also Schopenhauer's interest in the Buddhist *nirvana* (which in Nietzsche's scheme is a *post*-Dionysiac aspiration), but there is nothing corresponding to Dionysus and Apollo in Schopenhauer's account of tragedy. The place occupied by music in Nietzsche's book presupposes Schopenhauer, but again there is no counterpart to the Nietzschean theory of 'musical tragedy' in his writings. Schopenhauer's thoughts about Italian opera are as remote from *BT* as his valuation of Weimar classicism above its Greek exemplars or his preference for explicit verbal articulations of the 'moral' of a play. Nietzsche's attitude to origins, the chorus, myth, his antithesis of tragic and Socratic, almost all the obvious features of his theory – *except* the doctrine of the will – are entirely his own.

In the perspective of Nietzsche's whole career, his relationship with Schopenhauer seems like an unending *agon* in which he either follows his predecessor or attacks him. In *BT* this kind of relationship is visible in respect of the tragic effect. Tragedy, says Schopenhauer, gives the spectator a premonition of 'a different kind of existence'. Nietzsche agrees, but asks what kind of existence, and answers: *not* some *nirvana*, but the 'eternal life' (§ 16) which we glimpse through our 'knowledge' that despite the destruction of individuals – *because of* the destruction of individuals – we share in the underlying and indestructible unity of being. Tragedy, says Schopenhauer, gives its spectator 'an exalted pleasure'. Nietzsche agrees again, but asks what kind of pleasure, and answers: *not* the pleasure of mystical resignation from the world ('how far removed I was from all this resignationism', he observes, quite accurately, in the *Self-Criticism*),[45] but a 'higher joy' (§ 22), an overwhelmingly affecting experience which is capable of reconciling the mystical and the worldly instincts (§ 21). This is the crux of Nietzsche's first overt argument with Schopenhauer, and it is the model of all subsequent arguments with him. In Nietzsche's last active months in 1888 he is still minded to conduct the argument on this ground:

> ...tragedy is a *tonic*. The fact that Schopenhauer did not *want* to grasp this, that he posits a general depression as the tragic condition, that he made it clear to the Greeks (who to his annoyance did not practise 'resignation') that they were not up to the highest view of life, all this is merely *parti pris*, system-logic, the system-maker's false coinage; one of those base coinages which gradually corrupted Schopenhauer's whole psychology – wilfully, destructively, he misunderstood genius, art itself, morality, pagan religion, beauty, knowledge, and more or less everything.[46]

10

Style and philosophy

§ 1

The opening paragraph of Nietzsche's book is rich in substance yet succinct; self-confident yet provocative. So characteristic is it of his style and form of argument, and so full of anticipations, that we may use it as a pattern for the book as a whole:

Wir werden viel für die ästhetische Wissenschaft gewonnen haben, wenn wir nicht nur zur logischen Einsicht, sondern zur unmittelbaren Sicherheit der Anschauung gekommen sind, dass die Fortentwickelung der Kunst an die Duplizität des *Apollinischen* und des *Dionysischen* gebunden ist: in ähnlicher Weise, wie die Generation von der Zweiheit der Geschlechter, bei fortwährendem Kampfe und nur periodisch eintretender Versöhnung, abhängt. Diese Namen entlehnen wir von den Griechen, welche die tiefsinnigen Geheimlehren ihrer Kunstanschauung zwar nicht in Begriffen, aber in den eindringlich deutlichen Gestalten ihrer Götterwelt dem Einsichtigen vernehmbar machen. An ihre beiden Kunstgottheiten, Apollo und Dionysus, knüpft sich unsere Erkenntnis, dass in der griechischen Welt ein ungeheurer Gegensatz, nach Ursprung und Zielen, zwischen der Kunst des Bildners, der apollinischen, und der unbildlichen Kunst der Musik, als der des Dionysus, besteht: beide so verschiedne Triebe gehen nebeneinander her, zumeist im offnen Zwiespalt miteinander und sich gegenseitig zu immer neuen kräftigeren Geburten reizend, um in ihnen den Kampf jenes Gegensatzes zu perpetuieren, den das gemeinsame Wort 'Kunst' nur scheinbar überbrückt; bis sie endlich, durch einen metaphysischen Wunderakt des hellenischen 'Willens', miteinander gepaart erscheinen und in dieser Paarung zuletzt das ebenso dionysische als apollinische Kunstwerk der attischen Tragödie erzeugen.

We shall have greatly advanced the science of aesthetics once we have established not only through the perspective of logic but also by intuitive certainty that continuity in the development of art is bound up with the duality of the *Apolline* and the *Dionysiac* in a similar way as procreation depends on the duality of the sexes, involving them in perpetual strife and only intermittent reconciliation. These names we borrow from the Greeks, who intimate the profound mysteries of their vision of art to the discerning mind not through concepts but through the arrestingly clear figures of their gods. Associated with these two art deities, Apollo and Dionysus, is our knowledge of the gigantic conflict, in origins and aims, between the Apolline work of the visual artist and Dionysus' imageless art of music: these two differing instincts proceed side by side, mostly in open conflict, inciting each other to ever more vigorous births, so as to perpetuate that antagonism which the common term, 'art', only superficially reconciles; until at last, through a miraculous metaphysical act of the Hellenic 'will', they appear united and in this union finally produce a work of art equally Dionysiac and Apolline – Attic tragedy.

The first sentence assigns the work its place within an acknowledged academic discipline – 'the *science* of aesthetics' – by which Nietzsche means not only the study of works of art, but also their genealogy and their effects within the culture and life of the nation as a whole. The conditional clause, 'once we...', then goes on to distinguish between conviction based on logical argument and conviction based on intuition, strongly implying a preference for the latter; the methodological question, how this might affect the 'scientific' status of the inquiry, is not considered. The cardinal distinction is brought in apodictically, without further ado. It is subtly supported by the recondite contrast between *Einsicht*, with its rationalist connotations, and *Anschauung*, from a verb traditionally connoting perception of a non-rational, intuitive, occasionally mystical kind. This kind of verbal play is a good deal less emphatic than Hegel's exploitations of the peculiarities of German etymology; Nietzsche will often use it to support a philosophical argument, rarely to clinch one. Next, the idea of the continuous development (not 'progress') of art is introduced, with the implication that this *Fortentwicklung* goes on into the present, and the idea is then associated, in a manner as yet unexplained, with that grand dichotomy round which the whole book is constructed. And the sentence concludes with a simile, designed to strengthen the connection of the dichotomy with that 'development' of art by likening it to the process of human generation, a process said to 'depend' on a permanent battle between the sexes. In this first sentence the connections between various parts of the argument are left indeterminate; but clearly, strife, of whatever kind, emerges as the fundamental principle of creation, of whatever kind. The sentence leaves us in no doubt that Nietzsche's conception of an 'aesthetic science' will be anything but antiquarian or narrowly academic.

Nietzsche's way of invoking his two pivotal terms, 'Apolline' and 'Dionysiac', is peremptory and unargued. It is not that the terms are arbitrary, yet neither here nor later on in the book are we given adequate philosophical or historical grounds for his use of them. Their metaphorical – or metaleptic – status is theirs from the start. On being told, in the second sentence, that we simply 'borrow' these two names from the Greeks, the reader is likely to be left with the erroneous impression that they were common and accepted terms of classical aesthetics. Nietzsche does nothing to discourage this impression. His present purpose in referring to Greek sources is to emphasize the venerable pedigree of that preference for instinct and intuition, as against rationality and logic, which was already implied in the first sentence and which will be reiterated many times throughout the book. The profundity of those esoteric doctrines in which the Greeks enshrined their view of art is enhanced (we are to suppose) by being expressed, not in the conceptual language of logic, but in the figurative language of Presocratic myths. The point Nietzsche is making has a good deal of polemical significance. It is the opening shot in the first of those many attacks on the style and mode of contemporary scholarship and *Wissenschaft*, which he will continue in his second book, *Thoughts Out of Season*, in the dialogue 'On the Future of our Educational Institutions', and elsewhere. Moreover, in pointing to the (apparently self-evident) superiority of figurative and mythic language over conceptual language, Nietzsche is defending – here as yet only by implication – his own work and the mode of communication to which it too is committed. This self-referential element in his style is one of the things that make for the profoundly paradoxical nature of his undertaking. His intention is to place his own work as close as may be beside those profound esoteric doctrines of old and to transmit rather than explain their mysteries; yet at the same time his polemical acknowledgement that this is what he is trying to do puts the stamp of an inescapably modern, 'sentimental' self-consciousness on his undertaking. This paradox persists throughout his enquiry.

A third sentence, of considerable length and complexity – displaying the sort of ungainly 'scientific' syntax which Nietzsche will avoid in his later writings – concludes the opening paragraph. Apollo and Dionysus are now named explicitly as the tutelary gods of art, or rather of the visual and musical arts respectively. A brief and unconvincing query, whether it is appropriate to use the unitary term 'art' for the warring tendencies presided over by the two gods, is raised and dismissed – Nietzsche's language criticism in *BT* is almost always perfunctory – and from now on the weight of his rhetoric is on contrast and conflict. What distinguishes these two kinds of art in respect of their 'origins and aims' is (he suggests) the presence or absence of a sensuous, image-making quality; and the distinction is then embodied in the etymological play on *-bild-*, where the work of *der Bildner* (an uncommon word, chosen with a view to the pun) stands for the plastic and visual arts, and *die unbildliche Kunst* for music. With these stylistic devices Nietzsche induces us to accept the dichotomy which, in its various forms, will provide his argument with its vital contrasts. At the same time he invites us to assume a close relationship between the work of art and its 'origins and aims', particularly its origins. The 'union' of the two deities produces a work 'equally Dionysiac and Apolline': the formulation prefigures a discussion which cannot be said to be *either* about tragedy *or* about the birth of tragedy, but takes in both without formally distinguishing the one from the other. As much as anything else, it is this conflation of 'generation and subsistence' (to use Hobbes' terms) which gives us the curious impression that no sooner have we entered 'the science of aesthetics', Nietzsche's chosen field of inquiry, than we are being pushed out of it at the other end, into rudimentary psychology and genetics. For the dichotomy which he enthusiastically dramatizes into a 'gigantic [*ungeheuer*] conflict', is suddenly represented as a contrast between two different *instincts;* and *Triebe*, like the play on *-bild-*, is intended to emphasize the *physical* basis of the contrast. It is a conflict which, like the battle of the sexes, incites to ever new 'births', and as that battle is kept going (the old-fashioned *perpetuieren* sits oddly in what has now become an impassioned modern tirade), so the quality of the outcome is enhanced. Once more we return to the aesthetic plane: the contrasting and conflicting 'instincts' now come to be united in, and make their appearances as, a work of art. For now, in a sense each rhetorical device urges us to call literal, Attic tragedy is born. It is born from an energy-enhancing conflict which culminates in a 'miraculous' pairing of the two deities in whom the concrete instincts and the abstract metaphysical principles are embodied.

The source of this vocabulary of love and war, procreation and conflict, is Schopenhauer; and the dialectics of the passage, too, owe more to Schopenhauer than they do to any Greek sources. And if Nietzsche himself had not acknowledged his intellectual obligation in the *Self-Criticism* of 1886, the quotation marks he puts round the Hellenic 'will' which brings about the 'pairing' of the two instincts would serve as the first of his many explicit indications of discipleship. The differences between the two thinkers are important, but (as we have seen) they occur within the same kind of universe. Schopenhauer advocates the negation of the world of the will, Nietzsche now proposes the fullest possible assent to it. What he will eventually propose is a revaluation (or perhaps we had better use his own term, *Umwertung*, *trans*-valuation) of Schopenhauer's scheme: and this, even in the present context, is the purpose of his sketchy allusions to genetics. His notion that 'strife' leads to 'ever more vigorous births' – in itself no better than a tag of fashionable Darwinian folklore – does more than supply the text with a handy metaphor. It sets in train a revaluation of Schopenhauer's 'will', which now becomes something positive, a creative principle in art and life alike.

This is the first paragraph of the first work in which Nietzsche addresses a general public. Looking back on it, we note three stylistic devices on which the argument is heavily dependent: imagery, often unresolved or only partly resolved; the insistent play on words; and the dramatization of dichotomies and contrasts. All three devices are ultimately related to the subject-matter of the book: they evoke the art with which it deals.

The opening of the second paragraph shows Nietzsche at his most characteristic. Pairs and parallels dominate the passage and produce the desired emphasis. A way of coming closer to what his two deities stand for (he begins) is to think of them as analogous to 'the two physiological states' of *dream* and *ecstasy*. First comes the explication of the Apolline principle of dream. In the course of it, what began as an analogy very quickly turns into 'an important part of poetry' itself. Lucretius, Schopenhauer and Richard Wagner are mentioned as witnesses to the dream-origin of poetry: Hans Sachs, true hero of *Die Meistersinger*, describes the poet as one who 'notes down and interprets' his own and mankind's dreams. 'Real' dreams – and metaphorical ones. Nietzsche depends on the ambiguity for the coherence of his argument: 'dream', initially no more than an analogy, has become substantial cause, yet it continues to be available as metaphor.

Art in its Apolline mode is the content of dreams *and* a commentary on those dreams. It is the calm look and the recognition of images amidst the desolation and chaos of a universe hostile to man, the imposition of form and pleasing shape upon inchoateness. Yet there is nothing unnatural about this imposition. In order to explain man's readiness to respond to the prompting of Apollo, god of form and light, Nietzsche next alludes to a famous poem of Goethe's, in which the human eye is described as 'sun-like', and this quality is seen as the necessary condition of the eye's ability to perceive whatever is illuminated by the sun. Nothing unnatural? Mortal peril belongs to the very nature of the life of man, and without it man is incomplete. With a quotation from Schopenhauer's highly dramatic simile of man in his fragile boat calmly contemplating his own exposure to the hostile seas of fate, Nietzsche exults in man's marvellous capacity for creating those harmonious images 'which alone make life possible and worth living'.

From dreams Nietzsche proceeds to intoxication, ecstasy and the Dionysiac; the transition is effected by a second reference to the Schopenhauer quotation. Before leaving the Apolline, however, he offers a striking characterization of the dream experience of 'the artistically sensitive man' and his awareness that he is in fact dreaming. It is not only 'agreeable and friendly images' that he experiences:

Auch das Ernste, Trübe, Traurige, Finstere, die plötzlichen Hemmungen, die Neckereien des Zufalls, die bänglichen Erwartungen, kurz die ganze 'göttliche Komödie' des Lebens, mit dem Inferno, zieht an ihm vorbei, nicht nur wie ein Schattenspiel – denn er lebt und leidet mit in diesen Szenen – und doch auch nicht ohne jene flüchtige Empfindung des Scheins; und vielleicht erinnert sich mancher, gleich mir, in den Gefährlichkeiten und Schrecken des Traumes sich mitunter ermutigend und mit Erfolg zugerufen zu haben: 'Es ist ein Traum! Ich will ihn weiter träumen!'

The serious, the troubled, the sad and the sinister, the sudden arrests of experience, tricks of fortune and anguished expectations – all this, the whole 'divine comedy' of life, the inferno included, passes before him: not like a mere play of shadows on the wall – for he lives and suffers with these scenes – and yet not without that fleeting sense of illusion. And perhaps many will, like myself, recall how, amid the dangers and terrors of a dream, they have sometimes called out to themselves in self-encouragement and not without success: 'It is a dream! I want to go on dreaming it!'

What is remarkable about this characterization is that here for once the image-making faculty is *not* contrasted with consciousness, or indeed self-consciousness, and the observations it produces. With hindsight it seems almost as if Nietzsche is anticipating his conclusion (§§ 21–22) that the 'aesthetic response' to tragedy includes *both* empathetic acceptance of the drama *and* an alienated distance from it. As yet, however, there has been no reference to the Dionysiac component of that response, nor is the passage overtly concerned with drama or even with art (in the ordinary sense) at all. In any event, this sudden appeal to personal experience in a context of philosophical generalization has all the force of the *vidi* – 'my own eyes are witness to it' – of a Dante or a Lucretius. Few of Nietzsche's insights are more accurate and more profound, and few formulations more beautiful.

After the introduction of the Dionysiac and 'the analogy of intoxication', Nietzsche confronts us with a view of medieval German mob scenes and the *orgia* of Greece and Babylon. This in turn makes possible a quick side-swipe at pallid 'enlightened' intellectuals who fail to respect the dark chthonic forces which still slumber in all 'authentic' [*ursprünglichen*] peoples. He brings the section to a close with the Schillerian rhapsodic chorus of the Ninth Symphony: in adoration and wonder the host of mankind bow to their creator. Is he Dionysus, the god of self-forgetting and violent ecstasy? Schiller *would* have been surprised.

The first section of the book makes it amply clear why Nietzsche's undertaking cannot be accommodated within any established genre or category, and why in particular this is no scholarly treatise of the accepted kind. There are, for one thing, the vivid and varied scenes from life. For another, the allusions to Goethe, Schopenhauer, Wagner and Schiller point to Nietzsche's intention to accompany the classical argument by a critique of contemporary German culture; the special status of Schopenhauer is very evident, and it is noteworthy that, as if by some inverted parody of classical scholarship, the only page references provided by Nietzsche in the whole book are for his works (there are more in § 16). Nor can there be any question of personal detachment or cool reporting on the results of disinterested academic research where all is either enthusiastic advocacy or condemnation. Above all, there is Nietzsche's method of allowing his arguments to be guided and determined by the very metaphors, analogies and myths which are, or are derived from, the material of his inquiry. Schopenhauer is concerned to establish the *concept* of individuation, which he *illustrates* with an image. For Nietzsche, Dionysus and Apollo are neither logical entities nor Greek gods. They are cast in a middle mode of language: they evoke, not a specific genre, or a specific context or time, but a fundamental mood – *Urstimmung*, *Grundstimmung* – of mankind.

In 1873, the year following the publication of *BT*, Nietzsche dictated to an old school-friend, Carl von Gersdorff, a speculative essay of some fifteen pages, entitled 'On Truth and Falsehood in an Extra-Moral Sense',[1] which contains his most fully considered observations on language and its place in experience; the ideas in the essay – some original, some not – remain essentially unchanged in his later writings. Language is seen as a referential and descriptive medium, an entirely conventional – and thus, for Nietzsche, an entirely arbitrary – system of sounds and signs; it names and describes a 'reality' to which it does not belong. Wherever, in our uncertain existence, certainty may reside, it is not in language, which can never connect us with each other or the world of things. Its relationship with that world (Nietzsche tells us) is neither consequential (things are not the causes of words) nor mimetic, but merely arbitrary; and so is all knowledge which comes to us in the form of words. At this point it becomes clear that what Nietzsche is concerned with is less a theory of language than of *words*, and in particular nouns functioning as names.

Is nothing else to be said about this relationship between words and world except that it is contingent and unreliable? These are deprecatory terms and depressing thoughts, of course: they proclaim man's solitary condition and the vanity of the obvious means to true knowledge; yet should it not be possible to see the relationship in a different light, to attach different expectations to it? By an extraordinary leap of the imagination – but we have to get used to the fact that Nietzsche's philosophical muse proceeds not by steady jog-trot but by leaps and bounds *and* by intermittent commentary on its own procedure – he now appeals to a central concept of *BT* and identifies the relationship as an aesthetic one. Language, he asserts, has its origin in

ein *ästhetisches* Verhalten, ich meine eine andeutende Übertragung, eine nachstammelnde Übersetzung in eine ganz fremde Sprache: wozu es aber jedenfalls einer frei dichtenden und frei erfindenden Mittelsphäre und Mittelkraft bedarf.

an *aesthetic* attitude, by which I mean the merest intimation of transference – a sort of halting, stammering translation – into an entirely foreign language: for which purpose we need a freely poeticizing, a freely inventive middle sphere and middle faculty.[2]

Nietzsche's claim that the nexus between words and world is established by 'transference – a sort of halting, stammering translation' is his way of saying that the relationship is a *metaphorical* one. Hence the next question:

Was ist also Wahrheit? Ein bewegliches Heer von Metaphern, Metonymien, Anthropomorphismen, kurz eine Summe von menschlichen Relationen, die poetisch und rhetorisch gesteigert, übertragen, geschmückt wurden und die nach langem Gebrauch einem Volke fest, kanonisch und verbindlich dünken: die Wahrheiten sind Illusionen, von denen man vergessen hat, dass sie welche sind.

What then is truth? A mobile army of metaphors, metonymies, anthropomorphisms – in short, a sum of human relations which, poetically and rhetorically intensified, became transposed and embellished, and which after long usage by a people seem fixed, canonical and binding on them. Truths are illusions which one has forgotten *are* illusions.[3]

Every man (Nietzsche believes) has to organize these 'illusions' purposefully in order to be able to attend to the practical business of life. But as soon as he has freed himself from the pressure of material needs, as soon as he is free to become truly, that is 'aesthetically', creative, he need no longer follow the order of common discourse, he need not go on building those 'purposeful' conceptual structures of long petrified metaphors and metonymies which we call 'science', and may abandon his illusory search for 'truth':

Jenes ungeheure Gebälk und Bretterwerk der Begriffe, an das sich klammernd der bedürftige Mensch sich durch das Leben rettet, ist dem freigewordnen Intellekt nur ein Gerüst und ein Spielzeug für seine verwegensten Kunststücke: und wenn er es zerschlägt, durcheinanderwirft, ironisch wieder zusammensetzt, das Fremdeste paarend und das Nächste trennend, so offenbart er, dass er jene Notbehelfe der Bedürftigkeit nicht braucht und dass er jetzt nicht von Begriffen, sondern von Intuitionen geleitet wird. Von diesen Intuitionen aus führt kein regelmässiger Weg in das Land der gespenstischen Schemata, der Abstraktionen: für sie ist das Wort nicht gemacht, der Mensch verstummt, wenn er sie sieht, oder redet in lauter verbotenen Metaphern und unerhörten Begriffsfügungen, um wenigstens durch das Zertrümmern und Verhöhnen der alten Begriffsschranken dem Eindrucke der mächtigen gegenwärtigen Intuition schöpferisch zu entsprechen.

That gigantic structure of planks and timberwork of concepts to which indigent man clings for dear life is for the freed mind no more than a scaffolding and a plaything on which to practise its most daring tricks; and when he breaks it in pieces, disarranging its order and putting it together ironically again, joining the things farthest apart and separating those closest together, he thereby reveals that he has no need of those makeshift contraptions and that now he is guided, not by concepts, but intuitions. No regular way leads from such intuitions to the land of ghostly abstractions; it is not for them that the word was created; seeing them, man falls silent or speaks in forbidden metaphors and extravagant combinations of concepts, so that by demolishing and mocking the old conceptual boundaries (if in no other way) he may show himself equal to the impression with which the mighty intuition seized him.[4]

Taken all together, these observations must serve as Nietzsche's theory of language. We are not concerned with the truth of this theory, but with the light it throws on his practice as a writer:

(i) Metaphor (along with comparable linguistic modes) is the essence of language and the heart of the aesthetic activity. All language is metaphorical, and metaphor, though a lie,[5] constitutes an approach to truth.

(ii) This is Nietzsche's apologia, in unusually explicit form, for allowing imagery to dominate his style, for refusing (or being unable?) to confide his insights to a purely 'scientific' mode of discourse. Neither the language of plain facts nor conceptual language is better, or more reliable, than metaphorical language: conceptual language is the same thing, only devitalized and even further removed from 'reality'.

(iii) The implication of this argument is that truth must ultimately be sought beyond language: Nietzsche's low view of language remains essentially unqualified. Truth (to reverse Hobbes' theorem) 'is of' anything but 'proposition'. The realm to which *meta*phors or 'transferences' point cannot be charted by words; it is, as *BT* puts it, below articulated discourse in the reach of primordial reality, *im Urgrund des menschlichen Daseins*.

(iv) The closing description of the artist at work among 'forbidden metaphors', untoward combinations of concepts and isolated intuitions contains the most accurate account we have of Nietzsche's own future philosophical and literary undertaking. What makes it so revealing is its suggestion of the discontinuities, *aperçus* and aphoristic turns that will come to characterize his writing. Although these features are not given free rein until his later books of *pensées* and extended reflexions, they are already present in *BT* – for instance in that passage where the whole 'comedy of life' is likened to a dream with its 'sudden arrests of experience, tricks of fortune and anguished expectations'. For Nietzsche life, still more than drama, is not so much an Aristotelian *praxis*, as a series of disconnected scenes, moods, discrete 'forbidden' metaphors.

Nietzsche himself recalls his undertaking in the *Self-Criticism* of 1886. At the end of § 2 he interprets that 'impossible book' as an attempt at mediation between 'art' and 'science'. His self-imposed task had been '*to perceive science* [which includes all the fruits of academic scholarship and research] *in the perspective of the artist and art, moreover, in the perspective of life*'. In § 3 of the *Self-Criticism* he proceeds to dismiss the style of *BT* as a worthless hybrid. There is no suggestion that its hovering between metaphorical and literal, between myth and ordinary 'reality', had itself been part of that meritorious, if immature, attempt to mediate between the two spheres; but whatever Nietzsche felt able to remember of his motives fifteen years later, we can hardly doubt that the style is just that. Such an undertaking, however, is still open to the criticism that, whatever its original purpose, its actual effect is likely to be confusion between fact and fiction. Which, then, is it: mediation or muddle? The only way to answer the question is to step outside the framework Nietzsche has constructed and to ask what he has done for the standing (and not merely the *under*standing) of the cultural experiences he is concerned with, especially the Greek experience, in our age. And to this question, the unambiguous answer is that no single modern book has done more.

To say this is not to invalidate the criticisms made by Wilamowitz and others; it is rather to suggest how far the overall condemnation to which such criticisms usually belong is mistaken. Nietzsche's book does not contain significant 'contributions to scholarly knowledge' about the ancient world, even if it does contain important interpretations, or reinterpretations, of what others had discovered. The ultimate concern of his presentation of Greece is not classical scholarship. It is one and the same as the purpose of his hybrid style: to make available to us a moment in Greek culture; to do it in terms evocative of those in which that moment was experienced; and thus to show us *our* world and *our*selves 'in the perspective' of antiquity.

§ 2

The purpose of the brief historical section which now follows is to show that the barbaric Dionysiac rites of the Near East had to be moderated by Apollo before they could become an integral part of Greek culture; and again the section concludes with a dithyrambic invocation of the splendour – at first threatening, eventually enriching – of the Dionysiac dithyramb.

While this argument is proceeding apace, a stylistic peculiarity of the young

Nietzsche, amounting to an unconscious mannerism, begins to obtrude itself on the reader. In almost every sentence, and often three or four times in succession, one stumbles across the particle *als*, 'as', with which one function is substituted for another, one use or rôle for another. The first sentence of the section begins with one such substitution –

> So far we have considered the Apolline and its opposite, the Dionysiac, *as artistic energies* [*als künstlerische Mächte*] –

and there are two more in the same sentence. On occasion the mannerism even runs against the syntactic conventions of the language.[6] The overall impression is that nothing is quite itself, and everything represents something else. And when the plethora of 'as'es' and 'as ifs' is conjoined with one of Nietzsche's summary reinterpretations of history (as here), or one of his attempts to subsume a whole area of inquiry into an aphorism or two (as elsewhere), he writes like one whose existential exploration needs every possible path left open.

Though it is especially marked in this historical section, the stylistic tic is evident throughout the writings of Nietzsche's first period and, less obtrusively, it becomes an integral part of his mature style. And again the essay of 1873 and its view of truth as 'a mobile army of metaphors' helps us to understand the prominence of these substitutions in Nietzsche's style. Like a metaphor, an 'as' or 'as if' implies the inadequacy of the bit of language to hand. For Nietzsche such devices confirm the inadequacy – the limited capacity for truth – of language as such. And yet language is still the medium of his existential experiment.

§ 3

We can find no better example of Nietzsche's mediation between reality and myth – of his showing up the modern world in the perspective of antiquity – than in his retelling of the story of King Midas' search for Silenus, boon companion of Dionysus.

The tale is introduced with a sharp disclaimer: anyone contemplating the Olympian gods with expectations derived from Christian ideals is in for a grave disillusionment. Life under these gods – and the life *of* these gods – is 'beyond good and evil': the phrase, alluded to here for the first time, will become the title of the first and in some ways most accomplished book of Nietzsche's last phase. Asceticism of any kind is wholly alien to the Olympian world: it is all 'luxe, calme et volupté'. The only modern analogue that occurs to Nietzsche is the Faustian scheme of values: hence a passing allusion to

Faust's magic potion (*Zaubertrank im Leibe*) and his conjuration of Helen, 'floating in sweet sensuality' (*in süsser Sinnlichkeit schwebend*).[7]

But once made, the allusion to Faust is abandoned. Nietzsche addresses himself again to his contemporaries, who are bound to approach the myths with Christian values in mind –

> Do not turn your back [on these mysteries], but hear first what the popular wisdom of the Greeks has to say about this life, which unfolds itself with such inexplicable serenity before your eyes –

and, without change of mode, he turns this apostrophe into the story of King Midas, culminating in the terrible disclosure which Midas forces Silenus to make:

> Oh wretched race of ephemera, children of trouble and chance, why do you force me to tell you what it is least beneficial for you to hear? The best is quite beyond your reach, for the best of all things is not to be born, not to be, to be nothing. But the second best thing for you is – to die soon!

This is no mere re-telling of ancient myth but an address to the modern reader, and thus a complex act of mediation. What began as a warning against moralizing anachronism ('Anyone contemplating these Olympians with another religion in his heart...') becomes a leap across centuries, cultures and planes of reality. The terrible wisdom of the Greeks, their god and his attendant, are all presented – made present – to *you*, the modern unbeliever and 'Christian' sceptic, because it is *your* life, too, which Silenus is condemning, and which art, in the argument that is now introduced, will redeem.

Nietzsche is not (to emphasize it once more) writing an academic disquisition on a genre called 'tragedy'. Nor is he writing a defence of pessimism, as Schopenhauer was when he quoted these same lines from *Oedipus at Colonus*,[8] as one of so many literary confirmations (from Heraclitus to Byron)[9] of his central philosophical doctrine. Nietzsche's aim is different. He quotes the lines as a prelude to a rhapsodic affirmation of the creative spirit of man in the face of his inevitable doom. Now (he continues) and now only, 'the Olympian magic mountain opens up for us and shows us its roots.' The metaphor somewhat miscarries, but its allusion to Mount Venus and Tannhäuser,[10] aided by the assonance that follows (*Zauberberg ...die Traumgeburt der Olympischen*), takes him to the centre of his interest: death is present at all times, the ephemeral alone is perennial. To make men face this predicament *and* hide it from them, *but* not too much, is the far from naïve task and justification of art as Nietzsche sees it (and the message, too, of a later *Magic Mountain* story).

Once more the 'classical' argument is interrupted by a wholly modern polemic, this time against the Romantic cliché of identifying Homer's 'naturalness' and 'naïvety' with Rousseau's *faux-naïf* Emile. Even 'Homeric' naïvety is a complex Apolline illusion, and the art which Schiller calls 'naïve' is 'natural' only in the sense of being the embodiment of nature's complex ruse, her design for the protection not of the living but of life itself. Art and the Olympian gods issue from the same life-protecting instinct and answer the same vital need.

There is little enough about Christianity in *BT*; and nothing about that lurid illocutionary maxim of the 1880s, 'God is dead'. (The rhythm of that phrase, however, is prefigured in the 'shattering cry' once heard by passing sailors in Tiberius' time, 'Great Pan is dead', § 11.) Yet it is from these observations on the vital nature of Greek religion that Nietzsche's increasingly bitter anti-Christian polemics will take their cue. Against the Greeks' deep *need* of the Olympian gods, and the genius that enabled them to satisfy that need by means of their creations, Nietzsche will set his assessment of Christianity as a mere convention which no longer satisfies any genuine human need and is redundant and sterile through and through. Against his present praise of gods which are freely created and 'neither an imperative nor a reproach' to their creators, he will set his indictment of Christian eschatology for being just that – a collection of impossible imperatives and insidious reproaches.

§ 4

The importance of Schopenhauer's influence on Nietzsche was evident from the first sentences of the book. The long opening paragraph of this section shows how deeply his thinking is still involved, through Schopenhauer, in Kant's philosophical idealism. In the earlier parts of the book Nietzsche has made considerable a-logical use of the ambiguities of the German word *Schein*, which means 'appearance' and 'illusion' and also, in the repeated phrase *der schöne Schein*, suggests brightness and beauty.[11] We realize now – with something of a shock, it may be – that *Schein* points us not simply to an Apolline world of appearances and beauty, but to idealist assumptions about life. The claim is that we are so constituted as to experience life

> als das wahrhaft Nichtseiende, das heisst als ein fortwährendes Werden in Zeit, Raum und Kausalität, mit anderen Worten: als empirische Realität.

> as the truly non-existent, that is, as perpetual becoming in time, space and causality; in other words, as empirical reality.

'Empirical reality' – the world itself – as 'the truly non-existent': the author of *Twilight of the Idols* (1888) could hardly find a handier target for his anti-idealist tirades than this. As yet, however, the incongruity of vindicating 'life' against other-worldliness with the negative terminology of German idealism has not struck home: an indication, this, of how dramatic Nietzsche's changes of heart will be during his philosophical career.

§ 5

'We now approach the real goal of our investigation', the section begins: that is, the question how tragedy emerges – 'is born' – from the spirit of music. This time we shall look at the structure of Nietzsche's argument.

The two founders of Greek literature (*Dichtung*) are named as Homer and Archilochus. In the terminology of 'modern aesthetics' they are apt to be described as the 'objective' and the 'subjective' poet respectively, but Nietzsche rejects this distinction as irrelevant (*blosse Einbildung*) and indeed anti-poetic. The so-called 'subjective' artist is simply the bad, inadequate artist. This argument is now left hanging in the air, while Nietzsche turns to music: to the 'musical mood', which Schiller alleged to be 'the mental condition preceding the act of creation'; and music proper, which expresses the inchoate, pre-linguistic oneness of the Dionysiac artist (*das Ureine*) with the world of suffering, *Urschmerz*. When the images that fill the Apolline dream are imposed on the Dionysiac world of music, lyric poetry ensues. And 'lyric poems in their highest development are called tragedies and dramatic dithyrambs'.

The question can hardly be avoided: what is it that enables Nietzsche to make, and to urge on us as plausible, these transitions from music to lyric poetry and from lyric poetry to tragedy? The obvious answer is the accepted history of the Greek genres: Greek lyric poetry was words *and music*, and lyric (in the shape of the dithyramb) developed into Attic tragedy. As the allusion to Schiller reminds us, however, even when ostensibly concerned with Greek music, Greek lyric poetry and Greek tragedy, Nietzsche is also concerned with music, lyric poetry and tragedy *per se*; and for these larger entities some link is required. There is, of course, Wagner, whose work conjoins the three, but even for Nietzsche, Wagner is not quite the whole of music, lyric and tragedy; and so far Wagner is not even an explicit part of the argument.

There is one other possible answer. Could it be that music and lyric poetry and tragedy are all closely related as *mood*? We gather from the Schiller anecdote that the preliminary to lyric – and presumably to tragic – composition is a musical mood, and we recall that the art-work of life is a series of disconnected scenes or moods (§ 1). Moreover, as we have seen,[12] the German tradition tends to respond to tragedy as mood, and Nietzsche is sometimes inclined to forget the – Apolline – action and treat tragedy as – purely – Dionysiac mood himself. As an answer to our question, this one by itself is even less adequate than the others. Nevertheless, we may well feel that all three answers are involved here. They are not mutually exclusive, and they have one thing in common: they all eschew formal proof, and their logic is the logic of metonymy and metaphor. And metonymy and metaphor (we recall from the essay of 1873) constitute the only true relationships between language and 'the real world' which Nietzsche considers; they yield the only kind of 'truth' there is.

Now the conundrum of 'modern aesthetics' – the question of the lyrical poet's 'subjectivity' – is taken up again. Nietzsche introduces it as a concession to a mode of discourse which he disapproves of, yet cannot quite avoid. He turns it into a distinction between 'the empirically real person of the artist' (T. S. Eliot's notion of 'the man who suffers'), and 'the lyrical genius' who is 'pure medium' (Eliot's 'the mind which creates').[13] Only the latter is the creator, the true *poet* Archilochus. Only the poet is capable of 'redeeming' passion, anger and suffering, including those of *the man* Archilochus, by endowing them with form and symbolic meaning. This is the vocabulary and the tone in which, seventeen years later, Nietzsche will be describing his own rôle as recipient of the Zarathustrian vision: 'Has anyone living at the end of the nineteenth century a clear notion of what poets of vigorous epochs called *inspiration?* If not, let me describe it. Anyone who was the least bit superstitious would find it hard to reject the impression that he was mere incarnation, mere mouthpiece, mere medium of superior forces...'[14]

Whereas the epic artist, under Apollo's protection, faces the world and views his creations with detachment, the lyric poet is inseparably at one with them. They are no more than 'different objectivizations' of himself, but they also constitute the world of which he is the centre.

The ontological question, 'What is art?', coincides with the existential question, 'What is the meaning of life?' And the answer is the famous metaphysical and meta-aesthetic apothegm,

nur als *ästhetisches Phänomen* ist das Dasein und die Welt ewig *gerechtfertigt.*

'Only as an aesthetic phenomenon is existence and the world eternally...' – justified? vindicated? However we translate the phrase, the characteristic Nietzschean paradox remains. Nietzsche's starting point is the aesthetic conceived as a sphere beyond all moral considerations, self-sufficient, an alternative form of existence. How is this to be brought into a meaningful relationship with the world in which we live? Evidently, only by some vindication or justification of this world which cannot itself be aesthetic – that is, by some kind of redemption. All his writings are marked by some attempt at an aesthetic re-casting of the world of human experience, yet any such attempt is foiled by the requirement that, if it is to be more than 'a phantasmagoria', it must be anchored to that activity of ours which endows the world with value. A redefinition of the word 'aesthetic' to bring it closer to this value-giving activity is implicit in *BT* – surely an admission of the dilemma.[15] Even as an aesthetic phenomenon the world must be *justified*: language itself, it seems, reflecting accurately what is possible in the world of our experience, leaves Nietzsche no choice.

How can we know any of this? Where do *we* stand? The world we belong to is an 'aesthetic phenomenon'; specifically, it is an 'art-world' and a 'comedy of art', and to these definitions Nietzsche now adds a comparison with a modern, Kleistian ring which more pointedly confounds the two spheres of life and art. We know no more about the world around us than the soldiers painted on a canvas know about the battle raging around them, except that... Only the creative act of the Dionysiac artist, which unites him with the prime artist and creator of all things (*Urkünstler der Welt*) gives him – and so, eventually, us – a glimpse of the true foundations of existence. What he sees is the whole world (*Dasein und Welt*) as his own creation and himself as part of it. For Schopenhauer this 'coincidence of object with the subject' is the ineffable mystical anchorage of his philosophy. Nietzsche is content to add one more comparison: it is 'just like that eerie image in the fairy tale, which can turn its eyes inward and behold itself...'.

The strength and weakness of Nietzsche's argument seem inseparable. Only by claiming an identity between the Dionysiac artist and his world can the central importance and surpassing value of art be established: its status not as an 'aesthetic' phenomenon alongside other phenomena, but as the only full mode of existence itself. But no sooner is this done than two incongruities, of which Nietzsche seems unaware, threaten to destroy the entire argument. On the one hand, the distinction between 'the empirically real self' and the artistic self is apt to lead to a loss of all idea of selfhood and the disappearance of any human agent at all. This impression is reinforced by highly impersonal metaphors of creation which lean heavily on the tendency to abstraction inherent in German verbal constructions: the Dionysiac–musical enchantment to which the sleeping Archilochus has succumbed *emits* sparks of lyrical imagery; poems in their highest *unfoldings* (of what?) become tragedy; lyric genius feels a world of metaphors *growing out of* its metaphysical condition of oneness and self-renunciation. And the impression is confirmed by the quasi-religious vocabulary of redemption through self-sacrifice in which the whole argument is cast.

The second, closely connected danger is that of solipsism, a danger which, in one form or another, will beset many of Nietzsche's later philosophical arguments. *BT* in general, and passages like the present one in particular, belong to his critique of the fragmentation of modern man, which will be given its fullest and most explicit statement in *Zarathustra*. Here Nietzsche's barely acknowledged inspiration is the great Romantic dream of the oneness of art and life. Yet it is this visionary dream, too, which threatens to turn the whole world into a monstrous extension of the self. Many a reader will suppose that here Nietzsche is 'simply being German', doing no more than following the mainstream of 'German' thinking. It is proper to remind ourselves that it was the greatest of the German Romantics who viewed this tendency with apprehension and recognized in it 'the root of evil':

> woher ist die Sucht denn
> Unter den Menschen, dass nur Einer und eines nur sey?
>
> wherefore, among men, the passion
> That *one* man alone should exist, and *one* thing alone?[16]

Nietzsche's first book is 'out of season' – much more than the four essays which follow it. It aims not to analyse, but to recreate: above all, to recreate the Greek world into which tragedy was born. This explains the non-discursive nature, the absolutism, of some of its positions. This absolutism is not always present. There are passages in which Nietzsche cannot help using a different, more seasonable mode of discourse. But wherever, as in this section, the absolutism is dominant, there his various arguments, weak or strong, fuse in a single assertion, irrefutable only because it is, in fact, unargued.

§ 6

Schopenhauer is concerned with the world of the will, which (he maintains) is redeemable by being recast in the medium of music. Nietzsche, intent on showing the superiority of music over all other forms of experience, reverses the argument. Music (we are now told) makes its appearance in the world in the form of the will; its essence, however, remains inexpressible, and its true habitat is presumably some other world than our own. In his capacity as Apolline artist, the lyric poet's task is to find a verbal equivalent for music. To do this he must be like Stephen Dedalus' ideal artist, 'indifferent, paring his fingernails'.[17] He must withdraw from the world of the will so that he may use his 'empirically real self' ('his own willing, yearning, groaning and rejoicing') as an image (*ein Gleichnis*) to intimate that which must remain 'essentially' beyond the sphere of language. The allusion here is perhaps to the penultimate lines of *Faust II*, in which the old Goethe reviewed the whole of Faust's life – that strange enigma in whose company he had lived for more than half a century – and in a single poetic *aperçu* named it, as part of all that is ephemeral, 'an image, no more': *Alles Vergängliche ist nur ein Gleichnis.* What Goethe was expressing is more than an isolated poetic idea, but very much less than a consistent philosophical theme. There are critics who have attempted to read his life's work by the light of this epigraph, with not very illuminating results. To Nietzsche, on the other hand, the idea of life as 'an image' is fundamental – even if he, like Goethe, never consistently pursues it.

Goethe too had occasionally expressed doubts about the efficacy of language as a means of conveying the deepest of man's secrets, but for him the expression of such doubts was merely an additional way of coming closer to those secrets and a part of the rhetoric of conveying them.[18] Nietzsche's argument, however, simply by being an argument, lands him in difficulties of an altogether insoluble kind; this must surely be one of the passages he had in mind in 1886 when he suggested that the style of the book was still too prosaic for the new vision it was meant to convey.[19] The claim that the essence of music lies beyond – not just to one side of, but beyond – the sphere of language is an essential part of that new message. Yet such distinctions as the one between 'the essence' and 'the appearance' of music, or between language as 'an imitation of the world of images and appearances' and language as 'an imitation of the world of music', belong to the conventional terminology of the German Platonic and idealist tradition; they owe everything to the 'rationalistic' and 'scientific' philosophy whose Socratic roots are attacked later in the book. Nietzsche, of course, was no stranger to this vocabulary – no more than any student or teacher at a German university in his day or in ours. Nor did he ever free himself entirely from the schematization it imposes on his thinking about the world. Yet this must be almost the last time that he allows it to involve him in such logical circularities and verbal awkwardnesses as

> Music in its essence cannot possibly be the will, because as such it would have to be banished entirely from the realm of art, the will being the unaesthetic *per se*; rather, music *appears* as the will...

The ghostly terminology is the best he can do: he offers it without any irony. Small wonder, then, that 'language' is repeatedly denigrated, for its inability to 'approach' (*beizukommen*, almost 'get the better of') the essence of music and its 'world-symbolizing' function.

§7

The birth of tragedy – here Nietzsche agrees with the scholarly tradition – is in the tragic chorus: but what is the chorus? Two hypotheses are quickly disposed of. The democratic hypothesis which sees the chorus as 'a constitutional representation of the people', is not so much refuted as ridiculed out of existence. To take it for that, says Nietzsche curtly, is blasphemy, if only because such representation was unknown to the Greeks of the archaic age. Behind this dismissal lies a wholesale contempt for politics, which Nietzsche shares with the bulk of the German middle classes in the century between 1848 and 1948 – the dates that mark the defeat and the successful reinstitution of the parliamentary system. The discussion ends oddly:

Eine konstitutionelle Volksvertretung... haben sie hoffentlich auch in ihrer Tragödie nicht einmal 'geahnt'.

It is to be hoped that [the Greeks] did not have so much as an 'intimation' of a constitutional representation of the people in their tragedy.

The peculiar solecism of a retrospective hope is evidently intended to add irony to the dismissal. One wonders whether it is not also a sign of the author's uneasy awareness that the Greeks of the tragic age were, in Aristotle's phrase, political animals, and that disdain or despair at traditional politics is first articulated in the works of the arch-enemy of tragedy, Plato.

The second hypothesis is August Wilhelm Schlegel's idea that the chorus is really 'a quintessence and extract of the crowd of spectators', recreated in an 'idealized' form by the dramatist. This idea Nietzsche dismisses at first by making play with the German tendency to 'idealize' anything, even a crowd of Athenian ruffians rushing on stage and interfering with the action.

Implicit in Nietzsche's discussion of Schlegel is his awareness of the shape of the Greek theatre, in which the chorus in the *orkhēstra* stands between the audience and the 'stage'.[20] And though the point is only made explicit in the next section (§8), it underlies Nietzsche's positive appraisal of Schiller's view of the chorus, to which he now turns. Schiller, offering a justification for introducing a chorus into a modern 'tragedy of fate', described the classical chorus as 'a wall which tragedy builds around itself, thus protecting its ideal ground and freedom' – that is, its status as a work of art. The separateness of stage and auditorium Nietzsche sees at one and the same time as a physical fact, an aesthetic phenomenon and a metaphysical–religious condition. It alone provides that free space beyond the tyranny of empirical life within which tragedy is enacted and without which no true culture is possible.[21] With a contemptuous allusion to 'the painstaking [otiose?] copying of empirical reality', Nietzsche castigates every kind of naturalism which intrudes on that space.

Primitive tragedy is a world erected on 'the scaffolding of a fictitious natural state' peopled by the satyr-chorus, 'fictitious natural beings'. And as such it is *real*. These Dionysiac heights have 'the same reality and credibility as Olympus with its inhabitants had for the [ordinary] Greek believer'. All this talk of 'reality' is more than a little bewildering, for we now have a hand with three, or perhaps four, realities to play: the empirical (just discarded, but soon to be brought back into the game), the religious (Olympian), and the dramatic, which is at this moment indeterminately religious (Dionysiac) too. But the complications arise only because Nietzsche cannot even here do without the problematic vocabulary of German idealism, in which 'reality', even when it is ostensibly unreal and not of this world, is always trumps.

The last three paragraphs are among the subtlest and most vital in the book. The presentation of Schiller's idea of the chorus can now be seen as an introduction to what is closest to Nietzsche's heart; and there follows, without any technicalities, an apodictic statement (not, indeed, a discussion) of the relationship between tragedy and action, drama and life, life and knowledge. Tragedy (we say) is designated as 'real'. It is an aesthetic phenomenon, yet it has a purpose. As with many other important points in Nietzsche's mature philosophizing, this point is made in a kind of syllogism of his own devising, (*a*) → (*not-a*) → (*A*):[22]

(*a*) Tragedy has a positive purpose, which is to reveal the full horror of life. What it tells us is not merely that a particular time is out of joint and that a particular man must fail to put it right, but that no human action whatever can fundamentally alter the true essence of things.

(*not-a*) This purpose, however, would seem to be ultimately negative. If tragedy compels a recognition that all endeavour is illusory, it must therefore induce a negation of the will to live. Nausea grips Hamlet, not (as the simplistic view goes) because 'thinking too hard, he doesn't get a chance to act': 'no – it is no mere "reflecting", it is true knowledge of and insight into the horrible truth [which] outweighs any motive for action, in Hamlet as well as in Dionysiac man'. This is the conclusion at which Schopenhauer's discussion of tragedy is content to rest. Nietzsche does not explicitly challenge the conclusion – only towards the end of his philosophical career will he identify it as a sure sign of Schopenhauer's 'nihilism' – but passes on to the third stage of his syllogism which is a negation of the second and a higher form of the first.

(*A*) Tragedy's full purpose is not the overpowering of the will and the negation of life. On the contrary, tragedy *preserves* the will and thus the life instinct. It does this by virtue of its Apollinity – or, as Nietzsche simply expresses it here, by virtue of *art*. The effect is to 'turn' (the word *umbiegen* is weak for the burden of meaning it has to carry) the horror and absurdity of being into 'ideas' (but *Vorstellung* has little that is abstract about it and includes products of the imagination): into 'ideas with which it is possible to live'. In the face of 'the truth about life', consolation and comfort are manifest in the symbolic immortality of the chorus as it lives on, behind the mere foreground of civilization, beyond all catastrophe, as life's timeless embodiment.

Is this, one wonders, an empirical account of tragedy after all – endless survivals of a hypostatized 'life itself'? Or is it a first inkling of the great metaphysical fiction of Nietzsche's last works, the doctrine of 'the eternal recurrence of the same'? In a passage of great beauty the young Thomas Mann has captured this moment of consolation, the most comprehensive of illusions that supervenes all illusion and disillusion alike. It takes the form of a dream in which Thomas Buddenbrook, the earliest of Mann's strenuous heroes, is granted a vision of the 'true' purpose of his unhappy, apparently purposeless life. The whole world that Thomas Buddenbrook has reared around him is about to collapse. The family firm and reputation threatened with disaster, his succession worsted, his health undermined, he chances upon a chapter of Schopenhauer's great work[23] and therein discovers – not Schopenhauer's assuaging doctrine of the annihilation of the will, but Nietzsche's vision of the recuperation of life:

> And behold: it was as though suddenly the darkness were rent before his eyes, as though the velvet wall of night parted and disclosed an immeasurably deep, eternal vista of light...*I shall live!* said Thomas Buddenbrook, almost aloud, and felt his breast shaken with inward sobs. This, this is the thing: I shall live! *It* will live...and that this *it* is not *I* is merely an illusion,[24] an error which death will rectify. This, this is how it is...
>
> To live on in my son – was that my hope? In a personality yet more timid, weaker, more flickering than my own? Arrant, childish folly! What is a son to me! I need no son! Where shall I be when I am dead? But it is so brilliantly clear, so overwhelmingly simple! I shall be in all those who have ever, do ever or ever shall say *I* – but especially in all those who say it most fully, vigorously, joyfully...[25]

Supremely sensitive and endowed with a supreme 'capacity for suffering', Nietzsche's Hellenic man is rescued from despair 'on behalf of life' and its mysterious ends. This is the true teleology of tragedy and all legitimate art. Italics and a coy dash mark the author's sense of achievement:

Ihn rettet die Kunst, und durch die Kunst rettet sich ihn – das Leben.

Act rescues him, and through art – life.

The cogency of the argument may be less than complete; its concluding insight takes us to the depths of the human predicament.

§ 8

While Nietzsche continues his account of the satyr chorus of primitive tragedy, his underlying concern with 'reality' is seen to have a special significance.

He begins by showing how difficult it is for us to see, or rather to experience, the unity of feeling and being incarnated in the satyr chorus; how much our civilization has alienated us from that unity; how abstract and complicated we are bound to think the relationship of chorus to the Apolline world of dramatic action; how distant we are from Nature and true 'reality'. The attitude of which Nietzsche accuses us is that which Schiller had designated as 'sentimental', because it excludes the poet from the natural, unreflecting world by placing between him and that world (and even between him and his own feelings) his capacity to reflect on both; by contrast, the 'naïve' poet and his utterance remain within the charmed circle of natural creation. To be a poet (Nietzsche concludes – *con brio ma non giudizioso?*) is to live poetically, amidst poetry's creations.

In Greece (Nietzsche hypothesizes) there was a literal identity between original chorus and original audience, and, by virtue of their Dionysiac capacities, an effective oneness between original chorus and original poet. All – audience, chorus, poet – ultimately participate in the Dionysiac act of total, ecstatic affirmation. Nietzsche's argument is rich in comparatives: the chorus depicts the being of man in the world (*Dasein*) 'more truthfully, with greater reality, more completely' than does the 'lying' art of our civilization; and this is so because the chorus is 'older, more original, indeed more important' than the dramatic action itself, where 'more original' (*ursprünglicher*) stands, as so often in German, for something like a mystic closeness to the origin of all things, and therefore for greater authenticity and truth. In brief, the chorus 'is the only "reality"' there is.

German poetry, more than any other, abounds in attempts to intimate this ontological oneness, this unity of all being and all things. Nietzsche recalls it now in some words from the dithyramb with which Goethe's 'Spirit of Earth' addresses Faust.[26] And it is significant that Goethe's description of that

Spirit's own Protean activity recalls to the reader's mind Luther's translation of *Acts* 17. 28. Goethe wrote:

> Ein ewiges Meer,
> Ein wechselnd Weben,
> Ein glühend Leben
>
> An eternal sea,
> A weft of changes,
> A glowing life

And Luther:

> denn in ihm leben, weben und sind wir
>
> for in him we live, and move, and have our being.

Goethe (for Schiller the 'naïve poet' of the modern world) had no qualms about recreating the ontological unity with any material, even Christian material, that came to hand.

All this 'movement' is Dionysiac in origin and inchoate in effect: once again the German notion of a non-dramatic drama comes into view. Dramatic action and any coherent form become possible only through individuation, that is, when the chorist in his ecstatic state sees a specific, Apolline vision of the god Dionysus outside himself and distinct from himself, and (later) comes to impersonate the god, or eventually (as Nietzsche makes explicit in §10) some heroic surrogate of the god in individual form. Henceforth the single, 'epic' hero separates himself from the chorus, and through that separation a new, contrasting tonality enters the drama. Even so, the world under this second, Apolline aspect, too, is '*more* distinct,... *more* poignant' than our world; and here Nietzsche's preoccupation with 'reality', half polemical and half philosophical, re-emerges.

There are more references, implicit and direct, to Goethe's *Faust* in Nietzsche's book than to any other modern work, partly because it is with *Faust* that the hunt for 'reality' enters German and European literature. This is the dominant theme of Goethe's dramatic poem. When we ask what precisely it is that Goethe's hero is intent on purchasing from Mephistopheles (which is really another way of asking how he and his times differ from earlier Fausts and *their* times), the answer can only be given in terms of that peculiar quasi-moralistic vocabulary on the borderlines between philosophy, psychology and aesthetics, made up of such phrases as 'greater reality', 'more concrete experience', 'richer life', 'more poignant feeling' and the like. This is Nietzsche's constant philosophico-polemical concern: to present the Greek poets, their creations and their public alike to our impoverished 'reality' in terms of these comparatives. Only thus are the Greeks able to offer us the exemplary spectacle of their 'richer' existence. The aerial roots of this argument are in Hölderlin's *Hyperion*, its flowering is to be in Wagner's mythopoeia. This is what Wagner will be called on to contribute to German culture, and this too, after the rejection of Wagner, will be Zarathustra's message.

What is Nietzsche's talk of a 'greater reality' worth? We can hardly avoid asking the question, even if this is not the place to offer a definite answer. For some, this vocabulary seems to hold great promise. It may be elusive; it may, in Nietzsche's case, be entangled in dubious idealist notions; nevertheless, it searches out a range of feeling and ideas hinted at, but not articulated, in earlier Western thought. It evokes religion and religious perspectives; but it points to a religion-without-god, a *via media* between discredited religion-*with*-god and a futile, or arrogant, secular humanism. In these terms, it represents a first attempt to reinterpret the valuable part of an otherwise untenable complex of known religious attitudes. The coloration of the new vocabulary derives in part from Christian–Platonic mystical feeling, via the Romantics, though its impetus is rather associated with the immanent religio-tragic *Weltanschauung* of ancient Greece which Nietzsche understands so well.

For others, any such attempt is doomed from the start; the whole notion of a religion without god is an evasion and a contradiction; and the supposed 'reality' for which Nietzsche yearns is nothing but a Will-o'-the-wisp, a piece of fishy metaphysics without adequate support from ancient thought or modern experience (let alone logic or epistemology), the kind of verbal indulgence of which even the anti-idealist Nietzsche of the 1880s will never quite rid himself.

Both sides may at least agree that, unlike so many of his followers, Nietzsche himself does not pretend that his 'greater reality' (whatever its ultimate derivation) has anything to do with Christian values. The only other unambiguous thing about it is the 'pathos' of his presentation of it.

§9

The notion of 'Greek serenity' had dominated the German understanding of Greek culture since Winckelmann's days, and Nietzsche too does not wish to do without it. His aim is to reinterpret and salvage it by giving it a serious content. His reinterpretation is set in train with the aid of a metaphor. Whenever we force ourselves to contemplate the brilliant core of the sun, we are saved from its blinding effect by forming dark patches in our eyes around that core: whenever we expose ourselves to the full impact of tragedy, the dramatist saves us from annihilation by the luminous patches which his art forms round tragedy's dark core for our protection. These luminous patches include the lucid dialogue, the elegant unravelling of a tragic knot, and the tones of reconciliation at the drama's end. These are, quite literally, tragedy's saving graces. They delight us, and we experience this delight whether, as in Sophocles' *Oedipus at Colonus*, the tragedy is the outcome of the hero's passivity and endurance or whether, as in Aeschylus' *Prometheus* (with which Nietzsche associates Goethe's early eponymous poem), the issue is 'the glory of activity'.

Set in motion by a metaphor, the argument now continues by way of a curious grammatical conceit. The Goethean–Aeschylean portrayal of the artist-like creator is designated the 'quintessential hymn of impiety' and exalted as a celebration of 'sacrilege' (*der Frevel*); and once that word is uttered, its supposed antonym, 'sin' (*die Sünde*), is summoned to the argument, and with it a whole clutch of all too readily related ideas heaves into view. *Sünde* is feminine and evil; it suggests lust, curiosity and deceit; its archetypal myth is the Semitic story of the Fall. *Frevel* is masculine and therefore manly and Aryan. It is a bitter thought, he tells us (indulging in the sententious and melodramatic connotations of the phrase *herber Gedanke*), that sacrilege should be a virtue, dignity incarnate, the source of all that is highest and finest among the achievements of humankind.

Again Goethe's *Faust* is put in the service of the argument, this time, however, with somewhat unfortunate consequences. The passage which Nietzsche quotes from the witches' chorus has no very recondite meaning:

> Wir nehmen das nicht so genau:
> Mit tausend Schritten macht's die Frau:
> Doch wie sie sich auch eilen kann,
> Mit einem Sprunge macht's der Mann.
>
> We don't mind where the journey leads:
> A thousand steps the woman needs;
> Though she makes haste as but she can,
> A single leap brings home the man.[27]

To enquire how Nietzsche comes to connect this mild joke (which perhaps adverts to one of Goethe's less successful affairs) with the dialectic of Aryan sacrilege and Semitic sin, might be revealing; what it would reveal is not only how much Nietzsche knew about women, but how much he knew about jokes.

That this whole racial vocabulary has, not undeservedly, fallen on evil days is too obvious to need emphasizing. More interesting is the question how

Nietzsche has got himself landed with a set of concepts so much closer to a Judaeo-Christian than a Greek view of life. The answer takes us to the basis of his later philosophy.

He is not content with the 'luminous patches', the pleasure of the aesthetic contemplation. He insists on finding value in catastrophe itself; or rather, in a hero's sacrificial stand – regardless (it seems) of what he stands *for* – in the face of the clearly perceived lawlessness, unreasonableness and inhumanity of all that surrounds him. By this argument, suffering itself is made into an absolute value.

Seeing the law of reason dissolved, Nietzsche imposes on reason what he calls the 'necessity of sacrilege'. Sacrilege, then, is an action, unreasonable but chosen by man, which will accord with the unreasonable nature of the cosmos in which he happens to find himself. When, in some notes for *Human, All Too Human*,[28] Nietzsche praises Heinrich von Kleist for braving the rigours of 'irremediable' tragedy (at the expense of the 'conciliatory' Goethe who had refused to contemplate the 'dark patches'), he recognizes in Kleist the one German dramatist whose work rests on the same premise as his own notion of 'necessary sacrilege': the premise of a fundamental disharmony between the setting within which man's existence is enacted and his reasonable expectations of it.

Necessary sacrilege, sacrifice, suffering: these absolutes are among the elements which will eventually come to constitute Nietzsche's philosophy of strenuousness. This philosophy will be asserted as the venture of a single man, independently of any established tradition. In *BT*, where the absolutes are still associated with a specific cultural experience and belong to a considered attitude rather than a philosophy, Nietzsche is trying to fit them into a tradition, to give them a habitation and a name. 'Aryan' is the name he finds for them and 'Semitic' is the name of their mirror-image. It is, in the age of Gobineau, a fashionable terminology. Hearing it used by others, especially of his sister's anti-Semitic company, he will find it worse than embarrassing. The time will come when he will have good reason to be distrustful of names.

§10–11

The Birth of Tragedy is the only one of Nietzsche's books in which he is intent on establishing continuities: between metaphorical and literal meaning, between myth and history, between the metaphysical and the secular. This last opposition, already invoked earlier on in the book, is reintroduced in these two sections and invested with a momentous literary-historical significance. Nietzsche opens the argument with the opposition in a slightly disguised but very black and white form. On the one side stand the idealized characters of tragedy, on the other the individuals of ordinary experience. The tragic heroes (he argues) are as remote from such individuals as the Platonic forms are from their earthly copies: ordinary individuals are unworthy of serious attention and merely comic. Only because it is founded in the myth of the dismembered Dionysus can individuation become tragic. It is always Dionysus who, appearing each time in a different guise –

> Seine Metamorphose
> in dem und in dem. Wir sollen uns nicht mühn
> um andre Namen
>
> His metamorphosis
> In this and in this. We should not labour
> for different names[29] –

remains the only hero of tragedy and the true substance of its 'mystery doctrine'. Once Dionysus makes way for ordinary individuals, tragedy dies.

It is at this point that one of the richest arguments of the book is set up: out of the metaphysical comes the secular; the death of ancient tragedy is the birth of modern 'literature'. It is of course Euripides to whom this cataclysmic development is ascribed, and Euripides himself is presented as a suitably modern figure, secularized and 'scientific'. Divided between educating the rabble and despising that same 'public' that he himself had called into being, between obsession and disenchantment with the traditional norms of his art, Euripides is the world's first victim of the 'anxiety of influence'.

From the ruins of tragedy arises New Comedy, and with it that naturalistic concern for verisimilitude which takes from the spectators – and no longer from the myths – the norms of the drama. The spectator himself now struts upon the stage; and the action is given over to the trivia of his daily life, to the petty concerns of 'bourgeois mediocrity'. And this process, which amounts to a secularization and democratization of the noblest art, imitates the democratization of politics, 'the rule – at least in sentiment – of the slave'; the rule of what, in *Beyond Good and Evil*, Nietzsche will call 'slave morality'. Abandoning his belief in an 'ideal past' and an 'ideal future', the Greek sinks into a light-hearted contentment with the passing moment: this is what the early Christians saw and condemned as 'Greek serenity'.

It is no disparagement of Nietzsche's originality to suggest that there is a precedent for this apocalyptic sweep through six centuries. The pattern he has designed is analogous to a Protestant pattern characteristic of the religious histories of seventeenth-century Pietism. In his evangelical childhood Nietzsche will have become familar with these histories and, through them, with those quiet rebels against clerical orthodoxy who are dismissed in one of his last books as 'Pietists and other cows of Swabian provenance'.[30]

The Pietists' attitude to the history of Christianity is dominated by their belief in the original, pristine vision of the divine mystery, perceived and voiced by the true prophets of the Faith, of whom Christ was the first. And this vision the Pietists saw betrayed in the course of its dissemination and propagation, in each new century of Christianity's decline, as its ineffable mysteries hardened and degenerated into contentiousness and lifeless dogma. Literal-minded utterance, fixed statement and rationalization, the widening of the circle of uninspired initiates leading to impiety and worldliness: these are the causes of religious degeneration as the Pietists portrayed them; and these, too, are the causes Nietzsche sees underlying the decline of Dionysiac tragedy and *its* mystery doctrine. 'The word kills, everything that is fixed kills', Nietzsche will write,[31] in order to explain how the unity of personal being that was incarnate in the living Christ came to be destroyed. The fixity of the rational word kills, he is saying in *BT*, for it destroys the unity of vital experience which was incarnate in tragedy – an art that was not born out of criticism and words, but out of the spirit and reality of music.

Nietzsche himself does not mention the Pietistic parallel, yet the subsequent course of his philosophical thinking confirms its relevance clearly enough. For underlying one major aspect of his philosophy, and eventually emerging into the clarity of explicit statement, is the analogy between Dionysus and Christ the Crucified. At the end of his conscious life, Nietzsche tries to place these two figures in absolute opposition to each other, affirming the sacrificial death of Dionysus as the Earth's most bountiful enhancement, rejecting the death of Christ as the symbol and source of a life-denying nihilism. The antithesis is made melodramatically, as though to drown an inner voice of doubt. It is the kinship of the two – the theme of Hölderlin's *Bread and Wine* – that remains uppermost in the reader's mind.[32]

§ 12

The central sections of Nietzsche's book are given over not to the birth, but to the death, of tragedy. In § 12 we meet for the first time the portentous association of Euripides, who 'fought the death struggle', and Socrates, the 'newborn *daemon*' who, through the agency of Euripides, usurped Dionysus' place on the Attic stage. The new Euripidean drama is not merely naturalistic: it is a self-defeating 'dramatized epic', self-conscious and rationalistic.

This brings us to what Marxist critics have called Nietzsche's 'irrationalism'. The accusation is too sweeping to stand up to examination. Nietzsche does not say that early tragedy was the epitome of Greek culture because it was irrational, but he does say that the Euripidean era was an era of decline because its drama was a product of conscious contriving. It follows that any drama which sets out to expose a problem of human existence or co-existence to reflection and which emphasizes the possibility of solving it; which deliberately separates – 'alienates' – the spectator from the action, so as to cool his response to it and thus inculcate in him an attitude of critical detachment; and which offers to take *its* 'bright patches' from strenuous but exhilarating ratiocination – in brief, 'epic drama' as Bertolt Brecht conceived of it – would, for Nietzsche, be a symptom of cultural disorder yet more profound than he felt able to identify a century ago. And to invoke Brecht is hardly to prove Nietzsche wrong.

§ 13

Nietzsche is no Spenglerian determinist. The agencies which bring this life-cycle of Greek culture to an end are not anonymous 'historical forces'. Yet his 'Euripides' and especially his 'Socrates' are not presented as ordinary personages either: this 'Socrates', *agent provocateur* and instigator of an age of prose, philosophy and *Wissenschaft*, is the archetype of a force greater than himself *and* a human being at its mercy.

What is so remarkable about Nietzsche's portrait of him is its deep ambivalence. Socrates, privileged to belong to a world 'whose very hem' we long to touch, nevertheless presumes to 'correct existence':

Dies ist die ungeheure Bedenklichkeit, die uns jedesmal angesichts des Sokrates ergreift und die uns immer wieder anreizt, Sinn und Absicht dieser fragwürdigsten Erscheinung des Altertums zu erkennen.

This is what we feel to be so immensely problematic whenever we consider Socrates; again and again it impels us to seek the meaning and purpose of this most questionable phenomenon of antiquity.

This opening and the series of rhetorical questions that follow it –

Wer ist das, der es wagen darf, als ein einzelner das griechische Wesen zu verneinen, das als Homer, Pindar und Äschylus, als Phidias, als Perikles, als Pythia und Dionysus, als der tiefste Abgrund und die höchste Höhe unserer staunenden Anbetung gewiss ist? Welche dämonische Kraft ist es, die diesen Zaubertrank in den Staub zu schütten sich erkühnen darf?

Who is it who dares single-handed to deny that quintessence of the spirit of Greece which, in the guise of Homer, Pindar and Aeschylus, Phidias, Pericles, Pythia [priestess of Apollo] and Dionysus – as deepest abyss and crowning peak, is assured of our astonished veneration? What daemonic power is it that dares to spill this magic potion in the dust? –

rising to the spirits' imprecation –

Welcher Halbgott ist es, dem der Geisterchor der Edelsten der Menschen zurufen muss:

> Weh! Weh!
> Du hast sie zerstört,
> Die schöne Welt,
> Mit mächtiger Faust,
> Sie stürzt, sie zerfällt![33]

What demigod is it, to whom the chorus of mankind's noblest spirits must call out:

> Woe and despair!
> You have destroyed it,
> A world of things fair,
> Brought low by your might,
> It falls through the air! –

and finally to the solving of the riddle –

Einen Schlüssel zu dem Wesen des Sokrates bietet uns jene wunderbare Erscheinung, die als 'Dämonion des Sokrates' bezeichnet wird

It is that wonderful phenomenon known as 'the *daimonion* of Socrates' which offers us a key to his character –

all this is designed to teach us the 'meaning and purpose' of *modernity's* 'most questionable phenomenon'. Socrates is condemned for his excessive reliance on logic and 'science', and the major project of his life – the attempt to 'correct Being by Knowing' – is condemned for the impiety it is – *and yet* it is not entirely his contingent, individual self that determines his course, but his *daimonion*. That *daimonion*, however, was (as Plato makes clear)[34] a negative thing: it inspired Socrates not to act, but to hold back from action. In Nietzschean terms this negativity is a sterile perversion – *and yet* Socrates' inability to turn this instinct against himself in criticism of the rational process is commended as a proof that his rationality itself must have been an elemental force and evidence of a 'divine vocation'. And so 'logical Socratism' turns out to be impersonal, 'an immense driving wheel behind Socrates', and Socrates himself to be a mere shadow through which we see the force that moves him and mankind in the ages of enlightenment and science. All this Socrates *knows*. His rational awareness was such that he could understand and explicate his own unique gift. It was even such that at his trial he could wittingly ensure his own death, and not regret it. Here again Nietzsche closely follows the ancient sources,[35] but here too condemnation is implicit in his version. Socrates passed sentence on himself 'without any natural terror of death'. Perverse and unnatural to the last, then – *and yet* even this does not prevent Nietzsche from concluding the section with a peroration on the dying Socrates, in whom the noble youth of Greece, with Plato in the van, worship their new ideal. (A new ideal? In Nietzsche's last books this will be seen as the moment of history when the modern ascetic ideals were born.)

Ambivalence embodies and preserves, but does not resolve, Nietzsche's dilemma. His is the dilemma of a modern mind seeking redemption among myths acknowledged as myths (and thus demythologized); seeking for truth among metaphors soon to be unmasked as lies; seeking 'reality'. . . Nowhere in all his stylistic experiments has Nietzsche proved to be more influential than in such displays of energetic ambivalence as he shows here.

And yet, in the course of any continuous argument and especially at its junction with the next, ambivalence cannot maintain itself. Such is the nature of all context-bound statements – all statements with some claim to meaning – that any ambivalence they may contain must resolve itself into a yea or a nay, however qualified. And so it is here: 'Socrates' too – reason itself – is a *daemon*. Destroyer of a culture and its gods, he is yet the bearer of a divine vocation. From which god? There can be no answer for one who seeks to preserve the divinity of man in an age – Socrates' age and Nietzsche's age – which has destroyed the divine.

§§ 14–15

The Marxist attacks on Nietzsche's 'irrationalism' are not only indiscriminate, they are also in a sense not radical enough. Even Georg Lukács, whose early work[36] shows beyond doubt that he should have known better than to join in the monotonous chorus of accusations,[37] fails to see the characteristically Nietzschean turn that leads from the death of tragedy to the birth of science: the sudden reversal that enables Nietzsche to claim, not only that Socrates – the voice of reason itself – is a *daemon*, but that the impetus which leads to and sustains the scientific spirit is unreasoning 'instinct'.

What Nietzsche means by 'instinct' is, for once, clear enough: it is that capacity in man which enables him to co-operate with 'life' in life's essential task of perpetuating itself.[38] And this 'instinct', Nietzsche argues, is at work in science in the same way as it was in tragedy, and takes science towards the same strange goal. Socratic optimism – the uncompromising search for knowledge and truth, and thus the hubristic desire to correct existence – marks only the first stage of man's scientific search; so too do the rationalist and secularist attacks on art, the prosy concern with 'poetic justice' and the invention of 'optimistic' literary forms, beginning with the Platonic dialogue. All these phenomena are symptoms of that new species represented by Socrates, which Nietzsche calls 'theoretical man'. The new species also has its own myth, which is embodied in the death of Socrates, and its own form of 'Greek serenity': the love of the created world as the repository of the objects of man's scientific passion. But this is not the end of man's 'universal hunger for knowledge'. His avidity is unappeasable. What drives him on and on, to ever new exploration and inquiry, is not the prospect of a final truth, not (as it seems at first) 'possession of the naked goddess', but the passion inherent in the *striving* after truth. At this point (§ 15) Nietzsche alludes to Lessing's famous credo:

Not the truth which any man possesses or thinks he possesses, but the honest effort he has applied to discover the truth, is what constitutes the value of man. For it is not through possession but through the search after truth that man's powers are increased, and in this alone does his ever growing perfection consist. Possession makes calm, inert, proud.[39]

Lessing here follows Leibnitz's *Monadology* in taking it for granted that, by virtue of its very intensity, this striving is directed toward a religious – though not exclusively Christian – goal. The strenuous effort glorified in Goethe's *Faust* is no longer linked to a recognizable religious goal, but it is – eventually – directed towards an existential value with religious overtones. Minimizing the religious aspects of Lessing's scheme, Goethe intends us to see that this unsparing effort justifies its own end. Nietzsche looks to the next step in the process: he reveals the scientific quest as a self-validating activity, which pays no regard to what it is striving for. The profound, if unacknowledged, purpose of this activity, meanwhile, is to provide *homo Socraticus* with a reason for living. The quest for knowledge gives thinking men 'a spur to existence'; and since science lacks an attainable goal, the quest and the incentive it provides seem to be guaranteed in perpetuity. But science has its limits. There comes a point in the pursuit of Socratic-scientific knowledge where *that* kind of knowledge is shown up as an illusion. In earlier sections Nietzsche has intimated, in more or less plain language, what this revelation must amount to: the laws of causality seem to stop working (§ 1); the cosmos with all its apparent order and sobriety is seen as an infinity of 'excess' and 'contradiction' (§ 4). The moment of revelation is now conveyed more pungently by imagery. Thought is a huge circle; the thinker starts at the centre and works onwards, that is outwards, towards the circumference. Anyone gifted enough to reach a point on the circumference finds not a point of rest, but the edge of reason itself, past which he can only 'stare out into what defies illumination' and 'see with horror how logic coils up and finally bites its own tail'. When this happens, Socratic optimism recognizes its illusoriness and 'topples over into tragic resignation and [a recognition of] the dire need for art'.

The verb, *umschlagen*, 'topple over', is used twice at the conclusion of this argument. It defies all attempts at translation. What it conveys is something important, a familiar yet often chilling part of our experience. It is the sudden reversal that accompanies the completion of a process: the moment when supreme good fortune turns into disaster; when the convex surface of the liquid in an overfull vessel is disturbed and overflows, re-forming not in a horizontal level but in a concave surface; or when 'all the digits in a sum/cancel out to nothing'.[40] Such sudden and often dramatic reversals mark the crucial stages in Nietzsche's history of European culture; his style, it need hardly be added, is uniquely suited to convey them.

§16

It is in this section that it becomes clear, if it was not clear already, why Nietzsche's ideas about the instinctive basis of the scientific spirit and his theory of the birth of tragedy belong together in one book: the connecting link is his hopes for tragedy's rebirth. Tragedy is derived from the deepest instincts, which science seeks to deny but must ultimately defer to. These deep instincts express themselves most immediately in music, which is a direct representation – *re*-presentation – of the true ground of all being. Tragedy was born from them and its rebirth in our world depends on them once again.

This argument, if not entirely dependent on Schopenhauer's aesthetics, certainly presupposes them. We are not surprised, then, to find that Nietzsche should now resort to a very long quotation from Schopenhauer's account of music and its relation to the 'universal will'.[41] Richard Wagner too is called to the witness box, and Nietzsche hints excitedly at a rebirth of tragedy *and* 'perhaps other blessed hopes for the German genius'. For the moment, however, Schopenhauer's theory of music (its 'eternal truth' corroborated by Wagner) holds our attention. Music and music alone among the media of art is both *general* (it represents all there is) and *concrete* (it is free from all conceptual abstractions).[42] And the Schopenhauerian argument comes full circle as Nietzsche quotes it in support of his own special plea for 'tragedy and the tragic' as the 'highest objectivization [of music] in images' (*höchste Verbildlichung*). The question of the relative values (measured in 'heights' or depths) of the various arts is as much on Nietzsche's mind here as the rebirth of tragedy from music; and the two issues go closely together.

Schopenhauer's metaphysical scheme (the cogency of which cannot be our present concern)[43] and Nietzsche's uncritical reliance on it are prime instances of that nineteenth-century German exaltation of music which we have already discussed.[44] The peculiarly, self-consciously German quality of the attitude, and its habit of translating itself into hierarchies of the arts like Nietzsche's own, are nicely spoofed in Heinrich Mann's *The Man of Straw*.[45] The context is a discussion between the jingoistic anti-hero and his wife:

'The highest form is music, therefore it is the German art form. Then comes drama.'
'Why?', asked Guste.
'Because it can often be set to music, and because you don't have to read it, and particularly –'
'What comes next?'
'Portrait painting, of course, because of the pictures of the Emperor. The rest are not so important.'
'What about the novel [*der Roman*]?'
'That's not an art form at all! At least, thank God!, not a German one. You can tell by the name.'[46]

§ 17

A defence of tragedy against the spirit of literature: does such a thing make sense? Nietzsche conducts it on four fronts: (i) He suggests that (by comparison with myth, stage symbolism and music) the *words* of tragedy are its most superficial component. (ii) He attacks all programmatic, 'tone-painting' music, in which the Dionysiac art is reduced to an imitation of phenomena and thus to a condition of 'superficiality' in its turn. (In this connection, it is ironic to recall that the most distinguished act of musical homage subsequently paid to Nietzsche, Richard Strauss's *Also sprach Zarathustra*, is among the most programmatic and *tonmalend* of modern compositions.) (iii) He interprets the prosaic stock characters of New Comedy as the consequence of Euripides' trivialization of myth and music. (iv) Finally he repeats his criticism of the glib way that the new drama replaces 'metaphysical consolation' with the painless *deus ex machina*.

The most far-reaching of these arguments is the first, which, as we have already noted, invites comparison with one of T. S. Eliot's early contributions to critical theory.[47] In the essay 'Hamlet and his Problems' Eliot argues that '*Hamlet*...is full of some stuff that the writer could not drag to light, contemplate, or manipulate into art. And when we search for this feeling...' (no 'feeling' has been mentioned before; throughout the essay Eliot himself seems to be struggling with the difficulties he identifies in Shakespeare) '...search for this feeling, we find it...very difficult to localize. You cannot point to it in the speeches...not in the action, not in any quotations that we might select.' And Eliot then goes on to criticize the play for lacking 'an objective correlative' capable of evoking 'that *particular* emotion' which should have been conveyed if the tragedy was to have been 'intelligible, self-complete, in the sunlight'.[48]

Nietzsche's comment is both wider in its application and more succinct:

the heroes [of Greek tragedy] speak as it were more superficially than they act: the myth does not find its adequate objectivization in the spoken word at all. The structuring of the scenes and the vividness of the images reveal a deeper wisdom than the poet himself can put into words and concepts; the same may be observed in Shakespeare, for instance in Hamlet, who similarly talks more superficially than he acts.

The principle articulated here comprehends Eliot's, but goes far beyond it.

In our comparison two fundamentally different kinds of critical thinking are revealed. Eliot is concerned with problems internal to the play itself, which come to a head in Shakespeare's striking inability (as Eliot sees it) to express, through his hero's speeches and actions, the emotion by which that hero is apparently possessed. Is this emotion really inexpressible, something one may feel but no one can put into words? Eliot calls the play 'an artistic failure', and claims that 'Shakespeare tackled a problem which proved too much for him'.[49] Does this mean that another dramatist might have succeeded where Shakespeare failed, or is Eliot suggesting that Shakespeare has overstepped the limits of art itself? Proposing, as always, 'to halt at the frontier of metaphysics or mysticism',[50] Eliot leaves the questions open. What he has given us is an illuminating consideration of a central problem in *Hamlet* and, arising from that and as a quasi-technical answer to it, a major concept in literary criticism.

What Nietzsche is saying is not that certain plays by Sophocles or Shakespeare are 'artistic failures', but that language, even in the hands of the greatest dramatists, is an inadequate medium for expressing 'the full depth of our being in the world'. He too is concerned, at least initially, with a problem in dramatic art, but the standard he applies is not, as it is with Eliot, some other play. For Eliot, Shakespeare's inability to express Hamlet's emotion is striking because 'if you examine any of Shakespeare's more successful tragedies',[51] you *do* find emotion adequately expressed. Nietzsche's ultimate standard is music, which is unverbalized because it cannot be verbalized, and myth, which arises from music and shares its pre-verbal power. Once again the notion of unarticulated mood seems to colour Nietzsche's view of tragedy, and once again it is clear that he sees tragedy as a *Weltanschauung* rather than a literary genre.

Language itself, Nietzsche is saying, is inadequate (to which Eliot might reply, 'I've gotta use words when I talk to you...').[52] As long as we see in the Greek tragedians mere poets, *Wortdichter*, we are bound to experience their work as impaired by a fundamental flaw, 'the incongruity between myth and word'. It is true that Nietzsche's argument, like Eliot's, has its origin in a concrete experience, our perfectly plausible feeling that the Greek 'heroes speak more superficially than they act'. But in seeking to explain that experience, Nietzsche ignores all literary and technical considerations and turns to philosophical reflection on the value of language as such – a movement not towards 'mysticism', but certainly towards 'metaphysics'.

The inadequacy of language: expressed in a rich variety of metaphors and carrying with it a rich variety of implications – philosophical, stylistic, personal – this thought will accompany Nietzsche throughout the next sixteen years: as an irritant in the face of his achievements, as a consolation in the face of his failures. In Eliot 'the inexpressible' is a single emotion, in Nietzsche 'the inexpressible' contains all that really matters:

> Our real experiences are not at all garrulous. They do not communicate themselves even if they wished to. That is because they lack the right word. In all talk there is a grain of contempt. Language, it seems, has only been invented for the average, for the middling and the communicable. Language vulgarizes the speaker.[53]

§§ 18–20

The brilliance *and* the exasperation of this extraordinary book stay with the reader to the end.

Section 18 begins with a restatement of Nietzsche's cultural history. The premise of the argument remains Schopenhauer's conception of the world as the illusory product of 'the insatiable universal will', where only 'the will itself' has, or rather is, complete 'reality'. In the most explicit indication we have that the Socratic mode is to be seen as fully equal to the Apolline and the Dionysiac, Nietzsche represents the modes as the three great illusions by means of which the will seeks to perpetuate itself. Under these three headings, historicized as Alexandrian, Hellenic and Buddhistic, the entire history of human culture is to be subsumed. By contrast with Nietzsche's periodizations of ancient Greece, it is not clear how literally this attribution of historical periods should be taken (the same goes for Spengler's, which largely derives from it). The value of the scheme, like the value of so many of Nietzsche's insights, lies in its reappraisal of established categories: looking towards history, it also looks towards psychology. It provides a designation of three fundamental tendencies or dispositions of the human mind; and there is some reason for thinking that the scheme may have influenced Freud's threefold analysis of the self into the *super-ego*, corresponding to the paramount rationality of the Socratic mode; the *ego*, equivalent to the dominance of the Apolline and artistic; and the dark, chthonic *id*, which rules the kingdom of Dionysus.[54] The true matrix of Freud's categories, however, is rather to be sought in the Platonic image of the psyche as a team of two horses and a charioteer ('reason').[55] Unlike Freud and Plato, Nietzsche is not schematizing the dispositions of the mind 'as such', but in historical time.

But even on the psycho-historical level, Nietzsche is not really concerned with a characterology of the whole human race. The psyches that concern him are those of 'the more nobly formed men', those who 'experience the burden and the heaviness [*die Schwere*] of existence with a deeper aversion' than the rest of mankind; and it is implicit that he regards culture – its creation and maintenance – as the province of this select minority. The question of how to characterize the standard of excellence by which the minority may be defined will be posed explicitly in one of his next works, the second of his *Thoughts Out of Season;* and this essentially moral question (which we for our part have not solved by turning the word 'élitist' into a term of abuse) will remain one of his chief philosophical concerns. This normative aspect also serves to distinguish his thinking from Freud's, of whom it has been well said that he 'found...that there was more to know and less to judge than most thinking people had imagined';[56] Nietzsche's view is more likely to be, 'tout comprendre, ce n'est rien pardonner'. Yet in their assumptions the two men differ from each other less than in their procedures or their declared aims. Freud too, as impatient with social issues as Nietzsche, takes it for granted that culture is the creation, burden and reponsibility of a minority; and although the three-layered psyche he describes is intended to be valid for the entire human race, those who exemplify it in the pages of his writings seem all to come from a few *gut bürgerlich* districts of Vienna.

The bulk of § 18 and the two sections that follow is made up of lengthy polemics directed against Socratism in the modern world. By way of a transition to these sorties, Nietzsche anticipates one of his favourite ways of philosophizing in later life, and lets an anecdote make his first and least controversial point for him. The point, made with affection and warmth, is that modern 'theoretical man' finds it absurdly difficult to ascribe value and significance to experience of a non-theoretical kind. And the difficulty is given its ironic put-down by Goethe in his conversations with Eckermann when, calling Napoleon 'one of the most productive men who have ever lived', he adds, 'Indeed, my dear fellow, one doesn't have to confine oneself to making poems and plays in order to be productive – there is also a productivity of deeds, and in many instances this is of a considerably higher order!'[57]

Once the peculiarly modern paradox of this charming story has been established, and before we reach the profoundly perceptive tribute to 'musical tragedy' in §21, we have to make our way through the invective against 'Socratic man' and his contemporary ascendancy. It has to be said that these sections are not calculated to persuade the uncommitted. By Socratic man Nietzsche means something much wider than the 'pure' thinker. In later years he does indeed single out the thinker for one of his inimitable deconstructions, identifying the 'will to reason' which informs Socrates with the 'will to make the world thinkable', and unmasking this in turn as an all-too-impure passion for dominance over others – theoretical man's form of the 'will to power'.[58] But in *BT* 'Socratic man' represents a more sweeping category. The phrase covers the journalist and the academic, the novelist and the critic, the admirers and the composers of pre-Wagnerian opera (which is belaboured at length in § 19). It is not that these professions are beyond reproach, or that Nietzsche is wrong to point an accusing finger at the essential bookishness of modern high culture. Nor is the expanded category of Socratism in itself suspect: that large category, or something very like it, is needed, if only as an evaluative key to the changes in Greek art during and after the fifth century. But to dismiss so much requires something more than an intemperate and frequently ill-tempered tirade full of abstractions and largely innocent of detail, amounting to little more than a string of indignations.

Nietzsche's animus against Socratism is understandable enough. It reflects not only his personal dissatisfaction with scholarship, but also his persuasive reading of the history of German classical studies as a fall from a national and cultural rôle to a purely academic one; hence some bitter words about the modern educator's 'sceptical abandonment of the Hellenic ideal' in §20. But such personal and particular grievances, once again, cannot justify the scope of his assault.

Despite a reminder of the stature of Kant and Schopenhauer in § 19, the dignity of the Socratic pursuit of knowledge (tragic implications and all) gets lost in the stampede, and Nietzsche's control of style seems to go with it. There are some sharp observations, like the one in § 18 on the internal contradictions of modern culture, whose continued existence depends on 'a slave class', but whose optimism 'denies the necessity of such a class'. The rest is a series of more or less hoarse attacks on largely generalized enemies: on the Rousseauist appeal to 'natural man', which is associated both with the opera and, more vaguely, with 'socialist movements' and the impending insubordination of the masses; on the German educational system; on all intellectual and humanistic panaceas. Nietzsche will certainly write harsher polemics, but none so arid as the attack in §20 on 'the circles of teachers in our institutions of higher learning' (*die Kreise der Lehrer an den höheren Bildungsanstalten*) – a bureaucratic cliché, repeated almost verbatim a few lines later, and worse than any of the fashionable jargon for which he will shortly be castigating David Friedrich Strauss.[59]

Much of Nietzsche's venom is directed against the superficiality of modern culture, typified (as usual) by traditional opera and also by the modern artist's indiscriminate appropriation of past idioms and alien cultural forms (§18). Here the kindest thing to say is that he spoils a good case – the undoubted case for cultural absolutism – by an assault as indiscriminate as the practices he abhors. How (to quote a single example from §19) is the reader to react when Nietzsche caps his lengthy ridicule of opera for its 'fantastic triviality' and the 'sickly seductive column of scent' that rises from it with the exhortation, 'He who would wish to destroy opera must take up the fight against Alexandrian cheerfulness'? The 'he' is the uncritical disciple of Wagner, and the effect of Nietzsche's sudden equation of his 'nobly formed' reader with such a 'he' is to make even the most superficial cheerfulness a welcome alternative to this ponderous solemnity. The future admirer of Bizet and the light touch will one day deplore precisely this kind of writing and see in it 'the bad manners of the Wagnerite'.[60]

So much for Socratism: what of the Dionysiac values on the other side of the argument? The invocation of the tragic view of life is certainly less arid. It includes a memorable comparison of Schopenhauer to Dürer's 'Knight with Death and Devil';[61] and the transition to the climax of the book *ad maiorem Wagneri gloriam* is underscored by a passage of high rhetoric:

> But how suddenly does the...desert of our exhausted [Alexandrian] culture change on being touched by the Dionysiac wand! A tempest seizes everything that has outlived itself, everything decaying, broken, withered...Yes, my friends, believe with me in the Dionysiac life and the rebirth of tragedy (§20).

There follow two immensely effective alliterations, of which the first – *Leben, Leid, Lust* ('life, suffering, joy') – is a first allusion to Act III of *Tristan und Isolde*, while the second – *Wahn, Wille, Wehe* ('illusion, will, woe') – recalls Hans Sachs' song from Act III, scene i of *Die Meistersinger*.[62]

These purple passages continue the panegyric to Dionysus to which so much of the book has already been devoted, but they are cast in an uncomfortably negative tone. We are told that the proper task of art, and of tragedy above all other arts, is 'to redeem the eye from gazing into the horrors of night and to deliver the [human] subject through the healing balm of appearance [*Schein*] from the spasms of the activated will' (§19) – yet for the moment we hear little about the delivering and the redemption, and rather more about 'the horrors of night'. At the end of §20, again, Nietzsche summons the votaries of Dionysus to 'prepare yourselves for harsh strife, but believe in the miracles of your god', where the strife sounds real enough, but the miracles hypothetical. In this preoccupation with horrors and strife there is something of a strange 'reversal', an ominous process of *Umschlagen* unnoticed by the author. In the *Self-Criticism* (§7) Nietzsche detects a nihilistic 'relish for destruction' (*Vernichtungslust*) in the book, which he repudiates as a 'romantic' response to life, recommending (convincingly or not) 'Zarathustra's laughter' instead. This is not a candid criticism. What is wrong with *these* passages, at least, is not that they are romantic, but that they are heedlessly destructive. The 'disturbing' power of Nietzsche's thinking, which adds so much to his account of Greek religion and his theory of tragedy,[63] has no such positive tendency here.

Is it really inevitable that the positive side of the 'Dionysiac life' should be so elusive? For modern man, it is 'a new form of existence, whose substance we can only divine from Hellenic analogies' (§19) – in other words (as Nietzsche makes clear at the beginning of §21), from the 'tragic age' of Aeschylus and the Persian wars. But both Aeschylean drama and the victories over Persia presuppose Apolline 'redemption': it is, indeed, explicit in §21 that the patriotic instincts (such as those shown in the Persian wars) are *wholly* Apolline. Nietzsche assumes, of course, that if we want Apollo, we must have Dionysus first. It is, nevertheless, disconcerting that the 'tragic age' should now be equated with a 'Dionysiac life', and that Nietzsche should suddenly be inviting his nobly formed readers to worship Dionysus – who is, by himself, destructive – with hardly any mention of redemptive-creative Apollo at all.

In these anti-Socratic sections there is another new emphasis. Nietzsche talks repeatedly of *German* music, *German* philosophy, and the *German* spirit, which will soon be 'renewed by the fire-magic of music' (§20). His conviction is that 'the birth of a tragic age' is synonymous with 'the German spirit finding itself again' (§19). It might be supposed that his confidence in the imminence of this new age rests partly on a tacit analogy between the Athens of the Persian wars and the Germany of 1870, but only a single equivocal sentence (in §23) points that way.[64] We recall that during the war of 1870 he had not been disposed to take much patriotic comfort from his own experiences of the battlefield; we may add that a year after the publication of *BT*, he will dismiss any idea that the military victory over France can be seen as a cultural achievement and will call it 'the defeat, indeed the extirpation, of the German spirit by the "German *Reich*"'.[65] But for the moment he allows at least a brief evocation of the 'victorious fortitude and blood-stained glory of the recent war' (§23) as a possible augury of the new dawn.

Nietzsche voices his hopes for a new beginning: when did German thinkers *not* voice such hopes? He is not presenting any kind of programme for political action. Neither here nor in any of his later writings does he show any sustained interest in politics or any sign of understanding the possible political implications – or of anticipating the possible political uses and perversions – of his own views. He is the archetypal 'non-political' man of letters; but then, from Leibnitz to Heidegger, German philosophers have often ignored 'all that is the case' in the ordinary social world in order to concentrate on building an alternative world in the mind instead. In later life Nietzsche may ridicule the members of this tradition as 'makers of veils' (*Schleiermacher*),[66] just as Marx and Engels will dismiss them as 'ideologists',[67] but, like Marx and Engels, Nietzsche is no stranger to their ranks, and (unlike Marx and Engels) not least in his essential innocence of the political aspect of life. And so here too he addresses his hopes not to a politically minded public, but to the few who, like himself, 'experience the burden and heaviness of existence with a deeper aversion' (§ 18), and who, as 'contemplative men' (§ 15), perhaps deplore, but certainly do nothing to diminish, their isolation from the contemporary political world.

With hindsight, however, it is difficult not to ascribe a political significance to Nietzsche's 'a-political' ideas. The 'romantic' acceptance of destruction, the readiness for 'harsh strife', the association of 'tragic' with 'German', the sense of the imminent downfall of the existing order: taken in combination and out of the context of *BT*, these anti-Socratic notions evoke a particular conservative ideology, not at first always explicit or aggressive, to which large numbers of German intellectuals contributed in the decades before 1914. It reached its apogee in Thomas Mann's *Meditations of a Non-Political Man* and Oswald Spengler's *Decline of the West*, both written in the decade of the Great War; and it was eventually appropriated by a regime only too eager to exploit the spirit of sacrifice and destruction for its own hideous ends.

This is not to say that *BT* breathes the same air as (say) Wagner's theoretical writings or the nationalistic vapourings of the numerous *fin de siècle* 'cultural philosophers' and self-appointed prophets of doom.[68] Even the 'German' element in Nietzsche's book (which he will soon view much more critically) is not a sign of nationalism so much as one of his attempts to find some concrete form – 'a habitation and a name' – for a recurrent mythopoeic dream. It *is* to say that, in a political world, it is impossible for a man of letters to remain a-political, and, in a world of 'enormous battles and transitions' (§ 15), it may be irresponsible to try.

§21

In the most influential of his books of cultural criticism, Sigmund Freud quotes from a letter in which a friend had reproached him for 'failing to appreciate the true source of religious feelings [*Religiosität*]'.[69] 'This source', Freud reports with a touch of irony, 'is said to be a special feeling which (so my friend assures me) never leaves him, the existence of which he finds confirmed by many others and feels justified in assuming exists in millions of people. It is a feeling which my friend is inclined to call "a sensation of eternity", a feeling as of something limitless and unbounded, as it were 'oceanic'... It is the source of the religious energy which is seized on by the various churches and religious systems... On the basis of this oceanic feeling alone one may call oneself religious, even though one might wish to reject every belief and every illusion.' Confessing ruefully that he does not share this emotional experience, Freud nevertheless adds a helpful definition of his own: 'a feeling of indissoluble connectedness with and participation in the totality of the external world'. In short: for 'oceanic' read 'Dionysiac'.

Nietzsche, however, does not admit any doubt about the 'reality' of this 'feeling', and what concerns him is not its place in religion, but its place in art – above all (in these late sections of the book), in music. It is here, we recall, that the latent confusion about the existence of any wholly Dionysiac art rises to the surface.[70] We can restate our earlier conclusion by noting that Nietzsche *does* believe in the 'reality' of such wholly unarticulated and unspecific art, in (that is) the Dionysiac equivalent of 'pure beauty unadulterated by anything beautiful',[71] but *also* allows, however obliquely, that no such art has ever existed, or in ordinary experience ever could exist. Such art – which must be music – is *theoretically* possible. It is Nietzsche's equivalent of a body travelling at the speed of light: if it ever happened, the consequences would be extraordinary. The body in motion would – literally – attain infinite mass: an audience exposed to the full potential force of music would – literally – 'expire in a spasmodic unharnessing of all the wings of the soul'. The most that Nietzsche can offer to exemplify this total music is (of course) the music of Wagner which affects him so potently. But even that, *as it stands*, is inadequate for the purpose. What he envisages is a more concentrated potency, and he attempts to evoke this by imagining Wagner's music *without* its obvious Apolline elements. Hence the formula: it is inconceivable that anyone could apprehend the third act of *Tristan* without the aid of word and image *and not expire*...

However extravagant it may seem, then, the formula is meant literally, and we must not let the abundance of rhetorical exaggerations in this part of the book mislead us into supposing that here is yet another hyperbole. It is quite false to claim (as one critic has claimed) that it is 'the rhetorical mode of [Nietzsche's] text' which creates 'the myth of...the "deadly" power of music', and that the whole argument 'has all the trappings of the statement made in bad faith'.[72] There is no rhetoric here, no myth, and no bad faith. There is, on the contrary, a simple syllogism: *if* the ultimate – Dionysiac – truth about the world is an unbearable revelation of suffering and pain; and *if* music is (or rather tends towards the condition of) a wholly Dionysiac art; *then* it must follow that undiluted music is (or rather tends towards the condition of being) an unbearable representation of that suffering and pain in another medium. The fact that the undiluted music of a Chopin Nocturne or the Andante of Schubert's Quintet in C major produces no such unbearable effect hardly invalidates Nietzsche's argument – even if it does make us wish that Nietzsche himself had been a little more forthcoming with the 'tends towards' and a little less with the 'is'.[73]

The place of the 'oceanic' feeling in art is determined by the imposition of Apolline form. In the case of 'musical tragedy' it is drama which imposes particularity on what would – or might – otherwise be pure, limitless emotion and as such the undoing of individuality. Nietzsche's three examples offer immediate illumination. Where 'all we seemed to perceive was a hollow sigh from the very centre of being', we now hear no more than a man's words, *öd und leer das Meer;*[74] where we seemed overwhelmed by a convulsion of undirected feeling, we now *see* a hero mortally wounded, we now *hear* his despairing cry, a commingling of longing and death; and where the jubilation of the horn had a poignancy which cut across the difference between torment and joy, we now have the jubilant Kurwenal welcoming Isolde's ship into the harbour.

This argument (it might be said) takes us to the point we had already reached by pondering the lesson of Hamlet and the insufficiency of the word (§ 17). Nietzsche now goes one step further, to complete the three-stage pattern of his thinking:

(*a*) In the beginning, unindividuated, was Dionysiac music.

(*not-a*) Imposing the distinctness of form – 'words and ideas' – upon the music is the Apolline mode of drama whose individual characters are illuminated by melodic and harmonic patterns, whereby the impression is created that it is music which explicates, individualizes and assists the portrayal of the characters and the action.

(*A*) This impression is actually only an illusion. The truth (to the extent that theoretical man can make it out) is that Apolline characters as well as Apolline distinctness of action are no more than 'externalized copies' (*veräusserlichte Abbilder* – the pejorative lies heavy on both terms) of music's own totality of undifferentiated, 'oceanic' feeling. Hence Nietzsche's triumphant but justified conclusion, that in the perfect symbiosis of music and drama 'Dionysus speaks the language of Apollo, and Apollo, at last, the language of Dionysus.'

§§ 22–23

In § 22 Nietzsche announces the rebirth of the 'aesthetic listener' and analyses – or, as so often, recreates – that listener's complex response to 'true musical tragedy'. During the course of the discussion, it becomes apparent that in addition to 'tragedy' and 'musical tragedy' there is a third tragic entity, 'tragic myth', in the foreground of Nietzsche's thoughts. And even if he is somewhat evasive about the exact distinction between these three,[75] he makes it amply clear that the mythic, like the musical, aspect of tragedy is vital to its metaphysical task: '*tragic myth* [very often in this book italics provide our only introduction to a new topic] is to be understood only as Dionysiac wisdom become image by means of Apolline artifices; it leads the world of phenomena to its limits where it denies itself and seeks to flee back again into the womb of the sole true reality.'

In § 23 the new topic is dealt with more fully, but now simply under the heading of 'myth'. The metaphysical properties of true myth are still in evidence – Nietzsche sums them up in terms of its 'timelessness' – but in the first instance his attention is given to the cultural politics of myth and, thereby, to the large question of the relation between art and the state. Whereas myth, at least 'tragic myth', belongs substantially to the Dionysiac, the state (as we learn from § 21) is a creation of the Apolline genius for individuation. Nietzsche is not concerned with the mere survival of the state, or its significance as a source of power or riches or material amenities: he is preoccupied with its cultural value. If it is to flourish as the ground from which man may reach his highest potential, if it is to be the home of the highest culture, its spiritual life must be co-extensive with its art, and its art must derive from a commonly valid mythology: 'Without myth, every culture loses its healthy natural creativeness; only a horizon bounded [*umstellt*] by myths unifies a whole cultural movement.'

In what follows we are taken through much of that 'organic' vocabulary of 'natural and national', 'myth and custom', 'unconscious metaphysics', alien influences and improper cultural and ethnic transplants, which was prefigured in the critique of Socratism in § 18 (and which will eventually become part of the vocabulary of the Wilhelmine conservative intellectual).

During this argument, Nietzsche repeatedly deplores 'the historical sense' of Socratic man, the 'critical-historical spirit' of our culture, the secularization that ensues 'when a people begins to comprehend itself historically'. It will not be long before he has decided that 'both the historical and the unhistorical [points of view] are equally necessary for the health of an individual man, a nation, and a culture',[76] but in *BT* he is insistent that the historical sense is purely destructive – notwithstanding his own reliance on it throughout the book. What the historical sense destroys is myth and the timelessness of myth, and the remedy suggested for such destruction is the creation of a new mythology, or rather (with Wagner and 'the German spirit' in mind) the *re*-creation of an old one. The section ends appropriately with another nudge to the reader, this time to heed 'the blissful luring call of the Dionysiac bird' – a 'centripetal' allusion to Act II of *Siegfried*.

The paradoxes – how does one repair 'a people's break with its unconscious metaphysics'? how does one *create* myths? – may be exasperating, but what they intimate is a profound modern need for a sanctified collectivity. There is, no doubt, a venerable archetype for this creative or recreative activity in Plato's conception of the 'noble lie' which would serve as a foundation myth for the Ideal State: if existing mythologies have been discredited (partly by Plato himself), new myths are needed; the first generation of citizens will be sceptical; their successors may believe.[77] But Plato's prescription was designed to help a utopian society at its birth. The need which *BT* articulates is one felt by an all too imperfect old world.

How profound, and how universal, this need was to become is perhaps attested most fully by the disturbed literature of the 1920s and thirties with its search for roots, for a definition of authentic culture, and for experience patterned on common myth. It is this search which characterizes writers in other respects as different as T. S. Eliot and Ezra Pound, Ernst Bertram and Theodor Haecker, Simone Weil and Jean Giono.

Nietzsche's concern for the 'German spirit' and its need for myth is by definition a nationalistic concern, and yet (quite apart from the ambiguous terms of his reference to Sedan)[78] it surely is a very odd 'nationalism' which argues that a nation's glory lies, not in power and conquest, but in the renouncing of its 'worldliness' (*Entweltlichung*) as a condition of having 'the stamp of the eternal' pressed upon its history. There is certainly nothing remotely *realpolitisch* or programmatic about any of these statements; and if the founding of the Bayreuth festival theatre four months after the publication of *BT* seemed like a realization of Nietzsche's high mythopoeic hopes, it was precisely the worldliness of the venture, as well as his increasing awareness of the sheer expediency of Wagner's 'religious' attitude, which was soon to lead to that estrangement and eventual hostility in which Wagner came to figure as the corrupter of everything genuinely 'German'. In the era of Germany's political unification, military expansion and industrial development – when the Ruhr and the Hamburg wharves, Siemens, the chemical and the rayon industries are soon to become some of the greatest industrial complexes in the world – Nietzsche's eyes are fixed on the 'deep' unworldly potentialities of the German soul. Once more his 'nationalism' appears as part of that never-ending search for a 'real' accommodation of an 'ideal' existential project; and 'German' comes to mean what it meant to Hölderlin:[79] a word that would tie the writer's soul to a piece of the earth, to prevent it being consumed by a disembodied 'longing for eternity'.

Our conclusion may be expressed as a three-stage argument like one of Nietzsche's own:

(*a*) Nietzsche's theory of myth, set as it is in his own 'timeless' m... terminology, seems at first to point us to the cal... 'eternal' truths of aesthetics.

(*not-a*) Seen in the context of its age, however, the th... notoriously modern malaise. A troubled awareness of ... deprivations of mass civilization is silenced by dithyran... for an undefined, but mythologically enriched, commu... and *by* which (though not *for* which) the individual ca...

(*A*) But at bottom the problem of 'the individual and the co... for Nietzsche at least, more than a temporal matter. It is ma... concern – more recently tricked out with various comp... Heidegger's conception of *Angst* – at discovering that his tr... and destination are in the unbounded oneness of an anonym... indifferent universe, in relation to which his individuality is n... than an error and a regrettable exception.

Nietzsche's assessment of life is prefigured by at least one of his heroes of the Presocratic age. Take an aesthetic theory designed to promote a national rebirth and an aggressive-sounding nationalism whose end purpose is a tragic philosophy of life. Could there be anything more Heraclitean – more backward-looking *and* less conservative, more modern *and* more archaic – than this impertinent rejection of the commonly accepted categories of that world of 'perpetual becoming' which we call 'empirical reality' (§4)?

§§ 24–25

'Dionysus speaks the language of Apollo, and Apollo, at last, the language of Dionysus': that formula for tragedy was offered in §21, but in the same section Nietzsche also assured us that 'in the overall effect of tragedy the Dionysiac predominates once again'. The two statements are not incompatible, but there is an apparent difference of emphasis between them. As Nietzsche brings his book to its close, this question of emphasis takes on a new interest.

In §24 Nietzsche reasserts that 'the Dionysiac, with its primordial joy sensed even in pain, is the common birthplace of music and tragic myth'. In our response to tragedy (again he alternates between the designations 'tragic myth' and 'tragedy') and in our response to music, there is a 'striving for the infinite' which points to the Dionysiac basis of both arts. All this is familiar. But at this late stage in the book he suddenly combines these now familiar ideas with a new one. The Dionysiac is the common source of music and tragic myth, and 'the joy roused by tragic myth has the same source as the joyful sensation of dissonance in music'.

Dissonance – according to one modern theorist – is 'the primary means of musical expression', at least in Western music since the Renaissance; it is 'any musical sound that must be resolved, i.e. followed by a consonance'. A consonance is 'a musical sound that needs no resolution', a sound defined by an 'effect of ending', by a 'cadential function'.[80] The essential character of dissonance, therefore, is that it evokes a need for a resolution which it cannot itself satisfy. Since it does not satisfy the need, it evokes the feeling of *pain*;[81] and since it is without resolution, it evokes *infinitude*. It is consonance, resolution, that removes the pain by imposing limits. Dissonance, therefore, is Dionysiac; consonance, Apolline.

Is this in fact what Nietzsche has in mind? Its relevance to his argument seems obvious, but the terms in which he – briefly – relates 'musical dissonance' to tragedy point a different way:

> Is it not possible that by calling the musical relation of dissonance [? = the relation between consonance and dissonance] to our aid we may, incidentally, have made the difficult problem of the tragic effect much easier? For we now understand what it means to want to see tragedy and at the same time to yearn for something beyond sight: in respect of the use of dissonance in art we would have to characterize the corresponding state by saying that we want to hear and at the same time yearn for something beyond hearing. That striving for the infinite, the wing-beat of yearning, which accompanies the highest delight at the clear perception of reality, reminds us that in both states we must recognize a Dionysiac phenomenon.

It may still be inferred that resolution is Apolline and that the sense of relief associated with resolution is an Apolline pleasure. But the real significance of the new image is now seen to lie elsewhere: it is dissonance itself that is keenly – *painfully* – pleasurable; and that painful pleasure is such as to create a longing to escape from the medium that is its source – to escape not into finite consonance, but into infinite silence. In the case of that hypothetical entity conceived of as 'pure' Dionysiac music, this longing would, no doubt, be irresistible.

It is this second reading that more fully accords with Nietzsche's theory as we have already encountered it. Even so, the ('centripetal') use of a purely musical phenomenon to characterize tragedy tends to put a new emphasis on tragedy's Dionysiac component, while the negative tone of *Dissonanz* tends to emphasize that component's destructive power. The first reading, on the other hand, would imply an exact equivalence between Dionysiac and Apolline, contrary to the supposed predominance of the Dionysiac 'in the overall effect'. On both counts, then, the range of implications which the image of dissonance carries with it exceeds the limits of Nietzsche's explicit theory, whether he realizes it or not. It seems not inappropriate that at the very last the apparent stability of a Nietzschean theory should be threatened by hints of a new 'becoming'; and not inappropriate either that this threat should come from a 'forbidden metaphor'.

The new image is followed by another, equally large in its consequences. From music and tragedy we jump, once again, to all life:

> That striving for the infinite...reminds us that in both states we must recognize a Dionysiac phenomenon: again and again it reveals to us the playful construction and destruction of the individual world as the overflow of a primordial delight. Thus the dark Heraclitus compares the world-building force to a child at play who places stones here and there, builds sandcastles and knocks them down again.

One particular implication should not pass unnoticed. The pattern, dissonance followed by its consonant resolution, is not alluded to.[82] Life is *not* like the *Oedipus at Colonus*, closing with 'tones of reconciliation from another world' (§17). The pattern is reversed: construction, *then* dissonance-destruction. In a world of perpetual becoming, is this difference significant? Is the answer perhaps that there can be no true end and thus no true resolution, simply because the process is perpetual?

The new image of dissonance thus seems to reinforce the dominance of the Dionysiac in tragedy and in the tragic universe which man inhabits. In §25 Nietzsche summons up the image again as if with this thought in mind: 'If we could imagine dissonance become man – and what else is man?...' But now comes the final reversal: 'If we could imagine dissonance become man..., this dissonance, to be able to live, would need...' – would need its resolution, its Apollo; and Nietzsche, being man, duly concludes with an image of Greece at its most resolved and its most Apolline. He exhorts his reader to let himself be carried back, if only in a dream, into an ancient Hellenic existence: to walk beneath lofty Ionic colonnades, to look up to a horizon defined by pure and noble lines, flanked by images of his transfigured shape mirrored in the shining marble; while all around him human beings are walking in solemn procession or moving delicately, speaking a language of harmonious sounds and rhythmic gestures...

The Dionysiac is not forgotten, but the dominance of the Apolline is preserved in the last commandment of all:

Sacrifice with me in the temple of both deities!

Both deities are invoked, but Dionysus is to be worshipped in an Apolline temple, in Apollo's domain, as he was at Delphi.

Apollo's temple harbours no wild ecstasies, no overwhelming powers of nature – and no cruelties or horrors such as Nietzsche's most devoted disciple conjures up for us:

The bronze door of the sanctuary stood open, and the poor fellow's knees all but gave way beneath him at what he saw inside. Two grey women, half naked, with matted hair, hanging witch-like breasts and dugs as long as fingers, were about some horrible business there between the flaming braziers. Over a bowl they were tearing a little child to pieces, tearing it with their hands in savage silence...and devouring the pieces, so that the brittle bones cracked between their teeth and the blood ran down from their foul lips...[83]

This is *not* how *BT* ends; but if man is dissonance, if all the consolations of science and art and religion really are illusory, and if this world really is so horrific that it can only be justified as an aesthetic phenomenon, surely it *should* have ended like this. Nietzsche chooses not to: like his anonymous art-deity which builds or destroys wilfully, he chooses in the end to build; should we say, wilfully?

Notes

In these notes N. = Nietzsche, and E.F.-N. = Elisabeth Förster-Nietzsche. For bibliographical abbreviations, see below, pp. 429ff.

1 Germany and Greece

1 For its earlier history, see D. E. R. George, *Deutsche Tragödientheorien vom Mittelalter bis zu Lessing: Texte und Kommentare*, Munich, 1972.
2 A characterization by N. (with our italics) of, in fact, German *philosophy*. The words come from the N. of the 1880s (*Will to Power*, 419).
3 The work that made him famous was *Gedanken über die Nachahmung der griechischen Werke in der Malerei und Bildhauerkunst*, 1755.
4 The group is Greek, but hardly 'classical' in any strict sense. It was carved in the late first century B.C. and then, or soon afterwards, brought to Rome where it was rediscovered in 1506 in the ruins of the Baths of Titus. Winckelmann saw a copy of it in Dresden; see C. Justi, *Winckelmann und sein Jahrhundert*, Leipzig, 1943, I, 490f.
5 Miss E. M. Butler's translation, from *The Tyranny of Greece over Germany*, Cambridge, 1935, p. 46; German text in J. J. Winckelmann: *Ewiges Griechentum, Auswahl aus seinen Schriften*, ed. F. Forschepiepe, Stuttgart, 1943, 21f.
6 *Faust*, I, 3238.
7 Friedrich Schlegel, *Über das Studium der griechischen Poesie*, 1795, ed. P. Hankamer, Godesberg, 1947, 222f.
8 'Denn, ihr Deutschen, auch ihr seid/Tatenarm und gedankenvoll...'
9 *Hyperion*: Hölderlin, *Sämtliche Werke*, ed. F. Beissner, Stuttgart, 1946–, III, 82.
10 *Ibid.* III, 50.
11 See e.g. R. W. Meyer, *Leibnitz and the Seventeenth Century Revolution*, Cambridge, 1952, 110 (with n. 281). A. D. Momigliano, *Studies in Historiography*, London, 1966, 1–39, dates the rise of the idea to this period, with reference to the study of the ancient world.
12 J. E. Sandys, *A History of Classical Scholarship*, III, Cambridge, 1908, 54.
13 Sandys, 60. Without disparaging Wolf's achievement, many students of the history of scholarship would now wish to give some of the credit for these developments to his predecessor Christian Gottlob Heyne (1729–1812).
14 Principles qualified, but not negated, by recent work on 'open' and 'closed' manuscript traditions.
15 Cf. U. von Wilamowitz-Moellendorff, *Erinnerungen 1848–1914*, Leipzig, 1928, 99ff.
16 Elegie, *Hermann und Dorothea*, 27f.

2 Biographical background I: Nietzsche and his early interests

1 For futher details or documentation concerning the external aspects of N.'s life, see K. Schlechta, *Nietzsche Chronik*, Munich, 1975, and C. P. Janz, *Friedrich Nietzsche*, Munich/Vienna, 1978 – (in progress).

2 All collected in *GA*² XVII. Most, but not all, of this work was done before N.'s move to Basle.

3 See *HKG* II, III, IV.

4 *HKG* II, 364ff.

5 Initially as 'extraordinary' professor. In April 1870 he was promoted to 'ordinary' (i.e. full) professor. The *Habilitationsschrift* was the dissertation required of a prospective university lecturer.

6 Letters to Gersdorff, 7 April 1866 (*KGB* I, 2, 121), and 11 April 1869 (I, 2, 386); to Rohde, Jan. 1870 (II, 1, 94); to Gersdorff, 11 March 1870 (II, 1, 105); and to Rohde again, 15 Dec. 1870 (II, 1, 165).

7 *KG* V, 1, 500.

8 *HKG* II, 55.

9 *KGB* I, 2, 61 (11 June 1865).

10 Schlechta, III, 133.

11 *KGB* I, 2, 160 (to Gersdorff, August 1866) and I, 2, 229 (to Deussen, Oct./Nov. 1867).

12 *HKG* III, 352–61.

13 See N.'s letter to Rohde of 9 Nov. 1868 (*KGB* I, 2, 342) and above, p. 30.

14 See *BT* §20.

15 *HKG* IV, 213, part of a note of 1868.

16 *KGB* I, 2, 195 (to Gersdorff, 16 Jan. 1867).

17 Schlechta, III, 51f. and 73.

18 Schlechta, III, 117f.

19 19 Oct. 1861. The letter (Schlechta, III, 95–8) is seemingly fictitious, a school-exercise.

20 See *HKG* II, 89, 114, 171f. and 220; and *ibid.* 255–61.

21 *KGB* I, 1, 239 (2 May 1863).

22 N. himself once (Schlechta, III, 135) dated his 'becoming a philologist' to the time of Ritschl's commendation of his Theognis paper – i.e. to Jan. 1866, *after* the discovery of Schopenhauer; but that 'becoming' refers to his first achievement as philologist, not to the actual decision to specialize in philology.

23 Schlechta, III, 118.

24 Schlechta, III, 151.

25 *KGB* I, 2, 209f. (to Gersdorff, 6 April 1867) and I, 2, 344 (to Rohde, 20 Nov. 1868). For N.'s later thoughts on classical scholarship, see below, p. 399, n. 93.

26 *KGB* I, 2, 275 (3/4 May 1868).

27 Letter to Gersdorff, 11 April 1869 (*KGB* I, 2, 386).

28 *HKG* V, 271.

29 Schlechta, III, 117. Our discussion of N.'s early musical activities and interests is indebted to the lucid study by F. R. Love, *Young Nietzsche and the Wagnerian Experience*, N.C., 1963. The book is ignored – perhaps because its evidence and arguments would inconveniently obstruct various of his tidy conclusions – by N.'s learned disparager, Vogel (see p. 386, n. 43 below).

30 Letter to Rohde, Dec. 1871 (*KGB* II, 1, 257).
31 Cf. Schlechta, III, 151.
32 See Love, 4–50, esp. (for Liszt) 29.
33 Cf. N.'s letter to Rohde of 9 Dec. 1868 (*KGB* I, 2, 352).
34 *Ecce Homo*, II ('Why I am so clever'), §6.
35 By Love (n. 29 above).
36 On these points see Love, 12–17 and 21–7.
37 See below, n. 48.
38 On these points see Love, 31–6. A letter to Gersdorff of Oct. 1866 (*KGB* I, 2, 174) finds 'great beauties' and positive features in *Walküre* offset by equal ugliness and shortcomings.
39 Above, p. 57.
40 *KGB* I, 2, 305f. (6 Aug. 1868).
41 *Gesammelte Aufsätze über Musik*, Leipzig, 1866.
42 *KGB* I, 2, 322 (8 Oct. 1868). In their correspondence N. and Rohde use *die Gesunden* as shorthand for the philistines of their day; so too Rohde in *Pseudo-philology* (Gründer, 68, 70: see below, p. 396, n. 16). 'Provincial' is our rendering of *Grenzbotengeist*. The word alludes to a journal called *Der Grenzbote* to which Jahn contributed highly critical articles on *Tannhäuser* and *Lohengrin* in 1853–4; both are reprinted in his *Gesammelte Aufsätze* (n. 41 above), pp. 64ff. and 112ff.
43 N. had actually used this association publicly as early as 2 July (letter to Frau Ritschl, *KGB* I, 2, 299).
44 *KGB* I, 2, 332 (27 Oct. 1868).
45 See remarks in his letters to Rohde of 8 Oct. (*KGB* I, 2, 321) and 9 Nov. (I, 2, 337f.).
46 *KGB* I, 2, 335ff. (9 Nov. 1868).
47 *KGB* I, 2, 346 (25 Nov. 1868).
48 Cf. Love 8, 16f., 86.
49 See e.g. his letter to Gersdorff of 18 Jan. 1869 (*KGB* I, 2, 364).
50 See N.'s letter to Rohde of 20 Nov. 1868 (*KGB* I, 2, 344).
51 On these points, cf. Love, 43–60.
52 Letter to Rohde, 9 Dec. 1868 (*KGB* I, 2, 352).
53 Letter to Lou Salomé, 20 July 1882 (*Nietzsche in seinen Briefen und Berichten der Zeitgenossen*, ed. A. Baeumler, Leipzig, 1932, 268): 'es war eine ganze lange *Passion;* ich finde kein anderes Wort dafür.'
54 *KGB* I, 2, 356f. (10 Jan. 1869).
55 See e.g. his letters to Rohde of 3/4 May 1868 (*KGB* I, 2, 272ff.) and 16 Jan. 1869 (I, 2, 358) and to Gersdorff, 8 Aug. 1868 (I, 2, 309).
56 *KGB* I, 2, 337 (9 Nov. 1868).

3 Biographical background II: the genesis of *The Birth of Tragedy*

1 Letter to Deussen, Feb. 1870 (*KGB* II, 1, 98).
2 Letters to Gersdorff, 28 Sept. 1869 (*KGB* II, 1, 60), and 11 Apr. 1869 (*KGB* I, 2, 386). Admittedly, though, in his letters to this particular friend, N. often showed a more formal Schopenhauerian face than elsewhere. He was most himself in his correspondence with Rohde.

3 *KGB* II, 1, 52 (3 Sept. 1869) and II, 1, 42 (17 Aug. 1869).
4 *KGB* II, 2, 44 (23 Aug. 1869).
5 Letter to Krug, 4 Aug. 1869 (*KGB* II, 1, 37).
6 *KGB* II, 1, 52 (3 Sept. 1869).
7 *Ecce Homo*, II, §5: *KG* VI, 3, 286.
8 *HKG* II, 376.
9 *Die griechischen Lyriker*. These lectures were given during the summer semester of 1869, starting at the beginning of May (*KGB* I, 2, 371 and II, 1, 7). N. had decided on them by February (*KGB* I, 2, 372 and 379). The notes are reasonably dated by the editor of *HKG* (V, 441) to the time between the appointment and the move to Basle – i.e. between January and April. For full details of Nietzsche's lectures at Basle see J. Stroux, *Nietzsches Professur in Basel*, Jena, 1925, 94ff., and C. P. Janz, *Nietzsche Studien*, 1974, 196–203.
10 See *HKG* V, 337–9.
11 *KGB* II, 1, 63 (7 Oct. 1869) and II, 1, 98 (to Deussen, Feb. 1870).
12 See *HKG* III, 116.
13 *KGB* II, 1, 63.
14 *HKG* IV, 118; IV, 210; V, 183–6.
15 First in Baumgarten's thesis *Meditationes philosophicae de nonnullis ad poema pertinentibus* §16 (1735). On Kant, see above, pp. 301f.
16 *Das griechische Musikdrama* (18 Jan.) and *Sokrates und die Tragödie* (1 Feb.) (*KG* III, 2, 1–41); the notes for these lectures are in *KG* III, 3, 5ff.
17 *KGB* II, 1, 313 (letter to Rohde, 30 April 1872) and Schlechta, III, 174.
18 *KG* III, 2, 13.
19 'Socratic rationalism': *KG* III, 2, 32. 'Terror' and 'absurdity': *KG* III, 2, 38.
20 The lectures were published shortly afterwards: see below, p. 395, n. 3.
21 The preference is implicit in the letter to Rohde (Sept. 1869) quoted above, p. 33: the representative creative figures are not (e.g.) Sophocles and Plato, but Aeschylus and Pindar.
22 Various other English equivalents have been used at one time or another, including Apollinian, Apollonian, Apollinesque, Dionysian.
23 *KG* III, 2, 36 and III, 2, 16; a preparatory note for the latter passage is extant from autumn 1869 (III, 3, 28 [70]).
24 See *KG* III, 3, 54 (*l.* 23), 62f. [12], 66 [21], 67 [25, 27], 69 (*ll.* 6f., 19–22), 70 (*l.* 5), 72 (*ll.* 1f., 17). Cf. also the plan discussed above, pp. 43f., and also p. 215 with n. 86.
25 Letter to Deussen, Feb. 1870 (*KGB* II, 1, 98f.).
26 *KGB* II, 1, 95 (15 Feb. 1870).
27 Stroux 33, 36.
28 Letters to N., shortly before 12 Feb. 1870 (*KGB* II, 2, 146) and 4 Feb. 1870 (II, 2, 137f.).
29 The first time was in her first biography: E. Förster-Nietzsche, *Das Leben Friedrich Nietzsches* II, 1, Leipzig, 1897, pp. 22 and 53. That publication postdates GA^1 IX, whose editor, Fritz Kögel, refers to such a large-scale *Griechenbuch* without any emphasis (p. 375) and only in connection with the plan 'Socrates and Instinct' of 1870 (see above, pp. 43f.). Kögel was writing in 1895 (p. 373). The editors of GA^2 IX, writing in 1903 (p. 449) *after* Elisabeth's assertion was in print, were more in line (pp. 451f.).

30 See above, pp. 41, 43f., 47–9, and the following notes to Ch. 3 below: nn. 31–2, 55, 78–81, 91, 93, 102, 104, 112, 122, 127–8.

31 *KG* III, 3, 12f. [23] (*Zur griechischen Philosophen- und Dichter-geschichte*, autumn 1869) and the plan 'Socrates and Instinct' (above, pp. 43f.). The editors of *GA*² IX (451f.) took the first of the *Altertümliche Betrachtungen* plans (n. 32 below) as relevant here, but that plan is for a miscellany, not a coherent book.

32 *KGB* II, 1, 65f. The miscellany in question corresponds to (*a*) the plan headed *Altertümliche Betrachtungen* ('Reflections on Antiquity') (*KG* III, 3, 39, autumn 1869) or (*b*) a list of topics without a heading (p. 43 [2]). There is also (*c*) another plan for a miscellany headed *Altertümliche Betrachtungen* (p. 45 [7]). List (*b*) and plan (*c*) belong to the beginning of a notebook dated 'winter 1869/70–spring 1870' in *KG* III, 3, but the notes immediately following plan (*c*) (p. 45 [8]) look very like the calculations on which N. based his remarks about lectures etc. in his letter to Ritschl.

33 *KGB* II, 2, 75f. (5 Nov. 1869).

34 Unless we count the idea N. played with during the winter of 1870–1, of adding to a tragedy–aesthetics book philological sections on Homer, language, or metre (below, p. 389, n. 81).

35 To Gersdorff, 28 Sept. 1869 (*KGB* II, 1, 60f.).

36 The three plans/lists mentioned in n. 32 above all contain relevant items.

37 By Colli and Montinari in the *Kritische Gesamtausgabe* (*KG* III, 3), superseding *GA*¹ IX and *GA*² IX (= *Musarion* III). However, the promised commentary on this material (in a *Nachbericht* for *KG* III) has not yet appeared (although we have had the use of Professor Montinari's preliminary account of N.'s manuscripts between 1869 and 1874, which he kindly sent us in 1977), nor have the volumes containing N.'s philologica, including the philological *Nachlass*, some of the contents of which are certainly relevant to the genesis of *BT* (see e.g. below, pp. 45 and 393, n. 127). For the early *Nachlass*, including philologica, up to 1869, we have *HKG* I–V (1933–40); for the philologica thereafter, we must for the time being make do with the selection in the early and defective edition *GA*² XVII–XIX (1910–13). On the inadequacies of the early editions, see M. Montinari, *The Malahat Review*, 24, 1972, 121ff.

38 *KG* III, 3, 3–400. The relevant notebooks are those numbered 1–14 in *KG* III, 3, 447.

39 In *KG* III, 3 all this manuscript material is presented with a minimum of editorial interference. By contrast, the early (and very shoddy) editions, *GA*¹ IX and *GA*² IX, offer ascriptions of items to given plans with given dates without any indication of how speculative the attributions are.

40 A list with a title or numbered sections or a word like 'Introduction' (*Einleitung*) is presumably a plan for a book; a list of topics without any of these may or may not be. Notes that clearly have no bearing on *BT* include those associated with *Homers Wettkampf* (title of a fragment written up in 1872, *KG* III, 2, 277ff.) and ascribed to 1871 (presumably *late* 1871, *KG* III, 3, 419–34).

41 For likely examples, see below, pp. 387, n. 49; 389, nn. 81, 84; 389f., n. 90. The simple distinction between dating a manuscript and dating its contents seems to have eluded those who have discussed the background of *BT* hitherto.

42 See e.g. Schlechta, III, 1383–1432; W. Kaufmann, *Nietzsche: Philosopher,*

Psychologist, Antichrist, ed. 4, Princeton, N.J., 1974, 424–58; M. Montinari, *The Malahat Review*, 24, 1972, 121–33 and C. P. Janz, *ibid.* 93–102.

43 Thus: E. Förster-Nietzsche, *Das Leben F. N.'s* II, 1 (1897), 53–64; *Der junge N.*, Leipzig, 1912, 273–86; *Wagner und N. zur Zeit ihrer Freundschaft*, Munich, 1915, 71–9; *Nietzsches Werke* (Naumann's *Taschenausgabe*), Leipzig, 1906, intro. by E. F.-N. to vol. 1. E. Newman (*The Life of Richard Wagner* IV, London, 1947 (Cambridge, 1976), 332–4), E. F. Podach (*Ein Blick in Notizbücher Nietzsches*, Heidelberg, 1963, 73–6), M. Vogel (*Apollinisch und Dionysisch*, Regensburg, 1966, 149f.) and others, all more or less following E. F.-N., attach great significance to a visit paid by N. to Tribschen in April 1871, seeing here the cause of the book's 'Wagnerization'. The most circumstantial of these accounts is one of Elisabeth's (*Wagner und N.*, 72), which runs as follows: after a holiday in Lugano (see above, p. 52) N. made a detour to Tribschen to show his new manuscript to Wagner and Cosima. During this visit he perceived that Wagner had been hoping that the new book would 'somehow serve to glorify his own art. For all my brother's enthusiasm for Wagner and his art, his scholar's conscience jibbed at the thought of combining anything so disparate in a book which at that time bore the title, *Greek Serenity* [*Griechische Heiterkeit*]. But consideration for his friend prevailed, for as soon as he returned to Basle he zealously set about revising the book, by cutting out several chapters and confining himself strictly to the problem of Greek tragedy, so as to be able to bring in the reference to Wagner's art.' This visit certainly took place (3–8 April, see Cosima Wagner, *Die Tagebücher*, 1, ed. M. Gregor-Dellin and D. Mack, Munich, 1976, 375f; Newman, IV 341; Vogel, 150), but most of the detail is either suspect or demonstrably false. The book was not at *this* time called 'Greek Serenity' (above, p. 48), but 'The Origin and End of Tragedy', as is shown by N.'s letter of 29 March to Rohde (see above, p. 51) and by an item in Cosima's *Tagebuch* for 5 April: 'Prof. N. reads to me from a work (Origin and End of Gr. Tragedy) which he wants to dedicate to R.; great joy at this.' The Wagner household may indeed have had self-centred expectations (Cosima's very next comment is: 'one sees here a very talented man imbued with R.'s ideas in an individual way'), but it is evident from the title that the book was *already* centrally concerned with tragedy – if not, by implication, with Wagner too.

44 In 1885 Elisabeth married Bernhard Förster, who committed suicide in 1889. A few years later she adopted the double surname.

45 Quoted by Kaufmann, *Nietzsche*, 4f.

46 Podach, 69.

47 E.g. pp. 108, 150 (n. 43 above), 153 (p. 395, n. 146 below). This reliance is shown even – absurdly enough – by Podach, for all his contempt for her testimony (above, n. 46).

48 E. Förster-Nietzsche, *Wagner und N.*, 72.

49 *Sokrates und der Instinkt*, *KGB* II, 1, 120 (30 April 1870). The title, with accompanying plan, is set out in N.'s notes during this period (*KG* III, 3, 79f., 'winter 1869/70–spring 1870). Earlier in the same notebook (*KG* III, 3, 66 [22]) we find an item consisting of three titles: *Die Geburt der Tragödie*, *Die Philosophen des tragischen Zeitalters*, *Über die Zukunft unserer Bildungs-*

anstalten. The third is the title of a series of public lectures which N. was to give in early 1872 (below, p. 388, n. 78). The second is virtually the title of a long unpublished work produced in 1873 (above, p. 109). The first is the short version of the eventual title of *BT* itself, on which N. settled no earlier than 1871 (see pp. 58 and 392, n. 122). Had the items in N.'s manuscripts been written in strict chronological order, the eventual title of the book would actually have been N.'s first title for it. Plainly, they were not (cf. above, p. 41). For whatever reason, this item must have been inserted in 1871 or later.

50 N.'s uncertainty of mind is confirmed by the tone of an earlier remark in the same letter: 'new ideas [*sc.* for the book] keep coming to me'.

51 *KG* III, 3, 79f. (see n. 49 above).

52 Above, p. 39.

53 *KG* III, 3, 84 [88].

54 See below, p. 393, n. 127.

55 *KG* III, 3, 71 [38] has a plan for a book in fourteen chapters, entirely on drama, ancient and modern (the modern items include opera, French tragedy, Goethe and Schiller). There is another plan in which tragedy predominantes in III, 3, 75 [53].

56 See above, pp. 48f.

57 This title seems to have no better authority than N.'s sister and the early editors. In *GA*² IX, 212–29 *Über Musik und Wort* is the title given to a compressed version of what *KG* III, 3 shows to be two separate fragments on that subject written in early 1871 (pp. 193–200 [127] and 377–87). At all events, these continuous pieces stand with a few others (*KG* III, 3, 187ff. and 300ff.) which were excluded from *BT* in 1871, but whose subject-matter is not incompatible with it.

58 *Homers Wettkampf* (above, p. 385, n. 40); for the philological work, see above, p. 16.

59 *KG* III, 3, 84 [87].

60 *KGB* II, 1, 120.

61 *Die dionysische Weltanschauung* (*KG* III, 2, 43–69). See N.'s letter to Rohde of 23 Nov. 1870 (*KGB* II, 1, 159f.). A shortened version of the essay, retitled 'The birth of tragic thought' (*Die Geburt des tragischen Gedankens*) was given to Cosima Wagner for Christmas 1870 and is dated, in manuscript, June 1870 (*KG* III, 2, 72) – on the significance of which, see above, p. 214.

62 *KGB* II, 1, 156 (10 Nov. 1870).

63 See *GA*² XVII, 291ff. The rest of the introduction was apparently devoted to Sophocles' life and, presumably, work. The lectures were given in the summer semester and therefore, doubtless, prepared in the spring (like those on Greek lyric a year earlier – cf. p. 384, n. 9, above). With reference to N.'s supposed plans for a book 'about Greece', it is significant that these lectures take in nothing outside tragedy – especially nothing of a socio-political nature. Introductory lectures on *Oedipus Rex* could easily have been made the occasion for discussing some such topics (e.g. religious ethics or the relation between the individual and the state), if N. had wanted to pursue his thoughts about them as much as his ideas on tragedy.

64 *GA*² XVII, 316f.

65 *GA*² XVII, 297.

66 'You will recall [the preface is addressed to Wagner] that it was during the period when your masterly *Festschrift* on Beethoven came into being, amid the terrors and sublimities of the war that had just [*eben*] broken out, that I collected myself for these reflections' (*KG* III, 1, 19): the war broke out in mid-July. Likewise, still more flamboyantly, from the first paragraph of the 'Attempt at a Self-Criticism' of August 1886: 'As the thunder of the battle of Wörth [6 August] was rolling over Europe,...[the author]...sat somewhere in an Alpine retreat...and wrote down his thoughts about the Greeks – the core of the...book...' (*KG* III, 1, 5). This evidently refers to 'The Dionysiac Philosophy', which was written, or finished, on holiday in the Swiss Alps (see E. Förster-Nietzsche, *Das Leben F. N.'s*, 31f.). In a letter to Brandes, 10 April 1888, N. put it more succinctly and explicitly: '*BT* was written between the summer of 1870 and the winter of 1871' (*GB* III, 1, 298).

67 29 August, 1870 (*KGB* II, 1, 138).

68 To Gersdorff, 12 Dec. 1870 (*KGB* II, 1, 160).

69 *Ecce Homo*, IV, §1: *KG* VI, 3, 308.

70 To Gersdorff, 21 June 1871 (*KGB* II, 1, 204).

71 To Gersdorff, 21 June 1871 (*KGB* II, 1, 203) and Rohde, 23 Nov. 1870 (*KGB* II, 1, 160) and 19 July 1870 (*KGB* II, 1, 130) respectively.

72 *KGB* II, 1, 144 (11 Sept. 1870). Unlike N., Wagner found some humour in the war, sufficient to inspire a pseudo-Aristophanic doggerel comedy (published anonymously) called 'A Capitulation'. N.'s more complicated attitude towards Germany was relatively recent. In 1866, for instance, after the Austro-Prussian war, his doubts about Prussia seem to have been confined to the purely practical: 'Bismarck's...policy...can be just as much cursed as worshipped, depending on how far it succeeds' (letter to Gersdorff, August 1866, *KGB* I, 2, 159). Wagner's attitudes, conversely, had been more complicated in his earlier years.

73 In a note dating from 'end of 1870 to April 1871' (*KG* III, 3, 166 [88]) N. tries to persuade himself that the Venus de Milo in the Louvre could be seen as a 'second Helen' and its capture by Germany as the 'spiritual interpretation' (*pneumatische Auslegung*) of the war. Contrast his tone on hearing the reported fate of the Louvre a few months later (p. 46 above).

74 Letter to Gersdorff, 11 March 1870 (*KGB* II, 1, 105).

75 A note of 1862.(*HKG* II, 68).

76 See above, p. 17.

77 *Die Tragödie und die Freigeister*, *KG* III, 3, 97 [1]. N. added a subtitle, 'Reflections on the ethical-political meaning of musical drama' (*Betrachtungen über die ethisch-politische Bedeutung des musikalischen Dramas*, *KG* III, 3, 101 [22], 107 [42]). This was not strictly the first plan to go so far beyond Greece: the first was the drama plan produced a year earlier (*KG* III, 3, 71); see above, p. 387, n. 55.

78 For the details of the plan, see *KG* III, 3, 107f. [43], to which pp. 130 [119], 135 [1] and 137f. [9] seem to be alternative extensions. Education was a subject which N. eventually dealt with in separate lectures 'On the Future of our Educational Institutions' (1872: *KG* III, 2, 133ff.).

79 See *KG* III, 3, 107 [41], a modified title, and 114 [75], a new set of subdivisions.

80 'Tragic Man' (*Der tragische Mensch*, *KG* III, 3, 128 [114]); 'Tragedy and Greek

Serenity' (*Die Tragödie und die griechische Heiterkeit*, p. 130 [120]); for 'Greek Serenity', see n. 81 below.

81 *Griechische Heiterkeit:* the title and various versions of the plan are set out in *KG* III, 3, 141 (*l.* 21) – 142, 147 [14–16], 156 [41], 161 [64], 171 [109], 204 [142], 217 [176]. The last note expresses the intention to add 'something philological' to the book, 'e.g. a section on metre, Homer'. That this is a gloss on the book in its 'Greek Serenity' stage is shown by the fact that beside the explicit plan on p. 142 N. added a list of three items, 'Homer. Language. Metre.' Several months later, the phrase 'Greek Serenity' is alluded to in letters from Cosima Wagner to N. (13 April 1871, *KGB* II, 2, 356; 5 June 1871, II, 2, 383), but as a slogan rather than a prospective book title. It also occurs several times in the February preface to Wagner (below, p. 391, n. 105).

82 *KG* III, 3, 141 (*l.* 22)–142.

83 *Ibid.*

84 'The Greek State' (*Der griechische Staat*) is the name assigned to § 10 in the thirty-section plan (*KG* III, 3, 142). In the older editions of the *Nachlass* the four fragments are printed as one (e.g. GA^2 IX, 144–76). In *KG* III, 3 they are printed separately: (*a*) pp. 175–8 [121], (*b*) pp. 178–84 [122], (*c*) pp. 184–7 [123], (*d*) pp. 347–63. There is a small overlap (indicating interconnection) between (*b*) and (*d*) (on pp. 178 and 363). Fragments (*a*)–(*c*) belong to a manuscript dated 'end of 1870–April 1871', fragment (*d*) to one dated 'beginning of 1871'. The latter dating follows a superscription by N. himself, 'Fragment of an expanded form of "The Birth of Tragedy", written in the first weeks of the year 1871' (*Fragment einer erweiterten Form der 'Geburt der Tragödie'*..., p. 346). That heading is obviously a retrospective addition, presumably made in 1872. In that year N. wrote up what he called 'Five prefaces to five unwritten books' as a Christmas present for Cosima Wagner (*KG* III, 2, 245ff.) One of the 'prefaces' was a modified form of (*d*), which N. now entitled *Der griechische Staat*, whence the casual use of the name for the reconstructed sequence as a whole.

85 Variously emphasized in her versions of the genesis: see the references on pp. 384, n. 29, and 386, n. 43 above.

86 In the pagination of *KG* (n. 84 above) they cover about 28 pages, as compared with the 131 of *BT* itself (*KG* III, 1, 21–152, not counting the preface or the *Self-Criticism*): the comparison is slightly artificial in that parts of the fragments were actually included in *BT* itself (below, n. 88).

87 Subsume: *KG* III, 3, 147 [14–15]. Rewrite: III, 3, 232 [8]. Omit: III, 3, 142, *ll.* 25ff., where, however, the sections may be subsumed under the second heading, 'Presuppositions of the tragic work of art', as in the plan on p. 147.

88 Notably part of the section on the mysteries (*KG* III, 3, 184–7) for *BT* § 10.

89 According to H. J. Mette, *FN: Socrates und die griechische Tragödie*, Munich, 1933, 26, 86ff., 107–9, the long fragment at *KG* III, 3, 847 ff. was for a time envisaged as following *BT* § 4.

90 The differences are in fact confined to three of these four fragments, (*a*) (*b*) (*c*) (*d*) (n. 84 above). In (*c*), the fragment on the mysteries which was eventually worked into *BT* § 10 (n. 88 above), the differences are not apparent. In the other three fragments, however, they are such as to make one wonder whether the sequence might not be a reworking of much earlier drafts, now lost. If so, the

memorandum to rewrite the sequence (above, p. 48) might refer to that earlier work, which would presumably have been done with reference to part IV of 'Socrates and Instinct' (cf. above, p. 43, and see *KG* III, 3, 80) in early 1870. There are, however, notes for various parts of the extant fragments in the front of the manuscript [7] which contains three of them, (*a*) (*b*) (*c*) (*KG* III, 3, 145ff.), and which is dated in *KG* to 'the end of 1870'.

As for the idiosyncratic features of (*a*) (*b*) (*d*), the first is negative: the general absence of the 'poetic' idiom of *BT* (see above, pp. 188–204) and especially of the terms 'Dionysiac' and 'Apolline', in contrast to *BT* as we have it, to 'The Dionysiac Philosophy' of summer 1870, and to fragment (*c*). That short piece, three pages long, has seven instances of the adjectives (e.g. 'zwei Grundtriebe des Apollinischen und des Dionysischen, *KG* III, 3, 187). Fragment (*a*), slightly shorter in length, has none. Fragment (*b*), twice as long, also has none – until its last, page-long paragraph (pp. 183f., 'Alle diese...des Demos'), which has six. Fragment (*d*), seventeen pages long, has no fewer than fifteen in its first two-and-a-half pages (to p. 349, *l*. 28), including instances like 'dionysisch–apollinische Kunstwerk' (p. 349), but none thereafter. (The names 'Dionysus' and 'Apollo' are not included in these counts.) The Dionysiac–Apolline construct is the hall-mark of all N.'s work on tragedy since the spring of 1870 (above, pp. 37f., 45). The impression given by the three fragments is that they were conceived without reference to it, and subsequently modified for inclusion in a book now inseparable from it; hence the curious fact that all the explicit instances are concentrated at the beginning of one fragment and the end of another. Moreover, all three fragments have moments when the Apolline terminology is, as it were, latent and could easily have been used, but seems to have been avoided. Examples include discussions of the political instinct and art (pp. 176–8) and individuation and Apollo himself (pp. 182f.), as well as single phrases like 'die olympischen Frauen (p. 179), 'die künstlerische Kultur' (p. 351), 'die olympische Existenz' (p. 362). Either N. was deliberately avoiding his construct, or he had originally envisaged these sections without reference to it, i.e. before he had fully evolved it. Either conclusion makes it hard to see the fragments as a viable part of the book, and the discrepancy is the more striking in that three notes – pp. 231 [6], 232 [8], 232f. [9] – attempt to subsume fragments (*a*) (*b*) (*d*) and (*c*) under the respective headings of Apolline and Dionysiac 'particulars' (*Einzelne*).

The other alien features of (*a*) (*b*) (*d*) concern their attitudes on a variety of important questions. (i) The sexual act is seen as inherently 'shameful' (p. 352); contrast *BT* §8. (ii) Primitive Christianity is given a very positive valuation (pp. 354f.); contrast N.'s mixed feelings in *BT* (above, pp. 114, 121, 287). (iii) Plato is given an amazingly high valuation, being credited with 'poetic intuition' and a 'sure hand' (pp. 362, 178), and emerging as one of 'the wisest of men' (p. 181, without irony), while his exclusive worship of the Socratic intellectual is likewise deferred to ('the genius of wisdom', p. 363); contrast *BT* §§13–14.

91 After the notes in *KG* III, 3 discussed in nn. 84–90 above, the 'Greek State' topics are hardly referred to again. The only other consequential reference is at *KG* III, 3, 217 [178] ('end of 1870–April 1871'), where 'The Greek State' and 'The Greek Mysteries' are apparently separate book titles.

92 This is implicit in the superscription discussed on p. 389, n. 84 above.
93 As early as 1868 N. had speculatively envisaged an essay on Wagner (*HKG* IV, 120), but presumably as a self-contained study. One of the 'Greek Serenity' plans also envisages a preface to Wagner (cf. below, n. 105).
94 *KGB* II, 1, 165f. (15 Dec. 1870).
95 To Gersdorff, 12 Dec. 1870 (*KGB* II, 1, 162).
96 *KGB* II, 1, 174–7, addressed to W. Vischer-Bilfinger, a fellow-Professor of Greek and head of the cantonal education department, who had supported N.'s original appointment there.
97 Above, p. 16.
98 See *KGB* I, 2, 269, 274, 289f., 318.
99 Above, p. 35.
100 Stroux, 36.
101 It was not until 1881, for instance, that he looked at Spinoza: see his letter to Overbeck of 30 July 1881 (Schlechta III, 1171f.). To the end of his conscious life he saw European history either through the eyes of Presocratic Greece or through those of eighteenth- and nineteenth-century Europe.
102 *KGB* II, 1, 189f. (29 March 1871). During the winter N. also toyed with the idea of a book on aesthetics as a whole (see *KG* III, 3, 221 [197]).
103 The title is recorded in the *Nachlass*, *KG* III, 3, 175, as well as in Cosima Wagner's *Tagebücher* (p. 386, n. 43 above).
104 The details are uncertain, because apart from the specification of a preface to Wagner, there is no plan attached to the title on its single occurrence in the *Nachlass* (n. 103 above). There are, however, four closely associated plans, on which our account is based: *KG* III, 3, 164 [78] (entitled 'From Homer to Socrates', and ending with the 'Rebirth of Greek Antiquity'); p. 175 [120] (immediately after the 'Origin and End of Tragedy' plan, but entitled 'Tragedy and Dramatic Dithyramb', and ending with 'Richard Wagner'), to which p. 331 [122] is similar; p. 249 [44] (no title, ending with 'Rebirth of the dithyramb'). In GA^2 IX, 456f. the editors cite a plan beginning with 'The birth of tragic thought' and ending with 'Rebirth of Tragedy' (*Wiedergeburt der Tragödie*). There seems to be no such plan anywhere in *KG* III, 3, and one is left to conclude that the editors of GA^2 IX gratuitously conflated p. 249 [44] with one of the 'Greek Serenity' plans (p. 142, *ll.* 25ff.). (For good measure, they added two snippets from p. 204 [143], *ll.* 19f. and 22f.)
105 *Vorwort an Richard Wagner*, dated 22 Feb. 1871 (*KG* III, 3, 367–73). Newman's assertion (IV, 337–40) that N.'s preface does not suggest a book about tragedy and Wagner (but rather one about 'himself and German culture') is transparently absurd. More to the point is whether the preface was in fact written for the book at its 'Greek Serenity' stage. One of the various 'Greek Serenity' plans makes provision for a preface to Wagner (*KG* III, 3, 171 [109]), and the phrase *griechische Heiterkeit* occurs several times in the preface, but the tone of the piece is more compatible with a book ostensibly concerned with the 'end' or 'goal' of tragedy and part-oriented towards modern culture.
106 See Love, 67–76 and (for the drama, *Empedokles*) *KG* III, 3, 243–7.
107 And so does not require any of Elisabeth Förster-Nietzsche's *ad hoc* explanations apparently invented to justify her brother's 'change of plan' (see p. 386, n. 43, above).

108 See Love, 63–5.

109 See his depressed letter to Rohde of 10 April 1871 (*KGB* II, 1, 192f.).

110 Even before the result of his application was known, he had put it to Rohde that even the chair of philosophy only attracted him 'for your sake' (*KGB* II, 1, 191: 29 March 1871), but the remark smacks of hyperbole *ad hominem*.

111 Specifically, the final part will have been far from finished: see n. 122 below. This aspect of the genesis remains obscure, because there is no certainty about the plan for that part anyway (see p. 391, n. 104 above), and because most of the copious material in *KG* III, 3 (about three hundred pages of which belong to some part of 1871) cannot be dated with any precision.

112 The letter survives only in a draft: *KGB* II, 1, 193f. (20 April 1871). For the plan in the *Nachlass*, see *KG* III, 3, 296–300.

113 See J. M. Stein, *Richard Wagner and the Synthesis of the Arts*, Detroit, Mich., 1960, 149ff.

114 *Briefwechsel zwischen Wagner und Liszt*[4], ed. E. Kloss, Leipzig, 1919, II, 43. The 'English critic' was John Oxenford, in an article entitled 'Iconoclasm in German Philosophy', which appeared in *The Westminster Review* of April 1853, pp. 388–407.

115 *Die Welt als Wille und Vorstellung*, trans. based on that by E. F. J. Payne, New York, 1969, I, 260.

116 One of Wagner's more honest comments on *Opera and Drama* is reported by Cosima (*Tagebücher* I, 490: 11 Feb. 1872): 'I know what N. didn't like in it, it's also what...made Schopenhauer hostile to me: what I said about language [*das Wort*]; at that time I didn't yet dare to say that music engendered drama, though in my heart I knew it.' Even here, however, Wagner's urge to vindicate himself is as strong as ever.

117 *Gesammelte Schriften* XII, 293. See above, pp. 214 and 218ff.

118 *Gesammelte Schriften* VIII, 187.

119 *Gesammelte Schriften* VIII, 195.

120 *KGB* II, 1, 156f. (10 Nov. 1870). Wagner would not have been entirely unused to a critical attitude from N.: cf. the comment in n. 116 above.

121 Cf. a remark in N.'s letter to Rohde of 9 Dec. 1868 (*KGB* I, 2, 352).

122 This is suggested by the list of Wagner topics in *KG* III, 3, 299 [40] and confirmed by two other notes, presumably from the same period: p. 330 [117], an alternative title, 'Richard Wagner and Greek Tragedy'; and p. 331 [124], presumably the corresponding list of chapters. N. was still eager to experiment with titles and plans. We find 'Opera and Greek Tragedy' (p. 281 [1]); 'The Birth of Tragedy from Music' (p. 281 [2]); the eventual title, 'The Birth of Tragedy from the Spirit of Music' (p. 281 [3]); 'Tragedy and Music' (p. 306 [51]); 'Greek Tragedy and Opera' (p. 322 [95] = 326 [108]?). Besides these, there is a plan with opera near the beginning, but no overt sign of Wagner (pp. 290f. [16]), and another 'Birth of Tragedy' plan, the beginning of which looks to a new tragic age, while the end considers the philologists of the present (p. 293 [27]).

As N. was only able to send Engelmann the first part of 'Music and Tragedy' (p. 53 above), and as there is no trace of a continuous draft for the 'whole last part', it may be inferred that much of that part was never written (i.e. except for the parts used for the later sections of *BT* and the parts later discarded: see p. 44 with n. 57). The same conclusion may be assumed (*a fortiori*) for the Wagnerian part of 'The Origin and End of Tragedy'. However, it is certain (*pace* e.g. Newman IV, 335) that some of the 'whole last part' of 'Music and Tragedy' was written, not only because of the existence of the discarded 'music and words' fragments, but also because N.'s letter to Engelmann mentions the impact that some of the passages in that 'last part' had already made on his friends (*KGB* II, 1, 194). In fact, the first – few – relevant notes on Wagner (*KG* III, 3, 238f.) date from the winter of 1870–1, to judge from their context: they are set out in a notebook shortly after a series of 'Greek Serenity' notes (pp. 229–35) and shortly before a series of 'Empedocles' notes (pp. 243ff.), both of which belong to the winter of 1870–1 (above, pp. 48 and 52, n. 106). However, most of the notes on Wagner and associated modern topics in *KG* III, 3 (scattered over pp. 283–96, 315–43, 391–400) seem to belong to the spring, summer or autumn of 1871.

123 *KG* III, 2, 64–9.

124 Cf. above, p. 44. The editors of *GA*² IX (p. 460) contrived to see the deletion of these generally undistinguished pieces of theorizing as a *sacrifizio dell' intelletto* – in deference (one is left to gather) to Wagner, presumably on the grounds that they discussed music without simply aping or adulating Wagner's own ideas: cf. *GA*¹ IX, 378.

125 See N.'s letters to Engelmann in that month, *KGB* II, 1, 200 and 205f.

126 *Sokrates und die griechische Tragödie* (*KG* III, 2, 93–132); cf. N.'s letters to Rohde (one of its recipients), 7 June and mid-July 1871 (*KGB* II, 1, 197 and 211).

127 See his letter to Rohde of 4 Aug. 1871 ('...wenn die ganze Schrift zusammenhängend vorliegt...', *KGB* II, 1, 215). In this period N.'s propensity for devising alternative plans seems at last to come to an end. In *KG* III, 3, 343 we find a sketch for a book on Aeschylus, but not one relatable to *BT* at all. The editors of *GA*² IX (pp. 459f.) assigned to this period a two-part plan from the *Nachlass* of N.'s philologica (therefore not in *KG* III, 3), of which part I deals with tragedy (without the name) and part II with metrics. This must rather belong to the winter of 1870–1. That was the time when N. toyed with the idea of adding a section on metrics to his book (p. 389, n. 81 above). It was also a time when he lectured on, and thought hard about, metre and rhythm (see Stroux 96; N.'s letter to Fuchs, July 1877, Schlechta, III, 1137; and above, p. 33): the lecture notes are set out in *GA*² XVIII, 269ff.

128 See N.'s letter to Deussen, 16 Oct. 1871 (*KGB* II, 1, 231). The full title first appears in N.'s notes early in 1871 (*KG* III, 3, 281 [3]; see above, p. 392, n. 122 and cf. pp. 386f., n. 49) and reappears later (p. 419 [1]).

129 See the letter from Fritzsch of that date (*KGB* II, 2, 455f.).

130 See Fritzsch's letter of 16 Nov. (*KGB* II, 2, 455f.) and N.'s reply of 18 Nov. (II, 1, 241); also n. 134 below.

131 See N.'s letters to Fritzsch of 27 Nov. (*KGB* II, 1, 250) and to Gersdorff of 14 Dec. (II, 1, 254). The preface is dated by N. himself to 'end of year 1871' (*KG* III, 1, 20).

132 See his letters to Wagner of 18 Nov. (*KGB* II, 1, 245f.) and to Rohde of 23

Nov. (II, 1, 248). In that month N. is on record as having borrowed books on both subjects from Basle University Library (Max Oehler, *N.'s Bibliothek*, Weimar, 1942, 50). He was also heavily committed to other academic work during this period (cf. *KGB* II, 1, 250).

133 *GA*[1] IX, 376; E. Förster-Nietzsche, *Das Leben F. N.'s* II, 1, 64.

134 It is not possible to infer from N.'s notebooks when the last part of the book was composed, except that most of it will have been later than April 1871 (above, pp. 392, n. 111, and 392f., n. 122). The idea that it was all done as a late afterthought doubtless commended itself to his sister (under whose authority the first editors worked) for the reasons discussed above, pp. 41f. In a letter of 3 Dec. to his mother and sister (*KGB* II, 1, 250) N. mentions the need to 'complete' (*abschliessen*) the book, but nothing can be inferred from this beyond the revision that we know of. In a letter to Rohde shortly before Christmas, N. writes: 'the entire last part, which you do not know, will certainly astonish you' (*KGB* II, 1, 256). This again tells us nothing new: all that Rohde had seen was §§8–15 ('Socrates and Greek Tragedy'), which was finished earliest anyway. The bearing on this question of Mette's remarks about the development of *BT* (*FN: Socr. und die gr. Trag.* 107–9) is unclear. The general thrust of Mette's argument is that §§16 (*sic*)–25 were the last to be composed, but his concluding paragraph (p. 109), though not pellucid, appears to suppose that *BT* was indeed submitted to Engelmann in more or less its eventual form – i.e. that §§16–25 (*vel sim.*) were composed in or by April 1871, and §§1–15 completed (*vel sim.*) somewhat earlier.

135 Cf. pp. 392f., n. 122 above.

136 In all N.'s many later comments in writing on *BT* or (especially) on Wagner, there is no hint of any major late addition to the book, although he would have had reason enough to mention it after his estrangement with Wagner and repudiation of the book's Wagnerian aspect (see above, pp. 111–25), when he went out of his way to make large criticisms of the book's form and content (above, pp. 18ff.). The only relevent comments, for what they are worth, point, the other way. A letter to Brandes of 10 April 1888 says (Schlechta, III, 1284) that the book was written 'between the summer of 1870 and the winter of 1871', but immediately adds, 'finished in Lugano', i.e. in March–April; while N.'s *Selbstkritik* of 1886 assures us (§ 1) that he 'finished the final draft' in 'that month of profoundest suspense when the peace treaty was being debated at Versailles' and he himself was convalescing, i.e. (again) March–April.

There has, in general, been too much in the way of glib assumptions about which parts of *BT* were written when. The difficulties involved in dating specified parts of the book are illustrated in miniature by the partial reappearance at the end of *BT* §17 (*KG* III, 1, 111) of a sentence from a note of early 1869 (?) (*HKG* v, 269), 'Die Wissenschaft...erkannt zu werden'.

137 Letter to Gersdorff, 18 Nov. 1871 (*KGB* II, 1, 244).

138 One of the most respected German publishing houses in the field of classical scholarship, now associated particularly with scholarly editions of classical texts.

139 Letter to Rohde, 23 Nov. 1871 (*KGB* II, 1, 248).

140 Letter of 4 Aug. 1871 (*KGB* II, 1, 215).

141 See n. 134 above.

142 *KGB* II, 1, 256.

143 *Ibid.*
144 Above, p. 39.
145 The book was in fact thus nicknamed in the Wagner household: see Wagner's letter to N., *KGB* II, 2, 146 (Feb. 1870).
146 'Heavy clouds' is *Contristationen*, a nonce-form derived from the Latin 'contristare', whose predominant classical use is of cloudy weather. This remark has been unwarrantably taken to imply that N. reluctantly suppressed material in deference to Wagner – that the 'task', in fact, was an embarrassment to him (so e.g. E. Förster-Nietzsche, *Wagner und N.*, 78, and Vogel, 153). There is no evidence for any such 'reluctance' or indeed for any large scale 'suppression' (see above, pp. 42f.). The real implication is that the 'task' – the task of dispassionate appraisal – was so great that N. hardly knew how to fulfil it, as the continuation of the letter (not quoted by Förster-Nietzsche or Vogel) shows.
147 Letter to Rohde, 4 Feb. 1872 (*KGB* II, 1, 288f.).

4 The argument of *The Birth of Tragedy*

1 Above, p. 109.
2 See Schiller's letter to Goethe, 18 March 1796, and a note on Klopstock in his *Über naïve und sentimentalische Dichtung* (1795), ed. O. Walzel, *Sämtliche Werke*, Stuttgart and Berlin, 1905, XII, 209.
3 A. W. von Schlegel's *Vorlesungen über dramatische Kunst und Literatur* (1816²), ed. G. V. Amoretti, Bonn and Leipzig, 1923, I, 54f.
4 Hegel's *Ästhetik*, ed. F. Bassenge, Berlin, 1955, 1083f.
5 E.g. in his preface to *The Bride of Messina* (1803).
6 'Epic poet' is the least misleading translation of *der Rhapsode*, which strictly refers to the professional reciter of epic poetry, who might also be its composer. W. Kaufmann (*FN, The Birth of Tragedy and the Case of Wagner*, New York, 1967, 64) and others translate the word opaquely as 'rhapsodist'.
7 Athenaeus, *Deipnosophistae*, I. 22a.
8 E.g. in the Demeter ode, *Helen*, 1301–68.
9 N.'s words for 'be an artist' are *treibe Musik*, which by itself means 'practise music' and is generally, but unintelligently, taken in some such way. In fact, *Musik* has a wider sense here, the sense of the Greek word from which it derives and which, in this context, it evokes: *mousikē*. This word usually means poetry sung to music (as so much of Greek poetry was) or music in particular, but also the arts in general. In a famous passage from Plato's *Phaedo* (60c–61b), which is N.'s source for this anecdote, Socrates is told, *mousikēn poiei kai ergazou* ('make and practise *mousikē*'), and his belated compositions are described generally as *poiēmata* ('poetry') and specifically as a *prooimion* (say, 'hymn') to Apollo and some versified Aesopian fables (*mūthous*). N.'s own description, which is virtually a literal translation of Plato ('...dichtet er ein Proömium auf Apollo und bringt einige äsopische Fabeln in Verse'), should have made it obvious in any case that this *Musik* is not 'music' in our limited sense, but something wider that includes, above all, poetry.
10 See *Eine Duplik* from Lessing's controversy with Goeze (*Gesammelte Werke*, Berlin and Weimar, 1968, VIII, 27).
11 The German word *Wissenschaft* would not normally be thought of as an

equivalent to 'philosophy', but in *BT* might be said to *include* philosophy, at least in its logical and epistemological aspects (cf. especially § 18). N. has perhaps been influenced by the wide range of the Greek word *epistēmē* (derived from *epistasthai* = German *wissen*.)

12 Goethe, *Generalbeichte* (1802).

13 In *Über naïve und sentimentalische Dichtung*, *Sämtliche Werke*, XII, 201f.

14 See above, pp. 27, 248. N. is also thinking of Hanslick's *Vom Musikalisch-Schönen*, Leipzig, 1854.

15 From N.'s formulation of the point, one might suppose the 'fashionable' view was that drama was the body and music the soul, but a parallel passage in § 19 proves the contrary. The source of the notion seems to be the *Discourse on Ancient Music and Singing* by Giovanni de' Bardi (*c.* 1580): 'just as the soul is nobler than the body, so the words are nobler than the counterpoint [i.e. the music]' (O. Strunk, *Source Readings in Music History*, New York, 1950, 295). Bardi was at the centre of the Florentine 'Camerata' responsible for the invention of opera (cf. above, p. 240), and N. quotes his discussion in a note of 1871 (*KG* III, 3, 283). Whether N. had any basis for suggesting that the notion was still current, let alone a cliché (in § 21 he attributes it to 'our aestheticians', 'unsere Ästhetiker'), is doubtful.

16 See above, pp. 307–9, 302f., 298f.

5 The aftermath

1 *KGB* II, 1, 271f.

2 23 Nov. 1871, *KGB* II, 1, 248.

3 Edited by Zarncke; see letter from Rohde to N., 27 Nov. 1871, *KGB* II, 2, 466.

4 *KGB* II, 2, 493 (Wagner) and 510 (Cosima).

5 Cosima Wagner, *Tagebücher* I, 476–8 (3–7 Jan.).

6 *Tagebücher* I, 477. For a similarly revealing comment on Rohde's published review, see *Tagebücher* I, 525 (26 May).

7 See the letter from Liszt to N., *KGB* II, 2, 557f. (29 Feb.), and the reaction of Malwida von Meysenbug quoted in E. F.-N., *Das Leben F. Ns* II, 72.

8 Letter to N., *KGB* II, 2, 525 (29 Jan.).

9 *Tagebücher* I, 482 (18 Jan.).

10 *KGB* II, 1, 279.

11 *KGB* II, 1, 281f.

12 *HKB* III, 461.

13 *KGB* II, 1, 279 (28 Jan.).

14 Letter to N., *KGB* II, 2, 541–3 (14 Feb.).

15 See his letter to Rohde of mid-Feb. (*KGB* II, 1, 295).

16 See Rohde's letters to N., 9 and 29 Jan. (*KGB* II, 2, 502, 524f.). The text of this and the other central contributions to the controversy over the book is readily available in *Der Streit um Nietzsches "Geburt der Tragödie"*, ed. K. Gründer, Hildesheim, 1969. Much of the other relevant documentary evidence is cited, with or without misinterpretation, in Vogel's *Apollinisch und Dionysisch* of 1966, since when some new material has been published: correspondence between N. and Wagner, in *Archiv für Musikwissenschaft*, 1970, 173ff.; and

between N. and Rohde in *Nietzsche Studien* 1976, 321ff. The whole N. correspondence is meanwhile appearing in *KGB*, the latest relevant volumes of which go as far as May 1872.

17 Letter to Gersdorff, *KGB* II, 1, 286f.
18 *KGB* II, 1, 293f. (mid-Feb.).
19 Above, p. 53.
20 Letter to Rohde, 25 Oct., *HKB* III, 303.
21 *KGB* II, 1, 294 (mid-Feb.).
22 Above, p. 53 (Engelmann); p. 51 (Rohde); p. 92 (Ritschl); letter to Malwida von Meysenbug, *HKB* III, 313 (7 Nov.).
23 *KGB* II, 1, 293 (mid-Feb.). It seems also to be implicit in N.'s remarks to Rohde on June 18 (*HKB* III, 250–2) that *BT* was addressed to their fellow-classicists.
24 Cosima Wagner, *Tagebücher* I, 507 (3 April); letter from N. to Fritzsch, *KGB* II, 1, 312 (29 April); the review is reprinted in *HKB* III, 470f..
25 See N.'s letter to Fritzsch, *KGB* II, 1, 310 (April).
26 On 26 May; text in Gründer, 15ff.
27 Gründer, 25.
28 Text in Gründer, 27ff. In a note of 1869 (*KG* III, 3, 40, *l.* 1) N. actually invokes 'Philologie der...Zukunft' himself.
29 Quotations: Gründer, 31, 32, 55.
30 See his letters to Gersdorff, 3 June (*HKB*, III, 245f.), and 10 June (*HKB* III, 248); and to Rohde, 8 June (*HKB* III, 246f.).
31 See N.'s letters to Rohde, 8 June (*HKB* III, 247) and 18 June (III, 251).
32 For Wagner's initiative, see Cosima's *Tagebücher* I, 533 (10 June). The letter is reprinted in Gründer, 57ff.
33 Gründer, 60.
34 Newman IV, 369. Cf. N.'s remarks to Rohde about Ritschl, 16 July (*HKB* III, 260).
35 Above, pp. 38 and 91f.
36 See N.'s letters to Rohde, 18 June and 16 July (*HKB* III, 251f., 260–2).
37 See N.'s letter to Rohde, 16 July (*HKB* III, 259f.).
38 Text in Gründer, 65ff.
39 Letter from N. to Rohde, 18 June (*HKB* III, 251f.).
40 *Ibid.*
41 *Ibid.*
42 Gründer, 72.
43 Gründer, 73–5.
44 *Antike und Abendland*, 1954, 14.
45 *Journal of Roman Studies*, 1948, 29.
46 See *Greek, Roman, and Byzantine Studies*, 1974, 362.
47 *Ibid.*, 361f.
48 '*Greek Historical Writing*' *and* '*Apollo*', tr. Gilbert Murray, Oxford, 1908, 25.
49 *Human, All Too Human*, II, 126.
50 See Otto Crusius, *Erwin Rohde, ein biographischer Versuch*, Tübingen, 1902, 65 and 175.
51 Crusius, 62.
52 Crusius, 58 and 237.

53 See above, pp. 129f.
54 U. von Wilamowitz-Moellendorff, *In wieweit befriedigen die Schlüsse der erhaltenem griechischen Trauerspiele?*, ed. W. M. Calder III, Leiden, 1974, 3–7.
55 See respectively Gründer, 54, referring to N.'s recent lectures on Aeschylus, and 33, 'da kann man nur den Schulknaben des Pastors von Laublingen citieren.' N. reserved his own abuse about Wilamowitz for letters to his friends (e.g. to Krug, 24 July 1872, *KGB* II, 3, 30).
56 Gründer, 36.
57 See above, pp. 163f.
58 Letter to Rohde, Oct. 25 (*HKB* III, 301).
59 See N.'s letters to Wagner, mid-Nov. 1872 (*HKB* III, 322) and Rohde, 25 Oct. (*HKB* III, 303).
60 For Ribbeck, see Rohde's letter to N., 1 Aug. 1871 (*KGB* II, 2, 406); his essay was *Anfänge und Entwickelung des Dionysoscultus in Attika*, Kiel, 1869. For Leutsch: N. to Rohde, 25 Oct. 1872 (*HKB* III, 302). For Burckhardt: N. to Rohde, mid-Feb. 1872 (*KGB* II, 1, 293f.); his *Griechische Kulturgeschichte* was published posthumously, 1898–1902. For Bernays: Crusius, 58 and K. Gründer, 'Jacob Bernays und der Streit um die Katharsis', in *Epirrhosis* (*Festgabe für Carl Schmitt*), ed. H. Barion et al., Berlin, 1968, 520f., and cf. below, p. 415, n. 97. Bernays' monograph was *Grundzüge der verlorenen Abhandlung des Aristoteles über Wirkung der Tragödie*, Breslau, 1857.
61 25 Oct. 1872 (*HKB* III, 302).
62 Letter to Malwida von Meysenbug, 7 Nov. 1872 (*HKB* III, 313).
63 Mid-Nov. 1872 (*HKB* III, 320).
64 Gründer, 113ff.
65 Gründer, 135: '...sollte ich hie und da die Grenze des Erlaubten in meiner Polemik überschritten haben...'
66 Gründer, 134.
67 Letter to Rohde, 22 March 1873 (*HKB* III, 366).
68 Letter to Gersdorff, 13 Dec. 1875 (*HKB* IV, 249).
69 See Stroux, 97ff. It was in fact at the *Pädagogium*, rather than at the University proper, that N.'s success in these years was most marked: see Janz, I, 518ff.
70 *Bursian's Jahresbericht* for 1873, I, 613–20, reviewing N.'s *Der Florentinische Tractat über Homer und Hesiod*, published as two articles in *Rheinisches Museum* for 1870 and 1873 (though most of the work for both was done before N. came to Basle in 1869). The reviewer was H. Flach, then at Tübingen.
71 Cf. N.'s remarks about Wilamowitz himself in two letters to Gersdorff, 3 June and 10 June 1872 (*HKB* III, 245, 248).
72 *Homers Wettkampf* (above, p. 385, n. 40) and *Die Philosophie im tragischen Zeitalter der Griechen* (*KG* III, 2, 293ff.).
73 See a previously unpublished letter from N. to Wagner, 25 July 1872, in *Archiv für Musikwissenschaft* 1970, 178.
74 Alluded to once in *Human, All Too Human* (I, 219); once in the course of his discussion of *BT* in *Ecce Homo* (above, pp. 123ff.); and once in the third lecture *Über die Zukunft unserer Bildungsanstalten* (*KG* III, 2, 194), which was delivered in Feb. 1872 before the composition of the two Greek essays. It is specifically

discussed only once, in the ninth part of *Twilight of the Idols* ('Skirmishes of a man out of season', aph. 10). Elsewhere there are a few inexplicit allusions to the antithesis, and a few more explicit references in the *Nachlass*, including that part used by E. F.-N. for the collection entitled 'The Will to Power' (*Der Wille zur Macht*); see aphs. 798–9, 1049–50. See further above, p. 118.

75 *Wir Philologen*, *KG* IV, 1, 90ff.

76 *KG* IV, 1, 95, 165f., 197.

77 Other factors were Rohde's marriage in 1877 and a certain 'cowardice' (*Feigheit*) that he felt in the face of N.'s deteriorating physical condition (cf. a comment in his letter to E. F.-N., 28 March 1894, first published by H. Däuble, *Nietzsche Studien*, 1976, 347).

78 25 April 1877 (*HKB* IV, 339). Cf. Karl Jaspers, *Nietzsche*[2], Berlin, 1947, 91–117.

79 Most fully, if not most reliably, by Ernest Newman in *The Life of Richard Wagner*, volume IV; a useful corrective is provided by R. W. Gutman, *Richard Wagner*, London, 1968, 426–509; see also F. R. Love, *Nietzsche Studien*, 1977, 154–94, and Janz, I, 699ff.

80 Above, p. 90.

81 Letter to Gersdorff, 1 May (*KGB* II, 1, 317).

82 See e.g. Cosima's *Tagebücher* for 3 Jan. 1872 (I, 476), 2–3 Jan. 1873 (I, 623), 9 Apr. 1874 (I, 810f.).

83 *Ibid.* 28 Sept. 1873 (I, 733).

84 See e.g. *Tagebücher* I, 595f. (9–10 Nov. 1872) for Cosima's sleepless night on hearing that N. had no student enrolments.

85 Newman, 326. The Wagner household, however, had always suspected that N. could not be 'theirs alone': cf. Cosima's comment on 3 Aug. 1871 (*Tagebücher*, I, 424) on N.'s reserved manner, which she interpreted as self-defence against Wagner's forcefulness.

86 *Tagebücher* for 11 July 1876 (I, 994).

87 Letter to Rohde, 11 April (*KGB* II, 1, 304f.).

88 *Ecce Homo*, II, §5.

89 Above, p. 386, n. 44.

90 As is evident from the tone of various comments about 'Freund Nietzsche' in Cosima's *Tagebücher:* 2 Nov. 1876 (I, 1012), 13 Oct. 1877 (I, 1077), 23 Oct. 1877 (I, 1078), 2 Dec. 1877 (I, 1091). The change comes in April 1878 (II, 87–9).

91 In a letter to von Seydlitz, 4 Jan. 1878 (Schlechta, 3, 1146f.).

92 See above, n. 90.

93 Letter to Malwida von Meysenbug, 13 March 1885 (Schlechta, III, 1230). For the 'eccentricity' of N.'s scholarly existence, see his letter to Fuchs, 14 Dec. 1887 (Schlechta, III, 1273). A list of references to N.'s views on scholars is given by D. S. Thatcher, *The Malahat Review*, 24, 1972, 43, n. 44.

94 Letter to Gast, 19 Feb. 1883 (Schlechta, III, 1201).

95 *Ibid.*

96 *Ecce Homo*, II, §6 and a letter to Gast, 21 Jan. 1887 (Schlechta, III, 1249). On N.'s continuing receptivity to Wagner's music, cf. F. R. Love, *Nietzsche Studien*, 1977, 190–4.

97 Letter to E. F.-N., 3 Feb. 1882 (*GB* V, 479).

98 Letters to Overbeck, 22 Feb. 1883 (*Nietzsches Briefwechsel mit Franz Overbeck*, ed. R. Oehler and C. A. Bernoulli, Leipzig, 1916, 202), and to Malwida von Meysenbug, 14 Jan. 1880 (Schlechta III, 1161).
99 Letters to E. F.-N., 3 Feb. 1882 (*GB* v, 480) and to Lou Salomé, 20 July 1882 (Baeumler, 268).
100 *The Wagner Case*, § 5 and Preface.
101 Letter to Mathilde Maier, 15 July 1878 (Schlechta III, 1152).
102 Letter to Fuchs, 27 Dec. 1888 (Schlechta III, 1347).
103 Letter from Rohde to Overbeck; see Crusius, 150.
104 The *casus belli* was the French positivist Taine; see N.'s letters to Rohde, 21 May, 23 May, 11 Nov. 1887 (*GB* II, 580–3) and to Overbeck, 3 Feb. 1888 (Baeumler, 447). For Rohde's formula for the breach, see Crusius, 168, n. 1 and cf. Däuble, 327.
105 See especially his letter to E. F.-N., 28 March 1894, quoted by Däuble, 348.
106 Crusius, 116f.
107 'Originalität des Humbugs' was Rohde's dismissive phrase for Wilamowitz's *Antigonos von Karystos* which he reviewed in the *Litterarische Centralblatt* for 1882. Cf. R. Pfeiffer, *History of Classical Scholarship: from the Beginnings to the End of the Hellenistic Age*, Oxford, 1968, 247, n. 1.
108 *KG* IV, 3, 348 (a note of 1878). There are even a few passages in which 'the Greeks too have to be overcome' (*Gay Science*, 340) – i.e. we have to outgrow their example altogether.
109 *Twilight of the Idols*, x, § 2.
110 On N.'s various attitudes to Socrates, see most recently W. J. Dannhauser, *N.'s View of Socrates*, Cornell U. P., Ithaca, N. Y., 1974, and cf. above, pp. 360ff.
111 See above, p. 246 with n. 37.
112 See above, pp. 125, 226, 331.
113 Notably *Gay Science*, 370; *Will to Power*, 91. See also below, p. 294 with n. 138.
114 See above, p. 114, and cf. p. 287. In N.'s notes of 1870–1 Christianity is in fact specifically described as Dionysiac (*KG* III, 3, 122 and 147).
115 *KG* VI, 3, 307ff.
116 Though nothing on the scale of one of N.'s last letters (to Gast, 22 Dec. 1888, *GB* IV, 434), where reinterpretation has reached the stage of uncritical euphoria: 'Now I am absolutely convinced that they are all successful productions from start to finish – and that one and all they aim at the same object. Yesterday I read *BT*: it is something indescribable, deep, subtle and happy...'
117 The *Ecce Homo* comment on Christianity in *BT* concludes: 'there is one allusion to Christian priests as "a vicious kind of dwarfs"'. This is also wrong. The 'dwarfs' (§ 24) are, if anything very specifiable, Socratic optimists.
118 Cornford, 111. His reasons for admiring *BT* are not necessarily the right ones; see above, p. 144.
119 See Crusius, 160, 167–9; Däuble, 347.
120 'Welch herrlicher Mensch und wie eine neue Offenbarung menschlichen Wesens war damals der arme Nietzsche!', from a letter by Rohde to Overbeck in 1890 (Crusius, 175).
121 Although he was against publication in the end (Däuble, 348f.).
122 Crusius, 169f., 57, 152.

123 Crusius, 183–6 and above, p. 246 with n. 37.
124 *Psyche*[2] (Tübingen, 1897), Ch. VIII ('Der thrakische Dionysosdienst'), §3; translation based on that by W. B. Hillis, London/New York, 1925 (pp. 260f.).
125 The material, though not quite the nub, of the two reasons is given by Crusius, 188f. (cf. 160, 176ff.) and Däuble, 333f. respectively.
126 *Psyche*, Ch. IX ('Dionysische Religion in Griechenland').
127 Part of a letter to E. F.-N. quoted by Däuble, 350, shows beyond doubt that Rohde shrank from publicity above all else.
128 Walter Kaufmann, introduction to translation of *BT*, p. 6.
129 For German literature, see B. Hillebrand, *Nietzsche und die Literatur*, Tübingen, 1978; for English, P. Bridgwater, *Nietzsche in Anglo Saxony*, Leicester, 1972 and D. S. Thatcher, *Nietzsche in England, 1890–1914*, Toronto, 1970.
130 *RE*, 6A 2075. The writer was Konrat Ziegler.
131 Translation based on that by G. C. Richards (U. von Wilamowitz-Moellendorff, *My Recollections*, London, 1930, 150–2), from *Erinnerungen* 128–30.
132 In *BT* §19. See above, p. 104.
133 See above, p. 218.
134 *The Idea of Progress in Classical Antiquity*, Baltimore, Md., 1967, 87.
135 Snell, *The Discovery of the Mind*, trans. T. G. Rosenmeyer, Harvard, 1953, 121; Jaeger, *Paideia*[2], Berlin, 1935, I, 340; Else, *The Origin and Early Form of Greek Tragedy*, Cambridge, Mass., 1965, 10.
136 In *Studies in N. and the Classical Tradition*, ed. J. C. O'Flaherty, T. F. Sellner and R. M. Helm, Chapel Hill, Univ. of N. Carolina, 1976, 9.

6 Nietzsche's account of Greece

1 See Hugh Lloyd-Jones in O'Flaherty, 1.
2 See above, pp. 130f., and Lloyd-Jones in O'Flaherty, 6–13. To the discussion and references given there, one might add that the young N.'s philological standing is confirmed by the academic offers made to him: in 1866 Dindorf invited him to work on an Aeschylus lexicon (*KGB* I, 2, 153 and 157), and in early 1872, before *BT* was properly known, Susemihl sounded him out about a possible transfer to the chair at Greifswald (*KGB* II, 1, 277f.; II, 2, 513). Even as a purely textual critic, N. is not entirely forgotten: see e.g. R. Führer, *Nachrichten der Akademie der Wissenschaften in Göttingen* I, 1976, 4. 115.
3 Ed. Fraenkel, *Aeschylus, Agamemnon*, Oxford, 1950, I, 60.
4 See above, pp. 106, 160, 163, 175, 267, and below, p. 402, n. 13, and cf. Crusius, 60.
5 Satyrs: see the passage quoted above, p. 149, and cf. Wilamowitz in Gründer, 46. Pindar: above, p. 152.
6 See p. 138. This is one of a number of instances in which the notes or earlier studies for *BT* are in fact more detailed or more accurate. Cf. below, pp. 402, n. 11, 403, n. 16, 404, n. 47, 408, n. 113, and above, p. 280.
7 See p. 160.
8 Lloyd-Jones in O'Flaherty, 8.
9 It is not clear what lies behind the blithe plurality of 'sculptures, gems, etc.', but N. appears to be thinking specifically of a double herm that he discusses

briefly in the notes for his lectures on Greek lyric poetry in 1869 (*HKG* v, 312f.): 'Archilochus...mit Homer zusammen dargestellt auf einer Doppelherme des Vatikan[ischen] Museums.' The note goes on to quote F. G. Welcker's description of the piece (*Kleine Schriften*, I, 73). The ascription to Archilochus, however, is not Welcker's, but Visconti's in 1808. G. M. A. Richter (*The Portraits of the Greeks*, Brussels, 1965, I, 68) comments: 'The head in a double herm in the Galleria Geografica, Vatican, coupled with Homer, was identified as Archilochus by Visconti (*Ic. gr.* I, pp. 80ff. [a mistake for 8ff.]...), but is today recognised to be Aeschylus.' The fact is that Archilochus portraits in any medium are very rare, and from early Greece quite unknown. It is actually only in recent years that evidence has come to light of one dating back even as far as the fourth century B.C. (see Richter, *Greek Portraits IV*, Brussels, 1962, 22f.). A generation ago, K. Schefold (*Die Bildnisse der antiken Dichter, Redner und Denker*, Basle, 1943) knew of no earlier instance than a first-century B.C. coin of Paros, depicting Archilochus on one side and – interestingly – Dionysus on the other (pp. 138, 172f., 195). One point of interest about Visconti's ascription is that opposite his representation of the alleged 'Archiloque et Homère' he added a note explaining the association of the two poets in remarkably proto-Nietzschean terms: whereas Homer had invented epic, Archilochus was regarded by antiquity as the father of lyric, and though 'il n'a pas, à la vérité, été l'inventeur de la poésie dramatique,...il en a été regardé comme la première source' for a variety of reasons, including his exercises in choral lyric. Whether N. would have known Visconti at first hand, however, is unclear.

10 *Dithyramb Tragedy and Comedy* (A. W. Pickard-Cambridge), rev. Webster, Oxford, 1962, 10. Archilochus' literal Dionysiac connection is attested by the coin cited in n. 9 above. For Archilochus and the dithyramb, see above, pp. 151ff., 138f., 141ff. Apropos Dionysus' cult, we should mention that, for better or worse, the concept of 'fertility deity' is at present out of fashion among social anthropologists. Readers familiar with contemporary anthropology will note that in discussing N.'s categories, we make no attempt to invoke those currently in vogue: it remains to be shown that structuralist insights supersede, rather than simply bypass, earlier terms of reference.

11 As is evident from the discussion of Greek music in his lecture on 'Greek Music Drama' (1870); cf. n. 16 below.

12 Much of the scholarly writing on Greek music veers excessively towards the later Greek theorists and their mathematical preoccupations. There is a lucid account of various less mathematical aspects in W. D. Anderson, *Ethos and Education in Greek Music*, Cambridge, Mass., 1966. See further T. J. Mathieson, *A Bibliography of Sources for the Study of Ancient Greek Music*, Hackensack, N.J., 1974.

13 Wilamowitz (Gründer, 38–40, 123–5) attacked N. for implying a musical origin for these genres. In fact, such an origin is now widely assumed for both, and for the historic period we have evidence of both musical accompaniment and singing of elegy (M. L. West, *Studies in Greek Elegy and Iambus*, Berlin, 1974, 5–19).

14 Pratinas (*fr.* I. 6–8 Page *PMG*) in the fifth century, Plato (*Rep.* 398c–d) in the

fourth. Cf. above, p. 243. In a note of 1871 (*KG* III, 3, 335 [134]) N. denies the relevance of the Pratinas passage.

15 See Anderson, 135, 251, 269.

16 As N. knew perfectly well: *KG* III, 2, 16 and 20 ('Greek Music Drama', 1870), and III, 3, 17 (a corresponding note from 1869). There has been a long-standing theory that a limited exploitation of 'different tones' *was* practised and that this was associated with Archilochus. N. might have had this theory in mind (cf. his notes from 1869, *HKG* V, 314, 335). Were it not for this, one might suppose that when he writes *Harmonie*, 'harmony', he is thinking of Greek *harmonia* ('mode', see p. 139), just as his *Musik* in § 14 means *mousikē*, not 'music' (above, p. 194.).

17 See Pickard-Cambridge-Webster, 32 and above, p. 143.

18 There is perhaps a trace of this idea in Proclus, *Chrestomathia* 48–9 Severyns, where we are offered a surprising contrast between the 'simplicity' of dithyrambic diction and the language of the nome (cf. Severyns' comments, pp. 154–6, 159).

19 Anderson, *Ethos and Education*, provides a comprehensive discussion.

20 Most explicit in ps.-Plutarch, *De Musica*, 8, but apparently already presupposed by Ion of Chios (*fr.* 32 West) in the fifth century.

21 Aristotle, *Politics* 1290a. The principle is perhaps implicit in Plato, *Laches* 188d, where the Dorian is pronounced (though not by Socrates) the only Greek mode – which would seem to presuppose a classification into Greek and barbarian.

22 Phrygian for the dithyramb: Aristotle, *Politics* 1340b. 4–5, 1342a. 32–b. 3. Dorian for the nome: Proclus, *Chrestomathia*, 44 Severyns. Mixolydian for tragedy: Aristoxenus, *fr.* 81 Wehrli. Other modes for tragedy: ps.-Plutarch, *De Musica*, 17; C. Lord, *Hermes*, 1977, 175–9. According to Aristoxenus (*fr.* 79 Wehrli), Sophocles was the first tragedian to use the Phrygian. On music in tragedy as a whole, see A. W. Pickard-Cambridge, *The Dramatic Festivals of Athens*², rev. J. Gould and D. M. Lewis, Oxford, 1968, 156–67 and 257–62, and more recently M. Pintacuda, *La musica nella tragedia greca*, Cefalù, 1978.

23 For which see H. Schönewolf, *Der jungattische Dithyrambos*, Giessen, 1938; Pickard-Cambridge–Webster, 38–58; and for a succinct summary, *OCD*² 711.

24 On this point see Anderson, 49–53.

25 Pickard-Cambridge–Webster, 51.

26 Vogel, 37–40, 360.

27 See the discussions of earlier work in Else, 9–31; Pickard-Cambridge, 87–218 *passim;* C. Del grande, *Tragoidia*, Naples, 1952, 255–89; F. R. Adrados, *Fiesta, Comedia y Tragedia*, Barcelona, 1972, 21–77; H. Patzer, *Die Anfänge der griechischen Tragödie*, Wiesbaden, 1962, 39–88; A. Lesky, *Die tragische Dichtung der Hellenen*³, Göttingen, 1972, 17–48.

28 Else, 9f.

29 *Ouden pros ton Dionuson.* See Pickard-Cambridge–Webster, 124–6.

30 Pickard-Cambridge, 87–220, esp. 218f. (except that he [p. 87], like most scholars until recent years, assumed an earlier date for Aeschylus' *Suppliants*).

31 On Ridgeway see Pickard-Cambridge, 174–85 and on Murray, 185–208.

32 Else, 10.

33 Though cf. Pickard-Cambridge–Webster, 34.

34 The quasi-dramatic form of Bacchylides' dithyramb xviii (*Theseus*), which dates from the mid-fifth century, is more likely to reflect the influence of contemporary drama than some primeval tradition.

35 Pickard-Cambridge–Webster, 128. On Dionysiac religion in Mycenean Greece, see above, p. 163.

36 Pickard-Cambridge–Webster, 60–129, summarized on 129–31.

37 Above, p. 126. For Jane Harrison's 'discipleship' to N., see *Themis* (ed. 2, Cambridge, 1927), viii and cf. 476.

38 Pickard-Cambridge, 186f. (= Jane Harrison, *Themis*, 342f.).

39 Cf. e.g. E. R. Dodds, *The Greeks and the Irrational*, Berkeley, 1951, 66f., 271f.

40 G. M. Sifakis, *Parabasis and Animal Choruses*, London, 1971, 7–14 denies that impersonation in Greek drama involved identification on the actors' (or the spectators') part with the characters they impersonate. Plato, among others, would have been pleasantly surprised to hear it: cf. *Ion* 535, *Republic* 395–6 etc.

41 Kranz (*Stasimon*, Berlin, 1933, 25) in fact affirmed the importance of the principle for all Greek drama, comedy as well.

42 J. W. Donaldson, *The Theatre of the Greeks*, ed. 7, London, 1860, 6f. and 35f.

43 Donaldson, 23f.

44 J. A. Davison, *From Archilochus to Pindar* (published posthumously, London, 1968), 1–27; W. Schadewaldt, *Wege zu Aischylos* (ed. H. Hommel), Darmstadt, 1974, I, 104ff.; W. Burkert, *Greek, Roman and Byzantine Studies*, 1966, 87ff.; F. R. Adrados, *Fiesta, Comedia, y Tragedia*, 1972; O. Szemerényi, *Hermes*, 1975, 300ff.

45 Else, 9f.

46 See e.g. W. F. Otto, *Theophania*, Hamburg, 1956, 116.

47 See further, pp. 176f. Contrast a note of 1869 (*KG* III, 3, 27), where N. essays a derivation of tragedy from the mysteries *as opposed to* the dithyramb.

48 Else, 15f.

49 *Gründer* 32, 46f. On satyrs and Sileni see the *OCD*² article *s.v.*; Pickard-Cambridge–Webster, 113–18; M. P. Nilsson, *Geschichte der griechischen Religion* I³, Munich, 1967, 232–5. One notorious problem concerning the creatures, especially the satyrs, is whether they were originally horse or goat demons – the point being that *tragōidia* (tragedy) has generally been etymologized to mean 'goat-song'. On this, compare and contrast Pickard-Cambridge–Webster, 114f.; Burkert, *GRBS*, 1966, 90f.; Lesky, *Trag. Dicht. Hell.*³, 33f. In *BT* N. takes them to be goats.

50 *OCD*² *loc. cit.*

51 *BT* § 13; Plato, *Apol.* 21a–b (cf. Xenophon, *Apol.* 14). The later form of the oracle is numbered 420 in H. W. Parke and D. E. W. Wormell, *The Delphic Oracle*, vol. II (*The Oracular Responses*), Oxford, 1956, and is classified by the editors as a fabrication from the period between 300 and 190 B.C. For the Wilamowitz–Rohde argument on the point, see Gründer, 49, 101, 129f.

52 See M. L. West, *Classical Quarterly*, 1973, 179ff.

53 Formally: Dio Chrysostom, 33. 11; *Anth. Pal.* 11. 20 (Antipater); Philostratus, *Vit. Soph.* 27. 10. Less formally, Heráclitus, *fr.* 42; Aristotle, *Rhetoric*, 2. 23. 11; Cicero, *De Finibus*, 2. 115.

54 As is particularly clear towards the end (Schlechta III, 170–2). Much of the lecture is concerned precisely with the status of the traditional equation between 'Homer' and 'epic'.

55 Gründer, 37.

56 As in *fr.* 31 Lobel–Page; cf. D. L. Page, *Sappho and Alcaeus*, Oxford, 1955, 26–8.

57 Gründer, 49f. On the question of Socratic influence on Euripides, see the references in Stanford's note on Aristophanes, *Frogs* (London, 1958), *v.* 149.

58 In O'Flaherty, 9. For a summary of the links between the two men, see T. B. L. Webster, *The Tragedies of Euripides*, London, 1967, 25–8, and cf. above, pp. 260f.

59 Thuc. 1. 22. 1.

60 See M. R. Lefkowitz, 'Pindar's Lives', in *Classica et Iberica* Festschrift for J. M.-F. Marique, ed. P. T. Brannan, Worcester, Mass. 1975, 73.

61 G. S. Kirk, *The Nature of Greek Myths*, Harmondsworth, 1974, Ch. 12, especially pp. 279ff.

62 *Republic*, 607b. The earliest attested use of *philosophia* or related words is in Heraclitus, *fr.* 35 (the adjective, *philosophos*, which Pythagoras too is said to have used: see LSJ *s.v.* I. 1; W. K. C. Guthrie, *A History of Greek Philosophy* I, Cambridge, 1962, 204; W. Burkert, *Hermes*, 1960, 159ff.; C. J. de Vogel, *Pythagoras and Early Pythagoreanism*, Assen, 1966, 96–102).

63 Cicero, *De Divin.* 2. 117. Contrast Dodds *GI*, 75.

64 Dodds *GI*, 243f. In full, Dodds writes, 'no one except a few intellectuals' – which under the circumstances is perhaps not the ideal turn of phrase.

65 Above, p. 132.

66 See M. Robertson, *A History of Greek Art*, Cambridge, 1975, I, 128.

67 Gründer, 47.

68 Dodds *GI*, 103ff. Cf. Bernard Knox (reviewing G. Devereux, *Dreams in Greek Tragedy*) in the *Times Literary Supplement*, 10 Dec. 1976, 1534f. and A. H. M. Kessels, *Studies in the Dream in Greek Literature*, Utrecht, 1978, 157ff.

69 Lloyd-Jones, 160. In a note of 1869/70 (*KG* III, 3, 72 [42]) N. makes the central point about immanence himself.

70 *Pythian* 3. 61f.

71 *Acharnians* 665–702.

72 Along with his friends Burckhardt and Rohde. Cf. J. C. Opstelten, *Sophocles and Greek Pessimism*, Amsterdam, 1952, 7 and Lloyd-Jones in O'Flaherty, 9f.

73 Gründer, 35f.

74 On Dionysiac worship in Mycenaean Greece cf. above, p. 144.

75 *HKB* III, 260f. (16 July 1872).

76 In O'Flaherty, 9f. It is worth noting that N.'s interesting thoughts on Greek religion are virtually restricted to *BT*. His lectures on the subject in 1875–6 (GA^2 XIX, 1–124) are, by comparison, tame and conventional (cf. Otto Gruppe, *Geschichte der klassischen Mythologie und Religionsgeschichte*, Leipzig, 1921, [published as a supplement volume to W. H. Roscher, *Ausführliches Lexicon der griechischen und römischen Mythologie*], 226) – a reminder that by the mid-seventies N.'s philosophical thinking and his classical studies were two separate things (cf. above, p. 110).

77 Lloyd-Jones, 156f.

78 The orgiasm interpretation is now widely accepted. Among the most vocal

dissenters in recent times has been Karl Kerényi (e.g. in *Dionysos, Archetypal Image of Indestructible Life*, tr. R. Manheim, London, 1976, 138).

79 Nilsson, *Geschichte* I, 611.

80 Cf. above, pp. 126ff.

81 See W. K. C. Guthrie, *The Greeks and their Gods*, London, 1950, 106–8.

82 See e.g. *OCD*[2] s.v.

83 Above, p. 130.

84 On Apollo in general see Nilsson, *Geschichte* I, 205ff., Guthrie *GG*, 73ff., 145ff., 183ff.; further references in *OCD*[2] and *Kl.P. s.v.*

85 Aeschylus, *Prometheus* 22. The sun-Apollo equation may go back in some form to the sixth century and the Orphics. See J. Diggle, *Euripides, Phaethon*, Cambridge, 1970, 147 and in general G. S. Farnell, *The Cults of the Greek States* IV, Oxford, 1907, 136ff., 316f. There *was* a general tendency in the early Greek poetic world for Olympians as a whole to be bright/white as opposed to the dark/black chthonians (see E. Irwin, *Colour Terms in Greek Poetry*, Toronto, 1974, Ch. 4, especially pp. 178, 182–7), but not such as to associate any single Olympian, or even the Olympians as a whole, with the sun.

86 *Iliad* I. 9–52.

87 Guthrie *GG*, 73.

88 In *Hermes*, 1903, 575ff. and *Der Glaube der Hellenen* I, Berlin, 1931, 324ff. More recently W. Burkert (*Rheinisches Museum*, 1975, 1ff.) has traced Apollo in part to a Peloponnesian god of the assembly (*apellai*).

89 On N.'s *extra*ordinary authorizations for his extensions, see above, pp. 208f. The historical support for the three functions as they stand is as follows:

(i) Dreams. Apollo is the prophetic god, but his prophecy is not characteristically mediated through dreams, although 'tradition said, probably with truth, that the original Earth oracle at Delphi had been a dream-oracle' (Dodds *GI*, 110). In later classical times oracle-dreams were supposed to be inducible by sleeping with the god's emblem, a branch of laurel, under the pillow (on the authority of Antiphon – Dodds, 126, n. 46 – on whose identity see *id.* 132f., n. 100). The late fifth century Hippocratic treatise *On Regimen* shows how little Apollo was distinctively associated with dreams. At IV. 87 the author divides dreams into divine (predictive) and physiologically explicable, and (IV. 89) mentions prayer as one of the appropriate responses to the dream-experiences. The deities listed include Apollo – but also Athene, Hermes, Earth, Zeus *et al.*

(ii) Appearance and illusion. There is even less ancient authority for this. The most N. offers (as Wilamowitz [Gründer, 34] sarcastically pointed out) is a German pun. 'Der Schein' is both '[glimmer of] light' and 'illusion/appearance'. N.'s claim for the latter is allowed to depend on its homonymy with the former.

(iii) Visual art. In so far as Apollo is an art-deity, it is as god of music. He is not a god of visual art – sculpture or any other – even if Guthrie (above, p. 169) allows himself (ultimately under Nietzschean influence) to refer to him as such. Similarly the Muses, who are frequently associated with Apollo, have no particular connection with the visual arts. In fact, apart from the interests of Athene and Hephaestus in handicrafts, there *was* no god of visual art at all.

90 See B. C. Dietrich, *The Origins of Greek Religion*, Berlin, 1974, 116, n. 283;

Nilsson, *Geschichte* I, 863; and the discussion of J. Puhvel in *Mycenaean Studies*, ed. E. L. Bennett Jr., Madison, Wisc., 1964, 164–70.

91 *Dionusos* < * Diwos-sūnus: Szemerényi, *Journal of Hellenic Studies*, 1974, 145 and *Gnomon*, 1972, 665.

92 See above, p. 404, n. 35; Dietrich, 116f., 175f.; *Cambridge Ancient History* II, 2^3, 865f. and 887. In sum, we know that the religious experience of Mycenaean Greece included (1) the name Dionysus, (2) chthonic worship (see above, p. 183), (3) ecstatic dancing. We have no evidence of the full Dionysiac paraphernalia of omophagy, *sparagmos*, etc., but (3) does likewise indicate *possession* which is the crucial aspect of historic Dionysiac worship. There is no proof that (1) was connected with (2) and (3), though it must be more likely than not. In the volatile world of Greek religion it is always possible that a name may be in use without its 'essential' functions, or the essential functions without the name. This point may have a bearing on the Mycenaean status of an Apollo-deity. At Delphi, for instance, it is clear that there had been a cult of some kind since the Bronze Age, although no connection with 'Apollo' is demonstrable until the eighth century; see further Dietrich, 308f., 223f.

93 Above, p. 144.

94 *Iliad* VI. 264f. On the aristocratic correlation, see Dodds *GI*, 94, n. 80 and his commentary on *Bacchae* (ed. 2, 1960), *vv*. 421ff.; Dietrich, 270–5; and cf. above, pp. 173, 181. G. A. Privitera, *Dioniso in Omero e nella poesia greca arcaica*, Rome, 1970, suggests instead that there was an independent tradition of Dionysiac poetry in the epic period (so H. Jeanmaire, *Dionysos*, Paris, 1951), which was known to the poets of the Homeric tradition, but unsuited to heroic epic.

95 On Dionysus in his different guises see Dodds, *Bacchae*, xi–xxv, Nilsson, *Geschichte* I, 564ff. It is not clear whether, or how far, the different guises reflect a multiple origin (Phrygian/Thracian/pre-Greek Mediterranean/? proto-Greek), but for us the question is by the way.

96 See Dodds, *Bacchae*, xxviii–xxxvi.

97 On Corybantism see I. M. Linforth, *Univ. of Calif. Publ. in Class. Phil.* 13, 1946, 121ff. and Dodds *GI*, 77ff. The 'Corybantes' were ministers of the Phrygian mother goddess, whose rites they performed with wild music and dancing. In the sophisticated world of fifth-century Athens, the rites seem to have been sought out by those with morbid psychological conditions, from which the heightened proceedings offered a psychotherapeutic 'catharsis'. For the view that Dionysiac worship itself had once been like that, see Dodds *GI*, 76f.

98 Hesiod, *Works and Days* 614.

99 Nilsson, *Geschichte* I, 567f.

100 See Dodds, *Bacchae*, xxii on the Lenaea; on Dionysus and obscenity, J. Henderson, *The Maculate Muse*, New Haven, Conn., 1975, 13–17.

101 Plutarch, *Moralia* 365a, translated by Guthrie *GG*, 156.

102 Cf. n. 92 above and Guthrie *GG*, 30–2.

103 *Bacchae* 861.

104 Dietrich, 273f.

105 *Bacchae* 699–711.

106 Above all in C. A. Lobeck, *Aglaophamus*, Königsberg, 1829.

107 See Dodds, *Bacchae*, xiii.

108 See Gründer, 41f. and cf. *Erinnerungen*, quoted above, p. 130.

109 From Plato, *Laws* 672c–d one might suppose Dionysus *was* regarded as a deity of music, but the passage refers back to 653d where it is clearly not so: he is simply a god associated with festivals and festivity. For the late and/or limited evidence for Dionysus as a musical god in cult, cf. Roscher, I, 1082, L. R. Farnell, *Cults* v (1909), 143–9.

110 For discussion and references to further literature, see Nilsson, *Geschichte*, I, 678–99, Guthrie *GG*, 307–32.

111 A date not later than the sixth century for this Titan myth is argued for by Dodds *GI*, 155f.

112 Aristotle, *fr.* 10 sp. Rose. For Pythagoras and Orphism, cf. Dodds *GI*, 143, 149.

113 At the end of §12 there is a 'centripetal' image (above, p. 200) involving Orpheus and in §19 a passing reference to Orpheus as singer. Orphism is explicitly associated with tragedy in N.'s notes, however, e.g. *KG* III, 3, 101, *ll.* 13ff. (September 1870–January 1871).

114 *RE* v, I, 1042.

115 Cf. Rohde, *Psyche*, 419; Nilsson, *Geschichte* I, 599. For the Orphic mysteries, see Kern, *Orphicorum Fragmenta*, 1922, *testim.* 173–219 and W. Wili in *Papers from the Eranos Yearbooks* II (ed. J. Campbell), London, 1955, 77ff. In *RE* XVI, under the heading *Mysterien*, Kern provides detailed discussion of both 'die orphischen *teletai*' (1279ff.) and 'Dionysosweihen' (1290ff.). Wilamowitz (Gründer, 42) accused N. of conflating early Dionysiac worship with *post-classical*, syncretistic mystery religion; however, the charge presupposes a degree of scepticism about early Orphism and its Dionysiac character which Wilamowitz never lost (cf. *Der Glaube der Hellenen* II, 1932, 192ff., 379), but which one is not obliged to share.

116 Dodds on *Bacchae* 72–5. For mysteries of the Eleusinian type we have it on the authority of Aristotle (*fr.* 15) that initiation involved experiencing something (*pathein*), not learning anything (*mathein*).

117 For the connection, cf. Guthrie, 316–20 and Wili, 75. On 'the one and the many' see further M. C. Stokes, *One and Many in Presocratic Philosophy*, Cambridge, Mass., 1971.

118 Above, p. 147. For details of the Eleusinian ritual, see G. E. Mylonas, *Eleusis and the Eleusinian Mysteries*, Princeton, N.J., 1962, 261–72.

119 Guthrie *GG*, 202.

120 On the *thyrsus* see Dodds on *Bacchae* 113.

121 M. P. Nilsson, *A History of Greek Religion*², trans. F. J. Fielden, Oxford, 1949, 194 and 208f.

122 Aeschylus, *frr.* 82–9 Mette. Cf. the discussion in Guthrie *GG*, 314–16.

123 Cf. Guthrie *GG*, 314–18.

124 Dodds *GI*, 156.

125 In fact there is no evidence for taking the story to be as old as that, although it may be older than seemed conceivable to Wilamowitz at the time. (Fifth century at the earliest, he supposed: Gründer, 32, 120.) It has a complicated tradition (discussed most recently by M. Hubbard in *Proceedings of the Cambridge Philological Society*, 1975, 53ff.). The saying 'not to be born is best' is attested first in the sixth (?) century (Theognis 425), but probably goes back to the (? late) epic tradition (see van Groningen on Thgn. *loc. cit.*). The first literary

allusion to the story associating Midas and the trapped Silenus is by Herodotus (viii. 138), but depictions are found on black-figured vases of the sixth century (cf. J. Boardman, *Athenian Black Figure Vases*, London, 1974, 233). The story and the saying are first found together in Aristotle, *fr.* 44. N.'s own scholarly thoughts on the saying are on record in his essay on the *Contest of Homer and Hesiod* (*Rheinisches Museum*, 1870, 528ff. = GA^2 XVII, 215ff.).

126 Above, p. 165.

127 Plato, *Laws* 828c. For a concise account of the distinction, see Guthrie *GG*, 205–53.

128 Although various of Homer's uranian deities are suspected of having had a chthonic origin (Dietrich, 277f.).

129 *Cambridge Ancient History* II, 2 (ed. 3), 1975, 852f. (with 'chthonian' for 'chthonic').

130 W. den Boer, *Harvard Studies in Classical Philology*, 1973, 4.

131 Above, pp. 171, 173.

132 Above, p. 172. On the predominance of women in Dionysiac cult, see Farnell, V, 159–61.

133 J. P. Vernant, *Mythe et Pensée chez les Grecs*, Paris, 1965, 268f.

134 Dodds *GI*, 76f.

135 There is no need to discuss here Wilamowitz's attempts to undermine the chthonic–Olympian antithesis itself; cf. Guthrie, *GG* 209f., 218 and generally 205–23.

136 See e.g. Guthrie *GG*, 189–93.

137 See B. C. Dietrich, *Hermes*, 1961, 42ff.; Nilsson, *Geschichte* I, 594–8.

138 Heraclitus, *fr.* 15. See A. Lesky, *Wiener Studien*, 1936, 24ff.; cf. Dodds *GI*, 196.

139 Perhaps (in the light of the provenance of the Dionysus-rebirth myth) under Orphic influence. For the evidence and general discussion see H. Metzger, *Bulletin de Correspondance Hellénique*, 1944–5, 314–23; Pickard-Cambridge–Webster, 7, 103f.; further references in nn. 138 above, 140 below.

140 See K. Schauenburg, *Charites* (Festschrift Langlotz), Bonn, 1957, 174, n. 27.

141 The phrase is Jane Harrison's (*Themis*[1], xiii). Her notion of an undifferentiated, functionary, non-personalized 'eniautos-daimon' (to which her phrase refers) seems to have been vindicated as a meaningful formula for the *pre*historic period: see Nilsson, *Geschichte* I, 321, cf. Dietrich, 13f., 235. The assumed historical shift toward differentiation (on which cf. Guthrie in *Cambridge Ancient History*, II, 2^3, 869–71, 878) seems to evoke N.'s vision of the development from oneness to individuation, but that development is not directly to do with man's representation of deities, but his interpretation of all existence.

142 Dietrich, 276, referring to Nilsson, *Geschichte* I, 611ff.

143 *Psyche*, Chs VIII §2, IX §§3–4.

144 E.g. from Kern, *RE* V, 1017f.; W. Nestle, *Vom Mythos zum Logos*[2], Stuttgart, 1942, 60.

145 So e.g. Guthrie *GG*, 198–201.

146 Alcman, *fr.* 51 Page *PMG*. Cf. Vogel, 78f.

147 As remarked above, p. 178. One must be cautious here, because our evidence for most things is much more extensive for the fifth century than the centuries preceding, but the signs seem clear enough. The literary evidence includes: (1) Exchanges of attendants (e.g. Muses for Dionysus, Soph. *Ant.* 965). (2)

Exchanges of symbolic properties (e.g. Aesch. *fr.* 86 Mette not only gives Apollo ivy, but calls him *Bacchic*). (3) Exchanges of artistic forms (e.g. Bacchylides at Delphi writes a dithyramb [xvi] to Apollo). The new-musical switches in mode between the Apolline nome and the Dionysiac dithyramb are also relevant here (above, p. 140 with n. 24).

148 *Orat.* xxxi. 11. On syncretism, see in general Nilsson, *Geschichte* II[2] (1961), 242ff., 581ff. and cf. above, p. 215 with n. 85.

149 Plutarch, *Moralia* 388–9. For the association of the paean with Apollo, see e.g. *Iliad* I. 472; *Homeric Hymn* III. 518; Proclus, *Chrestomathia* 41 Severyns.

150 Vogel (pp. 69–93) chooses to ignore the point. Contrast e.g. Farnell, *Cults*, IV, 249.

151 These propositions are inferred from the evidence discussed above, pp. 138–40, 184 (with notes 17–22, 149), together with the following:

(1) Dionysiac and Apolline lyric are opposed by name (and associated with intoxication *versus* calm and order) from *c.* 300 B.C. (Philochorus 172 Jacoby *FGH*). The opposition between paean and dithyramb is probably implicit in Plato, *Laws* 700b, d.

(2) Aristotle, *Politics* 1340–2 presupposes an elaborate opposition between the two types: on the one side, dithyramb, 'flute', Phrygian mode, religious ecstasy; on the other, Dorian moderation and sedateness (and implicitly nome/paean and lyre). That opposition may underlie such passages as Pindar, *fr.* 67 and Euripides, *Hercules* 878f. from the fifth century.

(3) We gather from an unknown musicologist *c.* 380 B.C. that in some circles (apparently the 'harmonicist' school associated with Damon) some melodies (*melē*) were regarded as relatable to 'the laurel', others to 'the ivy' (*Hibeh Pap.* I, 13, 31f., see Anderson, 149–52, 277, n. 10). Laurel and ivy were symbols of Apollo and Dionysus respectively since the archaic period (Homeric Hymn III. 396, VII. 40; Hesiod, *Theogony* 30 [cf. West *ad loc.*]; Boardman, *Athenian Black Figure Vases*, 217f.).

152 One might expect that N.'s responsiveness to politics etc. would be shown in the 'Greek State' fragments (above, pp. 44, 48f.). Rather, the mediocrity of those pieces and N.'s willingness to put them aside (above, p. 49) testify to his fundamental lack of interest in such matters. Cf. also J. P. Stern, *A Study of Nietzsche*, Cambridge, 1979, 130, 132f.

7 Mode and originality

1 Above, p. 39.

2 Above, pp. 103, 119f.; and *KGB* II, 2, 511 (Cosima Wagner to N., 18 Jan. 1872). From Stefan George to Martin Heidegger and Gottfried Benn, the sentence, 'Sie hätte singen sollen, diese "neue Seele" – und nicht reden!', has been quoted innumerable times.

3 A. H. J. Knight, *Some Aspects of the Life and Work of Nietzsche*, Cambridge, 1933, 9.

4 Above, p. 51.

5 Above, pp. 395f. (nn. 9 and 11), 403 (n. 16).

6 '...ästhetische Abstraktionen': above, pp. 130, 168.

7 E.g. Tragedy, *HKG* II, 155–64, 364–99, IV, 118f., 210; Orphism, *HKG* IV, 10,

68, 135f., 566–95 (*passim*), v, 94f.; Homer, *HKG* iv, 9–31 and *passim*; Democritus, *HKG* iii, 246–79, 327–64 (*passim*), iv, 36–104. Cf. above, pp. 33–5 and 16, and n. 15 below.

8 *HKG* iii, 348f.

9 *KG* iii, 2, 8, 13.

10 *HKG* iv, 213.

11 Crusius, 237.

12 Kaufmann, *Nietzsche*, 395. Cf. Knight, 175: why does N. hate Socrates? – 'because (1) he disapproves of Socrates, (2) he feels that he is very like him'.

13 Above, p. 395, n. 9. In a note of late 1870/early 1871 (*KG* iii, 3, 210 [131]) N. actually identifies his artistic Socrates with Shakespeare ('Shakespeare...ist der musiktreibende Sokrates'). However, a little later (?) (*KG* iii, 3, 334 [132]), he decides that, as one would suppose, Shakespeare is Dionysiac ('ganz dionysisch') after all.

14 Above, pp. 189f. In a note of 1869 (*KG* iii, 3, 37) Socrates and Democritus are specifically compared.

15 *HKG* iv, 59; similarly iii, 348f., iv, 44, 47, 78.

16 *KGB* ii, 2, 34 (26 Aug. 1869). Cf. e.g. N. to Rohde, 3 Sept. 1869 (*KGB* ii, 1, 52).

17 N. to Lou Salomé, 16 Sept. 1882 (Schlechta, iii, 1189). On occasion N. applies the principle to his own works, sometimes in bizarre fashion, as in *Ecce Homo*, 'The Birth of Tragedy', §4, where he tells us that in *Richard Wagner in Bayreuth* 'one need not hesitate to put down my name or the word "Zarathustra", where the text has the word Wagner'. That particular self-dramatization is relatable to his final equation of himself with Dionysus (cf. above, p. 118) and its partial prefiguration in a curious fantasy of his involving himself, Wagner and Cosima, in the mythological roles of Dionysus, Theseus and Ariadne (Kaufmann, 32f., Vogel, 325–40).

18 *Will to Power*, 549, 552.

19 *Agamemnon* 41. Cf. Fraenkel *ad loc.*

20 It also tends to involve 'interaction' as defined in M. S. Silk, *Interaction in Poetic Imagery*, Cambridge, 1974.

21 Gründer, 45.

22 See F. Brommer, *RE*, *Suppl. Band* viii, 1001.

23 See W. K. C. Guthrie, *Socrates*, Cambridge, 1971, 82–4.

24 Above, p. 179.

25 See M. L. West, commentary on Hesiod, *Theogony* (Oxford, 1966), on *v*. 509.

26 Above, p. 121.

27 See Newman, iv, 260 and more recently Gutman, 23–32.

28 *KGB* ii, 2, 117 (16 Jan. 1870). Later N. used his knowledge to mock Wagner's anti-Semitism by making insinuations about his real origin: 'Was W. a German at all?...His father was an actor by the name of Geyer. A Geyer is practically an Adler' (Postscript to *The Wagner Case*). Geyer and (especially) Adler are often found as Jewish surnames.

29 On the differences between the Aristophanic, the Platonic, and the real Socrates, see Guthrie, *Socrates*. On the Dionysiac Silenus, Apollo as sun-god, and the Orphic oneness, see above, pp. 148, 169, 177.

30 On the anecdote, see above, pp. 148, 408f. (n. 125).

31 See Roscher, *Lex. Myth.* I, 1087–9; J. Noiville, *Revue de Philologie*, 1929, 245ff.

32 See the summary in S. Reinach, *L'Origine des Aryens*, Paris, 1892; and for recent discussions of the I.-E. homeland, M. Gimbutas and W. H. Goodenough in *Indo-European and Indo-Europeans*, ed. G. Cardona, H. M. Hoenigswald, and A. Senn, Philadelphia, Pa., 1970, 155–97, 253–65. The idea that Sanskrit was the mother language (*vel sim.*) itself, goes back to Friedrich Schlegel's *Über die Sprache und Weisheit der Indier* (1808).

33 *Ion* 534a.

34 Aristotle, *Poetics* §6, 1449b. 24–8 and *Politics* 1341b.32–42a.15. On Bernays see above, pp. 105, 217, and below, p. 415, n. 97. On the Aristotelian passages and the question as a whole, see J. Croissant, *Aristote et les Mystères*, Liége, 1932; Jeanmaire, 316–21; Dodds *GI*, 77ff.; F. Susemihl and R. D. Hicks, comm. on *Politics* I–V (London, 1894), pp. 641ff.; D. W. Lucas, comm. on *Poetics* (Oxford, 1968), pp. 273ff.; the bibliography in G. F. Else, *Aristotle's Poetics: The Argument* (Cambridge, Mass., 1957), 225f.; and pp. 420f., n. 86 below.

35 *Frogs* 816 and 1259.

36 *Deipnosophistae*, X. 428f. and Plutarch, *Quaest. Conv.* 715d–e; cf. other passages cited in Wilamowitz's edition of Aeschylus (Berlin, 1914), 14f. The Aeschylus-wine anecdotes may be regarded as special instances of a more general biographical *topos* that goes back to Archilochus' *auto*biographical comment cited above.

37 Pausanias I. 21. 2.

38 Above, p. 154.

39 Above, pp. 171, 181.

40 Above, p. 140. There was also a tradition, popularized by K. O. Müller (cf. Wilamowitz in Gründer, 33), that Apollo was a deity with particular Dorian connections (e.g. Müller, *Die Dorier*, 1824, II, 1, §1). On Müller and N., cf. E. Rawson, *The Spartan Tradition in European Thought*, Oxford, 1969, 322f., 329f.

41 Herodotus 2. 144.

42 Pliny, *Nat. Hist.* X. 7; Pausanias X. 5. 7; Strabo IX. 3. 5; Artemidorus, *Onirocrit.* II. 9, IV. 2 (pp. 114, 243 Pack). On the dream-book, see further F. Susemihl, *Geschichte der griechischen Litteratur in der Alexandriner Zeit*, Leipzig, 1891, I, 299–301 and *RE* VIA 2, 2236f.; D. del Corno, *Graecorum de re onirocritica scriptorum reliquiae*, Milan, 1969, 73f., 154.

43 Antisthenes, *fr.* 3 Jacoby *FGH* (508), cf. Stobaeus, *Flor.* 21. 26, Proclus, *Chrestomathia* 13, *Et. Magn.* 357. 52 (and other *testimonia* in Severyns II, 34). The idea that the hexameter was invented at Delphi (see e.g. Plutarch, *Moralia* 402d) was one that interested N. sufficiently to be still in his mind as late as 1882 when he was writing *The Gay Science* (II, 84).

44 A. S. Riginos, *Platonica: The Anecdotes Concerning the Life and Writings of Plato*, Leiden, 1976, 10, whose discussion (pp. 9–32) should be consulted for details. For N. and Diogenes Laertius, see above, p. 16.

45 *Symposium* 215a–b.

46 The Platonic Socrates on Dionysiac (*aulos*) music, *Republic* 399e; on tragedy, *Republic* 394b–398b (cf. Aristophanes, *Frogs* 1491–5); on Apolline music, *Republic* 399d–e and *Phaedo* 60c–61b; on Apolline religion, *Republic* 427b–c, *Laws* 759c, 945e–947d.

47 For Wagner's letter to Ludwig (24 Feb. 1869), see O. Strobel (ed.), *König Ludwig II und Richard Wagner: Briefwechsel*, II (Karlsruhe, 1936), 261. It is apparent from a comment in a letter to Rohde (16 July 1872, *HKB* III, 262) that N. not only knew the painting well, but actually 'had it in mind' on at least one occasion when writing the book. Vogel (pp. 142, 147) sees fit to make a song and dance about this small point. See further, above, pp. 214f.

48 See e.g. L. Curtius, *Merkur* (*Deutsche Zeitschrift für europäisches Denken*), 1947, 363ff. and n. 60 below. N.'s knowledge of the statue and its art-historical significance derived partly, at least, from Feuerbach's *Der vaticanische Apollo* (see below, p. 416, n. 99).

49 Above, pp. 169f.

50 Above, pp. 195, 207.

51 The Orphic association: above, pp. 176f. The struggle between Olympians and Titans (the Titanomachy) is first set out in detail by Hesiod, *Theogony* 617ff. (see West *ad loc.*).

52 Above, pp. 207 (with n. 40), 140, 171, 185.

53 Above, pp. 171–7. This distinction is perhaps also assisted by Aristotle's correlation between the Dorian mode and oligarchy as against the Phrygian mode and democracy (*Politics* 1290a.19–29), although N. himself is insistent on the apolitical character of the Dionysiac (§21, cf. §7 and above, pp. 181f.).

54 The voluminous discussions of N.'s precursors by Andler I³ (1920), *passim*, and II² (1921), 219–74 have not been superseded. Later attempts to underline the relevance of particular names on the list or to add to the list itself tend to make much of coincidence of views without reference to the likelihood of any borrowing on N.'s part. A representative instance is provided by H. Wagenvoort (*Mnemosyne*, 1959, 13ff.), who attempts to ascribe *BT* to the influence of the French historian Jules Michelet; contrast the sensible remarks by A. Momigliano on N.'s relationship with Burckhardt in *Essays in Ancient and Modern Historiography*, Oxford, 1977, 301 (cf. above, p. 163 with n. 72). A more important influence is that of Eduard von Hartmann's *Philosophie des Unbewussten* (cf. H. M. Wolff, *FN: Der Weg zum Nichts*, Bern, 1956, 43ff.). N.'s Greek influences are discussed erratically by Knight 13–92; his Greek *sources*, however, are nowhere systematically treated.

55 Heraclitus, *fr.* 10.

56 *A Midsummer Night's Dream* V, I. On the antithesis in antiquity, see the summary by C. O. Brink in *Horace on Poetry: The 'Ars Poetica'*, Cambridge, 1971, 394f.

57 E.g. *frr.* 54, 50. Cf. the emphasis N. puts on Heraclitus (and the terms of his discussion) in 'Philosophy in the Tragic Age of the Greeks' §§5–9.

58 Letter to Böhlendorff, 4 Dec. 1801 (*Hölderlin, Sämtliche Werke*, ed. F. Beissner, Stuttgart 1946–, VI, 426, no. 236).

59 The letter was included in the 1846 edition of Hölderlin's works (ed. C. Schwab, Stuttgart and Tübingen, II, 86–8) which N. may well have used in the early 1860s when Hölderlin was his 'favourite poet' (above, p. 22).

60 See H. Zeller, *Winckelmanns Beschreibung des Apollo im Belvedere*, Zürich, 1955.

61 Cf. Rohde's letter to N. on the 'Göttingen' Apollo, 22 April 1871 (*KGB* II, 2, 361). For a recent instance of the same, cf. above, p. 169.

62 See M. L. Baeumer in O'Flaherty, 165–89.

63 Cf. Baeumer, 171–5 and also Stern, *A Study of N.*, 180f.

64 Here rather than in the celebrated comment by Friedrich Schlegel on Sophocles, to the effect that the poet's *psyche* blended 'the divine intoxication of Dionysus, the profound resourcefulness of Athene, and the quiet reflectiveness of Apollo' (*Über das Studium der griechischen Poesie*, 133).

65 F. W. J. von Schelling, *Sämtliche Werke*, II, 4 (Stuttgart and Augsburg 1858), 25f. (trans. Baeumer, 186).

66 So, rightly, D. Jähnig, *Schelling: Die Kunst in der Philosophie*, Pfullingen, 1969, II, 157, 342. Contrast Baeumer, 186, notwithstanding his summary of Schelling's view of Apollo a page earlier.

67 So O. Kein, *Das Apollinische und Dionysische bei Nietzsche und Schelling*, Berlin, 1935, pp. 14 and 18, followed by Vogel, 96, Baeumer, 186, Jähnig, II, 342.

68 J. J. Bachofen, *Gesammelte Werke*, ed. K. Meuli (Basle, 1943–8), IV, 238f., trans. Baeumer, 187.

69 *Gesammelte Werke*, II, 59–61, trans. R. Manheim in *Myth, Religion and Mother Right, Selected Writings of J. J. Bachofen*, London, 1967, 114f. and 116.

70 See above, p. 121.

71 See Andler, II, 259, Vogel, 99.

72 Oehler, *N.'s Bibliothek*, 49, and above, pp. 53, 59f.

73 Cosima Wagner, *Tagebücher*, I, 243 (11 June 1870).

74 See Vogel, 147f., following K. von Westernhagen, *Richard Wagner*, Zürich, 1956, 145–61. The direct evidence for the discussion of Apollo and Dionysus, however, consists of the word of sister Elizabeth (*Wagner und N.*, 67f.) – i.e. it may be no more than speculation.

75 Above, pp. 37f., 45.

76 Above, p. 387, n. 61.

77 *HKB* III, 262 (16 July 1872) and Gründer, 90.

78 Cf. above, p. 56.

79 So Vogel, 95–148; Baeumer, 189; Podach, *Ein Blick in Notizbücher Nietzsches*, 72.

80 *Gesammelte Schriften*, x, 14f.

81 As even Vogel (121) admits, despite doing his best to represent the reference to Dionysus in an Apollo-context as proto-Nietzschean.

82 See Vogel, 142 and plate 41.

83 Full details in Vogel, 125–48 (with plates).

84 *Saturnalia* I. 18. 1, 'Aristoteles, qui Theologumena scripsit, Apollinem et Liberum patrem unum eundemque deum esse...asserat' ('Aristotle, author of the *Theologumena*, declares that Apollo and Father Bacchus are one and the same god'); on the precise date of Macrobius' work see Alan Cameron, *Journal of Roman Studies*, 1966, 25ff., and on the passage itself, see n. 85 below.

85 See above, p. 184. Vogel, 66f., with a certain lack of historical perspective, uses the syncretistic Macrobius passage as evidence for his contention that the Dionysus–Apollo relationship was one of affinity, not opposition, all the time. What is worse, he claims Aristotelian authority for his case by asserting in his text, 'In seinen *Saturnalien*...führte M. aus, schon Aristoteles habe gesagt...', without any indication that 'Aristoteles qui Theologumena scripsit' (n. 84

above) is *not* Aristotle, but refers to a pseudonymous work or collection from late antiquity (see W. von Christ and W. Schmid, *Geschichte der griechischen Litteratur*, I, 1[6], Munich, 1912, 768). That is, he quite properly cites the full Macrobius text in his note, but allows his readers (few of whom will be classicists) to suppose that Aristotle himself is on his side. If Vogel knew that this was not the real Aristotle, his procedure can only be called unscrupulous. If he did not know, he had no business posing as an authority on these matters in the first place. It is unfortunate, but true, that in non-classical circles Vogel's study *has* attained an authoritative status – witness, for instance, Baeumer, 165, where we are assured that in his 'philologically and historically precise investigation' (*precise* perhaps, *accurate* no) Vogel 'provides clear proof for the fact that N.'s Dionysus and his antithetic concepts "Apollonian–Dionysian" are completely un-Greek'. Vogel does no such thing, much as he would like to have done – nor, incidentally, does E. R. Dodds (as Baeumer suggests in the next sentence) support Vogel's 'rejection of the antithesis'.

86 Above, pp. 38, 45.

87 *HKG* v, 339; the formulation appears to derive from J. A. Hartung, *Die griechischen Lyriker* IV, Leipzig, 1856, 197.

88 *HKG* IV, 10 and 28. Cf. also IV, 30, where N. goes out of his way to comment on the Dionysiac–Apolline connections of the mythological figure Maro, and IV, 32–5 (immediately following the notes on epic chronology), where he has an unexpected textual comment on Aristophanes, *Thesmophoriazusae* 126ff., a passage dealing with song and Apollo.

89 As catalogued by Oehler, the eventual list takes up forty-three pages (pp. 2–44).

90 Above, p. 23.

91 *Gay Science*, III, 248 and *Ecce Homo*, II, §8.

92 Cf. above, p. 413, n. 54.

93 Above, pp. 36f.

94 'What I Owe to the Ancients', §§1–2: *KG* VI, 3, 148f.

95 Lloyd-Jones in O'Flaherty, 15.

96 *Friedrich Nietzsche und die klassische Philologie*, Gotha, 1920, 1.

97 On Lobeck and Bernays see above, pp. 407 (n. 106) and 207 (with n. 34). As the scholar responsible for establishing a link between the 'cathartic' effect of tragedy and that of the music of 'enthusiastic' ritual, Bernays, it may be said, also partially anticipated the reinterpretation of the Dionysiac aspect of tragedy (hence his reaction to *BT*: above, p. 105). N.'s debt to Bernays, however, should not be overstated (as it rather is by A. D. Momigliano, *Jacob Bernays*, Amsterdam, 1969, 17, and K. Gründer in *Epirrhosis*, 519–22). *BT* is not about *katharsis* and it is not as if N. even accepted that tragedy has a 'cathartic' effect. It is also worth noting that Bernays' book (*Aristoteles über Wirkung der Tragödie*) is one of those that N. borrowed from the Basle University Library at a late stage in his work on *BT* (May 1871: Oehler, 49) – i.e. only after much of the book, and his thoughts as a whole, were already formed; cf. pp. 213f. above and n. 98 below. However, he certainly knew and valued Bernays' interpretation of Aristotle before that: see a note of 1869–70 (*KG* III, 3, 71, *ll.* 6–9).

98 It is possible, for instance, that Creuzer may have influenced N. in respect of the association between India and Greece (above p. 206). There is no published evidence that shows that N. had read Creuzer until June 1871, when he

borrowed the third volume of the *Symbolik* from the Basle University Library (Oehler, 49). In later life he possessed a complete set of the *Symbolik* (Oehler, 10), but presumably did not at the time of the genesis of *BT*, or else there would have been no need for the borrowing. Podach, however (*Ein Blick in Notizbücher Ns*, 73), reports that N.'s (? philological) notebooks of 1869–70 contain extracts from this work among others. On Creuzer see further Sandys III, 65–7, Baeumer, 179–81, Vogel, 97f. In his later years Rohde developed an interest in Creuzer's life, the fruit of which was *Friedrich Creuzer und Karoline von Günderode* (1896).

99 *Der vaticanische Apollo* also contains a substanitial discussion of Greek drama in terms of visual representation. In January 1870 N. quoted admiringly from the book in his lecture on 'Greek Music Drama' (*KG* III, 2, 8f.). He had borrowed the book from the Basle University Library in November 1869 (Oehler, 46) – according to one hypothesis (Westernhagen, 152, followed by Vogel, 43) on Wagner's recommendation.

Apart from unwittingly assisting the Apollo-sculpture association, Feuerbach may have helped to shape N.'s Apollo–Dionysus antithesis, insofar as he puts forward tragedy as an interaction of two elements. His two, however, are sculptural-formal ('Plastik', 'Gestalt') and verbal ('Poesie', 'Wort') (p. 295), *both* of which belong on the Apolline side of N.'s antithesis. More to the point, perhaps, are Feuerbach's comments on 'Bacchic inspiration' ('die bacchische Begeisterung', pp. 300–2), which half suggest N.'s association of ecstatic possession and dramatic impersonation (esp. in *BT* §8).

One other devious classical influence on N.'s antithesis is worth noting: the classification of arts by a scholiast on the grammarian Dionysius Thrax (II. B.C.) into *praktikai* and *apotelestikai* (*Grammatici Graeci* I, iii, ed. A. Hilgard, Leipzig, 1901, 119, 122). The distinction is apparently between arts that consist in *action* (like dancing) and those that involve a *product* (like sculpture) (cf. Quintilian, II, 18, 1), but it was interpreted by the historian and theorist of Greek music R. Westphal (*Geschichte der alten und mittelalterlichen Musik* I, Breslau, 1865 and elsewhere) as a distinction between performing arts (like music) and arts which need no performer (like visual art): cf. the discussion (not entirely accurate) by W. Tatarkiewicz, *Journal of the History of Ideas*, 1963, 234–6. N. at this time was well-acquainted with Westphal's work, including the *Geschichte* (he owned a copy [Oehler, 16], and cf. his letter to Rohde, 16 July 1872, *HKB* III, 261), and in his lectures on Greek Lyric Poetry (early 1869) he employs Westphal's interpretation of the antithesis: 'Die Griechen unterschieden nämlich apotelestische und praktische Künste', specifying these as 'Orkhestik Poesie und Musik' and 'Architektur Plastik und Malerei' respectively (*HKG* V, 307). The editor of *HKG ad loc.* (V, 480) cites Westphal's *Die Metrik der Griechen* I[2] (of which N. also owned a copy [Oehler, 16] as N.'s immediate source. N. does not on this occasion refer to Westphal by name.

100 Above, pp. 126f.

101 Above, p. 130.

102 Göttingen was the centre of activities of such distinguished scholars as K. O. Müller (1819–40, above, p. 412, n. 40) and E. Curtius (1856–68), to whom Crusius (55, 2f.) refers the dictum.

103 22 April 1871 (*KGB* II, 2, 361).

104 Crusius, 54f.
105 Crusius, 221–4, numbers 7, 8, 11, 12.
106 Especially with the note on the death of tragedy (number 12), which is dated 22 June 1870 (Crusius, 224) – that is, soon after a holiday the two friends had spent together (29 May to 13 June: Schlechta, *Nietzsche Chronik*, 35) which included the visit to Tribschen, discussed above, pp. 214–6. The other notes listed in n. 105 above are not dated to the month.
107 Letter to Elisabeth Förster-Nietzsche, 16 June 1894 (Däuble, 350).
108 Above, pp. 40, 43, 111.
109 R. Wagner, *Mein Leben* I, 468f. (ed. W. Altmann, Leipzig, 1923). For Wagner as Hellenist, see W. Schadewaldt, *Hellas und Hesperien*², II, Zürich, 1970, 341ff. and H. Lloyd-Jones, *Times Literary Supplement*, 9 Jan. 1976, pp. 37–9.
110 *Gesammelte Schriften*, X, 117.
111 *Gesammelte Schriften*, X, 16 and 227 ('Geburt aus der Musik: Äschylos. Décadence–Euripides'). N.'s eventual title was also prefigured by a talk given by Wagner's brother-in-law, Oswald Marbach, in 1868 on 'the rebirth of dramatic poetry through music', which N. may conceivably have heard (Love, 54).
112 Vogel, 121–3. Cf. above, p. 32.
113 Cf. above, p. 256.
114 Above, pp. 21, 24, 33.
115 *Gesammelte Schriften*, VIII, 154.
116 Above, p. 58.
117 Newman, IV, 371.
118 Newman, IV, 707, Vogel, 119. The latter is a prime specimen of the Wagnerian bent on denying N.'s originality.
119 Letters to Wagner, 2 Jan. 1872 (*KGB* II, 1, 271f.) and 10 Nov. 1870 (II, 1, 156).
120 Letter to Gersdorff, 7 Nov. 1870 (*KGB* II, 1, 155); cf. above, p. 383, n. 2.
121 *KGB* II, 1, 270f.
122 Wagner to N., 4 Feb. 1870 (*KGB* II, 2, 137) and 10 Jan. 1872 (II, 2, 504). Cf. also Cosima's letters to N., 5 Feb. 1870 (II, 2, 138f.), 24 June 1870 (II, 2, 223), 18 June 1871 (II, 2, 389).
123 Cosima Wagner, *Tagebücher*, I, 542 (1 July 1872).
124 Above, pp. 56, 214.
125 *KGB* II, 2, 377 (28 May 1871).
126 Cosima Wagner, *Tagebücher*, I, 338 (5 Jan. 1871).
127 Above, pp. 34f., 215.
128 *HKG* II, 375–7 and II, 89, 172. See above, pp. 33, 22.
129 Cf. Love, 15–17.
130 Cf. Brown, 218.

8 Tragedy, music and aesthetics

1 Classicism and France: e.g. *Will to Power*, 849. Hostility to the theatre: e.g. *Gay Science*, 86. Convention as the condition of art: *Will to Power*, 809. Art as the cult of the untrue: *Gay Science*, 107.
2 *Human, All Too Human*, II, 171.

3 *Katharsis: Human, All Too Human* I, 212; *Gay Science*, 80; *Twilight of the Idols*, 'What I owe to the Ancients' §5; *Will to Power* 851.
4 Tragedy as action: *The Wagner Case* §9 (footnote). The Aristotelian principle is already criticized in the notes for *BT*: *KG* III, 3, 69 (1869–70), 120 (1870–1).
5 Cf. above, p. 157, and Lucas on *Poetics*, Ch. 25, 1461a.1. In a note of 1869–70 (*KG* III, 3, 78) N. himself criticizes Aristotle for sanctioning closet-drama (*Lesedrama*).
6 *BT* §§3, 4, 10 and especially 9; *Poetics*, Chs. 11, 13, 14, 15, 16, 26.
7 Cf. p. 355 above.
8 Reservations confirmed elsewhere, e.g. *Poetics*, Ch. 15, where four separate Euripidean plays (*Orestes*, *Melanippe*, *Iphigenia at Aulis* and *Medea*) are criticized on four separate grounds.
9 *Poetics*, Ch. 13 (1353a.28–30).
10 The categories are those of M. H. Abrams, *The Mirror and the Lamp*, Oxford, 1953.
11 *Preface to Lyrical Ballads.*
12 Chs. 17 and 22.
13 *Almost*, because one of the mentions of 'genius' noted above (n. 12) shows that Aristotle took at least one facet of literature to be uninducible: mastery of metaphor (Ch. 22, 1459a.5–8).
14 Above, p. 159.
15 Above, p. 125.
16 Plato, *Ion* 533d–e.
17 'The Study of Poetry', in *Essays in Criticism*, Second Series, 1898, 1f.
18 See above, p. 157.
19 See e.g. G. M. A. Grube, *The Greek and Roman Critics*, Toronto, 1965, 354f.
20 J. G. Herder, *Sämtliche Werke*, ed. B. Suphan, Berlin, 1877–1913, XV, 539.
21 Above, p. 150, cf. 163f.
22 See above, p. 148.
23 *Essay on Criticism* (1709). For the ancestry of the conceit, see D. A. Russell, '*Longinus*', *On the Sublime*, Oxford, 1964, xliif.
24 Above, pp. 40, 42f.
25 Gutman, 19.
26 Above, p. 54.
27 Translated by Charles Burney, *A General History of Music*, 1789 (second edn.), ed. F. Mercer, London, 1935, II, 515.
28 Perdita in *The Winter's Tale*, IV, iv.
29 See Love, *The Young N.*, 15–17 and *Nietzsche Studien*, 1977, 158f., and above, pp. 21f. At some point N. had, perhaps, also been influenced by K. Fortlage, *Das musikalische System der Griechen*, Leipzig, 1847, which includes a discussion of the problematic relation between word and music in the western world.
30 Above, pp. 56f.
31 See above, p. 138 with n. 14.
32 Above, pp. 140, 184f.
33 *Human, All Too Human*, II, 171. N. is opposing the formula set out in Schopenhauer's *Parerga und Paralipomena* (ed. Grisebach, Leipzig, 1891), II, xix, 218.

34 Elliott Zuckerman in the course of a useful discussion of 'Nietzsche and Music' in *Symposium*, 1974, 19.
35 Cf. W. S. Allen, *Accent and Rhythm*, Cambridge, 1973, 96–102.
36 The conclusion is correctly drawn by Zuckerman, 18f. On the place of the Dionysiac in music, see further below, pp. 378f.
37 Other important differences are that in *BT* the Dionysiac is defined by antithesis with the Apolline, later by the antithesis with Christianity (above, p. 118); and that in *BT* Dionysus (like Apollo) is essentially an art impulse, rather than, as later, a life force. The changed quality of the Dionysiac in N.'s later thinking is epitomized by the fact that he can associate Goethe with it (*Twilight of the Idols*, IX, 49): contrast pp. 357 above and 422 (n. 117) below.
38 See above, pp. 178f.
39 In a note of 1869–70 (*KG* III, 3, 69) N. in fact does say it: 'also ist der reine Dionysismus unmöglich'. Even in a case like this, however, we must beware of putting his notes on a par with his book. The book, after all, is what he finished and published, and often the notes imply positions which he abandoned while writing it: cf. e.g. below, nn. 49 and 112 (p. 422).
40 Letter to Rohde, after 21 Dec. 1871 (*KGB* II, 1, 256f.).
41 *Will to Power*, 810.
42 C. A. Bernoulli, *N. und die Schweiz*, Leipzig, 1922, 107f. The intriguing news of a few scrawled personal notes from these years (see Ronald Hayman in the *Observer* Magazine, 29 April 1979, pp. 34ff.) hardly affects the point.
43 Letter to Ludwig Senfl at Munich, 4 Oct. 1530.
44 E.g. in the Preface to *The Bride of Messina;* on Schiller, see above, pp. 301ff.
45 *The Prelude*, VII, 636.
46 On N.'s interest in musical form see F. R. Love, *Nietzsche Studien*, 1977, 158–71.
47 See above, p. 52.
48 See the discussion by F. R. Love, *Nietzsche Studien*, 1977, especially 155f.
49 Cf. above, pp. 140f., 258, 262; and for Wagner's music as 'literature', see *Will to Power*, 829. These reversals should be distinguished from what we find in (e.g.) several notes of 1871 (*KG* III, 3, 319, 341f.), where Wagner is represented as the climax of the modern idyllic-operatic tradition. This is contrary to *BT* §19, but evidently because N. is still in the process of formulating his terms of reference.
50 *Human, All Too Human*, II, 134.
51 F. R. Love, *Nietzsche Studien*, 1977, 166f., summarizing various of N.'s notes.
52 *Will to Power*, 852 (our italics).
53 *The Death of Tragedy*, London, 1961, 133.
54 Unless we take *Rhesus* to be non-Euripidean or *Prometheus* to be non-Aeschylean; recent discussions in W. Ritchie, *The Authenticity of the Rhesus of Euripides*, Cambridge, 1964 and M. Griffith, *The Authenticity of Prometheus Bound*, Cambridge, 1977.
55 Above, pp. 36f.
56 Pickard-Cambridge–Webster, 62. See, however, the sceptical comments of Griffith, 16.
57 C. J. Herington, *The Author of the Prometheus Bound*, Austin, Texas, 1970, 87; against such interpretations is the *caveat* by A. F. Garvie, *Aeschylus' Supplices:*

Play and Trilogy, Cambridge, 1969, 183–5. See also T. Gantz, *Classical Journal*, 1979, 289ff.

58 But see the comments of Griffith, 13–16, 249–52.

59 See above, p. 125.

60 This is acknowledged in a note of 1869–70 (*KG* III, 3, 81): 'Greek religion higher and deeper than all later religions...Its high point Sophocles: its goal love of *this* world (among pessimistic thinkers)' Cf. also III, 3, 335, *ll.*1f. (1871).

61 The *Seven Against Thebes*, originally the final play of an otherwise lost trilogy, is not, as it stands, overloaded with reconciliation, but its end has been extensively tampered with at a later period. Recent discussions include O. Taplin, *The Stagecraft of Aeschylus*, Oxford, 1977, 169ff. and R. D. Dawe in *Dionysiaca* (*Festschrift* for Sir Denys Page), Cambridge, 1978, 87ff.

62 John Jones, *On Aristotle and Greek Tragedy*, London, 1962.

63 Other reasons are that the concept of the hero is latent in Aristotle's *Poetics* and explicit in his pupil, Theophrastus, as Jones belatedly (p. 276) admits; and that no theorist, ancient or modern, is infallible (cf. above, p. 306).

64 B. M. W. Knox, *The Heroic Temper*, Cambridge, 1964, 1.

65 Knox, 45–50.

66 See above, n.54.

67 In *Philosophy in the Tragic Age of the Greeks*, § 19 (*KG* III, 2, 363) and implicitly in *Human, All Too Human*, I, 170, where Euripides is paired with Aeschylus.

68 *OCD*[2], 419.

69 As in the celebrated *fr.* 292 Nauck.

70 *Adv. Math.* I. 288 (*ho skēnikos philosophos*).

71 'Euripides the Irrationalist', *Classical Review*, 1929, 97ff.

72 In 'Homer's Contest' (1872) (*KG* III, 2, 277–86).

73 *Poetics*, Ch. 25; G. M. A. Grube, *The Drama of Euripides*, London, 1961, 7; Jones, 245–73.

74 Gründer, 51.

75 Parodied by Aristophanes, *Frogs* 1335f., 1352ff.; full details in W. Breitenbach, *Untersuchungen zur Sprache der Euripideischen Lyrik*, Stuttgart, 1934, 214ff.

76 Above, pp. 156ff.

77 As is shown by (e.g.) his use of 'serious' lyrics; see M. S. Silk, 'Aristophanes as a Lyric Poet', in *Yale Classical Studies*, xxvi, 1980, 99ff.

78 Above, p. 141.

79 Above, p. 28.

80 Xenophon, *Symposium* 3. 11; *Vit. Aesch.* 9, Pollux iv. 110.

81 Above, pp. 402f. (n. 14). On the general question of music in Greek tragedy, see above, pp. 140, 403 (n. 22).

82 *Ein Blick in Notizbücher Ns*, especially p. 73.

83 Gründer, 35; Dodds, *Bacchae*, xvi.

84 Plato, *Philebus* 48a; for Aristotle see n. 85 below.

85 *Poetics*, Chs. 14 (1435b.10–13), 4, 9. See further above, p. 300, and for further evidence of Aristotle's interest in the question, cf. Bywater on *Poetics*, 1448b.10.

86 Unless we identify the 'pleasure that springs from pity and fear' with *katharsis*, and like L. Golden (see *Hermes*, 1976, 437–52) interpret *katharsis* as intellectual clarification. But Golden's theory is untenable. The idea that the pleasurable

effect of tragedy is an intellectual one would certainly be an answer to Plato's question and it would square with Aristotle's other intellectualist positions. But quite apart from the total discrepancy with the parallel passage in the *Politics* (above, p. 207), 'achieving through pity and fear the clarification of such emotions' makes no sense, and Golden's attempt to interpret the phrase to mean 'achieving, through the representation of pitiful and fearful situations, the clarification of such incidents' (after Else, *Transactions of the American Philological Association*, 1962, 58) is at odds with the Greek. (It is also at odds with a post-Aristotelian discussion of *katharsis* in *Pap. Herc.* 1581, on which see M. L. Nardelli, *Cronache Ercolanesi*, 1978, 96ff.)

87 *Antigone*, 332–75.

88 N.'s own definition in a note of 1870–1 (*KG* III, 3, 121): 'Pathological interest...We feel as if we had had the experience' ('Das pathologische Interesse...Wir fühlen als ob wir es erlebten'). On the 'pathological', see above, pp. 277f.

89 Contrast a note of 1871 (*KG* III, 3, 285): 'the spectator of Aeschylean tragedy [responded]...as whole man, not as aesthetic man ('als ganzer Mensch, nicht als aesthetischer Mensch').

90 *Procs. Arist. Soc.* (supplementary volume) 1960, 145–64; the quotation comes on p. 145.

91 Quinton, 160.

92 See above, pp. 162f., 271, 285f. A similar error is made by Dodds *GI*, 68f.

93 Quinton, 161.

94 Quinton, 162.

95 Quinton, 161.

96 Above, p. 255 (our italics).

97 F. R. Leavis, *The Common Pursuit*, London, 1952, 127.

98 Leavis, 132.

99 Leavis, 133.

100 Leavis, 126.

101 Leavis, 126–8.

102 Leavis, 130.

103 Leavis, 292 (our italics).

104 Leavis, 130.

105 Bridgwater, 68ff.

106 Leavis, 131.

107 Steiner, 241.

108 Letter of 9 Dec. 1797: 'Without a lively pathological interest [cf. n. 88 above]...I too have never succeeded in elaborating a tragic situation...' This might imply that Goethe simply lacked the 'pathological interest', but the continuation of the passage ('the mere attempt to write tragedy might be my undoing') suggests that he was not prepared to try the experiment. With respect to this letter, at all events, Nietzsche's assertion, 'Goethe admitted that he wrote pathologically' ('...dass er pathologisch dichte', *KG* III, 3, 318, a note of 1871), is unwarranted. On Goethe, cf. further above, p. 281.

109 Some critics see a special relevance in the *Iliad*. Steiner (p. 5) goes so far as to call the poem 'the primer of tragic art'.

110 One of the N.'s later redefinitions of the tragic (*KG* IV, 3, 371) offered without reference to Homer.
111 Leavis, 132.
112 See e.g. *KG* III, 3, 31f., 100f., 201, 251, 334, 340f. (mostly on Schiller, Goethe, Kleist and Shakespeare). The tentative character of these notes is exemplified by contradictions about Shakespeare and Schiller (above, p. 281, and below, n. 117).
113 *KG* III, 2, 5f. and 16; III, 3, 201 and 334.
114 *The Sacred Wood*, London, 1928 (ed. 2), 100f. (see further above, pp. 365ff.) and *Gay Science*, 98.
115 He even found the language hard to deal with: C. A. Bernoulli, *Franz Overbeck und FN: eine Freundschaft*, Jena, 1908, I, 154.
116 Erich Heller, *The Disinherited Mind*, Cambridge, 1952, 42.
117 For the notes, see *KG* III, 3, 331 and 341, where Schiller is bracketed with Shakespeare and Wagner respectively, and 109, where he is said (in contrast to Goethe) to 'point the way to a tragic culture'. (How much of this refers to Schiller as dramatist, however, is unclear. Cf. above, p. 304). On Schiller's drama: GA^2 X, 280f. (a note of 1873). Kantian ethics: *KG* VII, 3, 291 (a note of 1885). Beauty: *Dawn*, 190.
118 Above, pp. 152f.
119 Above, p. 55.
120 See e.g. N.'s letter to Overbeck, 23 Feb. 1887 (Schlechta III, 1250); *Human, All Too Human*, II, 109; *Twilight of the Idols*, ix, 45; *Ecce Homo*, II ('Why I am so clever'), §3.
121 Above, p. 159.
122 Above, pp. 162, 186.
123 In the notes of 1870–1 there are in fact signs that N. was inclined to equate the 'artistic Socrates' and 'tragic man': *KG* III, 3, 122, *ll.* 21–3 (on Empedocles), 201, *ll.* 3–9 (on Shakespeare).
124 *Gay Science*, Second Preface (1886); reprinted in the epilogue to *Nietzsche Contra Wagner* (1888).
125 Above, pp. 203f.
126 Above, pp. 189f., 194f.
127 *KG* III, 2, 36f. (N.'s italics).
128 Cf. above, pp. 185, 193. In several notes of 1870–71 N. suggests that 'theoretical man' is the product of 'unlimited Apollinity' (*KG* III, 3, 140 [13], cf. 146 [7]) and that 'all *Wissenschaft* is in a sense Apolline' (166 [86], cf. 169, *ll.* 14f.).
129 See e.g. Ruth Benedict, *Patterns of Culture*, Boston/New York, 1934, 78f.
130 '...a predominantly *Socratic* or *artistic* or *tragic* culture...[i.e.] an Alexandrian or a Hellenic or a Buddhistic culture'. Kaufmann in a note to his translation (p. 110) observes: 'All editions published by N. himself contain these words...[but] the standard editions of [his] collected works substitute "an Indian (Brahmanic) culture" for "Buddhistic culture". According to volume I (p. 599) of...[GA^2], this change is based on "a pencil correction in N.'s own hand in his copy of the *second* version.' It would seem that both "Buddhistic" and "Brahmanic" depend on some misconception; neither seems to make much sense.'

131 Above, p. 121.
132 Above, pp. 212f.
133 *Epistle to the Galatians*, 3, 28.
134 For further discussion of these matters, see C. M. Barrack, *Nietzsche Studien*, 1974, 115–30.
135 Above, p. 46.
136 *Will to Power*, 822.
137 References in LSJ *s.v.* IV, 1.
138 *KG* IV, 3, 388 [51], a self-contained fragment: 'Damals glaubte ich, dass die Welt vom aesthetischen Standpunkt aus ein Schauspiel und als solches von ihrem Dichter gemeint sei...' At IV, 3, 391f. [68] there is another retrospective comment on *BT*, longer but rather incoherent and without the 'aesthetic phenomenon'.
139 Above, p. 120.
140 C. M. Barrack, *Nietzsche Studien*, 1974, 129.
141 *Will to Power*, 796.
142 *Gay Science*, 107.
143 The link is confirmed incidentally by a sentence in *Gay Science*, 143 on the products of polytheism, which refers to 'the invention of gods, heroes, and *Übermenschen* of all kinds'.

9 Nietzsche and earlier German theories of tragedy

1 *Thoughts Out of Season*, I, 4.
2 *Poetics*, Chs. 6ff.; cf. W. Schadewaldt, 'Furcht und Mitleid', *Hermes*, 1955, 129ff.
3 Above, p. 267.
4 J. D. Denniston and D. L. Page, *Aeschylus, Agamemnon*, Oxford, 1957, xxxi.
5 *Tragedy: Serious Drama in Relation to Aristotle's Poetics*, London, 1928, 118. N. himself (*BT* § 14) says much the same.
6 Cf. above, p. 35.
7 Above, pp. 227f.
8 Cf. e.g. the end of the first half of Schiller's essay *Über Anmut und Würde* (1793).
9 Though cf. above, p. 282, with n. 117.
10 *Libation Bearers*, 899–902 (translation ours): E. Staiger, *Aischylos, Die Totenspende* (*Orestie* II), Stuttgart, 1958, 45–7.
11 A formulation of his ideas is to be found in the section on tragedy in his *Philosophy of Art*, reprinted in *DLER*, Reihe *Romantik*, iii, 1931.
12 Snell, *Die Entdeckung des Geistes*, Ch. 1.
13 Jones, 196f. on Sophocles' Antigone.
14 Note e.g. the tendency in classical Greek, which goes back to Homer and, no doubt, beyond, to oppose an individual to aspects of himself in idioms comparable with the modern English 'I was struck by a thought', 'I restrained my anger'. Such idioms have been very sensibly discussed by K. J. Dover, *Greek Popular Morality in the time of Plato and Aristotle*, Oxford, 1974, 125f. In themselves they imply no more about their speakers' conceptual equipment than their English counterparts do.
15 Snell, 36ff.

16 For the Orphics see above, pp. 175ff.; for Heraclitus, n. 15 above; for the inscription, Guthrie *GG*, 262f.
17 *Dawn*, 240.
18 *Ecce Homo*, 'The Wagner Case' §3.
19 Preface to the *Philosophy of Right*.
20 A. C. Bradley, *Oxford Lectures on Poetry*, 1909, 71 (= Paolucci [see n. 21 below], 369).
21 Hegel, *Ästhetik*, IV, 1082 = *Hegel on Tragedy*, ed. A. and H. Paolucci, New York, 1962, 63: this is a useful collection of Hegel's writings in English, to which we provide references where appropriate, though without necessarily following the editors' translations.
22 *Ästhetik* IV, 1082ff.; Paolucci, 63ff.
23 Above, pp. 267f.
24 *Ästhetik* IV, 1082; Paolucci 64.
25 *Antigone* 905–12; Aristotle, *Rhetoric* III. 16. 9; Goethe, *Conversations with Eckermann*, 28 March 1827.
26 There is a tendency among recent classical scholars to regard the Hegelian position as entirely indefensible: see e.g. G. Müller, *Sophokles, Antigone*, Heidelberg, 1967, 9–11. Contrast Knox (n. 28 below) and, by implication, J.-P. Vernant and P. Vidal-Naquet, *Mythe et tragédie en Grèce ancienne*, Paris, 1972, 34f.
27 *Antigone* 454f., 199.
28 Knox, 102 and (on Hegel) 179, 182.
29 Demosthenes xxi. 34: cf. Dover, *Greek Popular Morality*, 306–9.
30 *Antigone* 368ff.: *pareirōn* ('weaves together'), the reading of the manuscripts, has been doubted, but the point at issue is not affected.
31 Cf. Lloyd-Jones, *Justice of Zeus*, 113–17.
32 *Antigone* 856ff.
33 Hegel's *Philosophie der Religion*², ed. D. P. Marheineke, Berlin, 1840, II, 133f.; Paolucci, 325.
34 Bradley, 74f.; Paolucci, 372.
35 *Ästhetik*, II, 541; Paolucci, 197.
36 *Antigone* 781ff.
37 *Ästhetik*, IV, 1095; Paolucci, 83.
38 *Antigone* 875.
39 *Ästhetik*, IV, 1086; Paolucci, 69f.
40 In *Die Welt als Wille und Vorstellung* I, iii, §51 and the corresponding passage II, iii, §37.
41 *Ibid.* I, iii, §51.
42 Transl. Philip Wayne, Harmondsworth, 1950.
43 *Die Welt als W. und V.* II, iii, §37; translation based on that by Payne, II, 433–6.
44 In Goethe's *Tagebuch für Charlotte von Stein*, Bologna, 19 Oct. 1786 (see the *Hamburger Ausgabe* (ed. 9, 1982), V, 407).
45 See above, p. 122.
46 *Will to Power*, 851.

10 Style and philosophy

1 *Über Wahrheit und Lüge im aussermoralischen Sinne*, *KG* II, 2, 367ff. See also Stern, Ch. 10.
2 *KG* III, 2, 378.
3 *KG* III, 2, 374f.
4 *KG* III, 2, 382f.
5 '...in an extra-moral sense', whatever that may mean: in the absence of any social context its meaning is indeterminable.
6 E.g. in the second sentence of §2: '...zugleich Rausch- und Traumkünstler: als welchen wir uns etwa zu denken haben...' See also Stern, 186.
7 Goethe's *Faust*, I, 2604. The quotation N. applies to Helen is in fact from *Wilhelm Meisters Lehrjahre*, I, iv, 14, where it is said of Ophelia.
8 *Die Welt als W. u. V.* II, §46; *Oed. Col.* 1224ff.; cf. above, pp. 408f., n. 125.
9 Schopenhauer (*WWV* I, 4, §63) also quotes Calderón's famous wording, 'the greatest guilt of man is to have been born at all', from *Life's a Dream*. All of this – the pessimism and the unreality of life – becomes a favourite topic in mid-nineteenth-century German (especially Austrian) literature.
10 Another favourite topic. Wagner in his opera of 1845 derived his interest from Heine's eponymous satirical poem of 1836.
11 Above, p. 406, n. 89 (ii).
12 Above, pp. 226, 230.
13 *The Sacred Wood*, 54.
14 *Ecce Homo*, 'Zarathustra', §3.
15 'Phantasmagoria': *KG* VII, 3, 376. Redefinition of 'aesthetic': above, pp. 269ff., 294.
16 Friedrich Hölderlin, *Wurzel des Übels*, 1795.
17 'The artist, like the god of the creation, remains within or behind or beyond or above his handiwork, invisible, refined out of existence, indifferent, paring his fingernails' (James Joyce, *A Portrait of the Artist as a Young Man*, Ch. 5).
18 Both in the third scene of *Faust*, I (*l.* 1226, where Faust rejects 'the word' as a translation of *Logos*: 'Ich kann das *Wort* unmöglich so hoch schätzen') and in the famous catechization scene with Gretchen (*ll.* 3456–7, where 'a name' is contrasted with 'feeling': 'Ich habe keinen Namen/Dafür: Gefühl ist alles;/Name ist Schall und Rauch') the low opinion of language has a purely dramatic function.
19 *Self-Criticism*, §3.
20 Above, p. 70.
21 This argument is similar to Matthew Arnold's in 'The Function of Criticism at the Present Time' (1865), but differs from it in ignoring the political implications of a lack of this 'freedom from the practical considerations of things'.
22 See Stern, 160f.
23 I.e. §41, 'Über den Tod und die Unzerstörbarkeit unseres Wesens an sich' in vol. II of *Die Welt als W. u. V.*
24 I.e. 'the veil of Maya' of individuation.
25 Thomas Mann, *Buddenbrooks: Verfall einer Familie*, X, Ch. 5.

26 *Faust*, I, 505ff.
27 *Faust*, I, 3982ff.
28 Above, p. 421, n. 108.
29 Rilke, *Sonnets to Orpheus*, I, 5.
30 *Antichrist*, §52.
31 *Antichrist*, §32, presumably alluding to 2 *Corinthians* 3. 6, 'the letter killeth, but the spirit giveth life'.
32 Cf. above, p. 211.
33 *Faust*, I, 1607ff.
34 Primarily, but not only, Plato: see above, p. 411, n. 23.
35 See Guthrie, *Socrates*, 63f.
36 His essays on Laurence Sterne and on 'The Metaphysics of Tragedy' in *Die Seele und die Formen* of 1911 are heavily influenced by *BT*.
37 E.g. in Lukács' *Die Zerstörung der Vernunft* of 1954.
38 In his later writings, especially those of the 'middle period', the terms *Instinkt* and *Trieb* cease to have any circumscribed meaning; even here, though, it must be said that whatever clarity attaches to *Instinkt* is attained at the expense of *Leben* ('life'), which Nietzsche will represent as necessarily indefinable (e.g. in *Human, All Too Human*, I, 32f., *Twilight of the Idols*, V, 5).
39 Above, p. 395, n. 10.
40 R. M. Rilke in the 'Fifth Duino Elegy'.
41 *Die Welt als W. u. V.* I, iii, §52.
42 The paradox is familiar from the Marxist argument about types. Lukács tried to solve it in his last writings by creating the category of 'speciality'; see B. Kiralyfalvi, *The Aesthetics of György Lukács*, Princeton, N.J., 1975, Ch. 5.
43 See J. P. Stern, *Re-Interpretations: Seven Studies in Nineteenth-Century German Literature*, London, 1964, Ch. 4, 'The Aesthetic Re-Interpretation'.
44 Above, pp. 248f.
45 Said to have been begun in 1906, though not published until 1916.
46 Heinrich Mann, *Der Untertan:* quoted by G. A. Craig, *Germany 1866–1945*, Oxford, 1978, 222.
47 Above, p. 281.
48 *The Sacred Wood*, 100.
49 *The Sacred Wood*, 98, 102.
50 *The Sacred Wood*, 59.
51 *The Sacred Wood*, 100.
52 *Sweeney Agonistes*, 'Fragment of an Agon'.
53 *Twilight of the Idols*, IX, 26.
54 We are indebted to Kai Arste who, in an unpublished essay, 'Nietzsche and Freud', draws an extended analogy between Nietzsche's three archetypes and what Freud calls 'the three provinces of [man's] mental apparatus'. Freud himself was clearly not aware of the analogy. Only in respect of 'the id', he says, does he 'follow a verbal usage of Nietzsche's, taking up a suggestion made by Georg Grodeck': *New Introductory Lectures on Psycho-Analysis*, in *The Standard Edition of the Complete Psychological Works of Sigmund Freud*, XXIII, p. 72. See also *The Ego and the Id*, in *ed. cit.* XIX, 23, and Ernest Jones, *Sigmund Freud: Life and Work*, III, London 1957, 303.
55 *Phaedrus* 246ff.

56 Peter Gay, *Freud, Jews and Other Germans*, London, 1978, 73.
57 Goethe to Eckermann, 11 March 1828. Nietzsche regarded the *Conversations* as 'the best German book there is' (*Human, All Too Human*, II, 109).
58 *Zarathustra*, II, 12, 'On Self-mastery'.
59 In *Thoughts Out of Season*, I.
60 *Self-Criticism*, §3.
61 Nietzsche had already associated this etching with his conception of Schopenhauer in the letter to Rohde (8 October 1868) discussed above, p. 27.
62 'Tragedy is seated amidst this excess of life, suffering, joy . . . listening in sublime ecstasy to a distant melancholy song that tells of the Mothers of Being whose names are Illusion, Will, Woe.' Nietzsche refers (both here and in the first paragraph of §16) to the myth of 'the Mothers', which Goethe found in Plutarch's *Life of Marcellus* (Ch. 20) and used freely in *Faust*, II (Act I, *ll.* 6216–20) to represent the mysterious origin of all being beyond time and space. It has since become a bit of higher-cultural patter.
63 See above, pp. 174f., 273ff.
64 See below, n. 78. In his notes of 1870–1 N. states the analogy, then seems to go back on it: 'we have reached the Persian war period' (*KG* III, 3, 101), but 'our Persian wars have hardly begun' (*KG* III, 3, 392).
65 See above, pp. 46f., and the first page of *Thoughts Out of Season*, I.
66 *Ecce Homo*, 'The Wagner Case', §3.
67 In their notes of 1845–6 entitled *The German Ideology*, left uncompleted, and first published in 1932.
68 Men like Paul de Lagarde, Julius Langbehn and Houston Stewart Chamberlain. *Kulturpessimismus* is a curiously enduring part of the German politico-intellectual scene. After being appropriated by the powerful extreme right, it now seems to have become the property of a minute, but equally extreme, left. Friedrich Hölderlin's fragmentary verse drama, *Der Tod des Empedokles* (begun in 1797), contains an apologia for the Presocratic philosopher's fabled suicide; in an early draft of the poem, this is seen as a revolutionary political act of self-sacrifice on behalf of the unenlightened masses. A rumour current in Federal Germany at the time of writing has it that an open copy of Hölderlin's poem was found in Ulrike Meinhof's cell in Stuttgart after her suicide in 1978.
69 See the second paragraph of Freud's *Civilization and Its Discontents* (1930); the quotations come from a letter of Romain Rolland in criticism of *The Future of an Illusion* (1927).
70 Above, pp. 245ff.
71 Ludwig Wittgenstein, *The Blue and the Brown Books*, Oxford, 1964, 17.
72 This particularly regrettable formulation occurs on p. 51 of Paul de Man's not always scrupulous and frequently opaque 'de-construction' of N.'s argument ('Genesis and Genealogy in Nietzsche's *The Birth of Tragedy*', in *Diacritics*, Winter 1972, 44–53). Among de Man's other failings is a misleading account of N.'s theory of metaphor; he ignores the 1873 essay (above, pp. 338ff.) which illuminates N.'s view of language as well as his stylistic practice.
73 Cf. above, p. 246.
74 'Desolate and empty the sea' – words which thanks to Eliot's *The Waste Land* (*l.* 42) have a more canonical status in English than in German.
75 Cf. above, pp. 250f., 279.

76 *Thoughts Out of Season*, II, § 1. The dictum may be compared with Eliot's appeal to the 'historical sense which is a sense of the timeless as well as of the temporal' ('Tradition and the Individual Talent' in *The Sacred Wood*).

77 Plato, *Republic* III. 414–15.

78 'Perhaps there are those who may think that this [German] spirit must begin its struggle by ousting everything Romance; and they may see in the victorious fortitude and blood-stained glory of the recent war an external preparation and encouragement for that struggle. Its inner necessity, however, must be sought in the ambition to be ever worthy of the sublime champions in this field – of Luther no less than of our great poets and artists.'

79 In poems like *Brod und Wein* (last stanza), and *Mein Eigentum*.

80 Charles Rosen, *Schoenberg*, London, 1976, 32f.

81 Rosen (n. 80 above) demurs at this notion, but as he himself indicates, the notion is widespread – which means that the evocation it rests on must be widespread too: N., at least, appears to presuppose it.

82 N. avoids the word *Konsonanz* in this part of *BT*, although he does use it in § 17 (deprecatingly, of the 'earthly consonance' favoured by Socratic man), where the phrase 'the tragic dissonance' is also used, but without explanation.

83 Thomas Mann, *The Magic Mountain*, vol. II, Ch. 6, 'Snow'. Even in Mann this terrible vision is in fact a dream, whose dreamer (Mann's young hero) does not want to go on dreaming it: contemplating the scene, he resolves to return to life. Immediately preceding this 'Dionysiac' passage is an Apolline scene which closely resembles the one we have just quoted from *BT* § 25. For a critical view of Mann's Nietzschean passage, see R. D. Gray, *The German Tradition in Literature 1871–1945*, Cambridge, 1965, 166ff.

Bibliography

ABBREVIATIONS

Baeumler	*Nietzsche in seinen Briefen und Berichten der Zeitgenossen*, ed. A. Baeumler, Leipzig, 1932.
GA^{1}	*Nietzsches Werke: Gesamtausgabe in Grossoktav*^{1}, ed. E. Förster-Nietzsche and others, Leipzig, 1894–1904.
GA^{2}	Second edition of the same, 1901–13.
GB	*Friedrich Nietzsches Gesammelte Briefe*, ed. E. Förster-Nietzsche and others, Leipzig, 1900–9.
HKB	Friedrich Nietzsche, *Historisch-kritische Gesamtausgabe, Briefe*, ed. W. Hoppe and K. Schlechta, Munich, 1938–42.
HKG	Friedrich Nietzsche, *Historisch-kritische Gesamtausgabe, Werke*, ed. H. J. Mette, K. Schlechta, and C. Koch, Munich, 1933–40.
KG	Nietzsche, *Werke, Kritische Gesamtausgabe*, ed. G. Colli and M. Montinari, Berlin and New York, 1967– .
KGB	Nietzsche, *Briefwechsel, Kritische Gesamtausgabe*, ed. G. Colli and M. Montinari, Berlin and New York, 1975– .
Kl.P.	*Der kleine Pauly*, ed. K. Ziegler and W. Sontheimer, Stuttgart, 1964–75.
LSJ	H. G. Liddell and R. Scott, *A Greek-English Lexicon*^{9}, rev. H. S. Jones, Oxford, 1925–40.
LSJ, *Supp.*	*A Supplement* to the above, ed. E. A. Barber and others, Oxford, 1968.
Musarion	Nietzsche, *Gesammelte Werke, Musarionausgabe*, ed. R. Oehler, M. Oehler and F. C. Würzbach, Munich, 1920–9.
OCD^{2}	*The Oxford Classical Dictionary*^{2}, ed. N. G. L. Hammond and H. H. Scullard, Oxford, 1970.
PMG	D. L. Page, *Poetae Melici Graeci*, Oxford, 1962.
RE	Pauly–Wissowa, *Real-Encyclopädie der klassischen Altertumswissenschaft*, Stuttgart 1894–.
Schlechta	Friedrich Nietzsche, *Werke in drei Bänden*, ed. K. Schlechta, Munich, 1954–6.

CLASSICAL TEXTS

Texts and abbreviation of works and authors generally follow the practice of LSJ or LSJ, *Supp*. The fragments of Greek iambic and elegiac poetry, however, are cited from M. L. West, *Iambi et Elegi Graeci*, Oxford, 1971–2.

OTHER WORKS

The following works are referred to in the notes by the author's name or in some other abbreviated form:

Adrados, F. R. *Fiesta, Comedia y Tragedia*, Barcelona, 1972.
Anderson, W. D. *Ethos and Education in Greek Music*, Cambridge, Mass., 1966.
Andler, C. *Nietzsche, sa vie et sa pensée*, Paris, I³ 1920, II² 1921.
Bachofen, J. J. *Gesammelte Werke*, ed. K. Meuli, Basle, 1943–8.
Baeumer, M. L. 'Nietzsche and the Tradition of the Dionysian', in O'Flaherty, *Studies in N.*, 165–89.
Boardman, F. *Athenian Black Figure Vases*, London, 1974.
Bradley, A. C. *Oxford Lectures on Poetry*, London, 1909.
Bridgwater, P. *Nietzsche in Anglosaxony*, Leicester, 1972.
Brown, John. *Dissertation on the Rise, Union, and Power, the Progressions, Separations, and Corruptions, of Poetry and Music*, London, 1763.
Bywater, I. *Aristotle On the Art of Poetry*, Oxford, 1909.
Cornford, F. M. *From Religion to Philosophy*, London, 1912.
Crusius, O. *Erwin Rohde, ein biographischer Versuch*, Tübingen, 1902.
Däuble, H. 'Friedrich Nietzsche und Erwin Rohde', *Nietzsche Studien*, 5, 1976, 321–54.
Dietrich, B. C. *The Origins of Greek Religion*, Berlin, 1974.
Dodds, E. R. *Euripides, Bacchae²*, Oxford, 1960.
The Greeks and the Irrational, Berkeley, Calif., 1951.
Dover, K. J. *Greek Popular Morality in the Time of Plato and Aristotle*, Oxford, 1974.
Eliot, T. S. *The Sacred Wood²*, London, 1928.
Else, G. F. *The Origin and Early Form of Greek Tragedy*, Cambridge, Mass., 1965.
Farnell, L. R. *The Cults of the Greek States*, Oxford, 1896–1909.
Förster-Nietzsche, E. *Das Leben Friedrich Nietzsches*, Leipzig, 1895–1904.
Wagner und Nietzsche zur Zeit ihrer Freundschaft, Munich, 1915.
Fraenkel, E. *Aeschylus, Agamemnon*, Oxford, 1950.
Griffith, M. *The Authenticity of Prometheus Bound*, Cambridge, 1977.
Gründer, K. *Der Streit um Nietzsches "Geburt der Tragödie"*, Hildesheim, 1969.
Guthrie, W. K. C. *The Greeks and Their Gods*, London, 1950.
Socrates, Cambridge, 1971.
Gutman, R. W. *Richard Wagner: The Man, His Mind and His Music*, London, 1968.
Harrison, J. E. *Themis*, Cambridge, 1912 (ed. 1), 1927 (ed. 2).
Hegel, G. W. F. *Ästhetik*, ed. F. Bassenge, Berlin, 1955.
Jähnig, D. *Schelling: Die Kunst in der Philosophie*, Pfullingen, 1969.
Janz, C. P. *Friedrich Nietzsche*, Munich and Vienna, 1978–.
Jones, J. *On Aristotle and Greek Tragedy*, London, 1962.
Kaufmann, W. *Friedrich Nietzsche, The Birth of Tragedy and The Case of Wagner* (trans. with comm.), New York, 1967.
Nietzsche: Philosopher, Psychologist, Antichrist⁴, Princeton, N.J., 1974.
Knight, A. H. J. *Some Aspects of the Life and Work of Nietzsche*, Cambridge, 1933.
Knox, B. M. W. *The Heroic Temper*, Cambridge, 1964.
Leavis, F. R. *The Common Pursuit*, London, 1952.

Lesky, A. *Die tragische Dichtung der Hellenen*[3], Göttingen, 1972.
Lloyd-Jones, H. *The Justice of Zeus*, Berkeley, Calif., 1971.
Love, F. R. *Young Nietzsche and the Wagnerian Experience*, Chapel Hill, N.C., 1963.
Mette, H. J. *Friedrich Nietzsche: Socrates und die griechische Tragödie*, Munich, 1933.
Middleton, C. *Selected Letters of Friedrich Nietzsche*, Chicago, 1969.
Newman, E. *The Life of Richard Wagner* IV, London, 1947 (reprinted Cambridge, 1976).
Nilsson, M. P. *Geschichte der griechischen Religion* I[3], Munich, 1967.
Oehler, M. *Nietzsches Bibliothek*, Weimar, 1942.
O'Flaherty, J. C., Sellner, T. F. and Helm, R. M. *Studies in Nietzsche and the Classical Tradition*, Chapel Hill, N.C., 1976.
Paolucci, A. and H. *Hegel on Tragedy*, New York, 1962.
Payne, E. J. F. *Arthur Schopenhauer, The World as Will and Representation*, corrected edn., New York, 1969.
Pickard-Cambridge, A. W. *Dithyramb Tragedy and Comedy*, Oxford, 1927; rev. T. B. L. Webster, Oxford, 1962.
Podach, E. F. *Ein Blick in Notizbücher Nietzsches*, Heidelberg, 1963.
Quinton, A. M. 'Tragedy', *Proceedings of the Aristotelian Society* (supplementary volume), 1960, 145–64.
Rohde, E. *Psyche*[2], Tübingen, 1897.
Sandys, J. E. *A History of Classical Scholarship* III, Cambridge, 1908.
Schelling, F. W. J. von *Sämtliche Werke*, Stuttgart and Augsburg, 1858.
Schiller, F. *Sämtliche Werke*, ed. O. Walzel, Stuttgart and Berlin, 1905.
Schlechta, K. *Nietzsche Chronik*, Munich and Vienna, 1975.
Schopenhauer, A. *Die Welt als Wille und Vorstellung*, 2 volume edn., Leipzig, 1859.
Severyns, A. *Recherches sur la Chrestomathie de Proclos* II, Paris, 1938.
Snell, B. *Die Entdeckung des Geistes*[3], Hamburg, 1955.
Steiner, G. *The Death of Tragedy*, London, 1961.
Stern, J. P. *A Study of Nietzsche*, Cambridge, 1979.
Stroux, J. *Nietzsches Professur in Basel*, Jena, 1925.
Vogel, M. *Apollinisch und Dionysisch*, Regensburg, 1966.
Wagner, Cosima *Die Tagebücher*, ed. M. Gregor-Dellin and D. Mack, Munich, 1976–7.
Wagner, Richard, *Gesammelte Schriften*, ed. J. Kapp, Leipzig, 1914.
Westernhagen, K. von *Richard Wagner*, Zürich, 1956.
Wilamowitz-Moellendorff, U. von *Erinnerungen 1848–1914*, Leipzig, 1928.
Der Glaube der Hellenen, Berlin, 1931–2.
Wili, W. 'The Orphic Mysteries and the Greek Spirit', *Papers from the Eranos Yearbooks* II (ed. J. Campbell), London, 1955, 64–92.
Zuckerman, E. 'Nietzsche and Music', *Symposium*, 1974, 17–32.

Index